Growth and Empowerment

Munich Lectures in Economics
Edited by Hans-Werner Sinn

The Making of Economic Policy: A Transaction Cost Politics Perspective, by Avinash Dixit (1996)

The Economic Consequences of Rolling Back the Welfare State, by A. B. Atkinson (1999)

Competition in Telecommunications, by Jean-Jacques Laffont and Jean Tirole (2000)

Taxation, Incomplete Markets, and Social Security, by Peter A. Diamond (2003)

The Economic Effects of Constitutions, by Torsten Persson and Guido Tabellini (2003)

Growth and Empowerment: Making Development Happen, by Nicholas Stern, Jean-Jacques Dethier, and F. Halsey Rogers (2005)

In cooperation with the council of the Center for Economic Studies of the University of Munich

Martin Beckman, David F. Bradford, Gebhard Flaig, Otto Gandenberger, Franz Gehrels, Martin Hellwig, Bernd Huber, Mervyn King, John Komlos, Richard Musgrave, Ray Rees, Bernd Rudolph, Agnar Sandmo, Karlhans Sauernheimer, Klaus Schmidt, Hans Schneeweiss, Robert Solow, Joseph E. Stiglitz, Wolfgang Wiegard, Charles Wyplosz

Growth and Empowerment

Making Development
Happen

Nicholas Stern, Jean-Jacques
Dethier, and F. Halsey Rogers

The MIT Press
Cambridge, Massachusetts
London, England

MIT Press books may be purchased at special quantity discounts for business or sales promotional use. For information, please e-mail special_sales@mitpress.mit.edu or write to Special Sales Department, The MIT Press, 5 Cambridge Center, Cambridge, MA 02142.

This book was set in Palatino on 3B2 by Asco Typesetters, Hong Kong.
Printed and bound in the United States of America.

Library of Congress Cataloging-in-Publication Data

Stern, N. H. (Nicholas Herbert)
Growth and empowerment : making development happen / Nicholas Stern, Jean-Jacques Dethier, and F. Halsey Rogers.
    p.   cm. — (Munich lectures in economics)
Includes bibliographical references and index.
ISBN 0-262-19517-8 (alk. paper)
1. Economic development. 2. Economic policy. I. Dethier, Jean-Jacques, 1952–
II. Rogers, F. Halsey III. Title. IV. Series.
HD75.S7625   2005
338.9—dc22   2004057878

10 9 8 7 6 5 4 3 2

Contents

Series Foreword   vii
Preface   ix
Acknowledgments   xix
A Brief Guide to These Lectures   xxiii

Lecture I   Experience   1

1   **Living Standards and Poverty**   3

2   **Development as a Process of Change**   33

3   **Lessons of Development Policy**   83

4   **Lessons from Development Theory**   109

Lecture II   Strategy   125

5   **A Strategy for Development**   127

Lecture III   Research   165

6   **Data and Measurement as Drivers of Change**   167

7   **The Dynamics of the Investment Climate**   199

8   **The Dynamics of Empowerment**   225

9   **The Dynamics of Preferences**   243

10   The Dynamics of Political Reform   267

Lecture IV Action   285

11   The Challenge   287

12   Domestic Action: Public Finances and the Role of the State   315

13   International Action: Trade and Aid   357

Conclusion: A Strategy to Guide Policy, a Program for Learning, and a
Plan of Action   387
Notes   391
References   405
Index   441

Series Foreword

Every year the CES council awards a prize to an internationally re-nowned and innovative economist for outstanding contributions to economic research. The scholar is honored with the title "Distin-guished CES Fellow" and is invited to give the "Munich Lectures in Economics."

The lectures are held at the Center for Economic Studies of the Uni-versity of Munich. They introduce areas of recent or potential interest to a wide audience in a nontechnical way and combine theoretical depth with policy relevance.

Hans-Werner Sinn
Professor of Economics and Public Finance
Director of CES
University of Munich

Preface

This book originated in a set of lectures that I gave in Munich, Germany, in November 2002, on the occasion of my appointment as Distinguished Fellow at the Centre for Economic Studies at Ludwig-Maximilian University. It is part of the annual series of those lectures published by the MIT Press. Jean-Jacques Dethier and Halsey Rogers, two of my close colleagues at the World Bank, have collaborated with me throughout the research and writing of this book.

Although the ideas offered here were presented in the lectures, they have evolved in many ways since the lectures were given. They have also grown from the three authors' many years of work on development economics and are reflected in our publications over that time. In addition, the ideas were strongly influenced by the three and a half years I spent as chief economist and senior vice president at the World Bank (from spring 2000 to autumn 2003) and by the six years before that when I was chief economist at the European Bank for Reconstruction and Development (EBRD). While this book is influenced by my having spent a decade in international institutions, it is not a book about either the EBRD or the World Bank. It is a book about development, drawing on experience way beyond those two institutions.

The book retains the style of a set of lectures. It is not a treatise and does not attempt to be exhaustive on the subjects it examines. The purpose is to present the ideas in a structured way and to point to some of the evidence underpinning them. My departure from the World Bank in autumn 2003, to work at the U.K. Treasury, led us to offer the book as it is now rather than continue developing and revising it as we otherwise might have done. There are some parts, especially in lecture III, which are more technical than others, but the reader who is less enthusiastic about this kind of material can skip it without detracting from the understanding of the main arguments of the book.

The Opportunity and Agenda for Development

The past twenty-five years have been remarkable. In the late 1970s China emerged from the nightmare of the Cultural Revolution and embarked on reforms initiated by Deng Xiao Ping. As a result more than 1 billion people—one-fifth of earth's population—have experienced a period of sustained growth and poverty reduction that has no precedent in human history. In the late 1980s the Berlin Wall came down, setting 400 million people in Central and Eastern Europe and the former Soviet Union on a transition from communism and a command economy to, for most, democracy and a market economy. By 2004 the European Union was welcoming as members many countries once separated from the rest of Europe by an iron curtain. India's growth began to pick up in the 1980s, and in the early 1990s it initiated far-reaching economic change. Today India is seeing growth and poverty reduction on a scale that would have been dismissed as highly improbable by many analysts in the 1970s and early 1980s. Twenty-five years ago just one-third of the world's countries could be described as democratic; now that share is closer to two-thirds.

Remarkable too has been the improvement in living standards, including those related to health and education. In the past forty years the average life expectancy in developing countries increased from the mid-forties to the mid-sixties—whereas the move from the mid-twenties to the mid-forties took from the early 1800s to the mid-1900s. Over the past thirty years the share of illiterate people in the developing world declined from around one-half to one-quarter, with particularly strong progress for girls and women. And in the last quarter-century the number of people living on less than $1 a day fell by about 200 million, the first sustained drop since the early nineteenth century—or, indeed, since as far back as we can construct data. This decrease has occurred at a time when the population of the developing world rose by 1.5 billion.

Sadly, such progress has not been universal: far too many people have been left out. In rich countries, mortality for children under age five is 7 deaths per 1,000, but in poor countries the average is 84 deaths per 1,000—and in sub-Saharan Africa, it is a shocking 162 deaths per 1,000. Half the women over age fifteen in South Asia and sub-Saharan Africa are illiterate. More than 1 billion people in developing countries lack access to safe water for drinking and personal hygiene. Since the 1950s nearly one-quarter of the world's croplands, pastures, forests, and woodlands have been degraded, with one-sixth so severely degraded that it is too costly to reverse. Sub-Saharan Africa has suffered seemingly endless tragedy: the scourge of HIV/AIDS, failings in the battles against malaria and tuberculosis, the devastation of widespread conflict. This region has also seen little or no growth in average incomes for the past forty years.

Reaching those left behind presents many challenges, including overcoming disillusionment in countries where growth has failed to take root despite difficult reforms. Although developing countries still have substantial barriers to trade, they cut average tariffs in half between 1980 and 1998 (from 15 to 7 percent), and inflation has been brought under control. Yet many Latin American and sub-Saharan countries have not seen the expected results in terms of growth and poverty reduction.

The Doha round of trade talks of the World Trade Organization, launched in November 2001, put developing countries' needs at the top of the agenda. Yet more than three years later, there is a real possibility that developed countries will retreat into protectionism. Developed countries continue to impose substantial obstacles on imports from developing countries, despite pledges to remove or reduce them. High-income countries provide more than $300 billion a year in domestic agricultural subsidies—six times the amount of aid to developing countries—and block or discourage agricultural exports from developing countries in many other ways. Developed countries have tariffs and quotas on textile imports that cost developing countries an estimated 27 million jobs. Other tariffs and nontariff barriers further undermine manufacturing and employment in developing-country industries. Thus even as developed countries preach the benefits of trade to developing countries, they erect barriers to trade.

While we should not be under any illusions about the magnitude of development challenges, we have a special opportunity to do something about them. With accumulated evidence from our successes and failures, we understand better than ever before what works and what does not in development strategies and assistance. We have the resources to make more of a difference than at any other time in human history. There is growing understanding that the development of poor countries and people is not only a moral imperative; it is also in the interests of all the world's citizens.

The optimism that accompanied the arrival of a new millennium generated an unprecedented international commitment to promoting development and fighting poverty, a commitment manifested most clearly in the Millennium Declaration adopted at the United Nations in 2000. The Millennium Development Goals (MDGs) contained in that declaration provide a framework for measuring progress toward honoring that commitment. They offer specific targets for reducing income poverty; improving health, education, and the status of women and girls; protecting the environment; and strengthening international development cooperation. At the United Nations Conference on Financing for Development in Monterrey, Mexico, in spring 2002 and again at the World Summit on Sustainable Development in Johannesburg, South Africa, in August 2002, leaders of many nations committed themselves—and held themselves mutually accountable—to finding ways to achieve these goals. One purpose of this book is to contribute to a better understanding of the opportunity created by the events of recent years and how we can rise to the challenge of achieving the great advances in development embodied in our commitments. The slow progress in the year and a half since Johannesburg underscores the importance of sharing and deepening this understanding.

The understanding that we seek requires careful reflection on the experience of development, what the analytics of development can offer, and where further study should go. This book argues that this reflection must take us to a much more dynamic theory of development— one that looks at the underlying dynamics, the processes of structural change, and the meaning of development itself. Contributing to and helping to chart this new approach is the second purpose of this book. Taking this approach involves an extended, difficult work program. But it also provides a way of looking at development that, while building on what we know, generates a more productive perspective than was prevalent a few years ago.

This approach leads to a strategy and analytical structure that not only offer new perspectives and a new research agenda but also help shape a program for action now. This book makes no attempt to provide an exhaustive account of where this new approach will take us in developing ideas. And while the arguments are evidence based, the book does not provide extensive detail on the evidence supporting them.

My Journey

This book, and the lectures on which it is based, reflect my experiences over thirty-five years of study and work on development economics. My empirical research journey though the landscape of development began in 1969 in the tea gardens of smallholders in Kenya. It continued in the wheat fields of India, where I spent many months in 1974 and 1975 living in the northern Indian village of Palanpur. My collaborators on Palanpur (Christopher Bliss, Jean Drèze, Peter Lanjouw, and Naresh Sharma) and I have been returning over the years. Looking back, Palanpur has probably been the strongest influence on my understanding of development. Watching the village change over thirty years provides insights that would never be available from aggregated analysis of macroeconomic statistics, however lengthy and intense.

One might ask why someone trained as a mathematical economist would go tramping around in fields. The answer is that I believed that sound theory was not only intellectually rewarding but, when combined with serious evidence and reflected in policy, it also had the power to improve lives. Work in the field strengthened that belief, and my experiences in Kenya and India foreshadowed lessons that would recur often in later work. First, successful development requires both a dynamic private sector and an active and efficient public sector to provide a climate conducive to investment and growth. Second, if our goal is to live in a world without poverty, we must take action to empower poor people to participate in that growth.

I spent a good part of my professional life in various academic positions at Oxford University, the University of Warwick, the Massachusetts Institute of Technology, the Ecole Polytechnique, the Indian Statistical Institute, and the London School of Economics, which remains my intellectual home. I also had the pleasure of teaching at the People's University of Beijing in the first half of 1988 and am now an honorary professor there. What I discovered firsthand in China, and through my study of the Chinese economic transition, were the huge dynamic returns that can come from removing obstacles to market-driven development and the importance of adapting and building on existing institutions as well as building new ones. Indeed, the Chinese often remind us that fostering development requires taking cultural factors into account.

After my time in China, I spent six years focused on the transition economies of Europe and Central Asia as chief economist at the EBRD. In those economies, investment climate problems were paramount. Firms suffered from bureaucratic harassment and both grand and petty corruption, which reduced rewards to entrepreneurship and diverted energies into rent seeking and self-protection. The tragic experience of much of the former Soviet Union in the 1990s tells us that government must take direct action to create a good investment climate for the private sector rather than withdrawing and hoping that such a climate will emerge in the resulting vacuum. Government must also recognize and act on the costs of change, particularly for poor people. In addition, the former Soviet Union provides striking evidence that behaviors, not just institutions and policies, are crucial to economic performance. The experience of much of Central and Eastern Europe outside the former Soviet Union, while difficult, has been much more positive, largely because new and liberated states and polities have functioned much better.

In 2000 I became chief economist at the World Bank. My experience there sharpened the many lessons I had learned and helped me build from them a strategy for development. This strategy rests on two pillars: building an investment climate that facilitates investment and growth and empowering and investing in poor people so that they participate in that growth. As it unfolds in this book, I hope that this strategy sounds plausible—indeed, almost obvious. And I hope to show that it leads directly to policy. But this strategy and its policy implications are fairly new and not universally accepted. When I received the great honor of the invitation to give the Munich lectures in autumn 2002, it was this approach to development that I wanted to set forth. The elaboration of the ideas presented there is the substance of this book.

Although the strategy proposed in this book does not directly contradict other approaches to development, it differs strongly from many in its direction and emphasis. It is very different from the command economy, central planning, and protectionism models popular in the 1950s and 1960s. It is also very different from the dogmatic and naive market fundamentalism of much of the 1980s and 1990s, where some analysts appeared to believe that all government had to do was get out of the way and leave everything to markets. And it is not a middle way, built from bits and pieces of those two misguided approaches. Further, it is not an extension of the redistribution with growth story told in the mid-1970s by Hollis Chenery and others, which emphasized accumulation, human capital, and labor intensity.

This book's focus is elsewhere. It emphasizes growth and development as dynamic processes that are shaped by, as well as shape, history, learning, and institutions. It is not simply about aggregates; it emphasizes the importance of change—changing structures, behaviors, and institutions. Central to the story is empowering and investing in people. Empowerment, an idea that runs through the book and is developed at some length, goes beyond assets to the influences and constraints on behavior arising both socially and internally, in terms of an individual's perception of what is appropriate and possible. Empowerment is an idea that should be central to discussions of development policy, both as an end and means of development.

Neither is this book's strategy akin to the Washington consensus, as originally defined by John Williamson (1990), which emphasizes fiscal discipline, market-determined exchange and interest rates, protection of property rights, liberalization, privatization, openness to trade, and redirection of public spending toward education, health, and public infrastructure. There is nothing fundamentally wrong with the principles that Williamson articulated—as far as they go. Indeed, it would be dangerous to reject them. But that story leaves out so much of what is important that it is in many ways dangerously misleading. It says little about governance and institutions, the role of empowerment and democratic representation, the importance of country ownership (that is, involvement in the design of and commitment to policies) for effective policy, or the social costs and pace of transformation. Just as it learned from the failures of central planning, the development community has learned the hard way—through the setbacks of structural adjustment programs in developing countries in the 1980s and the transition in Central and Eastern Europe and the former Soviet Union in the 1990s—that these elements are at the heart of the development challenge. It has also learned the dangers of simplistic dogmatism of the market kind. And all too often, poor people have incurred the costs of the learning process.

Any intellectual journey is influenced by other thinkers and colleagues in addition to direct experience. Here, the influences of Joseph Schumpeter and Albert Hirschman, in their approaches to entrepreneurship and innovation and dynamic processes, and Amartya Sen, on the objectives of development, will be clear to most readers. And it is very much in the spirit of John Maynard Keynes, the intellectual and in many ways practical founder of the Bretton Woods institutions (the World Bank and International Monetary Fund), in that it sees good theory as contributing directly to changing the world and the importance of institutions and international collaboration in so doing. Looking back, I am struck that the first books my supervisor, and strong influence, James Mirrlees encouraged me to read were by Schumpeter and Keynes. I have also been strongly influenced by those

I have collaborated with over the years on public economics and development, notably Tony Atkinson and Mervyn King (during my London School of Economics years) on public economics, Ehtisham Ahmad on public finance in developing countries, and my Palanpur colleagues.

Action and Research

The overarching lesson I have drawn from my varied experiences and influences is that development is a dynamic process of changing structures, behaviors, and institutions and that this process can be influenced, shaped, and driven by better policies and understanding—with powerful benefits, particularly for poor people. Growth theory, development economics, and public economics offer a solid foundation for analyzing development as change, but we need to go much further than those theories take us in important areas: changing structures and institutions, changing preferences and behaviors, and the processes of learning.

The real story of the development process is too complex to be captured by standard theories of growth, many of which represent economic activity using simple aggregates and focus only on steady states. Anyone who has spent time in the developing world will appreciate that there is little steady about it. A more fruitful approach is to focus on the processes and structures that drive the decisions of households, firms, and farms. Such an approach looks at what really works (or does not) on the ground. It sees growth as a process of structural change and of learning. Like most other successful conceptual and theoretical frameworks, it cannot abandon simplicity if it is to have traction in shaping policy. The key is to focus on the right issues.

Action and research based on these ideas should be designed to guide public efforts to reduce poverty and improve well-being in developing countries. The challenge is to turn the solemn commitments contained in the Millennium Declaration into effective actions commensurate with the scale of the challenge. The strategy offered in this book can provide guidance in developing a framework for action and show us where we have more to learn.

The prospects for success depend on two factors. The first is an acceleration of learning. We cannot, however, wait for more learning before taking action. We know enough to act effectively now. Moreover, acting and learning at the same time are the essence of what development is all about.

The second factor determining the success or failure of our actions is political leadership and commitment. Developing countries must play the lead role in shaping their futures, creating locally owned strategies that reflect their priorities. But the responsibility for success is not theirs alone. Leaders of developed countries will not have the political space to deliver on their commitments unless they make development a central domestic issue. A fundamental ethical case can be made for all of us to play our part in overcoming suffering wherever it occurs. Poverty anywhere is a responsibility everywhere. We share our existence as human beings and share a single planet.

Less altruistic, but also relevant, is the incentive of enlightened self-interest. Five billion of the world's 6 billion people live in developing countries. They are the growing markets and producers of the future. Developed countries have every incentive to help ensure that developing countries achieve strong growth. In an integrated world, we can all benefit from having trading partners with growing economies. Further, problems of crime, terrorism, illegal drugs, and communicable disease feed on the hopelessness of extreme deprivation and collapsed states. Yet their effects are not confined to poor societies.

Beyond simple moral imperatives to help our fellow human beings and enlightened self-interest, we should surely be thinking of the kind of world, economy, and society we should be building for our children. Will it be a world of cooperation, mutual responsibility, and prosperity broadly shared? Or will it be one of conflict, narrow-mindedness, and wealth for just a few?

We are at a special moment in human history—one replete with risks and opportunity. We have the understanding and resources to win the fight against poverty and make a profound change in the world where we all live. But we must move from commitment to delivery. That will not happen without both strong leadership and the engagement of people around the world. These, in turn, will require strong evidence of what works and what does not. However we look at it, if we are to take this historical opportunity to fight poverty, no one has a greater responsibility than those of us who study economic development.

Nicholas Stern

Acknowledgments

Ideas are influenced by many things, including experiences, intellectual traditions, and colleagues. The authors of this book began working on development in the 1960s and have direct experience in countries ranging from Egypt, Ethiopia, Kenya, and Mali to China, India, Indonesia, and the Republic of Korea, to Albania, Hungary, Russia, and Turkmenistan, to Brazil, Ecuador, Mexico, and Peru. The intellectual traditions to which we have been exposed and the universities we have been affiliated with are similarly rich and varied. It is impossible to do justice to them all.

We are extremely grateful to the many colleagues who helped us with various aspects of this book. Shahrokh Fardoust has been a wise friend, colleague, organizer, and guide throughout. David Ellerman has generously shared his extraordinary scholarship and was closely involved in the preparation of early drafts. Greg Fischer's collaboration in summer 2003 was of enormous value, particularly for chapters 6 and 9. The sections on poverty owe much to Peter Lanjouw and Martin Ravallion. The sections on the investment climate and on small and medium-size enterprises owe a lot to Caralee McLiesh. Ehtisham Ahmad, a long-time collaborator with Stern on public finance, wrote a draft of the section in chapter 12 on that subject. The section on privatization in chapter 12 owes much to work we did with David Rosenblatt. Ines Garcia-Thoumi, Coralie Gevers, Stuti Khemani, Lawrence MacDonald, Priya Mathur, Joyce Msuya, and Mark Sundberg made valuable contributions to the book in many different but complementary ways. Lucie Albert, Jean Ponchamni, and Kerrie Quirk have provided warm support and guidance over the years.

The substance of the lectures owes much to our discussions and work with a number of World Bank colleagues, including Paul Collier, Shanta Devarajan, David Dollar, and Ian Goldin. We also received

valuable advice on a number of important issues from Monica Dasgupta, Asli Demirguç-Kunt, Daniel Kaufmann, and Michael Walton.

Under the World Bank's president, James Wolfensohn, the institution has shown tremendous leadership in ideas and action on development. We are deeply grateful to him for his inspiration, his
extraordinary commitment to fighting poverty, and his warm personal
support.

We have drawn extensively on World Bank publications, data, and
experience, and we are grateful for the creativity, dedication, and professionalism of our colleagues who conduct this work. In particular,
we have used material and ideas from the *World Development Reports*
produced in whole or part during Stern's tenure as chief economist:
the 2000/2001 report on attacking poverty, the 2002 report on building
institutions for markets, the 2003 report on sustainable development in
a dynamic world, the 2004 report on making services work for poor
people, and the 2005 report on the investment climate. We have also
drawn on the Bank's valuable Policy Research Reports, particularly
those on aid, gender, infrastructure, globalization, and land policy,
and on the *Global Economic Prospects* and *Global Development Finance*
series. This book takes forward some of the ideas set out in *A Strategy
for Development* (Stern 2001).

We have been fortunate to receive constructive comments from
many reviewers, including Philippe Aghion, Sudhir Anand, Abhijit
Banerjee, Timothy Besley, François Bourguignon, Robin Burgess,
Angus Deaton, and Peter Diamond. Angus Deaton contributed a generous *laudatio* when the lectures were presented in Munich, and he
and Peter Diamond provided great intellectual and moral support to
Stern during his time in the United States.

We are also grateful to Hans-Werner Sinn and his colleagues from
the Center for Economic Studies at the Ludwig-Maximilian University
in Munich, particularly Ulrich Hange and Martina Grass, for the great
honor of the Distinguished Fellow award given to Stern, as well as for
the warm hospitality and constructive scholarly interaction during our
pleasant visit in November 2002.

The London School of Economics has been generous in many ways
over the years. St. Catherine's College, Oxford provided valuable support in the final stages of producing this manuscript. Many of the ideas
presented here were strongly influenced by Stern's colleagues and
experiences at the EBRD. The British Academy kindly asked Stern to
give the Keynes Lecture in November 2002, and this provided an op-

portunity to discuss some of the ideas with academic and other colleagues in the United Kingdom. Further details of other practical and intellectual influences appear in the preface. We are grateful to all these institutions for their important contributions.

Paul Holtz has done a splendid job editing the manuscript. We also thank Carlos Rossel, from the World Bank, and the editors at the MIT Press for their help and advice.

We should emphasize that the World Bank, the other institutions mentioned, and the U.K. Treasury (where Stern now works) are not responsible for any of the views expressed here. That responsibility is ours alone.

Finally, we thank our families for their deep understanding and support throughout this work.

A Brief Guide to These Lectures

The purpose of this book is to propose a strategy for development. The basis of that strategy is the experience of development, development policy, and development assistance, particularly over the past half-century of extraordinary transformation. This experience tells us that we must understand development as a dynamic process of continuous change in which entrepreneurship, innovation, flexibility, and mobility are crucial. If individuals, and particularly poor people, are to be included and participate in that process, they must equip themselves, and be helped to do so, with the abilities to shape their lives.

The strategy that follows from this view of development comprises two mutually supporting ideas and sets of actions: building an investment climate that fosters entrepreneurship, innovation, productivity, and jobs, and empowering and investing in people, particularly poor people, so that they can participate in the economy and society. Small enterprises—including small farms, the most important small enterprises in developing countries—must be at the center of this strategy. It is there that most poor people earn their livings. The strategy focuses on people's ability to live their lives in the private sector and in civil society. But it also requires an active, dynamic state that fosters and invests in the economic environment and empowers and invests in its people.

This strategy builds on many theoretical ideas and is broad enough to include a great deal of existing thinking about development. But it also goes beyond many standard models and approaches, leading to new perspectives and emphases for research. The research agenda based on the strategy is large and challenging, and we identify some possible directions rather than explore them in detail.

The strategy also provides new perspectives on action. If we are correct about the strategic drivers of development, we should be asking of any action on domestic policy or external assistance what it does to advance the investment climate or to empower and invest in people. Any plan of action is, of course, dependent on where one starts, and toward the end of this book, we propose an action plan for world development based on the strategy and where we are now. We have a special opportunity in the next few years to make major breakthroughs in the fight against poverty, but we will have to act effectively on a large scale. To do that, we must base our actions on sound lessons about what works and what does not. We hope that the principles of the strategy will help us draw these lessons not just for now, but also over the future.

 This book argues that reducing poverty requires creating an environment where growth is strong and poor people can take charge of their lives—where they are their own agents of change. It is this perspective that lies behind the title: *Growth and Empowerment: Making Development Happen*. It is a dynamic story in that structural change is central, history counts, and institutions and behaviors are part of the process of change.

As Amartya Sen has argued, we can view the objectives of advancing development and raising living standards in terms of enhancing people's capabilities to act and choose as well as improving outcomes determined partly by individual or household choices. Here we suggest an approach that involves both opportunities and capabilities, or ex ante possibilities, and outcomes or ex post occurrences.

The book develops a set of ideas, drawing on the authors' experiences as students and practitioners of development. Because it is essentially a set of lectures rather than a treatise or textbook, we point to where many of these ideas could go, but do not develop those directions as far as we would have liked, had there been more time for research. We hope that interested readers will take forward some of the suggested research. In developing these ideas, we relate them to existing literature where we are aware of it and where it is relevant. But no attempt is made to be exhaustive, and no literature review is offered. In many cases, we have undoubtedly overlooked relevant, important contributions.

The book has four parts, or lectures, roughly corresponding to the structure of the Munich Lectures in Economics presented by Stern at Ludwig-Maximilian University in November 2002. Lecture I (chapters 1–4) presents evidence on the experience of development, and Lecture II (chapter 5) proposes a strategy based on our understanding of this experience. Lecture III (chapters 6–10) sets forth a research agenda arising from this strategy, while Lecture IV (chapters 11–13) shows how the ideas in the strategy can be translated into action.

Lecture I

Lecture I presents evidence on progress in developing countries over the past fifty years. It emphasizes the radical, rapid changes during this period and sets out the lessons that can be drawn from this experience in a way that forms the basis for the proposed strategy. Chapter 1 examines objectives for development and related indicators. We take it that the broad purpose of development is to raise living standards and, in particular, reduce poverty. We adopt a definition of living standards, and thus poverty, that includes income but also encompasses social and human dimensions—including empowerment, gender, education, and health.

Chapter 2 examines some of the key drivers of changes in living standards, particularly those shaping income. Thus, we analyze historical evidence on economic growth, inequality, economic structure, the environment, and international trade. We begin with growth, showing that the past fifty years have seen extraordinary growth for countries, regions, and the world. At the country level, we find that strong economic growth during one or two decades has been fairly common but that such growth is difficult to sustain for longer periods. Growth is a key driver of poverty reduction, but its influence on poverty is strongly intermediated by inequality. Accordingly, after examining growth, we look at the interrelationships among growth, poverty, and inequality. A focus on aggregate growth can obscure what is happening within an economy. Thus, we also examine the profound transformations in economic and demographic structures that are changing the face of the developing world, including shifts from agriculture to manufacturing and services, radical changes in population size and structure, and rapid urbanization.

While much of the discussion is at the country level, international influences are crucial to the development process, and these are covered in the next section of chapter 2. Radical changes in international structures of production, trade, capital flows, migration, and technology have both shaped and been determined by the development process. There is a strong link between growth and expansion of trade; openness to trade is fundamental to a competitive and creative investment climate, and access to markets is a vital determinant of economic opportunity. The extraordinary growth of the past half-century has been accompanied by powerful, often damaging change in many aspects of the environment. Going forward, a fundamental challenge will be managing environmental change along with the physical and human capital of development. Thus, the environment is a key strand in understanding the historical experience of growth, and is discussed in this chapter.

The final section of chapter 2 draws together lessons on the drivers of growth from both the preceding discussion and some of the empirical literature. The growth story that we tell is not one of steady or balanced growth. Rather, it is one of bursts, accelerations, and often slowdowns, and one of radically changing economic and social structures. Thus, what we are trying to explain and how we explain it look very different from many standard models that focus on the simple economics of savings and capital and steady and balanced growth. That is not the picture that history offers us. And at the center of the story of what drives growth we place institutions, behavior, and governance. Economic growth and structure are both profoundly influenced by institutions and governance, so the chapter concludes by reviewing the evidence on these crucial dimensions.

Chapter 3, on lessons from development policy, attempts to distill the past fifty years of development into a few key lessons. First, as described in chapter 1, we have learned that if we are to understand the purpose of development, we must look beyond income growth to advances in health, education, and human development more broadly—and beyond these, to empowerment. Second, we have learned that development is a dynamic process in which change is central, history matters, and structures are endogenous. Third, the state is not a substitute for the market but a critical complement. The challenging questions concern not so much the balance of the market relative to the state but how they combine to support development. Fourth, effective institutions and governance are crucial for growth. Failures here have often undermined or, as in cases of conflict, devastated development prospects. Fifth, global integration and openness have proven to be powerful forces for sustained growth. Sixth, growth provides the most powerful engine for reducing poverty, and trade is a crucial element of that engine. Seventh, effective development depends on the ability of people, particularly poor people, to get involved in the decisions that matter to them and to participate effectively in the economy and society and shape their lives. We refer to this ability as empowerment. Eighth, and relatedly, at a more aggregate level, reform programs imposed from outside with weak societal commitments are likely to fail.

For the purpose of understanding development and development policy, we can see these eight lessons as falling into four groups. The first, captured in the first lesson, concerns the purpose, meaning, and goals of development. The second group, comprising the second and third lessons, deals with the nature of development and the role of policy. It emphasizes the state's substantial role in catalyzing the development process. The third group, consisting of lessons four, five, and six, involves growth, its determinants, and its importance for reducing poverty. It emphasizes the centrality of institutions and governance for growth, the importance of openness and integration as engines of growth, and the link between growth and poverty reduction. Finally, the fourth group, made up of lessons seven and eight, is about empowerment, its role in effective development, and the importance of national ownership of and commitment to reform (as opposed to externally designed and imposed programs). The precise number of lessons is not important—one can always combine, separate, and add. But the broad grouping of the lessons does matter. In trying to understand the meaning of policies to shape development, we must be clear about both the nature of the processes we are examining and which approaches to analyzing them are likely to point to successful policy. And we should try to set out the lessons in a way that leads us to the specifics of a strategy.

Evidence on how we can foster development and fight poverty comes not only from structural analysis of empirical experience but also from the theoretical analysis we bring to that experience. Clearly the two must be combined, but in chapter 4 we focus on theory. Ideas about development have profoundly shaped policies and outcomes. For example, the ideas of Karl Marx, John Maynard Keynes, Joseph Schumpeter, and Friedrich Hayek have had an extraordinary influence on the policies that have been followed around the world over the past century. Our purpose in this chapter is not, however, to present the history of ideas relevant to development, but to examine some theoretical foundations in areas of direct relevance to the arguments put forth in this book. These come mainly from development economics, growth theory, and public economics. The proposed strategy draws on these ideas, but to pursue the ideas at the heart of the strategy, we need to develop a theory of public economics more focused on the processes and drivers of growth than have been the theories used until now. One part of that theory should go beyond standard microeconomic theory and venture into an analysis of the public policy of changing preferences, which seem central to the process of development.

Lecture II

Lecture II, consisting of chapter 5, presents the strategy. It is a two-pillar strategy that follows directly from the lessons of lecture I: first, build an investment climate conducive to entrepreneurship, innovation, investment, productivity, and job creation, and second, empower and invest in poor people so that they can participate in the economy and society. The strategy's emphasis on the combination of states and markets and the crucial role of institutions and governance, is based on the third group of lessons from chapter 3. The two pillars support each other and are interrelated. It would be a mistake to see the first pillar as referring only to growth and the second only to empowerment. Both focus on promoting both growth and empowerment. And both pillars derive their rationale directly from development goals, as well as from the instrumental role of those goals in driving the processes that influence other such goals. The promotion of activities that are both goals in themselves and means to other goals is a recurring theme in these lectures.

The language of the investment climate should be taken to refer to all forms of economic activity and all sizes of enterprise. We emphasize investment because we are thinking in particular about the dynamics of change, but its use has a much broader scope than a narrow interpretation of the term might bring. The first pillar is all about changing the structures in which economic activity, including investment, occurs.

Thus, in thinking about the strategy, it is important to recognize that while the pillars are distinct, they are also mutually reinforcing; they cover both development objectives and instruments for promoting those objectives, and they are about changing structures. On the distinctiveness of the pillars: while improvements in the investment climate and empowerment generally come together, there are societies where the investment climate is positive but sections of the community are largely disempowered, as with indigenous people in many countries from the United States to Guatemala. On mutual reinforcement: a strategy that improves the investment climate, and thereby growth, will often provide more economic opportunity and thus choice and empowerment for more members of society. A strategy that directly empowers poor people so that they can participate effectively—for example, through education and training—will enable them to become a force for growth. On objectives and instruments: this comes through most strongly for empowerment. Empowerment is, or should be, an explicit goal for development, but there is also growing evidence that it is a driver of development. This is particularly clear for the role of women. The report *Engendering Development* (World Bank 2001d) shows that many activities and mechanisms—including credit, education, health, agriculture, and governance—operate much more effectively when women participate strongly. On changing structures: for both pillars there is a strong emphasis on changing the structures in which entrepreneurs and individuals take their decisions; the whole approach is based on a view of development as involving processes of profound structural change and of development policy as focused on how to influence these processes.

Lecture III

The details of the strategy set the stage for the research agenda and action plan that are the subjects of lectures III and IV. Lecture III provides a sense of direction for research based on the strategy. A particular conceptual approach to development, such as the one offered here, carries implications for measurement in terms of objectives and in terms of the characterization of the processes driving development. In turn, the evidence generated feeds back into our understanding of the forces and mechanisms of development and policy. Evidence guided by and informing sound theory is a powerful force for change and should be the basis of good policy. Hence, in chapter 6, we examine how the strategy points to the data sets we should use and try to construct. First among these are household surveys designed to track the living standards of households in different circumstances. These surveys also provide information on characteristics that can help identify differences in household circumstances that are relevant for policy and on how households might change over time.

Attempts to measure a variable often lead to questions about the meaning of concepts to be measured. This applies to both the investment climate and empowerment. On the former, we have made considerable progress by asking structured questions directly of firms about the obstacles they face. Many of these data come from surveys generated in partnerships with the World Bank. These data are based on samples of firms, small and large, within a country. The evidence is quantitative—for example, number of days to get goods through customs or number of hours electricity is out—which allows comparisons across regions or countries. Basic data on outputs, inputs, sales, and the like are also collected.

Measuring empowerment poses particular challenges. The concept is likely to mean different things to different people, and many different aspects will have some relevance. For us, the central issue is people's ability to participate effectively in the economy. Thus, we look at obstacles facing individuals. Many of these arise from problems involving the transparency, functioning, and accountability of local institutions, particularly governments. Empowerment can be strongly affected by local customs, including discrimination on the basis of ethnicity, caste, or language. In many countries, positions and opportunities for women and girls are the most important empowerment issues.

Of special importance to an individual's ability to participate are education and health, the key elements of human development. Data on these areas come from both surveys and administrative sources but are often weak. Basic infrastructure for water, electricity, and transportation is crucial for development. How these services are delivered and to whom are central to empowerment. The World Bank and its partners recently embarked on a new set of surveys focused on the delivery of basic services such as health, education, and water, on how poor people are involved or excluded, and on how services can be improved (see World Bank 2003a). In some of these surveys, investigators arrive unannounced at schools and clinics and check for the presence, or often absence, of teachers, doctors, and nurses.

Taken together, the three types of surveys—of households, firms, and units delivering basic services—can provide powerful tools for implementing the strategy and understanding the role and impact of policy. This illustrates how policy can shape data collection and use and how results from the data and its analysis can shape policy. The data sets that are emerging are also valuable tools for further research.

The analysis of measurement and evaluation in chapter 6 indicates that while much of the theory and empirical work on the investment climate and empowerment are at an early stage, theory lags behind the empirical work in both cases. The next four chapters of lecture III are more theoretical, focusing on the dynamics of change along dimensions highlighted in the strategy. Chapter 7 covers the investment climate, including how we should model the processes and consequences of change in the environment for entrepreneurship. It also looks at the relationship between the investment climate and growth. And it examines in general terms how firms react to changes in the investment climate and how enterprises and other agents might influence changes.

Chapters 8 and 9 focus more on individuals than enterprises, particularly issues raised by empowerment. Chapter 8 examines the dynamics of empowerment, especially how individuals actually change their circumstances and the role that empowerment plays in this process. We examine three sets of issues. What is the role of empowerment in facilitating and accelerating the participation of disadvantaged groups in economic and political life? What role do small and medium-size enterprises play in the development and empowerment of poor people? And how can public policies facilitate the empowerment of poor people? As part of the discussion of public policy, we examine the role played by income and wealth transfers in the dynamics of empowerment and poverty reduction. The research agenda covered by chapter 8 is crucial to a key question for policy: In the fight against poverty, what is the appropriate combination of redistributive policies and of investments in opportunities for and empowerment of poor people?

Chapter 9 raises some difficult questions that go beyond standard microeconomics and briefly discusses some of the positive and normative issues raised by changing preferences. We suggest that changes in preferences are a fundamental part of the development story, particularly in education, health, migration, and gender relations. Theories of public policy based on an examination of individual incentives and welfare usually assume that preferences are given. The conceptual and theoretical challenges that follow from relaxing this assumption are not straightforward but are, in our view, unavoidable if we are to come to grips with some of the major policy questions of development.

In chapter 10 we examine some of the underlying mechanisms shaping the investment climate and empowerment from a political perspective, particularly the political economy of reform. We have argued that institutions and governance, and how they change, are at the heart of the development story—and examining how they change takes us directly into these areas. The issues that arise include the political changes that may be involved in changing participation, exclusion, and inequality. In some cases, the ability of some individuals to shape their lives can increase without reducing the empowerment of others. But in other cases, there is likely to be serious political opposition. Changes in the investment climate and empowerment are inherently political, and we are led to examine constituencies for and against change and how they might change over time. At their extreme, political and economic differences can generate violent conflict that is profoundly damaging to development.

Lecture IV

The final part of the book, lecture IV, concerns action. This lecture has two purposes. The first, in the immediate term, is to argue that we are at a special point in time where we have a unique opportunity—in relation to international understanding, commitment, and resources—to accelerate development. We have an opportunity to include many people who have been excluded and to make substantial inroads into poverty. The second purpose, less dependent on a point in time, is to show how the ideas behind our development strategy can be translated into relevant, practical policy and to identify policy directions in which these ideas lead.

The first task in chapter 11 is to assess the challenge in terms of where we start and the Millennium Development Goals (MDGs). These goals, established in 2000 by a large gathering of heads of state at the United Nations, set explicit, time-bound targets for 2015 based on a multidimensional view of development, in the spirit of lecture I. We argue that these goals can be achieved only if we move to a larger scale in our actions, in terms of both effectiveness and resources. Achieving the goals will also require strong partnerships between rich and poor countries and between the state, the private sector, and civil society. In addition, we will have to measure progress carefully, including delivery on commitments of different participants in the partnerships, and design that measurement in a way that allows us to constantly learn and adapt. If we are to act effectively and on a large scale, we will have to learn quickly and apply what we learn. The ability to learn is much stronger if it is designed into policies and action from their inception.

Chapter 12 examines what developing countries can do to improve their policies, institutions, and governance. It does this from the perspective of public finances: we look at macroeconomic balance and the expenditure and revenue sides of the budget. In large measure, the role of the state and the scope of public action are defined by the powers to tax and spend and how these powers are exercised. The organization of economic activity into public or private, and how the sectors relate, is also a key factor shaping the role of the state in economic life. Privatization has been a subject of changing enthusiasms in the economics profession and has often been marked by dogmatism. The chapter argues that the issues are not simply how much privatization, where, and how, but how to build appropriate combinations of private and public action. In this analysis, we need a careful approach differentiated by country and history, sector and type of activity, and the nature and balance of objectives. From the broad perspective of the public finances, the approach of the strategy highlights dynamism and inclusion in assessing issues, taking us beyond standard theoretical approaches, which focus on revenue, incentives, and efficiency.

Chapter 13, the last in the book, looks at international issues, particularly trade and aid. For developing countries, involvement in world trade is crucial to the competition and openness needed for a strong investment climate. Such involvement can bring ideas, creativity, technology, and benchmarks. Access to the markets of developed countries is a central element of economic opportunity, particularly markets where developing countries have a comparative advantage. The Doha round of international trade negotiations, launched in November 2001, puts developing countries' needs at the top of the agenda and provides a unique opportunity for advancing development. It is an opportunity that could be squandered, resulting in severe disillusionment, or one that could be grasped—greatly accelerating development, to the benefit of all. This is a challenge for multilateralism.

The second part of the chapter examines aid. The MDGs will not be achieved without a substantial increase in aid, as this chapter documents. Aid is just one part—and one of the smaller parts—of international flows. Foreign direct investment and worker remittances, both strongly influenced by the investment climate, are currently bigger parts of the story of generating the resources, technology, and ideas required for development. However, aid is a crucial complement to the recipient country's improvements in policies and institutions, including those that promote integration.

Some brief concluding remarks are offered after the four lectures. They argue that this is a special time for researchers and practitioners. As researchers, we face a hunger for knowledge about development from people (including ourselves) anxious to change the world. And we have a growing body of theory, exciting new intellectual challenges, and a world that is taking evidence and data more seriously. There has never been a better time to be a researcher in development.

As practitioners, we have a special opportunity to make the world a better place. Taking this opportunity will require international commitment and partnership. It will require changing policies and resources. But extraordinary gains are available to all of us. It is a time for learning—but also a time for action.

Growth and Empowerment

Lecture I   Experience

The past half-century has been an extraordinary period, economically, socially and politically. During that time, we have seen remarkable changes in the global landscape: the fastest economic growth in the world economy in human history; decolonization and a dramatic expansion in democracy around the world; rapid urbanization and far-reaching structural change; great strides in literacy and life expectancy in most countries; and profound changes in social relations. At the same time, hundreds of millions of people have been left out of progress or have seen deep declines in living standards, and many millions have had their lives cut short by poverty, ignorance, and disease.

Chapter 1 explores the goals of development and how we have fared in combating poverty. Development is not solely a matter of increasing a country's income-generating capacity. It is also about education, health, security, opportunity, empowerment, and other measures of well-being. Chapter 2 examines development viewed as a dynamic process of changing structures and institutions, and reviews the experience of developing countries over the past fifty years. Chapter 3 outlines policy lessons that can be drawn from development experience, setting these out in a way that underpins the strategy proposed in lecture II. Finally, chapter 4 describes the theoretical antecedents of the strategy, drawing on Hirschman, Schumpeter, Sen, and the modern theories of growth, development and public economics.

1 Living Standards and Poverty

Development is about people changing their lives for the better; it is about expanding their ability to make choices about the things that matter to them. Important as income is for the ability to shape one's life, development is about much more than that. Indeed, over the past twenty years, the development community's concept of development has broadened from a narrow focus on income and spending to include education, health, and social and political participation. Poverty, as the absence of development, must be understood from a similar perspective. Accordingly, poverty is now generally defined as the inability to achieve basic prescribed standards in most or all of these areas.

There have been many influences on this broadening perspective of development and poverty, and prominent among them has been the work of Amartya Sen. He has consistently emphasized that poverty entails the inability to achieve standards rather than simply whether standards are achieved. Poor people, he argues, lack fundamental freedoms to live lives they value (Sen 1999). They often do not have adequate food, shelter, education, and health care. They are extremely vulnerable to illness, violence, economic dislocation, and natural disasters. They are poorly served by institutions of the state and society. And they often find themselves powerless to influence key decisions affecting their lives.

It is poor people themselves who can best provide an understanding of the meaning of poverty, and they identify the same type of issues that have been increasingly emphasized in the literature over the past two decades. For the World Bank's *World Development Report 2000/ 2001*, researchers interviewed more than 60,000 poor people in sixty countries, asking them to articulate the meaning of their poverty (Narayan and others 2000). The researchers summarized what they heard from poor people in terms of development—and its absence, poverty—being about opportunity, empowerment, and security.

There is deep moral imperative to fight poverty, as we argue in lecture IV. But if we are to provide a serious strategy for promoting development and fighting poverty, we must go beyond passionate commitment, important though that is, and show both what we mean by development and poverty and what forces and mechanisms shape them. This chapter is devoted to the first of these tasks. In this first lecture (chapters 1–4), we place special emphasis on opportunity and empowerment. These are not only goals in themselves, as highlighted by poor people, they are also means to overcome poverty as measured, for example, by income and health. Indeed, the strategy described in chapter 5 is largely about creating opportunity and enhancing empowerment. But this approach to policy does not neglect security: the policies and strategy we propose also work to enhance security.

The coincidence of ends and means, or goals and instruments, is clear when we think about poverty in terms of education and health. Both are ends in themselves in that they enhance people's lives and capabilities. But they are also means to income, inclusion, and security.

With this evolution in our understanding, assessing development progress has become more complex. If we adopt a notion of well-being that extends beyond income and consumption levels, then we are arguing that poverty too has multiple dimensions. Because measures of the various dimensions of poverty do not necessarily change tightly together, it is possible for individuals, communities, and countries to do quite well in some dimensions and less well in others (Drèze and Sen 1989).

This chapter charts development progress along its various dimensions, motivated by the conceptual basis just described. It shows that over the past few decades, there has been remarkable progress in many countries, containing most of the population of the developing world. But that progress has been far from uniform, and some countries and communities, particularly in Africa, have fared very badly. Moreover, progress has varied enormously across different dimensions.

Income Poverty

Any broad assessment of development progress must make use of income and consumption measures of poverty, but even these more narrow measures are not straightforward. We have to decide what is included in income; dealing with returns to assets such as housing and nonmarket labor can be difficult. We have to decide how to measure household income or consumption when households often earn and consume as a unit and vary in their demographic composition (often, "equivalence scales" are used to address this issue). We have to specify the period for income, which can vary considerably across months. In examining change in incomes over time, we also have to take careful account of price indexes, often a difficult task (see Deaton 2005). And we have to specify poverty lines. These are often specified at the country level in relative terms (see Fields 1980 for a discussion of work on this issue in developing countries of the 1960s and 1970s), but for the most part we will be examining absolute poverty.

Poverty is commonly measured as the percentage of the population with incomes below an absolute poverty line defined in local currency. National statistical agencies use various methods to set poverty lines, including cost of basic needs and food-energy intake methods. Other measures of poverty differentiate between people located near the poverty line and those far below it.

The absolute poverty line generally used to monitor global poverty trends, involving comparisons across countries, was first defined in the World Bank's *World Development Report 1990* and was recently updated by Chen and Ravallion (2004). That line currently stands at just over $1 a person per day in 1993 consumption purchasing power parity prices. To make comparisons across countries, purchasing power in local currencies must be converted to dollars. This generally involves comparing the cost of an appropriate basket of goods in the two currencies. This is called purchasing power parity, and it poses major challenges in choosing the basket and getting comparable price data.

The original derivation of this international poverty line is explained in Ravallion, Datt, and van de Walle (1991). It was chosen as being representative of the poverty lines found in low-income countries. Specifically, it is the median of the official poverty lines for Bangladesh, China, India, Indonesia, Nepal, Pakistan, Tanzania, Thailand, Tunisia, and Zambia. Absolute poverty lines in such countries are generally constructed to represent the incomes needed to purchase a very basic basket of food items, chosen to meet minimal nutritional requirements, and a similarly minimal set of essential nonfood items.

Lanjouw and Stern (1998) note that in the early 1980s, the most common poverty line for India translated roughly into the income needed to buy about 1 kilogram of wheat a day in the northern village of

Palanpur. That was only about one-quarter of what an agricultural laborer, the poorest member of a poor village, would have been able to earn with a day's work in the village. Although agricultural laborers cannot find work every day and have dependents, it is clear from this example that poverty rates based on such low poverty lines must be deemed conservative estimates in that there are many people with incomes above this level living in extremely difficult circumstances.

When poverty is viewed as a *relative* phenomenon, the focus is on the well-being of a given individual (or group of individuals) against the standard of the broader reference group of which he or she is part. This contrasts with the absolute notion of poverty, which focuses on the ability—or lack of it—to buy a given bundle of goods. From the relative perspective, a person might be described as poor if his or her income falls in the bottom fifth of the population distribution. In general, if one is interested in a snapshot of poverty in a specific place, the transparency and ready intuition of the relative notion of poverty have much to recommend it. But it is clearly more difficult to adopt a relative notion of poverty when the goal is to compare poverty across regions.

Even when specified in absolute terms, poverty lines in rich countries and regions typically have greater purchasing power than do poverty lines in poor areas. Thus, in practice, there seems to be a relative concept at work. Often this is made explicitly relative, and poverty is defined, as in the United Kingdom, relative to the median. This approach may be partly influenced by a notion of poverty in terms of exclusion: people are poor if they cannot afford the patterns of activity of the society in which they live. But it may also be that individuals evaluate their own consumption by reference to the consumption of others, so that relative deprivation is an important and direct determinant of welfare and behavior.

Adopting a relativist approach has much to be said for it in understanding poverty in a given society. But it does cause problems for comparisons over time and across societies. If the poverty line is set proportional to mean or median income, as is often the case in Western Europe, then it behaves a lot like a measure of inequality. If everyone's income went up in proportion, there would be no reduction in poverty even when poor people's absolute living standards had risen.

Income poverty is best measured using data from household surveys. Over the past decade, there has been a rapid, and very welcome, expansion of household survey data in developing countries. The global poverty estimates produced by the World Bank in 1990 were based on 22 surveys for 22 countries, while those produced a decade later were based on more than 400 surveys for 96 countries. Many countries today have multiple surveys across different years. Still, even though we have come a long way in our ability to measure global poverty, severe difficulties remain, and we must be cautious when interpreting evidence.

One of the problems is consistency between consumption levels calculated from household surveys and final consumption as estimated from national accounts. Consumption estimated from surveys is typically lower than consumption from national accounts. Deaton (2005) calculates that the average ratio of the two is 0.860 (with a standard error of 0.029), or an even lower 0.779 (S.E. 0.072) when weighted by population. The major exception to this rule is sub-Saharan Africa, where the average ratio of survey to national accounts consumption is unity in the unweighted, and greater than unity in the weighted calculations. But for member countries of the Organization for Economic Cooperation and Development (OECD), where survey and national accounts quality is presumably the highest, household surveys pick up only a little more than three-quarters of the national accounts consumption. And other developing regions also show the discrepancy, with India exhibiting particularly low ratios. These discrepancies pose major problems in assessing growth rates of consumption over time, because the ratios of the two consumption measures do not stay constant (see Deaton 2005 for a discussion of some possible reasons).

Having examined some of the challenges in defining and measuring poverty, it is time to look at the numbers themselves. The best assessment of recent global progress comes from Chen and Ravallion (2004), who examine progress in the period from 1981 to 2001. The authors draw on 454 national surveys spanning 97 developing countries and on the most recent price data possible. They find that the percentage of the population in the developing world living on less than $1 a day was 21 percent in 2001 (table 1.1). In absolute terms, at the turn of the century about 1.1 billion people—one in five in developing countries—lived below the $1 a day poverty line.[1] If the $2 a day line is used instead, the number in poverty rises to 2.7 billion, or more than half the population of the developing world.

During the past two decades, the developing world has made dramatic progress in reducing income poverty, notwithstanding the size of the challenge that remains. Chen and Ravallion estimate that the $1

Table 1.1
Absolute poverty

Region	$1.08 per day			$2.15 per day		
	1981	1990	2001	1981	1990	2001
Number of poor people (millions)						
East Asia	795.6	472.2	284.3	1169.8	1116.3	867.9
of which China	633.7	374.8	211.6	875.8	824.6	593.6
Eastern Europe and Central Asia	1.1	2.3	17.6	8.3	56.4	93.5
Latin America and Caribbean	35.6	49.3	49.8	98.9	124.6	128.2
Middle East and North Africa	9.1	5.5	7.1	51.9	50.9	69.8
South Asia	474.8	462.3	428.4	821.1	957.5	1059.1
of which India	382.4	357.4	358.6	630	731.4	826
Sub-Saharan Africa	163.6	226.8	315.8	287.9	381.6	516
Total	1,479.8	1,218.5	1,103	2,438	2,687.3	2,734.6
Head count index (percent)						
East Asia	57.7	29.6	15.6	84.8	69.9	47.6
of which China	63.8	33	16.6	88.1	72.6	46.7
Eastern Europe and Central Asia	0.3	0.5	3.7	1.9	12.1	19.7
Latin America and Caribbean	9.7	11.3	9.5	26.9	28.4	24.5
Middle East and North Africa	5.1	2.3	2.4	28.9	21.4	23.2
South Asia	51.5	41.3	31.1	89.1	85.5	76.9
of which India	54.4	42.1	34.7	89.6	86.1	79.9
Sub-Saharan Africa	41.6	44.6	46.9	73.3	75	76.6
Total	40.3	27.9	21.3	66.4	61.5	52.9

Note: The head count index is the percentage of the population living in households with a consumption of income per person less than the poverty line.
Source: Chen and Ravallion (2004).

a day poverty rate has dropped from 40 percent in 1981 to 21 percent in 2001. This means that the number of desperately poor people in the developing world dropped by more than 375 million between 1981 and 2001, notwithstanding an increase in population of around 1.5 billion over that period.

This decline resulted largely from the reduction in the number of poor people in China and, to a much lesser extent, in India (figure 1.1). In the 1980s the number of poor Chinese fell by a remarkable 260 million. Most of this reduction occurred in rural areas as a result of the program of market-oriented reforms in agriculture and elsewhere promoted by Deng Xiao Ping. This must be regarded as the most important event of poverty reduction in human history (see below). In India

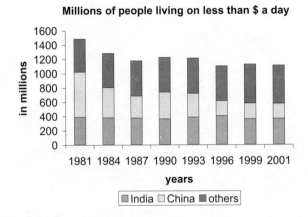

Millions of people living on less than $ a day

Figure 1.1
China has achieved dramatic reductions in poverty. *Source:* Chen and Ravallion (2004).

the number of poor people declined by an estimated 25 million between 1981 and 2001 (and there are some—such as Bhalla (2002)—who would argue that the decrease was much greater than this).

Though very significant, the fall in global poverty was not always steady. Between 1987 and 1993, poverty appears to have increased slightly, after agricultural setbacks in both India and China and macroeconomic difficulty in India. Nevertheless, on average since 1990, the global $1 a day poverty rate has fallen by 1.16 percentage points a year. Sustained progress at this rate would be more than enough to halve the 1990 aggregate poverty rate of 28 percent by 2015—meeting, at the global level, one of the Millennium Development Goals set by the international community.

Regional variations have been considerable, however. The number of poor people has fallen in East Asia and South Asia but risen in Eastern Europe, the former Soviet Union, the Middle East, Latin America, and sub-Saharan Africa. Changes have been especially dramatic in countries during periods of severe macroeconomic crises, such as in Argentina and Indonesia.

Assessments of longer-term poverty trends are necessarily more tentative, but Bourguignon and Morrisson (2002) apply roughly the same poverty line to data from thirty-three countries for the past two centuries. (Given the length of their time period, their data sets are inevitably less comparable than those used by Ravallion and Chen for the 1980s and 1990s.) They find that global poverty rates have declined

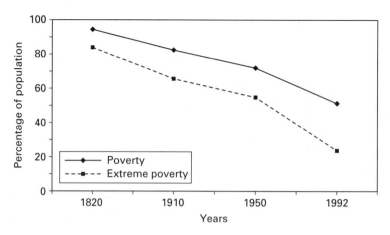

Figure 1.2
Around the world, the share of poor people has declined since 1820. *Source:* Bourguignon and Morrisson (2002).

steadily, from a high of 84 percent in 1820 to around 24 percent in 1992 (figure 1.2). Their analysis indicates that after World War II, poverty rates fell fastest in the 1950s and 1960s (from 55 to 36 percent) and less rapidly in the 1970s (from 36 to 32 percent).

Overall this is a picture of remarkable achievement, driven largely by poverty reduction in Asia—by far the most populous continent and the one about which so many commentators were pessimistic forty to fifty years ago. Still, it is crucial to recognize that poverty has increased sharply elsewhere, particularly in sub-Saharan Africa.

Looking beyond the global picture, country-by-country monitoring of poverty offers an alternative view on the evolution of poverty over time. It also generally provides a higher level of statistical reliability. An analysis of country-level experiences with poverty reduction confirms the strong link between economic growth and poverty reduction. But across countries, there is wide variation in the degree to which poor people benefit from a given growth rate. Ravallion (2001) points out, for example, that while on average across countries, poverty declines by about 2 percentage points for every 1 percentage point increase in economic growth, the 95 percent confidence interval around this average ranges from 0.5 to 3.5 percent. (The confidence interval reflects the range in which the value can be expected to fall with a given probability. In this case, there is a 95 percent chance that the actual poverty reduction will fall between 0.5 to 3.5 percent—or, to put it another way, a 5 percent chance that it will fall outside even that broad range.)

Nearly all of this heterogeneity can be accounted for by differences in countries' initial levels of inequality. The inequalities that limit poor people's participation in economic activity are related to social, sectoral (for example, urban or rural), spatial, and other factors. Even within countries, there may be considerable heterogeneity across regions in the extent to which poverty responds to growth. Datt and Ravallion (2002) show, for example, that India's economic growth in the 1990s did not take place in the states where it would have the biggest impact on poverty nationally. States with relatively low initial levels of rural development and human capital were less able to translate economic growth into significant reductions in poverty.

Assessments of the rate of global poverty reduction are controversial. Our statements and judgments here are based almost entirely on the work of Ravallion and Chen for the 1980s and 1990s and Bourguignon and Morrisson for earlier periods. In our view, these are the most careful analyses and painstaking assembly of available data. There will always be problems of measurement and definition, some of which are discussed briefly above. And there will always be problems of data comparability given that surveys vary in the quality of their execution and that different definitions and measurement techniques are adopted by different countries at different times. That is why great care, skill, and judgment are needed in assembling data for international comparisons and changes over time.

We should note, however, that there are others who take a different view of how the numbers have changed over time. Surjit Bhalla (2002), for example, argues that poverty rates have fallen faster than some analysts and organizations (such as the World Bank) have suggested. The basis of his argument is that the growth of consumption in national accounts is likely to be a more reliable indicator of growth in consumption than are the aggregates from household surveys. If consumption within the surveys is scaled up for this effect then, given that consumption in the national accounts has been growing faster than in the surveys, poverty falls more rapidly than indicated by the surveys. But it is not clear that the national accounts figures are more reliable or that they can be applied within the surveys to scale up uniformly across the distribution. Income distribution may have changed, and the accuracy of recording of consumption and survey response may vary across the distribution. Others, such as Reddy and Pogge

(2003), argue that the World Bank has been overestimating falls in poverty. Their arguments appear to be based in large measure on the specification and adjustment of poverty lines over time.

Our purpose here is not to evaluate these other claims but to present what we believe to be the best data available—while warning of the difficulties of measurement. (For other careful and considered evaluations of the difficulties of measurement and movements in poverty, readers should consult Deaton 2005 and Ravallion 2003.)

Profiles of Income Poverty—People and Regions

To understand poverty and design policies and interventions to combat it, we need to understand not only how poverty has changed over time but also the characteristics of poor people, including where they live. In other words, we need to construct a poverty profile. Such a profile is key to understanding deeper questions about why people are poor and what factors will enable them to escape poverty (Lipton and Ravallion 1995).

Poverty profiles for developing countries have improved steadily thanks to the growing number of data sources and increased ability of analysts to apply statistical and qualitative techniques to the data. What these profiles show is that, unsurprisingly, the characteristics of poverty vary across countries as a result of differences in geography, population, history, government, institutional structures, and many other factors. But there are also many common features.

First, in most countries, households with high dependency ratios (non-working-age family members relative to working-age family members) are more likely to be poor than is the general population. High dependency ratios are often found among households with young children, but also among the elderly and among households headed by women, particularly widows.

Second, in most countries, poor people have less education than the population average. In areas with very low average education levels (such as parts of India), the poorest people are generally completely illiterate. In countries where average education is higher (such as Latin America), poor people are those with only primary or lower secondary schooling.

Third, disabled people make up 15 to 20 percent of the population in poverty in developing countries (Elwan 1999). Much of the disability in these countries stems from preventable impairments, and in many cases disability could be eliminated through treatment or alleviated though rehabilitation. Conflicts and accidents are also important causes of disability. During conflicts, both soldiers and civilians are at risk from active hostilities, as well as from unexploded ordnance and land mines. Exclusion and marginalization reduce opportunities for the disabled to contribute productively to the household and the community and increase the risk of falling into poverty. Attitudinal barriers, physical inaccessibility, and lack of learning opportunities can block access to education and employment opportunities, reducing opportunities for income and social participation.

Countries vary considerably in their social composition, but a fourth common feature of the poverty profile is that in many countries, certain population groups suffer a much higher risk of poverty (see below). In India scheduled castes and tribes (the lowest-status groups, including those formerly labeled "untouchables") are poorer than higher castes. In many other countries, certain ethnic groups are highly represented among the poor. These groups are not always small minorities in their countries. Groups defined in terms of religious belief or language can also vary markedly in poverty within countries.

Fifth, in most countries, poverty is higher in rural than in urban areas. Moreover, these sectors are heterogeneous. For example, rural populations living in relatively densely populated areas, with access to a modicum of infrastructure services (particularly transportation and irrigation), tend to be less poor than populations in remote regions and dispersed settlements. In urban areas, poverty tends to be higher in small towns and cities than in major metropolitan areas. Almost three-quarters of the world's poor people live in rural areas. In the fifty-two countries for which separate rural and urban income data are available, 73 percent of poor people live in rural areas compared with just 63 percent of the population. In fact, all developing countries, whatever their income level, show high rural poverty. In the least developed countries, where most of the population is poor, the rural poverty rate is nearly 82 percent (World Bank 2003g). These numbers must be taken with a grain of salt because definitions of urban and rural differ markedly across countries, and this makes comparison difficult (Lanjouw and Lanjouw 2001). Nonetheless, the broad point that the incidence of poverty is higher in rural areas is robust.

Sixth, geographical variation in poverty is generally quite marked. Even in small countries like Guatemala, Malawi, and Nepal, spatial heterogeneity in poverty is significant, as shown by poverty mapping techniques that combine household survey data with population census data. Demombynes and others (forthcoming) show that the greater the degree of spatial disaggregation at which poverty can be measured in a country, the more heterogeneity one generally observes. That said, poverty maps should be interpreted with caution, because there is no way to display standard errors on the maps. These estimation techniques are still in their infancy, and the maps tend to be inaccurate at a very disaggregated level.

Finally, in many countries, casual wage employment is an important correlate of poverty. Poor people are typically not employed by government or by large, formal sector enterprises. Instead they work in small private enterprises, usually in the informal sector. In rural areas, casual agricultural wage laborers on small farms tend to be poor. The analog in urban areas is informal sector casual labor in microenterprises. Overall, much of poor people's employment occurs in the service sectors. An analysis of household surveys across developing countries provides useful information on where poor people work (Dethier and others 2003).

Consider the evidence for these points. First, the wealth of household data that we have shows that private enterprise is the main source of economic opportunity for poor people. Of the world's 1.1 billion people living on less than $1 a day, only a small fraction work in the public sector. In Bangladesh, for example, only around 1 percent of people in the poorest income quintile are employed by the public sector, compared with more than 10 percent of the richest quintile. A similar pattern holds across countries. Within the private sector, small and medium-size firms account for by far the largest share of employment (table 1.2). In a dozen countries studied, employment in large firms— those with more than 100 people—ranges from just 1 percent in Madagascar to 36 percent in Uzbekistan. This finding is consistent with studies of formal sector enterprises, which find that small firms are more prevalent in developing countries (Snodgrass and Biggs 1986, Tybout 1999). Small and medium-size enterprises are an especially important source of employment for poor people.

Among small enterprises, poor people are concentrated in microfirms and individual entrepreneurship, much of it in the informal sector. In Panama, for example, 88 percent of people in the poorest quintile work in firms with fewer than ten employees, compared with 43 percent of those in the richest quintile. By contrast, jobs in large firms are mainly for the better off: in Pakistan, people in the richest

Table 1.2
Employment distribution by firm size for selected countries: Evidence from household surveys (in percent, for adult employed population)

Country	Small			Medium			Large		
	Total	Poorest quintile	Richest quintile	Total	Poorest quintile	Richest quintile	Total	Poorest quintile	Richest quintile
Ecuador	74	90	58	13	7	15	14	3	26
Guatemala	77	90	61	13	7	22	9	3	18
India	83	88	74	6	6	8	11	6	19
Kyrgyz	46	45	38	43	45	45	11	10	17
Madagascar	99	100	95	1	0	3	1	0	2
Nicaragua	75	89	65	14	9	18	12	3	17
Pakistan	57	88	50	30	12	35	13	1	15
Panama	57	88	43	18	7	22	25	4	36
Paraguay	81	97	68	11	2	18	8	1	15
Russia	12	16	12	45	46	46	42	40	42
South Africa	52	81	36	22	10	29	26	6	31
Uzbekistan	15	19	13	49	51	43	36	30	44

Note: Firm sizes: Small = less than 10 employees; medium = between 11 and 100 employees except for South Africa and Paraguay (between 11 and 50) and India (between 11 and 20); large = more than 100 employees except for South Africa and Paraguay (more than 50) and India (more than 20). Firms include nonagricultural as well as agricultural firms.
Source: Dethier and others (2003), using country household surveys.

quintile are fifteen times more likely to be working in a large firm than are people in the poorest quintile (see table 1.2).

Moving beyond these common features, how has the poverty profile changed over time? Some countries have made concerted efforts to raise incomes of groups that poverty analyses highlight as particularly poor. Although some countries have made progress, the general poverty profile does not tend to shift dramatically over time. Safety nets and other social policies that target poor people can make a difference, but they have not always succeeded in changing the underlying process that generates poverty in the first place.

The common features described above show that overcoming poverty requires expanding opportunities for work in rural areas and small and medium enterprises. For that to occur, we argue throughout these lectures, it is necessary to have a climate that, first, gives private individuals confidence in the future, thus inducing them to invest; and second, empowers poor people, allowing them to participate and be included in the economy and society.

Poverty beyond Income

As argued in the introduction to this chapter, poverty is about much more than income. Accordingly, economic growth is not the only source of poverty reduction. Of special importance in reducing poverty—as both ends and means—are education and health. Both are, quite rightly, central to goals for and assessments of progress in poverty reduction.

Many developing countries have made major progress in improving education and health outcomes by targeting these goals directly and applying new approaches, knowledge, and technology rather than just waiting for the effects of income growth to improve these indicators. For example, during the twentieth century, infant mortality fell sharply all along the income spectrum, including in the poorest countries. In 1950 a typical country with per capita income of $8,000 (measured in 1995 dollars) would have had an infant mortality rate of about 45 per 1,000 live births. By 1970 a country at the same real income level would have had an infant mortality rate of about 30 per 1,000 live births—and by 1995, 15 per 1,000 (World Bank 1998c).

Such improvements in health indicators are remarkable by historical standards. Table 1.3 shows the secular increase in life expectancy at

Table 1.3
Birthrates and life expectancy by country or region, selected years

	Births per 100				Population life expectancy at birth (in years, average for both sexes)			
	1820	1900	1950	1998	1820	1900	1950	1999
France	3.19	2.19	2.05	1.26	37	47	65	78
United Kingdom	4.02	2.93	1.62	1.30	40	50	69	77
West Europe	3.74	3.08	1.83	1.00	36	46	67	78
United States	5.52	3.23	2.40	1.44	39	47	68	77
Japan	2.62	3.24	2.81	0.95	34	44	61	81
Russia	4.13	4.80	2.65	0.88	28	32	65	67
Brazil	5.43	4.60	4.44	2.10	27	36	45	67
Mexico	n.a.	4.69	4.56	2.70	n.a.	33	50	72
Latin America	n.a.	n.a.	4.19	2.51	27	35	51	69
China	n.a.	4.12	3.70	1.60	n.a.	24	41	71
India	n.a.	4.58	4.50	2.80	21	24	32	60
Asia	n.a.	n.a.	4.28	2.30	23	24	40	66
Africa	n.a.	n.a.	4.92	3.90	23	24	38	52
World	n.a.	n.a.	3.74	2.30	31	31	49	66

Source: Maddison (2001).

birth for a selected number of developing countries and regions. For the world as a whole, life expectancy more than doubled (from thirty-one to sixty-six years) in the twentieth century, after increasing only slightly over most of the nineteenth century. (Unless otherwise noted, the data in this section are from Goldin, Rogers, and Stern 2002.) In developing countries, life expectancy increased by more than twenty years in the fifty years after 1950, rising from the forties to the mid-sixties. Education improvements have also been remarkable. Whereas in 1970 nearly two in four adults in developing countries were illiterate, now it is only one in four. Table 1.4 shows illiteracy data broken down by gender, primary school enrollment rates, fertility rates, child mortality rates, and immunization indicators for the past three decades. The extraordinary health and education achievements depicted by table 1.4 contradict those who claim that there have been few achievements in economic development or who argue that things have been getting worse. Still, there have been important divergences from the overall picture, as with the decline in life expectancy in many African countries due to HIV/AIDS.

Table 1.4
Education and health indicators

Education	School enrollment, primary (%) (gross)				Illiteracy rate, adult females (% of females ages 15 and above)				Illiteracy rate, adult males (% of males ages 15 and above)			
	1970	1980	1990	2000	1970	1980	1990	2000	1970	1980	1990	2000
East Asia and Pacific	89	111	121	106	57	42	29	21	30	20	12	8
Europe and Central Asia	—	99	98	95	8	7	5	4	4	3	2	1
Latin America and the Caribbean	107	105	106	132	30	23	17	12	22	17	13	10
Middle East and North Africa	70	87	96	95	83	73	60	49	56	45	34	26
South Asia	71	77	90	98	82	75	66	58	55	48	41	35
Sub-Saharan Africa	51	80	74	79	82	72	60	48	62	51	40	31

Health	Fertility rate (total births per woman)				Disease prevention immunization DPT (% of children under 12 months)				Under 5 mortality rates (per 1,000 live births)			
	1970	1980	1990	2000	1970	1980	1990	2000	1970	1980	1990	2000
East Asia and Pacific	5.72	3.06	2.44	2.12	—	38	90	85	125	77	58	44
CEE/CIS and Baltic States	2.65	2.47	2.26	1.57	—	~90	77	93	76	58	44	38
Latin America and the Caribbean	5.25	4.09	3.14	2.56	—	38	71	87	123	84	54	36
Middle East and North Africa	6.74	6.17	4.75	3.41	—	~35	86	88	196	132	81	62
South Asia	5.98	5.26	4.06	3.29	—	6	67	57	206	176	128	100
Sub-Saharan Africa	6.62	6.63	6.07	5.20	—	16	57	46	223	194	180	174

Note: Data for education for 2000 actually refer to 1999.
Sources: World Bank (2003c, 2003g), WHO/UNICEF Joint Monitoring Programme (2001), Hill, Pande, and Jones (1997), and Hill and others (1998).

Advances in education and health have greatly improved the welfare of individuals and families throughout the developing world. Not only are education and health valuable in themselves, they also increase income-earning capacity. Although macroeconomic analyses of the effects of education on growth have been somewhat ambiguous, microeconomic evidence on the returns to education is overwhelming and robust. Each additional year of education increases the average worker's wages by 5 to 10 percent. And educating women is a particularly effective way to raise the human development levels of children. Better-educated mothers have healthier children, and their greater productivity in the labor force raises household income and so increases child survival rates—partly because, compared with men, women tend to spend additional income in ways that benefit children more.

The dramatic improvements in life expectancy are attributable to changes in education and the physical and social environment, but are also partly the result of public health actions. The control of diarrheal diseases, including the development of oral rehydration therapy to reduce child mortality, is one example. Another is education, particularly of women, on how to recognize the need for and use of such therapies and more generally on hygiene and how to use improved water supplies. Smallpox eradication, made possible by advances in public health research and effective program management, is another example of a successful twentieth-century public health effort.

In the poorest countries, increases in average incomes are strongly associated with increases in life expectancy. But as per capita income rises, this relationship flattens out and even disappears in richer countries. If we plot the international relationship between life expectancy and national income in current purchasing power parity dollars for 2000, we discover a nonmonotonicity around $5,000 per capita, driven by two factors: the collapse of life expectancy in Russia in the 1990s (reflecting the stresses of transition from the command economy) and the spread of AIDS in Africa, particularly South Africa. Neither of these reversals in life expectancy stemmed primarily from falls in income and so do not undermine the basic relationship. But they do remind us that health is shaped by much more than income (Deaton 2003c).

Many economists believe that the association between income and health reflects the operation of a third factor, particularly education or behavior, including time preferences and attitudes toward risk. People who are impatient or lack self-control are less likely to invest in their health and acquire the skills that generate higher income. Such arguments also focus on the role of health-related behaviors—such as smoking, drinking, and lack of exercise—often correlated with both low income and poor health.

The numerous studies cited by Angus Deaton (2003c) in a recent survey of, among other things, results derived from household data show convincingly that infant and child mortality in developing countries results primarily from poverty. Saying that poverty is a major determinant of health does not, of course, imply that the social environment is not important for individual health, let alone that individual health is unrelated to individual characteristics and the provision of personal medical care. Deaton cites several cases where reductions in deprivation in one dimension not only benefited individuals directly, they also helped relieve other deprivations, including poor health. Examples include land ownership (see Bliss and Stern 1978),[2] democratic rights (England in the 1870s, southern United States in the 1960s), women's agency (health and fertility in India), and income (through better nutrition or freedom from stress). This type of argument is central to Sen's (1999) thesis in *Development and Freedom*.

Studies in the United Kingdom, United States, and elsewhere show that an individual's position in social hierarchies affects his or her health status (see the references cited in Deaton 2003c, p. 151). The reasons are not entirely clear. It may be that ethnic, race, or gender discrimination is so severe that it is actually a health hazard. It may also be that such outcomes are the result of lower-quality health care in (for example) areas with large minority populations. Nevertheless, it appears likely that some social mechanism—perhaps the ability to control one's life—not only has direct effects on welfare but also affects health outcomes.[3]

Vulnerability

The discussion so far has emphasized poor people's low levels of income, health, and education. But volatility around these low levels is also a great concern. Poor people are extremely vulnerable to sudden drops in income or increases in spending—for example, as a result of illness, natural disaster, or economic shock. Responding to these unexpected occurrences requires material resources; without them, households are often forced to devise coping strategies, such as taking children out of school and putting them to work. But these coping strategies often increase the household's long-run vulnerability and deprivation on nonincome dimensions. Thus, many of the elements that reduce a household's vulnerability are linked to its ability to diversify resources and reduce risk.

In practice it is a combination of capabilities, markets, and institutions that best allows households to protect themselves against diverse risks (World Bank 2001c). By "capabilities" we mean the opportunities and freedom that a person has to live the life that he or she chooses (Sen 1999). For example, households with more education are usually better able to manage risk: they have more opportunities to diversify income, are often more able to adapt to changes, have better access to information, and usually have better access to credit markets. Similarly, stronger basic health not only provides greater resistance to disease, it also provides more reliable income through the ability to perform different tasks and be a more attractive employee.

A household's physical assets, such as a vehicle or a plot of land, are a measure of its capacity to self-insure. Physical assets can be sold to compensate for a temporary loss of income or to cover unexpected expenses such as health care. Physical assets can also be put to alternative uses as circumstances change. What matters here is not only the value of the asset, but also its liquidity.

A household's vulnerability is greatly reduced if it has access to credit (formal or informal) or the ability to save in liquid assets; either will help the household absorb income shocks and smooth consumption. Access to credit can also prove important in the face of a health shock that requires unexpected large expenditures. Households with liquid savings can also cope with such shocks.

A household's vulnerability is also reduced if it has access to social assistance, unemployment insurance, pensions, and other publicly provided transfers, or to workfare or similar employment programs. The effectiveness and credibility of such transfers are extremely important. In some countries these transfers are so low as to be meaningless; in others they do not get paid. In such cases, these benefits do little to reduce vulnerability and deprivation. The lack of credibility and reliability of the transfers simply adds to the uncertainty already facing households, including the need (often present in such circumstances) to invest time, effort, and bribes in increasing the probability of obtaining them.

In the face of adverse shocks, family-based networks, remittances, and transfers from friends and relatives (whether in cash or in kind) are important sources of support for poor households. Links to such informal support networks can thus greatly reduce a household's vulnerability to shocks. But when shocks are systemic, as they were in many countries of the former Soviet Union during the transition to a market economy, such informal links can break down.

Catastrophic illness or injury, which can throw even better-off families into poverty, is a major risk factor for the poor. People who are disabled or become disabled during conflicts are particularly vulnerable to deteriorating health. Useful summary measures are disability-adjusted life expectancy and disability-adjusted life-years (DALYs) compiled by the World Health Organization (WHO). These measures take into account both years of life lost because of disease and injury and years of healthy life lost to long-term disability. Ghobarah, Huth, and Russett (2003) find that civil wars significantly reduce these aggregate measure of national health performance. They use information on the major twenty-three diseases for categories of the population distinguished by gender and five different age groups. They find important effects of civil war in increasing the postconflict incidence of death and disability caused by particular infectious diseases and conditions among different population subgroups. As an example, in 1999 WHO (2000) estimates that 8.44 million DALYs were lost as a direct effect of all wars that were ongoing at that time. That same year, a further 8.01 million DALYs were lost as a result of civil wars that had ended during the period 1991–1997, but had increased the incidence of persistent infectious diseases. Thus, the legacy effect of civil wars on DALYs was approximately as large as the effect during conflict (Ghobarah, Huth, and Russett 2003).

Poverty and infectious disease feed on each other. Poor people are at higher risk of infectious disease, and sickness can deepen poverty, creating a vicious cycle of illness and poverty. The risk of and vulnerability to poverty-related health threats are compounded by hunger, malnutrition, and environmental threats, especially lack of clean drinking water and sanitation. The numbers are staggering. (The data in this section, unless otherwise stated, are taken from Wagstaff 2003.) Almost 11 million children died before their fifth birthday in 2000. Just 79,000 of these 11 million deaths (1 percent) occurred in high-income countries, compared with 42 percent in sub-Saharan Africa, 35 percent in South Asia, and 13 percent in East Asia. Of the estimated 140 million children under the age of five who are underweight, almost half (65 million) are in South Asia. In 1998 an estimated 843 million people were considered to be undernourished on the basis of their food intake. One of the greatest health risks is HIV/AIDS, which in just two decades has become the world's fourth leading cause of death. In sub-Saharan Africa life expectancy is fifteen years less than it would be without AIDS. There have been 22 million deaths from AIDS, and more than 40 million people are HIV infected (Commission on Human Security 2003). Of the 3 million people who died from HIV/AIDS in 2001, the great majority (99 percent) were in the developing world— 73 percent in sub-Saharan Africa alone. Tuberculosis claimed 2 million lives, with the epidemic worsening where economic and social crises have emerged.

Illness and death in a household reduce income and lead to potentially impoverishing expenses on medical care. In Vietnam, for example, health expenses are estimated to have pushed around 3 million people into poverty in 1993 and 2.7 million in 1998 (Wagstaff and Van Dooerslaer 2003). The vicious circle is evident at the country level as well. With a daily per capita income of $1.17 (PPP$5.60) in 2000, it is scarcely surprising that coverage levels of key preventive and treatment interventions are so low in low-income countries. Barely 40 percent of the births in low-income countries take place with the assistance of a medically trained person. Barely 60 percent of children have DPT3 immunization. And only a third of infectious patients ill with tuberculosis are using effective treatment. These low coverage levels translate into high rates of child and maternal mortality and low levels of nutrition. That, in turn, acts as a brake on economic growth and contributes to income poverty. Children who are ill and malnourished are less likely to be in school, and they learn less when they are in school. Their productivity in later life is reduced as a result. It is estimated that $1 invested in an early child nutrition program in the Philippines would yield at least $3 return in the form of higher earnings due to better educational outcomes (Glewwe, Jacoby, and King 2003).

Illness and malnutrition reduce the productivity of current workers too, as well as the hours they can spend working. A recent study from Indonesia finds that the loss of the ability to undertake a typical activity of daily living (such as sweeping the floor or walking five miles) leads to a loss of earnings equivalent to 10 percent of average earnings, and a loss of ability to undertake any activity of daily livings would wipe out earnings altogether (Gertler and Gruber 2002).

Complications from childbirth are another leading cause of death for women in many developing countries. Each year more than 515,000 women die during pregnancy or childbirth, and 99 percent of these deaths occur in developing countries. The risk of dying from childbirth is 1 in 1,800 in rich countries and 1 in 48 in developing countries (Commission on Human Security 2003). This gap implies that countless pregnancy-related deaths in developing countries could be prevented with adequate resources and services. Moreover, for every woman who dies from childbirth, ten to fifteen more become incapacitated or disabled due to complications from it. As a result more than a quarter of women in the developing world—about 300 million women—suffer from short- or long-term complications of childbirth. And because women in developing countries bear more children than women in rich countries, they are exposed to the risk of pregnancy-related death or disability more often.

Identifying causes of vulnerability requires being able to provide workable measures of vulnerability. The discussion until now has rested on the implicit assumption that we can do so, but measuring vulnerability is difficult. Vulnerability can be defined as the risk that a person or household will experience a significant fall in welfare. From an income poverty point of view, vulnerability can be more narrowly defined as the risk that a person or household will fall below the income (or consumption) poverty line over a defined period. The higher the risk, the more vulnerable the person or household.

Ideally, we are looking for indicators that allow us to predict which individuals or households are at risk of poverty and how severe the risk is. This is complicated because a household's risk depends not only on its own characteristics—such as the level of education, employment status, and assets of household members—but also on how well markets function and the extent to which the household can rely on formal and informal safety nets. These variables may be much harder to measure or proxy, and thus harder to analyze. To measure the determinants of household vulnerability satisfactorily, it is usually necessary to use panel data or data sets with repeated observations over time.

The strategy proposed in this book focuses on increasing opportunity and empowerment. As we have seen from the examples presented, such increases will reduce vulnerability and increase security. Their effectiveness in doing so will largely reflect poor people's ability to use available family, community, and social insurance mechanisms. This in turn will be determined by how these mechanisms function. That story is a continuing theme in these lectures.

Discrimination and Social Exclusion

Although there have been great improvements in living standards for many people in developing countries over the past half-century, large segments of the population have failed to benefit. All too often this is because of discrimination or social exclusion. Different social groups— whether differentiated by ethnicity, race, caste, religion, gender, or socioeconomic status—experience different outcomes.

For instance, in many countries, ethnic minorities have lower living standards than majority groups. Van de Walle and Gunewardena (2001) document these differences in Vietnam using household survey data for 1992–1993. Differences in living standards in northern rural Vietnam partly reflect geography: minorities live in less productive areas that have poor infrastructure and are farther from markets. But disparities are not just a matter of where groups live. Within the same region, even after controlling for household characteristics such as household size and education, large differences persist between minorities and the majority in Vietnam.

The extent of inequalities in developing countries appears to be determined largely by disparities in opportunities. Discrimination against and (outright or implicit) exclusion of some groups may in turn explain inequality of opportunities.

A recent survey of the evidence on exclusion establishes that poverty among minorities and indigenous peoples is a global problem (Justino and Litchfield 2003).[4] Drawing on many sources, such as World Bank country poverty assessments, the authors present voluminous evidence of ways in which exclusion manifests itself in five key areas: income poverty, education, health, employment, and housing and shelter. In each of these areas, minorities and indigenous peoples typically lag well behind other groups, in developed and developing countries alike.

Consider just a few of the indicators of minority deprivation and exclusion cited by Justino and Litchfield. In the area of income poverty, 93 percent of the indigenous population of Guatemala lives below the national poverty line; and in China, 40 percent of poor people are members of ethnic minorities, even though those groups make up only 8 percent of the population. In health, more than 90 percent of children under 5 years of age in one heavily indigenous area of Peru were chronically malnourished in the early 1990s, compared with 27 percent for the country as a whole. In housing, the authors note that only 10 percent of Dalit (formerly untouchable) households in India have access to sanitation, and that rates of electrification in Dalit households are only half those of other households—in part because in some cases "the state deliberately excludes Dalits from basic amenities" (Justino and Litchfield 2003, p. 13).

It is not always easy to establish that the lower achievements of certain minorities are the result of social exclusion and discrimination. But there is strong evidence in many societies to suggest that these are powerful forces. In many societies there is a high and persistent correlation between race and socioeconomic status. For instance, in public surveys conducted in 2000, half of the respondents in Brazil perceived blacks to be the group most discriminated against, while in Guatemala almost 60 percent stated that Indians face the greatest discrimination (Behrman, Gaviria, and Székely 2003). The correlation between race and status can be taken as one sign of discrimination.

Other differences between races may also provide clues to the existence of exclusion and discrimination and to how they reproduce themselves through social capital—that is, the extent and density of social networks—and access to opportunities. Differences in political participation, for example, may help explain political biases in favor of one group and against another. Moreover, low political participation by one group may be self-reinforcing: if group members do not participate because they have been excluded in the past, then their lack of participation will typically deepen their exclusion. Differences in social capital may help explain differences among racial and ethnic groups not only in socioeconomic outcomes but also in life satisfaction and other subjective indicators of well-being.

Different groups usually display differences in subjective well-being. In the Latin American surveys mentioned above, the share of individuals reporting satisfaction with their lives was at least 5 percentage points lower among Indians and blacks than among individuals from other races. Furthermore, controlling for interracial differences in education and socioeconomic status reduces this difference only marginally, which suggests that minority groups in the region have even lower levels of life satisfaction than their low socioeconomic status would indicate.

Although it is tempting to interpret these differences as reflecting the psychological costs of exclusion, they may also be driven by differences in material possessions, employment status, and social mobility. Using survey data from Brazil, Bourguignon, Ferreira, and Menéndez

(2003) try to measure the extent to which inequalities in individuals' observed backgrounds—as summarized by their race, region of origin, and the education and occupation of their parents—translate into inequalities in per capita income. They find that own education and parents' education may be responsible for a substantial proportion of total inequality—12 percentage points in the Gini coefficient for individuals. Inequality of observed opportunities shapes the household income distribution not only through the earnings of household heads or spouses, but also through other channels, particularly fertility and, to a lesser extent, labor force participation and nonlabor income. Of course, successive cohorts faced different situations in terms of inequality of opportunities. In Brazil intergenerational educational mobility has increased over time, especially at the bottom of the income distribution, so children's education levels now depend less on their parents' education level.

Gender

The second half of the twentieth century saw great improvements for women in both their living standards and key dimensions of gender equality.[5] Female education levels improved markedly, with girls' primary enrollment rates roughly doubling in South Asia, Africa, and the Middle East. Because this growth was faster than that of boys' enrollment, the initial large gender gaps in schooling fell substantially. In health, women's life expectancy increased by fifteen to twenty years in developing countries. And women's labor force participation has risen—by 15 percentage points since 1970 in East Asia and Latin America, for example. Because men's labor force participation grew more slowly, the gender gap in employment also narrowed over this period, as did gender gaps in wages.

Despite this progress, huge gender inequalities in rights, resources, and voice persist in all developing countries, and in many areas progress has been slow and uneven. In no country do women and men have equal social, economic, and legal rights. In many countries women still lack the right to own land, manage property, conduct business, or even travel without their husband's consent. Women continue to have less control over a range of productive resources, including education, land, information, and money. In South Asia women have only about half as many years of schooling as men, and girls' enrollments at the secondary level are still only two-thirds of boys'. Many

South Asian women cannot own land, and those who do generally command smaller holdings than men. Finally, in most developing regions, enterprises run by women have worse access to machinery, fertilizer, information, and credit than do male-run enterprises.

Partly because of these limits on their access to resources and ability to generate income, whether in self-employed activities or in wage employment, women are also constrained in their ability to influence consumption and investment decisions in their homes. And in the public arena, women's unequal rights and lower socioeconomic status limit their ability to influence decisions in their communities and at the national level. Women remain vastly underrepresented in local and national assemblies of democratic countries, accounting for less than 10 percent of seats in parliaments (except in East Asia, where the figure is about 19 percent).

Gender disparities in education and health are often greatest among poor people. A recent study of forty-one countries indicates that gender disparities in enrollments are often greater among poor people than among less poor people. In health, mortality rates for children under age five show similar patterns across poor and nonpoor households, with larger gender discrepancies among poor households.

Gender inequalities impose large costs on the health and well-being of men, women, and children, and affect their ability to improve their lives. Gender inequalities also reduce productivity in farms and enterprises and weaken a country's governance. Low investment in female education has been a barrier to growth in South Asia, Africa, and the Middle East—compared with East Asia, which closed gender gaps more rapidly. Even after controlling for income and other factors, more equal rights and greater participation by women in public life are associated with lower corruption and better governance, which promote growth. Thus, greater gender equality not only is a goal in itself that has direct benefits for women, it can also accelerate growth and poverty reduction for all.

Parts of East and South Asia illustrate the pernicious, far-reaching effects of gender inequalities. In China, northern India, and the Republic of Korea, traditional kinship systems generate gender discrimination, depriving girls of proper nutrition, health care, and education. These countries have some of the world's highest proportions of girls "missing" (relative to the number of girls that would be expected in the absence of discrimination) because of neglect, selective abortions, or female infanticides. The proportion of "missing" girls rose sharply in these countries during times of war, famine, and declining fertility. The resulting shortages of wives improved the treatment of adult women but did little to reduce discrimination against daughters or increase women's autonomy. Those goals can be achieved only with fundamental changes in women's family position—changes that are occurring slowly.

Das Gupta and Li (1999) document this story in detail, showing how war, famine, and declining fertility—all of which constrained household resources—increased the excess mortality of girls between 1920 and 1990. Of the three countries examined, China experienced the most crises (civil war, invasion, famine) during this period. The resulting excess mortality of girls in China offset the usual demographic forces making for longer life expectancy for women, implying a shortage of wives as overall mortality rates declined in more stable times. India had the quietest history during this period, and consequently experienced a growing surplus of available wives—the normal demographic pattern given natural male-female differences in mortality rates.

The divergent Chinese and Indian changes in sex ratios had substantial social ramifications. In the arena of marriage institutions, Das Gupta and Li hypothesize that these demographic factors encouraged the continuation of bride-prices in China, while in India there was a shift to dowries. At the same time, the extent and manifestations of violence against women diverged in the two societies. An "oversupply" of women eases constraints on domestic violence and is associated with neglect of girls' nutrition and health care, as well as abortion of female fetuses. By contrast, women in short supply receive better treatment, because men become more careful not to lose a wife.[6] Ironically, then, higher discrimination against girls can lead, over the long run, to a reduction in violence against women. But these "market-driven" changes in treatment of women are agonizingly slow.[7]

Economic Mobility and Employment

Different households experience economic growth and change in different ways. The fortunes of individual households depend not only on their country's economic growth, but also on factors such as the growth rate of their region or community and the health of the industries or firms that employ household members. At the level of the individual, many other factors have important economic consequences, including schooling, marriage, birth of children, health status, and advancement at work. Studies of economic or socioeconomic mobility track changes in these factors over time. One important objective of such studies is to understand how individuals escape poverty.

Given what we know about employment patterns of low-income households, the route out of poverty for many poor people starts in a small, private firm or farm. But although they are an important source of employment and income for poor people, there is little evidence that small firms contribute more to growth—through higher productivity, job creation ratios, wages, labor intensity, or the like—than do large firms (see, for example, Biggs 2002, Hallberg 2000). A notable exception can be found in transition countries that were able to impose market discipline and create favorable climates for private investment in the 1990s. These countries witnessed a substantial increase in the share of small and medium-size enterprises in employment, more foreign direct investment, and an accelerated return to growth following the transition-induced recession (Mitra and Stern 2002).

Empirical studies of mobility show that exiting from poverty and improving the well-being of oneself and one's family are consistently and significantly associated with three variables: employment of one or several household members, change in residence, and number of children in the household.

Grootaert, Kanbur, and Oh (1999), using panel data from Côte d'Ivoire for 1985 through 1988, find that important factors explaining welfare changes over time were region of residence, socioeconomic status, and endowments of human and physical capital. In urban Côte d'Ivoire human capital was the most important factor explaining welfare changes over time. Households with well-educated members suffered less loss of welfare during a period of macroeconomic decline than did other households. What really seems to have mattered, though, is the skills learned through education, not the diplomas obtained. In fact, diplomas may even have worked against some households in that they oriented workers too much toward the formal labor market at a time when employment growth came almost entirely from small enterprises.

In rural areas, physical capital—especially the amount of land and farm equipment owned—mattered most. Smallholders were more likely to suffer welfare declines than other groups. Households with diversified sources of income managed better, especially if they had an important source of nonfarm income.

In both urban and rural areas, large households suffered greater declines in welfare. Households whose heads worked in the public sector maintained welfare better than other households did. Interestingly, migrant non-Ivorian households did better at preventing welfare losses than did Ivorian households, while households headed by women outperformed those headed by men (after controlling for differences or changes in endowments).

Employment offers the best opportunity for socioeconomic mobility. Case studies from countries as diverse as Brazil, Costa Rica, Indonesia, and Taiwan show that the labor market plays a critical role in transmitting economic growth or responding to a lack of growth (Fields and Bagg 2003). And growth leads to higher wages, more productive and higher-paying jobs, and a more educated labor force.

The extent of long-term labor mobility depended on the roles and integration of public and private labor markets. Of the four countries examined in the study (covering the period 1970–2000), Taiwan comes the closest to a nondualistic labor market. There, the private sector was the engine of growth in employment. In Indonesia most workers are employed in the private sector, and the percentage of employees working as civil servants fell over time. Thus, the private sector was the stimulator of employment growth in Indonesia. In Costa Rica wages in the public sector are almost twice those in the private sector, yet in the 1990s the private sector experienced higher employment growth, facilitating the upward mobility of workers. In contrast, Brazil's public sector played a disproportionate role in recent labor market gains. During the 1990s employment and earnings growth were both higher in the public sector, even as the private sector remained the country's dominant employer.

Poverty Reduction and the Process of Change

Thus poverty should be understood not only as a lack of financial resources but also as a lack of capabilities across a range of dimensions. The recent flowering of micro research on these many dimensions has shed light on the characteristics of poor people, as well as the material deprivation, vulnerability, and social exclusion that they suffer. But even as our understanding of these dimensions of poverty has grown, the developing world has seen unprecedented—but also uneven—improvements in some of them. Thanks largely to the remarkable growth in China and impressive increase in growth in India, the percentage of those in developing countries who live in extreme poverty has fallen from an estimated 40 percent in 1981 to 21 percent in 2001. Improvements along other dimensions of poverty, such as illiteracy and infant mortality, have accompanied and sometimes outpaced the reductions in income poverty. Yet while the pace of advance over the past few decades has been unique in human history, too many have been bypassed by this progress, especially in sub-Saharan Africa.

Chapter 2 explores the processes of change that make this poverty reduction possible. Even if we consider only the dimension of income poverty, poverty reduction does not result merely from increases in production in an economy and society that are otherwise static in structure. Development involves dramatic change in virtually every facet of life: to take just a few examples, societies become much less agricultural, more urbanized, more educated, and more integrated with the global economy. In short, development is not just growth; it is fundamental change in the way people work and live.

2 Development as a Process of Change

The history of development is one of acceleration and deceleration, of stops and starts, of rapid advance in some areas and slower progress in others. This has profound implications for how we analyze growth and development. Our choice of analytical tools should depend on the type of process we are analyzing, and in this chapter we provide data intended to show that models of aggregate growth—of broad dimensions moving closely together, or of steady state—are not well suited to the experience of growth and development. It would require another large book to present evidence for all countries over a long period; here we offer just enough to establish the essence of this argument.

This chapter examines growth in aggregate income, the relationship between income growth and inequality, structural changes in the economy and demography, the environmental implications of growth, changes in political institutions and governance, and international dimensions of growth, including trade, capital flows, aid, and migration.

Together this chapter and the previous one summarize some of the empirical foundation of the strategy offered in chapter 5 and establish some basic features of development over the past fifty years. These features include the fact that, first, development is a process of fundamental change. That might seem an obvious point, but it is often overlooked or downplayed in formal analyses of growth.[1] Second, the past fifty years have seen extraordinary achievements for some regions—as well as tragedy and stagnation for much of Africa. Development *is* possible, and there are many examples of successful development on grand and small scales. But there are also many examples of setbacks and even catastrophic failures. Third, many of these achievements and failures are associated with change and damage to the physical environment, which implies that some aspects of future development efforts will have to be very different from those of recent decades. Finally, this chapter examines the changing structure of the international economy, focusing on trade and capital flows. We shall see that rapid, sustained development is associated with movements toward markets and international integration. Subsequent chapters explore what all this change implies for development strategy; here, we concentrate on establishing these patterns of development of change.

Patterns of Growth

A look at long-term economic growth reveals a significant turning point in the world economy around 1820. (Our ability to present and understand long-run growth patterns depends heavily on the pioneering work of Angus Maddison; see, for example, Maddison 2001.) During the second half of the twentieth century world growth accelerated strongly and a wider range of countries participated in it. Between 1000 and 1820 the world's per capita GDP growth averaged less than 0.1 percent a year, and from 1820 to 1950 it averaged 0.9 percent a year (excluding the difficult period between World Wars I and II). But over the next fifty years, average annual growth accelerated to 2.1 percent. The years of recovery from the Great Depression and World War II, 1950–1973, saw exceptionally high growth, averaging 2.9 percent a year, or three times the average of the previous century (table 2.1).

Over time these improvements in growth have become more widely distributed across regions and countries. Until the late nineteenth century the acceleration in growth occurred mostly in early industrializing

Table 2.1
Long-run world per capita GDP growth, by region (in percent)

	1000–1820	1820–1950	1950–1998	1950–1973	1973–1998
Western Europe	0.14	1.00	2.90	4.10	1.80
Western offshoots	0.13	1.60	2.20	2.40	1.90
Japan	0.06	0.80	5.00	8.10	2.30
Asia (excluding Japan)	0.03	0.10	3.20	2.90	3.50
Latin America	0.06	1.00	1.70	2.50	1.00
Eastern Europe and former USSR	0.06	1.10	1.10	3.50	−0.70
Africa	0.00	0.50	1.00	2.10	0.00
World	0.05	0.90	2.10	2.90	1.30

Source: Maddison (2001).

countries active in the industrial revolution. Thus it was Europe-centric, with especially strong performance in the United Kingdom. But in the period that followed, population movements, growing international capital flows, and rapid expansion in international trade spread economic growth far more widely. The period of relative peace and market liberalization from 1870 to 1913 saw higher growth in Latin America and the "Western offshoots" (North America, Australia, and New Zealand). From 1913 to 1950, however, conflicts and recession led to increased autarky and a sharp retreat from liberalization, resulting in much lower growth.

The second half of the twentieth century began with growth's rapid restoration. In the period immediately after World War II, trade and capital flows surged, and higher growth rates spread to many developing countries and to Japan. After that golden age of postwar global growth, most rich countries and many developing countries saw a slowdown in growth—though East Asia's growth accelerated. Growth rates for the postwar period had no historical precedent. Until then no country had ever sustained per capita income growth averaging at least 5 percent a year over a fifteen-year period. But since World War II that feat has been achieved by more than thirty-five countries, three-quarters of them developing (table 2.2).

The establishment of more open trade and investment flows within a stable international environment was central to this transformation. Rich countries grew rapidly in the 1950s and 1960s in part because they were recovering from the tremendous dislocation of the war, but also because of the dismantling of the restrictive trade policies of the interwar years.[2] For many developing countries in Asia that saw rapid growth, the main catalysts were political independence together with policy changes that opened markets to new trade and investment flows. The experiences of Latin America, Eastern Europe and the (now) former Soviet Union, and Africa were all rather different. What they have in common is that all achieved rapid growth in the early postwar decades but later suffered major reversals.

Latin America
In the period following the Great Depression, Latin America embraced import substitution as the path to industrialization and growth, an approach supported by export pessimists such as Raúl Prebisch (1950). Much of the region grew strongly through the 1960s and 1970s, until the import substitution model, combined with heavy external

Table 2.2
Countries with sustained high growth

Country	Periods of sustained per capita income growth exceeding 5% p.a. since 1950[a,b]	Variability of output[c]	Income distribution for selected years (Gini coefficient)			
			First year	Value	Last year	Value
Algeria	1963–77	8.0	—	—	—	—
Austria	1953–67 to 1954–68	2.7	—	—	—	—
Barbados	1961–75 to 1967–81	6.2	1951	45.5	1979	48.9
Botswana	1961–75 to 1978–92	6.7	—	—	—	—
Brazil	1959–73 to 1967–81	3.7	1960	53.0	1989	59.6
Chile	1984–98	5.3	1968	45.6	1994	56.5
China	1977–91 to 1986–2000	4.7	1980	32.0	1992	37.8
Cyprus	1965–79; 1975–89 to 1978–92; 1981–95	7.6	—	—	—	—
Equatorial Guinea	1984–98; 1986–2000	20.7	—	—	—	—
Gabon	1961–75 to 1965–79	10.6	1975	59.3	1977	63.2
Germany[d]	1950–73	n.a.	1963	28.1	1984	32.2
Greece	1952–66 to 1965–79	4.0	1974	35.1	1988	35.2
Haiti	1983–97 to 1984–98	10.1	—	—	—	—
Hong Kong	1961–75 to 1980–94	5.1	1971	40.9	1991	45.0
Indonesia	1966–80 to 1971–85	3.9	1964	33.3	1993	31.7
Iran	1956–70 to 1960–74; 1962–76	8.0	1969	41.9	1984	42.9
Ireland	1984–98 to 1986–2000	3.1	1973	38.7	1987	34.6
Israel	1955–69; 1958–72 to 1960–74	5.0	—	—	—	—
Italy	1955–69 to 1956–70; 1971–85 to 1974–88	2.5	1974	41.0	1991	32.2
Japan	1951–65 to 1967–81	3.6	1962	37.2	1990	35.0
Jordan	1971–85 to 1972–86	8.9	1980	40.8	1991	40.7
Korea	1959–73 to 1986–2000	4.2	1953	34.0	1988	33.6
Luxembourg	1983–97 to 1986–2000	3.7	—	—	—	—
Mauritania	1962–76 to 1964–78	12.5	1988	42.5	1995	37.8
Portugal	1954–68 to 1964–78	3.3	1973	40.6	1991	35.6
Puerto Rico	1951–65 to 1953–67; 1955–69 to 1959–73	3.7	1969	52.3	1989	50.9
Romania	1961–75 to 1965–79; 1968–82 to 1975–89; 1981–95 to 1982–96	12.7	1989	23.4	1994	28.7
Saudi Arabia[e]	1961–75 to 1966–80	9.0	—	—	—	—
Singapore	1961–75 to 1979–93; 1982–96	6.9	1973	41.0	1989	39.0

Table 2.2
(continued)

| Country | Periods of sustained per capita income growth exceeding 5% p.a. since 1950[a,b] | Variability of output[c] | Income distribution for selected years (Gini coefficient) | | | |
			First year	Value	Last year	Value
Spain	1951–65 to 1962–76	4.3	1965	32.0	1989	25.9
Syria	1961–75 to 1962–76; 1967–81 to 1969–83; 1971–85	13.9	—	—	—	—
Taiwan	1952–66 to 1984–98	7.6	1964	32.2	1993	30.8
Thailand	1956–70 to 1957–71; 1959–73; 1975–89 to 1984–98; 1986–2000	7.1	1962	41.3	1992	51.5
Trinidad and Tobago	1951–65 to 1956–70	3.7	1958	46.0	1981	41.7
Zimbabwe	1956–70; 1958–72 to 1964–78; 1969–83	6.3	—	—	—	—

Note: Smaller countries are not included.
[a] Sustained high growth defined as average growth of 5 percent per annum or more for fifteen years.
[b] Period growth rates calculated as averages of annual growth rates over fifteen years using real GDP per capita (constant price: Laspeyres Index) series.
[c] Standard deviation in the annual growth rate for the available data over the period 1951–2000.
[d] Average annual growth rate approximated 5 percent per annum over the entire period 1950–73; Maddison (2001) due to unavailability of relevant data in Heston-Summers-Aten.
[e] World Bank database (SIMA) due to unavailability of relevant data in Heston-Summers-Aten database.
Sources: Heston, Summers, and Aten (2002).

borrowing, began to experience serious problems. First, import substitution was very patchy, in that Latin America continued to depend on imported capital goods for domestic production of manufactured goods. Growth was adversely affected if such goods could not be imported due to terms of trade shocks or other reasons. Over time the declining world prices of Latin America's principal exports (coffee, wheat, copper) adversely affected the terms of trade.

Another problem with the import substitution model was that domestic demand for manufactured goods was limited. This problem of limited markets might have been addressed by forming regional trade associations or common markets. But such approaches were hampered by the fact that, with many countries in the region following a similar industrial policy, industries in the region tended to be more competitive than complementary. In addition, the capital-intensive technology associated with this industrial policy resulted in weak industrial demand for labor. The result was a failure to reverse growing unemployment, which began to pose a serious threat of social unrest by the 1960s.

Latin America was able to sustain growth based on import substitution through the 1970s. The global shocks of the early 1970s—accelerated inflation, the collapse of the Bretton Woods international monetary order, oil price shocks—ushered in a period of slower growth in advanced capitalist countries but failed to change policies in Latin America. During this period most countries in the region continued to spend, borrow, and accumulate debt. But the 1980s brought higher interest rates as OECD countries pursued anti-inflationary policies. Mexico's debt default of 1982 damaged the credit-worthiness of Latin America as a whole, and the flow of private lending stopped abruptly. Together with the threats of hyperinflation and fiscal crisis, this forced a severe adjustment in these economies—leading to more open economies, lower fiscal deficits, and reduced government intervention. But the inevitable curtailment of domestic demons and reallocation of resources caused a severe slowdown in growth.

Eastern Europe and Central Asia

The Soviet Union and its satellite countries in Eastern Europe grew strongly between 1950 and 1973, more or less keeping pace with Western Europe if official data are taken at face value. In fact, the strong reported growth was probably in part a statistical artifact (Gros and Steinherr 1995). Nevertheless, growth in Eastern Europe and the former Soviet Union in this period marked a clear acceleration from the preceding period, when development had been slowed by the devastation of the war and the chaos arising from the Stalinist economic policies of the 1930s.[3] But this rapid postwar growth was short-lived: in the subsequent period, 1973–1990, it decelerated sharply as the economic and political system began to disintegrate.

Nor did the region's economic difficulties end with the transition to capitalism in the 1990s. These former socialist economies faced major obstacles in the transition: their capital stock was outmoded, workers needed new skills, legal and administrative structures had to be transformed, and in many cases weak governance was replaced by an unregulated struggle dominated by powerful and opportunistic vested interests. The countries of the region confronted these problems with varying degrees of success. Poland, for instance, weathered the transition relatively well, achieving rapid income growth after a short-lived recession in the early 1990s. At the other end of the spectrum, the former Yugoslavia was crippled by conflict, and many of the countries of Central Asia and the Caucasus became fiefdoms.

Sub-Saharan Africa

Sub-Saharan Africa also enjoyed an early period of rapid growth. During the first two decades of independence, a process that began in the mid-1950s, growth was as strong as in other regions. For many African countries, this growth was based on exploitation of natural resources. But in the late 1970s came a sharp deceleration. A major cause of this slowdown was worsening terms of trade—most notably, sharp declines in the prices of the commodities that Africa exported. For non-oil exporters in the region (excluding South Africa), these cumulative terms-of-trade losses over the 1970–1997 period amounted to 120 percent of GDP (World Bank 2000c). But these external shocks were greatly exacerbated by conflict and weak governance, as has been emphasized in various studies (Collier and others 2003, Ndulu and O'Connel 1999, Collier and Gunning 1999).[4]

Another factor, as Maddison (2001) points out, was debt overhang. In the years following independence, with the Cold War at its height, various countries poured resources into Africa without any attention to their effective use. As a result many African countries accumulated large debts without generating projects or programs with any significant development impact. When the Cold War began fading in the mid-1980s, foreign aid petered out as well, and increased foreign direct investment only partly replaced the decline in aid.

Of course, not all African countries shared this experience. For instance, Botswana has been one of the world's fastest-growing countries, with growth largely based on a natural resource (diamonds), even as other resource-rich countries (Nigeria, Zambia) have seen political instability and poor policies undermine growth. Yet given Africa's size, potential, and diversity, the prevalence of its decline and the associated hardship and distress have been a tragedy, as well as a failure of the international development community.

Global Patterns

Growth has been highly variable over time. Yet during the past half-century a number of countries, primarily in East Asia, have managed to sustain rapid growth over extended periods and make great progress toward the income levels of rich countries (see table 2.2). The range of effective growth strategies has been quite diverse, ranging from East Asian–style outward orientation combined with heavy-handed interventionism at home and a single-minded focus on exports to Latin American–style import substitution industrialization (Rodrik 2003b). Still other countries rode extended natural resource booms.

Table 2.3 shows consistency of a less welcome sort: countries that have experienced fifteen-year periods in which per capita income declined. Although there is no single explanation for these periods of decline, there are two prominent causes. In some cases, particularly in Africa, the main reason is prolonged conflict. In others, for example in Latin America, it is hyperinflation, populism, and chaotic economic management. Some examples combine both.

A few key points emerge from this brief account of the history of growth:

• The past fifty years have seen extraordinarily rapid growth worldwide.

• Many developing countries sustained rapid growth for extended periods and achieved substantial increases in the incomes of their populations.

• For the most part this growth came from policy reforms that provided macroeconomic stability, encouraged markets, and embraced greater openness to trade and investment.

• Although rapid growth (above 5 percent per capita income) has occurred for long periods (here we have highlighted fifteen years), maintaining such growth for much longer is rare. There are very few cases where that has been maintained for more than a quarter of a century (with Japan, 1951–1988, China, 1979–2003, and Korea 1954–1998 being the most notable examples). Thus, we should see the episodes as an acceleration sustained for a period of time rather than as steady states.

• Most of the extended declines in per capita income involve a collapse in governance.

One thing we do not do in this chapter is report in detail on the extensive literature based on cross-country growth regressions; we make only a few occasional references.[5] The reason is that while this approach can point to some interesting regularities in cross-country experiences, it does not help us understand what is shaping the

Table 2.3
Countries with declining standards of living

| Country | Episodes of growth below 0% per capita over 15 years since 1950[a,b] | Income distribution for selected years (Gini coefficient) | | | |
		First year	Value	Last year	Value
Algeria	1981–95; 1983–97 to 1986–2000	—	—	—	—
Angola	1961–75 to 1976–90; 1979–93 to 1982–96	—	—	—	—
Argentina	1971–85 to 1978–92	—	—	—	—
Bangladesh	1960–74 to 1966–80	1963	37.31	1992	28.27
Bolivia	1951–65; 1952–66; 1972–86 to 1983–97	—	—	—	—
Burundi	1971–85; 1978–92 to 1984–98; 1986–2000	—	—	—	—
Cameroon	1979–93 to 1986–2000	—	—	—	—
Central African Republic	1961–75 to 1984–98	—	—	—	—
Chad	1961–75 to 1964–78; 1969–83; 1970–84; 1980–94 to 1983–97; 1986–2000	—	—	—	—
Congo Rep	1984–98 to 1986–2000	—	—	—	—
Congo, Dem Rep	1963–77 to 1983–97	—	—	—	—
Costa Rica	1977–91 to 1981–95	1961	50.00	1989	46.07
Cote d'Ivoire	1972–86 to 1986–2000	1985	41.21	1995	38.00
Ecuador	1978–92 to 1986–2000	—	—	—	—
El Salvador	1967–81 to 1980–94	—	—	—	—
Equitorial Guinea	1964–78 to 1982–96	—	—	—	—
Ethiopia	1970–84 to 1984–98	—	—	—	—
Gabon	1974–88, 1979–93, 1980–94	1975	59.27	1977	63.18
Gambia	1977–91 to 1986–2000	—	—	—	—
Ghana	1971–85 to 1975–89; 1979–93; 1980–94	1988	35.90	1992	33.91
Guatemala	1978–92 to 1982–96	1969	52.32	1989	50.86
Guinea	1960–74 to 1970–84; 1972–86; 1977–91	—	—	—	—
Guyana	1951–65 to 1954–68; 1970–84 to 1973–87; 1975–89 to 1981–95	1956	56.16	1993	40.22
Haiti	1972–86 to 1976–90; 1978–92; 1979–93	—	—	—	—

Table 2.3
(continued)

Country	Episodes of growth below 0% per capita over 15 years since 1950[a,b]	Income distribution for selected years (Gini coefficient)			
		First year	Value	Last year	Value
Honduras	1979–93 to 1986–2000	1968	61.88	1993	54.00
Iran	1971–85 to 1979–93	1969	41.88	1984	42.90
Jamaica	1971–85 to 1975–89; 1967–81 to 1969–83; 1971–85	1958	54.31	1991	41.11
Jordan	1980–94 to 1986–2000	1980	40.80	1991	40.66
Kenya	1980–94	—	—	—	—
Lesotho	1979–93 to 1982–96	—	—	—	—
Madagascar	1961–75 to 1986–2000	—	—	—	—
Malawi	1978–92, 1980–94	—	—	—	—
Mali	1961–75, 1973–87, 1974–88, 1976–90 to 1982–96	—	—	—	—
Mauritania	1970–84 to 1985–99	1988	42.53	1995	37.80
Mauritius	1951–65 to 1958–72	1980	45.70	1991	36.69
Mexico	1981–95 to 1983–97	1950	52.60	1992	50.31
Mozambique	1962–76 to 1983–97	—	—	—	—
Namibia	1974–88 to 1980–94, 1982–96 to 1985–99	—	—	—	—
Nicaragua	1965–79 to 1986–2000	—	—	—	—
Niger	1961–75 to 1986–2000	—	—	—	—
Nigeria	1971–85 to 1975–89; 1980–94 to 1982–96; 1985–99; 1986–2000	1986	37.02	1993	37.47
Peru	1971–85; 1974–88 to 1983–97	1971	55.00	1994	44.87
Philippines	1978–92 to 1982–96; 1984–98	1957	46.14	1991	45.00
Poland	1980–94	1976	25.81	1993	33.06
Romania	1984–1998 to 1986–2000	1989	23.38	1994	28.66
Rwanda	1961–1975; 1979–93 to 1984–98; 1986–2000	—	—	—	—
Senegal	1961–75 to 1967–81; 1969–83 to 1971–85; 1973–87; 1976–90 to 1980–94; 1983–97; 1984–98	—	—	—	—
Sierra Leone	1964–78; 1965–79; 1969–83 to 1982–96	—	—	—	—

Table 2.3
(continued)

Country	Episodes of growth below 0% per capita over 15 years since 1950[a,b]	Income distribution for selected years (Gini coefficient)			
		First year	Value	Last year	Value
South Africa	1978–92 to 1986–2000	—	—	—	—
Tanzania	1969–83; 1974–88 to 1986–2000	1969	39.00	1993	38.10
Togo	1969–83; 1970–84; 1980–94 to 1986–2000	—	—	—	—
Trinidad and Tobago	1980–94; 1982–96 to 1984–98	1958	46.02	1981	41.72
Uganda	1953–67; 1965–79; 1966–80	1989	33.00	1992	40.78
Uruguay	1952–66; 1954–68 to 1958–72	—	—	—	—
Venezuela	1963–77 to 1986–2000	1971	47.65	1990	53.84
Zambia	1965–79; 1966–80; 1968–82 to 1986–2000	1976	51.00	1996	52.40
Zimbabwe	1984–98; 1986–2000	—	—	—	—

Note: Smaller countries are not included.
[a] Defined as average growth of 0 percent per annum or less for fifteen years.
[b] Period growth rates calculated as averages of annual growth rates over fifteen years using real GDP per capita (constant prices: Laspeyres Index) series.
Source: Heston, Summers, and Aten (2002).

processes of change that are at the heart of the development story. To achieve that understanding, we must look inside the aggregates, go beyond steady-state analyses, and ask about the drivers of institutional and structural change.

Poverty, Inequality, and the Growth Process

We have seen that many developing countries have managed to generate extended periods of strong growth. But given that development objectives are focused on reducing poverty, we must ask how inequality and poverty have been associated with the process of income growth. When economic growth benefits everyone in equal proportion, the incomes of poor people grow at the same rate as average income. The fraction of the population with incomes below a fixed poverty line must then decline, although the rate at which it does so depends on the position of the poverty line in the income distribution, with overall growth generating more rapid poverty reduction the greater the fraction of the population both below and near the poverty line. If instead economic growth is unequally distributed, growth will reduce poverty less (more) rapidly, depending on whether the incomes of poor people grow by less (more) than average (Datt and Ravallion 1992, Deaton 2005, Bourguignon 2003a).

What does the experience of developing countries over the past fifty years tell us about the relationships between economic growth, income inequality, and poverty? We can make three fairly broad statements to summarize the evidence:

1. There is a clear empirical relationship between rapid growth and reductions in absolute income poverty—that is, poverty defined by an absolute, constant poverty line. This relationship is relatively robust across countries and over time.

2. In contrast, the relationship between growth and inequality or income shares is much less clear. Although the income shares of poor and rich people change over time (usually slowly) in most countries, it is difficult to detect a systematic relationship across countries between growth and changes in the income shares of poor people.

3. The inequality of income among the world's people (embodying inequality across as well as within countries) increased for at least a century and a half from 1820, but appears to have stabilized in the past two decades with the rapid growth of China and, more recently, India.

The rest of this section elaborates on these points and offers supporting evidence.

There are two important observations about the first statement. First, the average growth elasticity of poverty reduction is high; thus growth should be at the center of poverty-reduction strategies. Based on a sample of developing countries, the growth elasticity of poverty (measured by the number of people living on less than $1 a day) was estimated by Ravallion (2001) to be around 2, as noted in chapter 1. That is, a 1 percent increase in mean income or consumption spending in the population reduces the proportion of people living in poverty by 2 percent.[6]

Second, there is great variation across countries in the relationship between economic growth and poverty reduction. Several countries have experienced only limited changes in poverty despite fairly strong growth, while poverty has fallen in some countries where growth had been disappointing. Understanding the causes of these differences is crucial for the design of poverty-reduction strategies. To cite one example, Martin Ravallion and Gaurav Datt have analyzed which Indian states have had the highest poverty-reduction elasticities from growth, and why. They conclude that "amongst the initial conditions we have found to matter significantly to prospects for pro-poor growth, the role played by initial literacy is particularly notable. For example, more than half of the difference between the elasticity of the headcount index of poverty to non-farm output for Bihar (the state with lowest elasticity) and Kerala (the highest) is attributable to the latter's substantially higher initial literacy rate" (Ravallion and Datt 1999, p. 20). In cases where the elasticity is lower than average, ambitious poverty-reduction strategies might have to combine economic growth with a range of policies targeted toward poor people (Bourguignon 2003b).

Turning to the second of our statements about growth and inequality, we should remind ourselves that poverty is about absolute levels of living—the number of people who cannot attain certain elements of living standards and given consumption levels. Inequality is about disparities in levels of living—how much more income or assets are accounted for by rich people than poor people. This concept is, in most measures, expressed in terms of ratios and shares; if everyone's income goes up by the same factor, measured inequality is unchanged.

Ravallion (2001) provides a detailed study for forty-seven countries examining changes in inequality for 117 pair-wise comparisons of surveys (where pairs are within a country). He finds no positive correlation (the coefficient is -0.06) between growth and changes in *relative* inequality, as measured by the ordinary Gini index. (See table 2.2 for examples of rises and falls in the Gini index among fast-growing countries.[7]) He notes that most studies (usually less detailed and careful) that have examined the relationship between growth and inequality have come to this conclusion.

Ravallion also shows that if instead one looks at absolute inequality (which measures differences across individuals or households using absolute rather than relative income), there is a positive relationship between growth and absolute inequality. This is not surprising given the result on relative inequality—because if everyone experiences higher incomes and relative incomes are unchanged, the absolute increase to someone earning twice as much as someone else is twice the size.

Our third statement concerns the distribution of world income. Here one has to be careful to distinguish between inequality across countries and inequality between people. For example, over the past few decades, the initially poorest twenty countries have grown much more slowly than the richest twenty (see, for example, Pritchett 1997). But of course, countries vary enormously in population size. When that is taken into account, the picture of rising inequality changes dramatically.

Total inequality between the world's people can be decomposed into two components: inequality between countries and inequality within countries. Since one naturally takes population into account when calculating overall inequality, the contribution of the between-country component is also weighted by population. Given the population weighting, the contribution of the between-country component has tended to fall even though the poorest countries have not tended to have higher growth rates (see, for example, Schultz 1998 and Bhalla 2002). The two largest countries naturally figure prominently in this finding: China and (more recently) India have enjoyed high growth rates, contributing strongly to lower global inequality. Combining the between- and within-country pictures, there is no convincing sign of a significant trend increase in world inequality between individuals over the past twenty years or so—and some indication that it has fallen.

However, if the same growth trends for China and India persist, they would not continue to be a force lowering world inequality indefinitely. Global inequality would continue to decline until 2015 or 2020 (depending on the measure of inequality), after which it would likely rise as both countries move toward or beyond world average per capita income. A large share of the world's poor people still lives in India and other Asian countries, so continued rapid growth there will be equalizing for another decade or so. But more and more, poverty will be concentrated in Africa, so if its slow growth persists, global inequality will eventually rise again.

So far we have focused our discussion of inequality on the past few decades. Let us briefly take a longer-term perspective. Indicators of world inequality as calculated by Bourguignon and Morrisson (2002) are given in table 2.4. Inequality in the world seems to have increased from the early nineteenth century until around 1980, with stability or possibly a modest decline since then (the declining trend after 1980 is not shown by Bourguignon and Morrisson, but it is clearly noticeable in the calculations of Chen and Ravallion). Africa's representation in

Table 2.4
World income distribution: Inequality and poverty, selected years

Index	1820	1910	1950	1992
Income shares (percent of world income)				
Bottom 20 percent	4.7	3.0	2.4	2.2
Bottom 40 percent	13.5	8.8	6.8	6.4
Bottom 60 percent	25.7	17.6	14.2	13.5
Bottom 80 percent	43.7	33.0	31.1	28.2
Top 10 percent	42.8	50.9	51.3	53.4
Top 5 percent	31.8	36.7	35.5	36.0
Mean world income (PPP $1990)	658.7	1,459.9	2,145.5	4,962.0
World population (millions)	1,057.0	1,719.0	2,511.3	5,459.1
Poverty head count (percent of world population)				
Poverty	94.4	82.4	71.9	51.3
Extreme poverty	83.9	65.6	54.8	23.7
Summary inequality measures				
Gini coefficient	0.50	0.61	0.64	0.66
Theil index	0.52	0.80	0.81	0.86

Note: The Gini coefficient is defined as

$$G = \frac{-(n+1)}{n} + \frac{2}{n^2 r}\sum_{i=1}^{n} ix_i$$

and the Theil index as

$$T = \frac{1}{n}\sum_{i=1}^{n}\frac{x_i}{r}\,ln\left(\frac{x_i}{r}\right)$$

where x_i = income, r = average income, n = total number of recipients.
Source: Bourguignon and Morrisson (2002).

the bottom 60 percent of the world income distribution has risen over the past half-century, while that of Asia has begun to fall (table 2.5). Nevertheless, Asia still accounts for nearly three-quarters of the bottom 60 percent.

Few countries have experienced a trend increase in inequality over the long term. China has sustained rising inequality since the mid-1980s, and, given its weight in the world population, it is an important exception. Many countries of the former Soviet Union have experienced sharply increasing inequality—though over a shorter period—but their weight in the world population is fairly small. Over such short periods one finds rising inequality in about half of developing countries, although, as we have seen, this is uncorrelated with growth

Table 2.5
World income distribution: Regional composition of world percentiles, selected years

World percentiles	Africa	Asia	Japan, Korea, and Taiwan	Latin America	Eastern Europe	European countries and offshoots	Total
1820							
Total	6.9	64.9	3.6	1.8	8.2	14.6	100
Bottom 60 percent	7.9	75.8	3.2	1.7	6	5.3	100
Mid-30 percent	5.8	55.3	4.4	1.4	12.5	20.5	100
Top 10 percent	4.1	32.5	3.5	3	8	48.9	100
1910							
Total	6.2	51.6	3.7	3.8	12.9	21.7	100
Bottom 60 percent	8.1	71.1	2.9	4.1	9.5	4.4	100
Mid-30 percent	4.6	25	5.6	4.1	21.2	39.6	100
Top 10 percent	0.9	25	1.8	1.9	6.3	64.1	100
1950							
Total	8.9	49.6	4.5	5.5	10.9	20.7	100
Bottom 60 percent	12.7	74.4	2.7	4.6	3.5	2.1	100
Mid-30 percent	4.2	18.2	8.7	8.3	25.8	34.8	100
Top 10 percent	1.2	4.4	2.1	3	8.3	81.1	100
1992							
Total	12	54.8	3.5	7.6	8.3	13.8	100
Bottom 60 percent	17.4	72.7	0	6.5	3.2	0.3	100
Mid-30 percent	5	36.2	5.3	11.1	19.7	22.6	100
Top 10 percent	1.4	6.1	18.2	3.8	4.1	66.4	100

Note: Reading across, each row gives the share of that group accounted for by each region. For example, Africa in 1820 accounted for 6.9 percent of global population, but only 4.1 percent of the top decile of the global income distribution.
Source: Bourguignon and Morrisson (2002).

in average household consumption per capita (Chen and Ravallion 1997).

So far, this section's discussion of trends and relationships in poverty and inequality has been fairly aggregated. Let us close it with a country example that shows the importance of looking more closely within a country in order to understand mechanisms at a level appropriate for guiding policy. The relationship between growth and income poverty reduction is complex, and average cross-sectional results conceal much that is important. We must take into account the heterogeneity in the relationship between changes in poverty and changes in income. We cannot just jump into regressions; mechanisms count. The following example, taken from Ferreira and Paes de Barros (1998), illustrates the complexity of these issues.

In Brazil GDP per capita increased 0.2 percent a year between 1976 and 1996, with no change in overall inequality (the Gini coefficient decreased from 0.595 to 0.591). Despite these improvements, poor people (in practice, the bottom 15 percent of the income distribution) suffered a sizable fall in relative income and rising absolute poverty. This increase in poverty can be explained mostly by changes in labor force participation or employment, depending on how the data are interpreted.

In effect, a more detailed analysis reveals that the main cause of these downturns was less employment and more informal sector activity among the poorest households. It is difficult not to relate these developments to Brazil's sluggish growth during this period. Within a dual-economy framework, which seems to be helpful in understanding some aspects of the Brazilian economy, the general story might be as follows. Slow growth led to a weak labor market, which may have caused an increasing differential between wage workers and the self-employed, as well as job losses and worker discouragement. Both the widening wage gap and the job loss, but mostly the latter, contributed to an increase in poverty in the bottom 15 percent of the population. This increase would have been greater had it not been for a fall in family size that was more pronounced at the bottom of the distribution.

Above the fifteenth percentile, urban Brazilians essentially "stayed put." But to do so, they had to survive some hard climbing along a slippery slope. To counteract falling absolute and relative returns in the formal labor market and in self-employment, they had to gain an average of two years of schooling—which still leaves them undereducated for the country's per capita income—and substantially reduce fertility.

As this example demonstrates, the distribution of income may interact with economic growth through various channels. Policies to fight poverty should be guided by analyses that take careful account of country-specific data and the structure of the economy and society.

Structural Changes in Economies and Societies

Over the past fifty years the developing world experienced changes that, in their speed and depth, have no precedent in human history.

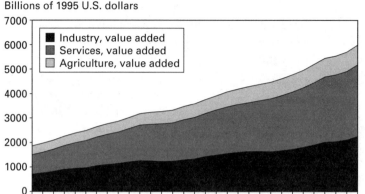

Billions of 1995 U.S. dollars

Figure 2.1
Services account for a growing share of developing countries' GDP. *Source:* World Bank
data.

This section briefly reviews the profound transformations that have
taken place in economic structure (agriculture, industry, and services),
demographics (population growth and age composition), urbanization, migration, and the environment. In its presentation and analysis
of changes, the section draws heavily on the *World Development Report
2003* (World Bank 2002d).

Changes in the Economy
Developing countries have shifted from depending on agriculture
as a primary source of employment and income to nonagricultural
activities—mostly manufacturing and services (figure 2.1). Hollis
Chenery and his collaborators documented this process of structural
change in a series of path-breaking studies (Chenery, Robinson, and
Syrquin 1986; Syrquin 1988; Syrquin and Chenery 1989). These studies
showed that structure and performance are intimately linked, and
Chenery's research described empirical regularities in development
patterns. He argued that large countries perform better than small
ones, that specialization in manufacturing outperforms specialization
in primary commodities, and that outward orientation exhibits higher
growth rates than inward orientation.

We do not attempt here to replicate that type of analysis. Rather, our
purpose is to draw attention to its focus on industrial change. If we
bring the basic description up to date, we see that the strong move-

Table 2.6
Sectoral composition of output, developing countries, in percent of GDP

	Low-income countries			Middle-income countries		
	Agriculture	Industry	Services	Agriculture	Industry	Services
1960	50	17	33	—	—	—
1970	43	23	34	16	40	44
1980	36	27	37	12	41	47
1990	30	30	40	13	40	47
2000	26	30	44	11	39	50

Source: World Bank database.

ment out of agriculture has been confirmed over the past few decades. In both low- and middle-income countries the share of manufacturing has stabilized, while that of services is still rising (table 2.6). In rich countries services usually account for more than 70 percent of GDP, and it seems reasonable to expect that the share of services will continue to rise in developing countries. It is important to recognize this pattern and to avoid the mistake of seeing development as being dominated by a move to manufacturing.

Population Changes and the Demographic Transition
A global demographic transition is well under way. The world's population is expected to stabilize by the end of the twenty-first century at 9 to 10 billion people, a level 20 to 30 percent lower than forecast in the 1960s and 1970s. Many factors have contributed to this slowdown relative to expectations, including:

• More educated, employed women, resulting in smaller families

• Greater off-farm employment opportunities, which encourage investing in children's education and so favor "quality" over quantity of children

• Widespread dissemination of modern contraceptive technology, making it easier for people to plan childbearing

Of the expected population increase before the world population stabilizes, 85 percent (3 billion people) will be born in the next fifty years. The speed of the transition, and the resulting population size and structure, will vary considerably by region (figure 2.2).

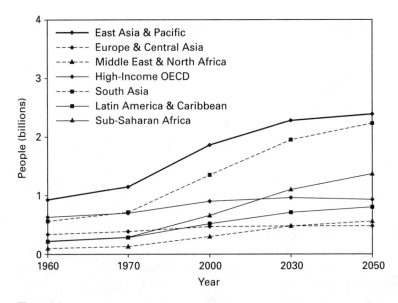

Figure 2.2
World population, actual and projected. *Source:* World Bank, Statistical Information Management and Analysis (SIMA).

If fertility rates do not fall as rapidly as projected, larger populations will put more pressure on natural resources and the social fabric. If fertility rates drop faster, many countries will have to deal sooner than expected with another problem: an aging population. This aging can have major consequences, especially for rural populations for whom formal social safety nets are nonexistent or underdeveloped. For example, one consequence of China's one-child policy, which dramatically lowered population growth, is that as much as one-third of the population may be older than age sixty-five by 2030.

Influencing demographic processes in many countries is the growing incidence of HIV/AIDS, malaria, and tuberculosis. Sub-Saharan Africa is losing huge numbers of working-age people to AIDS, and with HIV prevalence among working-age adults (ages 15–49) estimated at some 8 percent, the epidemic is projected to strengthen (UNAIDS/WHO 2003). Other regions too are seeing the epidemic spread rapidly, albeit not yet to the extent it has in Africa. Such high mortality would be tragic under any circumstances, but economically its effects are amplified by the loss of the private and public investments that have been made in these workers. The loss of their productive lives leaves large, unpredictable gaps in the labor force, and it robs many young children of their parents, inflicting heavy economic costs by depriving them of nurture and education. Unlike HIV, malaria does not kill most adults it infects. Still, it too inflicts heavy losses on labor productivity. Changes in the incidence of disease will have profound effects on health spending in African countries.

With declining fertility the age structure of the population changes, opening a window of opportunity in developing countries for a few decades. The fertility decline raises the size of the working-age population relative to the population of children (those under age fifteen) and the elderly (over age sixty-five; figure 2.3). This demographic shift enables societies to spend less, for example, on schools and old-age medical expenses and to invest the savings in economic growth.

But such benefits materialize only if members of the working-age population are gainfully employed and have opportunities to expand their assets. Eventually dependency ratios rise again as workers age, and the window of opportunity starts to close—as will soon happen in East Asia and Eastern Europe (see figure 2.3). Some countries, most notably in East Asia, have benefited substantially from the drop in dependency ratios. Investments in forming a skilled, healthy labor force, combined with policy and institutional settings conducive to using this labor force effectively, helped generate strong economic growth.

Because most developing regions will continue to experience relatively low dependency ratios for several decades, careful preparation now can help make the most of their windows of opportunity. Governments in both urban and rural areas can move from catching up with the quantitative need for infrastructure and human development services, to upgrading their quality. Lower rates of population growth will reduce pressure on natural resources, but this will be offset by increased per capita consumption, a trend that makes it essential to adopt technologies and growth paths for production and consumption that ensure sustainable use of natural resources. To benefit from the opportunities a stabilizing population provides, it is critical to anticipate problems and identify development strategies for getting through the transition period (the next twenty to fifty years) without creating conditions that generate conflict or degrade resources.

Urbanization

Over the past fifty years the world's population increased by more than 3.5 billion people, 85 percent of whom were in developing (including

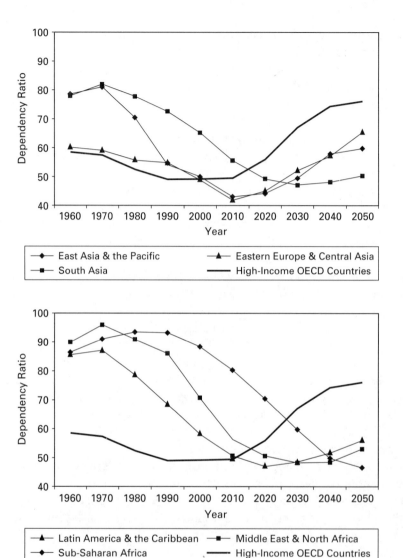

Figure 2.3
Dependency ratios are falling, but will eventually recover. *Source:* World Bank database
(SIMA). *Note:* The dependency ratio is the ratio of the non-working-age population (under fifteen years and over sixty-four years old) to the working-age population (ages fifteen to sixty-four).

transition) countries. The number of people living in fragile rural areas in developing countries doubled, in contrast to the declining number in this category in high-income countries. The number of megacities—cities with more than 10 million people—soared from zero to fifteen in developing countries, but only from one to four in high-income countries.

In the next thirty to fifty years the projected 2 to 3 billion increase in the world's population will occur almost entirely (97 percent) in developing countries—and nearly all of it will be in urban areas, in the sense that the urban population will grow by this amount. The continued growth of the urban population will be driven by natural increase, rural-urban migration, and the incorporation of high-density rural areas on the urban fringe. The number of megacities in developing countries is projected to increase to fifty-four, while it will stabilize at five in high-income countries (World Bank 2002d).

The developing world's urban growth offers many opportunities, in addition to the obvious challenges. Because it brings diverse peoples closely together, urbanization generally promotes social transformation and social innovation. Social norms restricting the role of women are often less strictly enforced in urban areas, for example, and urban households typically reduce household size because of space constraints. On the economic front, urban areas offer what economists call "agglomeration externalities"—productivity-increasing benefits from locating near other producers or economic activities. These productivity advantages explain the emergence of high-technology regions like Silicon Valley in the United States, but with a good investment climate they will apply also to developing countries. Urban areas often also offer more opportunities for employment, education, and other services for migrants. The challenge will be for developing countries to take advantage of these opportunities for learning and innovation—in a word, for development—while limiting urban congestion, crime, and environmental degradation.

Environmental Change

Despite rapid population growth, developing countries have achieved considerable gains in living standards. But development has also left a legacy of environmental problems that cannot be reversed. The increased scale and reach of human activity have put great pressure on local and global common property resources, and this pressure has manifested itself in various forms.

• *Air pollution.* Hundreds of cities in the developing world have unhealthy levels of air pollution. At the global level, the biosphere's ability to absorb carbon dioxide without altering temperatures has been compromised by excessive dependence on fossil fuels. Excess nitrogen—mainly from fertilizers, sewage, and combustion of global fossil fuels—has also begun to have adverse effects, ranging from reduced soil fertility to excess nutrients in lakes, rivers, and coastal waters.

• *Water pollution.* Fresh, safe water is increasingly scarce—while demand for it is rising quickly. One-third of the world's population lives in countries that are experiencing moderate to high water shortages. In 1995 a quarter of the world's population—more than 1 billion people in low- and middle-income countries and 50 million people in high-income countries—lacked access to safe water for drinking, personal hygiene, and domestic use.[8]

• *Soil degradation.* Since the 1950s nearly a quarter of all cropland, pasture, forest, and woodland has been degraded, meaning that it has suffered a temporary or permanent decline in its productive capacity. Of this nearly 2 million hectares of degraded land, 39 percent is lightly degraded, 46 percent is moderately degraded, and 16 percent is severely degraded (Scherr 1999).

• *Deforestation.* Deforestation has been proceeding at an unsustainable pace. Since 1960 one-fifth of tropical forests have been cleared. The developing world, where deforestation has been concentrated, lost nearly 200 million hectares between 1980 and 1995 (World Bank 2002d). By contrast, in developed countries forest cover is stable or increasing slightly, though forest ecosystems have been altered. Still, only about one-fifth of the earth's original forests remain relatively natural ecosystems (UNDP and others 1999).

• *Biodiversity loss.* One-third of terrestrial biodiversity, accounting for 1.4 percent of the earth's surface, is in vulnerable areas and threatened with extinction in the event of natural disasters or further human encroachment (Myers and others 2000).

• *Fisheries depletion.* About 58 percent of the world's coral reefs and 34 percent of fish species are at risk from human activities (UNDP and others 1999). Some 70 percent of the world's commercial fisheries are fully exploited or overexploited and experiencing declining yields (World Bank 2001e). Marine fisheries peaked in 1989 with a catch of about 85 million tons. Since then there has been almost no growth in the harvest of capture fisheries. Moreover, the composition of the catch has been shifting from high-value to low-value species. This change reflects the industry's relentless fishing down the food chain, from large predators like tuna, billfish, salmon, and cod, down to anchovies, squid, and jellyfish. Scientists estimate that the global ocean has lost 90 percent of its large fish predators since industrial fishing was introduced. There has also been a decline in the health of the world's coral reef ecosystems: nearly one-third are severely damaged.

Lest readers think that the past fifty years have produced only challenges on the environmental and land use fronts, we should note several important successes. During the 1950s and 1960s it was feared that many developing countries—particularly China, India, and Indonesia, the three most populous—would be unable to feed their rapidly growing populations. Gunnar Myrdal's famous book, *Asian Drama* (1968), was deeply pessimistic about the future of the continent where the vast bulk of poor people lived.

But these depressing scenarios did not materialize. Better policies and improving education led to rising incomes. The green revolution in agriculture also played a central role, introducing high-yielding varieties of wheat and rice and improving other enabling factors: government policies, irrigation, seed production, fertilizer use, pest management, and research and extension services. In part, this technological progress resulted from a donor-supported network of agricultural research centers (under the Consultative Group for Agricultural Research, or CGIAR) that has produced higher-yield food crops and improved farming systems. More than 300 varieties of wheat and rice and 200 varieties of maize developed through CGIAR-supported research are being grown by farmers in developing countries. Beyond improving yields, the new varieties have spurred environmental gains by allowing reduced pesticide use and releasing marginal lands from cultivation (Goldin, Rogers, and Stern 2002).

In the 1960s and 1970s the Club of Rome and many other groups forecast that the earth would rapidly run out of key natural resources. But so far that has not happened. If such outcomes were imminent, we would expect to see prices increasing with scarcity. Yet commodity prices have actually fallen, as changes in technology and demand have allowed new resources to be substituted for old—fiber optics for copper, for example.

Although markets have the potential to function well in addressing natural resource problems, for most environmental issues—such as biodiversity loss, global warming, land degradation, and fisheries depletion—collaboration, collective action, and appropriate institutions will be crucial to finding workable solutions. Here the record is mixed.

The response to ozone depletion provides an example of successful collaboration by the global community to address a global problem. Refrigerators began using chlorofluorocarbons (CFCs) around 1930. By 1970 the world used about 1 million tons of these substances each year as coolants, as propellants in aerosol cans, and for manufacturing. After many unsuccessful attempts by scientists to draw public attention to the problems created by ozone depletion, the issue was finally taken seriously. In 1985 the Vienna Convention committed the world's nations to address the issue but imposed no obligations. In 1987 the Montreal Protocol imposed obligations on developed countries to reduce the use of ozone-depleting substances and set up panels to assess the impact of ozone depletion and the technology and economics of mitigating ozone-depleting substances. In 1990, under the London Protocol, developing countries agreed to take on obligations, with a grace period, and developed countries underwrote a trust fund to assist them. Two more amendments to the Vienna Convention have been adopted, and the process remains dynamic. The likely result of this collaborative action is a reduction in the atmospheric concentration of ozone-depleting substances and an eventual recovery of the ozone layer.

Climate change initiatives offer another example of a search for collaborative solutions to a global problem. Concerned with climatic risks posed by the high atmospheric concentration of greenhouse gases, in 1992 most of the world's nations agreed to the United Nations Framework Convention on Climate Change. As a first step, the Kyoto Protocol was negotiated in 1997. It required developed and transition countries to accept specified limits on greenhouse gas emissions for 2008–2012. Unfortunately, this global initiative has run into trouble, including the unwillingness of the United States to participate, and has not entered into force.

Collaborative solutions are also being used to address local environmental problems. In India, for instance, in response to severe degradation of forest resources, recent attempts have been made to involve forest-dependent communities in managing forest resources. In states like Gujarat, projects in forest-dependent communities have succeeded in establishing a complementary relationship between the development and protection of the forest and the welfare of the people.

We have emphasized that development is about change. As economies, societies, cultures, institutions, and nature evolve at varying speeds, the changes generate new stresses. Moreover, in an era of globalization and rapid technological advances, the scale and speed of change have accelerated. Although faster change can offer many benefits, it can also have adverse side effects if institutions do not evolve fast enough to deal with the spillovers and dislocations. This process of change cannot be stopped, but it can be better managed, and it can be harnessed to create new opportunities. For instance, the flow of information and ideas, boosted greatly by technological innovations such as the Internet, can enable developing countries to learn more rapidly from each other and from developed countries, and even to skip over stages in the development process that rely on inefficient uses of natural resources.

The severity of the environmental stresses described here reflects the failure of institutions to develop fast enough to manage and provide public goods, correct spillovers, and broker differing interests in this period of rapid change. We will not attempt to identify specific policies to address environmental concerns. The institutions required to manage change are not static, and they need to evolve to keep pace with change. Many of the principles for shaping institutions and more detailed analyses of these issues are provided in the World Bank's *World Development Report 2003*. We have tried to bring out two main points here. First, change has been extremely rapid by historical standards, environmental damage has been severe, and a viable future cannot be presented as a simple extrapolation of the past. Second, effective responses will depend on building institutions that provide for collective action and collaboration, while at the same time integrating workable mechanisms for markets and incentives. These two themes run through many of this book's lectures and the strategy they present.

An Integrating World

Global economic integration—in terms of growing movements of goods, people, capital, information, ideas, and technology—has been going on for thousands of years. It has gone faster or slower in different periods, and occasionally backward, but it is a process that has been taking place since the early history of human beings. What is of special importance about the most recent wave of integration, which began around 1980, is how developing countries are integrating with developed countries.

As in previous waves, integration today is driven partly by deliberate policy changes and partly by technological advances in transportation and communications. But unlike in previous periods, this time most of the developing world's population lives in countries that have shifted from inward-looking to more outward-oriented policies. The term *globalization* is often used to describe this process of integration, and we occasionally use it here. It is a word that means different things to different people, but we shall use it largely in the sense of integration along various dimensions, including those just listed. Integration takes place along many other dimensions, including the environment, disease, crime, terrorism, and war. (This section draws on the policy research report on *Globalization, Growth, and Poverty*, World Bank 2002c.)

International Trade

The first great wave of modern globalization ran from about 1870 to 1914, a period when global growth accelerated and the world reached levels of economic integration comparable in many ways to those of today. Expansion in international trade was pivotal during this period, with the volume of trade (relative to world income) nearly doubling from 10 percent in 1870 to 18 percent on the eve of the World War I.

The surge in trade was driven by technological advances that sharply reduced transportation costs. New markets were opened, and trade expanded as use of the steam engine in rail and ship transportation sharply cut the cost of trade within and between North and South America, Asia, and Africa. There were also large capital flows to rapidly developing parts of the Americas, and during this period foreign asset ownership more than doubled, from 7 percent of world income to 18 percent. Probably the most distinctive feature of this era of globalization was mass migration: nearly 10 percent of the world's population relocated permanently in this era (Lindert and Williamson 2001, World Bank 2002c). Much of this migration was from poor parts of Europe to the Americas, but there was also considerable migration out of China and India (in the latter case, much of it forced).

It is important to keep in mind that while global indicators showed considerable integration from 1870 to 1914, this period was also the heyday of colonialism, and much of the world's population was highly restricted in its opportunities to benefit from expanding commerce. Colonies supplied raw materials to metropolitan powers and had limited freedom to develop modern economies.

Global integration took a big step backward during the period of World Wars I and II and the Great Depression. In a powerful reminder that policies can halt and reverse integration, governments retreated into protectionism and narrow nationalism during the interwar years. By end of this dark era, trade and foreign asset ownership were nearly back at their levels of 1870. Thus, the protectionist period undid fifty years of integration. The era of relatively free migration was also at an end, as virtually all nations imposed restrictions on immigration.

Between 1945 and about 1980 developed countries restored much of the integration that had existed among them. They negotiated a series of mutual trade liberalizations under the auspice of the General Agreement on Tariffs and Trade (GATT). The composition of trade has also changed significantly since World War II. Trade among developed countries, which continues to represent the bulk of global trade, has been increasingly dominated by trade in services and manufactured goods, often intra-industry trade.

For developing countries trade in the first few decades after World War II was similar to that in the nineteenth century, composed mainly of primary, often unprocessed, commodities. But this changed dramatically during the latest wave of developing country trade growth, which began in the late 1970s. Liberalization of capital flows proceeded more slowly, and not until 1980 did the level of foreign asset ownership return to its 1914 level. During this period, there was also modest liberalization of immigration in many developed countries, especially the United States.

In this second wave of modern globalization, covering the first three decades following the World War II, the story was largely one of integration among rich countries. Most developing countries were on the sidelines, often by choice. Many countries in Asia, Africa, and Latin America followed import-substituting industrialization strategies that kept their levels of import protection far higher than in developed countries. Most also restricted foreign investment by multinational firms. Still, in the 1970s quite a few developing countries turned to the expanding market for international bank borrowing and took on significant foreign debt.

The most recent wave of globalization started around 1980. The most significant feature of this wave has been China's dramatic economic reforms and opening to the outside world. China's opening roughly coincided with the second global oil shock, which contributed to external debt crises in Latin America and elsewhere in the developing world. In a growing number of countries, from Brazil to India to Mexico to many in sub-Saharan Africa, political and intellectual leaders began to fundamentally rethink development strategies.

What is distinctive about this latest wave of globalization is that most developing countries have shifted from an inward-focused strategy to a more outward-oriented one. The change in growth strategies adopted by major countries can be seen in the huge increases in trade integration between 1977 and 1997. China's ratio of trade to GDP more than doubled during this period, and countries such as Bangladesh, India, Mexico, and Thailand saw large increases as well (figure 2.4). Not all developing countries have followed this pattern, however. Quite a few—such as Egypt, Nigeria, Senegal, and Zambia—traded smaller shares of GDP in 1997 than they did two decades earlier.

It is not only how much developing countries trade, but also what they trade that has changed sharply (figure 2.5). In 1980, primary products accounted for some 75 percent of merchandise exports from developing countries. Thus, the stereotype of poor countries exporting tin or bananas had a large element of truth. But in recent decades the biggest increase in merchandise exports from developing countries has come from manufactured goods, which now account for 80 percent of such exports. Garments from Bangladesh, refrigerators from Mexico, computer hardware from Thailand, software from India, compact disk players from China—these are the face of today's developing-country exports. As noted, service exports from the developing world have also increased enormously. Growth has taken place in both traditional areas, such as tourism, and new ones, as exemplified by the software industry in Bangalore, India.

Manufactured exports from the developing world are often part of multinational production networks. Nike contracts with firms in the Philippines and Vietnam to make shoes, and automobile parts are produced in different countries before being assembled in a single location. What has fueled this integration? Part of the answer lies in the

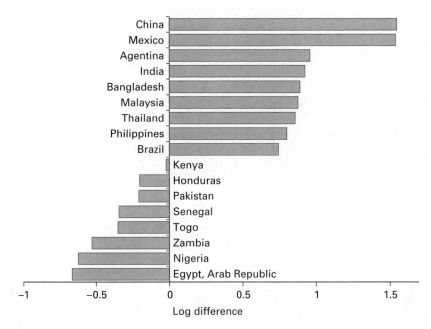

Figure 2.4
Some countries have seen big increases in the share of trade in GDP, 1977–2002. *Source:*
World Bank database (SIMA). *Notes:* Trade share = exports and imports/GDP. Log dif-
ference is the difference in the natural logs of the trade shares for 1977 and 2002.

technological advances that make integrated production feasible, notably the dramatic declines in the costs of air transportation and international communications (table 2.7). But another part of the answer lies
in the policy choices of developing countries. In the late 1970s China
and India had very closed economies. Thus, their increased integration
would not have been possible without the policy steps they took to
open up to trade and foreign direct investment.

These policy changes are reflected in average import tariffs for the
developing world. Such tariffs have fallen sharply in South Asia, Latin
America, and East Asia, less so in Africa and the Middle East (figure
2.6). But these tariffs capture only a small portion of trade policy
changes. Often the most pernicious impediments are nontariff barriers:
quotas, licensing schemes, restrictions on purchasing foreign exchange
for imports. In China reductions in nontariff barriers in the early
years of reform contributed to a dramatic surge in trade (figure 2.7).
In 1978 one government ministry monopolized foreign trade, but the

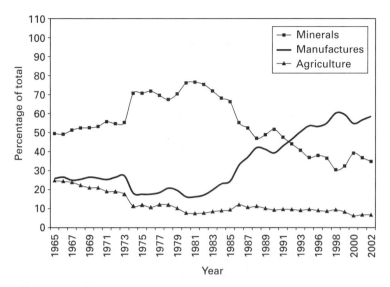

Figure 2.5
Manufactured goods account for a growing share of exports from developing countries. *Source:* UN COMTRADE. *Note:* Excludes countries that grew out of developing-country status during the period (e.g., Korea and Taiwan); inclusion would show even higher shares of manufactures than on this figure.

following year China began allowing a growing number of firms, including private ones, to trade directly. It also opened a foreign exchange market to facilitate this trade.

In many developing countries weak port and customs services are another major impediment to trade. For example, it is much more expensive to ship a container of textiles from the port of Mombasa (Kenya) to the east coast of the United States than it is to ship it from Asian ports such as Bombay (India), Shanghai (China), Bangkok (Thailand), or Kaohsiung (Taiwan)—even though Mombasa is closer (figure 2.8). The extra cost, which is equivalent to an 8 percent export tax, is due to inefficiencies and corruption in the Kenyan port. As noted, quite a few developing countries, including Kenya, trade less today (relative to GDP) than they did twenty years ago (see figure 2.4). This is largely due to restrictive trade policies, weak infrastructure, and inefficient customs and other administration. Developing countries that have become more integrated with the world economy have relatively well-functioning ports and customs, and improvement of those has often been a deliberate policy goal.

Table 2.7
Measures of global integration

| | (1) | (2) | (3) | (4) | (5) |
| | | | Transport and communications costs (constant US$) | | |
	Capital flows: Foreign assets/ world GDP (in percent)	Trade flows: Trade/GDP (in percent)	Sea freight (average ocean freight and port charges per ton)	Air transport (average revenue per passenger mile)	Telephone call (3 minutes in New York/ London)
1820	—	2[b]	—	—	—
1870	6.9	10[b]	—	—	—
1890	—	12[c]	—	—	—
1900	18.6	—	—	—	—
1914	17.5	18[bc]	—	—	—
1920	—	—	95	—	—
1930	8.4	18[bc]	60	0.68	244.7
1940	—	—	63	0.46	188.5
1945	4.9	—	—	—	—
1950	—	14[b]	34	0.30	53.2
1960	6.4	16[c]	27	0.24	45.9
1970	—	22.4[b]–20.0[c]	27	0.16	31.6
1980	17.7	—	24	0.10	4.8
1990	—	26[bc]–38.7[d]	29	0.11	3.3
1995	56.8	42[d]	—	—	—
2000	67.0[a]	49.9[d]	19[e]	0.07[e]	0.25[e]

Note: Trade flows represent the sum of merchandise exports and imports divided by the value of GDP, all in current US$.
Sources: Column (1) Crafts (2000); (a) UNCTAD (2001) for 2000.
Column (2) (b) Maddison (1995) and IMF (1997); (c) Crafts (2000); (d) World Bank database (SIMA); (e) Busse (2003).
Column (3)–(5) IMF (1997); (e) Busse (2003).

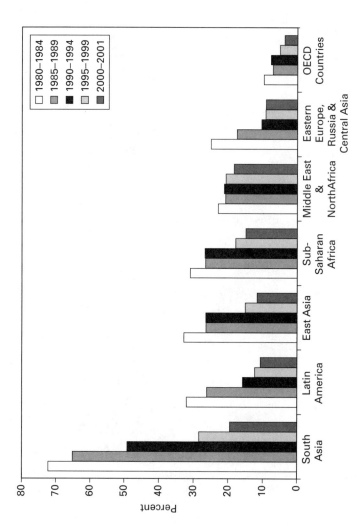

Figure 2.6
*Average unweighted tariffs have fallen in every region. Source: World Bank data.

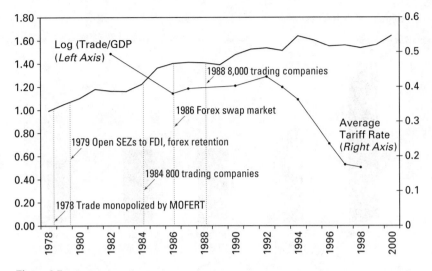

Figure 2.7
China's trade reforms have increased its openness with the global economy. *Source: China Statistical Year Book*, various issues.
Notes: Trade/GDP refers to imports and exports/gross domestic product
Forex = Foreign exchange
SEZs = Special economic zones
FDI = Foreign direct investment
MOFERT = Ministry of Foreign Economic Relations and Trade

Thus a key development in the current wave of globalization is the dramatic change in how many developing countries relate to the global economy. The developing world is now a major exporter of manufactured goods and services, many of which compete directly with products made in developed countries. The nature of trade and competition between rich and poor countries has been transformed.

These dramatic changes in the degree of integration of the developing world matter because of the links between integration, growth, and poverty reduction. There remains some debate about the degree of trade liberalization that is advisable for poorer developing countries—debate fueled by the observation that open domestic markets were not a precondition for rapid growth in the East Asian tigers, or indeed historically in much of Europe and North America. Yet it is clear that highly protected markets have not been a recipe for rapid growth in most developing countries, particularly those with smaller

Costs (share of export value)

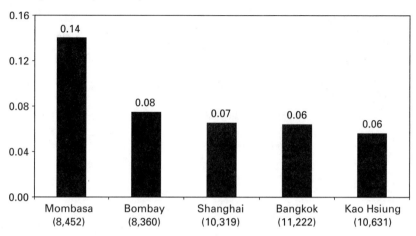

Figure 2.8
Maritime transport of textiles to the U.S. east coast is cheaper from Asia. *Source:* U.S. Department of Transport, U.S. Waterborne databank. *Note:* Distance in nautical miles between the city and U.S. (East Coast) in parentheses on the horizontal axis.

markets. Rather than nurturing the maturation of potentially productive infant industries, high trade barriers have typically created a preserved enclave for inefficiencies and rent seeking. More positively, it is also clear that most recent periods of rapid growth have also been periods of increased engagement with the international economy. In the 1990s, for example, developing countries that had fast export growth also had, on average, 1 percent higher annual growth in GDP than those with slow export growth; in the 1980s, the difference was even greater. The domestic investment climate and the actions of the domestic private sector are the key drivers of development, as we shall argue in chapter 5, but international engagement can play an important complementary role.

Note that it is the direction of change that is crucial. Even in historically closed economies such as China, which was far from completely open during the early reform period of the 1980s, the increase in access to international capital and markets during that period helped fuel rapid growth. Where local conditions for entrepreneurship and growth are good, exposure to international competition increases the productivity of domestic firms and lowers input costs for downstream users, while foreign direct investment brings with it new production and process technologies, organizational capacity building, and marketing networks.

These benefits of integration highlight the costs of continued restrictions on trade. Despite the large drops over the past fifty years, trade barriers remain high. For many products in which poor countries have a comparative advantage, such as textiles and agricultural goods, rich countries maintain high tariff and nontariff barriers. Moreover, developing countries maintain barriers much higher than those of rich countries and limit trade among themselves. We return to some of these issues in lecture IV.

International Migration
Periods of rapid global growth and globalization have coincided with major waves of international migration. The longest era of migration in history ran from 1870 to 1914, when an estimated 10 percent of the world's population—mostly unskilled workers—relocated permanently to other countries (Lindert and Williamson 2001). This was a time when transportation costs were falling and migration policies were relatively liberal, though barriers to immigration had begun to rise. In addition to the large wave of European immigrants to the United States and Latin America, it is estimated that migrations from China and India to less populated countries in Asia were of the same magnitude.

Massive migration to the Americas was a major force in making these countries among the world's richest after the turn of the century. It also helped expedite income convergence between destination and source countries, as wages rose as much as 30 percent in countries of origin and fell 8 to 16 percent in some destination countries in the Americas (Lindert and Williamson 2001). Indeed, it has been estimated that mass migration accounted for as much as 70 percent of the global convergence in living standards that occurred during the nineteenth century (O'Rourke and Williamson 1997, 1999; Taylor and Williamson 1997).

But like trade and capital flows, migration fell dramatically after 1914. The period through World War II saw much tighter immigration controls, apparently motivated by economic concerns—particularly fears that immigration of unskilled workers would lower unskilled wages and so increase inequality in destination countries (O'Rourke and Sinnot 2003). Recovery began in the 1940s but remains incomplete. In contrast to the late nineteenth century, the world stock of migrants today represents only 2 percent of the world's population. The composition of migrant flows has changed as well: skilled workers now make up a much larger share. Migration appears to be driven largely by wage differentials. Legal immigrants to the United States from Mexico see their wages increase ninefold on average. Indonesian immigrants to Malaysia see an increase almost as large (World Bank 2002c).

The contribution of migration to growth is complex and influenced by many factors. For recipient countries migration can provide scarce labor and new skills. Kaldor (1994) argues that it may have allowed such countries to overcome constraints on factor supply to increasing return industries and so increased the growth rate. Recent waves of migration motivated by large wage differentials often fill low-skilled jobs for which there have been increasing labor scarcity and wage pressures. Such migration depresses wages correspondingly in the recipient country, harming some types of workers even as it eases labor constraints and accelerates growth. Demographic changes associated with immigration—broadening the base of the population pyramid and raising fertility rates—have also enhanced growth by reducing the pension burden from aging populations in rich countries.

The impact of migration on labor-exporting countries is less clear. Remitted earnings have been a major source of income for families with members abroad, contributing scarce foreign exchange even when most such funds are used for consumption. In fact, worker remittances have become the second largest source, behind foreign direct investment, of external funding for developing countries.

Still, there can be offsetting detrimental effects for countries that lose skilled workers and entrepreneurs. These losses can weaken pressure to improve the investment climate, with long-term effects on growth opportunities.[9] One recent study argues that the tighter immigration controls of the twentieth century prevented mass migration from being a force for international convergence (O'Rourke and Sinnott 2003). It suggests that rich country policies favoring the immigration of high-skilled workers may have contributed to international divergence in incomes and worsening income distributions in the developing world.

Financial Flows to Developing Countries

The 1970s brought the beginning of a new era in the international financial system and an acceleration in cross-border financial flows. Intermediation of capital funds following the decade's oil shocks, together with the breakup of the Bretton Woods system of fixed exchange rates, flushed new liquidity into international capital markets and increased capital mobility. For many developing countries this led to the gradual easing of capital account restrictions.

Between 1970 and 1997 total capital flows to developing countries underwent an eleven-fold increase, reaching more than $300 billion (table 2.8).[10] During this period official aid fell to $35 billion in 1997, reducing its share from around half to about one-eighth of total flows (figure 2.9). Some of the reasons for the drop in official aid, and policies for its increase and better use, are discussed in chapter 13. Private capital flows, particularly foreign direct investment (FDI), surged to become the dominant source of foreign capital during this period. Between the early 1980s and mid-1990s FDI and other private flows (mainly loans) were of comparable magnitude. But starting in 1997–1998, and corresponding to the financial crises in East Asia and Russia, these other private flows fell sharply, becoming negligible or negative in 2001. FDI has been much more stable.

After FDI, worker remittances have been the second largest source of external funding for developing countries in recent years (see figure 2.9). In 2001 remittances reached $72.3 billion, far exceeding official aid and non-FDI private flows—and equaling 42 percent of FDI.

FDI appears to have been a key factor spurring rapid export growth, with many multinational corporations locating production for world markets in developing countries (particularly those in East and Southeast Asia). FDI has often brought with it access to technology, management techniques, and developed country markets. Recent World Bank estimates suggest that every $1 of FDI results in roughly $1 of additional domestic investment, which is much more than the estimated effects of portfolio investment and bank loans. Moreover, a 1 percent rise in the ratio of FDI to GDP is associated with a 0.18 percent rise in GDP growth—about 50 percent more than is true for domestic investment (Dollar and Kraay 2002, World Bank 2002b). Macroeconomic policies that generate high inflation, excessive government consumption, and economies highly protected from trade and direct foreign investment hamper growth.[11] The slowdown of growth in developing countries after the 1960s and early 1970s stemmed in part from macroeconomic instability, which reduced confidence in government and in its ability to maintain a stable climate for private firms. Stable macroeconomic conditions—meaning fiscal stability and transparency, low inflation, sound monetary and exchange rate policies—support the private sector by reducing risk, providing sound economic signals, and

Table 2.8
Long-term capital flows to developing countries (US$ billions, at constant 2002 prices)

	1985–1989	1990–1994	1995	1996	1997	1998	1999	2000	2001	2002
Official development finance	48.9	58.3	53.9	29.2	35.0	48.3	45.3	33.6	38.4	34.5
Concessional flows	37.6	48.5	44.9	37.0	32.9	37.8	41.5	36.1	38.1	43.0
Official grants[a]	20.0	33.1	32.3	26.6	25.7	28.3	29.6	29.3	29.7	32.9
Official concessional loans	17.5	15.3	12.5	10.4	7.1	9.5	11.9	6.8	8.4	10.2
Official nonconcessional loans	11.4	9.8	9.1	−7.7	2.1	10.5	3.8	−2.5	0.3	−8.5
Private flows	38.1	112.7	177.5	232.6	269.9	270.2	217.7	198.9	170.3	149.5
Private loans	20.1	32.5	53.4	78.2	81.0	87.8	22.1	14.3	−8.7	−2.9
Foreign direct investment[b]	17.0	55.3	104.1	122.2	163.2	175.0	180.6	158.8	172.9	143.0
Portfolio equity investment	1.0	24.9	19.9	32.1	25.7	7.4	15.1	25.7	6.0	9.4
Aggregate net flows	87.0	171.0	231.4	261.8	304.9	318.6	263.1	232.5	208.7	184.0

Note: 2002 numbers are estimates.
[a] Excludes technical cooperation.
[b] IMF data complemented by country sources.
Sources: World Bank (2003c) Country Tables and sources cited therein, World Bank Economic Model, OECD Development Assistance Committee's Geographic Distribution of Flows.

$ billion

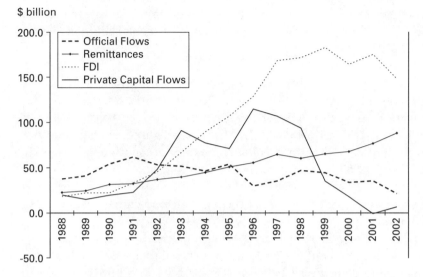

Figure 2.9
Capital flows and remittances to developing countries. *Source:* World Bank, Global Development Finance 2004.

promoting clarity. Openness to trade and foreign investment promote competition and incentives for innovation and entrepreneurship. Thus, better policies in developing countries have brought more FDI, which has brought faster growth.

In contrast, other private flows seem to be much more volatile and have many fewer beneficial effects on growth. Even worse, they can be destabilizing when combined with weak financial systems. International lending during the past two centuries occurred in surges, with each episode followed by a financial crisis—with crises in the 1820s, 1870s, 1890s, 1930s, 1980s, and most recently the 1990s. The lending wave in the 1920s was dominated by refinancing loans to cover debt service on prewar loans and loans to induce German recovery and reparations. This episode came to an end with widespread defaults in the early 1930s by most of Latin America and Eastern Europe, Turkey, and China.

The next big lending spree came in the second half of the 1970s, following the oil price shock of 1973. Between 1970 and 1980 developing countries as a group accumulated debt at a compound rate of 24 percent a year. Their borrowing was facilitated by low interest rates and the willingness of the international financial community, particularly commercial banks, to provide funds. The capital flows came to an abrupt halt with the onset of the global debt crisis that began in Mexico in 1982.

Several factors played a role in the onset of the crisis: higher interest rates, lower commodity prices, chronically large fiscal deficits, and overvalued exchange rates. After the Mexican crisis, external financing for developing countries plummeted—by almost 40 percent between 1981 and 1983 (Edwards 1989). Moreover, highly indebted countries were forced to close their collective current account deficit from $51 billion in 1982 to $9 billion in 1988 (Husain and Diwan 1989). This rapid adjustment was achieved by a severe reduction in imports and investment, which adversely affected growth and employment in these countries.

Despite the adjustment, developing countries continued to accumulate debt throughout the 1980s. For low-income countries total external debt more than tripled between 1980 and 1990, from $126 billion to $422 billion, or from 22 percent of GDP to 54 percent (table 2.9). For middle-income countries it jumped from $454 billion to $1,000 billion, or from 2 percent of GDP to 27 percent. Private and public lending continued to increase until the East Asian and Russian crises of 1997–1998, when it slowed (with much the same variation as in 1995–1997). Lending dropped somewhat in 2000. As before, rapid adjustment required a strong compression of imports and investment. This sequence of lending sprees and debt accumulation, followed by crisis, default, and depression, raises major questions about the wisdom of developing countries' relying on private external loans to finance their development. The first source should be their own savings, though foreign investment, aid, and remittances have substantial roles to play. We return to some of these issues in lecture IV, on action.

Implications for Analysis

Whichever dimension of development we examine, we see fundamental change over the past fifty years—in the income and nonincome dimensions of welfare (chapter 1), economic structure, demographics, environment, trade, and capital flows (this chapter). Surely this demonstrates (as has been a key purpose of these first two chapters) that any development policy or strategy must be founded in an analysis of the drivers of change and how they can be influenced. The policy challenge is to understand, anticipate, exploit, and facilitate the type of change we have described. The dynamic nature of the process implies that policy must embody learning and action at the same time.

We cannot be certain of the next changes, but it is clear that the pace of change has been accelerating in the past two decades, and there is little reason to expect it to stop or slow down. Development policy must be about guiding and fostering the dynamic processes shaping this change—and that is the subject of most of the rest of this book. In concluding this chapter, we confine ourselves to two further points: the type of comparative statistical analysis in our story and the role of institutions, politics, and governance.

Statistical Analysis of Growth

In describing the changing world and highlighting key features, we have made few references to cross-country regression analysis. It is certainly true that we should try to learn by comparing the experiences of developing countries, and cross-country regression analysis is one of the tools for doing so. It can indeed help advance our understanding, and regressions have highlighted, for example, the role of human capital, geography, and institutions in development human capital (see, for example, Knack and Keefer 1995; Gallup, Sachs, and Mellinger 1999; Hall and Jones 1999; Krueger and Lindahl 2001). But readers of the recent literature on development might be forgiven for thinking that regression analysis is the most powerful tool for the modern development economist. While recognizing its contribution, we do not share that view.

The kinds of processes we are describing involve looking inside the aggregates typically used in cross-country regressions, where the overwhelming concern seems to be "explaining" aggregate growth rates in terms of broad aggregate factor inputs and country characteristics. All too often the estimated equations are essentially econometrically unidentified, with powerful interaction effects between, for example, savings and growth, and growth and education (see also Stern 1989 for an early emphasis on this problem, a warning that went largely unheeded in the 1990s).

Rodrik (2003a) provides a helpful diagram to illustrate the issue (figure 2.10). Current income levels depend on both endowments— the capital, labor, and natural resources that a country has at its disposal—and the productivity with which those endowments are used. Both endowments and productivity are deeply endogenous,

Table 2.9
Evolution of external debt in developing countries, 1970–2001

	1970	1975	1980	1985	1990	1995	1996	1997	1998	1999	2000	2001
Debt outstanding and disbursed (DOD), (current US$ billion)												
Low-income countries												
Total external debt	23.7	54.4	126.0	224.5	421.5	554.0	550.7	545.0	581.0	578.1	552.8	533.4
Long-term debt	21.9	47.8	103.6	179.6	360.3	456.6	455.0	451.9	495.1	491.3	473.1	457.3
Public and publicly guaranteed debt	20.8	44.1	95.4	168.0	342.4	416.8	401.3	387.2	420.9	424.7	407.9	398.4
Private nonguaranteed debt	1.1	3.7	8.2	11.6	18.0	48.8	53.7	64.8	74.2	66.6	65.2	58.9
Use of IMF credit	0.3	2.2	5.3	13.7	11.3	15.3	15.0	16.9	23.8	24.9	23.7	21.7
Short-term debt	1.5	4.4	17.1	31.2	49.8	73.1	80.7	76.1	62.0	61.9	55.9	54.3
Middle-income countries												
Total external debt	46.5	133.0	453.6	763.1	1,000.1	1,511.6	1,575.3	1,643.8	1,814.2	1,848.9	1,809.8	1,798.8
Long-term debt	38.8	103.5	329.5	617.4	794.3	1,162.1	1,212.8	1,270.7	1,451.7	1,508.0	1,495.2	1,450.5
Public and publicly guaranteed debt	24.7	74.4	269.4	544.1	752.1	991.4	991.2	986.7	1,031.6	1,044.9	1,025.8	996.0
Private nonguaranteed debt	14.2	29.1	60.1	73.3	42.2	170.7	221.6	284.0	420.1	463.1	469.4	454.5
Use of IMF credit	0.4	1.9	6.2	24.4	23.3	45.8	45.1	42.9	53.2	47.9	34.7	53.6
Short-term debt	7.3	27.6	117.9	121.2	182.5	303.8	317.5	330.3	309.4	293.1	279.9	294.7
% GDP												
Low-income countries												
Total external debt	14.9	18.3	22.2	37.5	53.7	61.1	54.8	53.0	64.1	58.3	53.8	51.0
Long-term debt	13.7	16.1	18.3	30.0	45.9	51.3	45.3	43.9	54.6	49.5	46.0	43.7

Public and publicly guaranteed debt	13.1	14.9	16.8	28.1	43.6	46.0	39.9	37.6	46.4	42.8	39.7	38.1
Private nonguaranteed debt	0.7	1.2	1.4	1.9	2.3	5.4	5.3	6.3	8.2	6.7	6.3	5.6
Use of IMF credit	0.2	0.7	0.9	2.3	1.4	1.7	1.5	1.6	2.6	2.5	2.3	2.1
Short-term debt	1.0	1.5	3.0	5.2	6.3	8.1	8.0	7.4	6.8	6.2	5.4	5.2
Middle income countries												
Total external debt	1.5	1.8	2.1	7.6	27.1	33.6	31.8	31.5	36.1	39.4	35.5	34.9
Long-term debt	1.3	1.4	1.5	6.1	21.5	25.8	24.5	24.4	28.9	32.2	29.4	28.2
Public and publicly guaranteed debt	0.8	1.0	1.3	5.4	20.4	22.0	20.0	18.9	20.6	22.3	20.1	19.4
Private nonguaranteed debt	0.5	0.4	0.3	0.7	1.1	3.8	4.5	5.4	.8.4	9.9	9.2	8.8
Use of IMF credit	0.0	0.0	0.0	0.2	0.6	1.0	0.9	0.8	1.1	1.0	0.7	1.0
Short-term debt	0.2	0.4	0.5	1.2	5.0	6.7	6.4	6.3	6.2	6.3	5.5	5.7

Source: World Bank database.

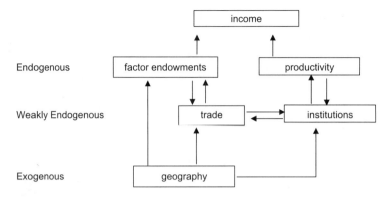

Figure 2.10
Endogenous and exogenous determinants of growth. *Source:* Rodrik (2003b).

meaning that they depend on other factors that need to be incorporated into any analysis of the sources of growth. But even if we take
another step back and examine such underlying "causal" variables as
levels of international trade and quality of institutions, we find that
these factors too are partly endogenous: they depend on each other
and on such truly exogenous factors as geography. Any regression
framework that treats institutions and integration as exogenous (fixed)
variables will therefore yield misleading results. Thus, although regressions have a role to play and can highlight broad regularities, understanding the processes at work requires looking into the details of
economic and social structures and dynamic processes.

Governance, Institutions, and Growth
In concluding this chapter, we must emphasize that an understanding of institutions and governance, and their change, is required to
understand virtually all the processes of change we have examined: in
economic structure, urbanization, environment, demographic, trade,
capital flows, and so on. These changes have been profoundly influenced by institutions and governance. These have themselves under-
gone extraordinary change, in many cases but not always generated
by the structural changes we have described. There are powerful interactions between institutions and governance on the one hand and economic structure and performance on the other. This is a recurring
theme in this book, and in closing this chapter, we examine the profound political changes that have occurred in developing countries in

recent decades, focusing on the quality of governance and democracy. These are difficult to measure, but some rough quantifications point to profound change over the past twenty years on these crucial dimensions for development.

Good governance has been widely recognized as fundamental to growth and development. After surveying more than a century of comparative development experience in forty developing countries, Reynolds (1983, p. 976)—before the era of cross-country regressions— concludes that "the single most important explanatory variable [of development] is political organization and the administrative competence of government." Going back still further, governance's importance is dramatically represented in the frescoes painted by Ambrogio Lorenzetti in the Palazzo Pubblico of Siena around 1340. What the viewer sees are *gli effetti del buon governo*, the effects of good government. Although the causes of good governance are difficult to explain, they are suggested by the painter with the allegories of three virtues—justice, common good, and concord—painted on the wall of the city council's meeting room.

Broadly speaking, governance refers to the traditions and institutions by which authority is exercised in a country. Though governance is not easily defined and measured with precision, the work of Daniel Kaufmann, Aart Kraay, and their collaborators is the current state of the art (Kaufmann, Kraay, and Zoido-Lobatón 1999, 2002; Kaufmann, Kraay, and Mastruzzi 2003). Governance is generally taken to include the processes by which governments are selected, monitored, and replaced; the government's capacity to formulate and implement sound policies; and the respect of citizens and the state for the institutions that govern economic and social interactions among them. Good governance implies a well-run state, but it involves more than just the state. It depends on how power is exercised in "all political, social, economic and cultural hierarchies," as Fernand Braudel (1982, p. 555) puts it. Institutions that protect the property rights of the broad cross-section of society, and constrain the power of politicians and rich elites, help create a climate conducive to growth and empowerment. By contrast, institutions that create political instability, concentrate political power in the hands of elites, confiscate property arbitrarily, and deny basic rights to the majority of the population are bad for growth and empowerment because they discourage investment in physical capital, human capital, and technology. They also prevent entry and investment by productive agents, including poor people.

The World Bank tries to capture some key aspects of governance in its Country Policy and Institutional Assessments (CPIAs).[12] Movements in this index over the period 1999–2003 for developing countries, by region, are shown in figure 2.11. In most regions, there has been a moderate increase in recent years in the components of the CPIA index that measures the quality of institutions (social inclusion, public sector management).[13] The component measuring macroeconomic and trade policies shows improvements for some regions and a deterioration for others. In general, countries that have had high growth have also seen strong improvements in governance. One word of caution, however: the mechanisms relating governance to growth are complex, and one should not conclude from the correlation between GDP growth and governance indicators that higher per capita income leads to improvements in governance. There is no such thing as an automatic virtuous circle in which good governance leads to higher incomes and higher incomes in turn lead to better governance. Indeed, while China and India have achieved strong growth in the past two decades, it would be difficult to argue that corruption has decreased.

Political stability and the political conditions under which governments promote—or retard—economic development are an important aspect of governance. Achieving economic growth depends on maintaining a modicum of political stability, whether stability is defined as the absence of episodes of social unrest (such as demonstrations, riots, coups d'état, and political assassinations) or the absence of frequent changes in the ruling party (whether by constitutional or unconstitutional means). Political instability affects growth because it increases uncertainty, which has a negative impact on many private economic decisions, such as those about investments and savings. The empirical literature suggests that political instability also retards economic reforms (Alesina and others 1996, Perotti 1996)

There has been a considerable improvement in some key measures of political governance in recent decades. Twenty years ago, only around one-third of developing countries were democratic (Freedom House 1999). Today that share is about two-thirds. We have seen the collapse of political and military dictatorships in Asia and Latin America and the political transformation of most of Eastern Europe and the former Soviet Union. According to Marshall and Gurr (2003), for example, the number of autocratic countries fell from eighty to twenty-eight between 1985 and 2002.

As democracy has spread, there has also been an increase in the number of political regimes with a mix of democratic and autocratic

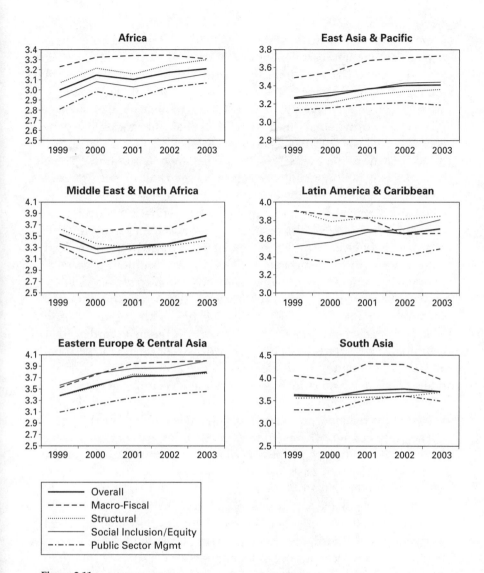

Figure 2.11
Country Policy and Institutional Assessment (CPIA) indexes. *Source:* World Bank data.
Note: y-axis = CPIA score.

features, and that increase should concern us (Zakaria 1997). These regimes are highly unstable, with more than 50 percent experiencing a major regime change within five years and more than 70 percent within ten years. Moreover, these polities are extremely vulnerable to armed civil conflict. They are about six times more likely than democracies and two and a half times more likely than autocracies to experience new civil wars (Marshall and Gurr 2003).[14]

Inconsistencies in governance are also common. For example, some countries may hold competitive elections for a legislature that exercises no effective control over the executive branch, or allow open political competition among some social groups while seriously restricting the participation of others.[15] There are many reasons for such inconsistencies. Some countries may be implementing a staged transition from autocracy to greater democracy. Others may be instituting piecemeal reforms in response to growing demands from emerging political groups. Social conflict often undermines democratic experiments: some regimes may be unable to fully institutionalize reforms due to serious disagreements among social groups, some may harden their institutions in response to increasing challenges or due to the personal ambitions of opportunistic leaders, and others may simply lose control of the political dynamics that enable (or disable) effective governance.

We have seen throughout this chapter the dramatic changes involved in the dynamic processes of development.

The processes are dynamic in the sense that history counts, learning takes place, institutions adapt and change, and the structures of the economy and society are transformed. We see these transformations across the whole range of human life, from demography and family structures to the shape and growth of the economy.

Drawing on the experience of development described and analyzed in chapters 1 and 2, the next chapter crystallizes some basic lessons that provide key elements of the foundation for the strategy set out in lecture II. As we will see, successful development depends on markets and incentives that function reasonably effectively amid all of this structural change—which depends in turn on a functioning government. The state has crucial roles to play in providing security, making social investments, ensuring provision of infrastructure, establishing legal and financial institutions, and conserving environmental resources. Chapter 3 turns to this question of the role of the state in development.

3   Lessons of Development Policy

The development experience of the past half-century, outlined in chapter 2, is at once heartening and disappointing. Determining the lessons of this experience is not easy, yet it is essential. To move forward, we must understand questions such as: Do we agree on what we are trying to achieve when we talk about promoting development? How have some countries—such as Botswana and the Republic of Korea—managed to increase their average incomes at such remarkable rates for so many years, while others—such as Haiti and Zambia—have suffered such sharp declines? What were the key forces driving such strong performance in the developing world in reducing child mortality and expanding literacy—sometimes even in countries where income growth had stalled? And most fundamentally, can we draw any broad lessons about spurring development? Or is each case so dependent on local history and circumstances as to make that impossible?

Based on our reviews of the development literature (Stern 1989, 2001) and our collective experience, working on and in developing countries for some seventy years, we strongly believe that it is possible to draw constructive general lessons. There are many ways to structure these lessons, but the broad outlines of most formulations have much in common. In a nutshell, the messages of this chapter are as follows:

· The first fundamental lesson from development experience and the literature is that the objective of development is not just to raise incomes, but also to enhance all individuals' ability to shape their lives.
· The second and third lessons deal with the nature of development and the role of policy. The second lesson is that development is a dynamic process that hinges on learning, history, and changing structures and preferences. The third lesson focuses on the state's substantial role in catalyzing and shaping this dynamic process.

• Lessons four, five, and six involve growth, its determinants, and its importance for reducing poverty. The fourth lesson emphasizes the centrality of institutions and governance for growth. The fifth stresses the importance of openness and integration as engines of growth. And the sixth makes the link between growth and poverty reduction.

• Lessons seven and eight are about empowerment. Lesson seven provides a definition of empowerment and emphasizes its role in effective development, while lesson eight emphasizes the importance of country ownership—that is, commitment to reform as opposed to externally designed and imposed programs.

These eight lessons from development experience are rooted in the empirical evidence presented in chapters 1 and 2 and in this chapter as well. When combined with the theoretical analysis set out in the chapter 4, these lessons will lead directly to the development strategy proposed in chapter 5.

Objectives of Development

In the early years after World War II, the study and practice of development focused on improving a country's capacity to generate income, and subsequently on ensuring that income growth was widely shared among the population. In recent decades the objectives of development have moved beyond income to encompass education and health. This emphasis recalls the extension of development into the goal of meeting basic needs in the 1960s, but goes well beyond that approach in both its ambition and its analytical foundations. We examined its scope and progress along different dimensions in chapter 1.

Amartya Sen has argued persuasively that the most appropriate way to look at development objectives is in terms of "the substantive freedoms—the capabilities—to choose a life one has reason to value" (Sen 1999, p. 74). This is not only an attractive philosophical principle, it is also the dominant view expressed by poor people all over the world. In interviews with more than 60,000 poor people from over 60 countries, one message came through very clearly: poor people seek not only income growth but also empowerment, participation, and inclusion (World Bank 2001c, Narayan and others 2000; see also chapter 1).

From this perspective the main goal of development should be to increase individuals' ability to shape their lives. It follows that including

poor people in processes to improve education and health outcomes—
and thus enhancing their capabilities to improve their lives—is an end
in itself, regardless of how it affects economic growth. It also follows
that empowering and including poor people goes beyond making
poor people targets of education and health investments, or redistributing the proceeds of growth to poor people. Empowerment requires
that poor people themselves be agents,[1] that they have choices and be
involved in the creation of wealth.[2]

Looking at development objectives in this way, we see that many
goals or ends are also means of achieving development. Education, for
example, raises individual incomes and economic growth, making it an
effective tool for development. But it is also an end in itself, because
being educated is a key capability. The same is true of governance
structures (such as arrangements that foster voice for people and increase the accountability of public officials) that create conditions for
poor people to participate in decisions intended to benefit them. In addition to leading to better outcomes, such participation gives people a
sense of control over their lives.

Recognizing broader development objectives allows us to better
gauge progress. The tendency of economists to focus on income
growth is understandable, but it has obscured progress in other areas.
Recent decades have seen historically unprecedented social progress,
as described in chapter 1: unprecedented gains in infant survival rates,
life expectancy, and literacy. Progress on social indicators has sometimes come even in countries and regions that have experienced little
or no per capita income growth in recent decades, such as sub-Saharan
Africa (Goldin, Rogers, and Stern 2002). This divergence underscores
the need to consider social indicators separately from, and in addition
to, income indicators. We cannot assume that these different dimensions move in lockstep.

Thus, development is fundamentally about enhancing opportunity.
But it is also about the ability to take advantage of opportunities, and
that depends on the constraints on an individual and on his or her
assets, physical and human. Empowerment, a concept central to the
strategy proposed in chapter 5, goes even beyond expanding opportunity, building assets, and reducing constraints, to the changing of
preferences.[3]

As we shall argue, the process of development involves substantial
changes in aspirations and attitudes. Education often changes not only
people's ability to achieve goals, but also their goals. Indeed, many

people embark on education for themselves or their children with the confidence that their preferences will change. They may not know for certain what this change will be or what it means, yet they are convinced that it is desirable.

This notion of preference change raises serious difficulties for the measurement of welfare change in policy assessments. For an external development partner, preference change greatly complicates the nature of collaboration because it raises difficult ethical and analytical questions. On what ethical basis is it desirable (or even acceptable) to work to influence preferences, and which preferences do we want to encourage? These are difficult questions, but there is no option but to grapple with them. Preference change is a fundamental part of the development process.

Development as a Dynamic Process

Development is a dynamic process in four key respects: change is central, history matters, structures are endogenous, and learning is at the heart of the story. Chapter 2 shows that two intertwined processes are crucial for development: the creation of an investment climate favorable for sustained growth, and the empowerment of all people so that they can participate fully in growth. Both of these are processes involving history, dynamic structure, and learning (see chapter 5 for further discussion).

When we say that investment climate and empowerment are dynamic processes, we are not talking about comparisons of two equilibria, about steady states, or about being on a production frontier—the comfortable concepts of standard theory. We are talking about processes of change, adaptation, creativity, and learning.

Technological change has been a basic element in the foundations of modern economic growth and in the progress that has reduced mortality around the world. In developing countries this progress is seen in both technological innovation and, more often, diffusion of existing technologies through learning by watching and learning by doing. These are a central focus of modern endogenous growth models, and they are part of the story we want to tell. Yet change in developing countries encompasses much more than technological advance and diffusion. Development requires fundamental changes in the organization of production, in approaches to and investment in infrastructure, in allocations of output and labor, and in institutions, organizations, and governance. It also requires, in many cases, profound changes in behavior. These changes extend beyond the shifts in production functions and growth of inputs underlying most modern growth theories.

The challenge for public policy is to better understand and influence these processes. Experience from developing and transition countries suggests that certain types of public actions can generate powerful virtuous circles or increasing returns. There are striking examples from around the world of direct public action under committed leadership achieving remarkable, sustainable success in promoting human development. Tendler (1997) describes one example, discussed later in this chapter, from the state of Ceará in northeast Brazil, where committed government leadership helped reduce infant mortality by one-third in just over a decade.

In the area of private sector development, too, public action can energize and coordinate investment and entrepreneurial activity. Government can facilitate private activity by ensuring that property rights and contracts are respected and by investing in education, health, roads, piped water, and so on. Moreover, government programs can reinforce each other. For example, if roads improve, reduced travel times may increase the demand for health services, and increased availability of alternative fuels may free up time of girls who collect firewood, enabling them to attend school. The challenge is to understand what kinds of policy change can generate strong, sustained increases in growth rates and large transformations in education, health, and other outcomes.

Markets and State as Complements

Private enterprise, operating through the market, has been the main force responsible for sustained economic growth. But the state has also played a major role in facilitating economic growth and improving well-being. When it has functioned well, the state's role in economic growth has been in providing the framework for effectively functioning markets and in facilitating services and coping with externalities in areas where the unaided market might perform badly, such as education, health, and environmental concerns.

As we have learned repeatedly—whether from the experiences of East Asia, Russia, Latin America, sub-Saharan Africa, or OECD countries—a productive and dynamic private sector does not emerge in a vacuum. One essential role of the state is to provide the right environment for entrepreneurial activity to flourish. That means an environment where contracts are honored and markets can function, where basic infrastructure is ensured, and, of particular importance, where poor people are enabled to participate. Without this role, private entrepreneurship may be diverted into rent seeking or other socially unproductive activities. Similarly, human development depends on state action to promote it. For instance, Easterlin (1996) makes the case that only the central administrations of nation-states have the ability to isolate regions from epidemics and contain subsistence crises, which contributes to economic growth.

Over the long term most development goals will not be achieved by the highly interventionist approach followed by many countries in the 1950s and 1960s, or by the minimal government free-market approach widely advocated in the 1980s and early 1990s. But choosing a better way is not a matter of striking the right balance between state and market or finding a middle way on some spectrum. These ways of defining the role of the state suggest that states and markets are substitutes, when in fact they are usually complements.

Take the example—recently very salient in the United States and elsewhere—of government regulation of securities markets. This is clearly a case where better regulation can improve the functioning of markets and increase the efficiency of private sector activity. As a second example, consider the effects of a well-developed financial sector on state activity. An efficient bond market can lower government borrowing costs, reducing the share of the government budget devoted to paying interest and potentially freeing resources for health, education, and other public services. Put simply, governments need markets and markets need governments. As we shall argue, that implies that a simplistic "small government" approach is not the recipe for rapid development.

This view is not universally held. Some authors have argued that the only role for the state should be to establish and preserve law and order and ensure national defense. To go much further, it is claimed, would constitute an unacceptable interference with freedom and liberty. This minimalist or "night watchman" view of the state (Nozick 1974) is typically inspired by views about individual rights and responsibilities and about justifiable (or unjustifiable) methods of transfer of resources. In that sense it is concerned with procedures and opportunities rather than consequences or ends—in terms of, for example, the production and allocation of goods.

A view of markets as processes is also part of the Austrian school of economics, which has experienced a revival in the past twenty years (Kirzner 1987). This school's central idea is that decentralized markets with individual decision making provide incentives for learning, discovery, and innovation. Beyond any ethical justification, markets in this view are crucial to economic advancement. The Austrian school shares some similarity of spirit with the neoclassical view that individual maximization in a competitive market context leads to economic efficiency. But the Austrians' emphasis on the unknown and the process of discovery is not easily captured by the standard extension of the competitive model to contingent goods and insurance markets.

Much of the discussion of markets and governments is dominated by the idea of market failure. The progress of theory—for example, the emergence of information economics—has provided much clearer insights into what constitutes market failure than was available to the influential early writers who saw market failure as a reason for comprehensive planning (see chapter 4). At the same time, experience and theory have contributed to a much keener appreciation of the problems of government intervention. Much of the theory of government failure is based on ideas about how governments actually function and the incentives they create for individuals inside and outside the government.

Our view, developed in these lectures, is that there is a substantial role for the state in economic affairs. This is not, however, the extensive government involvement in production envisaged by many movements and writers of the early twentieth century, who spoke of the need for the state to capture the "commanding heights" of the economy (Yergin and Stanislaw 2002). Rather, we argue, the state's activities should focus on health, education, infrastructure, protecting poor people, and nurturing the environment for productive entrepreneurship.

The importance of this role for the state is a point that Stern made repeatedly in writings in the late 1980s and early 1990s (see Stern 1989, 1991b, 1992), when economic thinking was dominated by a naive market fundamentalism. Such naiveté was associated, in its early stages, with many of the problems of the transition to market in the newly independent countries of the former Soviet Union. The role of the state and its effect on economic and social progress depends crucially on the quality of governance and institutions. That is the essence of the next section.

The Centrality of Institutions and Governance

In many countries the state is part of the problem, not part of the solution. In such countries the state is characterized by weak institutions and poor governance. Following the definition in the *Oxford English Dictionary*, here the term *institutions* refers to organization and rules, such as for public service provision. Institutions can be public, private, or social. *Governance* refers to the "manner of governing." It includes public institutions and their functioning as well as the behavior of all those—politicians, civil servants or otherwise—involved in government (see the discussion in chapter 2).[4]

Countries that suffer from poor institutions and weak governance are beset by government harassment of citizens and business, feeble public services and infrastructure, and poor policy design and implementation. The judiciary, and legal system more generally, are neither effective nor predictable, contracts are only weakly enforceable, and crime is widespread. Public officials steal public funds, receive payments on public contracts, and dispense administrative jobs for a price. Bribes have to be paid to officials as "incentive bonuses," as a means of lowering the costs of public goods and services, or as protection money for the police. In short, these societies have been unable to develop an environment in which even-handed, predictable, just rules form the basis for economic and social interactions, and in which there is basic provision of infrastructure and public services needed for productive economic and social activity. Put another way, such societies have neither the soft nor hard infrastructure for robust economic development.

Max Weber was probably the first social scientist to systematically and empirically examine the relationships among governance and economic development. He emphasized the rule of law (*Rechtsstaat*) and proposed a comparative analysis of the role of law in China and the West (Messick 1999).

There is indeed an important set of relationships between law, economic policy, and development. To illustrate, consider the changes in legal institutions in the Republic of Korea, Malaysia, and Taiwan between 1960 and 1995, the crucial growth period for these countries. Legal reform largely involved transplanting parts of Western legislation, including competition law, environmental and consumer protection, intellectual property rights, and securities and exchange regulations (Pistor and Wellons 1998). Legal reform occurred in response to specific crises—such as environmental disasters and abuses of monopoly power—generally under political or financial pressure from foreigners. The economic takeoff of the East Asian tiger countries went hand in hand with a strengthened role of the state, and legal change preceded the economic outcomes. During the 1980s policy changes prompted economic change that gave rise to the demand for new legislation, and the repeal of numerous laws shifted control rights from the state to the market.

China's rapid growth, by contrast, has not been supported by clear and enforceable legal structures: it has been said that there are rules but not much law. What matters is that economic actors have some confidence, through their understanding of the rules of the game and past practice, that they can reap the rewards of their actions. This crucial example emphasizes that we must take care not to be overly formal in our understanding of the enforcement of property rights and must avoid overworking the term *rule of law*.

There are many other areas where institutions and governance are important for growth. We highlight those that influence the strength and form of private sector competition. Freedom of entry and exit are crucial to entrepreneurship and the functioning of competition. Freedom of entry is well understood, but freedom of exit is also essential. Firms that cannot exit without great cost if things go wrong may be less likely to enter, and firms may be reluctant to enter markets if incumbents have protected positions (Djankov and others 2002 and World Bank 2003b provide ample evidence).

This is a case where good policies and institutions complement each other. For example, government efforts to provide an institutional structure to promote competition domestically can be made easier if markets are subjected to greater competitive forces from abroad. This is one reason that a developmentally sound trade policy is so important for growth.

The quality of governance can also shift the arena for private sector competition. If firm owners and managers are subject to extensive bureaucratic harassment, it may not only reduce their productivity directly, it can also send them the message that competing for political favors and privileged treatment is more lucrative than competing in the market for customers and profits.

The institutions and governance that affect inclusion and empowerment are also important for growth. One point that is often overlooked when the role of institutions is discussed is that they are relevant not only for efficiency but also for equity. As Rawls (1999 [1971], p. 242) puts it, "The main problem of distributive justice is the choice of a social system. The social system is to be designed so that the resulting distribution is just however things turn out." The *World Development Report 2004* highlights institutions that determine the effectiveness of service delivery in health, education, social protection, and infrastructure used by poor people (World Bank 2003a).

But formal institutions and governance are only part of the story— and often a small part. Social institutions fostering cohesion are also important for economic development. Where does this social cohesion come from? Low social polarization, and formal rules that constrain government from acting arbitrarily, are associated with the development of cooperative norms and trust (Knack and Keefer 1997). The term *social capital* is used to cover norms, associations, and networks that influence trust and individual and community responses to different kinds of incentives and opportunities. Poor people often depend on their networks to secure credit and share risks. At the community level, there have been innovative efforts to measure social capital and demonstrate its importance for provision of local public services (see Coleman 1990, Putnam 1993, Fukuyama 1996, Knack and Keefer 1997, Zak and Knack 2001, Narayan and Pritchett 1999, Dasgupta and Serageldin 2000, Grootaert and van Bastelaer 2002).

The most extreme examples of breakdowns in governance, erosion of institutions, and collapse of social cohesion are usually associated with a radical, sometimes catastrophic, decline in living standards. For example, independence generated a massive shock for Moldova, the Caucasus, and Central Asia. Politically, it resulted in authoritarian rule or highly unstable competition between factions. Nation-building efforts broke down because of lack of consensus on the state's new role, exacerbated by regional and national conflicts and other geopolitical factors. In a very short period, these newly independent countries— particularly Armenia, Georgia, the Kyrgyz Republic, Moldova, and Tajikistan, which are relatively poor in natural resources—experienced a massive decline in living standards (largely because independence meant the loss of significant fiscal and quasi-fiscal subsidies). Poverty skyrocketed, the distribution of assets shifted radically, and income inequality increased sharply (with Gini coefficients doubling).

Many of these problems arose because state institutions were captured by small, powerful interest groups—generally the former local Soviet nomenklatura and their allies. Economies remain in limbo, neither socialist nor market, because these elites have proven utterly inimical to reform. The disintegration of Soviet power contributed to weak state capacity, because under the Soviet system, administrative capabilities were concentrated in the center. Weak capacity has led to a breakdown in economic and social services and contributed to the increase in poverty (Dethier 2003).

Of course, we need not search inside the former Soviet Union to find cases where weak state capacity has led to dramatic economic decline. Consider Zambia, which is often cited as a textbook example of a country where aid perversely abetted weak policy during the 1970s and 1980s. Like many other countries, Zambia was buffeted by the 1973 oil shock. But it was also hit soon after by a major decline in the price of copper, its main export. In ensuing years, as a Zambian government document notes, "Zambia failed to make the necessary adjustments in economic policy in the wake of the declining economic environment" (Republic of Zambia 2000, p. 2). In attempts to maintain living standards, the country borrowed extensively from international lenders and imposed price controls on consumer goods.

This way of adjusting to new circumstances was unsuccessful. The result was that, as measured by a World Bank index of the quality of policies and institutions, Zambia's policies steadily worsened between the late 1960s and late 1980s (World Bank 1998a). Per capita income dropped sharply, from $438 in 1975 to $300 in 1997 (in 1987 dollars; Republic of Zambia 2000). Although external circumstances posed a severe challenge, government interventions magnified and delayed adjustment to shocks, rather than dampening them.

Moving beyond these examples of weak governance and a poorly performing state, in too many other cases the problem is a failed state or one ensnared in civil war. Few things are as detrimental to development progress as violent social conflict. Among the countries with the poorest economic performance since World War II are not only states that have failed to adjust to economic shocks, but also many that have been deeply enmeshed in civil conflict, including Algeria, Angola, Burundi, Democratic Republic of Congo, El Salvador, Mozambique, Nicaragua, and Uganda. Moreover, some states (such as Afghanistan) have failed so thoroughly that they have been unable to collect basic economic data.

If a state cannot provide basic security, let alone take steps to improve the investment climate and provide basic education and health care, then growth and development go into reverse. Although these conflict-prone countries were often poor growth performers even before their wars, one estimate is that "after a typical civil war of seven years duration, incomes would be around 15 percent lower than had the war not happened, implying an approximately 30 percent increase in the incidence of absolute poverty" (Collier and others 2003, p. 17). The relationship between conflict and growth highlights the importance of the lessons on governance and institutions, and on the complementarity between states and markets.

Openness as an Engine of Growth

During the 1940s and 1950s, as discussed in chapter 2, the vast majority of developing countries adopted development strategies based on protectionism and trade controls. The case for protectionism rested on four main arguments. First, capital accumulation could be expedited by limiting consumption of imported goods. Second, accelerated development required that investment outpace savings, with consequent pressure on the balance of payments, necessitating the direct restriction of imports. Third, the consequences of fluctuations in export earnings could not be handled through local institutions and markets, and necessitated import controls. Finally, development was essentially about industrialization, and "late starters" required infant industry protection to gain a foothold and grow (Little 1982).

These arguments, combined with the impressive growth achieved by some countries that took this approach, helped sustain development policies based on import substitution—even though the considerable costs of these policies were being recognized by the early 1960s. By 1970, when Little, Scitovsky, and Scott published their famous study on industry and trade in developing countries, there was growing agreement among economists—with the significant exception of the more radical underdevelopment and *dependencia* schools represented by Paul Baran, Samir Amin, André Gunder Frank, and Fernando Henrique Cardoso—that import substitution policies were inefficient and led to undesirable biases against exports. Most economists believed that greater economic openness would increase the demand for unskilled labor, contributing to greater equality. This argument is in line with a simple Heckscher-Ohlin analysis of comparative advantage in international trade.

This idea of international integration as an engine of growth has been bolstered by the experiences of numerous countries over the past three decades. Between the 1970s and 1990s more than twenty developing countries—led by China and India and including Bangladesh,

Mexico, and Thailand—rapidly integrated with the world economy. During the 1990s alone 3 billion people in these countries saw their per capita incomes rise by about 5 percent a year, compared with just 2 percent growth in rich countries—and a drop in nonintegrating developing countries (World Bank 2002b). These integrating countries greatly increased the share of trade in gross domestic product (GDP), and trade liberalization and openness have brought large benefits in terms of growth and well-being.

Does openness to foreign trade and investment, coupled with complementary reforms such as tariff reductions, necessarily lead to faster growth in developing countries? Not necessarily; without supporting policies and institutions on the domestic side, import liberalization could lead to a deluge of imports (benefiting consumers) without a corresponding healthy supply response on the export side (which is necessary to benefit workers). But coupled with improvements in the investment climate and human development, increased integration can be a powerful driver of growth and poverty reduction. Countries that have had large increases in trade integration (as measured by the ratio of trade to GDP) have also had accelerations in growth. This relationship persists in cross-country statistical studies even after controlling for reverse causality from growth to trade—which is likely to be important—and for changes in other institutions and policies.

Our focus here is not on the direct benefits to consumers from liberalizing foreign trade and allowing lower-cost imports, though these benefits are considerable. Rather, it is on the longer-term benefits to productivity growth that openness can bring. More open economies are more innovative and dynamic, and so more flexible and able to sustain accelerated growth over long periods. Powerful evidence supports this claim. First, developing countries often have large productivity dispersion across firms making similar things. High-productivity and low-productivity firms coexist, and in small markets there is often insufficient competition to spur innovation. A consistent finding of firm-level studies is that openness leads to lower productivity dispersion (Haddad 1993, Haddad and Harrison 1993, Harrison 1994). High-cost producers leave the market as prices fall. Assuming (as seems reasonable) these firms were less productive or were experiencing falling productivity, their exits represent productivity improvements for the industry.

Although destruction and creation of firms are normal parts of a well-functioning economy, too often attention is paid only to destruction—missing half the picture and the key element in the growth story. The increase in exits is only part of the adjustment. Granted, it is the first and most painful part. But if there are not significant barriers to factor mobility or other barriers to entry, there will be new entrants. Exits are often front-loaded, visible, and vocal. But in a dynamic, innovative economy, there can be substantial gains in employment and production over time, particularly for poor or unemployed workers without privileges or entrenched rights who depend on the buoyancy of the labor market.

Wacziarg (2001) examines competition and entry by analyzing eleven episodes of trade liberalization in the 1980s. Using data on the number of firms, he calculates that entry rates were 20 percent higher in countries that reduced barriers to trade than in those that did not. Although other changes beyond trade opening were taking place, this is a sizable effect, and it indicates that there was strong potential for new firms to respond to new incentives.

There is also evidence that while exit rates may be significant during periods of trade adjustment, entry rates may be of comparable magnitudes. Using plant-level data from Chile, Colombia, and Morocco spanning several years in the 1980s, Roberts and Tybout (1996) find that when these countries initiated trade reforms, exit rates ranged from 6 to 11 percent a year, and entry rates from 6 to 13 percent. Over time the cumulative turnover was substantial, with a quarter to a third of firms turning over within four years.

The higher turnover of firms is an important source of the dynamic benefits of openness. In general, dying firms have falling productivity, and new firms tend to increase their productivity over time (Liu and Tybout 1996; Aw, Chung, and Roberts 2000; Roberts and Tybout 1996). In Taiwan, Aw, Chung and Roberts (2000) find that within a five-year period, the replacement of low-productivity firms with new, higher-productivity entrants accounted for at least half of the technological advance in many Taiwanese industries.

Similarly, in a study of India's machine tool industry, Sutton (2002) finds that some firms were extremely competitive in the production of computer-numerically controlled lathes. Comparing the Indian firms to their competitors in Japan and Taiwan, he finds that the real productivity of the best Indian firms improved in the face of the increased international competition that resulted from India's lowering of trade barriers in the 1990s. Moreover, that productivity was close to that of Taiwanese firms, which lead the world market for such lathes. Since the wages for the skilled labor in this field are six times higher in

Taiwan, the best Indian firms are very competitive domestically and internationally.

Sutton also found huge variations in productivity among Indian producers—much more so than among Taiwanese firms. Large productivity differences among firms producing the same thing are common in heavily regulated, relatively closed economies. With a more open strategy, we would expect some shakeout in this industry. More successful firms would expand, perhaps taking over some competitors, and other firms would go out of business.

Although these studies shed some light on why open economies are more innovative and dynamic, they also remind us why increasing integration is controversial. There is more dislocation in an open, dynamic economy, with some firms closing and others starting up. Some currently employed workers will lose out in the short to medium term because of liberalization, either because of unemployment or a decline in their earnings (Rodrik 1997). And yet adjustment costs borne by some workers do not justify continued protection. In the protected status quo, someone is already paying the costs of the implicit subsidies: an import tariff is a production subsidy financed by a tax on consumption. The long-term losers under protection include consumers and potential workers in sectors that protection discriminates against. Their losses are greater than the benefits to those benefiting from protection, particularly when we consider the forgone economic dynamism.

How can countries ensure that trade openness translates into better outcomes for workers despite these dislocations? If workers have good social protection and opportunities to develop new skills, nearly everyone can benefit. By social protection, we do not mean that poor countries should emulate the unemployment benefit systems and social policies of OECD countries. It is illusory to imagine that poor countries with strained public finances can afford welfare systems like those in rich countries.

The best social protection is an economy where displaced workers can find employment; economies that promote a strong investment climate and empower poor people to participate are probably the most robust system of social protection. But targeted transfers can also play a valuable role. By avoiding long-term damage from short-run dislocation, which could take the form of displaced workers withdrawing their children from school, for example, and helping credit-constrained workers take on productive opportunities for self-employment, such transfers may contribute to growth and empowerment of poor people (see chapter 8 and Bourguignon 2003b).

Growth as an Engine of Poverty Reduction

Over the past fifty years the world has seen economic growth that is remarkable by historical standards, and poverty has declined significantly. The key lesson of this experience is that higher growth is generally accompanied by faster falls in poverty.

Poverty has fallen most sharply in countries that have grown rapidly, such as China, India, Uganda, and Vietnam, where the poverty rate appears to have declined by more than 5 percent a year between 1993 and 1999 (World Bank 2002c). This is not to say that growth always benefits poor people equally, or even that they always benefit. But global inequality has leveled off precisely because populous poor countries (notably Bangladesh, China, India, and Vietnam) have seen sharp accelerations in growth (see chapter 2).

The extent to which growth is shared has been the focus of a large literature. On average, periods of growth have not been accompanied by any worsening of the income distribution—meaning that on average, poor people have seen their incomes rise as rapidly (in percentage terms) as those of the population as a whole (Deininger and Squire 1996, Dollar and Kraay 2002). In the 1990s some countries saw inequality increase (China and the United States are two important examples), while others experienced declines. The number of growth episodes in which poor people's share of income fell roughly offsets the number in which it rose. But the large majority of growth episodes have raised poor people's absolute incomes. Growth also tends to contribute to progress on social dimensions of poverty, albeit less strongly and consistently than it does to progress on income poverty (see chapter 2).

An examination of the empirical evidence leads to three conclusions. First, looking across countries, there is little evidence of a relationship between growth and inequality. Second, faster growth means faster poverty reduction. Third, an increase in inequality tends to increase poverty. But a difficult issue in establishing a development strategy for a given country, as pointed out by Bourguignon (2003b), is whether growth and distribution are independent of each other or, on the contrary, are closely interrelated. Does faster growth tend to reduce or increase inequality in a given economy? Are there reasons to believe that inequality slows growth in that country? Recent microeconomic case studies indicate that the relationship between growth and inequality in a country can be strong and sometimes complex (Bourguignon 2002). For example, Latin America's growth experience over the past two decades suggests that faster growth has been associated with increasing demand for skilled (relative to unskilled) labor and a widening of wage differentials. It is possible to say more when specific reforms are considered individually. Specific policies and institutions also influence growth. For example, whenever fiscal reforms have led to price stabilization, a reduction in inequality has resulted (De Ferranti and others 2003). Labor market institutions (such as unions, minimum wage rules, and employment benefits) tended to reinforce inequality because they protect the interest of formal sector workers at the expense of informal workers and the unemployed. In almost all countries, the dominant majority of poor workers are employed in the informal sector, where they are not protected by formal benefits, minimum wage rules, or unions (De Ferranti and others 2003). So while promoting growth is almost always a sound strategy for poverty reduction, it is also important to focus on any associated effects on distribution.

Empowerment and Participation

Empowering people—by which we mean ensuring that they can participate effectively in the economy and the society—is central to an effective development strategy. Empowerment is both an end and a means of achieving other goals (see chapter 1), and it influences other valued outcomes in many ways. Most obviously, growth depends on a skilled and capable workforce (or at least one that is rapidly becoming more skilled), so empowering poor people to improve their health and education contributes to growth. Empowerment also increases a poor person's willingness and ability to take risks and innovate. Furthermore, empowerment contributes to improvements in governance. For example, where private sector development is held back by rampant corruption, empowerment helps give people access to information, assets, networks, and legal standing, which allows them to challenge corrupt officials and practices.

Empowerment is a term and concept unfamiliar to many economists, and departures from their standard frameworks can make them uncomfortable and dismissive. But in our view empowerment is a concept of great importance for understanding development and development policy. Here we shall illustrate with some examples, then turn to definitions and clarification. (Some of these issues are addressed further in lecture III, on research.)

Empowerment can mean increasing the ability of people to influence the management of their local school. It means that their voices are heard and that schools have some accountability to them as stakeholders. Similarly, people who rely on irrigation schemes are more empowered if they can participate in a water users' association that has some voice in how water is allocated. Otherwise they are at the mercy of officials, without any means other than bribes to influence their decisions. Empowerment is also about households being able to report the performance of and exercise influence over utilities that supply them with electricity or water. This includes involvement in determining where lines are located and in setting priorities for routings and allocations.

Empowerment is also about having some security over assets, such as the land or house that an individual occupies. If rights are secure, an individual is much more likely to have the confidence to invest in the land or house. He or she can rent it out if a decision is made to move temporarily in search of work. It can be used as collateral for loans to make investments. These examples show that secure property rights, particularly for land and houses, play a vital role in the ability of people—especially poor people—to shape their lives. Such rights are key aspects of empowerment. This is at the heart of the argument of Hernando de Soto (1989, 2000), who has made this point convincingly over the past two decades. He speaks of the "dead capital" in land and homes that can be unlocked and has offered calculations of its magnitude. He estimates that in sub-Saharan Africa this dead capital is worth roughly $1 trillion, or around three times the region's GDP (de Soto 2000).

There are also examples of communities that have acted in specific, practical ways to enhance empowerment. These not only show that the empowerment perspective can point us to practical policies that can make a big difference in people's lives, they also help identify key elements in institutional structures and arrangements that can enhance empowerment. Consider the following:

• In the EDUCO (Educación con participación de la comunidad) program in El Salvador, the government empowered community associations to hire and fire teachers in community-managed schools. As a result net enrollments increased significantly, standardized test scores improved, and teacher absenteeism fell. These results were driven by an increase in the accountability of schools to communities, combined with good local organizational capacity.

• In the late 1980s Ceará, a state of 7 million people in northeast Brazil, had very weak health indicators. The newly elected leader in the late 1980s responded by launching a publicity campaign for a public health program to inform communities of health opportunities and help them press local governments to adopt the program. The state government also dramatically expanded the use of community health agents, usually locally recruited, who provided information to families as well as some curative care and hospital referrals. This campaign led to a sharp fall in infant mortality, from 100 per 1,000 live births in the late 1980s to 25 per 1,000 in 2001. In this case successful community mobilization depended on access to information and on the way it was communicated.

• During a public expenditure tracking program in the mid-1990s, Uganda's government discovered strong leakages in funding intended for schools. The government began publishing and broadcasting the amounts of monthly education transfers to districts. In addition, schools were required to post information on their funding. The resulting public awareness of funding leakages helped increase the share of nonwage funds that reached schools from 13 percent to around 90 percent (Reinikka and Svensson 2001).

Although these examples focus on education and health care, we have also learned to look beyond these sectors when trying to understand education and health outcomes. For example, better water supplies reduce the time that girls must spend collecting water, and so can enable them to attend school. Improved nutrition enhances school attendance and concentration, contributing to better education outcomes. Thus, enhancing capabilities, or empowering, on one dimension can yield strong improvements in achievements on other dimensions.

These examples point to the key factors in institutional structures that foster empowerment: accountability, information, transparency, local organizational capacity, and participation (Narayan 2002)—with the first four elements determining whether the fifth, participation, is effective. Nominal participation by villagers in managing the village school, for example, is unlikely to be empowering if the school director is not accountable for results, if villagers have little information about what is going on in the school, and if villagers have no organization to help them engage with the school's management. These elements help us recognize and test whether institutional structures and arrangements are promoting empowerment. But they do not define empowerment.

Empowerment is defined at the individual level as having the ability to shape one's life. Let us examine this definition a little more closely and provide some extra specificity. First, some abilities arise from individual endowments and human development. Second, an individual exists in a family, economic, social, cultural, and political context that plays a powerful role in the ability to shape one's life and may impose strong "external constraints." Third, individuals have "internal constraints" on their actions associated with their preferences and perceptions of their role; Appadurai (2004) speaks, for example, of the "capacity to aspire." The three factors determining empowerment are illustrated in figure 3.1.

There are, of course, connections between these determinants, or dimensions, of empowerment. For example, a country's quality of governance greatly influences how assets can be accumulated and managed. In chapter 8 we discuss some aspects of the dynamics of empowerment: how these dimensions change over time, how individ-

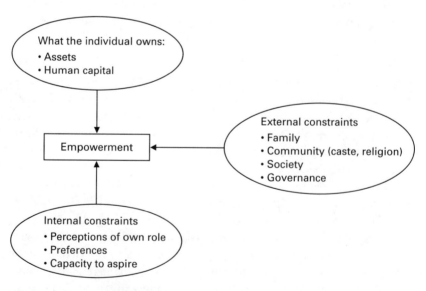

Figure 3.1
The determinants of empowerment.

uals act to change their lives, and how policies can enhance empowerment. In chapter 9 we look at the dynamics of preferences and how individuals develop the capacity to aspire.

The idea of empowerment is close in spirit to three other concepts in the literature: capability, inclusion, and participation. The rest of this section discusses each of these in turn.

Capability is an idea proposed by Amartya Sen that is very similar to that of empowerment. Sen sees an individual's capabilities as determining the freedom to live the life that he or she chooses. He points to a number of capabilities—including, importantly, health and education (Sen 1999). Our formulation of empowerment is similar, both conceptually and in terms of the kinds of policies it emphasizes. Although our discussion of empowerment in these lectures gives a little more emphasis to institutions, social relationships, and aspirations (that is, to the external and internal constraints in figure 3.1), we do not wish to exaggerate the difference. Our concern is examining the kind of strategy and operational policies to which this approach leads us.

On the second related concept, social inclusion (and exclusion), there are a number of different views about its meaning (Hills, Le Grand, and Piachaud 2002). Some observers stress the role of institutions and state systems in inclusion or exclusion. Others emphasize individual behavior and values in determining whether an individual is part of the mainstream. Still others emphasize the centrality of broader constraints, such as discrimination or lack of basic rights. But all these definitions implicitly view constraints on participation as an essential part of exclusion, in the sense that an individual is socially excluded if he or she cannot participate in some activities. Thus, social relationships and mechanisms—and not simply the level of consumption, income, or assets—are at the core of inclusion.

The concept of social exclusion differs from the concept of poverty in at least three ways, as Tony Atkinson argued in his 1997 presidential address to the British Association for the Advancement of Science (Atkinson and Hills 1998). First, we cannot judge whether a person is socially excluded by looking at his or her material circumstances in isolation. Whatever the merits of an absolute measure of poverty, it has no relevance to social exclusion. Assessing exclusion requires taking into account the circumstances and activities of others as well as the excluded. Exclusion may indeed be a property of groups of individuals rather than of individuals.[5] Neoclassical economics has traditionally considered individuals and their families in isolation—for example, taking little or no account of possible interactions among survey respondents who come from the same street or neighborhood. Yet social exclusion often manifests itself in terms of communities rather than individuals—for example, when financial institutions use postal codes for purposes of credit rating, thus excluding whole communities from an essential activity of economic life.

Second, exclusion implies an action taken by an agent or agents. In European countries, where social exclusion has become an important political issue, with a focus on unemployment,[6] unemployed people are shut out of many social interactions and often stigmatized. Researchers in Europe have also recognized that people may exclude themselves by dropping out of the market economy, or they may be excluded if banks or insurance companies refuse to provide them with credit or coverage. Similarly, people may refuse jobs, preferring to live on social assistance, or may be excluded from work by the actions of other workers, unions, employers, or government. For poor people in the developing world, the boundaries of exclusion are sometimes even starker than in wealthier countries. People are often excluded from acquiring certain jobs or from receiving benefits such as education simply because those advantages are reserved for men or for certain castes or ethnic groups.

Third, people may be excluded because they have few prospects for the future—both their own and their children's. That is, social exclusion may apply across generations, such as in a caste system. This is important because there may be ways of measuring this (see Roemer 1998). Thus, exclusion draws attention to dynamics, changes over time, and links across lives and between generations. Though such links are strong, they are not unbreakable. For example, the underclass in the United Kingdom and the United States is not permanently cut off from society, in that there is substantial social mobility through education and entrepreneurship. Even in India, where the caste system has historically reinforced social exclusion, government policy can improve the lives of those whom Gandhi called *harijans* and the law calls scheduled castes.

Differences between exclusion and poverty are real, but they should not be exaggerated. Focusing on exclusion does not transform the scale or nature of the problems to be addressed. What it does is shift the emphasis of policy responses and lead to a richer policy mix (Hills, Le Grand, and Piachaud 2002). For example, a focus on inclusion leads to a greater emphasis on gender issues than does a focus solely on poverty. In many communities empowering women is the most important challenge of the inclusion agenda. It is central to the objectives of development as we have defined them, because effective participation is impossible if half the population is excluded.

Like capability, the language and ideas of social inclusion and exclusion are similar to those of empowerment, and the concept of inclusion leads to an emphasis on the same kind of policies as empowerment. But inclusion leads us to believe that an individual is in or out, a zero-one notion, whereas empowerment is more a matter of degree. Further, empowerment, as we have seen in our emphasis on information and accountability, quickly leads to questions about how institutions function. Moreover, one could be included in a group but have limited power to affect its decisions. Empowerment can be low even if there is no problem of exclusion—for example, in a very poor but homogeneous community. But just as with capability, we have no desire to exaggerate differences when the approaches are so similar in spirit and substance.

Finally, there is the third related concept, participation. In many ways empowerment can be seen as effective participation. A person might participate in the sense of being present, but might be unheard or ignored. And we have seen that an important part of an analysis of institutional arrangements that can deliver empowerment involves determinants of effectiveness (including information and accountability). But again, the ideas are close.

The proximity of the ideas of capability, inclusion, participation, and empowerment means that for some purposes, they can be used interchangeably, and we occasionally do so in these lectures. Our decision to focus most heavily on empowerment embodies different areas of emphasis, as we have pointed out. These differences point to policy directions and analytical issues, such as questions about institutions and changing preferences, that are important for practical policy.

To conclude, let us briefly recognize some possible concerns about the concept of empowerment. We should acknowledge that the word itself has problems. It does not translate well into other languages: neither French nor Spanish, for example, has a corresponding word.[7] It can also be misused: members of particular groups that have suffered past injustices might use the term to justify violence or arbitrary intervention. This type of usage could undermine governance. But the possible misuse of a term should not prevent us from using an idea that seems central to the concerns of poor people. And empowerment does capture four important development issues. First, effective participation is essential to the development process. Second, the environment helps determine whether participation is possible. Third, effective participation depends on one's capabilities, and most important on health and education. And fourth, individuals can be constrained by their aspirations and perceptions of their role, so that development depends on relaxing those constraints.

Effectiveness of Foreign Assistance

The main lesson we have learned about the role of foreign aid in development is that it is most effective if it complements local development efforts rather than substituting for them. Successful development depends on local ownership, local involvement, and adaptation to local conditions. The term *ownership* is used to describe countries' choice of and commitment to reforms, as opposed to their reluctant acceptance. The success of reforms depends more on underlying political economy factors than on the direct investments made by outside actors such as private investors or international financial institutions like the World Bank. Aid from bilateral or multilateral sources can be a critical support to communities and countries where there is a genuine movement for change. But for reform programs to succeed, the country must be in the driver's seat.

Historically, aid has not been systematically targeted to countries with good reform records. The allocation of aid during the Cold War responded to political and military considerations. As the Cold War ended and fiscal pressures led donor countries to reexamine the use of taxpayer resources, they became more selective in their choice of countries, targeting those with the policy and institutional environments where aid would be most productive.

Action to increase aid effectiveness has been prompted in part by research findings that have led many donors to rethink their aid strategies. In the late 1990s a landmark study showed that aid contributes much more to economic growth and poverty reduction in countries with better policies and institutions (World Bank 1998a). This insight is confirmed not only by statistical evidence but also by detailed case studies of the role of aid in particular countries (Devarajan, Dollar, and Holmgren 2001).[8] Aid is most successful in countries that have shown commitment to reform by adopting improved policies, institutions, and governance—for their own reasons, rather than as a result of outside pressure. In addition, aid works better if it is based on a track record of reform rather than on promised reforms, even if there seems to be a window of opportunity. Judgments will always be needed on commitment to reform—and while a country's track record is the best guide, there are no certainties. Sometimes a donor has to take a chance and support strong reform efforts at times that look crucial. We return to some of these issues in chapter 13.

Other research findings have also influenced aid policies. Some research has emphasized that sector-specific aid, such as investment projects, is largely fungible (Devarajan and Swaroop 1998). In other words, aid can displace and redirect other sources of funds rather than complement them. Thus, while an aid-financed project to build schools can yield benefits in the education sector by transferring knowledge or building capacity, the marginal effect of the financial support would come elsewhere if education spending increased by much less than the project funds.

Fungibility has two implications for donors. First, donors should look beyond the rate of return on their individual projects to the quality of the country's overall public expenditure program. After all, it is that program that they are in effect supporting, and they should examine it directly. Second, the reasons for financing projects go beyond the productivity of a specific investment. As important is the generation of ideas, skills, and learning that spill over from projects. On average, aid is less than 1 percent of developing country GDP. But the ideas and innovations arising from aid can be much greater. We return to this important issue in chapters 11 and 13.

Another influential research finding is that traditional conditionality—whereby aid is given conditional on promises of policy reform—typically does not work. The number and frequency of conditions attached to adjustment loans and standby agreements from international financial institutions have little to do with whether policies are reformed. Case studies have shown that effective policy reform generally emerges from domestic political consensus—and conditionality from donors does not help, and sometimes hurts, consensus building (Devarajan, Dollar, and Holmgren 2001). There can be limited exceptions in the cases of "stroke-of-the-pen" reforms (such as exchange rate adjustments), where only a small number of decision makers need to be convinced of the benefits of a policy change. But even in these cases, policy reforms risk reversal if they do not command broad support. Having recognized these problems, donors by the start of the twenty-first century were shifting toward ex post conditionality—that is, aid based on jointly monitored results rather than promises (Collier and Gunning 1999, Collier and Dollar 2002).

Finally, at the microlevel, experience suggests that projects where people participate effectively yield better development results than those where they do not. We see this in examples from around the developing world, from communities running schools in El Salvador and Nicaragua to consumer scorecards for utility services in India and the Philippines, to village-level investment in infrastructure in rural Indonesia. Women's involvement is particularly important. For example, cross-country evidence suggests that when women have more rights and greater participation, a society suffers from less corruption (World Bank 2001d).

Two related lessons are clear: the positive effects of empowerment operate in donor-supported projects and programs as they do in development efforts more broadly, and donors benefit when they take participation seriously. Whether at the level of individual projects and programs or at the country level, success often depends on participation and ownership by the intended beneficiaries. Aid-financed projects and programs work better when beneficiaries are active agents of their own destinies.

4   Lessons from Development Theory

Lessons come from both theory and empirical evidence. In chapter 3 we drew some stylized lessons from development experience. In this chapter we examine some theoretical themes that will serve as both foundations and points of departure for the development strategy proposed in chapter 5. The goal of the strategy is to raise living standards, particularly for poor people, using the broad definition of living standards described in chapter 1. The two pillars of the strategy are, first, to create an investment climate conducive to growth, productivity, investment, and jobs, and, second, to empower and invest in people—especially poor people—so that they can participate in growth and take advantage of opportunities. The story told here is dynamic in its focus on growth in income, health, and education; on changes in lives, living standards, and activities; and on the roles of learning, history, and changing institutions.

The approach, strategy, and analysis presented in this book are influenced by contributions from many scholars of development, past and present, as well as our own experience and study. The ideas draw on the work of Joseph Schumpeter, Albert Hirschman, and Amartya Sen on how economies and societies change and on what the objectives of development should be. They have a foundation in modern theories of growth and public economics in the tradition of Paul Samuelson, Kenneth Arrow, Robert Solow, Peter Diamond, and James Mirrlees, who incorporate issues of objectives, dynamics, and information into a market-oriented analysis of public policy.[1] The ideas here also draw on some of the early post–World War II writers on development, including Paul Rosenstein-Rodan, Theodore Schultz, Esther Boserup, and Hollis Chenery. Nevertheless, this book's strategy departs from those works in important ways.

Foundations

The three strands of theory just mentioned—development economics, growth theory, and public economics—provide a strong foundation for the analytical inquiry generated by the two-pillar strategy presented in the next chapter. Yet none of them, separately or combined, yields the kind of dynamic public economics required to understand the dynamic processes at the heart of development. The strategy presented here raises theoretical and empirical challenges that go well beyond the existing literature. Dynamic economics is not static economics with a time subscript. The challenge is to understand how the key institutions and behaviors affecting development and their change can be influenced. We are finding renewed focus on the problems of dynamics in this sense. In particular, we see growing interest in the Austrian school of economics, particularly Schumpeterian analyses of processes and institutions. Our task here is to begin to sketch a response to this challenge.

Let us start with a brief look at the analytical foundations provided by early theories of development, growth, and public economics. Schumpeter's vision of development as a dynamic process of creative destruction has had a profound influence on the economics of the past seventy to eighty years, including recent theories of growth. Hirschman has greatly facilitated our understanding of endogenous processes of change in developing countries. And Sen has redefined the boundaries of development thinking with his idea of development as freedom, in terms of enhancing individuals' capabilities to improve their lives. More generally, human development and freedom are now seen as ends in themselves, regardless of how they affect narrower economic indicators of growth.

Development Economics
The strategy developed in chapter 5 has important antecedents in Rosenstein-Rodan's (1943) and Nurkse's (1953) idea of a "big push" to break out of a low-level equilibrium, in Schultz's (1964) emphasis on traditional agriculture as poor but efficient and on the role of technology in generating change, and in Boserup's (1965) seminal analysis of population pressures as the key determinant of agricultural change. Though varied in emphasis, each of these authors pointed to the need to understand and promote change—whether from agriculture to industry or within agriculture, and whether through resource accumula-

tion and allocation or technological change. From Schumpeter (1934, 1962) and Hirschman (1958) we draw our emphasis on entrepreneurship as the driver of innovation.

In stressing the investment climate, our focus is on obstacles to and incentives for entrepreneurship, particularly those associated with governance, institutions, and markets. Schumpeter and Hirschman were surely grappling with the right kind of issues. But there are significant differences in the analysis offered in this book. Schumpeter addressed the frontiers of capitalism in advanced societies, focusing on new products, new technologies, and creative destruction. That is not where our emphasis lies. And Hirschman, in our view, underemphasized the basic entrepreneurship of small farmers and small businesspeople. So while we salute Schumpeter and Hirschman as pioneers and identify and approach issues in a similar spirit, much of our emphasis is on the institutional, behavioral, and policy barriers to innovation and inclusion faced by small firms, farmers, and individuals—and on ways of overcoming these barriers.

In taking this view on the importance of entrepreneurship for growth, we have been strongly influenced by Nicholas Stern's work in developing and transition countries. Of particular importance has been his close involvement over several decades with China and India—two countries where the easing of constraints on entrepreneurship has produced a powerful response in terms of growth and poverty reduction. When China launched its reforms a quarter-century ago, it initiated the most important episode of poverty reduction in history. Work in India, including close study of one village (Palanpur) over several decades (with Christopher Bliss, Jean Drèze, Peter Lanjouw, and others), made Stern intensely aware of the country's long-standing barriers to entrepreneurship (Lanjouw and Stern 1998). Yet India's reforms, particularly since 1991, have begun to dismantle the "license raj" and have been associated with strong growth.[2] And however difficult the environment may be in a small, poor Indian village, one constantly finds examples of innovation and risk taking, such as farmers trying new varieties of seed or workers migrating to urban markets in search of new types of employment.

While at the European Bank for Reconstruction and Development for six years in the 1990s, Stern saw entrepreneurship stir in the former Soviet Union after seven decades of suppression—then saw failings in governance divert much of that entrepreneurial energy into destructive directions. Circumstances seem to be changing for the better, but the serious damage done in the early years continues to have an effect today. Those who seek to build well-functioning, market-oriented institutions and promote productive and civic-minded behavior (as opposed to rent seeking) in the former Soviet Union must take on powerful vested interests who grabbed positions in the 1990s. They must also conquer widespread cynicism about reform.

In his first applied project in Africa in the 1960s, which focused on tea farming, Stern witnessed the powerful entrepreneurship of smallholders (mostly women) in the highlands of Kenya, supported by public investments in infrastructure and agricultural extension. That experience convinced Stern that entrepreneurship can be the central creative economic force in all countries. Sometimes that force is expressed positively. Sometimes it is latent. And sometimes it is misdirected into rent seeking and crime. At the same time, government action is usually required to foster entrepreneurship. The challenge is to promote policies that redirect that energy into constructive, dynamic entrepreneurship (Jones and SaKong 1980; Tyson, Petrin, and Rogers 1994).

Growth Theory

Theories of growth try to model processes of change in a formal way. As ever, when we turn to formal approaches we gain something and lose something. Growth theory has helped us understand the roles of accumulation and technical progress, for example, and analyze the relationship between savings and growth. But with a few honorable exceptions, growth theory has failed to address something absolutely central: the growth engines of entrepreneurship and institutional development. Periods of strong growth in history bear little resemblance to steady state—notwithstanding Kaldor's (1961) misleading "stylized facts"—and the structural change that drives development is not well captured in an aggregate model, a point underlined by the review of development and change in chapter 2.

For a long time, economists influenced by Harrod-Domar and Solow models have focused on the savings rate and the capital-output ratio ($v = K/Y$) as determinants of the growth rate. Solow's influential model was built around an aggregate production function, with the economy assumed to produce a single good, Y. The model showed that the long-run growth rate of output, s/v, will come into equality with the natural growth rate of the labor force, n, through adjustment of the capital output ratio, v. (See Solow 2000 for a thoughtful review of the theoretical framework.) Increasing the savings rate will increase the growth rate in the short run but not the long run because v rises to bring growth back to the labor force growth rate n. A higher saving rate s will lead to higher long-run output per capita (at least if we ignore problems of excess saving connected with s being permanently above the "golden rule" level). But in these models long-run *growth* of output per capita is possible only if there is technological progress. If that progress is labor augmenting (that is, if it acts on output in a manner analogous to an expansion of labor input) at rate a, then it allows long-run growth with $s/v = a + n$ and output per capita growing at rate a.

Many researchers have expressed unease with using an aggregate production function with a single good to describe the accumulation and technological progress underlying a growth process. As usually formulated, its immediate implications include that technological progress is divorced from capital accumulation, that higher savings does not increase the long-run growth rate, and that learning does not occur. Arrow (1962) provides a seminal analysis of the economic implications of learning by doing. His model can produce steady-state growth with no exogenous technical progress. Formally, this looks similar to the steady growth rate in an ordinary neoclassical model embodying some increasing returns. This particular feature, where learning causes the benefits of investment in human capital to act like an externality, characterized the more recent upsurge of interest in growth and technical progress associated with Romer (1986) and Lucas (1988).

The growth literature that originated with the Harrod-Domar and Solow models has provided a valuable organizing framework for asking questions about the role of savings and capital accumulation for rich countries. Rich economies are dominated by the services sector (which has lower fixed capital requirements, presumably making capital investments more flexible) and have fairly flexible factor markets, so with enough hand waving and suspension of disbelief, one might be able to justify the one-good model. Yet even for these economies, the one-good model should not be pushed too hard as the right way of representing growth.

The assumption of an aggregate production function is even more questionable for developing countries. It misses most of what it is interesting and important for these countries (see the insightful comments on this in Solow 2001)—most notably, the differences in the nature of economic activity between sectors and the institutions and governance structures that often hobble the markets for factors, goods, and services.

Growth models have focused on aggregates, savings and investment, and steady states. More modern versions have incorporated the idea of learning and discussed issues of returns to scale. But they have not addressed issues of structural change and changing behavior—other than in a rather superficial way, such as by examining coefficients on poorly measured variables in cross-country regressions.[3] And most of these models have little to say about the roles of firms and government—again, other than as poorly measured variables in cross-country regressions. These are significant shortcomings when the purpose is to understand development. As earlier chapters explained, growth involves changes in the behavior of agents, the structure of preferences, and the structure of the economy, as well as institutions, governance, and policies.

A more Schumpeterian view of the growth process implicitly explains cross-country differences in growth rates as resulting from institutional differences, but does so at a high level of generality. The challenge is to go beyond general statements about the growth-enhancing effects of property rights protection, sound education systems, and stable economies. Aghion and Howitt (1992, 1998) imaginatively model the Schumpeterian process of creative destruction, with innovators taking over entire markets. The authors rightly see economic growth since the industrial revolution as embodying strong elements of social conflict, fueled by the obsolescence that technological progress inevitably causes. Many groups in society gain from progress, but they do so at the expense of those whose occupations, sectors, regions, skills, and capital goods were specialized to the products and processes being replaced by progress. Institutions and public policies determine who gains from innovations, who loses, and what the rents from innovations will be. The interaction between innovation and the institutional and policy environment helps us understand why those who stand to gain from growth prevail in some societies—while in others they are blocked by those who expect to lose out (Aghion and Howitt forthcoming).

Chapter 7 presents a simple endogenous growth model in which policy does more than just influence the investment rate and the output-capital ratio. The model shows how government and societal behavior can combine to increase the growth rate. Though simple, the model is rich enough to make at least two important points. First, growth is largely driven by public policies in areas such as education, regulation of competition, promotion of entrepreneurship, technological policy, and social policies that encourage participation. And second, government therefore has a crucial role to play.

At this stage let us emphasize one point. In modeling the growth process in most developing countries, the appropriate framework is not an economy on the technological frontier but one well inside it. Indeed, the position and shape of that frontier may not be the most useful basis for analyzing productivity and growth. Productivity improvements may be driven by better organization and management and by a public administration oriented toward overcoming obstacles to economic activity. If we do take a technological approach, productivity increases are likely to come from a mix of techniques—some leading edge, some local or traditional—with the combination depending on the society.

Aghion and Armendáriz (2002) and Hausmann and Rodrik (2003) argue that different institutions will shape different combinations of imitation (copying the leading edge) and innovation (adaptation and change starting from local or traditional technologies) in the process of technological diffusion. Thus, policies that will promote growth will vary across countries and over time.

Public Economics

Since the 1970s public economics has placed the formal analysis of incentives at the center of its agenda. It has shown how incentives and distribution—in crude terms, the size of the cake and its distribution—can be rigorously integrated with a discussion of public policy, both theoretical and empirical. This is an achievement of great importance.

What we need today is research that extends this analysis to more dynamic questions about the investment climate and about empowering and investing in poor people. Such an approach would focus on the structural and institutional underpinnings of growth and on whether poor people can participate in it. Thus, it would be a dynamic version of the size and distribution question, looking beyond the simple story of incentives to the difficulties, opportunities, behaviors, and perceptions that shape actions and outcomes.

Standard public economics made a vital step forward by going beyond traditional welfare theory and looking at constraints on policy arising from limitations on information. It has recognized that effective lump-sum transfers are usually impossible, because policymakers lack the information needed to calculate reform or optimality without the taxes ceasing to be lump sum, and it has gone on to analyze the implications of this fact for tax policy. It has helped us discuss the role of the state and the provision of public goods in a way that takes explicit and formal account of information constraints and limitations on tax instruments—and their implications for public policy. And it has given us an analytical framework for examining the costs and benefits of changes in taxes and policies. Prominent examples include Mirrlees (1971) on optimal taxation of labor income and Diamond and Mirrlees (1971) on taxation of commodities to finance public goods. Drèze and Stern (1990) make a presentation on the corresponding theory of reform and provide references. For examples of studies of this approach applied to developing countries, see Newbery and Stern (1987) and Ahmad and Stern (1991).

In these and many other ways, public economics has provided an analysis of the policy implications of market failure. That literature dates back to the nineteenth- and early twentieth-century work of Jules Dupuit, Knut Wicksell, Alfred Marshall, and Arthur Pigou. A more recent literature, including work by James Buchanan and others, focuses on government failure. Stern (1989) captures, from the perspective of development economics, the key causes of both types of failure (boxes 4.1 and 4.2).

Box 4.1
Reasons for market failure

---

1. Markets may be monopolized or oligopolistic.
2. There may be externalities.
3. There may be increasing returns to scale.
4. Some markets, particularly insurance and futures markets, cannot be perfect—and indeed, may not exist.
5. Markets may adjust slowly or imprecisely because information moves slowly or marketing institutions are inflexible.
6. Individuals or enterprises may adjust slowly.
7. Individuals or enterprises may be badly informed about products, prices, production possibilities, and the like.
8. Individuals may not act to maximize anything, implicitly or explicitly.
9. Government taxation is unavoidable and will not, or cannot, take a form that allows efficiency.

Source: Stern (1989).

Box 4.2
Reasons for government failure

1. Individuals may know more about their preferences and circumstances than does the government.
2. Government planning may increase risk by pointing everyone in the same direction. Governments may make bigger mistakes than markets.
3. Planning may involve complex decision making and so may be more rigid than private decision making.
4. Governments may be incapable of administering detailed plans.
5. Bureaucratic obstacles may inhibit private initiative.
6. Organizations and individuals require incentives to work, innovate, control costs, and allocate efficiently, and the discipline and rewards of the market are not easily replicated in public enterprises and organizations.
7. Different levels and parts of government may be poorly coordinated, particularly if groups or regions with different interests are involved.
8. Markets can constrain what government can achieve. For example, resale of commodities on black markets and activities in the informal sector can disrupt rationing and other nonlinear pricing and taxation schemes. This is the general problem of incentive compatibility.
9. Controls create resource-using activities that are influenced by lobbying and corruption. In the literature these are often called rent-seeking and directly unproductive activities.
10. Planning may be manipulated by privileged and powerful groups acting in their own interests. Furthermore, planning creates vested interests in planning, such as bureaucrats or industrialists who obtain protected positions.
11. Governments may be dominated by narrow interest groups interested only in their own welfare and sometimes actively hostile to large sections of the population. Planning may intensify the power of these groups.

Source: Stern (1989).

The list of market problems in box 4.1 comes from scrutinizing the assumptions of the two standard welfare theorems. The first theorem lays out the assumptions under which a competitive equilibrium is Pareto efficient—most notably, that all markets exist and are competitive and there are no externalities. The second theorem specifies the additional assumptions required to achieve a given Pareto-efficient allocation as a market equilibrium: convexity of production and preferences (that is, diminishing marginal rates of transformation and substitution), and the availability of lump-sum transfers to raise revenue and redistribute income. Box 4.1 is in effect a roll call of the many ways in which these assumptions may be violated.

Some of the problems listed in box 4.1, such as items 3 to 8, may make it difficult to establish or maintain equilibrium, and most of them can prevent efficiency even if equilibrium is established. Most of these points should be familiar or self-explanatory, with the possible exceptions of problems 4 and 9. As examples of problem 4 (imperfect markets), consider moral hazard and adverse selection in insurance markets, and bankruptcy and the possibility of default in capital and future markets.

With problem 9 (inefficient taxation) we simply recognize that taxes are required to raise revenue and that any non–lump-sum tax generates inefficiency. Further, any prima facie desirable lump-sum tax (that is, one related to ability to pay) ceases to be lump sum when its basis is recognized. For example, if income is the basis, then the tax is not lump sum, because the tax payment is affected by work input and so offers disincentives to work. Thus, where redistribution is a concern, taxation implies inefficiency, and the standard efficiency theorems cannot provide justification for an unfettered competitive market.

A typical response to a market failure is to propose a tax or bargaining mechanism to deal with it. One must be wary of this approach, however, because if several failures occur simultaneously, it can be misleading to analyze them one by one. A prominent example of a market failure concerns externalities. Standard solutions include Pigovian taxes or subsidies—for example, polluters may be taxed according to the marginal damage they cause—combined with an allocation of rights and an opportunity for Coasian bargaining (where an individual provides compensation if he or she damages another; Coase 1960). Yet these mechanisms will operate rather poorly in the typical developing country. Hence a common response to market failure is to propose state intervention.

This leads us to consider the problems described in box 4.2. Like box 4.1, this one should be largely self-explanatory, except possibly in the case of points 8 and 9. The problem of incentive incompatibility is important for both planning and the market. Indeed, it can be regarded as the central issue linking the two (Stiglitz 1994). It underlies both problem 9 in box 4.1 and problem 8 in box 4.2. A planning proposal or tax that fails to take into account the opportunities and incentives open to individuals (whether through markets or the political system) will fail to achieve its objectives. Rent seeking and directly unproductive activities (problem 9 in box 4.2) refer to actions by individuals to lobby, bribe, or threaten public officials to secure state-generated privileges. Such activities are difficult to quantify, but they are of substantial importance.

Boxes 4.1 and 4.2 were prepared fifteen years ago, before the extraordinary developments of the 1990s. Around that time Stern warned of the dangers of a simplistic market fundamentalism (Stern 1991b, 1992), or what Jean-Jacques Laffont (1992) called "*le libéralisme triomphant*," particularly as applied to the transition economies of Eastern Europe and the former Soviet Union. Such fundamentalism took its inspiration from an imbalanced concern with the problems of box 4.2, while ignoring many of the reasons for market failure enumerated in box 4.1. Though these boxes provide a useful starting point, the importance of institutional development, entrepreneurship, and behavioral change has become much clearer over the past fifteen years. In considering the implicit trade-offs suggested by the boxes, one also has to take political economy into consideration. Not all governments are incompetent or corrupt, and competent governments may or may not be manipulated by special interests. Markets and entrepreneurship appear to function better in some environments than others, whether or not governments are prepared to let them flourish. Thus we should be wary of taking a universal view on the relative force of the arguments embodied in boxes 4.1 and 4.2.

In sum, public economics has brought into the discussion the essential elements of externalities, information, and market failures. It has broadened our understanding of policy by providing a formulation and analysis of incentive and distribution issues. And it has provided a framework for discussing the role of the state. The challenge is to build on these insights by adding key dynamic elements of development.

Public Policy and the Dynamics of Development

The preceding sketch of theory in development economics, growth theory, and public economics shows that while these areas provide crucial insights and parts of a foundation, they do not capture the key dynamic factors that we have identified as drivers of growth and poverty reduction. We have argued that to understand those drivers, we need to focus on the processes of improving the investment climate and empowering people—processes that incorporate history, dynamic structures, and learning. The central challenge of development is to understand and influence these processes. We delve more deeply into the dynamic story in lecture III. The goal of this section is simply to introduce the issues and say a few words about their origins in the history of economic thought.

These two themes of improving the investment climate and empowering poor people, discussed at much greater length in lectures II and III, are intertwined as well as dynamic. In focusing on these two processes as key drivers of pro-poor growth, we are not talking about comparisons of two equilibria, about steady states, or about points along a production frontier. We are talking about processes of change, adaptation, creativity, and learning.

These unduly neglected themes in the dynamics of development go back at least to Adam Smith's thesis that the division of labor is limited by the extent of the market. Aspects of these themes appear in Alfred Marshall's notion of external economies—for example, in his treatment of industrial districts (1961)—and in Allyn Young's seminal 1928 paper on increasing returns.[4] Nicholas Kaldor studied with Young in the 1920s and was later one of the main proponents of Young's view that "increasing returns is a 'macro-phenomenon'" (in addition to any increasing returns at the firm level; see, for example, Kaldor 1994). In a survey of work on the determinants of growth, Stern (1991a, p. 131) predicted "a resurgence of interest in the work of Kaldor, including his emphasis on both static and dynamic increasing returns." In the development literature these themes were emphasized by Paul Rosenstein-Rodan (1943) and Ragnar Nurkse (1953).

Often theories are presented in terms of simple stories that serve as "intuition pumps" to illustrate the broader theme. Rosenstein-Rodan uses an example of a shoe factory. A new shoe factory might not be profitable in a small market. But if it were one of a number of firms in different industries that developed simultaneously, so that the firms and their workers could buy each other's products, the factory might become profitable.

Ideas about increasing returns were used by Rosenstein-Rodan and others in the concept of balanced growth. The idea of economic interdependence embodied in the notion of balanced growth was not controversial; it was the policy implications that generated controversy. Nurkse expressed it this way: "Whether the forces of economic progress are to be deliberately organized or left to the action of private enterprise—in short, whether balanced growth is enforced by planning boards or achieved spontaneously by creative entrepreneurs—is, of course, a weighty and much debated issue" (Nurkse 1953, p. 16). The subsequent thirty-five years of development and a deeper understanding of the history of the Soviet Union would now, we trust, lead few observers to propose a planning board as the main coordinator and driver of growth. But there is still much to learn about how to promote the creativity of the market and entrepreneurs, and how to enable poor people to be central to the process.

One line of thought was based on development planning using the idea of a "big push," an approach that today would find little support. Hirschman (1958) perceptively criticized the big push idea, noting that if a country had the capacity to carry out a big push industrialization program, then "it would not be underdeveloped in the first place" (p. 54). Nurkse (1967) broached an alternative to the centralized big push: "Schumpeter's creative entrepreneurs seem to have what it takes, and as they move forward on a broad front, their act of faith is crowned with commercial success" (p. 15). Hirschman agreed on the importance of entrepreneurship, and generalized the notion of entrepreneurship as induced decision making that mobilizes scattered and hidden development resources. He argued that the "inducing mechanisms" could be some of the same linkages or interdependencies that arise in the increasing returns literature.

For example, one developmental sequence of induced decision making was emphasized in rural development by Esther Boserup (1965, 1991). The pressure of population growth leads to changes in agricultural techniques, such as a shortening of fallow periods and the introduction of multicropping. This may be accompanied by improvements in work discipline and efficiency that, together with an increase in the number of workers, may lead to greater division of labor and new forms of work. That specialization will spur the development of off-farm enterprises, perhaps grouping together in new small market towns, and these enterprises will increase the efficiency of agriculture and broaden patterns of consumption and production (better fertilizer, seeds, feed, fencing, transport, irrigation, farming equipment, and so on)—continuing and repeating in a virtuous cycle of growth.

Where does that leave public policy? Hirschman found unduly pessimistic the notion of a vicious circle of poverty that would require a centrally coordinated big push to exit, arguing that it fed into the paralyzing attitude that nothing can be done except root-and-branch attempts to change everything at once. He argued instead for a "possibilism" based on "reform mongering" (1973). Whether they were early industrializers (like the United Kingdom and United States) or late industrializers (like Germany, Japan, and more recently the Republic of Korea), industrialized countries had found ways to develop using endogenous linkages, without all-at-once "big push" miracles. Thus, Hirschman said, public action should be able to expedite that process in today's developing countries (for example, through interventions with maximum backward and forward linkages).

Our goal in this book is not to suggest some new, unique answer to development. But experiences from developing and (more recently) transition countries suggest that certain types of public action have strong virtuous circle or increasing returns effects, based on the interdependencies emphasized in the intellectual tradition sketched above. The public goods aspects of the investment climate can have those effects too, so public action (or "reform mongering," to use Hirschman's phrase) to improve the investment climate can spur entrepreneurial activity, which can feed back into greater demands for a better investment climate.[5]

The challenge for students of development is to understand what kinds of change can generate strong, sustained increases in growth and large transformations in education, health, and well-being. This chapter has provided a brief explanation of why we have to go beyond the foundations in development economics, growth theory, and public economics to understand the dynamics of development. In lecture III (particularly chapter 7, on the dynamics of the investment climate) we return to this theme, showing how modest inputs can generate large returns or rapid growth.

The many important processes of change cannot be captured in a single model. Indeed, that is unlikely to be a sensible modeling or research strategy. We will need a collection of models. To understand the generation of large returns or rapid growth, we may think of acting in a way that tips a lever in the right direction or of moving to the steeply rising position of a logistic curve. A number of conceptual constructs can throw light on the process of accelerating growth, and we should make use of all of them.

The analytical challenge is to understand the different mechanisms and elements of the story. The conceptual challenge in formalizing policy is identifying which theoretical themes can provide useful guidance in any given set of circumstances. That requires knowledge of the theories, understanding of circumstances, and mature judgment. The type of theoretical focus we have described should therefore go hand in hand with empirical research. Only by combining theory with careful, detailed empirical research can we identify which, if any, of the above stories provide plausible explanations for the episodes of growth and decline we have observed in economic history.

Lecture II   Strategy

Drawing on the evidence, lessons, and foundation presented in lecture I, this lecture (chapter 5) proposes a strategy for development. It describes and analyzes the key elements of the strategy and distinguishes it from other approaches such as the Washington consensus, the neoliberal agenda, and redistribution with growth. The chapter also discusses the strategy's implications for research and for public policy and action, themes addressed in detail in lectures III and IV.

A Strategy for Development

The strategy for development proposed in this chapter has two key features: its objectives and its twin pillars. First, it is intended to promote development, with development understood to mean higher living standards—and higher living standards defined in terms of individuals' increased ability to shape their lives. This ultimate objective can be broken down into intermediate goals; we emphasize health, education, and people's ability to participate in the economy and society, all of which are affected by society's institutional and behavioral structures. We also, in lecture IV, discuss the Millennium Development Goals, a group of targets set by the international community for achievement by 2015. Second, the twin pillars are fostering an investment climate conducive to increased growth, productivity, and employment opportunities, and empowering and investing in people so that they can participate in the economy and society. This chapter describes and analyzes these pillars.

The strategy for development offered here differs in crucial respects from other approaches proposed in recent decades. Thus, this chapter also distinguishes the strategy from approaches such as the Washington consensus, the neoliberal agenda, the directed and protected economy, and redistribution with growth. In addition, we identify the strategy's implications for research (discussed in lecture III) and for public policy and action (examined in lecture IV).

The Strategy's Two Pillars

This chapter's strategy is based on the idea that development is fundamentally about change—changing institutions, changing governance, and changing behavior. Thus, the strategy's two pillars, guided by development experience and theory, embody the idea of an active state complementary to markets. Moreover, the processes embodied in the two pillars are mutually reinforcing in their effects on growth and poverty reduction (box 5.1).

The strategy could be described as one for "pro-poor" growth. But that term is unattractive, because it suggests a kind of growth that delivers something to poor people. The goal should be to enable poor people to participate in the processes of growth and to be key drivers of those processes. The following sections analyze each of the strategy's pillars in turn.

Improving the Investment Climate

The first pillar of development is creating a good investment climate —one that encourages firms and farms, small and large, to invest, create jobs, and increase productivity. This element is founded on the lessons from chapter 3 about the key roles that the private sector, trade, and growth play in poverty reduction. The approach taken here involves not just levels of investment, but also its process and the environment for entrepreneurship. In that sense it is essentially Schumpeterian.

This chapter's strategy defines the investment climate as the policy, institutional, and behavioral environment, present and projected, that influences the perceived returns and risks associated with investment. This perspective is much broader than that of investment interpreted simply as additions to physical capital stock. Here we think not only of the climate for investment, but also for pursuing new or enhanced economic activities more generally. Moreover, our emphasis is on the investment climate for small, domestic firms. In many developing countries the farm is the most important small firm, and in much of what follows *firms* should be understood to encompass farms (though for emphasis, we are occasionally specific on the use of *farm*). If the investment climate improves for small firms, it will likely improve for large and foreign firms as well. Moreover, a good investment climate not only makes life easier for incumbent firms, it also facilitates entry for new firms and promotes a competitive environment for all.

Improving the investment climate means strengthening the connection between sowing and reaping (both metaphorically and literally), as well as making it easier to sow. Key to investment decisions and productivity growth is investors' ability to get on with their efforts

Box 5.1
Links between the two pillars

The two pillars of this book's development strategy—creating an investment climate and advancing empowerment—share an intellectual symmetry. The first pillar focuses on the challenges facing firms, and the second is about the challenges facing individuals.

Because it is about the rules and processes governing the exercise of public authority, governance is at the heart of both pillars. Why is the exercise of public authority necessary in a market economy where private parties are autonomous and the invisible hand is supposed to allocate goods and services efficiently? The first reason is that private markets deal badly with public goods and externalities. Public mechanisms are required to ensure supply, payment, and regulation, whether in the supply of clean air or the control of traffic congestion.

The second reason is that economic transactions, private or public, always involve a degree of negotiation, understanding, or bargaining, and institutions (often public) are needed to support the procedures under which these interactions and agreements occur and the mandates of the parties involved (Zingales 1998). Institutions provide the rules of the game under which individuals and organizations operate—constraining and facilitating behavior and, together with endowments and technology, defining the economic opportunities in a society. Important institutions of governance include those defining norms of behavior, the reliability of information, commitment mechanisms, auditing systems, and effective enforcement. These institutions can be more or less formal. For example, China's legal system is rudimentary, and convention, reputation, and understanding are crucial bulwarks to markets, while India has a fairly litigious society (Dethier 2000).

One final connection between the two pillars is that the investment climate can be seen as a lens that brings into focus reforms that increase people's opportunities. Those reforms strengthen the link between sowing and reaping, but they also empower farmers, workers, entrepreneurs, and managers to build assets and shape their lives.

and see their rewards. If investors see their investments undermined by uncertainty, instability, and predation, they will be discouraged from pursuing them.

Government cannot guarantee against all the uncertainties of investment, but it has an obligation to ensure that investments are not arbitrarily disrupted and that investors are not robbed of their returns. This role is even more important than protecting property, because the creation of new assets depends on safeguarding the connection between investment and returns.

Too many societies have stagnated at a low-level equilibrium because of a dearth of investment opportunities and incentives. Government may protect static accumulated wealth (such as large landed property) but, with time, begin to act only as a rent-seeking bureaucracy. Similarly, some governments have—perhaps with the best intentions—acted as the first employer of educated youth. But that approach sends a signal that ambitious young people should look to a government sinecure rather than exploring entrepreneurship. The way that labor markets work is a critical element of the investment climate. Unless government encourages entrepreneurial investment in the private sector, or at a minimum avoids stifling or crowding out such investment, strong growth and poverty reduction are unlikely.

The investment climate is a function of several elements that can be grouped under three broad headings: macroeconomic and trade policies, infrastructure, and governance and institutions. Each of these elements is examined in detail in the sections that follow.

Stable macroeconomic conditions—fiscal stability and transparency, low inflation, sound monetary and exchange rate policies—support private sector activity by promoting clarity, reducing risk, and sending sound economic signals related to value and scarcity. (Political stability is important for the same reasons.) Moreover, openness to trade and foreign investment promotes competition and provides incentives for innovation and entrepreneurship. By contrast, unstable macroeconomic conditions undermine firms' ability to plan and produce. In addition, protection and weak competition in domestic markets—and trade barriers in foreign markets—suppress innovation and entrepreneurship.

But while macroeconomic factors are crucial to investment and growth, they do not tell the whole story. Growth requires improvements in the investment climate more broadly, including in the microeconomic areas of infrastructure and institutions. Without them, growth generated by macroeconomic reforms will likely falter. The microeconomic and structural improvements are commonly called second-generation reforms, but in our view, this term is misguided. Some microeconomic and institutional reforms may take longer to implement, but that does not mean that they should follow macroeconomic reforms.

The microeconomic and structural elements of the investment climate, including infrastructure and governance, are less understood than the macroeconomic factors. One reason for this is data limitations. To better understand these issues, we must go beyond inputs and outputs and ask how processes actually work and whether they are participatory. In particular, two types of survey data are needed to provide detail on the quality of the investment climate: first, firm-level data collected through surveys of firms, and second, national and subnational data also collected from surveys, on the institutions that affect firms. These surveys are discussed in chapter 6.

Macroeconomic and Trade Policies   The macroeconomic aspects of the investment climate have been well understood for some time. A large empirical literature shows that better macroeconomic conditions are associated with faster long-run growth. In particular, there is extensive evidence of a strong relationship between growth and low inflation, openness to trade, and openness to foreign direct investment (see, for example, Fischer 1993, Frankel and Romer 1999, Dollar and Kraay 2004). And it is well accepted that the slowdown of growth in developing countries in the early 1970s partly stemmed from macroeconomic instability, which reduced confidence in government and its ability to maintain a stable climate for private economic activity.

Most developing countries pursued macroeconomic stabilization and adjustment programs in the decades following the oil shocks of the 1970s. Many of these programs were designed to reduce external and internal imbalances, control debt, and contain inflation—policies that should encourage private investment. On average, developing countries have made impressive progress in reducing inflation over the past two decades. From 1974 to 1990 average annual inflation was 10 to 11 percent in every developing region except East Asia (where it was 8.2 percent) and Eastern Europe and the Soviet Union (6.5 percent). By 2002 inflation was 3 to 5 percent in every developing region except South Asia (1.8 percent).[1] Yet in many countries macroeconomic issues remained a persistent challenge throughout the 1990s, with exchange rate uncertainties and pressures on the balance of payments. In some countries the main problem has been unsustainable fiscal policies, resulting in balance-of-payments and currency crises.

Many developing countries have also made great progress in increasing openness over the past two decades. Since the first half of the 1980s average tariffs have fallen sharply in all developing regions, and in many countries the dispersion of tariffs has narrowed as well. Integration has brought enormous benefits. Growth rates for integrating countries generally accelerated rapidly in the 1990s, including in India, Mexico, Uganda, and Vietnam (see chapter 3). China's increased involvement in international markets—for both goods and capital—over the past quarter-century has played an enormous role in its extraordinary growth, which has aided its widespread reduction in poverty.

Protection of one industry or activity (usually those with weak performance) discriminates against others, inhibiting job creation in potentially high-productivity activities. It also results in higher consumer prices for the protected activities, usually hitting poor people particularly hard.

Where local conditions for entrepreneurship and growth are good, exposure to international competition increases the productivity of domestic firms and lowers input costs for downstream users. For example, allowing foreign competition in the financial sector can improve costs and service quality for other firms that rely on credit or other financial services (World Bank 2001f). Similarly, foreign direct investment brings new production and process technologies, organizational approaches, and marketing networks. Consider the Indian machine tool industry, discussed in chapter 3 (see Sutton 2002). When India lowered protection in the early 1990s, Taiwanese firms entered the Indian market and claimed around one-third of it. But after nearly a decade of more open policies, several Indian producers had adapted—dramatically increasing their productivity, introducing new and better products, reclaiming much of the market, and starting to export—benefiting all users, direct or indirect, of those products.

The extent to which such gains are realized depends on complementary actions by government. If the business environment is conducive to growth, the private sector will be better able to take advantage of opportunities from trade. But moving to greater openness may incur dislocation and adjustment costs, which should be recognized and managed. Seizing the opportunities of global integration requires reallocating resources and changing ways of operating. This can place serious pressure on national systems for social assistance and environmental protection, as well as on local communities and national values. And because gains are unlikely to be distributed equally and those who benefit most will be dispersed, change will likely face resistance—and may invite protection of special interests.

Infrastructure   The second crucial component of the investment climate is the quality and quantity of physical and financial infrastructure, including power, transportation, telecommunications, and banking and finance. Firms require physical links to markets, through ports and roads, as well as efficient communications. Many of these infrastructure services involve economies of scale (as with electricity) or pooling of resources (banking) and so imply a need for production far beyond the scope of individual firms. For such services public regulation of private production, or even direct public provision, is likely to be crucial, making them a major concern of public policy.

Bad infrastructure services force firms to expend more time, money, and effort acquiring information, obtaining inputs, and getting their products to market. These additional costs can easily eliminate firms' comparative advantages. Indeed, if they are high enough, they may deter firms from investing or entering at all. Firm surveys confirm the importance of infrastructure, often highlighting power reliability, transportation times and costs, and access to communications technologies as key determinants of competitiveness and profitability. These surveys also provide insights into countries' strengths in providing infrastructure services to entrepreneurs, as well as guidance about future challenges (see chapter 6).

For example, a survey in China found that infrastructure services there compare favorably with those in many other parts of the developing world. Chinese firms report losing an average of 2 percent of sales to power outages, compared with 6 percent in Pakistan. Similarly, in poor investment climates, unreliable electricity supplies force many firms to invest in their own generators. In India, where many states still have relatively poor investment climates, despite progress at the national level, 69 percent of firms report having generators, compared with 27 percent in China.

Moreover, many of the Chinese firms import materials or machinery; the typical firm got its most recent shipment through customs in eight days, comparable to the figure for richer countries such as the Republic of Korea and Thailand. In India, by contrast, customs clearance takes eleven days; and in Pakistan, eighteen days. The extremes on this measure come from the Middle East. In Algeria, for example, it takes twenty-four days to clear customs (see table 5.1).

Poor infrastructure is often particularly harmful for small firms. In Algeria small firms are 50 percent more likely than large ones to experience power disruptions (totaling eighteen days a year) and three

Table 5.1
Infrastructure indicators for selected developing countries

Country	Days of power outages from the public grid (average)	Losses due to power outages (% sales)	Days of insufficient water supply (average)	Losses due to insufficient water supply (% sales)	Days of unavailable mainline telephone service (average)	Losses due to unavailable mainline telephone service (% sales)	Firms with own generator (percent)
Albania 2002	47.5	—	15.9	—	8.8	—	—
Armenia 2002	4.5	—	26.7	—	7.9	—	—
Azerbaijan 2002	61.5	—	11.6	—	3.2	—	—
Bangladesh 2002	249.0	3.3	31.6	—	—	—	71.5
Belarus 2002	1.2	—	2.1	—	1.8	—	—
Brazil 2003	4.6	2.5	1.5	0.6	2.1	1.2	17.0
Bulgaria 2002	5.6	—	5.4	—	1.7	—	—
Cambodia 2003	5.7	2.9	3.5	1.9	4.6	2.6	39.0
China 2002	—	2.0	—	—	—	—	16.2
Croatia 2002	3.3	—	0.8	—	1.2	—	—
Czech Republic 2002	2.2	—	0.8	—	0.8	—	—
Estonia 2002	3.8	—	1.4	—	1.9	—	—
Ethiopia 2002	—	5.4	—	—	—	—	17.1
Georgia 2002	63.2	—	31.5	—	13.9	—	—
Honduras 2003	28.5	5.2	13.4	3.0	6.5	7.2	33.3
Hungary 2002	2.9	—	0.8	—	1.6	—	—
India 2000	—	—	—	—	—	—	68.5
Kazakhstan 2002	10.5	—	4.1	—	5.6	—	—

Kenya 2003	83.6	9.3	85.2	—	35.8	—	70.9
Kyrgyzstan 2003	12.4	2.5	1.8	0.7	2.2	0.2	8.9
Latvia 2002	2.7	—	1.6	—	0.8	—	—
Lithuania 2002	1.4	—	0.6	—	1.4	—	—
Moldova 2003	2.2	0.4	1.1	0.1	4.1	0.2	5.8
Nicaragua 2003	29.8	6.5	51.8	6.6	7.0	9.3	18.4
Nigeria 2001	—	—	—	—	—	—	97.4
Pakistan 2002	14.5	5.4	4.5	—	2.7	—	41.8
Peru 2002	8.9	3.2	13.7	—	6.7	—	27.6
Philippines 2002	6.0	7.1	9.9	5.7	1.9	—	36.6
Poland 2003	1.5	0.5	0.2	0.4	0.5	0.1	8.3
Romania 2002	7.2	—	10.6	—	2.0	—	—
Russia 2002	5.6	—	7.2	—	7.8	—	—
Slovakia 2002	2.6	—	0.6	—	1.4	—	—
Slovenia 2002	2.0	—	0.3	—	1.1	—	—
Tajikistan 2003	32.4	5.3	1.7	1.3	5.0	0.4	0.0
Tanzania 2003	67.2	9.7	105.0	3.1	49.6	0.7	55.0
Turkey 2002	2.7	—	0.9	—	0.8	—	—
Uganda 2003	70.8	6.3	6.1	—	17.8	—	36.0
Ukraine 2002	9.4	—	29.7	—	3.4	—	—
Uzbekistan 2003	7.7	4.8	2.0	20.0	1.8	5.0	4.0
Yugoslavia 2002	10.3	—	3.2	—	13.4	—	—

Note: Missing value indicates that the corresponding question was not asked in the survey for that particular country.
Source: World Bank Investment Climate Surveys.

times more likely to experience water disruptions (totaling fifty-four days a year). Moreover, small firms are less likely to have mechanisms for coping with inefficient infrastructure, such as their own generators.

In India energy capital costs are a severe problem for small and medium-size enterprises. The typical small and medium-size enterprise has its own generator, tying up one-sixth of its capital in an investment that should be largely superfluous. Poor infrastructure also imposes indirect costs on these firms. For example, it deters foreign investment, limiting opportunities to develop supply relationships with multinational investors, which can provide an enormous stimulus to small and medium-size enterprises.

Infrastructure services also affect firm performance. In India the share of firms with generators is twice as high in Uttar Pradesh as in Maharashtra, reflecting the less reliable electricity in Uttar Pradesh. Moreover, firms in Uttar Pradesh report twice as many visits from government officials. As a result Uttar Pradesh, the country's largest state and one of its poorest, has a higher capital intensity rate and lower growth rate than Maharashtra (World Bank and CII 2002).

Governance and Institutions   The third essential element of the investment climate is governance and institutions, particularly those that affect the creation and operation of businesses. Bureaucratic hurdles and corruption impose barriers to entry, raise operating costs, and create uncertainty for firms. Thus, these hurdles limit investment, increase risk, and reduce returns to investment. Although these problems affect both large and small firms, they are especially important for small and medium-size ones, which are less able to afford bureaucratic entry costs and less likely to have the political contacts required to cut red tape.

The story involves much more than the formalities of licensing, regulation, and taxation. It is largely about how people behave within a system. Systematic harassment can arise in any formal structure. For example, in many countries small businesses face endless and intrusive visits from tax officials, safety inspectors, and the like (World Bank 2003b). Taxation and safety inspection are essential functions of government, to be sure; indeed, both are often carried out less effectively than they should be. The problem comes when such interventions are motivated more by officials' desire to control and elicit bribes from firms than by the public welfare. Harassment is more likely if there are more entry points for official intervention in the operation of firms, but the behavior of officials is crucial whatever the structure.

Key factors determining the investment climate are the institutions shaping the:

• Competitiveness of output markets, particularly conditions for entry and exit

• Functioning of factor markets: labor and capital (including strong financial institutions)

• Application of legal structures, including for taxation and property rights

• Style of enforcement of rules that are in the public interest, such as those protecting the environment, health, and safety

Each of these areas involves relationships between government and private individuals and firms, including levels of corruption, arbitrary behavior, and harassment of entrepreneurs. They also shape the relationships between firms and between firms and households, as consumers or workers. They are complex areas; strengthening governance and institutions is no simple matter.

Our understanding of these issues has grown tremendously in recent years, allowing us to draw several lessons. One is that extensive bureaucratic harassment and intervention hamper entrepreneurship and productivity. This is not to say that regulation should be avoided. Rather, the question is what to regulate and how to do it. For example, regulation concerning transparency and safety can facilitate efficient outcomes and serve the public interest. But if regulation mainly serves as a lever for bureaucratic nuisance and corruption, it can cause tremendous damage to the investment climate.

Empirical research confirms this point. Cross-country studies have shown that indicators of governance and institutions are closely linked with development outcomes (see, for example, Kaufmann, Kraay, and Mastruzzi 2003; Acemoğlu and others 2001; Hall and Jones 1999). This applies to both large and small firms, but is especially important for small firms given their credit constraints and lack of political clout. In investment climate surveys, firm managers have been asked how much time they spend dealing with government bureaucracy and how much they pay in informal payments (bribes, in effect) to get things done. The results are striking. In Pakistan entrepreneurs report spending thirty-six days a year dealing with government inspections, compared with sixteen days in Bangladesh and ten days in India. In China firms in cities with high corruption and theft have lower performance. And across sixty-nine countries, the time that managers report dealing with government bureaucracy to obtain licenses and permits is associated with significantly lower foreign direct investment (controlling for market size), human capital, and macroeconomic stability (World Bank 2003d).

These surveys also tell us about the degree of competition in markets. One of the most telling indicators of the competitive vibrancy of a market is the productivity dispersion of firms within an industry. When less efficient producers are not being forced to improve their productivity or leave the market, productivity dispersion is high. As competition intensifies, firms are pressured to innovate, improve efficiency, adopt better technologies, or exit, and as a result productivity dispersion should shrink. The high performers in India's electronics industry are five times more productive than the low performers. Compare this with Korea, where the difference in productivity is only twofold. Studies show that productivity dispersion is closely related to entry and exit barriers: countries with higher barriers to entry tend to have more dispersion between the best and worst performers (World Bank 2003b, Djankov and others 2002).

Aside from reducing direct regulatory barriers to entry and exit, privatization can have a large impact on facilitating more vibrant competition, encouraging new entrants and productivity gains. Many studies and country experiences, particularly from transition countries, show that privatization can yield substantial gains (see chapter 12). But it is not a panacea. Successful privatization requires a strong institutional environment, and it delivers the greatest gains when combined with competition. Privatization in public services such as infrastructure differs markedly from privatization in ordinary competitive sectors of production, where it has been shown to bring the greatest benefits. Research for the financial sector shows that government ownership of banks tends to reduce competition, limit access to credit, and heighten the risk of crisis (La Porta, Lopez-de-Silanes, and Shleifer 2000).

Cross-country indicators of regulatory institutions also allow us to compare how different regulatory approaches affect entrepreneurial activity—for instance, showing how certain types of regulation increase the costs of doing business or encourage firms to join the formal sector, invest, and grow (table 5.2). Consider some findings from an analysis of regulatory institutions across the world (World Bank 2003b):

• *Entry regulations.* In 2003 it took 10 procedures, 44 days, and an amount equal to 92 percent of the country's per capita income to register a new business in Nigeria. By contrast, in Canada it took 2 procedures and 3 days; the process was entirely electronic and cost less than 1 percent of per capita income. In Denmark registration was free of charge. More extensive entry requirements are associated with higher corruption and a larger informal sector.

• *Contract enforcement.* Resolving a payment or other contract-related dispute through the courts takes on average 7 days in Tunisia, 39 in the Netherlands, 365 in Belgium and in India, 645 in Italy, and 721 in Lebanon. Higher procedural complexity is associated with less access to justice, lower contract enforceability, and more judicial corruption.

• *Labor regulations.* Egypt has much more rigid labor market regulations than other Middle Eastern, North African, and OECD countries, and in Egypt the unofficial economy accounts for a larger share of GDP (35 percent) than in the Middle East and North Africa (28 percent) and OECD countries (17 percent). More rigid labor regulations are associated with larger unofficial economies (Botero and others 2004).

Thus the ideas behind the investment climate and the first pillar draw from and build on our standard microeconomic theories of efficiency and productivity in markets, in that they emphasize the effects of monopoly power, externalities, and regulation. But the approach goes beyond the standard static micro in its emphasis on three key areas: understanding the institutional and governance determinants of the investment climate; promoting the dynamics of entrepreneurship; and constructing an empirical foundation based on data from surveys from firms, both domestic and foreign, on institutional and governance issues.

Empowering and Investing in People
The second pillar involves empowering and investing in poor people by increasing their capabilities to enhance their health, education, and security and by fostering mechanisms for them to participate in decisions that shape their lives. This pillar is founded on the lessons in

Table 5.2
Regulatory indicators

	Business registry (number of procedures)[a]	Time to register business (days)[b]	Cost of registering business (% of income per capita)[c]	Dispute resolution (days)[d]	Dispute resolution cost (% income per capita)[e]	Conditions of employment (index)[f]	Flexibility of firing (index)[g]	Share of unofficial economy (% of GDP)[h]
Best	2	2	0.2	7	10	22	1	9
Worst	19	215	1298	1460	521	95	73	67
India	10	88	50	365	95	75	45	23
China	12	46	14	180	32	67	57	13
Algeria	18	29	32	387	—	60	19	34
Egypt	13	43	61	202	31	83	61	35
Nigeria	10	44	92	730	7	76	36	58
Kenya	11	61	54	255	50	53	16	34
Cameroon	12	37	191	548	63	43	39	33
Pakistan	10	22	47	365	46	75	33	37
Indonesia	11	168	15	225	269	53	43	19
Korea	12	33	18	75	5	88	32	28
Brazil	15	152	12	380	2	89	68	40
Peru	9	100	25	441	30	81	69	60
Russian Federation	12	29	9	160	20	77	71	46
Serbia and Montenegro	10	44	13	1028	20	88	29	29

[a] A procedure is defined as any interaction of the company founder with external parties (government agencies, lawyers, etc.).
[b] Time is recorded in calendar days. Therefore, the time variable captures the average duration that incorporation lawyers estimate is necessary to complete a procedure.

c The text of the company law, the commercial code, or specific regulations is used a source for the costs associated with starting up a business.

d Estimate of the duration of the dispute resolution measured as the number of days from the moment the plaintiff files the lawsuit in court, until the moment of actual payment.

e Cost is inclusive of court costs and attorney fees as well as payments to other professionals like accountants and bailiffs.

f Covers working time requirements, including mandatory minimum daily rest, maximum number of hours in a normal workweek, premium for overtime work, restrictions on weekly holiday, mandatory payment for nonworking days, and minimum wage legislation.

g Covers workers' legal protections against dismissal, including grounds for dismissal, procedures for dismissal (individual and collective), notice period, and severance payment.

h This measures the output in the informal economy as a share of gross national income.

Source: World Bank (2003b).

chapter 3 on the roles of social inclusion and reform ownership in enhancing development effectiveness. It also promotes growth by bringing poor people's assets and energies into the process.

Empowering individuals means:

• Facilitating the development of their human capital (such as health characteristics and educational achievements) and physical assets

• Relaxing external constraints that shape their lives at the levels of family, community (caste, religion), society, and culture—by, for example, expanding women's rights to own property or participate in the management of public goods (such as schools) that affect their lives

• Easing internal constraints they impose on themselves, including their perceptions of their roles, preferences, and capacity to aspire (see chapter 3)

Chapter 3 has already explained the close relationship between empowerment and participation and inclusion. Using the terms *participation* and *inclusion* is often helpful. First, for many people the notion of participation is more concrete than empowerment—and may come with less political baggage. Second, *empowerment* does not always translate well into other languages, while *participation* tends to be a well-understood and easily translated concept. In the next section, we give examples of effective participation.

Like participation, the concept of inclusion can be useful if empowerment risks being misunderstood (again, see chapter 3). The many young people excluded from the job market by counterproductive labor market policies in Algeria, the many potential entrepreneurs prevented from making a decent living by predatory state policies in Russia, the many young girls prevented from attending school by discriminatory social attitudes—reinforced by bad policies—in Pakistan, the many poor people refused access to credit or given no voice in local affairs because of their caste or religious background in India: all are examples of social exclusion.

The issue of empowerment looms largest on gender issues. Many people, including us, see the empowerment of women as a goal in itself. It is a key part of equity and justice. But whether one accepts women's empowerment on ethical grounds, there is compelling evidence that attention to opportunities for girls and women not only improves their position in society, it also has a major impact on development effectiveness (World Bank 2001d). The education of mothers has a powerful effect on the health of their children by raising immunization rates, reducing malnutrition, and as a consequence reducing child mortality. Moreover, cross-country evidence suggests that lower investment in education for girls and women reduces growth performance.

Empowering women in other spheres also brings benefits. Transfer payments provided directly to women and women's control over income and productive assets more generally tend to increase household spending on food and clothing and reduce spending on alcohol and tobacco. And increasing women's involvement in public life reduces corruption. Demand-side interventions to close large male-female gaps in schooling promote women's empowerment. There are several successful programs of this type: for example, in Bangladesh stipends have dramatically expanded girls' enrollment in secondary school, and in Baluchistan, Pakistan, programs have had large effects in an area where few girls had attended school.

Empowerment and inclusion depend on the functioning of social networks and on individuals' location in them. The abilities that social networks confer on an individual or group are often encapsulated in the term *social capital* (Loury 1977, Coleman 1990, Putnam 1993). Further, families group themselves into social clusters, often based on ethnicity, in which local public goods are provided to young family members. Examples of such goods include peer influences, friendship networks, and contacts that generate information about employment. Under these circumstances historically generated differences between groups (in income, for example) will not disappear over time as they might otherwise be expected to do. Instead they will tend to persist, even where there are no underlying differences in tastes or abilities (Loury 1987). Many social constraints and individual attitudes and behaviors are founded in problems of uncertainty and a search for protection. Vulnerability is disempowering. Hence much of the policy aimed at increasing social protection can also be interpreted as policy to promote empowerment. It is possible, however, for some forms of social protection to limit empowerment if they foster a culture of dependency.

This discussion of ethnicity, gender, and social capital concerns the external element in the three factors shaping empowerment (assets, external constraints, and internal constraints). We now comment briefly on internal constraints, particularly the role of changing preferences and perceptions of one's role in society. (We return to this issue in chapter 9.)

Development is a process of change in both the structure of the economy and the structure of preferences. Preference change is obvious in areas of consumption goods: when an economy develops rapidly, consumers soon discover they have preferences for goods they had never before imagined, or at least imagined being able to own. For example, how many urban Chinese workers knew in 1980 what type of car they would like to own, much less their preferences for type and use of cell phones? One could try to invoke "basic" preferences in areas such as transportation and communications, but doing so would hardly cover the nature of the changes involved.

Moreover, development often involves more fundamental changes—for example, in preferences about gender roles and participation in decision making. Traditionally in economics, we model individuals as optimizing over a given pattern of preferences under fully specified constraints. Welfare analysis then rests on assessing outcomes in terms of individuals' given preferences. This is a powerful approach that has yielded real and enduring insights for policy. But to think of the assumption of fixed preferences as holding in a development context over the long term is deeply misleading. As economies and societies change, individuals and groups change their perceptions of their roles and what they seek. This is a vital consequence of change, but also a crucial determinant of it.

Take as an example the education of ethnic minorities (World Bank 2003a). Imagine that a government pushes to expand education opportunities for a minority group. The resulting increase in minority graduates may create an educated, engaged constituency that advocates further change, such as antidiscrimination laws in the workplace. The increase can also create visible role models who expand minority children's views of what they can achieve, giving them preferences in areas where they never had them, such as what type of professionals they want to become. With these preferences developing and old barriers breaking down, the children are equipped to take advantage of any increasing demand for their skills that come from a reduction in labor market discrimination.

Thus, there is a self-reinforcing dynamic of empowerment in which preference change is a key element. Just as with investment climate dynamics—in which improvements in the climate can create an entrepreneurial class, which then pushes for further improvements in the climate—empowerment gives people the tools and opportunities to push for further empowerment. Because disempowerment is also self-reinforcing, it may be a challenge to get such a positive cycle started. But once it begins, we may be surprised at its dynamism. If we doubt that, we need only consider what has happened to opportunities for women—and to both their attitudes and those of men—in the Western world over the past generation.

In understanding behavior—including the preferences that help drive it and the degree to which empowerment interacts with them—culture is central. Attention to cultural issues can lead to great advances in fighting poverty and in the general effectiveness of development projects and programs. A powerful example is of a birthing clinic in Peru that has dramatically increased rates of in-clinic births by changing its procedures and facilities to better suit local norms, such as by using a new kind of birthing table and providing a guest house for expectant mothers' families to stay in. This approach has been so successful that it has been emulated across the country. We must take care, however, with the lessons we draw from such examples. In particular, we should recognize the difficulties involved in "social or cultural engineering" (Scott 1998). (The discussion of changing preferences is taken further in chapter 9.)

That development involves major changes in preferences and behavior is not a new idea. Indeed, it was a fundamental insight of social scientists studying social change in the 1950s and 1960s. F. G. Bailey (1957), for example, described how changes in industrial structure—specifically, the growth and subsequent banning of the local distilling industry—raised one group from low to dominant caste in its Indian village. Esther Boserup (1965) examined how population growth led to technological innovation, which had widespread social effects. And Jane Jacobs (1969) explained how good city planning could feed positive externalities from human capital, fueling prosperity and raising the quality of urban life (through reduced crime and increased creativity, for example). We now understand that many anthropologists and social scientists were far ahead of mainstream economists.

Implementing the Strategy

Assume that one agrees that the two pillars constitute a structure for a development strategy. What do they mean in practice? How would a developing country, or an outside donor agency, act to strengthen the pillars? This section sketches out some answers to that question, examining each pillar in turn.

Investment Climate

Systematic investigation of the investment climate in developing (including transition) countries using firm surveys started in the 1990s at the World Bank and European Bank for Reconstruction and Development. Such efforts have gathered pace, and comparable surveys have been completed or are under way for about fifty countries, including Bangladesh, China, India, and Pakistan. These surveys cover large random samples of firms—some 1,500 firms in China and 1,200 in India, to take two examples—in selected sectors and cities.

The surveys collect the usual firm information on sales, outputs, inputs, capital, labor, finance, costs, and so on. But they also include specific quantitative questions about the infrastructure and governance aspects of the investment climate. Examples include: "How often are you visited by the authorities, and how much management time is spent with them?" and "How many days did your firm experience power outages in the past month?" The objective is to collect data that will allow researchers to link these investment climate indicators to outcomes such as firm productivity, investment, and growth. (The surveys are discussed in greater detail in chapter 6.)

Researchers have also begun to gather data on business regulation in more than 100 countries. (For an overview, see World Bank 2003b.)[2] These data include the procedures, time, and cost to register a new business, enforce a contract, and go through bankruptcy proceedings. With these data, we can benchmark country performance and analyze what drives cross-country differences in investment climate.

Investment climate surveys are useful for identifying areas that should be priorities for increasing firm productivity—whether macroeconomic and trade policies, infrastructure, or governance and institutions. The surveys allow us to translate these broad areas into precise definitions of specific barriers identified by firms and to link those barriers to firm productivity and other performance measures.

In the first area, macroeconomic and trade policy, developing countries have made major progress in the past two decades, reducing inflation, showing greater fiscal discipline, and slashing tariffs. Still, many developing countries maintain relatively high barriers to imports and protect domestic producers. The average tariff for low-income countries is 18 percent; for middle-income countries, 14 percent. Particularly in countries that maintain tariffs well above these average levels, the excessive protection, especially if combined with poor investment climates, is likely to reduce competitiveness and slow productivity growth. Moreover, tariff dispersion is high both across and within economic sectors, which probably creates significant distortions. Cumbersome customs procedures and often spurious quality standards further impede trade, insulating firms from competition and reducing the flow of ideas, both of which hurt the investment climate. And in highly protected environments, the energies of entrepreneurs are diverted from taking economic opportunities toward lobbying ministry officials and politicians.

In the second major area of the investment climate, infrastructure, the question is, What can governments do to improve infrastructure services for entrepreneurs? A primary reason for poor infrastructure services is that they are often provided by inefficient government monopolies that greatly underinvest in maintenance and expansion. Although experience is mixed and depends on the industry and country (see chapter 12), private participation in the provision of infrastructure services, supported by sound regulation, often helps enhance efficiency, increase investment, and expand access. Examples include:

• *Liberalizing entry for private providers.* For example, there have been substantial gains from allowing small firms and individuals to provide water services in Mexico and Paraguay and small enterprises to supply electricity in Yemen (World Bank 2003h, Rosenblatt and Stern 2003).

• *Privatization.* For example, impressive gains were achieved through the privatization of water services in Cartagena, Colombia. Service rose from seven to twenty-four hours a day, connections in poor areas jumped from 0 to 98 percent, and overall connections increased by 40 percent.

Private participation in infrastructure is generally most successful when accompanied by regulatory reform that aligns the incentives of private providers with the needs of consumers; encourages competition; provides for independent regulation of quality, price, and service coverage; and requires providers to make commitments on costs and service quality (World Bank 2003h).

Although private participation has an important role, the bulk of infrastructure provision will likely remain in the public sector in developing countries. The World Bank estimates that approximately one-fourth of developing-country investment in infrastructure involved private sector participation during the 1990s (World Bank 2003h). Thus, privatization should not be regarded as a universal solution. Moreover, the challenge of improving public infrastructure services remains— indeed, it is one of the key challenges of improving the investment climate.

Finally, in the third broad area of the investment climate—governance and institutions—data from investment climate surveys allow us to focus on the many dimensions of governance and institutions that affect firms' productivity and willingness to invest. These include labor laws, environmental protection, health and safety regulation, the availability and regulation of financial institutions, microeconomic policies that regulate the competitiveness of markets (entry and exit, subsidies), the legal and judicial framework for property, contracts, and bankruptcy, and other areas of public interest.

In all these areas a central concern is the relationship between government and private individuals and firms, including levels of corruption, arbitrary bureaucratic behavior, and harassment of entrepreneurs. Given the close link between the investment climate and firm productivity, reforms that facilitate the emergence of a highly competitive environment, reduce the bureaucratic burden and antibusiness practices, and improve public infrastructure are bound to improve prospects for growth. (These issues are discussed further in chapters 6 and 7.)

Empowerment

A favorable investment climate can promote growth, and where there is growth, poverty reduction is likely. But it is not certain. Growth can take many forms and can involve different types of changes in opportunities and outcomes for poor people. Thus the strategy's second pillar, empowering and investing in people, focuses on ensuring that poor people can participate in the growth process and are empowered with the capacities to shape their lives. These twin objectives are mutually reinforcing elements of a dynamic strategy for fighting poverty.

Statistics on income poverty are ex post indicators of poverty, in that they assess the success of the development process by looking at outcomes in terms of income. Our strategy of poverty reduction is based on both ex ante and ex post notions of poverty. We should not think of poverty only as an income-based concept, but should also recognize its capabilities dimension—that is, whether a person has the capabilities needed to escape from poverty, including sufficient education, good health, and the ability to take action within a community or society to improve her or his life. Fighting poverty depends not only on increasing the incomes of poor people, but also on helping them strengthen these key capabilities.

The challenge of empowerment and inclusion of poor people is in large measure the challenge of ensuring effective and efficient creation, availability, and delivery of basic health, education, and social protection services. Investments by society in health and in education enhance the employability of people and the health and education of their descendants, in addition to directly increasing their well-being. Investing in social protection allows poor people to take the risks inherent in participating in a dynamic market economy.

This focus on health, education, and social protection should not be taken to mean that actions to improve outcomes should be focused on these sectors. Progress in these areas depends heavily on the availability of infrastructure services such as roads, electricity, clean water, and sanitation, to name some of the most obvious. Acting across a range of sectors should be a key part of implementing the strategy's empowerment element.

Decentralization and Service Delivery   The challenge of making services work for people is examined in the World Bank's *World Development Report 2004*, on which this section draws heavily (readers are directed there for further discussion of this important issue). Simply increasing public spending on health and education is not enough. Cross-country evidence correlating public spending with health and education outcomes, after controlling for per capita income and other socioeconomic variables, does not indicate a strong relationship (Filmer, Hammer, and Pritchett 2000). That does not mean that, other inputs held equal, more spending on health and other social services has zero marginal effect. But it does highlight the importance of understanding how spending translates into outcomes. There are four ways that increased public spending can fail to translate into more services for poor people:

• Governments may misallocate budgets, spending resources on the wrong groups of people.

• Even when resources are allocated correctly, they may not reach their intended destinations if organizational and incentive problems in public agencies lead to misappropriation or theft.

• Even when resources reach a school or health clinic, providers may have weak incentives, motivations, or capacities to deliver services effectively.

• Social and cultural norms and individual preferences may result in weak demand for services.

The first type of failure, misallocation of budgets, can result from poor information and understanding of appropriate policy interventions. But we cannot ignore the role that political incentives and institutions play in this process. Political influences and pressures can skew public policies in favor of influential groups or systematically divert resources from budgets, reducing investment in essential public goods that benefit all citizens.

Recent empirical evidence on diversion of public resources from basic services is striking. Chapter 3 cited the evidence that only 13 percent of nonwage recurrent spending for primary education allocated in the Ugandan government's budget in the early 1990s actually reached primary schools (Reinikka and Svensson 2001). Similarly, surveys in India and Nigeria have found that many teachers and health workers did not receive their salaries for several months because local governments appropriated resources received from higher levels of government for their own purposes (World Bank 2003a).

In some environments powerful teacher and worker unions fight for higher wages, leading to underfinancing of nonwage recurrent spending. Service delivery surveys have found that because of this underfinancing, school buildings and health clinics often lack basic equipment, such as textbooks and drugs, needed to provide education and health services. A study on basic education in India reports that many school buildings have been abandoned for lack of simple furniture and teaching materials, and instead are used by local elites for personal purposes (PROBE Team 1999). Robinson and Verdier (2002) provide an analytical framework that accounts for such outcomes, with inefficient redistribution through public employment being the equilibrium political strategy under conditions of high inequality and low productivity.

Even where resources flow to intended points of delivery, incentives and support for high-quality provision may be weak. One manifestation of this is the widespread absenteeism among public service providers such as teachers and doctors. Service delivery surveys conducted for the *World Development Report 2004*, based on unannounced visits to primary schools and health centers, confirm the severity of this problem: provider absence rates range from 11 percent among Peruvian teachers to 67 percent among medical workers in the Indian state of Bihar (Chaudhury and others, forthcoming).

Numerous factors contribute to high absence rates, including insufficient monitoring of providers, weak rewards for good performance, and lack of local involvement in facility management—as well as difficult working conditions and low pay, which impede and discourage many service providers who have strong intrinsic motivation and professional pride. Providers sometimes do not receive their wages, and there are problems getting well-educated, trained individuals to move with their families to remote rural areas.

Innovative policies have helped get providers in places of need. For example, Nigeria's primary health care policy is founded on the model of community health workers, consisting of individuals drawn from local communities and trained to provide basic preventive and curative health care. India's polio eradication campaign, which sent doctors to villages for two days a month to perform immunizations, is another good example. The doctors provided this service effectively, presumably driven by both professional and patriotic motives, when they might not have been prepared to move to these villages for longer periods.

An intuitive and appealing argument that has recently gained ground is that creating institutions for active community participation in service delivery helps overcome many of the problems discussed above. Parent-teacher associations, water user associations, community health groups, and similar entities can play a powerful role in encouraging suppliers, tailoring services to needs identified by communities, and holding providers accountable for service delivery. Substantial evidence on and examples of these mechanisms are provided in the *World Development Report 2004*.

Still, we cannot jump to the conclusion that decentralization automatically empowers communities and improves service delivery. In fact, capture of public services by local elites may reverse the benefits for poor people. Bardhan and Mookherjee (1998) suggest that the benefits of decentralized service delivery for local governments and communities depend on the power of local elites and on the level and nature of local inequality. Platteau (2002) and Abraham and Platteau (2002) show that even though acting through local leaders enables international agencies and nongovernmental organization (NGOs) to channel considerable resources to rural communities in a short period, it can increase the probability that these resources will be misused by local elites. By virtue of their dominant position, elites can manipulate participatory methods by representing their interests as community concerns, expressed as project deliverables. In Senegal, for example, municipal bodies and rural councils used the new rights accorded to them under the country's decentralization scheme to engage in dubious dealings, such as sales of rural lands to tourist and other business interests, without consulting their communities.

Platteau (2002) argues that traditional elites are not the only group to benefit from newly channeled resources, since they often have tactical alliances with politicians and educated individuals operating outside the village domain. In sub-Saharan Africa it is common for chiefs to co-opt new elites in their village associations—for example, by creating neotraditional titles that are sold to the newly rich eager to acquire a political base in the countryside.

These offsetting benefits and risks of decentralized service delivery imply that policy design and implementation must take into account how policies are likely to work in given circumstances and ensure that monitoring and evaluation mechanisms are in place. One instance in which community participation has been rigorously evaluated is El Salvador's EDUCO (Educación con participación de la comunidad) program, briefly mentioned in chapter 3. The government provided financing to community-managed schools and empowered community associations to hire and fire teachers. Community participation led to higher enrollments, faster learning (as measured by standardized tests), and lower teacher absenteeism (Jimenez and Sawada 1999).

Evaluating the Impact of Public Programs There is need for much broader evaluation of the impact of community participation, including a stronger focus on the factors shaping its success or failure. For instance, India's District Primary Education Program, which encouraged community participation, has been widely cited as a success. But the absence of careful evaluation has made it difficult to make that claim unequivocally or to identify or understand reasons for varying performance in different environments and implementation methods.

It is important here to distinguish between different types of projects. Some may be too technical or large for communities to manage successfully, and local capacity constraints can limit the benefits from increased monitoring and participation. For example, Khwaja (2001) examines the performance of 132 community-maintained infrastructure projects in northern Pakistan and finds that project design is a critical determinant of success. Complex projects are poorly maintained and inequality in project returns has a U-shaped relationship with maintenance. Increased community participation in project decisions has a positive effect on maintenance for nontechnical decisions but a negative effect for technical decisions. Projects initiated by NGOs are better maintained than local government projects, as are projects made as extensions of old projects rather than anew. Although direct community involvement in management might not be sensible in many cases, in most cases community involvement in assessing services is likely to improve them.

Given the difficulty facing so many poor people in accessing or using public services, it is not surprising that they often bypass public service providers and seek out fee-based private services. There is enormous scope for the public sector to explore partnerships with the private sector in providing basic services. Though there is often a rationale for government intervention in basic service provision, constraints on effective public provision may imply changing the role of government from that of direct provider to facilitator and regulator. This is a big challenge because of both conflicting political incentives and lack of competitive private markets.

Bolivia and Colombia have experimented with contracting water supply to private firms. This arrangement was initially successful in Colombia, leading to better services and increased coverage in poor areas, but in Bolivia it led to a crisis—with farmers protesting against sudden tariff increases that were not accompanied by quality improvements. Further research is needed to cull lessons from such diverse experiences.

Even if public spending makes basic services available, historical and cultural norms may cause individuals and households to not respond to them—particularly disadvantaged groups such as women or ethnic, religious, and political minorities. In such cases financial incentives may be needed to boost private demand and supply. Mexico's Progresa program experimented with demand-side interventions by providing cash transfers to rural families that kept their children in school and took them for regular health care visits. This approach resulted in significant improvements in the health of both children and adults (Gertler and Boyce 2001). The program's achievements—and the careful evaluation documenting them—allowed it to survive changes in administrations and fostered its expansion across the country, including to urban areas.

Bangladesh's Female Secondary Scholarship program is another such example. Under this program a girl attending secondary school receives a stipend deposited directly into a bank account in her name. Schools also receive transfers proportional to the number of girls enrolled. Although the program has not been evaluated rigorously, preliminary findings indicate that it has contributed to the impressive increase in girls' secondary school enrollments.

There are many impressive examples of direct public action achieving remarkable, sustainable improvements in human development. Tendler (1997) and World Bank (2003a) describe how in the late 1980s, the newly elected leader of Ceará, a state in northeastern Brazil, launched a major public health program (see chapter 3). Like the Nigerian program, the Brazilian initiative recruited and trained local health care workers who then worked in their own villages rather than trying to convince trained people from cities to relocate to the countryside. One measure of this program's effectiveness is that between the 1980s and 2001, infant mortality in the state fell from around 100 to 25 per 1,000 live births.

In the Uganda case, when evidence of leakage of public school resources emerged, the central government launched an information campaign. It began publishing monthly transfers to school districts in newspapers, broadcasting them on radio, and requiring primary schools to post the information. As a result the information on leakage became a powerful driver of public action (Reinikka and Svensson 2001).

In these examples the commitment of specific leaders catalyzed community action and produced remarkable results. The challenge is determining how such advances can be generalized. Relevant institutions are those that inform citizens and spur the collective action needed to ensure that disadvantaged people can obtain the basic services so important to their empowerment. The power of independent and accessible media is highlighted in a study by Besley and Burgess (2001). The authors found that in India, government spending on food and disaster relief was significantly more responsive to citizen needs when there was wider circulation of newspapers, particularly in vernacular languages.

Service delivery surveys of providers and government agencies, along with household surveys on inclusion and participation, provide data for analyzing behavior and obstacles to investment in poor people's capacities. Dissemination of such data can empower communities, encouraging them to take action. The research agenda should answer such questions as:

• What kinds of institutional changes improve accountability in and provision of basic services?

• What kinds of incentives make service providers perform effectively?

• Under what conditions do public-private partnerships work well?

• What kinds of interventions influence individual and social demands for better services and opportunities, particularly for poor people?

Many countries are experimenting with innovative policies to bring about change. It is important that these be accompanied by systematic efforts to learn from them, including rigorous evaluations, so that we can develop a better understanding of what works and create a convincing basis for disseminating results and applying conclusions. Documentation and dissemination can reinforce better service delivery by preventing good policies from being overturned and allowing bad ones to be redesigned.

On the theoretical front, we need to better understand the social and political structures that arise in environments of inequality and extreme deprivation, and how they determine outcomes. Modern theories of organization and incentives can help identify which modes of service provision work better than others. Yet we must take care in applying these theories, because the success of innovative interventions is highly sensitive to broader political and social institutions—and can also be affected by the ethnic and cultural diversity and economic inequality that characterize many low-income countries (World Bank 2003a).

With the growing availability of different types of surveys—household, investment climate, service delivery—we are developing stronger databases to help us understand the dynamics of change that occur in even the most depressed communities (see chapter 6 for further discussion). Together with careful analysis of examples and experiments, these databases will allow us to identify policies that promote poor people's inclusion in the growth process and empower them to take control of their development.

Differences from Other Approaches

Development is a complex process of change, and no one single perspective or model can capture all the elements. This complexity and change imply that we should avoid assuming that we know the answers to the challenges of development. Understanding development requires advancing and assessing ideas, and learning what works and what does not in different circumstances. Development is shaped by historical circumstances and is intensely local. Thus, new ideas, however plausible and evidence based, should be applied cautiously in new settings.

In proposing a strategy for development, we do not seek to define a simple new economic model or recipe for action. Such an approach risks implying that we can collapse all our knowledge into a summary formula. Yet principles and theories are important for understanding development processes and guiding action. The strategy proposed here provides a structure for looking at development, and it is important to understand how it relates to other approaches.

In this section, we examine how the strategy we propose differs from those that dominated development thinking from the 1950s through the 1990s. Our main point is that while there have been clear development successes, the "direct-and-protect" approach popular in the 1950s and 1960s and the minimal-government, free-market approach advocated most strongly in the 1980s and early 1990s were dangerously simplistic and resulted in many failures. Our strategy draws on the lessons from those failures. The past fifty years have shown that growth, poverty reduction, and an effective private sector require a well-functioning government to provide a framework for governance, facilitate or provide physical infrastructure, invest in human capital, and ensure social cohesion. Institutional development has too often been neglected in past policy discussions, but has finally been recognized as essential to sustained poverty reduction.

Evolving Approaches to Development: A Brief History

In the 1950s and 1960s many economists argued that markets and incentives worked inadequately in developing countries and that therefore government should play a major role in determining the allocation of resources, particularly investment. In this the economists of the 1950s were responding to the terrible experiences of the preceding half-century, including wars, colonialism, and the Great Depression, which suggested that capitalism and external markets would not promote broadly based economic and social development in poor countries. These economists were also influenced by the apparent achievements of the Soviet Union (a perspective that changed over time as more accurate information emerged) and by the experience of wartime planning in the United Kingdom (see Little 1982). Although economists differed over strategies for government action—as with debates on balanced or unbalanced growth (see, for example, Rosenstein-Rodan 1943 and Hirschman 1958)—there was fairly broad agreement on the desirability of strong and fairly comprehensive government intervention in the economies of developing countries.

There were some voices against this seeming consensus. The economists Peter Bauer and Gottfried Haberler argued against interventionist states, for example, and political philosophers Friedrich von Hayek and Karl Popper made the case against central planning (see Bauer 1976, Haberler and Koo 1985, Hayek 1984, Popper 1962). Still, during this period many economists from both developed and developing countries were studying and advising on techniques for state planning. The predilection for planning and direct controls in the profession was often accompanied by pessimism about prospects for exports from developing countries, a pessimism closely associated with Hans Singer (1950) and Raúl Prebisch (1950). As a result many economists recommended industrialization based on import substitution, even though the motivations for planning and import substitution were logically distinct.

A central viewpoint on the macroeconomics of development was formalized in the two-gap model, in which Hollis Chenery played a leading role (see Bruno and Chenery 1962). The two gaps were, first, between saving and investment, and second, the balance of trade. Export pessimism was embodied in this model in terms of an assumed constraint on exports; domestic inflexibilities were incorporated through fixed import requirements for investment. Foreign aid, when viewed through these models, was seen as particularly productive: it would allow investment to expand by overcoming the constraint on its foreign exchange component. In both the planning and two-gap models, prices played a minimal role, and production techniques offered little choice, with fixed coefficients being a fairly universal assumption.

The 1950s and 1960s brought intense work on aggregate models of economic growth for both developed and developing countries. While the models applied to developed countries typically incorporated only one sector, those for developing countries gave a prominent role to dualism. Particularly influential was Arthur Lewis's (1954) model of economic growth with unlimited supplies of labor. In this model the process of development was depicted as a transfer of resources out of a traditional sector into an advanced sector, with the growth of the advanced sector driven by the investment of profits generated in that sector. Taking these various strands together, economic debate in the 1950s and 1960s can be seen as focused on growth through industrialization and import substitution, with government playing a central role in the process.

The late 1960s and the 1970s brought greater emphasis on applying basic microeconomic principles to analyses of growth and development. Concern about dubious industrial and project decisions made in the face of distorted domestic prices—or without reference to prices at all—led many economists to research the effects of those decisions. They worked on measuring price distortions and understanding the consequences and costs of the industrial and trade policies of previous decades. These new emphases for research led to a flowering of studies on topics such as effective protection, domestic resource cost, and shadow prices.

The late 1960s and 1970s also saw growing interest in the empirical study of poverty and income distribution. Robert McNamara, as president of the World Bank, made his famous Nairobi (Kenya) speech on income distribution and poverty in 1973 (McNamara 1981). The conceptual basis for measuring poverty and inequality was developed, with a focus on income, and income distribution began to be tracked in formal models. Development and growth economists turned their attention to the influence of income distribution on savings and growth, and conversely to the effects of growth on income distribution, with much of the discussion built on the work of Arthur Lewis (1955) and Simon Kuznets (1971).

At the policy level the concern with distribution was probably best expressed in the volume *Redistribution with Growth* (Chenery and others 1974) and in the *World Development Report* on poverty (World Bank 1990). Both focused on promoting labor-intensive growth and spurring investment in physical and human capital.

In the 1970s and early 1980s the debate on development was dominated by the inverted U hypothesis relating inequality and growth, formulated by Kuznets. The issue was whether this hypothesis—

describing the historical evolution of inequality and explained by the
sectoral reallocation of the population in the development process—
was a universal relationship, or whether instead the income distribution evolved in country-specific ways. Many economists believed,
based on data available in the 1970s, that the hypothesis held across
countries at different levels of development (see in particular Chenery
and his collaborators, including Ahluwalia 1976 and Ahluwalia, Carter, and Chenery 1976). But as more and better data became available,
particularly in the 1990s, the Kuznets hypothesis did not fit the evolution of inequality observed in a larger sample of countries (see Deininger and Squire 1998, Bourguignon 2003b).

In retrospect we know what was missing from this research: a recognition that economic growth depends not only on sectoral reallocation of resources, but also on institutional change—and that growth
tends to modify institutions, social relations, and culture. Institutional
change is likely to benefit some groups and hurt others, and in ways
likely to involve political responses by different groups. Thus, our
two-pillar strategy devotes more attention to the underlying determinants of development—particularly institutions, governance, and
behavior—than did the approaches that were prominent in the 1980s,
with their stronger emphasis on the workings of models in terms of
accumulation, factor intensity, choice of techniques, and demand and
supply.

In the 1980s perspectives on development policy shifted quickly and
strongly in response to the failings—in terms of growth and stability—
of statist policies. The direct-and-protect approach was replaced
by market fundamentalism (sometimes called neoliberalism), which
asserted that everything possible should be left to markets, that government should get out of the way, and that the role of the state should
be limited to defense, rule of law, and so on. Social protection was
often dismissed as social engineering, and it was argued that the private sector should take over a lot of public provision in infrastructure
and even education and health. Further, it was suggested that the private sector would create the demand for whatever institutions were
necessary.

Such views have often been associated with Milton Friedman (see,
for example, Friedman 1976). But an excessively market-oriented approach, which is only mildly caricatured here, is dangerously naive—
leading, for example, to many of the hardships encountered during
the transition in Eastern Europe and the former Soviet Union. Poor

people can fare extremely badly in a world driven by such a dogmatic approach (for evidence on the hardships they suffered, see World Bank 2000b, 2002f), which is far from the only way—or indeed, a reliable way—to produce growth. The obvious failings of the direct-and-protect approach should not lead us to jump to another simplistic, dangerous perspective.

The 1980s also brought new research on structural adjustment, driven by new data. Structural adjustment initially focused on achieving macroeconomic stability and promoting liberalization (for example, by getting prices right and privatizing state enterprises). But its many failures were associated with neglect of issues involving governance, institutional structure, policy ownership, and the social costs of adjustment (see World Bank 2001g)—precisely the reasons we must be wary of the mindless application of market fundamentalism.

The mid-1980s also saw renewed interest in theories of growth. This interest was fed on the theoretical side by developments in the theory of industrial organization and on the empirical side by research sparked by large, newly available cross-country data, particularly the studies of Kravis, Heston, and Summers (1983), and by advances in computing technology. Such cross-country regression studies were easy to carry out without much knowledge or work in developing countries, and the analyses often rode roughshod over delicate issues of identification (see Stern 1989). Nevertheless, the data expanded our ability to conduct comparative analysis, and complemented and spurred useful advances in growth theory.

At the same time, there was enormous empirical progress at the microlevel: data, computing, and econometric advances nourished a wealth of studies based on household survey data. These new data sets were multipurpose and applied to models of individual and household behavior, as well as to evaluations of the effects of different policies on income distribution and living standards. We began to accumulate valuable information on what was happening at the micro-level on important dimensions of poverty. As this research on structural adjustment, determinants of growth, and microlevel data on household behavior and poverty outcomes began accumulating in the late 1980s, it helped develop less dogmatic, simplistic approaches than those embodied by direct and protect or market fundamentalism.

In the early 1990s the dominant approach to development economics emphasized liberalization, privatization, fiscal discipline, openness to trade, protection of property rights, market-determined exchange and interest rates, and redirection of public spending toward education, health, and public infrastructure—an approach that John Williamson (1990, 1994) called the "Washington consensus." This term caught on quickly and was interpreted as a recipe for development mandated by international financial institutions such as the World Bank and International Monetary Fund. But in fact, the Washington consensus simply summarized key principles for sound economic management in small, open economies. It was not created exclusively by institutions based in Washington, D.C., and it did not represent a consensus. It combined the results of academic work and experience, taking stock of policy experiments in the 1970s and early 1980s that were characterized by overreliance on public sector intervention and investment and that led to debt crises and high inflation.

The Washington consensus principles are important elements of a good investment environment. But as a framework for development policy, they fall short in at least three vital areas. First, they devote insufficient attention to the policies needed to bring about poverty reduction. In recent writings Williamson himself has noted that the consensus is excessively narrow in this respect (see Williamson 2002, 2003 and Kuczinski and Williamson 2003). Second, certain principles of the consensus, such as those advocating capital account liberalization and privatization, were too general. They did not put sufficient weight on the value of a differentiated approach to reform sequencing and timing, to take into account vulnerabilities and gaps in institutional development. Simultaneous implementation of the Washington consensus principles can be disruptive. For example, privatization, trade liberalization, and deregulation can, in the short term, conflict sharply with maintaining fiscal discipline if an appropriate tax structure is not in place.

And third, even when viewed as a set of general principles for spurring growth, the Washington consensus is dangerously deficient. The problem is less what the consensus contains than what it leaves out—the most important and difficult dimensions of development. The consensus says nothing about governance and institutions, the role of empowerment and democratic representation, the importance of country ownership for successful policy reform, or the social costs and pace of transformation—four issues closely related to the political economy of reform. In retrospect, it was naive to think, as many did, that demand for institutions would create its own supply and that markets would work by themselves. The development community has learned the hard way—through the setbacks of structural adjustment programs in developing countries in the 1980s and early 1990s and the difficult transition in Eastern Europe and the former Soviet Union in the 1990s—that these elements are at the heart of the development challenge. They are what the strategy proposed in these lectures is all about.

How the Two-Pillar Strategy Differs

The preceding description of evolving ideas about development is intended to show how and why the strategy proposed here differs from them. Relative to the direct-and-protect approach, it involves a far bigger role for the private sector. Indeed, it sees the private sector as the engine of growth rather than government allocation, management, and centralized "picking of winners." And it sees poor people's participation as fundamental to their development and to overall growth.

Relative to market fundamentalism, the strategy recognizes the key role of governance and institutions in development. Further, in contrast to the minimal attention to distributional issues and social aspects of behavior and outcomes in the neoclassical framework, the strategy emphasizes the importance of poverty, inequality, empowerment, and inclusion.

Although the strategy is not inconsistent with efforts to achieve redistribution with growth, crucial parts of its emphasis differ considerably. The strategy focuses on underlying institutional and governance issues, as opposed to the simple accumulation of physical and human capital and factor intensity. And it places fundamental emphasis on policies that facilitate poor people taking control of their lives rather than simply having employment or human capital delivered to them.

Thus, the strategy proposed here is profoundly different from "direct and protect," market fundamentalism, and redistribution with growth. And it goes way beyond the Washington consensus. Certainly it shares features with all of these approaches: with direct and protect, recognition of market failure; with market fundamentalism, acknowledgment of the private sector's importance for growth; with redistribution with growth, emphasis on the importance of human capital; and with the Washington consensus, the need for fiscal discipline and openness.

But the strategy proposed here does not cherry-pick from those that preceded it and is not a middle way. It is based on a wholly different perspective—one that sees development as a dynamic process in which history, learning, and institutional change are central. It places institutions and governance at the heart of the story. Its main goal is to reduce poverty, and at its core is an interpretation of that goal in which empowering individuals to shape their lives is central.

We believe that this strategy involves a new and valuable perspective on development and policies to promote it. It can be expressed simply and intuitively enough to gain ready acceptance. Many of the ideas it embodies, such as the importance of institutions and empowerment, build on themes that have been gaining strength in recent decades, so we trust that it already has some traction in the development community.[3] Let us now examine where the strategy leads us for research (lecture III) and action (lecture IV).

Lecture III   Research

The strategy for development just proposed has numerous implications for work on public policy. The next five chapters focus on areas of research related to the strategy's key elements, particularly the dynamic processes of change in governance, institutions, policy, and behavior that are central to the strategy. A full analysis of development processes requires that these elements be built more securely into the analytical approach. Chapter 6 examines empirical research, with a focus on measurement surveys—information relevant to both processes and outcomes, particularly for poverty. Chapters 7 through 10 discuss the dynamics of four issues central to the agenda for public action that flows from the strategy: the investment climate, empowerment, preferences, and political reform.

6   Data and Measurement as Drivers of Change

Data collection is essential to analysis of development policy. A strategy is crucial to policy design and implementation. But so is evaluation: effective development depends on assessments of the effects of policies and the reasons for those effects. We must be able to understand what works, what does not, and why in order to learn, revise policies, and apply successful approaches elsewhere.

Data sets are driven by theories of and approaches to economics and development. After World War II, Keynesian aggregate theory helped shape the development of national accounts data. Later, the theory of planning and associated modeling of sectoral balances drove input-output data and tables. And now, the more micro and institutional approach embodied in our strategy and more recent approaches to development are putting energy behind survey-based approaches to data collection and development analysis.

The first two sections of this chapter examine the measurement of living standards, with a focus on household surveys. When designed and used well, household data can tell us not only about outcomes but also about drivers of outcomes. The next three sections analyze data that illuminate the two pillars of our strategy. The third section, on the investment climate, is focused on firm surveys (though much can be learned about the investment climate from other economic and administrative data). The fourth section looks at various dimensions of poverty beyond income—mostly empowerment and security. The fifth analyzes investment in human capital using emerging surveys on the effectiveness of public services such as health and education, which are key to empowering individuals. Together these three types of surveys—household, investment climate, and public services—provide an enormously valuable database for understanding development processes and outcomes.

In recent years statistical techniques for evaluating public policy have advanced considerably. There are many such techniques, but one of particular importance in current research is evaluation through randomized experimentation. This approach identifies a comparator or control population that differs from the experimental group only in the policy being applied (apart from random effects). The goal is to isolate the effects of the policy. Although it is not universally applicable, randomized experimentation is a powerful technique that is beginning to have a strong influence on policy assessments. Evaluation is the subject of this chapter's final section.

Much of the research and data gathering advocated in this chapter is ambitious. It is firmly based in our proposed strategy and directly related to enhancing policymaking. Moreover, precedents and examples exist for most of what we suggest. Implemented properly, these efforts can provide a framework for organizing research over an extended period and a benchmark against which the value of research can be judged.

Household Survey Data

Data from households have been the backbone of our understanding of poverty for centuries.[1] Modern household surveys appeared on a major scale in developing countries after World War II with the advent of India's National Sample Survey. Although household surveys are not a new development, recent years have seen a marked improvement in their coverage and quality. World Bank statistics on poverty in 1985 were based on data from only twenty-two of eighty-six developing countries (although those twenty-two countries accounted for 76 percent of the population of developing countries), while similar calculations currently under way cover seventy of one hundred developing and transition countries (and 88 percent of the population of these countries; Grosh and Glewwe 2000). The lag between collection and dissemination shrank from eleven years in 1974 to five years in 1997 (Ravallion and Chen 1997). Indeed, it can now often be measured in months, as increasingly powerful and portable computer technology moves into the field.

Household surveys typically provide data on spending for different kinds of goods. The questionnaires completed by households, with the help of investigators, usually also cover various household characteristics, such as the age, gender, education, and occupations of family members. Household data are particularly valuable for measuring income poverty and relating it to household characteristics. Many surveys also allow assessment of household food consumption in terms of calories and other nutrients—and in some cases, quality of housing.

Gathering these data poses many challenges. For example, much of the population of developing countries lives in rural areas. In addition, a substantial portion of consumption is produced at home, so quantities and value have to be estimated. Challenges of design and implementation extend into interpretation: surveys cover various aspects of consumption, income, and wealth, but great care has to be taken in choosing which of these concepts to use and which items they cover. Despite these complications, household surveys are the most valuable resource available for assessing economic outcomes, as well as some aspects of opportunity, and for understanding how those outcomes are associated with household characteristics.

Though great strides have been made on household surveys, there are many difficulties and problems with existing sources, particularly their suitability for examining changes over time and differences between regions and countries. Survey designs vary between countries and over time, making comparisons difficult. For example, some surveys ask respondents about their food spending over the past month, while others do so for the past week.

This is not a mere technical issue. When India experimented with different recall periods for the National Sample Survey, it found that relative to the traditional thirty-day recall period, a seven-day recall period increased reported food spending by 30 percent and consumption by 17 percent. Because so many Indians live close to the (local) poverty line, this statistical change was enough to remove almost 200 million people from poverty calculations (Deaton 2005).

Our ability to adjust for such differences is limited because many surveys lack thorough documentation. Moreover, many of the surveys in use were not designed to answer current questions about living standards. Instead, they were designed to complement national accounts calculations, project demands for economic planning exercises, or provide weights for consumer price indexes. In response, Deaton (1997) calls for a comprehensive inventory of existing surveys detailing coverage (for example, national or urban), measurement concept (consumption or income), and relevant aspects of design (such as how households are chosen, refusal rates, recall periods, and treatment of seasonality). Such an inventory would allow a much deeper understanding of key issues: what poverty levels are, what type of poverty is being measured, who poor people are, and how these numbers and characteristics of poor people are changing. It would also allow us to better address issues of comparability among countries.

Income and consumption data collected at the household level also suffer from the basic shortcoming that they reveal only indirectly the varying living standards of individuals within households. In particular, the conventional household survey does not allow direct measurement of consumption poverty among women, children, and the elderly. Data that can be collected at the individual level, such as on education and health, provide valuable gender- and age-disaggregated views of poverty. To understand intrahousehold dynamics better, future surveys should do more to isolate individual data.

There are also a number of technical issues to address in household surveys. Some are questions of linking household survey data with other data sources, such as census, administrative, and public service data, to provide a fuller picture of poverty. There is also a major challenge in reconciling survey data with data from national accounts, particularly to understand trends in consumption (Ravallion 2003a). As noted in chapter 1, in many countries consumption as measured by household surveys has grown less rapidly than consumption as measured in national accounts in recent decades. This problem is severe in developing countries but also occurs in developed ones. For example, Deaton (2005) notes that the divergence between consumption measures seems to be worse in the United States than in India, is particularly bad in China, and is less severe in the United Kingdom. As a result of the divergence, poverty as measured by surveys has fallen less than would have been predicted by measured growth in aggregate income or consumption in poor countries. There are a number of plausible explanations but no clear answers. A detailed exposition is beyond the scope of this chapter; here we highlight this puzzling and important phenomenon as an issue for further research.

Many of the issues raised in this chapter make further demands on household surveys while also increasing their usefulness. Some important questions will be best answered by adding data modules—covering topics such as education, health, and employment—to existing surveys. Others will seek to link household outcomes to other data, such as data on basic services, or make demands on survey methodology, such as requiring oversampling of minority groups to allow statistical analysis of discrimination and social inclusion. We are only beginning to realize the potential of household survey data in measuring outcomes and illuminating development processes. Such surveys are invaluable investments for both developing countries and the entire development community.

Panel Data

Development is a dynamic process, and data should reflect that dynamism. Panel data—that is, surveys that collect multiple observations from the same respondents over time—provide the most powerful data for understanding dynamics at the individual level. A number of excellent articles have discussed the design and use of panel data, as well as its advantages and disadvantages (Deaton 1997, Grosh and Glewwe 2000, Rosenzweig 2003). Here we offer only a sketch of how panel data relate to our two-pillar strategy.

Disaggregated within-country panels have been used to explore development topics in ways that go beyond what can be learned from cross-country data, carefully planned social experiments, or intensive fieldwork (Rosenzweig 2003). Particularly interesting examples include work on differential vulnerability to macroeconomic shocks in Peru (Glewwe and Hall 1995) and Indonesia (Frankenberg, Smith, and Thomas 2003), on the effects of education, health, and family planning in the Philippines (Rosenzweig and Wolpin 1986) and Indonesia (Pitt, Rosenzweig, and Gibbons 1993), and on the consequences of institutional change, such as local democratization, in India (Foster and Rosenzweig 2002). For our purposes panel data offer unique insights into vulnerability and mobility, which are key aspects of empowerment (as discussed later in this chapter and in chapter 8).

This is not to say that we are blind without panel data. Repeated cross-sectional surveys can be used to track changes in outcomes and behavior for groups of interest, such as women, scheduled castes, or ethnic minorities. Aggregate and administrative data can also contribute to understanding. For example, we know that agricultural output in India fluctuates with the monsoon, so data on the frequency of droughts in, say, Rajasthan offer insight into the vulnerability of Indian farmers. Administrative data on births and deaths or health status provide another perspective: from age-specific mortality rates and life expectancy calculations, we can learn a great deal about opportunities, or lack of them, at the individual level. Data from social security and pension schemes can tell us about prospects for particular groups.

Reporting systems in public health and education can also provide valuable information. In short, because developing countries often have poor data, we must be resourceful in using whatever is available.

But when we have them, panel data sets are a boon for the analysis of development dynamics. Beyond providing useful data for analyzing individual mobility and vulnerability, panel data have other advantages. Policymakers and researchers are often interested in the persistence of certain characteristics over time. For example, is a farm household with low productivity this year likely to exhibit low productivity next year, or is low productivity more likely the result of a temporary shock? Although repeated cross-sectional surveys can provide comparisons over time for groups (such as rural communities, unskilled and skilled laborers, or ethnic groups), panel data are required to address the movement of individuals. And from a technical perspective, panel data also allow surveyors to estimate aggregate quantities more accurately when unobservable (and hence unmeasurable) individual characteristics are correlated over time.[2] This benefit extends to correcting for some forms of measurement error—for example, when certain households tend to overestimate their income, and others underestimate. This same technical feature makes panel data particularly useful for estimating the effects of programs and policies; in effect, each respondent acts as its own control.

Panel data offer many advantages but are not without drawbacks. Tracking prior respondents can increase survey costs and impose administrative burdens beyond the capacity of a developing country's statistical office. International financial institutions should provide financial and technical assistance to mitigate these burdens, because such data are a public good both within countries and for those making comparisons across countries. The World Bank has been active in this regard, collecting valuable panel data through its Living Standards Measurement Study (LSMS) household surveys in many countries (table 6.1).

A serious difficulty with panel data is attrition, whereby respondents—whether firms, households, or household members—drop out of a survey. The problem is that those who drop out often have a considerable influence on survey findings. For example, if the dropouts are the least economically successful and return to rural areas to take advantage of informal safety nets, then the attrition bias in the sample will lead to an overestimate of the average income gains of the population. In this way, respondents who remain become increasingly unrepresentative of the original sample and the population as a whole. Rosenzweig (2003) uses an eighteen-year panel from Bangladesh to explore the effects of the common method of conditioning surveys on residence, where the panel includes only members of sampled residences who do not leave. He finds that this method generates substantial biases in estimates of economic mobility and that such biases are not eliminated by using proxy reports for household members no longer in residence, a common method of correcting for attrition.

One form of panel data is the repeated village study. In the early 1970s Scarlett Epstein returned to two villages in Karnataka (south India) that she had studied in 1944 (Epstein 1973). Similarly, one of the authors of this book (Stern) has been working on a village (Palanpur) in northern India since 1974. We have five 100 percent sample surveys of households in the village—one for each decade since the 1950s— that provide enormously valuable data for tracking changes over time (Lanjouw and Stern 1998). The design of the early surveys was not based on the assumption that there would be so many follow-ups. But given the 100 percent sample and the fairly standard and comprehensive questions, the surveys have allowed us to understand in depth how household circumstances have changed. Equally important, when combined with close personal and informal knowledge of households, they have given us insights into the reasons for changes.

If more researchers were to adopt this type of village panel approach, the effort would bring rich returns. Such studies are time intensive and require a certain amount of persistence (not to mention longevity) from researchers. And, of course, Palanpur, for example, is just one of the more than half-million villages in India, so the data are by no means representative of India as a whole. Still, they provide an opportunity to test, in a detailed microeconomic way, many of our core ideas and hypotheses about development.

Measuring the Investment Climate

Had we written this chapter ten years ago, we would have sounded a much more urgent call to improve measurement the investment climate. At that time economists were becoming more aware of the importance of institutions and the correlations between growth and institutional variables such as property rights, rule of law, and corruption (see Knack and Keefer 1995 and Kaufmann, Kraay, and Zoido-Lobatón 1999 for references). But such findings, based mostly on

Table 6.1
Panel data collection in developing countries

Country	Survey	Years of survey	Sample size (households)	Time between survey/rounds	Sample design	Attrition	Comment
Peru	LSMS	1985, 1990	1,200	5 years	Dwelling	43 percent of households after 5 years	Urban areas only, time of social unrest
Côte D'Ivoire	LSMS	1985–88	800	1 year	Dwelling	13 percent of households after 1 year	
Ghana	LSMS	1987/88, 1988/89	1,600	1 year	Dwelling	About 50 percent of households after 1 year	Did not explicitly ask about previous household members
Jamaica	LSMS	1988–present	2,000	1 year	Dwelling	About 50 percent of households after 1 year	Did not explicitly ask about previous household members
Tanzania (Kagera Region)	LSMS	1991–94	800	6 months	Household, but also followed individuals	10 percent of households after 2 years	Mostly in rural areas, one region only
Vietnam	LSMS	1992–93, 1997–98	4,800	5 years	Dwelling, but followed households that moved short distances	About 9 percent of households and 24 percent of individuals after 5 years	Relatively low mobility due to national restrictions on migration

India	ARIS	1968/69–1970/71	5,115	1 year	Household	19 percent of households after 2 years	Rural areas only
India	REDS	1970/71, 1981/82	4,756	11 years	Household	34 percent of households after 11 years	Rural areas only
India	ICRISAT	1975–84	120	Multiple interviews per year	Household	13 percent of households after 10 years	Rural areas only, interviewers living in villages, incentives provided to households to remain in the survey
Russia	RLMS	1992–present	6,334	6 months	Household	14 percent of households after 15 months	
Poland	HBS	1993, 1996	8,000	3 years	Household	37 percent of households after 3 years	
Malaysia	MFLS	1976, 1988/89	1,262	12 years	Individual	28 percent of women 12 years	
Philippines	CLHNS	1983–present	3,085	Varies (see text)	Individual	9 percent of children after 12 years	One region only
Indonesia	IFLS	1993, 1997, 1998	7,200	4 years (up to 1997), 5 years (up to 1998)	Household, but also followed individuals	6 percent of households and 9 percent of individuals after 4 years	13 provinces (out of 27)

Note: This list includes important panel data existing for major developing countries but is not exhaustive.
Source: Grosh and Glewwe (2000).

surveys of private businesses, do not lead directly to policy recommendations. The data from those surveys, while a major improvement over earlier proxies and instruments, were generally collected from small samples of large businesses. Thus, they did not allow a robust assessment of how the investment climate was perceived by small and medium-size enterprises, which form the backbone of most economies.

Moreover, most of the indicators of the investment climate used in these studies were relatively crude macro indicators and provided little guidance to countries on how specifically to improve the private sector environment. For instance, macro measures of the investment climate (such as rankings of rule of law, corruption, and infrastructure quality) are quite similar for China and India. Both countries have done relatively well compared to other developing countries. During the 1990s India grew impressively, at about twice the rate of OECD countries. China sustained growth almost twice as high as India and experienced much greater poverty reduction. Macro indicators fail to explain these differences. So while macro evidence may provide useful background and motivation, deeper analysis of the relationship between the investment climate, growth, and poverty reduction requires new surveys, with data gathered at the microlevel from large, representative samples of small and medium-size enterprises and other firms.

There has been considerable progress in conducting such surveys. Many of the data now available come from surveys conducted through partnerships between domestic business institutes, the World Bank, and the European Bank for Reconstruction and Development.[3] For example, drawing on uniform questionnaires distributed to more than 10,000 firms, large and small, in eighty countries, the World Business Environment Survey has generated comparable and quantitative measurements of the investment climate (Batra, Kaufmann, and Stone 2003). Its core questionnaire includes specific questions on obstacles to doing business, such as, "How many days does it take for imported materials to clear customs?" and "When firms in your industry do business with the government, how much of the contract value must they offer in additional or unofficial payments to secure the contract?" (Some of the findings from these surveys were discussed in chapter 5.) The results are also helping to target follow-up surveys in specific countries, such as most of those in Eastern Europe and the former Soviet Union. Let us illustrate with examples from India, China, Bangladesh, and Pakistan (table 6.2).

Table 6.2
A comparison of investment climate indicators in four countries (sample means)

	Bangla-desh	China	India	Pakistan
Inspections per year	18.6 (997)	28.1 (1,304)	7.99 (1,937)	32.7 (957)
Management time dealing with regulations	4.2 (985)	7.8 (1,456)	14.41 (1,667)	10.1 (963)
Unofficial payments (% sales)	2.5 (933)	2.5 (348)		2.2 (957)
Days to clear customs (imports)	11.7 (559)	7.9 (434)	9.06 (337)	17.2 (125)
Days to clear customs (exports)	8.84 (446)	5.41 (434)	6.55 (485)	9.72 (194)
Power loss (% sales)	3.29 (924)	1.99 (1,500)	8.7 (1,786)	5.42 (963)
Days for phone line	129.7 (277)	15.62 (1,454)	35.5 (643)	41.84 (927)
Have own generator (%)	71.1 (999)	27.3 (1,500)	61 (1,930)	42.1 (965)
Have own well (%)	55 (990)			44.1 (945)
Share with overdraft facility	0.66 (975)	0.18 (1,500)	0.57 (1,982)	0.23 (965)
Share with bank loan	70 (984)	44 (1,500)	12 (1,993)	19.8 (965)
Days to clear a check	2.9 (947)	4.3 (1,492)	10.9 (1,539)	1.9 (929)

Source: Dollar, Hallward, and Mengistae (2003).

Consider first India. Although its growth remains high by international standards, the strong performance of the late 1990s has softened since 2000. Moreover, relative to its market size and the quality of its workforce, India attracts a disproportionately small share of foreign direct investment—a mere 0.5 percent of GDP in 1999, compared with 3.9 percent for China, 4.5 percent for Brazil, and 5.0 percent for Thailand. An investment climate survey of more than 1,000 Indian firms carried out by the Confederation of Indian Industry and the World Bank identifies the microlevel roots of these phenomena (World Bank and CII 2002). Although we could identify a range of desirable reforms without a detailed survey, it is seldom feasible to pursue sweeping reforms across all dimensions of the investment climate simultaneously. Detailed surveys help identify bottlenecks and prioritize reforms.

India's survey singled out entry and exit procedures, transportation and communications infrastructure, and excessive regulation as binding constraints on productivity and growth.

Most people with extended experience with India and China would say that the investment climate in both countries has improved over the past two decades and would point to how the specifics of everyday business have become easier. In this respect, governance—the relationships between government and firms—has probably improved in terms of, for example, the time that firm managers spend with government officials even though, for example, corruption may not have decreased, according to some other indicator.

The last of these three factors further highlights the importance of detailed micro surveys. Cross-country indicators of governance and corruption show India in a relatively favorable light; India and China rank about the same in terms of corruption, but India is perceived as better in terms of rule of law (see World Bank 2003b, 2003e, and World Bank and CII 2002). But these subjective measures capture imperfectly the real costs of bureaucratic interference and corruption. Indian plant managers report spending 16 percent of their time dealing with government officials. In China the reported amount is 9 percent; in Latin America about 11 percent. Indian firms also face greater difficulties clearing goods through customs, reporting delays 50 percent longer than those reported by firms in the Republic of Korea and Thailand, and three times what many OECD firms report. Indian firms also report high variability in clearance times. Such difficulties force firms to keep on hand greater inventories of inputs, tying up resources that could be put to more productive use. These details, not visible in macrolevel data, point to specific policy recommendations, such as customs administration reform, that can directly improve the investment climate and foster growth.

Many of the reforms required to improve the investment climate must come at the subnational level. Recognizing this, the World Bank– Confederation of Indian Industry survey asked business managers to identify which states they thought had a better or worse investment climate than the one where they were based. Managers were also asked which of the ten states in the survey had the best investment climate and which had the worst. There was a pretty clear ranking of states, enabling the report to categorize Maharashtra and Gujarat as the "best climate" states; Tamil Nadu, Karnataka, and Andhra Pradesh as "good-climate" states; Delhi and Punjab as "medium-climate" states; and Kerala, West Bengal, and Uttar Pradesh as "poor-climate" states.

That entrepreneurs act on these perceptions can be seen in the investment rates for these states. In the sample the firms in the best states had high investment rates, increasing their capital stock by about 8 percent a year, while there was net disinvestment in West Bengal and modest growth of the capital stock (3 percent a year) in Uttar Pradesh. Macrodata on the location of foreign direct investment in India follow the same pattern: during the 1990s almost all such investment went to the states with the best and good climates. Also at the macrolevel, there has been significantly faster GDP growth in the best and good states (7.2 percent a year between 1992 and 1998) than in the poor ones (4.8 percent; World Bank and CII 2002).

The report also identified ways in which states vary and highlighted the impact of investment climate weaknesses on small and medium-size enterprises. For example, these enterprises receive twice as many inspections in the poor-climate states (averaging 9.5 visits a year) as in the best-climate ones (5.2 visits). In the best-climate states 31 percent of small and medium-size enterprises have their own power generator, compared with 73 percent in the poor-climate states, reflecting the severe problems with power supply in the poor-climate states. Moreover, it costs firms about twice as much to generate their own power as to buy it from the public grid.

There are also variations in Internet connectivity across states. In good-climate states 47 percent of small and medium-size enterprises use the Internet to conduct business, but in poor-climate states only 27 percent do so. One interesting anomaly is that use of the Internet is also low in the best-climate states (32 percent of small and medium-size enterprises), indicating that even the better states have investment climate problems in some areas.

Firms in all states reported overstaffing, but detailed inspections revealed different causes. In Karnataka and Andhra Pradesh, good-climate states, overstaffing was partly the result of labor hoarding in anticipation of growth. Still, nearly one in four firms even in these states reported that overstaffing was partly the result of labor regulations, and two in five indicated that it came from political pressure not to lay off workers. In Uttar Pradesh, a poor-climate state, there was very little reported labor hoarding; every firm said that it had too many workers because of labor regulations, and 94 percent said that they faced political pressure not to lay off workers.

From the perspective of expanding employment and providing income stability, overstaffing might seem desirable. But the Indian sample was of registered firms, meaning firms in the formal sector. Workers in these firms are far better off in terms of wages, days of employment, and job stability than the hundreds of millions working in agriculture and the informal sector. Chronic overstaffing seems likely to cost the economy much-needed dynamism, in return for supporting a (relatively) privileged group of workers.

Variation across regions is also substantial in China. The World Bank, in collaboration with the Enterprise Survey Organization of the Chinese National Bureau of Statistics, surveyed 1,500 firms in five cities: Beijing, Tianjin, Shanghai, Guangzhou, and Chengdu. The objective was to measure and exploit this regional variation to help prioritize and improve different dimensions of the investment climate. Like the World Business Environment Survey and the survey in India, the survey in China sought specific, objective measures of different aspects of the investment climate. For example, instead of asking if red tape is an obstacle, the survey asked managers how much time they spend with officials. And rather than asking if labor laws are restrictive, the survey gathered information on the share of temporary workers and extent of overstaffing.

By linking investment climate indicators to firm productivity and growth, we can throw light on the potential gains from improving the investment climate. For example, the Indian report found that if each state attained the best practice in India for infrastructure and relationships with officials, the Indian economy would grow two percentage points faster. These gains would be particularly large in poor-climate states, but even better-climate states fall well short of the best. And from comparisons with other countries and examining performance on particular dimensions, we can see that even the best-climate states could do much to improve their investment climates.

While understanding that the obstacles facing firms is a key component of understanding the investment climate, the goal of improving the investment climate is not simply to make life easier for firms. It is to help encourage the entrepreneurship, innovation, and economic activity that can lead to sustained economic growth and poverty reduction. In many cases that means intensifying competition and reducing barriers to entry and exit. In an industry dominated by a few firms with cozy relationships with government, those firms might proclaim themselves highly satisfied with the investment climate. Productivity data provide one way of correcting for this problem—since firms in the industry just described would likely have low or stagnant productivity—but we need other measures as well to help identify barriers to competition.

So to complement the data on obstacles identified by firms, we also need data on competition, openness to trade, barriers to entry, and the like. Some of this information is already available in existing surveys. When surveys include responses from many firms in different industries, we can use the problems identified as indicators of competitive intensity. Specifically, we can look for perception gaps between small and large firms, firms in different industries, new entrants and established players, and between exporters and the domestically focused.

Moving beyond firm surveys, we need to make use of supplementary data, such as macroeconomic data on concentration, price-cost margins, and industry-specific output and growth rates. Data from firm surveys and other sources should be linked. For example, survey questions about infrastructure (how many days it takes to get a phone line, frequency of electrical outages, and so on) can be matched against corresponding macrodata (on number of phone lines, electrical generating capacity, and expenditures) to flag obstacles to economic activity in a way that can be compared across countries.

Work on measuring the investment climate should build on the strong foundations provided by recent research. Existing surveys are already yielding insights—on the links between the investment climate and productivity, investment, and employment—that national accounts and sector-level data do not (Dollar, Hallward-Driemeier, and Mengistae 2003). There is much to be gained from using existing surveys to identify obstacles and design more detailed follow-up surveys. There is also a great deal to learn from increasing comparability across surveys.

The primary goal here is not to provide fodder for yet another cross-country regression. Part of the purpose is benchmarking: developing countries want to know how they rate against the best performers and learn from the comparisons. But more important, they want to identify specific micro and structural areas in which they need to take action.

Research is continuing at the World Bank for the *World Development Report 2005* (World Bank 2004a), which examines the investment climate, growth, and poverty reduction. The report focuses on the microeconomic conditions that shape firms' incentives to create jobs and invest productively. It has commissioned extensions of existing surveys in several developing countries, including China, India, and Brazil; to widen sampling to include smaller firms and unregistered enterprises; and to broaden sampling to include more rural and periurban firms.[4] Because the information is comparable with earlier surveys, the report is able to show how the investment climate differs between formal and informal enterprises, as well as how the informal sector compares across countries. Because countries differ considerably in the degree of churning of firms—that is, the extent to which existing firms die and others are born—the report has also commissioned work that links the investment climate survey data with firm census data from fifteen countries in Latin America, East Asia, and Europe and Central Asia. This linking of data allows an analysis of how the investment climate affects firm entry and exit, as well as job creation, job destruction, and productivity.

Measuring Poverty: Opportunity, Empowerment, and Security

Because living standards have many dimensions, so too does poverty. Poor people describe poverty in multidimensional terms that can be summarized using the ideas of opportunity, empowerment, and security described in the *World Development Report 2000/2001* and Narayan 2000. These ideas are consistent with the approach suggested by Amartya Sen in *Development as Freedom*, the ideas behind the *Human Development Reports* produced by the United Nations Development Programme, and the Millennium Development Goals adopted by the international community in 2000. The income aspects of opportunity are closely linked to the investment climate issues discussed in the first section of this chapter: improving the investment climate creates opportunities for entrepreneurship and employment, for rich and poor people alike. In terms of outcomes, the degree of opportunity is measured in part by the gains in income and consumption measured by household surveys, which are also discussed above. In this section, therefore, we discuss opportunity briefly but focus on measuring empowerment and security.

Opportunity
Opportunity generally refers to circumstances that lie beyond the control of the individual but that nevertheless significantly affect the results—and possibly the levels—of his or her efforts. By contrast, *outcomes* refers to the joint product of the efforts of a person and the cir-

cumstances under which that effort is made (Roemer 1998). This distinction between opportunity and outcomes, which builds on the work of John Rawls and Amartya Sen, is illustrated by the standard opposition between inequality and mobility. For example, the U.S. society is often presented as more unequal than European societies but at the same time more mobile from one generation to the next, a feature sometimes taken as a sign of a more equal distribution of chances or opportunities in the United States.

Bourguignon, Ferreira, and Menéndez (2003) use data from a 1996 Brazilian household survey, which included data on the education and occupations of the respondents' parents, to examine what kind of outcome inequality may be attributed to circumstances (in particular, family background) and what may be attributed to effort. Their analysis reveals a sizable inequality of opportunities in Brazil.

Parental education proves to be a powerful determinant of individual earnings or income, even after controlling for an individual's schooling. In addition, parental education is a strong predictor of children's schooling. In fact, older cohorts show a distribution of schooling that is nearly identical to that of their parents (with some increase in average schooling). The analysis also shows that the inequality that would remain after controlling for the inequality of all observed circumstances (parents' education, occupation, race, and region of origin) is very high—higher than the inequality of outcomes in many developing countries.

Parents' education, occupation, race, and region of origin are the most significant variables linked to opportunity. But there are many aggregate measures that can be indicative of the opportunities facing individuals. One indicator of the opportunities facing new cohorts of workers in a particular region could be, for example, the growth rate of towns or employment in rural areas or employment by industry in the broader economy.

The analysis of Bourguignon, Ferreira, and Menéndez illustrates the usefulness of household surveys in measuring and understanding poverty and living standards beyond income and consumption. We have already addressed some possible areas of improvement for these surveys, and there is a large literature, dating back decades, on methods and shortcomings of poverty measurement. Relevant topics include poverty line construction, definitions of relative and absolute poverty, income versus consumption data, incorporating assets such as the ownership of consumer durables, surveys versus national accounts, intrahousehold allocation, urban and rural differences, and international comparability and purchasing power parity adjustments. (For a detailed discussion of the research agenda in these areas, interested readers are encouraged to read Deaton 2005, 2003b and Chen and Ravallion 2001.) Next we turn our attention to two aspects of poverty where the research agenda is still being formulated: empowerment and security.

Empowerment

Empowerment is about choice and freedom. It is about not being constantly pushed around by officials and landlords. It is about being educated and having skills that provide opportunity. It is about being healthy. And it is about family and social structures that allow one to act with autonomy, to be one's own agent, which makes it clear that empowerment is fundamentally linked to the role of women and to discrimination based on color, caste, language, and religion.

This definition of empowerment is not an abstraction dreamed up by economists and international financial institutions. It comes from the true experts on poverty—poor people themselves, as recorded in interviews with more than 60,000 poor men and women from 60 countries (Narayan and others 2000). Much of what we define here as empowerment is based on how respondents to those surveys characterized poverty and what they identified as their priorities for development. We need to find indicators that capture these ideas.

The important and familiar human development issues of education and health are central to empowerment, and these would seem relatively straightforward to measure. After all, nearly every country reports basic indicators on educational progress and health status, such as student enrollment and infant mortality. By examining these indicators, we should be able to get at least a broad idea of the extent to which people—especially poor people—are being equipped with the education and health care needed to participate in growth and development.

And yet even in this well-defined area of empowerment measurement, the situation is less clear than it first appears. As discussed in the *World Development Report 2000/2001* (World Bank 2001c), these basic statistics are often of poor quality in developing countries. Because these countries often lack complete vital statistics registration systems, they are able to calculate mortality rates only on the basis of periodic censuses. In intervening years mortality rates must be estimated using interpolations and extrapolations.

The situation is not much better in education. There are problems, for example, with the main indicators of enrollment. The gross primary enrollment rate compares the number of enrolled students (of whatever age) with the number of students in the primary school age group. But this means that an increase in grade repetition will raise the enrollment rate, hardly a desirable property for such an indicator. An alternative is to use net enrollment, which restricts the analysis to children of intended school age, but this measure is available for far fewer countries. In any event, school attendance rates are sometimes quite low, so mere enrollment may not translate into human capital advances and empowerment.

But these measurement challenges pale beside those we face in measuring other aspects of (or constraints associated with) empowerment. In its emphasis on family, community, social, and governance constraints, the concept of empowerment goes well beyond levels of investment in human capital and physical assets (see figure 3.1). Empowerment centers on people's ability to act and make effective decisions on key aspects of their lives. It can also include an individual's perception of her or his role and expectations in life. Thus an individual's preferences and approach to behavior make up part of the story of empowerment.

Indicators to measure empowerment could be based on figure 3.1. They would thus be designed to capture constraints arising from family, community, society, and governance. Of course, one would not want to be rigid about the differences among these four elements, as there is some overlap. A number of indicators capturing gender and ethnic discrimination would come under the family and community categories, while social stratification and inequality issues should be seen as part of the society element. Our understanding of exclusion is improved by measuring differences in outcomes for people of different gender, ethnicity, caste, religion, and other characteristics. Some household surveys include data modules to identify these characteristics, but many other surveys do not. Here we suggest two examples where this disaggregation is particularly important:

First, social stratification and inequality are manifested not only in terms of income differentials, but even more in terms of access to resources such as land and credit. Standard economic statistics on average incomes across socioeconomic groups, average land holdings, and ownership of other assets can help illustrate the extent of this inequality. They can be supplemented by statistics on education, health, and other public services, disaggregated over the relevant groups. But there are no internationally comparable databases that contain such statistics, even though this type of disaggregated analysis is common in country-specific economic and sector studies and in poverty assessments. Further, these types of outcome indicators conflate constraints, assets, and efforts, and it is not easy to isolate the effects of the constraints.

As a second example, gender discrimination and the resulting inequality in economic, legal, political, and social outcomes is another important aspect of social stratification and exclusion. In the political arena, women almost always hold a much smaller share of elected office and political power than men do, as a result of both formal legal constraints and informal customs. Thus, one measure of gender inequality in the political sphere is the percentage of political offices, elected and nonelected, occupied by women. In the legal sphere, laws sometimes restrict women's rights in areas of divorce, inheritance, and ownership of land and productive resources. By examining laws, we can create indicators of the extent to which women have or do not have equal rights.

Distinguishing among the different types of constraints is important if countries are to act to remove them. For example, the United Nations Development Programme's gender-related development index and gender empowerment measure suggest that women in Eastern Europe and the former Soviet Union have achieved greater equality with men in terms of income, education, and health than in terms of political participation and the legal domain. Hence it may be desirable to monitor the latter two dimensions of gender equality as part of a core set of priority empowerment indicators.

Empowerment can be understood not only in terms of assets and capabilities acquired by people, and the social and family constraints on their use, but also in terms of the institutional environment in which people operate. What features of that environment does effective participation depend on? The responsiveness of institutions to poor people is a key element, and one that we need to be able to assess rigorously. One way to measure this responsiveness is to examine how well service providers such as schools and health clinics provide services to particular communities (that type of research is discussed below, in the section on measuring basic services).

Another set of institutional indicators measures political and civil liberties, democracy, rule of law, and corruption, generally in subjective fashion. For example, measures of corruption are derived from Transparency International's corruption perceptions index, which subjectively rates 102 countries in terms of the degree of corruption perceived among public officials and politicians. Political and civil liberties are measured using the subjective ranking of countries from a survey published each year by Freedom House. Political rights enable people to participate in the political process, while civil liberties are the freedoms to develop views, institutions, and autonomy apart from the state. The quality of government is often measured using subjective indicators, compiled by private service-rating agencies such as International Country Risk Guide (ICRG) and Business Environment Risk Intelligence (BERI), of risks facing (mainly foreign) investors.[5]

Other key elements of empowerment are transparency and access to information. Responsible citizens and a responsive government require a two-way flow of information between citizens and government. Informed citizens are better equipped to take advantage of opportunities, access services, exercise their rights, and hold state and nonstate actors accountable. Likewise, poor people and communities must be able to provide information about their preferences to public agents. Indicators on the role of the media are relevant in this regard (World Bank 2002g).

To advance our understanding of empowerment, we need more detailed surveys on the constraints that individuals face in shaping their lives. Like investment climate data five years ago, data on empowerment are at an early stage of development. We have a wealth of aggregate measures of key concepts such as the rule of law, accountability, and corruption, including qualitative governance indicators, data on budget transfers to local authorities, and indicators on the percentage of populations voting in national and local elections. But we need surveys that identify, as investment climate surveys do with firms, specific obstacles facing individuals such as measures of ethnic discrimination, and density of social capital networks and associations (see, for example, Alesina and La Ferrara 2000, 2002 and La Ferrara 2002), along with ideas for policy and institutional reforms.

At the moment there is relatively little we can say about the measurement of internal constraints. Doing so might involve systematic collection of data on, for example, aspirations. The surveys of people's perceptions of their own quality of life and of how they think people in their community in general are faring relative to other communities,[6] as well as the growing research on happiness (Easterlin 1996, Blanchflower and Oswald 2000, Eckersley 2000, Frey and Stutzer 2002), could be a good starting point for an empirical examination of the psychological and sociological constraints that individuals face in their endeavor to shape their own lives.

Security

Security is one of the core goals of reducing poverty, but it is often easier to define security by what it is not. Security is freedom from vulnerability, where vulnerability represents not only the risk that a household or individual will experience an episode of income poverty, but also the risk of a health crisis, crime, violence, natural disaster, and a number of other risks (see Commission on Human Security 2003). Measuring vulnerability is difficult because the concept is essentially dynamic. Panel data are useful in constructing a picture of volatility, as are data from multiyear recall surveys. Repeated cross-sections allow us to measure consumption or income fluctuations for particular groups (such as unskilled laborers). With so many poor people working in agriculture, we can get a sense of vulnerability by examining volatility in weather and commodity prices.

But with all these data, we must be careful not to assume that variation in income, consumption, health, housing, or other indicators of well-being presents a full picture of vulnerability. Simple measures such as standard deviations are flawed in several ways. They give equal weight to upward and downward fluctuations, but for those living close to the subsistence level there is an obvious asymmetry: downward fluctuations can be devastating. Standard deviations also lack a time dimension; ten years of alternating good and bad outcomes look the same as five good years followed by five bad, but the latter scenario would likely be much more difficult. Finally, all these methods measure vulnerability after the fact. Measurement efforts should include indicators that make it possible to assess the risks of an individual, household, or group beforehand and to assess how severe the risks are.

Among these indicators are physical assets, human capital, income diversification, links to networks, access to credit markets, and formal safety nets. Some progress has been made in collecting these data. For example, the World Bank's Local-Level Institutions Survey links asset data with questions on household links to local associations, and some of its Living Standards Measurement Studies incorporate modules measuring social capital. But many household surveys do not provide the needed information. Household surveys need to expand to include questions on assets, crime, links with networks, perceptions of sources of emergency assistance, participation in formal safety nets, and the effects of natural disasters. Such enriched surveys should be linked with panel surveys and aggregate data (such as census, registration, agricultural productivity, and national accounts data) to allow direct observation of how households deal with shocks and to link ex ante capabilities with ex post outcomes.

Security is not only a question of insurance against risks. It is also, for many poor people, a question of personal security. Poor people interviewed in Brazil, Russia, and elsewhere continuously return to issues of crime and physical security (Narayan and others 2000). The incidence of violence is probably underestimated by official crime statistics; in particular, many women are frightened of reporting to the police. A more reliable way of measuring vulnerability to crime is to use victimization studies—for instance, asking household survey respondents if they have been victims of serious crime (Bourguignon 1999). This approach also provides data on vulnerability that do not depend directly on intertemporal observations.

Assessing Multiple Dimensions

Defining poverty as multidimensional raises questions of how to measure overall poverty, how to evaluate policy trade-offs, and how to compare achievements. How does one assess the relative value of different dimensions? How much income are people willing to give up for, say, a unit improvement in health or voice? There are no easy answers, and indeed this may not be a helpful question for understanding and for policy. It is true that for policy, we need to have priorities and some understanding of rankings and intensity, but we can get this by asking survey respondents to identify the most important problems they face. That approach works well in the investment climate surveys.

We should recognize that there are many aspects to well-being and try to present them clearly. For analytical and policy purposes there is no need to aggregate them into a single indicator. Neither should we look for single indicators of the investment climate or empowerment, however useful such indicators might be in creating public interest in the approach.

Measuring Basic Services

To measure the effectiveness of the public services that are critical for empowering poor people and improving outcomes, we have another tool at our disposal: basic service delivery surveys. These surveys take service providers such as schools and health clinics as their units of observation (like firms in investment climate surveys), and they can be useful tools for understanding malfunctions in public service delivery.

Two main types of basic service delivery surveys have emerged: Public Expenditure Tracking Surveys (PETSs) and Quantitative Service Delivery Surveys (QSDSs).[7] (For details, see Dehn, Reinikka, and Svensson 2003.) Just as investment climate surveys can facilitate comparisons across countries and regions, PETSs and QSDSs provide microdata on the service delivery climate that are comparable across jurisdictions. Here we briefly describe each of these types of surveys.

If a government wants to invest in people, a necessary first step is ensuring that those funds are used as intended. PETSs follow the flow of public funds through various levels of the government bureaucracy and banking system to assess what share of the expenditure is reaching, or being used for, the intended beneficiaries. A multilevel PETS can help identify corruption, leakage, and capture of funds by political or bureaucratic actors. If publicized, the data from these surveys can both flag shortcomings in mechanisms for investing in and empowering people, and empower them directly by giving them information needed to act.

But even when funds are available, their ability to empower people largely depends on how efficiently they are used. This second step is the focus of QSDSs, which gather information on the quantity and quality of services that actually reach people. They ask, for example, whether people have access to clean water, children are being immunized, teachers are showing up at schools and doctors at clinics, schools have books and desks, and clinics have drugs and functioning equipment. They also measure staff incentives and efficiency and provide information on determinants of service quality (such as staff absenteeism) and qualitative data on corruption. Furthermore, they collect information on the institutional framework in which services are provided. Service delivery at a particular facility can thus be linked upstream to government agencies and the public decision-making environment in which services are located, or downstream to household surveys for more integrated analysis of supply and demand. These links allow a more comprehensive analysis of supply and demand factors than previously possible, as well as explicit analysis of political economy factors. By combining these sources of data, we learn more about what determines outcomes of interest—health, education, incomes, and opportunities for poor people—and what policy levers have greater potential impact.

Service delivery surveys can throw light on important empirical questions. For example, what is the relative importance of extrinsic and intrinsic factors motivating workers in these services, and how do they interact? How do professional norms, commitment, and trust affect the motivation and behavior of health workers? How can we approach the measurement of intrinsic motivation (such as professional ethical norms and moral commitment) and their impact on behavior? Is intrinsic motivation stronger or more important in certain types of organizations, such as NGOs or religious foundations?

There is little systematic evidence on these issues, particularly for developing countries.[8] Some research has tried to measure worker motivation and professional commitment through self-administered questionnaires with a broad range of questions about the worker's level of identification with the organization (such as a hospital) and its goals, willingness to exert effort on behalf of the organization, and general job satisfaction.

The PETS and QSDS were developed relatively recently, but earlier survey approaches, such as facility modules in household surveys and empirical studies to estimate hospital cost functions, have also tried to measure the provision of services. Living Standard Measurement Study household surveys have included health facility modules on an ad hoc basis. A number of the demographic and health surveys carried out in more than fifty developing countries have also included a service provider component. Similarly, the Family Life Surveys implemented by RAND have combined health provider surveys with household surveys.

The rationale for including a facility module in a household survey is to characterize the link between access to and quality of public services and key household welfare indicators. But because those surveys focus on households, they typically pay little attention to the determinants of service quality. In most cases the facility information collected as a part of community questionnaires relies on the knowledge of one or more informed individuals. Thus, information is heavily dependent on the perceptions of a few individuals and is usually not detailed enough to allow analysis of important service delivery parameters, such as operational efficiency, effort, or other performance indicators. To the extent that the information is based on perceptions, there may be additional problems attributable to its subjective nature and sensitivity to respondents' expectations. In contrast, the PETS and QSDS approach emphasizes and quantitatively measures provider incentives and behavior at the level of the service providing unit, such as the clinic or the school (Dehn, Reinikka, and Svensson 2003).

Central to these surveys are issues of participation, governance, and other key elements of empowerment, particularly its human development dimensions. The relationship between service provider and client is critical. For example, El Salvador's EDUCO program showed how parent associations and local communities, by visiting schools and monitoring teachers, can improve learning outcomes (Jimenez and Sawada 1999, World Bank 2003a; see also chapter 3). While one can construct game-theoretic models of community behavior, it is important to recognize that some types of community action arise spontaneously. Even if this phenomenon is difficult to model convincingly, it needs to be studied and documented. To that end, these relationships will often need to be examined in the context of policy experiments.

Effective Evaluation

The strategy proposed in this book points to the importance of evaluating economic and social policies ex ante and monitoring them ex post for their impact, particularly in terms of their consequences for poor people.[9] By *ex ante evaluation* we mean using quantitative techniques to predict the likely impacts on different groups of a change in policy (such as a new tax, subsidy, trade policy reform, or exchange rate regime) prior to its implementation. But it is also crucial to evaluate ex post the actual impact of a policy, as well as to understand differences between predicted and actual outcomes.

If we are to design policy and its implementation and learn from our activities, we should ask questions such as: What are the impacts of specific changes in public spending? How do changes in the delivery of public services, especially for health and education, affect poor people? How can public spending and revenue be better monitored and improved? What are the impacts of specific changes in taxation? How can the financial and administrative burden of taxation on poor people be reduced?

A second area for evaluation would focus on the impact of macroeconomic and structural reforms such as trade policy, privatization, agricultural liberalization, and price decontrol. How should these reforms be designed, implemented, and sequenced? What are the impacts of changes in the macroeconomic framework, such as fiscal, inflation, and exchange rate targets? What determines the trade-offs between objectives? What are the impacts of exogenous shocks, such as trade shocks, capital flows volatility, changes in foreign aid, and foreign payment crises? How can policy mitigate these effects?

Finally, a third group of evaluation questions concerns governance and the investment climate. What features of governance most affect investment and growth, and how can we measure the impact of governance on investment and growth? And what measures can improve governance and productivity?

These three sets of questions parallel three perspectives on poverty reduction. The first group of questions is microeconomic in nature, and in evaluation terms they call directly for incidence analysis of public spending and taxation. The second group of questions refers to two types of macroeconomic policies. One is concerned with policy-induced changes in the structure of the economy, in terms of either sectoral activity (as with trade or price policies) or firm ownership (private or public). The other type has to do with the management of aggregate demand and macroeconomic balances. It includes setting targets for the main macroeconomic instruments, as well as analysis of various types of shocks and the best way to cope with them (Lucas 2003). The third group of questions is more dynamic and essentially refers to changes in institutions and policies aimed at enhancing private investment and growth.

Evaluation in Multiple Layers

Thus, evaluation could involve a three-layer methodology for evaluating the effect that economic policies have on the investment climate and on poor people. The bottom layer would consist of a microsimulation model based on household survey data that permits analysis of the distributional incidence of public spending and taxation as well as the income-generation behavior of households. The top layer would include aggregate macroeconomic models that evaluate the impact of exogenous shocks and policies on aggregate variables such as GDP, its components, the general price level, the exchange rate, and the interest rate, in either a short- or medium-run perspective. The intermediate layer would consist of tools that permit disaggregating the predictions obtained with the top layer into various sectors of activity and various factors of production.

Ideally these three layers should communicate with each other in some consistent way. For instance, a major change in public spending on education at the bottom layer should modify the rate of economic growth in the top layer, as well as the structure of activity and factor remunerations in the intermediate layer. In turn those latter changes should affect the household income generation model in the bottom layer. The analytical tools for full integration of these three analytical layers are still being developed. (An overview is provided in Bourguignon and Pereira da Silva 2003.)

It should be possible to analyze medium-run growth and its effects on poverty and the distribution of living standards using this three-layer structure. An example of state-of-the-art micro-macro modeling of this sort is provided by Robilliard, Bourguignon, and Robinson (2003). This sort of exercise becomes difficult when the policy change being examined involves investments with long maturities, such as education (or more generally human capital) policies. An increase in public spending in these areas today is unlikely to affect income growth and distribution for another ten to fifteen years—which, from our modeling capabilities in an evaluation perspective, qualifies as the distant future.

Thus, a comprehensive analysis of these policies requires a truly dynamic framework that allows an evaluation of their effects on income distribution today—in particular, the negative effect of financing this policy on current income and poverty—as well as their effects a decade or more in the future. But the latter step requires projecting how the economy and the household population will change, which requires assumptions about economic and demographic growth. Such an analysis may rely on dynamic microsimulation analysis. Such techniques are available for a constant economic environment (as in Robilliard, Bourguignon, and Robinson 2003). But in this case the time horizon is much longer, and linking microsimulations with the evolution of the economy and the structure of economic growth is a much greater challenge. The logical structure we have described is too ambitious to be executed in detail in most environments. But its logic is largely forced by the nature of the problem and question. Thus, it is a useful framework for thinking about what we can do when we have to go for more rough and ready solutions. This is clearly an area where more research is required. (For a valuable assessment of where we currently stand, see Bourguignon and Pereira da Silva 2003.)

Several extensions to this type of evaluation are possible. One may think of extending incidence analysis and microsimulation to a population of firms—for example, using industrial survey data instead of household surveys. The first level of incidence analysis for a sample of firms would simply consist of measuring the subsidies and taxes on their income (profit) and investment. With simple assumptions about average tax rates, the average-incidence analysis conducted for households could be replicated: By how much is the tax system modifying the structure of prices, and possibly the investment and production decisions of firms? In addition, one could measure the direct effect of the cost of corruption (a quasi-tax) using information from investment climate surveys.

The next level would also replicate the path followed for households. Firms' output and demand for inputs (capital and labor) could be modeled as depending on levels of subsidies and taxes and costs of corruption. In particular, a relationship between firms' output and investment levels could be fed back into the economy's price levels and hence into the type of analysis conducted with households. A caveat in extending the household methodologies in this way, which would make the analysis more challenging, is that the dynamics of firm creation and destruction are more complex than the demographics of households.

The third level of the approach would consist of extending to firms the type of interaction with macromodels seen for households. It would be important to be able to disaggregate, by firm size, the productive sectors in the second layer. In particular, accounting for different investment, borrowing, or hiring behavior by firms of different sizes in the same sector would illuminate the interaction between small and medium-size enterprises and larger firms. This could have implications at both the macroeconomic level and for the distribution of income (for example, wage differentiation, profit distribution, exit and entry of firms).

Matching exactly for firms the approach followed for households may not be possible—as noted, the dynamics of creation and destruction are more complex—but one could envisage using the information on firm heterogeneity in the second layer of our framework. One could examine, for example, how large and small firms in the same sector react differently to macroeconomic policies and shocks. This type of analysis could also enable one to evaluate more precisely the effects of changes in the institutional environment facing firms. Based on the effects of specific investment climate variables on firms' investment, pricing, and hiring behavior, it would be possible to measure how different types of investment climates affect the level and structure of economic activity. Descending to the third layer, the effects of these changes on households could then be evaluated.

Randomization
Retrospective evaluations are often misleading. Consider a case where researchers observe that schools with more textbooks typically have better-educated children. It is possible that textbooks increase education quality and achievement. But there are good reasons to doubt estimates of that effect based on a simple retrospective evaluation. One reason is that the greater educational achievement might reflect other factors correlated with textbooks, such as income or parental interest in education, rather than being a direct causal effect of the textbooks. In this case there is a danger of overestimating the actual effects of textbooks. Yet if compensatory programs provide textbooks to problem schools and if it is impossible to control fully for the "problem school" effect in the statistical analysis, then retrospective studies may actually underestimate the effect of these programs.

Econometricians, most notably labor economists, have developed various techniques to try to get around these difficulties (see, for example, Angrist and Krueger 1999, 2001; Meyer 1995). But evidence suggests that omitted-variable bias remains a serious concern: estimates from prospective, randomized evaluations are often quite different from the effects estimated. For example, retrospective studies of Kenyan schools suggest that the provision of additional textbooks in schools with low initial stocks has a dramatic effect on test scores. Randomized experiments, however, suggest that textbook provision increases test scores by 0.2 standard deviations among the top students but does not affect scores for the bottom 60 percent of students (Glewwe, Kremer, and Moulin 2000).

In the epidemiological literature, where randomized trials have a richer history than they do in the social sciences, there is a catalog of cases where widely accepted retrospective statistical evidence was shown to be wrong once randomized trials were conducted (Deaton 2003b). In the retrospective framework, causality is almost always an issue. With random trials the question of causality is much more straightforward because the experiment is constructed so that apart from random factors, the only difference between groups arises from the variable whose effect is being examined.

Despite the importance of knowing whether development programs work as intended, randomized prospective evaluations constitute a tiny fraction of development evaluations. Prospective evaluations, with random assignment to treatment and comparison groups, revolutionized medicine, and they could have a similar impact on development. Recent history provides a number of successful examples. Several studies suggest that school health programs may be one of the most cost-effective ways to increase school participation (Miguel and Kremer 2003; Bobonis, Miguel, and Sharma 2002). A twice-yearly deworming program costs only $3.50 per additional year of schooling, compared with $99.00 per additional year of schooling induced by the provision of free uniforms and $36.00 per year induced by a school meals program.

Useful though they are, randomized experiments are no panacea. Often the questions of interest, such as macroeconomic policy, are economywide and not amendable to randomization. Other times the political process can limit attempts to randomize the "treatment" program. Withholding access to potentially life-saving health benefits or potentially life-altering education opportunities can be considered unethical or unfair. For example, Opportunidades, the urban version of Mexico's Progresa program, will not start with randomized evaluation because of strong opposition to delaying some people's access to the program (Duflo and Kremer 2003).

There are, however, ways to tackle concerns of this type, sometimes making a virtue of necessity. Financial considerations often necessitate phasing in programs over time, and randomization is often the fairest way to sequence phase-in. To evaluate a private school voucher program in Colombia, Angrist and others (2002) made use of the fact that the vouchers were awarded through a lottery. Comparing the outcomes of voucher winners with those of unsuccessful applicants, these researchers were able to distinguish convincingly the program's effects, and their results provided support for continuing and expanding the program.

It is also important to implement mechanisms to ensure that negative as well as positive results are disseminated. Evidence suggests a severe bias toward publishing only positive results (DeLong and Lang 1992), but randomized evaluations may be less susceptible to this problem than retrospective evaluations. Researchers obtaining negative results in retrospective evaluations are likely to try different approaches or not to publish. Once a structure for prospective evaluation is in place, results are usually documented and published.

Recently some attention has been paid to explaining why randomized evaluations are so rare. Pritchett (2002a) argues that program advocates block randomized evaluations because they would reveal programs' true impacts to decision makers. Kremer (2003) advances a complementary explanation in which policymakers are not systematically fooled but rather have difficulty gauging the quality of evidence.

Data and Measurement: Achievements and Possibilities

In short, the development community has made vast improvements in data gathering and measurement over the past two decades. At the household level, the rapid spread of household surveys across countries, and across time within countries, has greatly improved our ability to assess poverty reduction and changes in welfare. More recently, systematic surveys of firms have improved our understanding of what the sources of productivity and growth are, as well as what features of the investment climate hold firms back. These advances have helped anchor the first strategic pillar to an empirical foundation. Finally, despite obvious difficulties, the measurement and understanding of the second pillar, empowerment, have also improved greatly in the past few years. Service delivery surveys are now emerging to complement what can be learned from household panel data sets.

These achievements point the way toward the many possibilities for future data gathering and measurement. Beyond the areas just listed, much more can be done to make evaluation more effective as a guide to policy and program design. This chapter has highlighted some of those possibilities, including multilevel and randomized evaluation. But the strategy opens up research possibilities that extend far beyond new approaches to measurement and evaluation; chapters 7 through 10 explore these other new research directions.

7   The Dynamics of the Investment Climate

This book defines the investment climate as the policy, institutional, behavioral, and physical environment—current and expected—that influences the perceived risks and returns associated with investment. This definition is deliberately general, and we have made it even more general by emphasizing that we are concerned with the environment for changes in economic activity, not just for investments in physical assets. As a first step toward specificity we identified three broad elements of the investment climate: macroeconomic and trade policies, infrastructure, and governance and institutions (see chapter 5). To make these ideas more concrete, our discussion of firm surveys examined specific elements of the investment climate and how to measure them (see chapter 6). We have argued, based on the initial evidence offered in lectures I and II, that there is a powerful link between the investment climate and growth.

This chapter suggests directions for further research on the investment climate, particularly its dynamics. One strain of that research should aim at making the concept more precise, especially for the purpose of measurement. We began to discuss these issues in chapters 5 and 6, where, in basing our ideas and assessments on firms' views and quantifications of the obstacles they face, we adopted a strongly empirical view of the investment climate concept. The surveys we used highlight existing firms' views about barriers to productivity. Ideally, we would also interview potential new firms about obstacles to entry, since existing firms would be unreliable judges of this dimension of the investment climate. An investment climate that discourages entrepreneurship and innovation is typically less open to new entrants—yet it could be considered "good" by existing firms precisely because they are protected from potential competition. Thus, survey evidence should be complemented with data on various aspects of industry structure, including concentration, barriers to entry, and openness to trade.

One early research challenge is to examine more closely, conceptually and empirically, the concept of the investment climate. As with other general concepts, we will likely need to adapt the definition to the context in which we are working. Sometimes we will want to think in general terms—for example, when we interpret economic growth patterns. In other contexts, such as when analyzing policies to remove obstacles to entrepreneurship, we will want to work with specific definitions and details from firm surveys about the investment climate. More research will be needed to determine when a more specific definition is appropriate and to identify key elements of that definition. This definitional research should clarify two issues: how we make the concept of the investment climate more precise and how measure the investment climate in different circumstances for different purposes.

This chapter focuses on three additional research questions. The first section asks how we can better understand the relationship between the investment climate and economic growth. In the second section we take a more microeconomic perspective, analyzing the nature and extent of the investment climate's influence on entrepreneurship, innovation, and learning. It is through these processes that an economy generates changes in production and adapts to changes in the world, technology, and so on—in short, how it achieves flexibility in a changing world. An investment climate that promotes entrepreneurship will make the economy more likely to thrive in a dynamic environment. The final section examines how policy interventions can improve the investment climate. These interventions typically involve political as well as economic reform, and we return to challenges of political reform in chapter 10.

Understanding Growth

Economists since Adam Smith, David Ricardo, and Karl Marx have grappled with understanding the causes of growth. In the 1950s and 1960s there was a surge in such activity, both theoretical and empirical, in response to the strong growth after World War II in rich countries—but at varying rates—and the increasing availability of comparable national income statistics for these countries. There was particular emphasis on the role of capital accumulation and technical progress, with leading theoretical contributions by Robert Solow (1956, 1957) and

Nicholas Kaldor (1960, 1967) and empirical contributions by Edward Denison, who tried to decompose growth into contributions from various sources, leaning heavily on Solow's approach (see Denison 1967). Technical progress played a powerful role in most stories, theoretical and empirical, but was left as a largely unexplained, or exogenous, phenomenon. Notable exceptions include pioneering theoretical work by Kenneth Arrow (1962) on learning by doing and empirical work by Zvi Griliches (1958) on diffusion, or (mainly) learning by watching.

The past two decades have seen another surge in such research. This surge was also prompted by two phenomena: the rapid growth in a number of developing countries, particularly in East Asia, and the much broader availability of comparable data across developing countries. Irving Kravis, Alan Heston, and Robert Summers played an important role in making these data available in a way that allowed comparisons across countries using purchasing power parity (PPP; see Kravis, Heston, and Summers 1978, 1982; Summers and Heston 1991, 1994; Heston, Summers, and Aten 2002).

In the recent resurgence of the growth literature, the challenge of explaining growth differentials has moved to center stage, inspiring attempts to create models in which technological change is endogenous. These efforts have generated a range of theoretical models, most of which build to some degree on the Arrow and Griliches approach of learning by doing and learning by watching, but with a new emphasis on increasing returns, processes of innovation, and imperfect markets. On the theoretical side, Paul Romer's early work on increasing returns and on the production of ideas was of particular importance (Romer 1986, 1987). Of special importance to the more Schumpeterian perspective adopted here is the work of Philippe Aghion and Peter Howitt (see, for example, Aghion and Howitt 1998, forthcoming).

Our purpose here is not to review this theory in any detail, but to indicate where our emphasis on the investment climate might take us in research on modeling growth. We should be looking for ideas that will help us understand some of the central puzzles from the global experience of growth over the past century, particularly the past fifty years. Why have some countries been able to achieve surges of rapid growth lasting a decade or two (or in a few cases, three; see chapter 2), but others have not? Why is it difficult to extend these phases? Why have some countries, such as the Republic of Korea, been able to catch up rapidly with rich countries, while others that were once among the richest countries, such as Argentina, have slipped behind? Why has it been so difficult to generate growth in much of Africa? And why has growth been so strong in China for the past twenty-five years? We argue here that our growing understanding of the microeconomics of the investment climate will take us a long way toward answering those questions. The perspective of the investment climate exposes a rich vein of research for examining the structural, institutional, and behavioral aspects of growth, both theoretical and empirical. This research will build on many aspects of previous work on aggregate growth and move forward in new directions. Motivating this research is the powerful empirical relationship that is now emerging between firm survey data and growth performance. This relationship appears at both the national and regional levels: growth is strongest in countries such as China and India that now have relatively good investment climates, as well as in the Chinese provinces and Indian states that have better investment climates (see chapters 2 and 5).

As we have defined it, the investment climate is strongly dependent on governance and institutions. In the growth literature of the past decade, cross-country comparisons have emphasized differences in governance and institutions in their analyses of differences in growth rates. This new emphasis appears in both case histories of economic growth and studies based on cross-country regressions (see Acemoğlu, Johnson, and Robinson 2001; Banerjee and Iyer 2005; Hall and Jones 1999; Knack and Keefer 1997; Qian 1999; Rodrik 1999, 2003a).

Research has begun to delve into how institutions work and influence growth, and productive new directions are emerging. Such evidence is of great value, and it sits well with the investment climate approach. It is allowing us to go beyond the simple (but correct) statement that institutions are crucial for growth; we now understand that institutions that foster growth in some periods and circumstances may be less effective in others (Acemoğlu, Aghion, and Zilibotti 2002). In our view the most productive research directions are, first, those studying how governance and institutions affect growth and, second, those studying how public action can improve governance and institutions in ways that promote growth.[1]

Researchers are turning attention not only to explaining relative growth but also to how relative growth rankings change over time. For example, from the early 1950s until the mid-1970s, growth was higher and unemployment lower in much of Western Europe than in the United States. This stronger performance may have stemmed in part from Europe's more centralized and long-term relationship between the state and the private sector, from its consensual structures involving firms, employers, and governments, and from the longer-term relationships between individual firms and workers. But the 1970s and subsequent years brought major international shocks (including in oil prices and exchange rates), increasing international competition, and accelerating progress in information and communications technology.

These trends probably raised the returns to flexibility. The United States, with its more flexible labor and corporate institutions, returned fairly quickly to preshock unemployment rates and strong growth, while Europe now has much higher unemployment rates than the United States and experienced slower growth in the 1990s. Thus, we are tempted to conclude that institutions that served Europe well during postwar recovery and catch-up—a period of rebuilding, with slower technological and international change—may have served it less well in the more dynamic, turbulent period since 1973. Japan's situation may be similar, given the country's great difficulty in recovering from its depression of the 1990s.

This analysis points to important policy questions and directions:

• How do we model and measure an economy's flexibility and institutional adaptability? How does an economy become more flexible? Does, for example, the challenge of changing technology point to a need for greater emphasis on tertiary education? In this area there is already a growing literature on how developing countries can close the gap with developed countries in terms of productivity, skills, and technology (see, for example, De Ferranti and others 2002).

• What effects have new technology and trade liberalization had on the relative wages of skilled and unskilled workers, and more generally income distribution and poverty, in the developing world? Trade theory predicts that countries with an abundance of unskilled labor may see a decrease in wage inequality. But openness to trade and foreign direct investment often leads to the adoption of more advanced technologies, possibly more biased toward skilled labor, that could increase the demand for (and relative wages of) skilled workers. How are those mechanisms influenced by the investment climate?

Data from investment climate surveys and other firm data would be the most appropriate vehicles for investigating these issues, which in the past have generally been approached using household data.

Our emphasis on the investment climate, and on the role of institutions within it, is very much in the spirit of this recent research, but tries to get down to microeconomic and structural specifics. Which detailed problems in the investment climate are important for growth and distribution, and how can they be influenced by policy? The rest of this section examines some of the theoretical investment climate modeling issues that emerge from our perspective of development as change (lecture I) and our strategy for development (lecture II).

Modeling the Link between the Investment Climate and Growth
How does the investment climate influence growth, and how does the investment climate change over time? These questions should make it clear that our focus is not on aggregative models in steady state. We may, in modeling, need to work at a fairly aggregate level if we are to study aggregate growth. But our focus is on the underlying structural, institutional, and behavioral influences shaping and driving growth. And we certainly are not looking at long-run steady states. This chapter is looking at models, and then policies, that might explain the growth accelerations we have seen in recent decades and that policy should try to generate.

Our main hypothesis is that the investment climate affects economic activity throughout the economy, particularly incentives to invest. An improvement in the investment climate increases returns to current lines of activity and so increases investment in these lines. It generally also creates new possibilities—for example, through trade or access to new technology. It influences the psychology of entrepreneurs, affecting their assessment of whether innovation will pay off. It puts competitive pressure on firms that have enjoyed privileged positions as a result of import or other protection or special access to decision makers. As a result of greater competition, it may cause some firms, perhaps those close to technological frontiers, to shine—even as others fail. For example, India's 1991 liberalization led to higher productivity growth and profits in industries close to technological frontiers, as well as in states with less rigid labor regulation (Aghion and others 2003).

It follows that changes in the investment climate will affect different firms, industries, and regions in different ways. And these mechanisms indicate that the investment climate–fueled growth we are talking about here is not simply a shift toward some technological frontier. Instead the changes operate through the dynamics of innovation and competition, through relationships between firms and government, and through entrepreneurial enthusiasm or "animal spirits" (to use a term of which Keynes was fond). Whether the notion of a technological frontier is relevant for the economy as a whole, in most cases we are thinking of firms seeking innovations and improvements in a situation that is very distant from that frontier.

A weak investment climate may not only discourage investment, it may also lead businesses to take costly or counterproductive steps to defend themselves from the consequences of its weaknesses. If social order and control are weak, firms typically have to invest heavily in defensive measures such as private security (as they must in parts of Latin America or the former Soviet Union). If the power supply is unreliable, firms will invest in their own generating capacity (as in many parts of South Asia). If it is difficult to get goods through or to ports, trade is discouraged (as in many countries in sub-Saharan Africa) and larger, more costly inventories are held. Many such constraints on development are not quickly or easily reversed.

These features of the real-world investment climate suggest that a full description of its influence would, in principle, involve a vintage model with many productive sectors and types of capital goods. And we would want to know from empirical work about the nature of defensive capital. Is it, for example, proportional to output or capital, or does it act like a fixed cost? If the latter were the case, there would be a bias against small firms. Does a weak investment climate deter innovation more than it deters efficiency? Both policy and modeling are likely to be influenced by the answers to these empirical questions. These are all research questions for theory and applied work that are motivated by the perspective of the investment climate.

For several reasons we hesitate to offer a formal approach to modeling the investment climate in an aggregative growth model. First, such growth models almost inevitably involve production possibility frontiers, and most of our story concerns economies away from some hypothetical technological or efficiency frontier. The emphasis here is on overcoming or reducing all kinds of obstacles to efficiency, dynamic and otherwise, without any illusions that the economy will soon arrive at a frontier. The story is one of the dynamics of investment and growth rather than the marginal equalities that characterize efficiency. Second, as we have argued, the most interesting stories take place at the micro rather than the aggregate level. Third, in advancing our understanding of the investment climate and growth, we will want to appeal to many models, each with its own insights, rather than shoe-horning all interesting phenomena into any one particular model.

Still, for many people a little formality helps fix ideas. So at the risk of being misleading in the ways just described, we briefly describe a simple aggregative framework using approaches that are fairly standard in endogenous growth theory (see, for example, Aghion and Howitt 1998). Stephen Hawking, in his book *A Brief History of Time* (1988), warns that authors lose half their audience with each equation. Thus, we are living dangerously by having three equations in this book.

We start with a simple model, then discuss generalizations. We abstract from labor and suppose that output, Y, is a function of the capital stock, K, and the investment climate, as measured by a single variable M. We write this function, where t is time, as

$$Y = \exp(t \cdot \alpha(M))F(K, M). \tag{1}$$

As the function is written here, the investment climate affects both output and productivity levels, through the function $F(\ )$, and the rate of change of output, through the function $\alpha(\ )$. To keep things simple, we can portray the rate of change of the investment climate in the model as being governed by

$$\dot{M} = g(\mu, M, Y), \tag{2}$$

where μ is a vector of policy actions government can take and g is the function that converts these inputs into the change in M. This assumes that the policy acts through the rate of change of M rather than through an immediate discrete change in M. The rate of change of M can depend on both M itself and the level of income in the society (see below). Finally, we assume that

$$\dot{K} = sY, \tag{3}$$

where s is the aggregate savings rate, meaning that the capital stock increases with savings in the economy. These three equations describe a dynamic growth model with two state variables, K and M.

The growth rate can be increased by policy, captured in the vector μ, which improves the investment climate by shifting the rate of change of M. An increase in M can increase both the growth rate, through $\alpha(\ )$, and the level of productivity, directly through $F(\ )$. Improvements in the investment climate could generate further improvements through political economy mechanisms if they increase the number of people and firms with a stake in a better climate. (For example, if trade reforms create an export-oriented sector of the economy, that sector may increase pressure for further reforms to trade policy or trade-related infrastructure.) And higher incomes might lead to pressure for an improved investment climate in other ways, as people seek rules governing the protection of wealth or capital (hence function $g(\ )$ in equation 2).[2]

There is no general reason to suppose that this model has a stable long-run steady state. But that is not a drawback, because we have no great interest in modeling such a steady state. The model could in principle capture some of the phenomena we are seeking to incorporate, such as an endogenous investment climate and virtuous circles of growth (discussed below). Let us emphasize that it is not part of our argument to offer a formal model here as *the* portrayal of the investment climate. Instead it is offered as an illustration of some basic interdependencies, for those who like to work with production functions and formal growth theory.

We could generalize the notation to cover a vector of capital goods, vintage models, many dimensions of the investment climate, and so on. But we do not believe that this is the best approach. It is more likely that a series of simple but distinct models will provide different kinds of insights. Some possibilities are discussed below.

The Investment Climate, Dynamic Increasing Returns, and Accelerating Growth

A focus on the investment climate leads us in markedly different directions from those suggested by standard theories of investment. In conventional growth theory, investment is expected to lead to diminishing returns. As more investments are made in one area, marginal returns decline, and new investment seeks other outlets. The concept of diminishing returns thus implies that investment is self-limiting in each use, as long as other key inputs (including technology) remain unchanged.

The investment climate, by contrast, can be positively or negatively self-reinforcing, and thus can generate either growing prosperity or stagnation. Unlike most of the older stories of capital accumulation, the investment climate approach tries to capture some of the external spillover effects, the complementarities, and the nonrivalrous public nature of improvements in governance and institutions. As the investment climate improves, the frontier of opportunity expands:

existing investment becomes more productive, the rewards to productive behavior rise, the "animal spirits" of entrepreneurs are encouraged, and the economy tends to attract more investment rather than less.

These examples of the success of entrepreneurship and investment show other investors what is possible. But they also foster greater understanding of and commitment to a sound investment climate, strengthening the political and economic forces that work to improve it. Because there will always be vested interests that benefit from the status quo, strengthening the forces for change is a key part of the process. We should emphasize here that we mean there are increasing returns to improving the investment *climate* over some range, as opposed to increasing returns to investment. That is, this story is consistent with diminishing returns to *investment*, holding other factors equal.

A stronger investment climate leads to the kinds of sustained productivity improvements and vibrant entrepreneurship that induce a virtuous circle of investment, growth, and poverty reduction. In contrast, where the climate for productive investment deteriorates, these processes work in reverse—and replacement of capital and new investments can suffer as a pernicious downward spiral sets in. The kinds of dynamic reinforcement and increasing returns may not apply as strongly in rich countries, where more of the framework of a well-functioning market economy is in place. But even there they are unlikely to be entirely absent.

The challenge for students of development is to understand what kinds of changes generate strong, sustained increases in growth rates and large transformations in education, health, and other outcomes. The challenge of public action for development, in turn, centers on making these changes happen. Committed and prompt action is crucial if the Millennium Development Goals are to be approached even remotely (see chapter 11). These goals express a widely shared sense of the urgency of the development challenge, and the distance to them makes it clear that we should be striving for development results on a large scale. In part such efforts will require increasing the resources devoted to development (see lecture IV). But even more than that, we need to understand and generate dynamic processes that accelerate development and yield large-scale results even when the impetus or action is small. Thus, we have to try to understand both the dynamics of these self-reinforcing processes and the means of kick-starting them. Such processes lie at the heart of scaling up development results (see chapter 11).

How can modest changes in inputs generate large responses? From a visual standpoint, we might think of it as tipping a lever in the right direction, or moving to the steeply rising position of a logistic curve. Most of the relevant models that yield such responses are likely to be strongly dynamic in nature, though they may also embody standard notions of static increasing returns.

Let us briefly examine some of the circumstances and models that might generate these increasing returns and growth effects. First, in standard static production theory, there are commonly identified sources of increasing returns. One such source is set-up or fixed production costs—the fact that the volume of a sphere is proportional to the cube of its radius, whereas the surface area (or raw material for a container) increases with the square. Another source of increasing returns is network externalities, because the number of interactions in a network rises in proportion to the square of the number of activities or people in the network. If we build increasing returns into growth models, we can obtain accelerating growth rates (out of steady state) or steady states at growth rates above the growth rate of labor (in models where labor is an exogenous factor placing limits on growth; see, for example, Arrow 1962; Romer 1986, 1993; Lucas 1988; Barro and Sala-i-Martin 1995).

We should emphasize again, however, that our focus is decidedly not aggregate growth models in steady state. We should also consider models that might generate more extended acceleration of growth rates. Thus, our second example is of an improvement in the investment climate resulting from government policy that leads to major improvements in the productivity of resources and in the environment for entrepreneurship and innovation, which in turn could imply a jump in the growth rate. The past twenty-five years in China, or ten to fifteen years in India, might be examples. Schumpeterian or more broadly Austrian school theories of growth emphasize processes that can be understood using the notion of investment climate, while Hirschman has a similar spirit. Thus, there are well-developed strands of the growth and development literature that are in the spirit of this approach. From the perspective of the model presented above, we could understand such changes in terms of a sudden jump in M rather than the smoother process posited in equation 2.

Third, we have a class of models that can generate multiple equilibria. A disturbance of sufficient magnitude—a policy improvement and an injection of resources, for example—could initiate a movement from a lower-level to a higher-level equilibrium, embodying an acceleration of growth. Postwar development economics started with Rosenstein-Rodan's idea of a backward economy making a "big push" for industrialization by coordinating investment across sectors (Rosenstein-Rodan 1943). When domestic markets are small, a simultaneous expansion of many sectors can be self-sustaining through mutual demand support, even if by itself no sector could profit from an expansion. The presumption underlying this model is one of multiple equilibria, and for Rosenstein-Rodan the essential problem was to coordinate an escape from the low-level equilibrium trap to a higher-income equilibrium embodying industrialization. This idea was formalized in the model of Murphy, Shleifer, and Vishny (1989) in the context of an imperfectly competitive economy with large fixed costs and aggregate demand spillovers.

There is another, somewhat more dynamic, multiple equilibria argument based on the virtuous circles of innovation brought on by a diversified economic base concentrated in a locality. Innovation often occurs when a product or technique in one sector is found to solve a problem in a firm from another sector located "across the street." With a certain critical mass of diversity, this virtuous circle of cross-fertilized innovation can set in. Without it, isolated firms may spiral downward in stagnation as their procedures and routines prove insufficient to meet new challenges.

Fourth, there are a number of models that involve the diffusion of ideas or knowledge. There is an inherent increasing returns aspect to ideas because a new idea or piece of knowledge is nonrivalrous, meaning that it can be used across the whole economy. A small amount of resources that generate an idea can have a big economywide response (see Foster and Rosenzweig 1995 and Acemoğlu 1997). We should recognize, however, that technological change is more complex than simply transferring blueprints (or importing machines) to developing countries. There must be local investment in learning. Producers can make this investment through learning by doing, which involves experimenting with new technology to determine its applicability to local conditions. Alternatively, producers might learn from others—from either other producers engaged in learning by doing or local researchers or extension agents. An example is the green revolution, which transformed agriculture in large parts of Asia in the 1970s and 1980s. Indeed, the study of diffusion processes was a central issue in agricultural economies long before it became popular in modern growth theory (see, for example, Griliches 1958 and Stern 1996 for a review). The notions of ideas as public goods and learning by watching have been prominent in modern endogenous growth theory.

Fifth, we have political economy models in which the balance of politics is poised delicately on a metaphorical ridge at a crucial point in history, so that the right kind of external support at that time can nudge the economy in the right direction and launch a process that, once started, can gather momentum on its own (see Schelling 1978). The transition of Eastern Europe and the former Soviet Union from 1990 on provides examples where reform processes kept going despite opposition—and others where they did not (Roland 2000).

Sixth, there are models that stress the returns to skilled talent from rent seeking. When talented people become entrepreneurs, they improve the technology in the line of business they pursue, and productivity and income grow. In contrast, when they become rent seekers, most of their private returns come from redistribution of wealth from others and not from wealth creation. As a result, as Murphy, Shleifer, and Vishny (1991, 1993) point out, they do not improve technological opportunities, and the economy stagnates. The allocation of talent to rent seeking is damaging for several reasons. First, as rent-seeking activities expand, they absorb labor and other resources and so reduce income. The bloated government bureaucracies in some developing countries illustrate this effect. Second, the tax that rent seeking imposes on the productive sector reduces incentives to produce, and so also reduces income.[3] Finally, if the most talented people become rent seekers, the ability of entrepreneurs is lower, and rates of technological progress and growth will likely be lower. When rent-seeking sectors offer the most talented people higher returns than do productive sectors, the lure of the unproductive sector is likely to reduce income and growth.

We have offered six examples here, and there are undoubtedly other relevant conceptual constructs that illuminate the process of accelerating growth. Development research would be well served if it explored this area further, assembling and examining different potential models more rigorously. As we have argued, we should not be looking to select just one of these as an overarching model of the relationship between the investment climate and growth. The challenge is to get a number of these processes going at the same time—to understand and kick-start them. We will likely need a range of models, each capturing different aspects of the problem.

The Investment Climate and the Empirics of Growth

The type of theoretical focus described should go hand in hand with empirical research that tests how well these stories explain accelerations or declines in growth. There are a number of promising empirical approaches for doing so. For example, it would be valuable if we could devise tests to see whether improvements in the investment climate raised the growth rate for a long period or instead sparked a one-time productivity surge to a new higher level. The policy implications of the two cases would look somewhat different. The returns to an investment climate improvement would likely be higher in the former case, giving it high priority. If the latter case applied, we should focus on generating continued improvements in the investment climate. It may, however, be empirically difficult to distinguish between these two effects.

Some suggestive evidence might come from comparing states in India or provinces in China. If states and provinces with a better investment climate sustain higher growth over long periods—if, in other words, there is sustained divergence in incomes—and measured differences in the investment climate show little change, that would point to the strength of the effect operating through the growth rate of productivity rather than its level.

A second empirical challenge concerns the relationship between the investment climate and the type of investment. What kind of defensive measures or "coping" investments, such as expenditures on power generation or private security, does a weak investment climate require of firms? How costly are they? How do they vary across firms of different sizes and in different industries? This kind of problem is more tractable empirically, and current investment climate surveys—which marry investment climate information with standard production, investment, and cost information—are already producing results here (McMillan and Woodruff 2002; Batra, Kaufmann, and Stone 2003; Dollar, Hallward-Driemeier, and Mengistae 2003).

A third empirical challenge involves defining and measuring the flexibility and adaptability of firms in different investment climates. Why do some firms, and even whole economies, do better in turbulent environments than others? The challenge is to explore how far we can go in capturing this adaptability in empirical analysis (an interesting study dealing with this issue is De Ferranti and others 2003).

A fourth and related area concerns the management of economic transition. We have emphasized the importance of both history and change. All economies inherit institutional structures, often associated with a particular view of appropriate economic management. Thus, many countries in the 1970s inherited economic structures designed around protectionism and central planning. To varying extents this was true of China, India, and countries in Eastern Europe, the Soviet Union, large parts of North Africa, the Middle East, and Latin America, and many other parts of the developing world. The subsequent growth performance of countries has depended to a great extent on how they have managed the transition to a more market-oriented economy. Where the third area for empirical research focuses on ability to adapt to external shocks, this area concentrates on longer-term structural transitions that are necessary even in the absence of abrupt shocks.

Inherited institutions may have been appropriate for a certain phase of growth. We have already mentioned the example of public-private interactions and industrial relations in Western Europe, which were effective in sustaining growth in the postwar years but less well adapted to the environment after 1973. In other cases institutions may have been associated with ideologies that were misguided even at the time and might never have delivered sustained growth. Whatever the origins of inherited institutions, there will be periods when reigniting growth depends on changing them.

Many have argued, and we agree, that China owes some of its success in moving from a command economy to its ability to ensure that the transition was measured and controlled. That is not the same as a gradualist approach. Some changes in China, such as agricultural land reform, were dramatic and happened quickly. Nevertheless, change was controlled and not chaotic, even when it began as a bottom-up process. This approach contrasts with the experience of, say, the former Soviet Union, which was forced into fairly chaotic change through internal collapse, and with the experience of a number of Latin American countries forced into change by crises in recent decades. We return briefly to some of these issues in chapter 10, which covers the dynamics of political reform.

Policies to Improve the Investment Climate

All too often in developing countries, participants in the economy do not feel that the framework of policy, institutions, and governance engenders sufficient confidence in reaping returns for them to make the decisions and take the risks needed to make productive economic commitments. If they are frustrated in their efforts to establish practical arrangements for using assets, honoring contracts, and making financial commitments, that may confirm their fears. And if enough firms fail to invest and make long-term plans, the collective lack of commitment to the future will likely be a self-fulfilling prophecy.

The entrepreneurial spirit is suppressed by obstacles and hurdles often erected, operated, and maintained by those in privileged positions. This is not a new insight. After visiting China in 1930, the economic historian Richard H. Tawney (1966 [1932], p. 18) took note of the business climate:

The multitude of currencies; the variety of weights and measures; the absence of adequate machinery for investment; the existence till recently of over seven hundred tax barriers levying duties on goods in transit; the small volume per head of foreign trade; the preponderance of raw materials and food-stuffs among Chinese exports; the fact that the source from which great fortunes are derived is still almost as often official perquisites and military plunder as the profits of industry; the paradoxical sentiment which esteems the sage more highly than the millionaire—such phenomena point to the same conclusion.

The costs of such weaknesses in the investment climate have also long been recognized. For example, Lorenzetti portrayed the problems visually—and beautifully—in his fourteenth-century frescoes in Siena on good and bad governance, which contrasted life under the two types of regimes (see chapter 2). We can add to these insights data from investment climate surveys and other studies, which are starting to make the issues more quantitative and analytically tractable.

The challenge—and the dynamic question—is how to change governance for the better. We begin a brief discussion here. Because many of the issues are intensely political, we return to them in chapter 10 (on political reform) and lecture IV (on action). The research challenge is to identify key features of the investment climate and how to change them. We have discussed the first aspect at some length at various places in this book, including the two preceding chapters. Thus, we now focus on how to change the investment climate.

We look at this question in terms of three broad levels of the investment climate. The first is the governance framework and sense of direction of government. Does the population know where policies and the economy are likely to go, and are they reasonably confident in that this is the right direction? The second concerns the institutions that support the market relationships of business. Do people have confidence that contracts will be honored, and are they able to put their assets to work? The third level concerns the obstacles found in everyday economic activities, such as predatory behavior of officials and malfunctioning infrastructure. These are related to the institutional issues, but at a more detailed level.

Broad Framework and Changes in Government

As we argued in the first section of this chapter, changing approaches and, where necessary, institutions in response to a changing world is crucial to sustaining growth. Thus, our goal should be to identify institutions that promote responsiveness to change, as well as ways of changing institutions that have outlived their usefulness. Managing institutional transition is a real challenge. China, and more recently India, have embarked on this route in a fairly measured way. Although they have faced some turbulence, they have been able to chart their own courses rather than being forced into immediate change by internal collapse (as in the former Soviet Union) or by a crisis in external economic relations (as in the past two decades in several Latin American countries).

A key element in this story of managing transitions is leadership and role models. Who dominates society, and how do they behave? Is it warriors, thieves, or predatory bureaucrats who grab large parts of the pie and destroy incentives? Or is it entrepreneurs who help construct a bigger pie? The lessons of history, including that of the Balkans and parts of sub-Saharan Africa and the former Soviet Union, are clear: a society dominated by conflict and plunder has little future. In contrast, a society led by creativity generates hope and results. Conflict is often associated with official or unofficial plunder, so the causation goes both ways, and it can be hard to escape from the vicious circle (Collier and others 2003 is the most detailed analysis so far of civil war as it affects development policy).

Obviously one cannot in a single stroke banish thieves from leadership and install responsibility and creativity in their place. But neither is it impossible to promote change. In large measure, change has to come from within society. Ideally, it comes through democratic process. In other cases, a population can rise up and throw out a tyrant.

What research can do is try to inform argument and those who would seek change by showing which types of institutions and behaviors promote development, how these can develop over time, and how to promote such change. We return to some of these issues in chapter 10 and in the last part of this chapter.

Building Institutions for Markets

At the core of a sound investment climate are institutions that define and enforce property rights (see World Bank 2001a for further discussion and references on institutions for markets). When entrepreneurs are assured that their property is protected from expropriation by public or private interests, they have more incentive to make investments. Secure property rights can also increase access to credit, because assets can more readily be used as collateral, as well as facilitate trade, since the transactions costs of transferring property are lower when rights are well defined (Besley 1995, de Soto 2000). And stronger property rights can affect labor markets—for example, secure property titles in Peru led to a significant increase in hours of work, a shift from home to market work, and substitution of adult for child labor (Field 2002).

Informal networks and reputational effects are important ways of enforcing property rights and contracts, particularly in developing countries, where they substitute for a lack of formal enforcement institutions (Greif 1994, McMillan and Woodruff 2002, World Bank 2001a). But norm-based institutions are less effective as markets expand and the circle of trading partners grows or diversifies. Formal enforcement institutions, primarily courts, are needed to facilitate more complex and large-scale commercial activity. Some of the most promising improvements to the investment climate are court reforms: introducing expedited summary enforcement proceedings in Tunisia, simplifying judicial procedures in Argentina, and automating court administration records in the Slovak Republic are three examples that are bearing fruit for business activity (World Bank 2004a).

In many developing countries excessive regulation of factor and product markets is one of the greatest obstacles facing firms. World Bank (2003b) benchmarks the extent of regulation in more than 130 countries and finds that poor countries consistently regulate more heavily. For example, an entrepreneur in Belarus or Colombia has to go through nineteen procedures to register a business, which takes between sixty and one hundred days, whereas in Canada the process consists of two steps and takes on average only three days (World Bank 2003b). While some degree of regulation is necessary, most poor countries have less enforcement capacity and fewer checks and balances in regulatory agencies. As a result cumbersome regulation can become a source of arbitrary rent extraction and a deterrent to firm investment, productivity, and growth. Studies in OECD countries also show that heavy regulation in product markets (particularly entry regulation) is negatively related to investment (Alesina and others 2005) and productivity (Nicoletti and Scarpetta 2003).

Regulation redistributes rents (Blanchard and Giavazzi 2003). More often than not, excessive regulation protects the privileged and hinders the disadvantaged—small firms, unconnected entrepreneurs— the most. Heavy business licensing and entry regulation can protect incumbents from competition from start-ups. Heavy regulation also creates incentives for firms to operate in the informal sector. A study in India showed that proworker employment regulation led increased informal sector output, decreased formal sector employment, output, investment, and productivity, and higher urban poverty (Besley and Burgess 2003).

Across countries, regulatory obstacles to starting a business and more rigid employment regulation—such as higher costs and difficulties in shrinking the workforce or going out of business, restrictions on using part-time workers, and limits on working hours—are strongly associated with a larger informal sector (Djankov and others 2002, Botero and others 2004, World Bank 2003b). Informal sector workers generally do not have access to social benefits, and it is harder for informal firms to get utility connections and access to formal institutions such as those for credit and for dispute resolution. By encouraging small firms and individual entrepreneurs to participate in the formal sector, removing regulatory obstacles can simultaneously promote the goals of innovation and inclusion explored in these lectures.

Investment climate surveys consistently highlight the obstacles that businesses in developing countries face in obtaining finance. A large body of evidence tells us that proper regulation and supervision of financial markets, as well as a competitive market structure, including private ownership of banks, is important for a sound financial sector (see World Bank 2001a for a review). Other critical steps include reforming laws on collateral (as was recently done in the Slovak

Republic), improving the rights of creditors in insolvency laws, and encouraging the development of credit information bureaus. Such bureaus are especially important for expanding small firms' access to credit, because lenders are more likely to require collateral from and have less information on the creditworthiness of small business. These issues of finance emphasize that improving the investment climate is not always about deregulation. Rather, it is about reducing the wrong kind of regulation and increasing the right kind.

Institutions that foster learning are also key to market development. In developing countries industrial progress is partly driven by imitation, adaptation, and technology transfer. Hausmann and Rodrik (2003) emphasize that economic development includes an element of discovery, which is an additional cost for developing country enterprises. For them, change is innovation—as it is for a farmer trying a new crop or technique or a rural family sending a member to town for education or work. Technology transferred from abroad needs to be adapted to local circumstances, and the adaptation is by no means certain to pay off. Learning what you are good at producing requires an investment. The process of discovery (of physical or institutional innovations) and transfer (or transplant, as legal scholars call it) with adaptation to a developing-country setting has become an important theme in recent literature on development.[4]

The entry point for policy here is that the returns to discovery and transfer cannot be fully appropriated by the entrepreneur who makes the initial innovation. There is great social value to discovering when a country specializes in cut flowers (Colombia, Ecuador), software (India), hats (Bangladesh), or bed sheets (Pakistan), but the discoverer can appropriate only a small part of that value. Developing-country innovators who transfer technology and adapt it to local circumstances thus find themselves in a situation parallel to that of leading-edge innovators in advanced countries—but there are major investment climate differences between the two groups.

In advanced countries intellectual property rights, through patents, protect those who discover new goods. By contrast, developing-country investors who adapt goods or processes (for example, by figuring out that an existing good can be produced cheaply at home and how to do it) typically receive no such protection. Thus, policy might consider how to support first-mover innovators in developing countries, particularly when (as in the cases mentioned above) there is the potential for quick diffusion through spinoffs from first-mover firms. Business parks and enterprise zones are possible examples.

Obstacles in Everyday Life
Removing the specific obstacles in people's daily economic lives, such as poor infrastructure and bureaucratic harassment (see also chapters 2 and 5), usually requires institutional change, leading to an overlap with the policies suggested by the institutional analysis in the previous section. We do not separate these out in the policy suggestions that follow. Nevertheless, going to a more detailed level of specificity has some analytical advantages, as it lends weight to discussions of institutional reform that might otherwise sound airy or impractical.

Specific information from investment climate surveys not only identifies obstacles, it can also generate the public attention and government focus needed to steel the political will to remove those obstacles. In Pakistan, when a recent investment climate assessment highlighted the obstacles facing firms for the highest levels of government, it helped spur reform efforts embodied in the budget of the ministry of finance and elsewhere. Cities in China are now asking to be included in World Bank investment climate surveys so that they can benchmark themselves against others in China and elsewhere. This framework suggests reforms in three areas—institutions, information and transparency, and investment—that can both improve the investment climate directly and generate pressure for change.

Institutions

• Simplify business and tax regulations and make them transparent (less subject to bureaucratic discretion).

• Strengthen legal infrastructure for businesses and households, such as legal institutions for recognizing rights, enforcing contracts, and adjudicating conflicts.

• Build evaluation and checks into regulatory processes—for example, by requiring regulatory impact statements before new regulation is introduced or periodic reviews of the costs businesses face in complying with regulation.

• Reform public agencies that enforce regulations—for example, by aligning incentives between businesses and staff at tax inspectorates and automating business registration to minimize opportunities for arbitrary behavior.

Information and transparency

• Help businesses and business associations counteract bureaucratic and police harassment; providing information and points of contact can be powerful triggers for improvement in this area.

• Benchmark and publicize business climate indicators in different jurisdictions.

• Promote education institutions for business, including agriculture, and include business issues in more general education.

• Recognize and publicize entrepreneurial role models.

Investment

• Sponsor business incubators to help start-ups and spinoffs, and establish franchising procedures to multiply retail successes.

• Invest in, or promote investment in, physical infrastructure for business, including power, telecommunications, transportation, ports, and sanitation.

• Invest in, or promote investment in, financial infrastructure, particularly for small and medium-size enterprises.

All this is sound and sensible, but problems usually arise in choosing priorities when implementing the list. Investment climate surveys can be a great help in that process. And fortunately, there is experience with constructive methods to promote the kind of entrepreneurship, innovation, and learning we are discussing. The spirit has been expressed well by Hirschman (1971, 1984), who conceives of the development adviser (a role that could be filled at any level, from the village to the national government and could be domestic or external) as someone who operates through "entry points." The interaction begins by looking at the levels of families, villages, towns, cities, regions, or states for "where virtue appears of its own accord" (p. 204).

I began to look for elements and processes ... that did work, perhaps in roundabout and unappreciated fashion.... This search for possible hidden rationalities was to give an underlying unity to my work.... The hidden rationalities I was after were precisely and principally processes of growth and change already under way in the societies I studied, processes that were often unnoticed by the actors immediately involved, as well as by foreign experts and advisors. (Hirschman 1984, pp. 91–93)

The idea, then, is to reward, strengthen, and publicize these virtues rather than always be trying to create new ones. The message to others, when they see existing efforts rewarded, is: "If these families, villages, towns, cities, regions, or states can do this, so can you." Rivalry and local pride will play a role in motivating the diffusion of successful practices. Instead of starting with a given group of counterparts and puzzling how to motivate them to make deep-seated reforms, we start by looking where real change is afoot on its own and work to expand it.

Entrepreneurship, Innovation, and Learning

Entrepreneurship, innovation, and learning lie at the heart of development. They are actions taken by individual enterprises or individuals in their own environment: they are microeconomic and context specific. Thus, this section takes a much more microeconomic view than did the previous ones.

In a developing-country context, entrepreneurship and innovation do not necessarily require pushing out some global technological and knowledge frontier. Instead, innovation and entrepreneurship here refer to processes that lead to discrete improvements in welfare for individuals and households through the adoption of new ways of doing things, with *new* defined in terms of particular places and settings. The innovation is the change itself—the activity or approach that is new, and very different, for the organization, enterprise, household, or individual. By *entrepreneurship*, we mean the ability to identify and act on the innovation.

Some examples illustrate what we have in mind. Rural parents who send their son or daughter into town, whether to study or to work, may be making an economic innovation if others in their area have not done so before. A school that restructures itself in a way that sharply increases girls' enrollment is also innovating, as is a government that launches a successful program to reduce mother-to-child HIV transmission. Similarly, a firm is innovating when it enters a new market, embraces a new technology, or introduces new management processes that radically change its ways of working. Thus, innovation can come in both the public and private sectors and can be carried out by entrepreneurial households and individuals as well as firms.

The research challenge that flows from our development strategy is to identify the key determinants of entrepreneurship, innovation, and learning from the perspective of the investment climate and empowerment. Doing so will involve first sharpening our understanding of these processes. Here we are likely to be able to draw on case studies of how entrepreneurship and innovation actually occur. Are there identifiable characteristics of successful entrepreneurs and their environments? As ever, in this type of research there are sample selection problems, because it will be easier to identify successful entrepreneurs. It will be important to try to understand what distinguishes them and their environments from similar groups.

Social factors and individual characteristics are likely to be important determinants of entrepreneurial activity, and understanding entrepreneurship has long been a research subject for sociologists and psychologists. Sociologists emphasize that family, cultural values, political systems, and class structures influence whether and how entrepreneurial activity emerges (Cochran 1971, Young 1971, Dahms 1995). Psychologists highlight that entrepreneurship is associated with an individual's values and desire for prestige, achievement, autonomy, and risk taking (McClelland 1961, Rotter 1966, Liles 1974), although this literature does not link these personal characteristics to the social and institutional environment.

We also have to try to understand which institutions and policies are most conducive to entrepreneurship and innovation, and how to build them. Baumol (1968, 1990) and Kirzner (1979) offer conceptual frameworks and historical evidence on how laws, regulations, and social norms provide incentives for entrepreneurship. More recent research is focused on empirical relationships. Strong property rights protection and contract enforcement can sharpen incentives for creating new businesses (de Soto 2000, Field 2002), including through informal institutions such as reputational effects and social networks (McMillan and Woodruff 2000, 2002).

The World Bank's *World Development Report 2002* assembled evidence on social networks and social capital in information and learning, particularly information on trade partners and opportunities. A range of case studies—from Armenian traders in the seventeenth and eighteenth centuries, to fishmongers in Ghana, to female market traders in West Africa—shows that informal networks are a powerful way for entrepreneurs to exchange information about business opportunities. Such institutions can amplify the effects associated with learning by doing and learning by watching that were discussed above.

As we argued in our more macrodiscussion above, there is an inherent increasing-returns aspect to ideas, because a new idea or piece of knowledge can be used nonrivalrously across an entire economy. Burton Klein (1984, p. 17) gives an example of an S-curve that shows the bandwagon effect of learning and thus the diffusion of an innovation: "A few boys jump into a river; and, after they do so, more and more boys decide to take the risk and jump in too. So we get a curve that, though starting out slowly, rapidly rises; it finally flattens when only a few timid boys are left on the riverbank while the others are joyfully swimming in the river." Taking the "boys" to be farmers in a village or shopkeepers in a town, the example illustrates that after a few take a risk, many others will follow because they learn from the first-movers and want to join the innovative group. In this context, which may have some generality, they do not want to be seen as cowards or to miss out on something fun or rewarding.

There could be real returns to deepening our insight into the microeconomics of how small beginnings can lead to substantial accelerations of growth through the learning process. What are the main mechanisms through which entrepreneurs learn from each other? How are innovations diffused? We would want to know, for example, whether several small firms carry stronger learning externalities than a few large firms with the same output, as would be the case if a firm's visibility as an example was uncorrelated with its size. But one could also argue that if there are setup costs to new ideas, a large firm may be more productive in the creation of ideas. How important are these offsetting effects? Empirical answers would influence policies toward firms of different sizes.

As we have seen, these insights could come in part from looking at the role of the investment climate in enabling other mechanisms and in part from looking directly at the investment climate. As our understanding grows, we will be able to foster more effective policies and institutions to support entrepreneurship, innovation, and learning. There are fascinating possibilities for research—rich in their potential for insights and discovery and of real value for policies that promote growth and reduce poverty.

8   The Dynamics of Empowerment

Chapter 7 examined constraints on, actions of, and encouragement for enterprises and developed a research agenda aimed at understanding how a good investment climate accelerates growth and provides poor people with income-earning opportunities. The focus was on entrepreneurship and the obstacles facing entrepreneurs and enterprises. This chapter has a parallel focus on individuals—their constraints and actions, and ways of encouraging their empowerment. We concentrate on research related to the obstacles that individuals might encounter and the ways that they can be overcome. But many parts of the story are still unresearched, because research is even less advanced for this topic than for the investment climate.

This chapter takes steps toward addressing that research deficit, focusing on three areas. The first, analyzed in the first section of the chapter, concerns overarching questions on the dynamics of and policies toward empowerment. How does empowerment facilitate and accelerate the participation of disadvantaged groups in economic and political life? And how can public action promote empowerment? The second and third areas are based on our definition of empowerment: increasing an individual's ability to shape his or her life (see chapters 3 and 5). The key elements determining that ability are internal constraints, particularly individual perceptions, preferences, and aspirations; external constraints, such as discrimination and the family, economic, social, cultural, and political context; and assets, including human capital (see figure 3.1). Internal constraints are discussed in chapter 9. External constraints highlight the importance of small and medium-size enterprises (SMEs) in helping people escape poverty; thus, the second section of this chapter focuses on how to lower barriers to SME growth and employment of poor people. Finally, the third section focuses on the third element of empowerment: the role of assets and their redistribution (through income and wealth transfers).

How Empowerment Helps Poor People Participate in Economic Life

External obstacles may prevent individuals from taking advantage of economic opportunities and participating in growth. These obstacles range from discrimination based on gender, race, ethnicity, caste, religion, or language to corruption, cronyism, and capture of the state by powerful groups that exclude poor people from the benefits of public policies. The dynamics of empowerment are largely about reducing and overcoming these obstacles and promoting the acquisition of assets. (As noted, they are also about overcoming internal constraints; see chapter 9.)

A research program on the dynamics of empowerment would have to begin by carefully examining definitions of the concept. Chapter 3 offers a starting point, and we do not go into further detail here. Instead, our purpose here is to draw lessons from examples of empowerment and identify avenues for future research. We open with three examples.

Removing External Obstacles to Empowerment: Three Cases
Consider the Self-Employed Women's Association (SEWA), a union of eighty-five cooperatives based in Ahmedabad, India.[1] Its members are poor women working in the informal sector—which accounts for 94 percent of the Indian workforce—as construction workers, vegetable vendors, home-based workers, operators of small businesses, and so on. Most members belong to disadvantaged groups, including Dalits. SEWA empowers these women economically and socially by tackling problems surrounding their working and living conditions. The association offers many services, including banking, insurance, housing loans, training, health care, child care, and legal aid.

These efforts have been instrumental in changing the lives of these women and in some cases have resulted in policy changes at the national level. SEWA has provided poor, illiterate, vulnerable women with means and mechanisms that aid in their development and provide for their life cycle needs. Women's increased participation in activities such as training, banking, and decision making has also increased their confidence and self-esteem. And the participation of Dalit women in activities such as health care provision and savings groups has raised their status in their villages.

Moreover, thanks to its strong organizational capacity, SEWA has achieved policy changes through its numerous campaigns. For instance, the Ahmedabad Municipal Corporation has granted licenses to SEWA-affiliated street vendors and entitled them to receive bonuses from contractors as a result of a major campaign led by the organization. Similarly, SEWA members have been enabled to take on exploitative landowners and find better working conditions and wages. Poor women have also been aided in putting their children into school—and keeping them there.

The difficulty that Dalit groups find in moving out of poverty, as a result of social constraints, is illustrated by Stern's experience studying the village of Palanpur in northern India. The Jatabs (the main Dalit group) there were mostly illiterate and found it difficult to get jobs outside agriculture. Their children felt unwelcome in schools, increasing the likelihood that the Jatabs' inferior status would be replicated in the next generation. But as the local market for construction expanded, some of them have started to find work outside the village. With the increased opportunity, Palanpur's Jatabs are beginning to expand their horizons in terms of schooling for their children and quality of housing.

Consider next this example from the Philippines. In 2000 Social Weather Stations (SWS), an independent research organization, conducted a survey in metropolitan Manila and three other regions.[2] The survey, administered to 1,200 households, asked poor Filipinos about the constraints they encountered in accessing public services, their views on service quality and adequacy, and the responsiveness of government officials. In keeping with procedures developed elsewhere (see, for example, Paul 2002 on some Bangalore programs), customers filled out report cards indicating their feelings about public services. The survey revealed widespread dissatisfaction, provided insight into customer priorities and problems, and highlighted how different services could better meet poor people's needs. The report cards also enabled customers to play a part in holding agencies accountable for better services. For example, water supplied by all sources was considered unsafe for drinking. A third of the population had to look for their own water. Poor people who buy water from vendors consumed just 15 liters per day, close to the survival minimum. The government subsidy on rice benefited the nonpoor more than poor people. The Lingap Para sa Mahihirap (Caring for the Poor) poverty reduction program aimed to reduce the number of poor Filipinos from 24 million in 1997 to 17 million by 2004. However, after the first year of its implementation, the nonpoor received the bulk of the benefits of this program due to an ineffective beneficiary selection mechanism. According to the respondents these programs require a major overhaul or termination. The report card findings are being used by the government in revising the Philippines Medium Term Development Plan, crafting the new poverty-reduction strategy. By publicly articulating dissatisfaction, the report cards put pressure on service providers and the government. Steps are underway to address some of the constraints identified by the report card respondents.

Finally, consider the Kecamatan Development Project, a community-based project initiated by the government of Indonesia to reduce rural poverty.[3] The project is large, covering more than 30 percent of the country's rural *kecamatans*. (A kecamatan, or council, is an administrative unit made up of multiple villages.) A distinctive feature of the project is its highly decentralized nature. A significant portion of project funds are assigned to the kecamatan level and then allocated by communities. Villagers exercise full control over their development decisions, from identifying their needs (through discussions in public meetings) to implementing projects.

All transactions are carried out in public, and information is disseminated through notice boards, posters, and radio programs. The project also emphasizes gender equality and encourages women to participate in planning and decision making. Stern visited several kecamatans in 2000 and found remarkable local commitment to projects. Community members decide on projects together and maintain them well. And they include poor people in their actions—for example, helping a group with leprosy to start a viable brickworks and providing finance for home-based textile workers to replace exorbitant loans from buyers who had a considerable degree of local monopsony.

The first phase of the project, which was completed in 2002, financed roads, bridges, water supply systems, and school repairs in more than 21,000 villages in about 1,000 kecamatans throughout Indonesia. The project has been very successful in enhancing the participation of villagers, and Indonesia's Department of Home Affairs is implementing the second phase. The project is not without problems, however. In some areas high corruption has been reported in relation to the release of funds and procurement of materials. Some project funds are used to finance loans, which can be a powerful tool for empowerment, but in some regions repayment rates are as low as 50 to 60 percent. Thus, the project's financial sustainability is an issue, as is the support structure for procurement and financial management.

Making Empowerment Happen: Entrepreneurship, Leadership, and Participation

The above examples emerged in different ways. The use of report cards started in Bangalore, India, on the initiative of Samuel Paul (see Paul 2002). SEWA grew from small beginnings on the initiative of local individuals, notably Ela Bhatt, a labor organizer and a lawyer. And the Kecamatan Development Project started in the era of Soeharto as a top-down program but adopted a more transparent and participatory approach after the 1997 economic and political crisis. Thus, initiatives can arise through individuals, groups, or government.

How did the individuals and groups in these diverse environments develop the capacity to aspire to something different—and what made them effective? As these examples show, and as Appadurai (2004) makes clear, developing this capacity is closely linked to developing the voice of those who are poor and marginalized. Voice encompasses many crucial aspects of participation, such as the capacity to debate, contest, and critique. Entrenched social, political, and cultural inequalities often prevent poor people from availing themselves of economic opportunities. Thus, a key element in empowerment is public action that fosters social, political, and legal institutions to protect citizens (and their rights) and that provides voice and representation to poor people in public decision making.

Public action to enforce laws, safeguard rights, and influence policies to ensure that they protect the interests of poor people ultimately requires channels of political participation that force—through transparency and other means—politicians and other decision makers to act accountably. The state is an overwhelmingly important actor affecting the lives of poor people. Central to the challenge of increasing empowerment is structuring the incentives of decision makers so that their actions are oriented toward the general interest and well-being of all citizens. A state where citizens are disempowered is one where state officials, acting on their own behalf or on behalf of elite interest groups, harass or exploit the powerless and deprived. For example, in South Asia some poor, low-caste groups suffer from crime and violence committed by the richer, higher-caste groups that control the local police.

Democratic elections do not guarantee that politicians' incentives are aligned with citizen interests. The large-scale theft of state assets, particularly natural resources, by Russian oligarchs in the early and mid-1990s was carried out under a democratic system, and much of the theft was probably legal under the ill-defined legal structures in place at the time. More generally, elections can be manipulated and voters bought. The difficulty of coordinating multiple voters with different ideologies and interests creates opportunities for political rent seeking, waste, and capture by powerful interest groups.

Among democratic societies different types of political institutions have significantly different effects on policies. (Persson and Tabellini 2002; Milesi-Ferretti, Perotti, and Rostagno 2002; Besley and Case 2003) Political institutions affect welfare outcomes through their impact on both earned income and on taxes and transfers. For example, majority rule (first-past-the-post electoral formulas) often generates "unearned majorities" of parliamentary seats out of minority electoral support; collective bargaining frameworks affect the results of wage negotiations; property laws affect the assignment of responsibility for accidental losses; rules governing university admissions determine the class composition of the student body (Przeworski 1991). Conversely, countries without multiparty elections may have other institutions for collective action and accountability that ensure poor citizens have access to basic services and opportunities. Village committees in China, for example, exercise watchdog functions that limit corruption and promote transparency. Elections mandated by the Chinese National People's Congress in 1998 have resulted in positive changes in the village power structure. He (2003) reports that before these elections, it was the village branch of the Chinese Communist Party that held the most decision-making power, followed by the village committee (headed by the village chief), and the village representative assembly. But fieldwork carried out since 1998 has revealed a power shift:

The rise of elections for the village chief ... has allowed that individual to gain greater legitimacy.... [T]here is now a tacit acknowledgement of the growing power of village chiefs vis-à-vis that of the party secretary. Some elected village officials have also gained control of the use of the official village seals. Thus, the party branch is no longer the most important decision-maker in the village. A new power structure is emerging, in which the VRA [village representative assembly] is at the top, with the village chief and village party secretary as co-equals (He 2003, p. 2).

Several countries with traditional structures of inequality and deprivation have initiated political reforms to provide a voice for poor and disadvantaged people. India's 1993 Panchayati Raj Act created electorally accountable institutions of village governance, with seats reserved for women and members of disadvantaged groups. Chattopadhyay and Duflo (2004) evaluate the impact of such reservations through a survey of villages in the state of West Bengal. They find that in villages with women as heads of government, there is greater female participation in policymaking and greater provision of public goods preferred by women. Pande (2003) also finds that political reservations benefit disadvantaged groups, increasing spending on welfare programs targeted to them.

What determines participation in local governance? And how do people organize themselves for the common good? Some social science research has started on these questions, but more is needed. Further systematic household surveys measuring participation and its potential determinants would be useful. Poor people and disadvantaged groups may be stuck in a vicious circle: they have low income, suffer from poor education and health, and are socially excluded—all of which obstructs their participation in collective institutions that could ensure them access to basic services and opportunities. How can this circle be broken?

Evidence suggests that the path to increasing participation is sometimes circuitous. Lanjouw and Ravallion (1999), using 1993–1994 data from rural India, estimate the marginal odds that individuals from different income groups will participate in school and antipoverty programs. Their results suggest that most of the benefits of these programs are captured by the nonpoor, at least early on, when services are not widespread in their coverage. Evidence from Bolivia and Paraguay yields similar results, but suggests that as government expands access to services such as primary education, the marginal benefits begin to go more to poor groups (Ajwad and Wodon 2002). And over the past fifty years of democratic elections in India, poor people's participation in the political process has expanded significantly. Voter turnout in rural areas recently surpassed urban, and traditionally repressed communities have mobilized to influence state policies in their favor.

Chapter 5 provides several examples of public action that has achieved remarkable, sustainable improvements in human development. One (mentioned in chapters 3 and 5) is the public health program launched in the late 1980s by the newly elected leader of Ceará, a state in northeastern Brazil (Tendler 1997, World Bank 2003a). This initiative recruited and trained local health care workers who then worked in their own villages, rather than trying to convince trained people from cities to relocate to the countryside. One measure of the program's effectiveness is that between the late 1980s and 2001, infant mortality in the state fell from around 100 to 25 per 1,000 live births.

Research Challenges in Empowerment

In this Brazilian case, as well as the Ugandan schools example cited in chapter 5, the commitment of specific leaders catalyzed community action and produced remarkable results. These examples are highly instructive and point to the types of helpful action on information, organization, and accountability that we have identified. But as policy researchers, we cannot rely solely on a collection of individual achievements such as these. The research challenge is to build a body of systematic analysis of the kind illustrated here, identify key drivers of change in empowerment, and ask how they can be put into practice on a major scale. We want to identify methods and institutions that inform citizens and spur collective action to provide disadvantaged people with access to basic services and opportunities to shape their lives. Besley and Burgess (2001), on the role of independent and accessible media, is an example of analysis generalized to the state or country level. The authors find that in India, state government spending on food and disaster relief was significantly more responsive to citizen needs in states with wider circulation of newspapers, particularly in vernacular languages (see chapter 5).

The service delivery surveys of providers and government agencies and the household surveys on inclusion and participation discussed in chapter 6 provide data for analyzing behavior and obstacles to investing in poor people's capacities. As noted, dissemination of research results can empower communities with information that encourages them to take public action. The research agenda should answer such questions as:

• What kinds of institutional changes improve accountability in and provision of basic services?

• What kinds of incentives make service providers perform effectively?

• Under what conditions do public-private partnerships work well?

• What kinds of interventions change individual and social demand for better opportunities for all?

• How can government institutions act in a way that facilitates, encourages, and responds to social action, as opposed to simply imposing desired patterns and mechanisms from the top?

Many countries and governments are experimenting with innovative policies to bring about change. Research efforts include rigorous evaluations of these policy experiments to develop a better understanding of what works and to document and disseminate results (see chapter 6). Documentation and dissemination can reinforce better service delivery by preventing good policies from being overturned by vested interests or arbitrary government action and by allowing bad ones to be redesigned.

On the theoretical front, we need to better understand what shapes the social and political structures that arise in environments of extreme deprivation, how they determine outcomes, and how they can be changed. Modern theories of organization and incentives are helpful in identifying which modes of service provision work better than others. Our understanding of these issues has been greatly advanced by the *World Development Report 2004* (World Bank 2003a), but more research is required. The success of innovative interventions is highly sensitive to political and social institutions and can also be affected by the ethnic and cultural diversity and economic inequality that characterize many low-income countries. There are many lessons to be learned from developing societies that are undertaking bold experiments to transform their conditions and enhance the involvement of poor people.

One route to understanding these lessons is to combine the different types of surveys—household, investment climate, and service delivery—to understand the dynamics of change that can occur in even the most depressed communities. The first type of survey allows us to identify outcomes, the second the environment for entrepreneurship and opportunity, and the third the workings of investment in poor people and the mechanisms for their participation. If the survey design in each case takes into account the broader challenge of enhancing empowerment, we will likely make real advances in understanding the dynamics of empowerment.

Small and Medium-Size Enterprises as Paths out of Poverty

In examining the dynamics of change for poor people, we have placed special emphasis on the role of SMEs. Such enterprises are important determinants of empowerment in terms of the actions available to poor people. They comprise the vast majority of firms and provide most of the employment in developing countries (see table 1.2). This section emphasizes opportunities associated with off-farm SMEs.

For many rural households, off-farm SMEs provide the first route out of poverty. In rural areas, off-farm SME employment can play a vital role in income growth and stability (Lanjouw and Lanjouw 2001). In China, for example, the development of township and village enterprises fueled remarkable poverty reduction as rural labor shifted toward the nonfarm economy. And in India, although off-farm employment has played a smaller role in poverty reduction, about a third of rural households' income comes from nonfarm sources—much of it from micro, small, and medium-size firms. A similar fraction applies to incomes in the village of Palanpur, where data collected by Nicholas Stern and his collaborators go back to 1957 (Lanjouw and Stern 1998). Household incomes in the village come from a variety of sectors, including commerce, manufacturing, and services, and from regular and part-time wage employment as well as self-employment. Rural households value nonfarm income highly not only because it contributes significantly to overall income, but also because it can make households less vulnerable to the potentially devastating income fluctuations associated with bad harvests. Moreover, greater income security increases a household's willingness to innovate—whether by educating children, migrating in search of urban employment, or investing in agricultural improvements.

Any analysis of the dynamics of poverty reduction must pay special attention to rural development. Despite rapid urbanization, three-quarters of the poor people in developing countries are in rural areas. Most poor people in developing countries will remain rural and dependent on agriculture until at least 2035, even though a majority of the population will be urban by 2020 (International Fund for Agricultural Development 2001). Thus, despite the importance of off-farm SMEs in moving out of poverty, it would be a serious mistake to see empowering and investing in people only in terms of off-farm employment.

Within rural areas, poor people are more dependent on agricultural income than is the rest of the population. In India agriculture is the principal occupation for 82 percent of the poorest fifth of the rural population, compared with 65 percent of the richest fifth (Lanjouw and Shariff 2000). Most very poor countries are highly dependent on agriculture for household income; in Ethiopia and Malawi, for example, about three-quarters of household income is derived from agricultural activities. And across countries, most agricultural activity is organized in small farms.

Moreover, growth rates for agricultural and nonagricultural activities tend to be correlated. There is a strong complementarity between the two sectors in poor countries, because rising income leads to rising food consumption (though at a lower rate, since income elasticity is less than one). The correlation coefficient between growth rates in agriculture and nonagriculture in low-income countries was 0.169 for 1961 through 2001, but it was much higher in the latter half of the period: 0.299 for 1981 through 2001.[4] Thus it would be misleading to see a "competition" between agriculture and nonagriculture in terms of opportunities for poor people.

The role of different types of income varies across income groups, and the differences provide insights into channels for empowerment through work. Averaging across all income groups, nonfarm income in rural India contributed 34 percent of household income in 1993–1994, compared with 55 percent from cultivation and 8 percent from agricultural wage labor. The breakdown between nonfarm and farm income is fairly steady across income groups (table 8.1), but within those aggregates lie some important differences. Most important is the declining share of agricultural wage labor income as incomes rise: it contributes about a quarter of income for the poorest groups but is insignificant for the richest. (The incidence of nonagricultural employment is nearly twice as high for the richest quintile as for the poorest.) A similar pattern occurs in casual nonfarm wage income, which accounts for 15 to 16 percent of income for the poorest two quintiles but only 2 percent for the top quintile. Finally, nonfarm self-

Table 8.1
Nonfarm income shares in rural India

Quintile	Culti- vation	Agricul- ture wage labor	Non- farm labor	Non- farm self- employ- ment	Non- farm regular employ- ment	Total non- farm sources	Other sources	Real per capita income
Lowest	38.2	28.2	15.8	11.4	4.4	31.6	2.0	1,146
Q2	38.0	21.3	14.7	16.8	7.0	38.5	2.3	2,113
Q3	45.2	13.4	10.1	16.3	11.7	38.1	3.2	3,141
Q4	50.1	7.5	6.1	14.6	18.6	39.3	3.2	4,712
Highest	64.5	2.1	2.0	7.9	21.1	30.9	2.5	11,226
Total	54.9	8.0	5.9	11.5	17.1	34.4	2.7	4,468

Note: Quintiles defined at the national level. Numbers represent All India income shares by (real) per capita income quintile except last column, in rupees. Q2 represents the second quintile.
Source: Lanjouw and Shariff (2000). Data are from NCAER 1993/4 survey

employment income shares are highest for the middle three quintiles (around 15 to 17 percent) and lowest for the top quintile (Lanjouw and Shariff 2000).

What does all this imply for fighting poverty? It suggests a need to pay close attention to determinants of the real agricultural wage and to ways in which poor people can gain access to and equip themselves to earn various kinds of nonfarm income, including regular wage income. The real agricultural wage depends on farm and nonfarm investment, entrepreneurship, and growth, as well as demographics and investment in education. Poor people's access to nonfarm labor markets is an important research area for the dynamics of empowerment.

Off-farm employment is so important, especially as households begin to climb out of poverty, that it is worth exploring SMEs as a source of employment for poor people in greater detail, using India as an example. Data on the distribution of employment by firm size and consumption quintile strongly support the key role of SMEs (including farms). First, in rural areas most nonagricultural employment occurs in firms with five or fewer employees. Only a small percentage of the population works in firms with twenty or more employees, and the richest quintile is three times as likely as the poorest to be employed in such firms. The broad picture is similar in urban areas, with an even more pronounced underrepresentation of poor people in large firms. Second, in both rural and urban areas, rich people are vastly overrepresented in public employment and poor people vastly underrepresented. Small, private, often informal firms are the main sources of employment opportunities for poor people.

Beyond simply providing income for poor people, SMEs also help manage the risk of falling into poverty. Off-farm employment, largely in SMEs, enables diversification of household income. The distribution of nonagricultural employment by size of enterprise and income distribution in India is given in table 8.2. It shows that the heads of households in the bottom quintiles of the distribution work mostly in small enterprises. And SMEs are more flexible, in that they are able to substitute factors of production more efficiently than can bigger firms (Acs and Audretsch 1991). Thus, smaller firms are better able to cope with volatility and adjust to economic shocks. During recessions, job destruction is lower in SMEs than in larger firms (Davis and Haltiwanger 1999). Entrepreneurship is often a key coping mechanism for poor people (see, for example, de Soto 1989), so firm formation rates are often higher during recessions (Biggs 2002).

Table 8.2
Distribution of nonagricultural employment by enterprise size (number of workers) and distribution of income in India

Quintile	1 to 5	6 to 9	10 to 20	20+	Not known	Total
Rural						
Bottom	61.2	8.0	4.6	4.9	21.3	100
2	64.6	6.9	3.8	4.8	20.0	100
3	62.6	6.5	4.3	6.6	20.1	100
4	61.1	7.9	5.6	7.8	17.6	100
Top	53.4	6.6	6.9	15.5	17.5	100
Rural total	59.8	7.1	5.3	8.9	19.0	100
Urban						
Bottom	66.2	7.6	4.0	6.3	16.0	100
2	63.5	7.9	4.8	9.8	14.0	100
3	57.2	7.2	5.2	14.9	15.5	100
4	49.5	7.7	7.3	19.6	16.0	100
Top	35.9	7.3	8.5	31.3	17.1	100
Urban total	53.3	7.5	6.1	17.3	15.8	100

Source: India National Sample Survey, 55th round (1999).

There is also emerging household-level evidence that entrepreneurship is key to poor people's income mobility. Poor people involved in individual entrepreneurial activity are more likely to move up in rankings of income distribution in the United States (Holtz-Eakin, Rosen, and Weathers 2000). In Indonesia, South Africa, Spain, and Venezuela, the private sector is the primary source of employment for those who escape poverty—and most of the private sector is composed of SMEs (Fields and Pfefferman 2003). In Vietnam, too, households that operate nonfarm enterprises are more likely to make advances in living standards (Vijverberg and Haughton 2002).

This finding has been confirmed by poor people across the developing world: the 60,000 in sixty countries surveyed by World Bank researchers (see chapter 1) reported that entrepreneurial activity is the single greatest factor in moving out of poverty (Narayan and others 2000). Similar evidence on the private sector's importance for employment growth and economic mobility has been documented in Costa Rica and Taiwan (Fields and Bagg 2003). We must not forget that in many developing countries, family farms and private agricultural firms account for the largest share of employment. After the Chinese government let rural families make their own economic farming decisions, the world witnessed the most massive exit from poverty in human history. More recently, Vietnam has enjoyed similar benefits from allowing farm-level entrepreneurship to flourish.

Direct measures of economic performance may not capture some important externalities generated by SMEs. In particular, SMEs are likely to be an important source of innovation and ideas—the foundations for learning, change, and long-term growth. Creativity in firms is a visible example for other firms—an experiment that they can observe—so that 100 firms with 10 employees may create more externalities from learning by watching than 10 firms with 100 employees. Large firms may have fewer incentives for innovation because ownership and control are more likely to be separated, and thus principal-agent conflicts are more pronounced. Large firms may also suffer from the inertia of bureaucracy, which stifles efforts to innovate.

Individuals and small firms, in contrast, have the flexibility to rapidly seize opportunities and adapt to changes in their environment. With fewer free riders, workers in small firms are more likely to receive the full returns from their innovations. There is evidence that in developed countries, innovation rates are higher in small firms, especially in high-technology, skill-intensive industries (Acs and Audretsch 1987). But innovation is not just about new technology or large-scale investment in research and development; it also includes new processes. In many developing countries innovation through adaptation of ideas and processes has driven development, and much of this diffusion takes place through small firms.

Finally, the benefits of growth in SMEs extend beyond the provision of economic opportunities. Small firms give a breadth and depth to public voice, and thus can support the development of democratic processes over the long term. These firms provide a large fraction of the population with an ownership stake in society and can generate forces in favor of sound economic and political governance. So SMEs can be dynamic agents of change in an economy, putting pressure on larger firms and governments for innovations in institutions and processes.

To summarize, SMEs are a bridge between innovation and inclusion, between the investment climate and empowerment. They bridge the two pillars of our development strategy (and thus chapter 7 and this chapter). They account for a significant share of employment and GDP in developing countries and are a foundation for growth. Employment through SMEs provides a way out of poverty for many poor house-

holds. By creating these jobs, SMEs do much to empower those households, and they are a dynamic source of learning, ideas, and other
externalities for developing countries.

What research program emerges from these conclusions? Controversies about small-scale enterprises are still raging, partly because the evidence is fragmentary but also because we do not understand well the
dynamic stories involving SMEs. Not enough is known about where
poor people work and the links between poverty and enterprise size.
Our claim is that the dynamic stories that explain how SMEs can provide a path out of poverty are complex socioeconomic stories, involving household strategies of survival and mobility that contribute to
their empowerment. We are not claiming that SMEs are important for
developing economies because they increase output (and productivity)
and provide jobs; that they do, but so do large enterprises. What we
claim—and what requires more research—is that they may make a
disproportionately large contribution to poverty reduction and are
sources of innovations and ideas. Further, understanding how poor
people can get involved in employment and entrepreneurship in SMEs
is a key research challenge involving the dynamics of empowerment.

In this section we have shown the importance of SME policy and research for paths out of poverty. We have said less about the barriers
that poor people face in founding or gaining employment in SMEs.
Understanding these barriers is also key to the research agenda. One
part of the story is likely to be discrimination; another part the skills
and assets that poor people bring to the labor market; and a third part
the way that public and legal institutions work. For example, as has
rightly been emphasized by de Soto (2000), if poor people have clear
title to their assets, they are far more able to take risks and involve
themselves in entrepreneurship and the labor market.

Redistribution

Our analysis of the barriers to empowerment is based on three elements: external constraints, internal constraints, and lack of assets.
This section addresses the third of these, focusing on the role of redistribution in empowerment. Attempts at asset redistribution must take
into account several factors: the political forces that will resist redistribution, the administrative capacity of the state to carry it out fairly
and honestly, and fiscal constraints on the state. Some aspects of the
first issue are examined in chapter 10, and of the second and third in

chapter 12. Here we concentrate on the design and effectiveness of redistributive public policies that facilitate poor people's empowerment and participation. We shall look at these policies not simply or principally from the perspective of rebalancing existing distributions but from the perspective of their effects on the dynamic processes of growth and inclusion.

Redistributive public policy can facilitate moves out of poverty using various transfer mechanisms, typically financed by taxation. These include simple monetary transfers, transfers linked to performance (food-for-work programs, for instance) or human development (sometimes called smart transfers, described below), transfers of wealth (such as transfers of secure rights), land reform, and transfers of human capital (through education). Often policies involve a mix of income and wealth transfer. Wealth transfer policies that focus on the social function of the assets (such as secure property rights or child nutrition or health) tend to have stronger dynamic effects.

A growing body of research systematically evaluates redistributive programs. Examples include Banerjee, Gertler, and Ghatak (2002) on tenancy reform in West Bengal, Carvalho (2001) on Brazil's pension program, Case and Deaton (1998) and Duflo (2003) on South Africa's pension program, and Field (2002) on land rights in Peru.[5] This literature has identified a number of programs that have had very positive effects. Dynamic redistribution is possible, notwithstanding occasional pessimistic claims about its political and administrative infeasibility. But a lot can go wrong. We have a rich research agenda ahead of us, trying to understand which policies work and why.

In general, policies that redistribute income from the rich to the poor—and thus contribute to a decline in inequality—do not mechanically lead to a virtuous circle of progressively faster growth and accelerated poverty reduction. In fact, one effect of income transfers is the opposite: by reducing incentives to work, it dampens growth. It is almost impossible to make lump-sum redistributive income or asset transfers in a credible way. Transfer recipients who would otherwise work to earn higher incomes or accumulate wealth will recognize (and may be deterred by) the higher tax burdens that come with doing so. Thus, such transfers, by lowering the expected return from acquiring physical or human capital, may reduce effort, asset accumulation, and growth.

Some theoretical arguments suggest that these disincentive effects are less costly when redistribution is focused on wealth rather than current income. This may occur, for example, because of the positive collateral effects of wealth: greater assets for poor people may help bypass credit market imperfections that inhibit productive investment (Bourguignon 2003b). But in many cases the political economy of redistributing property is such that it is possible only under unusual circumstances, such as after a war or independence—as in the land reforms in China, Japan, and Taiwan—or at the cost of political violence. Such special circumstances can hardly be considered economic policy options.

Increasingly, therefore, we are seeing examples of land reform that eschew forced reallocation. Instead these reforms are generally based on subsidized transactions in the land market. Typically, land is bought from large landowners at what is considered to be the market price. It is then sold to landless peasants or smallholders through some kind of subsidized credit scheme. The operation falls somewhere between a wealth and an income transfer. Taxes, which are levied on the whole population, finance the credit subsidy, which contributes to asset accumulation among poor peasants. For details, see the conclusions of World Bank (2003j). That report emphasizes that we have an imperfect understanding of the welfare benefits from land access through market transactions, the obstacles faced in the process, and the possible long-term impact of such access, and that this is an important area for future research. Land reform is a central aspect of the dynamics of empowerment for poor people in developing countries.

The example given shows, as Bourguignon (2003b) points out, that the theoretical arguments indicating that wealth redistribution may have lower efficiency costs need to be qualified when we recognize how wealth distribution is to be financed. We clearly have to take into account any disincentive effects associated with raising the tax revenue from current resources needed to provide the finance. And there are some arguments against wealth transfers: income transfers may provide for better nutrition (Duflo 2003) and thus enhance human capital accumulation among poor people.

Thus, while the form and organization of transfers are very important, we should be careful not to overemphasize the distinction between transfers of assets and transfers of income. In many market economies insurance markets are highly limited. By providing some insurance in volatile environments, targeted income transfers affect very positively the assets owned by poor people. At the economy-wide level they can protect and enhance asset accumulation and asset holding by poor people. For example, they can reduce the long-term damage of short-term fluctuations associated with taking children out of school. And they can help poor, credit-constrained people become more productive workers or take up productive opportunities for self-employment (see Ravallion 2003c) by mitigating the risks associated with this kind of innovation in their personal and family lives.

So-called smart transfers, such as those under the Progresa program in Mexico and the Bolsa Escola program in Brazil, are essentially means-tested income transfers with a built-in conditionality. Benefits are conditional on children under a certain age attending school and visiting a medical center twice a year. In effect, these programs are pure income transfers for households that would have sent their children to school and the doctor anyhow. Yet for other households, they contribute to human capital accumulation—provided the supply of education and health services matches the induced increase in demand.

Evaluations have shown that these programs were effective in raising school enrollments and health outcomes in targeted populations. The Progresa program, initiated in 1997 and now known as Oportunidades, had strong effects that helped it survive a change in political regime (Schultz 2000, Gertler 2000, Skoufias and Parker 2001). Bourguignon, Ferreira, and Leite (2003) discuss Bolsa Escola, which has also been successful. (On smart transfers in general, see World Bank 2003a.)

These examples show that appropriately designed and implemented redistributive policies can have powerful dynamic effects on future poverty and on asset and income distributions. They not only modify the distribution of physical and human capital in the economy now, they also create future growth opportunities for the poorest segments of society and enhance their ability to take advantage of them.[6] Research on redistribution has usually not used the language of the dynamics of empowerment. But this perspective adds value to this fruitful line of research and can help shape future research. To understand paths out of poverty, we have to focus not only on the growth of opportunity but also on external constraints on seizing opportunity, internal constraints on aspirations and behavior, and physical and human assets that limit poor people's ability to participate. Understanding and overcoming these barriers is the essence of the dynamics of empowerment.

9

The Dynamics of Preferences

The past few decades have seen extraordinary changes in the lives and livelihoods of people in the developing world.[1] There has been a huge expansion in education in developing countries. Billions of people have moved from rural to urban areas, changing their ways of life and occupations. Many women have become educated, chosen to have smaller families than their mothers did, and asserted their rights and those of their daughters. The list goes on and on. Such changes have been a major theme in these lectures, and their importance has shaped the approach and strategy that we have adopted. We expect many of these trends to continue—and indeed, should encourage some of them as part of the development process—and new types of changes to emerge.

It seems highly plausible that these shifts involve not only dramatic changes in people's economic and social circumstances, but also powerful changes in their preferences. In a process more often studied by anthropologists, sociologists, and psychologists than by economists, preferences form as a result of personal histories of economic and social experiences and interactions. Family, community, and schooling are crucial elements in the shaping of preferences. When development coincides with dramatic changes in those histories, communities, and schools, as well as in family size and structure, the standard economic assumption of constant preferences appears increasingly untenable.

The discussion of empowerment in chapters 3 and 5 emphasizes that it can be seen as a combination of three elements: assets, both human and physical; external constraints resulting from family, society, institutions, and so on; and internal constraints, including those associated with a perceived role in family or society and the capacity to aspire. Thus, changing preferences are an important part of the study of changing empowerment. In this sense this chapter should be seen together with chapter 8.

If changing preferences are an inherently important part of development processes, we should try to understand how those changes occur and how they should be treated in policy analyses. This subject takes us beyond standard microeconomic theory and standard theories of public economics, as indicated in chapter 4. In those theories preferences are taken as given, and the theory of policy is constructed on the assumption that an individual is better off if he or she consumes a bundle of goods and services ranked higher in the given preference ordering. If preferences change, then that key foundation of the theory of policy is removed. Milton Friedman (1976, p. 13) expresses the standard neoclassical view succinctly: "The economist has little to say about the formation of wants; this is the province of the psychologist. The economist's task is to trace the consequences of any given set of wants. The legitimacy of and justification for this abstraction must rest ultimately ... on the light that is shed and the power to predict that is yielded by the abstraction."

There is no intention here to discard that kind of theory. It has been enormously fruitful for analyzing competition, efficiency, taxation, and trade—indeed, much of the subject matter of normative economics. What we are suggesting is that we sometimes need to go beyond this theory in development policy. We will see clear examples from the areas of education and gender, both of which are central to the ideas of effective participation or empowerment.

The subject of changing preferences poses major conceptual challenges in understanding behavior and adapting theories of policy. What people actually do—their behavior—depends on their preferences, but also on their circumstances and constraints. Here we will not cover the latter, since expansion of opportunity sets is covered in detail elsewhere in these lectures, most notably in chapter 8. Instead we focus on investigating changes in behavior that stem from changes in preferences.

As with many of the cases analyzed in this book, there are two ways of looking at choice and behavior. One is to retain the formal idea of preference orderings and see individual welfare as being shaped by those orderings, so that an individual is better off if an outcome is ranked higher in the ordering. The analytics then concern how preferences change and how such changes should be treated in rankings. An alternative approach focuses less on orderings and more on an individual's opportunities, freedoms, capabilities, aspirations, and attitudes without insisting on any formalization of preference orderings. This provides a more ex ante approach. It is less formalistic in appraising changes in the welfare of individuals but does allow discussion of standard of living changes when aspirations, attitudes, and capacities change. When we talk about the dynamics of preferences, we include both approaches. The use of the phrase *dynamics of behavior* has its attraction but might be interpreted simply as the study of price or asset changes, which is not our main concern here.[2]

The analysis of this chapter, like the others in lecture III, does not try to make major inroads into what is conceptually and technically a difficult subject. Instead it underscores the importance of changing preferences and indicates some directions for research. In the first section we use examples to illustrate how preferences change and establish the importance of changing preferences in development. We also raise the problem of distinguishing between changing preferences and changing information.

In the second section we examine the challenge of forming individual and social rankings oː welfare when preferences are changing. We also argue that in making these assessments, we are not obliged to proceed through the route of preferences; we can also base assessments on the degree to which choice or opportunity has been expanded.

In the third section we discuss policy in a way that is based on that argument. We briefly consider some issues of (fairly) standard theory concerning information and merit goods. We examine paternalism— where the state takes the view that it should override certain preferences or that it knows better than an individual what is good for her or his welfare. We also point to approaches based on individual rights and liberties, such as those of Berlin (1977), Nozick (1974), and Sen (1999). Finally, in the fourth section we emphasize the importance of processes and institutions in helping to bring about social decisions in the context of changing preferences.

Why Do Changes in Preferences Matter for Development?

Given the description of the sources of preferences, it is clear that preference change may result from shifting economic conditions and experiences. It can also result from other forces causing sociocultural transitions: group-based action, as with social movements; changes in power and the ideology of leaders, which might be reflected in education programs or in laws that enshrine or prohibit discrimination; and exposure to new ideas and experiences. Before we turn to some examples from development, two general points should be emphasized.

First, the causal relationship between economic conditions and preferences flows both ways. On the one hand, the former can clearly affect the latter. For example, the availability of irrigation may lead farmers to start thinking of possibilities over a much longer term than they had previously envisaged, and these thought processes could lead, in the language of preferences, to a change in their rate of pure time preference. Elijah Anderson's (1992) famous study of the racially mixed neighborhoods of western Philadelphia gives the example of how the disappearance of some types of manual work—combined with the rise of opportunities for making money by selling drugs—contributed to the erosion of traditional structures of family authority in black communities in the United States. At the same time, causality clearly holds the other way: changes in preferences affect economic outcomes through the choices that individuals and households make. The advertising industry recognizes this link very well; indeed, without it, the industry would exist solely to provide information.

Second, preferences may partly reflect highly unequal socioeconomic conditions. For example, inequalities in opportunities along race and gender lines can become enshrined in preferences. Thus, the initial set of preferences may reflect an underlying equilibrium between power and economic conditions, on the one hand, and dispositions, practices, and behaviors, on the other.

A few examples may help clarify the assertion that dynamic and endogenous preferences are central to many development issues. We draw on examples from five areas: industrialization and urbanization, education and gender, work and gender, race, and political leadership. There is, of course, a literature in economics on these issues, some of which we will indicate with a few references. But there is a much bigger literature outside economics—in management, anthropology, sociology, law, philosophy, and psychology, for example—and while we draw on some of it, our references will be very partial and do not reflect any attempt at balanced coverage.

Why Preference Change Matters: Five Examples

Consider briefly the first example, industrialization and urbanization. The economic historian Richard Tawney made the issue of endogenous preferences central in his remarkable book *Land and Labor in China*

(1966 [1932]) written after visiting China in 1930: "The movement to industrialization is a growing force. Where it directly affects, for better or worse, the livelihood of one, it indirectly modifies the habits of ten. Its effect on the mind ... is ultimately more important than its visible embodiment in mills and mines" (p. 17). Tawney is referring to what French historians call a shift in *mentalité*—the mind-set through which an individual views the world and his or her place in it. The change from a predominantly agrarian society to an industrialized, urbanized one is so great that it would be surprising if it did not involve major changes in preferences. Many of these, such as preferences for education or attitudes toward time, seem likely to be self-reinforcing in this context, as the changes may result in economic gains for those who adapt their preferences most rapidly.

A second example concerns the education of girls. In many societies, particularly in South Asia, the school attendance of girls is much lower than that of boys. This is changing, largely as a result of active policy promoted by governments, nongovernmental organizations (NGOs), and the international community. In Bangladesh girls' share of primary enrollment rose from 37 percent in 1980 to 49 percent in 2000; at the secondary level the gains were even more impressive, from 24 percent to 50 percent. India and Pakistan have also seen gains, albeit much slower ones.

How should we understand these phenomena: the low levels of educational participation by girls (relative to boys) in the past, the changes over time, and the priority of girls' education among national and international development objectives? We might try to explain the first two using standard economic approaches. Opportunities for women in the workforce, once very limited in many countries, are now expanding, giving parents a greater incentive to educate girls. In addition, parents may be getting better information about the returns to education. There may be some mileage in these arguments, but they lead to other questions: Why have work opportunities for women changed (we return to this in a moment)? Was information on the returns to education so inadequate in the past?

Many noneconomists would take a different tack, arguing that the reluctance to educate girls stems from particular views, or preferences, that men and women hold about women's role in society. Such views would usually be culturally determined, and they can change over time even in the absence of changing economic conditions or new information. Indeed, many NGOs are devoted to changing those views. The Bangladesh Rural Advancement Committee (BRAC) is a strong example of an organization that has been working very hard, particularly in rural areas, to enhance girls' enrollments, but there are many more across the developing and developed world. The rapid increase in girls' education in Bangladesh suggests that such views can and do change as a result of interaction with others.

Das Gupta and others (2004) show that governments can also affect preferences over women's roles. The authors conducted a comparative analysis of gender roles and women's empowerment in China, India, and the Republic of Korea over the past half-century. All three countries entered the period with similar patterns of familial authority, where women (particularly young women) had little autonomy. By the end of the century, state or other activity to promote gender equity in China, and to a lesser extent India, had achieved considerable progress. By contrast, the authors argue that the Korean government took actions that slowed the pace of change in gender equity relative to what might have been expected given the country's rapid economic and social change in other dimensions. Although some of these changes in gender equity undoubtedly reflect changes in laws and enforcement, the authors conclude that government's effects on the preferences of the governed are important: "These case studies illustrate the subtle ways in which states influence the manifestation of cultural beliefs and values" (p. 258).

A government or NGO that tries to persuade parents to send their daughters to school will use information on the opportunities that education can open. It will point out the economic and social returns to education, explaining that when the average educated girl reaches adulthood, she will be healthier, have healthier offspring, and earn a higher income as a result of that education. But an important part of the argument is to persuade the parents—often particularly the father—to think differently about the kind of life they want their daughters to lead. Do they want to equip them for a less subservient role in the family and society? Do they want to expose them to the broader horizons that education can offer? The approaches adopted with some success by governments and NGOs, focusing on the role of women, strongly suggest that they believe changing preferences to be an important part of this effort, beyond simply providing information on rates of return. We return to the challenges for policy in the next section of this chapter.

Beyond gender roles, education systems can have powerful effects on preferences. Schools and teachers inevitably transmit values to students, and parents and students make decisions about education in the knowledge—or hope—that preferences will change. The values transmitted by schools may be explicitly religious, or they may be secular values connected with notions of nationhood and citizenship. Indeed, Pritchett (2002b) argues that traditional economic justifications for public delivery of education do not stand up to scrutiny and that the transmission of values must provide the rationale for government control of school systems.

Any assessment of the effects of the transmission of values through schooling is inevitably normative. Public schooling can result in behavior and codes that help build strong, creative societies—for example, by fostering trust, building a sense of common purpose that bridges social groups, and promoting civic involvement. Conversely, schooling can transmit more damaging values and preferences, as under the regimes of Joseph Stalin in the Soviet Union, Adolf Hitler in Germany, the Khmer Rouge in Cambodia, and more recently the Taliban in Afghanistan, all of which placed great emphasis on the education system in shaping young people's values.

A third example of preference change concerns the role of women in the workforce. Views on this subject can be changed dramatically by experience, often in fairly short periods. Strong examples from the United Kingdom reflect the effects of mobilization during wartime. In both World Wars I and II the United Kingdom saw a strong increase in women's involvement in the formal workforce. This increase changed society's perception of women's employment, resulting in permanently higher formal employment of women.[3]

A fourth example concerns race relations. Other social scientists have examined these issues more extensively than have economists, though there is also a considerable literature in economics, most notably Gary Becker's *The Economics of Discrimination* (1957) and Glenn Loury's *The Anatomy of Racial Inequality* (2002). The anthropologist Arjun Appadurai's view is of particular interest to the analysis developed here. He argues that the capacity to aspire, to see a different role for oneself with wider opportunities and scope for action, is culturally produced and embedded in group-based social processes, where the relationships between groups play a powerful role (Appadurai 2004). He writes of the importance of "terms of recognition"—the ways that the dominant group (or groups) recognizes (or stigmatizes) the less dominant. The language and concepts he uses and the evidence he offers clearly involve endogenous preferences:

The poor are frequently in a position where they are encouraged to subscribe to norms whose social effect is to further diminish their dignity, exacerbate their inequality, and deepen their lack of access to material goods and services. In the Indian case, these norms take a variety of forms: some have to do with fate, luck and rebirth; others have to do with the glorification of asceticism and material deprivation; yet others connect social deference to deference to divinity; yet others reduce major metaphysical assumptions to simple and rigid rules of etiquette which promise freedom from reprisal. (p. 66)

Appadurai himself applies these concepts in the context of class- and caste-based differences in Mumbai (formerly Bombay), India.

There are differences between how economists view culture and how anthropologists and sociologists view it. To the extent that economists consider culture at all, they tend to view it as an exogenous factor—either a source of observed preferences or a set of constraints on behavior, as opposed to an endogenous part of the process of social, economic, and political change. Social theorists, by contrast, do not make such a severe distinction between preferences and constraints. Some suggest that preferences are often the constraint. Culturally produced beliefs, dispositions, and behaviors can lead to what Rao and Walton (2004) call "constraining preferences." They cite the example of the Hindu caste system, which creates preferences that "may create an acceptance of hierarchy and constrain the motivation for mobility, but those beliefs are also simultaneously external constraints; individuals from lower castes who engage in any form of class struggle may face severe social sanctions" (p. 15). Rao and Walton continue with a discussion of the broader dynamics underlying this type of culture- and preference-based constraints. They draw on the sociologist Pierre Bourdieu's (1990) conception of cultural capital, which extends the idea of (physical, human, and social) capital to all forms of culturally derived power:

Cultural, social, and symbolic resources can be drawn on by individuals and groups in order to maintain and enhance their position in the social order. As in the case of physical capital, these are valued resources and often become objects of struggle.... Once cultural capital is embodied and institutionalized, it can be accessed by others within the group. It can also be used as a form of domination. Bourdieu calls this use of capital "symbolic violence," where dominant groups have the capacity to "impose the means of comprehending and adapting to the social world by representing economic and political power in disguised, taken-for-granted forms" (Swartz 2000, 89).

The example of the Hindu caste system reflects this.[4]

Within the domain of economics, too, some researchers have discussed the importance of preferences and beliefs in reinforcing power structures. Loury offers a detailed quantitative analysis of racial inequality in *The Anatomy of Racial Inequality* (2002). He concludes that one can understand the persistence of development disadvantage only in terms of historically produced and structural stigma. Drawing on analysis of street culture in black society by the sociologist Elijah Anderson (1992), he also discusses ways in which the stigma assigned by more privileged groups can influence the behavior of the less privileged. And as Becker points out in his discussion of preferences, "the *beliefs* of employers, teachers, and other influential groups that minority members are less productive *can* be self-fulfilling, for these beliefs may cause minorities to underinvest in education, training, and work skills" (Becker 1996, p. 142). This underinvestment, he argues, does make them unproductive.[5]

Fifth, behavior can change in response to examples set by leaders. Many would argue that individual behavior in Russia deteriorated in the 1990s in part because of the example set by well-connected interests as they looted state assets. Similarly, when Indira Gandhi financed election campaigns in the 1970s with funds obtained through corruption, she probably contributed to the erosion of ethical standards in Indian public life. Both developments made predatory behavior more respectable.

Leadership by example can also play a positive role. In some cases good policy depends on changing preferences, and leadership is fundamental in spurring such changes. The leadership of Mahatma Gandhi and his commitment to nonviolence had a powerful effect on shaping India's struggle for independence. The leadership of Nelson Mandela profoundly shaped attitudes toward reconciliation in the transition to the new South Africa. In Uganda the leadership of President Yoweri Museveni in the campaign against HIV/AIDS has been central to changing sexual behavior. He has spoken forcefully about the epidemic and championed the ABC message: "Abstain, Be Faithful, or Use a Condom." That leadership has been vital to Uganda's strong progress in the fight against HIV/AIDS, with its prevalence dropping from 19 percent in 1995 to 8 percent in 1999.[6]

The Empirical Challenge: Identifying Preference Changes

The examples from the five broad areas just presented share two characteristics: changing preferences are central to the story described, and the issues are central to development. In most, if not all, we will face a challenge of identification—of distinguishing the effects of changes in *information* available to an individual from the effects of changes in his or her underlying *preferences*. In some cases the distinction will not matter much for policy. If we are trying to persuade South Asian parents to send their daughters to school, we may be justified in using both the evidence that education improves job opportunities and the health of future offspring and the argument that parents might want to change their view of the appropriate role for their daughters in society. In this case we may not need to know which argument is more persuasive.

But in other cases disentangling the information versus preferences issue may be more important. If communication is of the essence and publicized messages need to be simple, then the choice of message will partly depend on an assessment of whether the problem is one of information or underlying preferences. For example, antismoking campaigns in the United States have recognized that it is not enough to provide teens with information about the dangers of smoking.[7] Thus, they have also tried to change young people's images of smokers by portraying them as dupes of scheming tobacco companies. Antismoking campaigns in the United Kingdom have emphasized that the smell of smokers' hair and clothing is very unattractive. Indeed, one U.K. government campaign advertisement closed with the words, "It is like kissing an old ashtray."

In another example, a study of contraception in rural Bangladesh by Munshi and Myaux (2003) concludes that "contraceptive prevalence changes slowly and there is wide variation in long-run levels of contraception across villages" (abstract) because "individual behavior is often socially regulated in a traditional economy" (p. 47). Information about contraception is necessary but insufficient; individuals change their behavior only slowly as they resolve their uncertainty about the new social equilibrium that their religious community will reach. Indeed, BRAC, the Bangladeshi NGO, has successfully focused on changing preferences as a means of increasing contraceptive use through portrayals of different kinds of family life in families of different sizes. Policy toward gender or racial discrimination may be an issue where changing preferences is central. In such cases we will likely want to analyze the role of education in values and restriction of certain behaviors as policy tools.

Empirically it will be a challenge to solve the technical question of identifying information versus preferences in most real-world cases. One problem is that the change being contemplated may be so radical for the individual or family that they find it hard to envision the results. Thus, they may be able to identify their preferences only after experiencing the changed environment. One might argue that this is learning about preferences from experience rather than changing them, and some relevant literature takes this approach (for an early example, see von Weizsacker 1971). But we suspect that this is a distinction of limited importance, and we are happy to include this type of learning under the heading of endogenous preferences.

To distinguish changing information from changing preferences, one would like to find data where, for example, apparently similar groups in terms of information showed very different changes in behavior. The school attendance rates of children in different states of India might be one example, though there would be a number of variables to adjust for, including the functioning of schools. The formal structure of econometric models of household supply and demand does include a random term; that term is often interpreted as differences in tastes, just as production functions include a residual that is often interpreted as technical change. But in both cases this is really an interpretation or labeling of the random term, and it does not resolve the identification problem. Thus, this remains a fascinating problem for further research.

How Do We Assess Well-Being When Preferences Change?

If preference change is an important part of the development story, how does it affect the way we assess different situations or development approaches? Such assessments will generally be an integral part of any policy analysis or recommendation. To reach policy conclusions, we will usually have to judge one state of affairs (including paths over time) as being superior or inferior to another. That judgment will, in turn, often be based on an assessment of how individuals or groups are faring in terms of some notion of well-being in the two states.

Let us begin with the problem of assessing how an individual is faring. If an individual's preferences may change over time, perhaps as a result of some endogenous action or event, then welfare assessment becomes very challenging. In assessing a woman's well-being, do we—and should she—use the preferences that she has now? Or do we use the preferences that she will hold in the future? Or some combination of the two?

There are, broadly speaking, two approaches to resolving this conundrum. In the first we try to struggle with different ways of making comparisons, while retaining the idea of preference orderings. In the second we cut the Gordian knot by abandoning preferences entirely and working instead with notions of choice, capabilities (à la Sen), or opportunity. The first approach lies more in the standard neoclassical, efficiency-oriented public economics tradition, while the latter we might think of as being closer to an Austrian school approach, with its focus on processes. As elsewhere in the book, both have useful perspectives to contribute. Where preference change is important, however, the Austrian approach may have more to offer (see Kirzner 1987). Nevertheless, we begin here by maintaining the neoclassical view of preferences and seeing how far it gets us.

Within the neoclassical framework, one approach, which Becker takes, is to advocate using a grand (or meta-) utility function (Becker 1996). This would entail using all the relevant explanatory variables (including, in principle, the entire history and current position of humankind) to determine the current preference ordering of an individual over all possibilities now and in the future.

There are a number of problems with this approach. Assume that in thinking about current and future choices, the individual is aware of how experience, argument, and interaction could shape her or his preferences over time, or at least had some notion of a reduced form defined over variables of choice. That might appear to be an impossibly strong assumption, but even then the resulting intertemporal utility function over the variables to be chosen by an individual would not be likely to have the usual properties (such as revealed preference and concavity) with respect to the subset of variables being chosen. Moreover, this approach would pose complex problems of dynamic consistency, because experience and interactions modify judgment. More fundamental, there would be extraordinary difficulties in identifying such a meta-utility function in a useful way. In essence this approach generalizes a representation until it includes virtually everything, and thus has lost its theoretical bite and practical usefulness. It is the proverbial map that not only fails to fit in the glove compartment, but is as large as the territory it covers.

Of greater interest, if we are to follow the preference route, is to be more specific in our theorizing and try to model in simple frameworks some of the key drivers and parameters of change. One approach might be to put experience into the utility function. Becker and Stigler (1977), for example, posit preferences over fundamental goods whose expression will depend on the relative price of the specific good, which will affect the individual's experience of that type of good. (This is summarized in Rao and Walton 2004.) For example, if a consumer has a fundamental preference for music and the relative price of production of a certain type of music (say, Indian classical music) falls, it becomes cheaper to learn about and consume. This is closely related to the literature on habit formation.

Within such frameworks, assessments of individual rankings could then take into account, for example, whether an individual would rank a particular bundle of goods higher with respect to preference orderings both before and after change. Becker (1996) takes this route, arguing that the difficulty of evaluating welfare when preferences change is not intrinsic, but rather due to inadequate incorporation of the endogeneity into welfare criteria. Becker's view is that "if the relevant utility function for welfare analysis includes personal and social capital, the effect on utility of advertising and public policies can be evaluated without ambiguity." Regardless of whether this is true in principle, in practice it will likely be impossible to identify the social and personal capital variables (personal experience, past consumption, culture, social history) needed to remove ambiguity. In such cases, the most one would expect is a partial ordering.

There is no denying that we are on shaky ground as soon as we move away from fixed preferences, which have long been the Archimedean point that gave economics its normative leverage. If preferences are taken as changeable, what is the foundation for our policy advice? If development involves changing preferences, should development agencies be in the business of trying to change preferences? We return to this question below; here we suggest another approach.

We do have an alternative to working with preferences. We can instead use the notion of opportunity, capability, or freedom, an approach that echoes both Sen and the Austrian school. Sen (1999) outlines a view of development as freedom—the expansion of the capability to shape one's life. This shift to a capabilities and process point of view reflects the shift from the neoclassical to the Austrian view of the market. The neoclassical view yields the result that a competitive equilibrium is Pareto optimal, where the latter notion is defined in terms of given utilities or preferences (that is, a state of affairs where no one can be made better off in terms of their preferences without making some-one else worse off).

The Austrian school (for example, Hayek 1984) emphasized the mar-ket as a process of exercising mutually compatible freedoms, not the end state of Pareto optimality. Such an approach would, for example, lead to a rejection of an authoritarian mechanism even if, in theory, authoritarianism would achieve Pareto optimality. Sen would endorse this view (see his Arrow lectures in Sen 2002), and he notes that even the neoclassical results about the market can be reformulated "in terms of individual freedoms, rather than utilities." With "a cogent charac-terization of individual freedoms, a competitive market equilibrium guarantees that no one's freedom can be increased any further while maintaining the freedom of everyone else" (Sen 1999, p. 117). If we embraced this alternative approach, we would have a basis for giv-ing policy advice about development in terms of expanding freedom, even though we know that preferences, attitudes, and aspirations will change as part of that process.

Under an approach based on freedom, therefore, welfare analysis of a policy requires an assessment of whether it will expand the range of opportunities of an individual or his or her freedom to act. The objec-tive would be to identify policies that expand freedom for many peo-ple. In this approach too, there is likely to be great ambiguity about whether opportunities or freedoms for an individual are wider under one state of affairs than another.[8] And since we are considering free-dom to choose a life one values, assessments of an expansion of free-dom will be related to an understanding of what is valued. Change in what is valued, as in changing gender roles, is in large measure the issue under discussion.

Nevertheless, we can at least begin to discuss what kinds of vari-ables we would use to assess such freedoms. Measuring opportunity is inherently difficult: we observe individuals' choices but rarely their choice sets. As Sen (1999) notes about capabilities, to measure op-portunity or freedom we typically need to rely on instruments and proxies, including achievements. Some of the indicators used to mea-sure vulnerability and the effectiveness of public institutions, discussed in chapter 6, may prove useful here.

The issue of assessing well-being when preferences change is a com-plex one, but we cannot afford to shrink from it. To make decisions on policy, we will need to adopt some form of assessment, however crude or implicit. We now turn to that issue.

How Should We Approach Policy toward Changing Preferences?

In parallel to the two approaches to assessing individual welfare, with and without the construct of preferences, we can think of forming policy with and without preferences. We consider these approaches in turn. This takes us, particularly in looking at the second, inevitably into a discussion of political philosophy. We shall not go very far down that road but simply draw attention to some of the issues.

When we consider policy in the context of changing preferences, we face the question of which, if any, of the relevant preferences of the individual should guide social decision making. Putting the question in this way can lead us quickly into paternalism, in the sense that we adopt the position that we favor one of the individual's possible preference sets over another in social decision making. This issue arises, for example, when the state or some other entity makes membership in a pension plan compulsory. In that case the state is acting in support (in this case by imposing compulsion) of what it considers the "higher self"—the one that concerns itself with the individual's well-being in retirement. In doing so it contravenes the wishes of the "lower self," which might take a shortsighted approach at the moment but regret it later. Making education compulsory until a given age, say sixteen or eighteen, also carries aspects of paternalism.

As suggested by the term *paternalist*, this approach arises most naturally in these and similar questions of "youthful" versus "mature" decision making. Economists often talk of merit goods in this context, meaning that an individual may not realize the value that he or she will derive from one good—or, conversely, the damage that will be done by another (such as tobacco). Some part of the argument on pensions has to do with moral hazard, in the sense that those who do not save rely on the state to bail them out. But as usually expressed, that is only part, and often a small part, of the story of compulsion.

One can also, and more controversially, invoke the paternalist argument to override certain practices on the grounds that they come from preferences that *should* be changed, as with female circumcision. Of course, a society can ban or override certain behaviors because it considers them morally wrong, whether or not those bans are explained using the language of preferences. Cockfighting, apparently a "sport" attractive to some, is banned in the United Kingdom, presumably on the grounds of immorality (though externality to those who might be disturbed by the idea is probably part of the story too). One example where both the moralistic position and endogenous preferences come in is addictive drugs, a case where there is already a literature addressing preference change. But regardless of what position society takes, we are left with the challenge of justifying the overriding of one set of preferences on the basis of another.

The alternative approach speaks more in terms of freedoms than preferences. In this case we would recognize that the difficulties in choosing among an individual's preferences are probably insurmountable, so we drop altogether the idea of utility maximization over a set of preferences. We have noted Sen's views on expanding freedoms. Nozick (1974) takes a strong position along these lines. He argues that certain individual rights and liberties are inviolable and thus dominate others, which to him implies the state's role should be a minimal one. Thus, not only would Nozick abandon utility maximization for the preservation of freedoms, his formulation would also make many policy choices easy. No weighing of the consequences of different actions would be necessary because steps that violate those freedoms would simply be off-limits. As the example of cockfighting illustrates, however, we would still have to cope with questions about the acceptability of exercising different kinds of freedom.

In his landmark lecture, "Two Concepts of Liberty," Isaiah Berlin (1977) argues forcefully for pluralism and warns against adopting a simple formulation or final solution to the problems of making social decisions or organizing for justice or liberty. Berlin's perspective provides a warning that abandoning the language of preferences does not by itself resolve problems of decision making. The problem of weighting preferences has a parallel in the freedoms approach.

This is not the place to take these philosophical discussions very far. Our purpose here has been to highlight the difficulties that endogenous preferences cause for social decision making and to emphasize that we have to face them directly. In our view it is better to recognize their central role in development and development policy and make our treatment of this issue explicit and subject to open discussion.

Changing Preferences and Social Processes for Social Decisions

An approach to action in the context of changing ideas and preferences alluded to in the previous section focuses not so much on policies or outcomes, but on processes for making decisions. (This approach is similar to that in the *World Development Report 2003*, on sustainable development; see World Bank 2002d.) An example from Morocco illustrates this theme.

The village of Ait Iktel in the High Atlas Mountains, about sixty miles from Marrakech, had a per capita income of less than a $1 a day, much of which came from remittances from those who had left to find work elsewhere. After several years of drought, two men from the village who had good employment in Fez and Casablanca returned to help organize the construction of a well. That collective action was successful, and it began a process of building trust and cooperation (social capital) that proved useful in addressing other problems. The two men who had returned to the village were able to serve as "cultural translators," enabling the villagers to develop enough trust to try new possibilities and ideas that were not imposed from the outside.

This emerging collaborative approach was embodied in a local development association, Ait Iktel du Développement, under the traditional authority structure of a village assembly. The association organized worker remittances for a variety of community development projects. After improving an access road, buying an ambulance, and providing electricity through a local generator and solar panels, the assembly agreed to build a school for girls. By the second year, attendance had risen to 90 percent and a second school was built. After graduation some girls received scholarships from a national NGO committed to rural girls' education, allowing them to continue on to higher education (World Bank 2002d).

In this case, success bred success, with knowledge, preferences, and the spirit of collaboration changing along the way—and resulting in a radical change of attitudes and aspirations in the community. Instead of receiving the new road, ambulance, electricity, and schools as gifts from the outside, the villagers used the process of acquiring these improvements to build a new organization, new ways of behaving, and new capacity to solve other problems. A national foundation has been established to scale up this experience in other villages.

A second example comes from anti-AIDS efforts in Sonagachi, a huge red-light district in Kolkata (formerly Calcutta) that is the workplace for more than 4,000 sex workers. Rao and Walton (2004) describe how a shift in approach in the early 1990s played a pivotal role in containing the spread of HIV (the virus that leads to AIDS). Until then social workers had concentrated on trying to get women to leave the sex industry. But their efforts were hampered by the stigma that followed

former sex workers and by the women's reluctance to give up relatively high earnings.

So, in 1992 the All India Institute for Public Health and Hygiene
adopted a new strategy. It focused first on gaining an understanding
of, and establishing rapport with, the sex workers. After laying a foundation of trust, the institute launched an education campaign, but with
a twist: instead of sending out health professionals, it trained a small
group of sex workers to educate their coworkers. When providing this
peer education, the trained workers wore green medical coats that "not
only distinguished them from other sex workers, it also gave them a
sense of self-worth and a 'respectable' identity." Rao and Walton describe the effects:

> Educating the sex workers and mobilizing them for the HIV-AIDS interven-
> tion, along with the media attention that success brought Sonagachi, led to a
> cultural transformation for the sex workers. Their vision of themselves
> changed, and they organized an effective union.... They routinely organized
> public events ... which contributed to the process of mobilization, the removal
> of stigma, and changes in identity and aspiration.... The program has been
> remarkably successful as a health intervention, with almost all sex workers us-
> ing condoms at least some of the time. As a result, HIV incidence in Sonagachi
> was about 6 percent in 1999 compared to 50 percent in other red-light areas
> (including Mumbai's) that have not pursued such a culturally attuned ap-
> proach. (p. 8)

The idea of building mutual trust in a society working together on
specific problems is relevant and important with or without changing preferences. Nevertheless, the acts of discussing and working
together can have preference change at their core. Such examples
suggest that we can approach the challenge of changing preferences
for social decision making by taking a broader approach based on
an examination of the processes for such decision making. This
approach focuses strongly on effective participation and thus is very
much in the spirit of empowerment—the source of our discussion of
changing preferences.

These perspectives connect to an older tradition. Many social
thinkers—among them Alexis de Tocqueville, John Stuart Mill, and
John Dewey—have emphasized that active social problem solving
writ large provides a social philosophy for democracy known as government by discussion (also called "deliberative democracy").[9] Government by discussion is generally government that makes decisions
as a result of interactions where preferences are formed and changed.

Although he does not use this language, Mill (1972 [1861], p. 262) comes close:

As between one form of popular government and another, the advantage in this respect lies with that which most widely diffuses the exercise of public functions ... by opening to all classes of private citizens, so far as is consistent with other equally important objects, the widest participation in the details of judicial and administrative business; as by jury trial, admission to municipal offices, and above all by the utmost possible publicity and liberty of discussion, whereby not merely a few individuals in succession, but the whole public, are made, to a certain extent, participants in the government, and sharers in the instruction and mental exercise derivable from it.

The active social processes wherein people form and re-form their preferences are not just a fact that researchers should recognize; they are at the core of empowerment and democratic activities. Social decision making should be seen not simply as the application of a certain aggregation rule for given preferences, but as a social process where the views and values of others come to be appreciated, where inchoate preferences are clarified, and where trust and norms of cooperation are built along the way so that collective action problems can be tackled. "More important—in theory and in practice—is the idea that the central concern of politics should be the *transformation of preferences* rather than their aggregation. On this view the core of the political process is the public and rational discussion about the common good, not the isolated act of voting according to private preferences" (Elster 1984 [1979], p. 35). This is not a field that economists should leave to other disciplines: it is at the heart of the story of economic development.

Indeed, the market itself is an important arena for this social process. The neoclassical notion of the market is rather thin gruel: individuals bring their "given" preferences along with their goods for exchange, but do not discuss common social problems or soften the edges of individual self-interest,[10] much less modify their preferences (as noted in Piore 1995). Game theory, social choice theory, and the new institutional economics (see Furubotn and Richter 1998) transfer the fixed-preference economic model of the marketplace to broader social and political settings. That leads, for example, to the idea of engineering the right contracts and incentives to generate a semblance of "calculated trust" through repeated prisoners' dilemma games. The idea from repeated games—that action to build reputation is a winning strategy—is useful but is a rather narrow slice of development story.

The alternative approach involves social processes in which the parties actively transform themselves through discussions and joint undertakings to construct cooperative solutions to collective action problems—as in the Moroccan village example.[11] These processes often require participants to remake or at least adjust their identities. A worldview defined by self and other may require redefinition, so that someone who was previously other becomes a tentative part of a broader group with which one more closely identifies. "The rules of [this approach] transform what contractarians see as a chain of exchanges or an infinitely repeated game into a continuous discussion of joint possibilities and goals, where the parties' historical relation defines their mutual expectations. . . . Just as in a discussion, they must accept the possibility that their views of themselves, of the world, and the interests arising from both—their identities, in short—will be changed unexpectedly by those explorations" (Sabel 1994, pp. 247–248).

Similar shortcomings in the conventional approach emerge in the treatment of organizations. The idea of redefining identity through social processes is starting to enter into economics (see, for example, Akerlof and Kranton 2002), but it has long been a topic in management theory. One person who bridged the gap between economics and management theory was Herbert Simon, who noted the problems that the new institutional economics confronts when dealing with organizational motivators such as identification with the firm. "The attempts of the new institutional economics to explain organizational behavior solely in terms of agency, asymmetric information, transaction costs, opportunism, and other concepts drawn from neo-classical economics ignore key organizational mechanisms like authority, identification, and coordination, and hence are seriously incomplete" (Simon 1991, p. 42). Simon goes on to identify pride in work and organizational identification as some of the most important motivators. Neither is controlled by the purse strings of managers, but both are endogenous to social processes ("government by discussion") within the firm.[12]

Trying to analyze and tackle the problems of policy in the context of changing preferences in this way is not about trying to engineer preferences. Instead, it is about social processes that empower people to actively participate, so that along the way they will transform their own identities, preferences, and beliefs. In this way social science can acknowledge and assess processes that have the effect of changing preferences and beliefs—but can avoid social engineering of preferences and beliefs.

Under this approach, to paraphrase the old joke, public action would not take the form of a social decision maker saying: "Hello, I'm from the World Bank [or some other agency, domestic or international] and I'm here to change your preferences." Public policy would instead aim to support opportunities and institutions where people interact and act together to reach decisions.

This orientation toward processes of social decision making has helped guide donor (including World Bank) support for developing countries in recent years. The Poverty Reduction Strategy Paper approach, which aims to provide a framework for coordinated donor support of a country, is supposed to be founded on "broad-based participation by civil society and the private sector in all operational steps."[13] This requirement could be viewed as merely an attempt to ensure that information is shared across sectors of society. But we think that it aims at something deeper: giving people a chance to work together to forge social decisions. This goes beyond mere aggregation of preferences. To contrast two metaphors, the goal is not to make a stew in which various preferences are mixed, but to forge an alloy superior to its constituent preferences.

The idea of preference discovery and change through social decision making risks sounding utopian, and it is important that we not be naive about social decision-making processes in unequal societies. If people come together with all the preferences, dispositions, and practices born of entrenched inequality, social processes for decision making may merely reinforce the status quo. In effect, we will be aggregating preferences with highly unequal preference weighting. Rao and Walton (2004) argue that a prerequisite for this idea to work is what they call "equality of agency," which means that "in addition to providing equal access to human and physical capital, people are also entitled to equal access to, using Bourdieu's terms, cultural and social capital. But because cultural and social capital are inherently relational concepts, these require group-based interventions ... that are different from the more individual-based interventions that derive from the equality of opportunity perspective" (pp. 29–30).

To participate effectively, previously excluded groups may have to be encouraged, and provided with the opportunity, to develop the "capacity to aspire," to return to Appadurai's term. Such intervention may involve external pressure on authorities uncomfortable with the idea of empowerment. The ethics of such an approach are not straightforward, and this challenge should not be downplayed. But neither should the difficulties of neoclassical policy choice under conditions of changing preferences.

In concluding this section, let us emphasize again that, as indicated by Isaiah Berlin, we will probably want to embrace a plurality of approaches in incorporating preference change into analysis and policy. In some cases we will want to overrule certain forms of preferences (for example, those of cockfight organizers or child molesters) rather than include them in social calculus. And in other areas, such as some details of tax policy, we will want to leave part of the design to those who understand modern public economics, incorporating as it does a preference approach. Our purpose in this section has been to draw the attention of economists and researchers to an additional, often fruitful approach to social decision making—one that clearly recognizes the importance of the social processes emphasized throughout this book.

Conclusion

Our focus on preference change suggests several directions for research. On the empirical front, we would like to better understand the dynamics of both avenues discussed in this chapter: preference change and freedoms (or capabilities) expansion. First, within economics we still know relatively little about when and how preferences change. The literature on behavioral economics has drawn on and advanced the empirical insights into preferences offered by experimental psychologists (see, for example, Kahneman and Tversky 2000). This is a welcome development, and there will likely be many further insights along the way.

Second, we need corresponding empirical research into poor people's understanding of freedom and empowerment. Just as the *World Development Report 2000/2001* used surveys to explore how poor people define poverty, including constraints on empowerment (World Bank 2001c, Narayan and others 2000), we may want to initiate a similar survey to research the dynamics of empowerment. How do people see these constraints changing over time, and which changes increase their freedoms the most?[14] How do people recognize changes in their preferences and aspirations—and how do they view them ex ante and ex post?

The ideas presented in this chapter also have implications for formal theory. First, there is the notion of endogenous preferences. Like the empirical work on preference change, this area has attracted increasing support in recent years with the rise of behavioral economics. Yet there is much room for further work here, especially in development, where, we have argued, the phenomenon is likely to be particularly important. Although we have highlighted the challenges of working with preferences when they are endogenous, some of these challenges might yield to better theory. Second, the social decision-making processes described are likely of great importance, and our understanding would benefit from more thorough theoretical analysis.

10   The Dynamics of Political Reform

The strategy proposed in lecture II is not feasible without political change. Improving the investment climate will usually require changing policies, institutions, behaviors, and economic relationships among firms and between firms and the state. Thus, it will almost inevitably result in confrontations with entrenched interests. Similarly, empowerment involves expanding choices and setting in motion a dynamic that gives many people more control over their lives—but often reduces the power of others. These processes of political change are rarely straightforward.

In this chapter we point to the political economy research that arises from the strategy. In the first section we examine the political economy of growth, looking in particular at the relationships between growth, political institutions, and income distribution. For example, we ask how political institutions develop in response to patterns of income distribution and how they influence—and are influenced by—future growth and income distribution. The analysis concentrates on investment climate issues, but it also raises issues of participation in growth, and thus of the strategy's second pillar.

The second section focuses on empowerment and participation. We discuss participation in terms of voting franchise and education, the political forces shaping their development over time, and feedback to the political process. We also examine exclusion, a strong form of disempowerment. Groups can be shut out of many forms of economic and social activity in many ways, including through exclusion from credit, housing, and employment markets. We also briefly look at groups likely to be excluded, such as women and certain castes, tribes, and nationalities. The chapter's third and final section, in the context of the preceding discussion, examines the difficulty of economic reform, particularly building constituencies for change. Thus, in this chapter we return to some of the political issues raised in chapters 3, 5, 7, and 8.

The emphasis throughout is on identifying important directions for research by citing examples and pointing to relevant existing work—but without pretending to be exhaustive. As with the other chapters in lecture III, we do not try to cover all possible avenues that flow from the book's strategy. Our main aim is to show that the strategy leads us into research in specific areas, and that such research could be extremely productive in shaping policy that contributes to inclusive economic growth.

The Political Economy of Growth

Growth patterns vary. Some growth episodes contribute to neither effective participation nor future growth. Others foster sustained growth but exclude many people. And still others generate sustained growth with participation of poor people. Research can help us understand the root of these different patterns and the obstacles that policy must overcome to achieve growth with widespread participation. In this investigation the two-way interactions between institutional development and patterns of growth—the endogeneity of institutions, if one wants to use this language—will be central.

Growth with large inequality today can lock in stagnation tomorrow. Initial winners can use their influence with or control of government to "kick away the ladder," limiting competition from other elements of society (Chang 2002).[1] Over the long term this strategy can strangle economic growth.

Incorporating into their work the insights of Ronald Coase, and Douglass North and other institutionalists, in the 1990s researchers like Daron Acemoğlu, Abhijit Banerjee, and Andrei Shleifer developed a framework for thinking about the political economy of growth (see, for example, Banerjee and Newman 1993; Shleifer and Vishny 1998; and Acemoğlu, Johnson, and Robinson 2001). Economic institutions that promote lasting and shared growth are those that encourage investment and protect the property rights of a broad cross-section of society while constraining the power of wealthy elites.

But other types of institutions can arise, particularly where there are rents from extractive industries or plantation crops. Institutions that concentrate political power in the hands of an elite—whether an absolute monarchy, corrupt tyrants, or big agricultural estates—and deny rights to the majority generally create adverse incentives and discourage investment in physical capital, human capital, and technology for both the elite and those excluded or oppressed. They foster restrictive practices and resource misallocations from the entrenched interests and prevent entry and investment by other productive agents, including poor people.

For an example of how endogenous institutional development can have long-term development consequences, compare North and South America in the nineteenth century (Acemoğlu, Johnson, and Robinson 2001; Engerman and Sokoloff 1997, 2002). Both continents had large tracts of land and raw materials and had been conquered and settled by Europeans. But better institutions—meaning those more conducive to growth and shared development—arose in the parts of the New World lacking a large population that could be taxed or coerced to work (Acemoğlu and others 2003). North America was populated by European settlers whose aim was long-term settlement. They built an investment climate that gave rise to many small and medium-size firms, creating a constituency for further improvements in the investment climate. (Lest we paint an overly rosy picture of this story, we should also note that these settlers nearly eliminated the Native American population, largely by force or subterfuge, and denied them the property rights they had practiced for centuries.)

In South America, by contrast, features of the political, economic, and physical landscape led to much greater inequality. Greater population density made predatory (as opposed to settling) strategies more profitable, and large amounts of natural resources promoted the theft of assets owned by indigenous populations by early settlers and encouraged extractive activities and corresponding institutions. This led to powerful vested interests that were able to capture states and restrict competition and innovation, hampering development. This scenario played out not only in South America but also in the plantation economies of the Caribbean, based as they were on slave labor.

Exploitive societies with rent-seeking institutions can prosper for a period of time. But when the world changes and new opportunities emerge—in terms of technologies, goods, and working methods— rent-seeking institutions can prove disastrous. In the nineteenth century, it was societies with more flexible, open institutions of private property and more broadly based governance that took advantage of opportunities to industrialize.[2]

Causality also flows in the other direction: growth modifies institutions as well as social relations, behaviors, and culture. Under some circumstances growth and development may give elites an incentive to facilitate the emergence of a middle class by providing education. This strategy allows them to reap the benefits of higher economic growth triggered by the accumulation of human capital—while mitigating the likelihood of expropriation when more democratic societies develop as a result.

Various hypotheses have been offered to explain how growth-induced institutional change occurs. One is through preferences, with changing patterns of demand as income rises, particularly the demand for services. On the production side the division of labor changes with the size of the market. And on the political front people become more active as their stake in the economy and society rises (see Gradstein and Justman 2002), changing the distribution of political power and the evolution of institutions. Thus, the process of economic and social stratification cannot be separated, in a historical perspective, from the process of political transition to greater participation.

Justman and Gradstein (1999) make the link between the concentration of the political elite (or its opposite, democratization) and economic development. Growth reduces the power of the elite. In static and poor societies the fight for power is largely over a cake of fixed size, and the machinery of government is likely to be controlled by a narrow elite. If voting exists, participation may be limited to a few rich people; the ruling elite is part of a small group that exploits its political power to appropriate output. If dynamic forces arise in the early phase of development, a rise in income may be accompanied by increased inequality as elites control the gains. But when growth starts to affect a greater proportion of society and is driven by broader sections of society, political participation becomes broader, and the political elite is recruited from a wider social spectrum. Government policies may become more progressive, leading to a decline in inequality.

Justman and Gradstein's model, emphasizing political participation and redistribution, offers one explanation of why inequality first increased (when growth was low in the first part of the nineteenth century) and then decreased (in the late nineteenth and early twentieth centuries) in England and other European countries. During the nineteenth century most Western societies underwent major political reforms. Britain, for example, was transformed from an oligarchy to a more participatory democracy as the right to vote was extended in

1832 and again in 1867 and 1884. The decades after these political reforms witnessed radical social reforms, unprecedented redistribution programs, increased taxation, and extension of education to the masses. Acemoğlu and Robinson (2000) argue that these political reforms should not be viewed simply as the result of power struggles or changing political philosophies. They were also strategic choices by the political elite, aimed at preventing widespread social unrest and revolution.

Political transition from oligarchy to democracy (as opposed to redistribution under existing political institutions) occurs because without it, the elite cannot commit to future redistribution—that is, current transfers do not ensure future transfers. By contrast, the extension of the right to vote changes future political equilibria and acts as a commitment to redistribution. Acemoğlu and Robinson's theory offers one possible explanation of the Kuznets curve that some Western economies experienced during this period, when democratization and redistribution were followed by a fall in inequality.[3] Still, the United Kingdom did not give women political franchise until 1919, and it took their involvement in the workforce in World Wars I and II to accelerate their participation in employment and society.

Political participation depends on education and income levels and is thus endogenous to the growth process. This hypothesis has been proposed by, among others, Huntington and Nelson (1976) and has been subjected to intensive testing in political sociology. It was recently reformulated by Bourguignon and Verdier (2000a). Massive investment in poor people's education, when it expands education access and quality, is one of the few tools that both accelerates growth and improves the income distribution. This strategy has been recommended repeatedly in the development literature of the past thirty years, from the well-known *Redistribution with Growth* (Chenery and others 1974) to the World Bank's influential 1990 and 2000/2001 *World Development Reports* on poverty.

Although an important (if not entirely conclusive) literature has developed on how education contributes to growth, relatively little is known about how it affects income distribution. Bourguignon, Fournier, and Gurgand (2001), using data from household surveys, studied the relationship between the expansion of education and the distribution of income in Taiwan between 1979 and 1994. Their framework decomposes changes in the distribution of individual income and earnings into those arising from sociodemographic changes (especially in education), changes in labor force participation and occupational choices, and changes in the structure of earnings resulting from the supply of and demand for various types of workers. They find that an increase in returns to education in Taiwan, which occurred despite dramatic growth in the supply of educated workers, contributed to higher inequality by widening the gap between the more and less educated. But this effect was offset by three other factors: a change in participation behavior that increased the weight of middle-income earners; the expansion of education, which made the distribution of schooling and earnings more equal; and a drop in the variance of unobserved determinants of individual earnings. Overall, these trends significantly reduced income inequality in Taiwan.

Fixed education costs and liquidity constraints prevent poor people from becoming educated unless public subsidies are allocated to invest in their human capital. The political elite control these subsidies and thus have some control over how fast the economy grows, how the income distribution evolves, and how the structure of political power changes. That control implies a fundamental trade-off for the elite. Do they choose widespread education, which spurs growth and leads to higher returns to their assets (physical and human capital)? Or do they forgo faster growth for fear of losing political power and having their assets expropriated?

Verdier (2000) points out that these mechanisms—political rights and education—are also relevant in other redistributive contexts, such as land reform. The political economy arguments developed here are, in fact, valid for any economic reform or policy that increases the economic payoff to the incumbent elite, for instance, by spurring growth, while also reducing its political power by enabling new segments of society to engage politically.

Economic research on the dynamics of economic and political change is in its early stages and tends to be rather general in its analysis. We should sharpen the range of questions. For example, why do inefficient institutions persist for so long? From an empirical point of view, we would benefit from research that integrates political institutions, income distribution, and growth into more detailed analyses of the workings of particular societies. What we may learn is that the relationship between democracy, economic growth, and income inequality is more complex than can be unearthed by simple cross-sectional regressions using large samples of countries, with the growth rate as the variable to be explored. The loose, often ambiguous reduced forms in these regressions may be strongly misleading, and the variables measures used are not suited to the subtle mechanisms at work.

Anthropologists, on the other hand, tend to be careful and often more creative in understanding the relationship between economic and political change and social change. For example, Bailey (1957) examined how caste relationships are affected by economic change in eastern India, and Epstein (1973) explored the role of new infrastructure (here irrigation) in changing societal relationships in southern India. Their work was based on intensive study of specific villages. In Palanpur, another village in northern India, studies by Stern and collaborators (see Bliss and Stern 1978, Lanjouw and Stern 1998) show how the rising status of the Murao caste, through more effective investment in agriculture, was associated with rising political power in the village. Going forward, we need stronger emphasis on more microeconomic studies if we are to deepen our insights into how these mechanisms work.

The Political Economy of Exclusion and Inclusion

A number of political and cultural factors may inhibit poor people's participation in the growth process—or, on the contrary, may create economic opportunities for their inclusion in the process. Political rights, political participation (which depends on the education and income levels of the population), and mass education all promote inclusion. But there are also cultural factors that affect people's ability to take advantage of economic opportunities.

Constraints on participation in an economy or society sometimes take the form of excluding certain groups from employment, education, housing, credit, and voting. This section examines some of these mechanisms. Although we use the language of exclusion here, a similar dynamic is at work when a mechanism inhibits effective participation rather than preventing it altogether. Exclusion, after all, is only an extreme case of failure to participate. Exclusion generally arises from discrimination on the basis of certain criteria, most notably gender, caste, race, religion, and language.

We have already discussed some issues of discrimination, and their dynamics, in chapter 9, when we considered gender and race and how culturally produced beliefs and behaviors constrain preferences. Here we concentrate on economic mechanisms of exclusion and their consequences for growth and distribution, drawing on path-breaking research on growth and inequality published in the 1990s (we draw here on Bourguignon 1998, Ray 1998, Ferreira 1999). In examining these mechanisms we shall see that when inequality and exclusion arise, there may be powerful economic mechanisms that maintain them. This helps us to understand the magnitude and the nature of the political action that may be needed to overcome exclusion.

The core assumption underlying much of this research on growth and inequality is that fixed costs or investments are required to gain access to some productive activity. The cost or investment could be a school fee, the price of a viable plot of land in an agricultural community, or the permit to operate a stall in a market. One can find everywhere people who would be engaged in more productive activity if only they had the capital required to enter it.

Several models have described these mechanisms. They usually feature a missing or imperfect market—for example, a credit market where repayment is not costlessly enforceable, leading to a higher spread between lending and borrowing interest rates (Galor and Zeira 1993) or to collateral requirements (Banerjee and Newman 1993). In either case a group of people will fail to invest in productive activities despite being as able and entrepreneurial as anyone else. Members of that group limit their investment because they are (at best) trapped in a situation of low rates of return and high borrowing rates, or do not have enough wealth for the collateral. In this class of models poor people are prevented from choosing the most productive activity available given their skills. To the extent that credit is necessary to start a small business, educate oneself or one's children, or buy farming inputs, poor people are excluded from those activities.

These models illustrate the link between exclusion and growth. Fixed setup or entry costs and missing markets influence economic outcomes by affecting the ability to choose freely among occupations or investments, and thereby affect the evolution of inequality and output. In the model of Banerjee and Newman (1993), if some individuals in the subsistence sector could have become entrepreneurs, they would have generated profits for themselves and pulled more workers into the industrial sector.

Thus, initial inequality in wealth, by hindering access to credit markets, creates inefficiency in the economy as a whole. This inefficiency need not persist: if there is no exclusion, the "credit trap" will not continue into the long run and inefficiencies will be temporary. People will save, and their wealth will increase over time. Sooner or later they will see a loosening of credit constraints because they will have sufficient collateral to be entrepreneurs if they so desire (Ray 1998).

But if political, social, or cultural factors exacerbate the exclusion of poor people from economic opportunities, this inefficiency can become a permanent feature of the economy. Further, attempts to overcome these constraints by channeling credit to poor people can be taken over by political and social elites appropriating such credit for themselves. That happened in Palanpur in the 1970s and 1980s (Bliss and Stern 1978, Lanjouw and Stern 1998).

These types of models tell us nothing about how high inequality comes about in the first place, the topic of some of the political economy models discussed in the first section of this chapter. But they do suggest that high inequality and production inefficiencies may persist and become politically difficult to change. Multiple development paths are possible for otherwise identical economies, depending on initial inequality. This suggests that the market system lacks a self-correcting device for large initial inequalities, such as when access to credit is constrained by the need for adequate collateral. We may need to look to government (and the international community) to take an active role in promoting better-functioning credit and asset markets as well as providing for infrastructure, health, and education.[4]

Lack of insurance can be another source of persistent exclusion. By preventing people from reducing their vulnerability to shocks, a weak insurance market can cause inequality to persist and lead to inefficiencies. Several models describe this situation, usually assuming risk-averse agents who wish to hedge the risk of their projects by diversifying—that is, attracting participation by others in their venture and participating in other ventures. For a given degree of risk aversion there will generally be a minimum level of project participation that the agent must sell before he or she is willing to take on the project. If we assume that the disutility of effort supply increases with wealth and is not easily monitorable, then it is possible that to make a credible commitment to supply effort, those in the upper end of the income distribution would need to retain ownership of a share of the project that is too large to be acceptable, given their risk aversion.

In that case this rich group becomes a class of rentiers, lending their wealth rather than investing. Thus, the insurance market prevents a group—in this case the rich—from investing in the most productive activity (Banerjee and Newman 1991). Of course, we know from the large literature on asymmetric information that insurance markets can never be perfect. But part of the research and policy challenge is to understand their implications and workings so that policy can be designed to overcome their effects on exclusion and growth.

The models of Aghion and Bolton (1997) and Piketty (1997) also belong to this "moral hazard in effort supply" class. But in these models it is the credit market that is imperfect and poor people who are excluded from the desirable activity. Effort is not fully observable. Again, effort depends on the share of returns to the project that accrues to the enterprising agent rather than to the lender. Hence the lower the initial wealth of the borrower (and thus the larger the loan required to launch the project), the less likely he or she will be to supply the required effort. This leads lenders to establish a maximum loan size (or minimum initial wealth) for lending. Agents poorer than that minimum wealth level are excluded from borrowing and, hence, from the most profitable sector.

Other models of exclusionary mechanisms lead to the same basic result: in the presence of capital and insurance market failures, greater ex ante inequality leads to lower efficiency. Ferreira (1996) investigates the possibility that in such circumstances, government action can promote both efficiency and redistribution. In his model, while richer agents can substitute private capital for public, poor people face greater market barriers and are more dependent on state expenditures in services like health, education, public transport, and basic infrastructure. Thus, in his model public expenditures can both bring more poor people into the story and overcome distortions.

Bénabou (1996a) also shows how government intervention may improve efficiency and distribution in models with multiple equilibria. He combines capital market failures with a political economy setting to show that political-economic systems may display multiple equilibria. If taxation and spending have a positive net effect on efficiency, there may exist both a high-inequality, low-redistribution, low-efficiency equilibrium and a low-inequality, high-redistribution, high-efficiency equilibrium.

It should be clear from this brief discussion of theoretical work in inequality and growth that numerous economic mechanisms can block opportunities for excluded groups. These mechanisms reinforce political and cultural mechanisms of discrimination. While excluded people may view the constraints that they face as inevitable and internalize them, as discussed in chapter 9, they may also view the status quo as unjust. The lack of overt activism by subordinate groups does not necessarily reflect acceptance of the existing social order, as argued in Scott's (1985) study of the beliefs and behaviors of Malaysian peasants. It is important to distinguish between what excluded groups view as just and what they view as possible. A sense of injustice, coupled with a recognition of the inevitability of fate, can result in subtle, everyday forms of resistance that undermine the authority of dominant groups without completely overturning the system.

This discussion tells us that the economic mechanisms behind exclusion can be subtle. Thus, it is important that we think carefully about policies and political action intended to overcome exclusion. There is a lot more work to do, but there is a substantial base of analytical work on the functioning of economic exclusion on which to build.

The Political Economy of Reform: Building Constituencies for Change

We have argued throughout this book that institutional change is at the heart of the dynamics of development. The endogeneity of institutions, combined with differences in initial conditions, helps explain persistent cross-country differences in inequality, the investment climate, and growth. Where powerful interests are able to capture the state and restrict competition, they can prevent innovation and development. On the empowerment side, formal and informal institutional barriers can come together to cause social and economic exclusion. Empowerment is generally a positive-sum game in that it is likely to benefit all groups in society. But it can also be a zero-sum game. Empowering an individual or a group can sometimes mean disempowering someone else. Development depends on inducing change that lowers barriers and building an investment climate that encourages change.

Constituencies for and against Reform, from Machiavelli to Moscow

Change will invariably face opposition, and driving it through requires leadership, commitment, and skill. In *The Prince*, Niccolò Machiavelli (1940 [1513], chap. 6) expressed this point eloquently at the beginning of the sixteenth century:

It must be considered that there is nothing more difficult to carry out, nor more doubtful of success, nor more dangerous to handle, than to initiate a new order of things. For the reformer has enemies in all those who profit by the old order, and only lukewarm defenders in all those who would profit by the new order. Thus it arises that on every opportunity for attacking the reformer, his opponents do so with the zeal of partisans, the others only defend him half-heartedly, so that between them he runs great danger.

Machiavelli saw clearly the relationship between prospects for change, on the one hand, and constituencies for and against change, on the other. The success of any attempt to promote improvements in the two pillars of our development strategy—the investment climate and empowerment—will hinge on understanding these constituencies and their interests. The defense of vested interests, political and economic, typically represents the largest obstacle to the changes in policies and institutions needed to make development happen.

For a powerful example, we need look no further than the former Soviet Union in the early 1990s.[5] Although many observers recognized that Russia and its neighbors lacked market institutions, many thought that market-oriented policy reforms would create demand for institution building. But potentially beneficial reforms were hijacked by what quickly became entrenched elites. Russia's loans-for-shares deal in the mid-1990s and other policies and schemes, earlier and later, allowed well-connected oligarchs to secure monopoly positions at very low cost. The oligarchs were close to those in political power and exploited the absence of countervailing forces (acting through political, judicial, or governance institutions) to grab the assets of the Russian state and people.

The resulting monopolies and entrenched interests have hampered attempts to move to a well-functioning, inclusive market economy. Equally important, the ascent of the oligarchs raised higher the barriers to future reform because with greater economic power came state capture and the political power to block reforms. The effective demand for institutional reform dried up. Those who had exploited institutional defects for such great gain now held most of the political purchasing power. Unsurprisingly, they did not campaign for the institutional and governance improvements required to rein in their activities.

Since the late 1990s—with the default and devaluation of 1998, the arrival of more effective leadership, and high natural resource prices—Russia has seen stronger growth. Some oligarchs have been controlled, and others are seeking more respectable roles. But there is no doubt that the damage to institutions and civil behavior from that early period of transition, and the extreme inequality that has arisen, have done deep and lasting damage.

The post-Soviet transition story illustrates a more general point: that a society's flexibility and ability to take on entrenched interests determine how quickly a crisis or opportunity leads to reforms. This issue arises whether reforms are aimed at stabilizing the macroeconomy or introducing structural changes such as trade liberalization or privatization, as was the case in Latin America and East Asia in the 1980s (Haggard and Kaufman 1992, 1995), or whether they are aimed at achieving a successful transition from a planned to a market economy. The Latin American and East Asian reforms were prompted by the macroeconomic crises of the 1970s and early 1980s, which were the result of external shocks combined with unsustainable policies. In the 1990s transition countries launched systemic reforms combining macroeconomic stabilization with profound structural and institutional change. We would like to be able to explain why certain societies are successful at implementing reforms during or after crises and while others fail. Why, for example, did the Republic of Korea respond so promptly to the onset of crises in the early 1980s and late 1990s, while Brazil seemed unable to produce effective responses in the 1970s and 1980s?

A large literature on the political economy of reform arose over the past two decades as researchers and policymakers tried to explain the spotty—often poor—record of reform implementation. Thanks to that literature, we now better understand the conditions under which major structural reforms (such as trade liberalization, privatization, and land reform) can be successfully implemented. The rest of this section briefly summarizes this understanding, drawing on useful surveys such as Persson and Tabellini (2000), Drazen (2000), and Rodrik (1996). This literature examines, among other things, the cost of delayed reforms and the complementarily and sequencing of reforms.

Understanding Political Barriers to Reform
In implementing reforms, developing countries face a phalanx of constraints—not just political but also administrative, economic, and informational. Administrative capacity constraints arise for lack of physical, human, and organizational capital (a topic to which we return in chapters 12 and 13). On the economic side, market and institutional failures are complex, and acting and interacting to overcome a problem in one area may have little effect or be counterproductive given failures in other parts of the economy. Finally, reform outcomes are uncertain, and people have incomplete information about how a

proposed set of policies will affect them. These uncertainties can give rise to reluctance to embark on change.

But the political barriers to reform are often the most daunting. Unsustainable policies (such as overvalued exchange rates and high import tariffs) often persist—even though they harm the overall economy—because interest groups, particularly vocal middle classes, benefit from them (Alesina 1998). These groups may have captured certain social spending, and they will try to protect it during stabilization programs designed to restore macroeconomic balance—even though doing so means, in effect, protecting patronage and clientelism. Redistribution targeted at the middle classes can make poor people poorer still; Alesina cites the example of Chile's pension system before 1973. Similar problems arose in Argentina in recent years. Resistance from the potential losers of policy reforms delays stabilization and efforts to scale back regressive programs. Such delay is costly: often, the longer a society waits, the harder and costlier the policy reversal will be.

Thus, distributional issues, and political conflict over them, shape prospects for reform. Policy and institutional changes that may have important long-run benefits may also carry major short-run costs. And these costs typically fall more strongly on one group than another. For instance, if an import quota or licensing requirement is removed, consumers—particularly future consumers—benefit at the expense of importers and import-competing firms. As Rodrik (1994, 1996) emphasizes, the prospect of a net welfare gain for society is not enough to get a reform implemented. A better predictor of implementation is the political cost-benefit ratio of the reform. This ratio compares the reform's expected efficiency gains with its expected costs, which are the sum of losses suffered by losers (whether protected industries or rentiers). The political influence of the groups that stand to gain or lose will be key determinants of the political assessment. Thus, a key issue in designing and implementing reforms is generating the required political change.

Conflicts of interest are intrinsic to the reform process. To succeed, a program must have sufficient support from those with political influence at crucial decision stages. But people are often uncertain about the benefits of reform, and their expectations can be manipulated. Part of the problem is the asymmetric information between government and voters. Governments have strong incentives to engage in time-inconsistent behavior. Thus, measures that are promised to help compensate the losers from adjustment may never happen. Electorates, often through bitter experience, understand this, so there are major credibility issues about proposed policies.

Surmounting Political Barriers

How can these political obstacles be overcome so that reforms can be enacted? Past experience, particularly in transition countries, shows that several avenues are possible (Roland 2000). One approach is to work within the constraints. Fernandez and Rodrik (1991) show, in the tradition of Machiavelli, that when individual benefits from reform are not known ex ante, there is a bias toward the status quo. So if there is no consensus for reform, agents of change may simply have to wait for deterioration in the status quo. When conditions worsen sufficiently, a majority of the population will become convinced that not embarking on reforms would be much costlier than acting.

But policymakers may also try to create policies that overcome the political constraints. One effective way to do this is to provide compensating transfers to losers to "buy" their acceptance of the reforms. In the context of simple majority voting, the poorer is the median voter relative to the average, the larger will be the redistribution that the majority of voters is likely to favor. As Rodrik (1994, 1996) pointed out, the problem with some reforms is that their political cost-benefit ratios are too high. Even if the efficiency gains from a reform are undisputable, the reform may imply massive transfers from one group to another, and the redistribution required to generate the necessary support will be very large.

This is a particular problem with trade policy reforms and is what makes comprehensive trade reform so hard to achieve. In this context it is in some ways remarkable that the large tariff reductions achieved throughout the developing world in recent decades (see figure 2.5) actually happened. It is possible to create institutions with a built-in commitment to compensatory transfers—for example, by extending to a larger population the right to vote (Acemoğlu and Robinson 2000). But as Rodrik (1996) argued, institutions for fully compensating losers are not common.

Another way that policymakers can work around political constraints is by carefully choosing the speed and sequence of reforms. Because of the systemic nature of many needed reforms and their urgency, reformers in transition countries debated during the 1990s whether it was preferable to have gradual reforms or a "big bang." Poland's reforms are often described as big bang and contrasted with

Hungary's gradualism during this period. But both were fairly successful in terms of growth, and both involved radical change in a short
time. Similarly, China's gradualism over the past twenty-five years,
with its extraordinarily achievements, is often contrasted with the trau-
mas of Russia's big bang in the 1990s. Yet the transformation of
China's agriculture between 1979 and 1983 was probably one of the
most rapid, profound changes in the twentieth century. Thus, in our
view generalized arguments about gradualism versus big bang are
often a waste of time.

There is, in some circumstances, a period of "extraordinary
politics"—as Leszek Balcerowicz (1995) describes it—when collective
decisions on radical change are possible that may not be possible at
other times. But some reforms of this nature, such as building new
institutions, take longer than others, such as establishing price stability.
To talk of big bang or gradualism in a generic sense usually adds little
analytical value. An analysis of reform paths must be in terms of the
issues at hand and the economic and political context of a country in a
specific period. The comparative costs and benefits of the two approaches are debatable, as shown by Poland and Hungary. Poland's
big bang reform succeeded in increasing growth and reducing poverty,
if we take a ten-year perspective. But Hungary, the epitome of gradualism, was also successful on those fronts (Dethier and Orlowski 1998).

A big bang has clear advantages in terms of political economy. The
expected payoff is unaffected by individual uncertainty. Under gradualism, by contrast, sequencing makes a difference. If the first reform
has a negative aggregate outcome, the average voter will not support
continuing the reforms under sequencing because he knows that the
reforms will be reversed in the next period (for instance, if a less
reform-friendly government is elected). If the first reform has a favorable aggregate outcome, the distribution of benefits may determine
whether the reform process will continue. Thus, appropriate sequencing can be crucial in building constituencies in favor of reform and creating political irreversibility.

Going forward, the research agenda on the political economy of reform should have at its center the creation of political and economic
institutions that favor innovation and adaptability. But we will need to
keep in mind the basic trade-off entailed by economic reform for those
in strong positions in societies. Although reform may increase economic payoffs for these incumbents, it will also reduce their political
power by enabling new segments of society to be politically effective

and to ask for, or insist on, more opportunities or resources. As suggested above, one way forward would be to find ways to increase the willingness of local elites to support opportunities for others through mass education and other investments that improve the investment climate and empower poor people. This kind of redistribution is more likely to increase economic activity and opportunity without threatening a change in political power that might induce elites to block reform. This would be an application of the dictum of R. A. Butler, minister of education in Churchill's government during World War II, that "politics is the art of the possible," but with a creative influence on what is possible.

In following this line of analysis, we must be careful not to suggest that only timid, gradual change is possible or desirable. There are many examples in history where radical, beneficial change has occurred in the face of opposition by elite groups. Such change is likely to involve strength and leadership as well as, and in the course of, building coalitions for change. A society must work out its own routes for reform, however hesitant or strong. But researchers must try to understand and inform such political change.

Lecture IV

Action

In recent decades the development community has learned a great deal about the meaning of development and the processes that drive it. Based on that learning, the previous chapters have offered a strategy for development and a program of research to help guide public policy. The three chapters in this lecture translate the learning and strategy into an action plan for the development community as a whole— rich and poor countries working in partnership. Although our discussion is oriented to what should be done at the time of this writing, the principles and lessons for effective action apply far beyond current circumstances.

11   The Challenge

The scale and depth of poverty around the world pose daunting challenges for development. But the next few years present a historic opportunity for progress on development. The global community has recognized poverty as a central moral challenge and committed to reducing it, with progress measured against a multidimensional set of targets. Recent history offers impressive achievements, as well as lessons about what works, and the development community has accepted that poverty reduction is a shared responsibility. This special opportunity to act implies special responsibility. We cannot let the opportunity pass.

There are many reasons for optimism about this opportunity:

• *Shared recognition of the importance of the poverty challenge.* Recent international conferences in Monterrey, Mexico (the United Nations Conference on Financing for Development, in March 2002), and Doha, Qatar (the fourth ministerial conference of the World Trade Organization, in November 2001), signaled that political leaders from a broad spectrum of countries recognize that reducing poverty is a fundamental challenge facing the world. To be sure, there are self-interested arguments for increasing development assistance. Especially with deepening global integration, disease and conflict born of poverty in one part of the world spread quickly to others. Even rich countries can never fully protect or isolate themselves. Still, these arguments seem less compelling than the moral imperative to overcome the suffering of other human beings. It is morally untenable to accept the persistence of desperate poverty—yet we live in a world where 1.1 billion people subsist on less than $1 a day, 120 million children do not attend school, and tens of millions of people die every year from effects of poor nutrition and disease that could easily have been prevented or treated (Goldin, Rogers, and Stern 2002).

• *An international commitment to act on this challenge.* Building on the optimism and good intentions accompanying a new millennium, the international community has made an extraordinary commitment to promoting development and fighting poverty and has reiterated this commitment several times. It was crystallized in the Millennium Declaration, adopted by world leaders in 2000. The declaration pulled together commitments made at various international conferences on specific subjects in the 1990s. The resulting Millennium Development Goals (MDGs) represent specific targets for reducing income poverty and improving health, education, the status of women and girls, the environment, and international development cooperation between 1990 and 2015. In Doha the international community agreed on a new round of trade negotiations (under the auspices of the World Trade Organization) and for the first time placed the interests of developing countries at the top of the agenda. In Monterrey world leaders reaffirmed their commitment to the MDGs. Developing countries committed to improving governance, institutions, and policies, and developed countries committed to increasing aid, opening their markets to trade, and supporting capacity building in developing countries. The World Summit on Sustainable Development (held in Johannesburg, South Africa, in August 2002) picked up on these themes and then looked further ahead, to address the challenges of achieving sustainable development and protecting the environment.

• *An agreed, multidimensional set of targets.* The MDGs are significant for several reasons. First, they are outcome targets, which focus efforts on results. Second, they are multidimensional, covering the key objectives related to income poverty, education, health, gender equity, and the environment. Third, they are time-bound and ambitious; if we see continued reforms by developing countries and stronger action by developed countries, the goals are attainable. Still, achieving them will be a challenge, and on some dimensions in some regions the prospects already look bleak. And fourth, they have commanded broad international agreement. That agreement is an important achievement, and the MDGs provide a powerful shared sense of direction. They are goals that can help unify development efforts.

• *A history of achievements.* The advances described in lecture I— especially the reductions in income poverty and the advances in health and education—are becoming more widely known. There is growing recognition that the developing world has made considerable progress and that it has done so in many cases by making effective use of development assistance. Even analysts who have historically been skeptical of aid are now taking a more nuanced position: they recognize that the effectiveness of aid depends on the environment in which it is used and that we can mold aid allocations and methods to these environments and can help improve them.

• *A set of lessons about development policy, development assistance, and the drivers of development.* Prominent among these lessons are the conditions for effective aid and the importance of country ownership. Aid is most effective in countries that have shown ownership of better policies and institutions—typically by improving them of their own accord, without large amounts of aid (see chapter 3). The donor community has internalized these lessons and reallocated aid accordingly. In the 1990s, once the end of the Cold War made it possible for major donors to shift away from geopolitically driven aid allocations, the targeting of aid to countries with reasonably good policies and institutions improved markedly. Yet during the same decade development assistance fell sharply as a share of donor countries' incomes, partly because of the same waning geopolitical motivations for aid. When they pledged to increase development assistance at the Monterrey conference, donor governments signaled that they recognized the inconsistency of—and missed opportunities associated with—rising aid effectiveness and falling aid levels.

• *Acceptance of responsibility, commitment, and mutual accountability.* Developing countries have accepted that their actions—their policies, institutions, and governance—will be the primary determinant of the pace of their development, no matter what external forces historically may have contributed to their underdevelopment. The New Partnership for Africa's Development is a concrete statement of this acceptance of responsibility. Moreover, many developing countries have already improved policies and governance, as argued in lecture I. Such improvements lay the foundation for all the progress envisioned here. At the same time, wealthier nations have committed to do their part for development, through increased aid and a more open trading regime. The terminology now used by both groups of countries stresses mutual accountability for outcomes. This is a welcome improvement over the past tendency to blame others for development failures.[1]

With these pieces in place, we are in a strong position to take effective action on development, but progress is far from guaranteed. We must have an explicit strategy and action plan. So far we have focused on the strategy and the research needed to nurture it. In this chapter and the rest of lecture IV, we turn to the principles and practicalities of the action plan.

The Millennium Development Goals

Although they were officially adopted only in 2000, the MDGs express a commitment forged in a series of international gatherings in the 1990s on various aspects of development.[2] As a result the goals express not only a determination to fight poverty, but also a recognition of the multidimensional nature of that struggle. The MDGs encompass targets and indicators ranging from reducing income poverty, to improving health and education, to advancing gender equality, to achieving environmental sustainability (box 11.1). The target for income poverty is cutting by half the share of people living in income poverty between 1990 and 2015. In health and education the MDGs aim to cut child mortality by two-thirds and achieve universal primary education by 2015, while eliminating gender disparities in schooling by 2005. In addition, the MDGs commit the international community to start reversing the spread of HIV/AIDS and malaria, as well as the loss of environmental resources, by 2015. Each target is associated with measurable indicators, so the MDGs also provide a framework for the development community to monitor progress in each area.

The multidimensional nature of the MDGs reflects a much broader definition and deeper understanding of poverty reduction than we would have seen fifteen years ago. This multidimensionality is crucial not only in concept but also in action: confronting poverty requires collaboration among partners, whether they are acting in the same areas or different ones.

Measurability is another important feature of the MDGs. The measurable results on which the MDGs are based can help manage, allocate, and coordinate activities and resources more effectively. The deadlines for meeting quantitative targets also lend an appropriate sense of urgency to the development challenge. Appropriate, but also sobering: we are now more than halfway through the 1990–2015 period covered by the goals, but well less than halfway toward meeting most of them. Thus, the MDGs underscore the need for stronger, more effective action.

Box 11.1
Targets and indicators for the Millennium Development Goals

Goals/Targets	Indicators
Economic Well-being	
Reduce extreme poverty and hunger Reduce by half the proportion of the population living on less than $1 a day between 1990 and 2015	1. Incidence of extreme poverty: population living on less than $1 (measured in terms of purchasing power parity, or PPP) a day 2. Poverty gap ratio: incidence times depth of poverty 3. Inequality: poorest fifth's share of national consumption
Reduce by half the proportion of the population suffering from hunger between 1990 and 2015	4. Child malnutrition: prevalence of underweight children (under-age five) 5. General malnutrition: prevalence of undernourishment, as measured by dietary energy supply in the general population
Social Development	
Achieve universal primary education Achieve universal primary education by 2015	6. Net enrollment in primary education 7. Proportion of pupils starting grade 1 who reach grade 5 8. Literacy rate of fifteen- to twenty-four-year-olds
Promote gender equality Ensure that boys and girls have equal access to primary and secondary education by 2005, if possible, and to all levels by 2015	9. Ratio of girls to boys in primary, secondary, and tertiary education 10. Ratio of literate females to males (fifteen- to twenty-four-year-olds) 11. Ratio of female to male employment in nonagricultural occupations 12. Proportion of women in national parliaments
Reduce infant and child mortality Reduce by two-thirds the under-five mortality rate between 1990 and 2015	13. Under-five mortality rate 14. Infant mortality rate 15. Immunization rate for measles among under-one-year-olds

Box 11.1
(continued)

Improve maternal health Reduce by three-quarters the maternal mortality ratio between 1990 and 2015	16. Maternal mortality ratio 17. Proportion of births attended by skilled health personnel
Combat HIV/AIDS, tuberculosis, malaria, and other major diseases Halt and begin to reverse the spread of HIV/AIDS by 2015	18. Prevalence of HIV/AIDS among fifteen- to twenty-four-year-old pregnant women 19a. Condom use rate during last high-risk sex 19b. Percentage of population age fifteen to twenty-four with comprehensive, correct knowledge about HIV/AIDS 20. Ratio of school attendance of orphans to nonorphans age ten to fourteen
Halt and begin to reverse the spread of malaria, tuberculosis, and other major diseases by 2015	21. Prevalence and death rates associated with malaria 22. Proportion of population in malaria risk areas using effective malaria prevention and treatment measures 23. Prevalence and death rates associated with tuberculosis 24. Proportion of tuberculosis cases detected and cured under directly observed treatment short-course DOTS (internationally recommended control strategy)
Environmental Sustainability and Regeneration *Ensure environmental sustainability* Integrate the principles of sustainable development into country policies and programs and reverse the loss of environmental resources	25. Proportion of land area covered by forest 26. Ratio of area protected to maintain biological diversity to surface area 27. Energy use (kilogram of oil equivalent) per $1 of GDP 28. Carbon dioxide emissions (per capita) and consumption of ozone-depleting chlorofluorocarbons (CFCs)

Box 11.1
(continued)

Reduce by half the proportion of the population without sustainable access to safe drinking water and sanitation by 2015

29. Proportion of population using solid fuels
30. Proportion of population with sustainable access to an improved water source, urban and rural
31. Proportion of urban population with access to improved sanitation

Achieve a significant improvement in the lives of at least 100 million slum dwellers by 2020

32. Proportion of households with access to secure tenure

Global Partnerships

Develop a global partnership for development

Develop further an open, rule-based, predictable, nondiscriminatory trading and financial system. Includes a commitment to good governance, development, and poverty reduction—both nationally and internationally

33. Net official development assistance (ODA), total and to least developed countries (LDCs), as percentage of OECD/Development Assistance Committee (DAC) donors' gross national income (GNI)

Address the special needs of the least developed countries. Includes tariff- and quota-free access for least developed countries' exports, enhanced debt relief for heavily indebted poor countries and cancellation of official bilateral debt, and more generous official development assistance for countries committed to poverty reduction

34. Proportion of total bilateral, sector-allocable ODA of OECD/DAC donors to basic social services
35. Proportion of bilateral ODA of OECD/DAC donors that is untied
36. ODA received in landlocked countries as a proportion of their gross national income (GNI)

Address the special needs of landlocked countries and small island developing states

37. ODA received in small island developing states as a proportion of their GNI
38. Proportion of total developed country imports (by value, excluding arms) from developing countries and from less developed countries admitted free of duties

Box 11.1
(continued)

	39. Average tariffs imposed by developed countries on agricultural products and textiles and clothing from developing countries
	40. Domestic agricultural support provided by OECD countries as a percentage of their GDP
	41. Proportion of ODA provided to help build trade capacity
Deal comprehensively with the debt problems of developing countries through national and international measures to make debt sustainable in the long term	42. Number of countries that have reached their heavily indebted poor countries (HIPC) decision points and number that have reached their HIPC completion points
	43. Debt relief committed under the HIPC initiative
	44. Debt service as a percentage of exports of goods and services
In cooperation with developing countries, develop and implement strategies for decent and productive work for youth	45. Unemployment rate of fifteen to twenty-four year olds, by sex and total
In cooperation with pharmaceutical companies, provide access to affordable essential drugs in developing countries	46. Proportion of population with access to affordable essential drugs on a sustainable basis
In cooperation with the private sector, make available the benefits of new technologies, especially information and communications technology	47. Telephone lines and cellular subscribers per 100 people
	48. Personal computers in use per 100 people and Internet users per 100 people

The goals are defined as global targets. For example, the goal for income poverty specifies halving the percentage of poor people in the world's population from 27.0 percent in 1990 to 13.5 percent in 2015. But they can also provide indicators of development progress at the regional and country levels.[3] For example, the development community should probably not claim success on income poverty if—as seems likely—the goal of halving the poverty rate is met at the global level but sub-Saharan Africa falls far short.

Interpreting the Goals: Three Cautions

As important as the MDGs are as indicators and instigators of development progress, they pose several hazards if our efforts are undertaken too literally. The first risk is that donors will become too prescriptive and insist that the indicators be applied at the country level. As noted, the global MDGs can be seen as applying at that level, but a formulaic attempt to impose objectives on a country from the outside would likely be counterproductive. It is important that a developing country set its own targets for development; if it does not, commitment to specific actions or approaches is unlikely to follow.

Concern for country ownership is not the only reason to be cautious about overly literal interpretation of the MDGs. A second caution is that although the MDGs are (appropriately) multidimensional, they by no means cover all desirable development changes and challenges. For example, the MDGs omit much of what is important about freedom and empowerment, which are key to our understanding of development and poverty reduction. And even within the dimensions they cover, the MDGs are narrowly specified.

Consider the goal for reducing income poverty. We care about raising the incomes of people throughout the bottom range of the income distribution, not just those living below a fairly arbitrary level such as $1 a day. We would surely value more highly an income increase that lifted one family's income by 10 cents a person from, say, an initial level of 60 cents than an equivalent increase that lifted another family to 105 cents. But only the latter would count toward the $1 a day poverty-reduction goal. Similarly, while rates for completion of primary school and for literacy are very important, there is much more to education than those numbers.

All this is not to detract from the MDGs as objectives; goal setting always requires specificity and cannot encompass everything. But we should view the MDGs as important and relevant summary statistics, not as rigid and exclusive criteria for success in development. They need to be supplemented by indicators of important dimensions of development that they do not fully cover, such as empowerment. Some indicators of empowerment are discussed in lecture III.

A third mistake of literal-mindedness would be to infer that because the MDGs highlight sector goals, the right response is a set of purely sectoral programs corresponding to each goal. The goals for health and education will not be achieved through action in the health and education sectors alone, yet too often a call to improve health outcomes is interpreted as a call for building more clinics and training more doctors. This point is crucial—and often overlooked in the aid debate—so we will spend most of the remainder of this section on it.

Recognizing the Cross-Sectoral Effects of Development Interventions

Consider what we know about the main drivers of health outcomes. One is income growth. When households have more income, they choose to spend some of it on sanitation, prevention, health care, and other factors that make them healthier, and they may take fewer risks that will imperil their income. As a result, income growth has historically generated major improvements in health outcomes, especially the early gains in Western economies (Fogel 1986, 2004).

But more direct interventions also contribute to better health outcomes, and many take place outside regular channels of health care delivery. Indeed, income growth alone explains relatively little of recent advances in health status in the developing world. Counter to widely held perceptions of Africa as an across-the-board development failure in the 1970s and 1980s, sub-Saharan Africans saw marked improvements in their health status during that period, even as their economies were stagnating or declining.[4] The explanation for this cannot simply be a rise in spending in the health sector, because health spending typically does not rise when national income is flat or falling (Wagstaff 2003).

So what other factors drive improvements in health status, if not higher incomes or health spending? Leading determinants of age-specific mortality rates include diet, stress, tobacco use, immunization prevalence, access to clean water, and women's education, with delivery of health care by doctors, nurses, and hospitals coming some way down the list. Take child mortality. At every level of constant per capita income, child mortality rates have fallen sharply in recent decades (World Bank 1998c). Detailed micro evidence leads to the following conclusions about what factors reduce the death rate for young children:

• Mothers' education reduces child mortality by raising demand for health care and increasing mothers' ability to seek out and use new approaches to preventing illness within the family.

• Access to clean water reduces the probability of child mortality by an average of 55 percent, according to an assessment of forty-two studies (Wagstaff 2003). Accessible safe water supplies reduce the incidence of diarrhea, a major cause of child mortality, and provide the water needed to maintain basic hygiene. Such access is less common in the poor communities where child mortality is highest. The effect of clean water on child mortality is stronger when combined with mothers' education.

• Infrastructure investments are also associated with reduced child mortality. Roads are important because they allow households to access services and provide a way to reach clinics. So are modern forms of energy, such as electricity, gas, and improved cooking stoves. Switching from wood and dung fires to these sources can improve household air quality and reduce respiratory illnesses, a leading cause of child mortality. Infrastructure investments can also have a powerful effect on education—for example, by freeing time for girls to attend school.

• Better knowledge and technology contribute to lower child mortality. The development and deployment of vaccines is one example. Another is the development and dissemination of oral rehydration therapy, a low-cost remedy credited with sharply reducing the death toll from diarrhea. A third is the spread of the understanding of the germ theory of disease, which helps clean water and sanitation translate into better outcomes (Wagstaff 2003).

In fact, the importance of cross-sector effects on health status may be one reason that the literature has been unable to find a strong correlation between levels of public spending on health and health outcomes.[5]

This is not to deny that health spending is important. Expenditures within and outside the health sector complement each other. If roads improve, the demand for health services will rise. Conversely, health policy has complementary effects on other sectors: students who receive good preventive health care are more likely to attend school regularly, increasing the returns to public investment in school buildings and teachers. It would be wrong to give the impression that we can pull the roads lever, or the water lever, or the education lever, and health improvements will simply happen. Achieving substantial improvements in health outcomes requires making concerted efforts across sectors and changing ways of doing things to increase productivity. Each country will have its own mix of interventions, and it is at that level that analysis and consultations to guide decision making should be conducted.

Our focus in this example has been on the health sector, where arguments about cross-sector effects and complementarities are particularly applicable. Similar issues apply in education. Improvements in primary school completion and in literacy depend not only on the supply of schools and teachers and textbooks, but also on whether a community has access to roads and jobs. Roads and other transportation infrastructure help students and teachers get to school regularly and on time, and the availability of gainful employment for parents can reduce the need for child labor. In working toward the MDGs—whether in health, education, or the environment—the development community should ask at each stage where it can achieve the highest returns from investment, within or outside the targeted sector (Jayasuriya and Wodon 2003 contains useful discussions on the issue of increasing the efficiency of reaching the MDGs with a given amount of available resources).

Progress toward the MDGs—and the Need to Scale Up

These caveats notwithstanding, the MDGs provide a much-needed metric for overall development progress—and a sobering one. It is unlikely that all (or even most) of the MDG targets will be reached in all regions by 2015, barring an enormous increase in development resources and in the pace of policy and institutional change (figure 11.1). The goal for reducing income poverty may be achieved for the world as a whole, thanks largely to growth in China and India, but will not be achieved in most developing regions. And the prospects for achieving many of the nonincome goals are dimmer still.

As might be expected given its slow income growth, sub-Saharan Africa faces the greatest MDG challenges. In the 1990s less than a quarter of the region's countries were on track to meet most of the MDGs, and in many countries conditions have deteriorated since then. On the

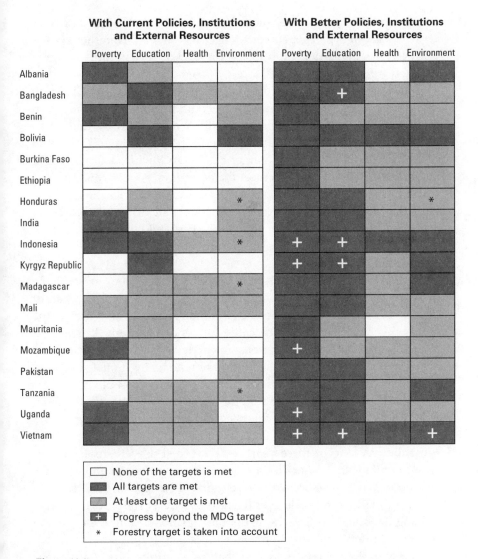

Figure 11.1
Prospects of meeting the MDGs. *Source:* World Bank (2003k). *Notes:* Each box shows progress in achieving MDG targets combined in four broad areas. Poverty: income poverty and hunger. Education: primary enrollment, completion, and gender equality in education. Health: child (under age 5) mortality, maternal mortality, and, where applicable, the prevalence of HIV/AIDS. Environment: improved access to water and sanitation, and where applicable, forestry.

income poverty goal alone, sub-Saharan Africa's GDP would have to grow by about 7 percent a year to meet the target. Given the region's growth rates in the 1980s and 1990s, this kind of growth surge is highly unlikely.

Other regions are projected to fall short of the goals as well. South Asia is on track to meet the MDG income poverty target, but even under optimistic assumptions, growth would lead to under-five mortality in the region dropping from 98 per 1,000 in 2000 to 69 in 2015—far short of the MDG target of 43. Worldwide, at least half of countries are not on track to meet the education, gender equality, and child mortality targets. For example, sub-Saharan Africa, South Asia, and the Middle East and North Africa are not expected to achieve universal primary education by 2015. The child mortality goal is especially remote and, in retrospect, seems to have been a very ambitious target.

In short, at current trends, the world will not meet most of the MDGs, especially when we apply them at the regional or country levels. Despite the caveats about the interpretation and use of the goals, this situation should be cause for serious concern. It is a clear indicator that while there have been great development successes in recent years, large swaths of the world are not sharing in the successes. Nor is success uniform across the various dimensions of poverty.

To achieve the MDGs, developing countries and the development community more generally will need to scale up their programs and projects. *Scaling up* is a term that has come into use at the World Bank over the past two or three years, and we shall use it here. It encompasses notions that otherwise are not easily summarized and captures the notion that development efforts—and their results—will have to be on a much greater scale over the next decade. A simple definition of scaling up would be "increasing both the quality (or effectiveness) and quantity of development efforts, to achieve results on a scale commensurate with the poverty reduction challenge and the agreed ambitions of the development community."

This is not a poorly camouflaged call to increase aid while otherwise continuing business as usual. While we believe that more aid is necessary, more aid alone will not achieve the MDGs. Aid, considered purely as a financing vehicle, will never be large enough to drive development. Total foreign aid from developed to developing countries is around $50 billion a year—about two-thirds of 1 percent of developing-country income. In contrast, foreign direct investment in the developing world exceeds $150 billion a year, and total investment in developing countries is $1.5 trillion a year. Even if donor countries were to double their aid, and even if all of the increase translated into new investment, investment would rise by only about 3 percent (not 3 percentage points of GDP). Clearly, aid alone is not going to solve the world's ills. Similarly, education lending by the World Bank, the largest external funder of education, is typically around $2 billion a year, compared with $250 billion in annual education spending by developing countries (Goldin, Rogers, and Stern 2002).

So aid will help countries achieve their development goals only if it contributes to self-reinforcing processes driving development—particularly government ownership, investment climate improvement, and empowerment. In other words, the development community must focus on increasing the effectiveness of aid in addition to increasing the quantity.

How can the development community scale up? As we argued in lectures I and II, the foundations of scaling up will have to be strengthening policies, institutions, and governance. Although policies, institutions, and governance are in the hands of developing countries, there is much that the broader development community can do to support progress on these key dimensions.

Achieving results on the scale of the MDGs will require greater efforts in at least two major areas, which we discuss in greater detail below. First, partnership among the various development players is essential. Developed and developing countries must dedicate themselves to making development happen through the governance, trade, and aid instruments at their disposal. We recognize that the word *partnership* is overused in some circles and can provoke much rolling of eyes. But here it has a concrete meaning. If donors are working at cross-purposes with each other and especially with recipient countries, or if their requirements impose excessive burdens on already overstretched recipient governments, then aid dollars will be wasted, and scaling up will be impossible. All partners need to work together to build the two pillars of our strategy: a strong investment climate and increased empowerment.

Second, scaling up depends on evaluation and learning. Even if they work in partnership the key development players cannot increase development resources by enough to meet the MDGs in the absence of learning. To scale up development results, recipient countries and donors alike will need to evaluate and learn lessons from their interventions and apply these interventions elsewhere. For example, imagine that a donor funds a pilot project to experiment with community management of schools in one province, and the project raises child and teacher attendance rates and improves test scores. While it is heart-warming to think that development takes place one life at a time, development assistance must have higher aspirations. Such a project will truly succeed only if the country's government has bought into the pilot and is willing to apply its lessons in other provinces and into the future. In all areas of development, we should stand ready to learn from projects—and indeed, design them for learning. And we should be careful not to confuse the application of learning with un-thinking cookie-cutter replication. The key is identifying which ideas and approaches were crucial and applying them with judgment in new circumstances.

The same considerations apply to policies. Indeed, improving poli-cies and governance across the whole economy is a key element of de-velopment, as we shall emphasize.

Beyond scaling up projects and programs, evaluation and measure-ment are essential in assessing the contributions of developing and developed countries to the partnership for development. We now turn to these issues of partnership and learning.

Acting Together: Implementing the Development Partnership

Developing countries must take the lead in scaling up efforts to fight poverty. The results of scaling up will occur largely by promoting and supporting changes in these countries' policies, institutions, and gover-nance. But strong support is required from developed countries if re-form efforts and changes in developing countries are to pay off as they should.

Developing Countries' Responsibilities

The compact that emerged from the Monterrey conference commits developing countries to work on implementing the policies, institu-tions, and governance needed to support the two pillars of our strat-egy. Because that is the subject of these lectures as a whole, it needs very little elaboration here. But the link to scaling up should be noted. If scaling up is about magnifying the effects of interventions—so that the lessons of a project or program have effects that, in terms of both time and space, extend well beyond the boundaries of that project or program—this commitment has a number of implications.

First, strengthened governance and institutional change are essential to scaling up. Policy improvements can be, and often are, reversed when it is no longer convenient for governments to stand behind a reform—often with damaging effects on the investment climate. For longer-lasting development progress, interventions must translate into sustained improvements in governance and institutions. This gets back to the notion of change processes, emphasized in chapter 2 and throughout these lectures. All the shifts in industrial composition and urbanization and income sources that come with development must be accompanied by steady improvements in governance and institutions. Strong governance and institutions are a key characteristic of developed countries, and they allow scaling up by ensuring sustainability and broad application of good practices.

Second, empowerment—providing voice to poor people and making institutions receptive to that voice—is also an integral part of scaling up. Empowerment promotes scaling up by allowing a society to tap into the energy and creativity of a class of people who otherwise would be able to contribute much less, or could even be a drag on the economy's development. The extraordinary increase in output in China's agriculture between 1979 and 1983 is one of the most striking examples of scaling up, and empowerment was central to it. The move from agricultural activity based on communes to households was very much a local initiative in response to serious failure. But it soared with the support of central authorities and spread across the country with remarkable results.

Third, evaluation and learning are essential. Interventions should have as their goal not only the direct achievement of results, but also the production of knowledge about what works, how, and why. Given that the public sector is weak in many developing countries, capacity building should be a sustained effort. This type of learning is a central element in building the capacity of institutions to take on more and bigger tasks. Capacity building is not a stand-alone training intervention but rather a strategically coordinated set of activities aimed at individuals, institutions, and sectors. Capacity building is fundamental to disseminating and applying ideas about what works and what does not. For example, lessons from building Shanghai's ring road were embodied in a road institute that guided the bidding for this type of road project across China.

In chapter 12 we discuss in depth the practical elements of implementing these ideas. Our strategy has outlined a rather substantial role for the state, which our discussion of scaling up reinforces. Chapter 12 discusses how to finance that role—a crucial point, since the state's ability to increase its role is ultimately limited by its budget. Underlying that discussion, however, should be a sense of the ultimate aim of these efforts: scaling up development results through the types of approaches discussed here.

Developed Countries' Responsibilities

Developed countries also have responsibilities under the compact agreed at Monterrey, because their actions are essential to ensuring that developing countries can reap the full benefits of improvements in their policies, institutions, and governance. Developed countries have major responsibilities in several areas that are crucial for development, such as environmental protection, international property rights, migration policies, and the international financial architecture. Most crucial are contributions involving trade and aid.

On the trade front, developed countries can make a major contribution to development by pulling down their trade barriers. Despite their low average tariffs, developed countries maintain substantial obstacles to imports in the sectors most important to developing countries, notwithstanding pledges to remove or reduce them. It is hard to miss the hypocrisy: developed countries preach trade as a driver of growth and poverty reduction, and they push for liberalization in areas such as financial services and technology goods—yet they erect barriers in precisely the areas where developing countries have a comparative advantage. The potential welfare gains to developing countries from trade policy reforms are enormous—conservatively estimated at $75 billion in real income from unilateral liberalization of merchandise traded by developed countries, plus another $120 billion from liberalization of developing countries' trade regimes. These estimates, if anything, tend to understate the gains from trade because they do not take into account possible dynamic gains from trade (Stern 2002b).

In terms of aid levels, donor rhetoric and commitment to the MDGs have not been matched by a significant increase in aid to developing countries. In nominal terms, net official development assistance fell from nearly $60 billion in the early 1990s to $52 billion in 2001. As a percentage of developed countries' GDP, it fell even further. Despite a small increase in 2002, much more aid will be required to reach results on the scale implied by the MDGs. Even with relatively optimistic assumptions about growth and policy improvements, increased aid of

$50 to $60 billion a year will be needed to meet the MDGs, which would mean at least doubling current official development assistance.[6]

Chapter 13 covers in detail the imperatives for trade and aid. Our purpose here is to point out that aid can either assist or undermine the scaling-up effort, depending on how it is designed. If we are to reach the MDGs, future aid will have to be qualitatively different from the past. Perhaps most important, the development community must provide its support in a much more collaborative, coherent, harmonious way. Efficient use of aid requires that donors both understand what other donors are doing and focus on their areas of comparative advantage. Recipient countries are in the best position to coordinate aid activities, in terms of knowledge about local needs and other actors, but they need help in doing so. If they are to increase aid effectiveness, donors should provide it in a way that supports country ownership more strongly.

One mechanism for this is country-led strategy efforts such as the process embodied in Poverty Reduction Strategy Papers (PRSPs).[7] These papers aim to coordinate donor efforts within the framework of strategies constructed and adopted by recipient country governments, with strong participation by the broader community. The PRSP process has become the primary vehicle for providing assistance to low-income countries, particularly those seeking broad debt relief. While this does not need to be the vehicle for coordination in all countries—large economies such as China and India may never adopt PRSPs—what is important is that the principle of country-led strategy setting and coordination be applied to all aid recipients.

A second mechanism for improving the quality of aid is reduced (or less intrusive) conditionality on loans and grants. Where countries have clear development strategies and are taking steps to implement them, donors should be willing to support them as a package rather than using constraining conditionality to micromanage development. Obviously, donors cannot support every proposal of every recipient government. But if they support the broad thrust of a proposed program, dialogue may be more effective than unwelcome conditionality as a tool for changing the elements they disagree with. The past experience summarized in chapter 3, particularly cases like Zambia where donors enabled bad policy choices that made poor countries even poorer, suggests that there is one appropriate broad condition for donor support. This condition is that *aid finance the costs of changing, and not the costs of not changing.* If a country fulfills this broad condition, in that it is willing to change to meet the MDGs or similar goals, then it should be given considerable leeway in choosing the means of doing so.[8]

Both of these mechanisms increase the probability of successful scaling up through aid. Donor coordination and country ownership reduce duplication of efforts and make it less likely that donor efforts will be undermined by government recalcitrance. Thus, they increase the returns to aid. They also increase the probability that the lessons from successful interventions will be applied more broadly throughout a country.

Learning, Evaluating, and Measuring Progress on the MDGs

Our understanding of development is sufficient to act now, and act effectively. Although there remain many unanswered questions, we cannot, like Hamlet, let the "native hue of resolution [be] sicklied o'er by the pale cast of thought." The agenda outlined above, for developing and developed countries, is a program for prompt and purposeful action.

Still, it is essential that the development community keep learning about what works and what does not. Just as learning cannot be an excuse for inaction, the fact that we are already acting does not justify an end to learning and adjusting course. We have identified new areas for long-term development research in lecture II, but the search for knowledge needs to go well beyond those areas, into real-time evaluation and measurement. As we have argued, scaling up depends on learning from innovative programs and projects, then applying what is learned on a much larger scale. Such programs and projects, if properly designed and evaluated, can have payoffs far greater than their immediate impacts because of the knowledge spillovers they generate. But learning is not enough for scaling up: energetic and committed dissemination and application of lessons are also crucial.

Because development is about change, we need to measure and learn how to promote change. Analytical work helps establish priorities and shows what can be done, helping policymakers shape action. Much of this work must be country specific: every country faces unique challenges, and it is these factors that need to be understood. This work must also be interdisciplinary, for neither economics nor any other social science has all the answers to reducing child mortality or achieving other MDGs.

Part of the task ahead involves making better use of data that are already available. Although those data are much weaker than we would like, that should not be cause for delay. We can get results quickly by applying what we know, while at the same time collecting complementary data. For example, suppose our aim is to better understand the processes of empowerment through health care delivery. In many countries we can use existing household surveys to examine, across the income spectrum and comparing urban and rural areas, whether consumers use public or private health facilities and how much they pay for services. We can use facility surveys to see how patients are treated, how long they must wait, when the facilities are open, and whether the providers actually show up (a serious issue in many countries). Case studies of users and providers can probe the question of which households are or are not included and can also examine the issue of roads and access. Finally, we could conduct community surveys to understand the interactions between household demand and supply, as well as the adequacy and appropriateness of supply.

With these data sources, we can ask such questions as: Do poor roads impede patient access and provider reliability? Do providers show up, and if not, why? Are there lapses in services due to utility breakdowns? Given the links between education and health outcomes, are children (particularly girls) in school, and if not, why? Do households have access to adequate water supplies, and is it safe for drinking (given that clean water is an essential element in health outcomes); if not, what are the impediments? By combining data to examine a problem from various angles, we can glean clear lessons on development effectiveness.

This research, evaluation, and learning will work best if it is a collaborative effort between researchers in developing and developed countries. On the research side, capacity in developing countries is improving. One indicator of progress is the success of the Global Development Network of research institutes in developing countries.[9] Supporting further improvement should be a major objective of development assistance. Similarly, on the data front, building statistical capacity to monitor and understand developments and their causes is crucial to well-targeted action by developing countries. Indeed, a major challenge in implementing the MDGs is that the basic statistics needed to assess progress are lacking in the poorest countries. As with institution building, in helping to build statistical capacity the development community must take care to build on what is in place and the progress that is being made, recognizing the importance of country ownership. Indeed, one of the first challenges for statistical capacity building is helping to develop local demand for data. When local decision makers see how data can help decisions and results, demand will grow.

In most countries government expertise is organized around ministries, which themselves are organized along sector lines. But as we have seen, outcomes are shaped by action across sectors. So while it is important that learning embrace existing institutions, sector priorities and issues need to emerge from a broader, multisector analysis. We do not want to suggest that road engineers should become experts on diarrhea, but rather that the portfolio of projects take into account cross-sector interactions. Once that is done, each project or program can get on with its job.

Measuring the Contributions of Developing Countries
Learning and adapting strategies require measuring progress. Each developing country needs to have indicators of its progress toward the MDGs, or toward whatever goals it adopts. Like the goals, metrics of success will generally be multidimensional, encompassing not just growth and income poverty measures but also measures of health, education, and the environment.

Learning will depend on using the right intermediate indicators of progress. Not all indicators of the MDGs are available in real time, and in any event MDG-related outcome indicators may give little insight into the dynamics of the processes that are supposed to give rise to them. Thus, intermediate and process indicators are needed. These should include measures of the investment climate, governance, and poor people's participation in growth, as described in chapter 6. Multilateral and bilateral development agencies are helping countries develop these, as with the recent upgrading of the World Bank's program for microlevel surveys. The Bank has led the way in developing careful, comparable household surveys focused on living standards and including data on consumption and income in their various dimensions.

More recently, systematic programs to develop surveys of processes have been launched, including investment climate surveys of firms (aimed at understanding where the major constraints on growth are) and basic service delivery surveys (which assess the quantity and quality of delivered services; see chapter 6). These process indicators complement household survey data by giving us insight into the processes that generate poverty reduction.

Measuring the Contributions of Developed Countries

Because development requires a partnership, it is not enough to measure policies and processes only in developing countries. Granted, it is in developing countries that we will look for the ultimate poverty reduction and development outcomes. But since the actions of developed countries affect those outcomes, they too should be measured and assessed. This is partly to ensure that developed countries are upholding their commitment to development, but it is also a tool for learning and adapting policies to make assistance more effective.

Many developed country policies and actions affect developing countries. The international environment determines the returns that developing countries can earn by improving their policies and institutions, so in that sense, developed and developing-country reforms complement each other. As an element of the partnership and mutual accountability discussed earlier, the international community should assess how developed-country actions affect development, in addition to developing-country actions.

We have discussed some of these areas and do so in greater detail in chapter 13. But to counter the perception that development progress is merely the responsibility of developing countries and that measurement should be confined to them, consider the following list. Each item reflects an area where developed-country actions affect development, and each can and should be measured:

- Volume and efficiency of aid, including the degree of harmonization of policies and procedures among donor countries
- Openness of developed country markets, including the extent of tariff and nontariff barriers to exports from developing countries
- International financial architecture and financial stability
- Extent of knowledge transfer from developed countries and effectiveness of capacity building
- Intellectual property regime and whether it primarily benefits or harms different parts of the developing world
- Migration policies

Developed countries also affect the following cross-border flows of international public "bads," and their involvement in these flows should be measured as well:

• Environmental degradation

• Spread of communicable diseases

• International flows of drugs and networks of organized crime

• Extent and effects of the arms trade

• Extent of conflict and the role of external forces in fueling it (for example, through the purchase of "conflict diamonds")[10]

• Bribery of developing country officials by developed country firms

In these areas measurement and learning are essential to improving developed-country policies. Even though international financial institutions, or whoever does the assessments, are unlikely to have direct financial leverage over developed countries, the embarrassment of low measured performance can be a powerful motivator. The fact that most donor countries are democratic probably increases the scope for knowledge to affect policy. Sometimes measurement can lead to strong, well-organized domestic constituencies for better policies in developed countries. One example is the recent Jubilee 2000 debt cancellation campaign, in which statistics comparing developing countries' debt repayments and spending on human development were powerful spurs to action by church groups and other NGOs—building momentum for debt relief programs for the world's poorest countries.

Some such measurement efforts are already under way. The Center for Global Development in Washington, D.C., for example, recently published a "development friendliness index" that ranks developed countries based on the degree to which their policies promote development.[11] An aggregate index, reducing everything to one number, can add confusion rather than insight (what does it mean to combine indicators on trade and aid, for example?), but the effort to bring attention to the individual indicators is a valuable one. The Development Committee (the joint ministerial committee of boards of governors of the World Bank and the International Monetary Fund on the transfer of real resources to developing countries) has mandated the staff of these institutions to carry out the global monitoring of policies and actions for achieving the MDGs and related outcomes.[12] Finally, NGOs like Transparency International publish useful tools such as annual corruption perception surveys, bribe payers surveys and, more recently, a global corruption barometer, which put pressure on political parties and governments to improve governance.[13]

Evaluating the Contributions of International Financial Institutions

International financial institutions and other donors should not be exempt from this increased emphasis on measurement. For donors, as for developing-country governments, hard-nosed analysis of what works is crucial to scaling up. Evaluation makes it possible to scale up by selecting the best projects as the basis for learning elsewhere. Note that this is different from measurement for accountability—though that too has a role—and that there will sometimes be tensions between the two.

Learning involves experimentation, and so sometimes failure. This is especially the case for international institutions, which must pilot new approaches that may have a significant risk of failure. Demonstration projects contribute to the international public good of knowledge about whether a given approach will work. The more innovative an approach is, the greater the learning externalities from trying it, which points to a role for a public institution—especially an international public institution—in accepting some of these risks. World Bank project success rates have risen steadily over the past decade, to 80 percent or more. But if they were ever to reach 100 percent, that would be a sign of timidity and therefore failure.

Project- and program-level evaluation is an element in increased measurement for learning, and the previous section outlines ways to strengthen our evaluation focus at those levels. But international financial institutions also need to be concerned with progress at the wider sector and economy levels. They should have outcome benchmarks in each area, such as education and health. Even though these institutions are never going to be the primary force behind achieving or missing those benchmarks, they need to know whether the programs they are supporting are part of a set of actions generating adequate progress.

We should emphasize here that while measurement is crucial for evaluation and learning, there are grave dangers in an international financial institution making excessive claims about its indispensability or key role in shaping outcomes. Development assistance is part of a partnership, and exaggerated claims by a single partner can undermine that method of working. In any case, attribution of success or failure to one party is usually misleading. An international financial institution should judge itself by asking whether it worked in partnership to create a good framework, whether it executed effectively its role in the partnership, and what the partnership achieved.

Conclusion: Putting the Pieces Together

In this chapter we have indicated the scale of the development challenge and the principles that should guide action as the development community works to build the two pillars of our strategy: the investment climate and empowerment. We have seen that the world is falling far short on its pledges to meet ambitious development goals by 2015. The standard response from development practitioners might be expected to be a call for more aid—and that is indeed one element of our response. But it is by no means the only one. More aid will have limited effect in poor environments. And even in reasonably good policy and institutional environments, its effectiveness will be hampered if we ignore the prerequisites of partnership and learning.

To make these notions more concrete, we close with an example of how these elements complement each other. In the past few years researchers have done analytical work to estimate the costs of the MDGs in terms of additional aid (Devarajan, Miller, and Swanson 2002; World Bank 2003k). These preliminary calculations take explicit account of the complementarities between developing-country policies and institutions and developed-country aid. They recognize that in the poorest policy environments, no amount of aid will achieve development targets in the medium term, because even massive aid flows are likely to be diverted or wasted.

Using relatively optimistic assumptions about growth and policy improvements, those researchers estimate that achieving the education, health, and water MDGs will require additional aid of $35 to $75 billion a year. Using the central portion of this range, a reasonable order of magnitude for an increase in foreign assistance is $50 to $60 billion a year, or doubling official development assistance to more than $100 billion a year.[14]

A more recent paper (World Bank 2003k) focuses on what the authors call "a broadly representative sample of 18 low-income countries with relatively good policies" (and institutions). This sample ranges from giants such as Bangladesh, India, and Indonesia to much smaller countries like Albania and Mauritania. Based on detailed examination of progress and projections, the study concludes that at current trends, none of these countries is likely to achieve all the MDGs. In fact, two countries, Burkina Faso and Ethiopia, are not projected to meet any of the goals.

What might be required for these relatively good-policy countries to achieve most or all of the MDGs? Taking into account the current and projected state of these countries' policy and institutional environments, the authors suggest that much can be achieved with a combination of better policies and more aid—a big part of the development partnership. The authors call for an immediate doubling or tripling of aid to the large Asian borrowers in the sample, and an increase of some 60 percent to the sample countries in sub-Saharan Africa and Central Asia. For the latter group of countries, the analysis calls for the increased aid to be phased in over time. The authors acknowledge that these countries' policies and institutions are not sufficiently developed for them to use large volumes of additional aid effectively right now. Increased aid needs to go hand in hand with its complement: policy and institutional reforms.

In the past, donors have been criticized for seeing aid as a substitute for good policy and country efforts rather than a complement. Easterly (2001) for example, argues that in trying to "fill financing gaps," multilateral and bilateral donors tried to hide (but probably exacerbated) the sins of bad or misguided governments. There has been some truth to this accusation in the past—as in Zambia, where steadily worsening policies were rewarded with equally steady increases in aid in the 1970s and 1980s (World Bank 1998a; Devarajan, Dollar, and Holmgren 2001). But financial gap filling does not motivate these recent analyses. The authors of the paper just mentioned (World Bank 2003k) recognize what we have argued in this chapter: that development is a partnership, and aid and good (country-owned) policies complement each other. To this recognition we would add an emphasis on evaluation and learning; without it, we cannot be sure that we are scaling up the right projects and approaches.

Domestic Action: Public Finances and the Role of the State

In proposing a strategy for development in lecture II, we drew attention to its implications for the role of the state and identified some of the kinds of government action that might flow from the strategy. In chapter 11 we described the development challenge embodied in the Millennium Development Goals. In this chapter we examine in more detail the implications of our strategy for action by a developing-country government as it seeks to accelerate poverty reduction. In Chapter 13 we will examine the role for international action, particularly the role of developed countries. Domestic and international actions are complementary and are most effective when they represent a partnership based on common goals and shared understanding of development policy.

The two pillars of our strategy—strengthening the investment climate and empowering all citizens—are challenging tasks for any government, and they imply extensive responsibilities for the state. How do all these responsibilities fit together? How should they be managed and organized? How can they be financed in a way that promotes a dynamic and entrepreneurial environment and an inclusive society? These are, in broad terms, the questions that we examine in this chapter. In proposing a strategy that implies a substantial role for the state, we would be remiss if we did not analyze how the strategy should be financed. All too often, discussions of the state's role are silent on this crucial point, and this silence undermines a large part of their validity. Hence this chapter's focus on public finances.

In the first section we outline, in the context of the proposed strategy, what the state should be doing. This issue is intimately intertwined with public finances, since revenue raising and spending responsibilities constitute much of the state's role. What should be the range of fiscal responsibilities, at what level of government should they be conducted, and how should accountability function? When a society answers these questions, it defines what it means by the role of the state. Thus, public finances shape the role of the state, and the role of the state shapes public finances.

A fundamental requirement for public action and public finances is that they display basic macroeconomic responsibility. At one level this simply embodies the observance of the laws of arithmetic: government can only spend the resources it has and cannot create resources for public infrastructure or public education through wishful thinking. There are, of course, issues of how to balance budgets over cycles and how to manage borrowing over time. These issues should be handled with some flexibility, but not in ways that conceal the fact that there are limitations on budgets. These constraints are the subject of this chapter's second section.

The third section examines the level, composition, and management of public spending. Over the past two decades we have learned a lot about how to improve public expenditure management—an essential task, given evidence that the quality of spending matters as much as the quantity. Quality depends on the details of organization, management, incentives, transparency, and accountability, as we discuss in this section. We also examine evidence on a further issue: Will management and efficiency improvements within current structures be enough to achieve ambitious development goals, or are new structures needed?

Expenditures are the drivers of public action. In most societies the main force for redistribution comes from the expenditure side of the budget. That force, or at least potential force, is a fundamental reason more egalitarian societies tend to have higher ratios of taxation to GDP. The way that expenditures are financed has profound implications for the functioning of the economy and society. The fourth section examines key issues related to the structure of the tax system in terms of indirect taxes, direct taxes, intergovernmental relations, and administration.

Finally, the fifth section looks at privatization, an issue that has been both contentious and politically sensitive over the past twenty years. What goods and services should government directly produce? How and when should government adjust the structure of its activities and privatize? Which activities are most likely to improve the investment climate and empower poor people?

As in previous chapters, we raise here broad, far-reaching issues that have been the subject of intense analysis and debate. We cannot hope to do full justice to the richness of that discussion. But it would be irresponsible—and, as we have emphasized, undermine our entire argument about the public action arising from our strategy—if we did not tackle directly the public finance and management issues that arise from it.

The Role of the State

What, in summary, is the policy content of our development strategy, and what does it imply for government? An active government is needed to create a favorable investment climate and to facilitate poor people's empowerment and their participation in economic life. This raises three general questions. First, what should government be doing? Second, which level of government should carry out these functions? Finally, and most important, what capacity does a government need to have to carry out these responsibilities? This section spells out briefly the principles involved in the answers to these questions.

What Is the Policy Agenda?

In broad terms, the policy agenda for building the first pillar of our strategy includes action that fosters an environment of trust and innovation, an environment where markets can function and contracts are honored. This requires the creation and maintenance of macroeconomic stability, infrastructure, defense, financial systems, and sound administrative, legal, and regulatory structures, at a minimum. In building the second pillar, the responsibilities of government include fostering health and education (which also influence the investment climate) as well as the social, political, and physical environment that helps people participate in the decisions that affect their lives in the economic and social realms.

An action plan to implement the strategy and deliver on the above responsibilities of the state would contain four elements. The first two have a powerful influence on both pillars of the strategy, the third is focused on the investment climate, and the fourth on empowerment.

The first element of the action plan is *good governance and public sector management*. It is the focus of the bulk of this chapter, with the second, third, and fourth sections dealing with responsibility for, and management of, the expenditure and revenue sides of the budget. Governance and public sector management shape both the investment climate and the efficiency of delivery of the basic services that are at the center of the empowerment agenda, particularly health and education.

The second element is *physical infrastructure*. Public transportation, power, telecommunications, and water have a vital influence on the ability of both enterprises (whether firms or farms) to operate effectively and individuals to participate. All these services depend on public action: government must either deliver them directly or create a regulatory and competition framework that channels private sector participation. The final section of this chapter, on privatization, raises issues critical for the delivery of infrastructure services. (Rosenblatt and Stern 2003 provides further details.) Infrastructure is crucial for growth—yet its contribution is often underestimated, and the sector's performance is often weak.

The third element of the action plan concerns the *institutional framework for markets*—information, property rights, legal systems, financial systems, and so on. Government should examine, and where possible reduce or remove, unnecessary administrative, regulatory, and policy barriers to doing business. That does not mean removing all barriers. Many, such as health and fire regulations and financial market supervision, are there for good reason, and some promote the functioning of markets. This institutional framework should promote competition, most notably by removing or reducing entry and exit barriers to economic activity. Thus, promoting a good business environment is not simply about making existing firms happy; it is also about exposing them to competitive pressure. Firm-level investment climate surveys, like those described in lectures II and III, can help identify many of the relevant barriers. A simple way of summarizing the policy agenda on this institutional side of the business environment is that most developing countries need more good regulation and less bad regulation. The story is not simply deregulation: it is not about getting government out of the way but about getting government to do the right things in the right way.

The fourth element in the action plan is the *organization of the provision of basic services*. We have learned much about how to provide services more effectively, particularly in education and health, which are central to empowerment. Transparency, accountability, and incentives are all crucial elements here, as we discuss in the section on public spending.

Who Does What?

At the center of our proposed development strategy are the twin ideas of enabling enterprises (first pillar) and individuals (second pillar) to have greater scope for action. Who should carry out which of the related functions, the public or the private sector? If the public, which level of government?

Some might infer that the proposed strategy implies decentralization to as low a level of government as possible. It can be argued that having the apparatus of the state closer to the individual brings two advantages. First, government will have a better understanding of the individual's tastes and needs. Second, government will be more democratically accountable and responsive. A third argument for decentralization, also important, concerns competition between regions. Benchmarking your community against others can help you assess its performance, which can improve accountability.

Although there is considerable weight to these arguments, we should be careful about jumping to the conclusion that the strategy always and unambiguously points, on empowerment or other grounds, to decentralization. On the question of matching individuals' tastes, in some cases central governments may be as able as local governments to tailor to local needs at lower levels—for example, by granting discretion to medical facilities or by maintaining strong databases. In other cases the central government may want to insist on uniform standards instead of varying services by community. Local accountability can go wrong, too, if local political barons, vested interests, or mafias take control. Moreover, there is no guarantee that small units have homogeneous populations. Many cities, for example, are very heterogeneous. In such settings certain cliques or communities may take over and pay little attention to the welfare of other groups.

Further, decentralization brings with it some basic costs and difficulties. First, there will be coordination costs, because in any locality some services will be consumed by out-of-jurisdiction households or firms that do not pay for them. Second, small jurisdictions may be at a disadvantage from a public finance perspective because there are increasing returns to scale for certain activities, such as tax collection and bond finance. Third, decentralization risks dynamic costs associated with a "race to the bottom" (excessive competition) among jurisdictions.

We have argued that the key features of authority in shaping empowerment (or effective participation) are information, transparency, accountability, and openness of local organizations, which combine with education, health, and property rights to determine the scope of action for individuals. These key features may be enhanced by decentralization to lower levels of local government, but that outcome is not certain. What matters most is how the organizations function. Can they deliver? Do they listen? Can they adjust to local needs? Decisions on the question of level of government must be based on answers to these questions rather than any prejudice for or against local control.

The allocation or assumption of responsibilities for action is not just a question of level of government. The private sector, NGOs, and civil society have roles to play, and effective action depends on cooperation among these sectors of society and government. We have touched on many of these issues elsewhere in this book, including most notably our discussion of empowerment (see chapters 3, 5, and 8). In the fifth section of this chapter, on privatization, we address some of the considerations used in deciding whether an activity should be public or private.

What Is the Capacity of the State?
The questions we have asked so far about the role of the state—about what it should do and at what level of government—have to be answered partly in terms of the capacity of the state. In both developed and developing countries there are many examples of governments that have taken on more than they can manage, given their administrative capacity to design and implement policy or to provide basic health and education services. These examples, together with weak revenue-raising capacity in many countries, have led some to argue that the state in developing countries should be extremely modest in its objectives and scope. There is some basis to this argument, but it must be set against the scale of the development challenge facing developing countries and the extensive range of state actions needed to foster inclusive growth.

How can we assess the capacity of the state in developing countries, and what can be done to improve it? One indicator of state capacity is the World Bank's Country Policy and Institutional Assessment (CPIA). This index, calculated annually for each of the World Bank's borrowing countries, is a subjective assessment by the experts working on a particular country. It grades the country's policy and institutional framework in terms of its ability to foster sustainable growth, reduce poverty, and make effective use of development assistance. The CPIA index is composed of twenty equally weighted criteria grouped in four clusters: economic management, structural policies, policies for social inclusion and equity, and public sector management and institutions.[1] The index is not publicly available; we believe that it should be moved into the public domain. Some people have argued for maintaining the status quo: they fear that with public dissemination, countries will lobby World Bank experts hard for higher ratings, which will reduce the accuracy and usefulness of the CPIA measure. But these arguments are likely outweighed by the benefits of transparency, as suggested by the IMF's recent experience with releasing many of its country macro-economic assessments (Glennerster and Shin 2003).[2] Other multilateral development banks have corresponding indexes that capture the capacity of a state, such as the African Development Bank's CPIA, the Asian Development Bank's Country Performance Assessment, and the European Bank for Reconstruction and Development Bank's Transition Indicators.

Macroeconomic Stability and Fiscal Discipline

A government concerned with promoting growth and fighting poverty must pay serious attention to macroeconomic stability and fiscal discipline. Indeed, the ability to control the fiscal position is a crucial test of good governance. Fiscal policy affects growth in two fundamental ways. First, prudent and sustainable policy—meaning low, stable deficit and debt over the long run—is associated with higher economic growth (Easterly, Rodriguez, and Schmidt-Hebbel 1994). Second, fiscal policy affects growth through its incentive effects on individuals and enterprises.

Macroeconomic instability—and its extreme case, macroeconomic crisis—usually has multiple causes, many of them interrelated. These include balance-of-payments deficits, often arising from overvalued fixed exchange rates; fragile banking systems, saddled with nonperforming loans arising from corruption, favoritism, or weak management; overexposure to financial risks by firms, financial institutions, and households (particularly mismatches of assets and liabilities in terms of foreign currencies, often arising from inadequate supervision); stagnation in the real economy; and unsustainable debt in the public and private sectors. Many of these causes have deep roots in the institutional structure of the economy or society—outdated industries kept alive by subsidies or directed credits, corrupt relationships tying bank or industry shareholders to government, opaque or undisciplined intergovernmental tax structures, and so on.

Although the precise combination of causes of macroeconomic instability varies by country, one cause appears in many crises, albeit with different roots: large, persistent government deficits that cause a buildup of debt that markets regard as unsustainable. But even that is not a universal phenomenon. East Asia's financial crisis of 1997–1998 was primarily a story of vulnerability to rapid capital outflows (a run on banks), and for the most part the crisis countries were not running unsustainable formal government deficits (Stiglitz and Furman 1998).[3] Whichever sector it manifests itself in, instability can be precipitated or intensified by open capital markets, a point underscored by the East Asian crisis.

Despite the macroeconomic progress highlighted elsewhere in these lectures, budget deficits and debt levels remain substantial in many developing countries, especially those classified as low income. In 2002 the (unweighted) average central government deficit for 142 developing and transition countries was 3.6 percent of GDP. For 61 low-income countries the deficit was higher still: 4.6 percent of GDP. In 30 developing and transition countries the average public debt was equivalent to 65 percent of GDP, while in 14 low-income countries the figure was 83 percent (International Monetary Fund 2002).[4]

These deficit and debt averages for developing countries would not be considered unmanageably high in a developed country; they are only slightly above the Maastricht criteria agreed (but not adhered) to in the Euro zone, for example. The problem is developing countries' vulnerability to macroeconomic crisis and the uncertainty of their future government revenues, together with the relatively high debt of low-income countries. In the face of macroeconomic instability in developing countries, the response of capital markets is often swift and severe, magnifying business cycles. Such punishment deepens the poverty of the many people in those countries already living on the margin. In addition to reducing these imbalances and vulnerabilities, developing countries may need to reorient the composition of their spending and improve its efficiency and targeting.

Among the challenges of fiscal discipline is divining its meaning. In downswings in a business cycle, revenue is likely to fall below trend and spending to rise above it. When deficits arise in this cyclical way, they can act as automatic stabilizers, which is often good macroeconomic policy. Thus, in assessing fiscal discipline, one must measure deficits over the entire business cycle.

At the same time, when making these structural deficit calculations, it is important to distinguish cyclical from secular downturns. Many sub-Saharan African countries treated commodity price declines in the early 1980s as temporary downtowns—when, as it turned out, the declines were permanent and required a major adjustment of revenues and expenditures. The region's indebtedness rose sharply as governments delayed this adjustment. Similar problems have occurred elsewhere. As an observer once said about Latin America (though it could apply equally well to other regions, developing and developed), "All bad news is temporary and all good news is permanent." The former requires no fiscal adjustment, and the latter allows increased spending or tax cuts.

Another point to consider is that deficits that finance consumption are likely to be more damaging than those that finance investment for growth. Indeed, government borrowing at reasonable rates for highly productive investment may make fiscal sense.[5] A final point is that if a country does descend into crisis, it must consider how any fiscal adjustment will affect short-term growth. In the East Asian financial crisis, governments had to relax their initially tight fiscal targets for fear that fiscal stringency would deepen an increasingly severe crisis.

Thus, any judgment on the appropriate fiscal stance at any point in time should be made with some subtlety—but not so much subtlety that we ignore the basic laws of arithmetic and economics. If a government is spending resources, those resources have to come from somewhere. Governments cannot indefinitely run deficits that increase debt faster than the growth of national income.

As noted, capital markets offer more leeway to countries that are richer and have better fiscal track records. If their governments say that they are allowing automatic stabilizers to work or are borrowing to invest in an extraordinary opportunity, these claims will likely be considered credible. By contrast, governments from poorer countries with weaker track records may find such borrowing much more difficult or costly.

Fiscal constraints can be very frustrating for governments trying to promote growth and poor people's participation in it. Many improvements in the investment climate, such as better infrastructure, place great demands on resources. So does investment in the education and health of poor people. Because of governments' inability to make tax systems strongly progressive in practice (no matter what the legislated marginal tax rates are), most redistribution takes place on the expenditure rather than the tax side of the budget (Burgess and Stern 1993). Thus, there are always pressures for spending. These pressures can degenerate into populist demands made by those who do not understand, or do not want to accept, the basic arithmetic of fiscal policy.

But ignoring fiscal constraints can plunge an economy into crisis, doing great harm to the living standards of poor people and the economy's prospects for future growth.[6] Pursuit of the strategy described here (or any other development strategy promoting growth and poverty reduction) requires fiscal discipline: careful control of expenditure levels, productive allocation and use of expenditures, and strong and predictable sources of revenue. In most cases the bulk of revenue will come from domestic rather than foreign sources, so raising revenue requires an efficient tax system. The next two sections of this chapter examine issues related to spending and revenues, respectively.

Public Expenditure

Our discussion of public expenditure in this section takes, for the most part, a macrofiscal perspective, in keeping with our emphasis on fiscal discipline at this point in the argument. But in some important ways the approach proposed here is reflected in our emphasis on the importance of the institutions delivering public services and how spending is organized—as in our discussions of health and education, particularly in the sections on empowerment (see chapters 3, 5, and 8). This point is also made powerfully in the *World Development Report 2004* (World Bank 2003a).

Level and Composition

Table 12.1 presents data on the composition of government spending (as a percentage of GDP) for a sample of developed and developing countries for the latest available fiscal year. (Because of data constraints, the table refers only to spending by central governments; it does not include municipal and local governments.[7]) The table shows that patterns of public spending vary greatly across developing countries. Some (such as Ethiopia and Jordan) suffer under a heavy burden of defense spending, while others (like Argentina and Costa Rica) spend little or nothing on defense. Spending on general public services—which includes the cost of police and other spending on public order, among many other activities—can be large but also varies considerably. Few developing countries spend much on agriculture and related activities; Botswana and Ethiopia are notable exceptions.

Health and education spending appears to be much higher in some countries than others. But education is often a local expenditure (though often financed largely by transfers from the central government), so comparisons based on central government expenditures may be misleading. When we examine changes over time, we find that health and education spending in the past two decades has been highly variable, but the trend is toward increased spending. Gupta, Clements, and Tiongson (1998), using a sample of 118 developing and transition countries, find that since the mid-1980s, average real per capita spending on education and health has increased in developing countries but decreased in transition economies.

In the context of our proposed development strategy, the question to ask is: To promote development and reach the targets set by the international community—the Millennium Development Goals (MDGs)—what should be the level and composition of public expenditure?

Consider first the level of spending. Is there a level that would enable a government to accelerate growth and achieve the MDGs? Put another way, is there a "right" size for government? Common sense tells us that the answers to both questions will depend on many variables, but we can learn some lessons by examining broad patterns and correlations.

One major determinant of the size of government is the extent of income transfers. Cross-country evidence shows that the amount of income transfers by government from high-income to low-income groups is highly correlated with per capita GDP. In the 1990s, for instance, transfers typically accounted for 55 to 60 percent of public spending in OECD countries, compared with 25 percent in sub-Saharan Africa. Low-income countries that are not former socialist economies (and for which data were reported) generally had small redistributive programs such as social security.[8]

Various theories have been offered to explain the size and growth of government, generally from a positive or descriptive perspective rather than a normative one. According to these theories the size of government results from a several elements: shifts in demands for government output, the costs of supplying that output, and the administrative costs of handling these demands or the political opposition to increased taxation. Explanations offered regarding government growth

Table 12.1
Central government: Expenditures by economic type (percent of GDP), selected countries

		General public services[a]	Defense	Education	Health	Social security	Agriculture and allied activities	Mining, manufacturing, and construction
Industrial countries								
Australia	1998	1.9	1.7	1.8	3.5	8.4	0.3	0.1
France	1993	3.6	2.5	3.2	10.0	17.9	0.1	0.1
Germany	1996	1.0	1.3	0.2	6.4	17.0	0.1	0.4
Spain	1997	1.8	1.0	1.1	1.9	12.9	0.2	0.1
Sweden	1999	3.5	2.2	2.6	0.8	18.2	0.6	0.1
United Kingdom	1999	2.8	2.6	1.3	5.5	13.1	0.1	0.1
United States	2001	2.3	3.0	0.4	4.3	5.5	0.4	0.0
Developing countries								
Argentina	2001	2.0	0.7	1.0	0.3	8.2	0.1	0.0
Botswana	1997	6.0	2.5	8.0	1.6	0.3	2.7	0.2
Brazil	1998	4.6	0.9	1.6	1.7	12.7	0.7	0.0
China (Mainland)	1999	1.2	1.3	0.2	0.0	0.4	0.8	0.3
Costa Rica	2001	2.1	0.0	5.0	5.2	5.0	0.4	0.0
Egypt	1997	2.4	2.9	4.5	1.0	0.1	1.6	0.0
Ethiopia	1999	2.7	8.8	3.5	1.3	0.4	3.1	0.3
India	2000	0.9	2.2	0.4	0.3	0.0	0.8	0.3
Jordan	2001	5.1	5.7	5.2	3.4	5.4	1.1	0.0
Kazakhstan	2001	2.6	0.8	0.6	0.4	4.8	0.6	0.1

Kenya	1998	5.1	1.5	6.7	1.8	0.7	1.5	0.3
Morocco	1999	5.8	4.2	5.8	1.0	3.0	1.2	0.0
Philippines	2001	2.2	0.9	3.3	0.4	0.8	0.8	0.0
Sri Lanka	2001	2.5	3.9	2.0	1.3	3.2	1.1	0.1
Sudan	1999	0.9	2.3	0.6	0.1	0.0	0.1	0.0
Thailand	2000	2.0	1.5	4.0	1.5	1.1	1.6	0.1
Turkey	2001	3.0	3.1	3.9	1.5	2.9	1.1	0.1

Data pertain to the latest available fiscal year. Data refers to consolidated central government for all extra budgetary operations for all other countries.

a Includes public order and safety.

Sources: Government Finance Statistics Yearbook 2002, IMF; *World Development Indicators*, various issues, World Bank.

include the income elasticity of demand for public services, or demand for public services linked to transformation of traditional society (Wagner's law); lower productivity growth in the public sector, with wages increasing at the same rate in both the private and public sectors, which leads to relative price shifts (known as "Baumol's disease"; see Baumol 1967); public employee voting that puts pressure on government to expand the bureaucracy; and the effects of fiscal decentralization.

Another major hypothesis to explain increases in public spending is that as GDP grows, the demand for social services changes. People become more active politically, changing the distribution of political power and causing institutional evolution. Another hypothesis is that with economic growth, it may become increasingly affordable to spend income on institutions that economize on transaction costs. More directly, as Jacobs (1969) remarked, it may also be that the process of urbanization that accompanies development is naturally accompanied by an evolution of social relations in the population—such as a greater need for coordination because of increased complexity. (These theories about the size of government and empirical tests of these theories are reviewed by Lybeck and Henrekson 1988, Mueller 2003, and Bourguignon 2004.)

These theories, while useful, do not necessarily provide much guidance on how large government *should* be. Our take on this question is to view it through the lens of our strategy on a country-by-country basis: If government is to deliver on the core investment climate and empowerment agenda, how large does it need to be? That agenda requires investing in infrastructure, public services such as education and health, social protection that allows risk taking, and so on. While the sum of these responsibilities will vary by country, together they imply a substantial role for the state. In subsequent sections of this chapter we lay out principles for financing this role and managing public spending. Combining an assessment of the state's responsibilities, revenue-raising potential, and management capacity should yield a judgment on its appropriate size and ambitions.

On the second point, the appropriate composition of spending to implement our proposed development strategy and meet the MDGs, it is clear that some countries will need to increase social spending, and possibly reduce spending on defense and law and order. But it is generally not true that all that is required to achieve satisfactory social outcomes is to increase spending on health and education (see chapter

11).[9] While it is difficult to generalize across countries, we would argue that improving the productivity of and institutional context for spending is typically more important than increasing overall spending. Although countries with good governance could in principle simply spend their way to the MDG targets, in practice this strategy is unlikely to be affordable given the scale of the targets and the productivity of expenditures. It would be even less affordable—and more likely impossible—in countries with weaker governance and lower ability to raise revenue and spending productivity.

These conclusions have two implications. First, building good policies and institutions is important for all countries; it increases the productivity not just of additional spending, but also of existing spending commitments. Second, in all countries the targeting of additional public spending is important. (See Wagstaff 2003 and World Bank 2003a for extensive treatment of these issues.)

To understand how governance and institutions can improve budget outcomes, consider health care. Wagstaff (2003) discusses examples of expenditure reallocations that can improve health outcomes. First, targeting resources to poor regions may benefit from the use of nontraditional mechanisms for priority setting and implementation. Social investment funds are one example.[10] A recent impact evaluation in Bolivia concluded that social investment funds were responsible for a statistically significant decline in under-five mortality, from 89 per 1,000 to 66 over a relatively short period (Wagstaff 2003). There is always a danger, however, that such funds will become creatures of a particular politician or group and used to dispense political favors.

Second, countries can benefit from coupling expenditure shifts away from secondary and tertiary hospital infrastructure and personnel with measures aimed at improving the performance of primary care facilities and district hospitals, together with measures aimed at raising household demand for health services. Third, targeting specific groups can increase the returns on some forms of public spending. Blanket subsidies fail to target interventions that generate externalities, such as the deworming program in Kenyan schools (Miguel and Kremer 2003). They also fail to benefit poor people disproportionately, despite the fact that poor people tend to bear a disproportionate burden of malnutrition and child and maternal mortality.

Finally, the productivity of resources can be increased through country-level assessments that identify the main impediments to faster health progress, suggest ways (and estimated costs) of removing them, and project how their removal will affect MDG outcomes. Work along these lines has begun in India, Mali, and several other African countries. In all these examples, it is important to pay attention to the institutional and governance dimensions of public spending, not just the level and composition.

Management

The budget is the main instrument for ensuring that all decisions about public spending are made within a consistent, sustainable framework. Given that spending decisions span more than one year, it has become common to take a medium-term perspective to assess the effects of both current policies and proposed measures. At a minimum this requires a medium-term macroeconomic framework to ensure the consistency of budget estimates with targets for economic growth, trade balances, inflation, and other economywide indicators. This macroeconomic exercise helps determine the overall budget envelope and is the starting point for the budget process.

The next task is allocation within the overall envelope. In principle, one would want to know, in a comparable way, the productivity of expenditures allocated to different uses. In a company, for example, there might be a rate of return that all projects should meet. This is a much more complicated exercise for government because it is not easy to bring all activities into a form where returns to expenditures can be calculated and compared. Still, some developed countries—Australia, New Zealand, the United Kingdom—have moved in this direction. They have all adopted forms of "budgeting for results," where ministries are funded and assessed based on specific measured results and objectives.

It is critical not only to be able to budget in an appropriate manner, but also to be able to track expenditures appropriately. Governments should be able to answer in a transparent way the questions of who used public money and what happened as a result.[11] Thus, the multilateral debt relief initiative (Heavily Indebted Poor Countries initiative, discussed in chapter 13) emphasizes the need for the most heavily indebted countries to track spending in areas, such as education and health care, that have a significant effect on poor people.

There are different models and experiences in establishing budget management systems. In some Western European countries, such as Norway and Sweden, line ministries are responsible for determining when budget appropriations need to be drawn down, as well as for accounting and reporting to the ministry of finance. Many developing and transition countries follow a more centralized model, where the ministry of finance establishes the spending calendar in consultation with the line ministries, taking into account cash flow constraints.

Regardless of whether there is centralized or delegated budgeting, almost all advanced and many developing countries have established a virtual or actual account, known as the treasury single account,[12] where all the government's cash is consolidated. This facilitates more effective cash and debt management and, more important, provides for transparency in spending by leaving an electronic or actual paper trail for the flow of public resources (both revenues and expenditures).

Transparency and Accountability
It takes time to build a credible budget process. In a politically stable environment the majority of players realize over time that the benefits of cooperation exceed the benefits of overspending and not abiding by the rules. During and after budget execution, credibility depends on three crucial elements: verification of expenditures, well-functioning control and audit institutions, and punishment of those who violate the law. Transparency and publicity during all phases of the budget process provide for better accountability and outcomes.

Transparency and accountability require not only an accurate and timely flow of information, but also the possibility of an audit—by both the ministry of finance and an independent audit agency that reports to parliament. These elements help ensure that public money is used effectively and not misappropriated.

Audit and accountability go beyond checking where the money has gone, to asking whether expenditures have achieved results. Managers of public spending should be asked to report on what happened as a result of the money spent in their charge. For example, at a first and basic level for education spending, one could ask questions about how many children went to school, what their educational attainments were, and so on. Or for a transportation budget, one could ask about the number, quality, and use of roads built.

More fundamentally, one would like to know whether budget funds could have been better spent relative to objectives. That leads us to the kinds of evaluation techniques discussed in chapter 6. For example, in 1994 India embarked on the District Primary Education Program that embodied a new approach to primary education. Key elements of the program include greater community involvement in running schools and incentives to get girls to attend school. From modest beginnings, the program now covers large parts of the country. And based on observations of some of the program's schools and experiences of seeing Indian schools in the past (including in Palanpur, a village in northern India that Nicholas Stern has studied with other colleagues since 1974), it seems likely that the program is benefiting children. But this type of casual empiricism is inadequate for assessing resource allocation on this scale; rigorous assessments are needed (on this point, see Case 2001). Unfortunately, the District Primary Education Program assessment was not set up in a way that allowed for sound statistical analysis of the program's effects.

At the beginning of the program it would have been possible to put in place mechanisms for rigorous assessments of the program's contributions relative to older methods of running schools. These mechanisms would have involved comparator groups, chosen with an eye toward statistical comparability and, where possible, random allocation of schools or villages into treatment and comparator groups. The District Primary Education Program is just one (albeit an important) example of a program where confidence in results was undermined by inadequate assessment. The statistical and experimental methods now available, including randomization, make it much more straightforward to establish what works and what does not (see chapter 6). Taking advantage of these tools is crucial not only to ensure accountability but also to allow scaling up of programs and policymaking.

Another set of problems is associated with the dependency of key outcomes on multiple causes. Health outcomes such as child mortality rates (prominent in the MDGs) depend on the education of parents (particularly mothers), nutrition, infrastructure (particularly water quality), environment (particularly indoor air pollution), and so on, as well as spending on and performance of health units such as hospital and clinics. Thus, it could be misleading to hold only health ministries accountable for health outcomes.

No simple formulas will provide easy answers to these challenges of evaluating results. And as noted, there are many complications beyond the difficulty of putting in place effective evaluations. Despite these complications, awareness of the analytical problems, buttressed by efforts to evaluate results, will likely make governments more responsible and resources more productive.

Public Sector Reform

We have tried to sketch methods for determining levels, allocations, and assessments of public expenditures. But public institutions in developing (and developed) countries are far from perfect. They often suffer from corruption and poor administration, and they are often staffed by people who are poorly paid and educated and have weak incentives for good performance. We should not pretend that such institutions and their employees can be transformed overnight into perfectly functioning organizations staffed by well-motivated paragons of efficiency and virtue. Reform of government administration is a major, ongoing challenge.

At the same time, we should not be overly negative about what can be achieved. Many countries have made impressive progress in fairly short periods. One example is Albania, which since 1999 has made significant strides toward establishing an effective civil service managed on the basis of merit. Competitive, transparent recruitment procedures are in place and are widely recognized to be functioning largely as intended. The share of civil service positions filled through competitive procedures rose from 38 percent in 2000 to 59 percent by 2002. And mechanisms to protect due process within the civil service have limited turnover following political transitions: quarterly turnover rates of civil servants between 2000 and 2002 show no evidence of spikes despite a cabinet reshuffling in mid-2001 (World Bank 2001h).

Budget discipline is another area where progress is difficult but not impossible. In many cases discipline is weak because politically appointed officials have no incentive to adhere to spending priorities and limits, institutional capacity to elaborate and implement realistic sector priorities is limited, especially in line ministries, and there are few incentives to ensure that spending programs are managed cost-effectively.

Our task in this section has not been to produce a mini-manual on budget and government reform. Rather, it has been to emphasize the importance of careful, responsible, accountable control over spending, and to illustrate what can be achieved through such control. This is an essential element of any strategy that implies a substantial and purposeful role for the state. So too is a discussion of revenue raising, to which we now turn.

Domestic Revenue as a Basis for Public Action

Government spending has to be financed through government revenue, borrowing, or printing of money, or through external grants. The costs of financing government spending thus fall immediately or subsequently on the people of the country (in the case of the first three) or on those outside (in the case of external grants). Being responsible requires that government statements about desired spending be accompanied by an indication of how the spending will be financed. In most countries the main source of finance is taxes. Because so many developing countries struggle to raise the revenue they need to operate, this section goes into detail on principles and approaches for raising revenue.

Challenges, Levels, and Choices

The level and allocation of spending have a profound influence on the investment climate and empowerment. They affect both the rate of growth and the extent to which poor people have a chance to participate in economic activity. As noted, though progressive taxation may seem an efficient mechanism for redistribution, in practice expenditures are usually a far more potent redistributive tool (Burgess and Stern 1993).[13] But expenditures must be financed. Thus, we should see the redistributional role for taxation largely in terms of financing the spending that will provide poor people with opportunities. A tax system that does not look very redistributional in terms of the way revenue is raised may nevertheless have strongly redistributional effects if it finances expenditures that go disproportionately to poor people.

At the same time, it would be a mistake to view the tax problem as simply one of financing a given aggregate expenditure (Burgess and Stern 1993). The tax system in developing countries is perhaps the most pervasive and far-reaching policy instrument available to the government. It is thus a crucial part of governance. When a government decides on its level of spending, the costs and difficulties associated with taxation should be central to the decision. We have to see the choices of taxation and spending as joint decisions. In this section we describe some of the challenges of taxation and illustrate what is possible in response.

On average, developing countries collect less tax revenue (as a percentage of GDP) than do developed countries (table 12.2). Central government tax revenue varies substantially by income level: for high-income countries it is about 30 percent, for middle-income countries about 20 percent, and for low-income countries about 15 percent. Developed countries find tax collection easier for two reasons: they have stronger administrative capacity to collect taxes, and, more important, the major economic activities in their countries are more straightforward to document and tax.

We should not conclude, however, that per capita income is the main determinant of government tax revenue as a share of GDP. There is great variation across countries with similar incomes, and some countries that are much poorer than others have similar or even larger ratios of tax revenue to GDP. For example, both Ethiopia and Thailand have ratios of about 17 percent, although Thailand's per capita income is around twenty times that of Ethiopia. And Brazil's ratio, at around 30 percent, is around twice that of its neighbor Argentina, although Brazil's per capita income is less than half that of Argentina. It is clear that the share of tax revenue in GDP, and thus to a large extent expenditure, is a matter of public choice. Those choices will be constrained by history, politics, constitutions, and the structure of the economy, but there are real choices that can be made.

Structure of the Tax System

As with overall levels of taxation, developing countries have substantial choice over the structure of the tax system in terms of the contribution and workings of individual taxes. This structure will be strongly influenced, but not uniquely determined, by the underlying structure of the economy and the development of administrative capacity. In this section we examine first how structures tend to change as development proceeds, then comment briefly on some underlying principles that should guide the choice of taxation.

The structure of taxation varies with the level of development (table 12.2). At low income levels, developing countries tend to rely more on trade and indirect taxes than direct taxes. Measurement of income, a necessary input for direct taxes, is more difficult in less developed economies; much of income comes from hard-to-measure peasant agriculture or small-scale services, for example. Thus, trade taxes have a more prominent role relative to consumption and sales taxes for countries at lower levels of development. Such countries have few "tax handles," and movement of goods across borders provides one of the few substantial opportunities to tax. Among direct taxes, the corporate income tax is more important (relative to income taxes and social security contributions) in developing than in more developed countries.

These differences among developing countries notwithstanding, what principles should guide the choice of tax structure and overall tax system, given the strategy proposed in this book? We provide below some general comments drawing on the vast literature on this subject for developing countries (see Burgess and Stern 1993 for a survey and Ahmad and Stern 1991 for a textbook treatment). Our purpose is

Table 12.2

Central government: Types of tax revenues (percent of GDP), selected countries

		Income taxes				Domestic indirect taxes				Foreign taxes			
		Individual	Corporate	Other	Total	General sales, turnover, VAT	Excises	Other	Total	Import duties	Export duties	Other	Total
Industrial countries													
Australia	1998	12	4	0.2	16.1	2.4	2.4	0.1	4.9	0.6	0	0	0.6
France	1997	6	2.1	0	8	8	2.7	1.1	11.7	0	0	0	0
Germany	1998	4	0.6	0	4.6	3.4	2.5	0.4	6.3	0	0	0	0
Spain	1997	6	2.4	0	8.5	4.3	2.5	0.2	7	0	0	0	0
Sweden	1999	2.4	3	0	5.4	6.7	3.5	0.4	10.7	0	0	0	0
United Kingdom	1999	10.5	3.8	0	14.3	6.8	4	0.4	11.2	0	0	0	0
United States	2001	9.9	1.5	0	11.4	0	0.5	0.1	0.6	0.2	0	0	0.2
Developing countries													
Argentina	2001	0.8	1.7	0	2.5	3.3	1.7	0	5	0.6	0	0	0.6
Botswana	1997	1.3	4.4	0.8	6.5	1.3	0	0.1	1.4	4.7	0	0	4.7
Brazil	1998	0.3	1.3	3.4	5	2	1.8	1.4	5.3	0.7	0	0	0.7
China (Mainland)	1999	0	0.5	0	0.5	4.3	1.1	0	5.4	0.7	0	0	0.7
Costa Rica	2001	0.1	2.9	0	3	5	1.9	2	8.9	0.8	0	0.1	1
Egypt	1997	0.6	4.5	0.6	5.7	0	4.4	0.1	4.5	3.3	0	0	3.3
Ethiopia	1999	1.1	2.7	0.5	4.3	2	0.9	0.4	3.2	3.4	0.4	1.2	5
India	2000	1.2	1.5	0.1	2.7	0	2.9	0.1	3.1	2.3	0	0	2.3
Jordan	2001	0.8	2.2	0.1	3.1	8	0	1	9.1	3.9	0	0.4	4.2
Kazakhstan	2001	0	2.8	0	2.8	4.6	0.5	0.8	6	0.5	0	0.2	0.8

Kenya	1998	n.a.	n.a.	n.a.	8	5	4.1	0.5	9.6	3.6	0	3.6
Morocco	1999	3.3	2.7	1.1	7.1	5.5	4.4	0.9	10.7	4.7	0	4.7
Philippines	2001	2.2	2.7	1.2	6.1	1.6	1.6	0.8	4	2.6	0	2.7
Sri Lanka	2001	1	1.5	0	2.5	3.3	3.2	3.1	9.7	1.9	0	1.9
Sudan	1999	0.4	0.8	0	1.2	0.8	1.4	0.6	2.8	2.3	0	2.3
Thailand	2000	1.8	2.8	0.2	4.8	3.1	3.4	0.4	6.9	1.7	0	1.8
Turkey	2001	7.2	2.3	0.7	10.2	7	4.3	0.3	11.6	0.3	0	0.3

[a] Data pertain to the latest available fiscal year.
[b] Data refers to consolidated central government for all developed countries, Argentina, Brazil, Costa Rica, Egypt, India, Kazakhastan, Morocco, Thailand and Turkey; and to Budgetary Central Government (and hence may exclude some extrabudgetary operations) for all other countries.
Sources: Government Finance Statistics Yearbook 2002, IMF; *World Development Indicators*, various issues, The World Bank 2003g.

to bolster our argument that sound taxes that raise substantial revenue are possible—but that they have to reflect sound economic and administrative principles and an assessment of administrative capacity.

Tariffs   Tariffs on imports can be a useful source of revenue in a poor developing country with few tax handles. Tariffs remain relatively high in a number of developing countries, and dispersion of tariff rates is high both across and within economic sectors. But tariffs carry some serious economic and administrative disadvantages. Import tariffs raise prices for both consumers of a good and producers using that good, while protecting domestic producers of that good. Thus, they are a subsidy to certain sectors of the economy, paid for by consumers buying from that sector and by other sectors that use the good as inputs. Tariffs therefore distort economic incentives in the sense that resources are diverted from nonsubsidized sectors to activities that are profitable only at prices higher than those on world markets. That is the traditional static inefficiency argument, and it is important.

There are also some dynamic investment climate issues of great importance in assessing import tariffs. Openness to world markets and the ideas and competition it brings can stimulate entrepreneurship and allow for the recognition and adoption of new opportunities. Further, customs administration is notoriously one of the most corrupt activities in the governance of developing countries (Rose-Ackerman 1999). In a large portion of the investment climate surveys carried out by the World Bank and its partners, customs administration was one of the biggest obstacles to business activity (Batra, Kaufmann, and Stone 2003; World Bank 2003b). Simple structures of import tariffs with moderate, fairly uniform rates could help limit corruption in customs administration.

On the other hand, it has long been argued that tariffs are useful for encouraging new industries that might provide strong lessons for others—that is, that might produce externalities for which they are not rewarded. And capital markets may not supply finance to industries that engage in essentially profitable activities but will incur losses in their early years as learning occurs. These so-called infant industry arguments should not be dismissed out of hand, given the number of countries that have grown rapidly while protected by significant import barriers. We reviewed briefly in chapter 2 the history of intellectual support for import-substituting industrialization, which relied heavily on tariffs. More recently, arguments emphasizing learning externalities and the challenges faced by new industries have been offered by Hausmann and Rodrik (2003).

From a revenue-raising perspective there are good arguments for keeping moderate tariffs in place in low-income countries where other tax instruments are relatively weak. While doing so will provide some protection for tradable sectors, infant industry arguments for protection should be handled with great care. They do not lead directly to the conclusion that tariffs are the appropriate instrument. It may be better to subsidize the education or other skills that are clearly related to the externalities. Or it may make sense for the state to invest in infrastructure that allows connections and exchange of information among firms as they learn and grow.

Similarly, problems in capital markets should be tackled directly, where possible—for example, with corporate tax systems that allow for the carry-forward of losses. Such measures can contribute directly to the investment climate, and to economic opportunity more generally, while causing fewer political and administrative problems than tariffs.

Although tariff protection has gone hand in hand with successful growth in East Asia and elsewhere (and some researchers argue for a causal relationship), it is important not to downplay the costs imposed by high levels of protection. Not only do tariffs create distortions, they are also self-reinforcing: the erecting of tariff walls creates and nurtures a powerful lobby for continuing protective privileges, and thus diverts resources from entrepreneurship into rent seeking. (Little, Scitovsky, and Scott (1970) is the classic reference here.) As has often been noted, it is remarkable how long infant industries can remain uncompetitive and go on proclaiming their infancy (see, for example, the description of India's strategy in Bhagwati 1998 and Srinivasan 1998).

From the point of view of reflecting our proposed strategy in the tax system, developing countries are thus well advised to move away from excess reliance on import tariffs and to build alternative sources of revenue. But it takes time to build alternative sources. Industrial adjustment can also take time. Even firms that would eventually adapt to life without the tariff, and thrive in the new setting, may fail if the adjustment is too sudden. Of course, there will be other firms that should not survive; if they cannot operate profitably at the new prices, after due allowance for pace of adjustment, then they are wasting resources by producing goods or services at higher costs than they are worth. It is better for the economy and general well-being if these resources are allocated elsewhere and if workers devote their time to more productive activities. But these alternative opportunities do not appear by magic, and helping to stimulate them is precisely what improving the investment climate and empowering and investing in people are all about.

Indirect Taxes Indirect taxes cover sales, production, value-added, and excise taxes. As much as possible, it is best to avoid taxation of intermediate goods. With such taxation, firms using those goods in further production are paying more than it cost to produce them, which distorts production levels and techniques. There are formal demonstrations that such intuition is robustly correct (Diamond and Mirrlees 1971). This principle is one of the reasons many economists recommend moving to a value-added system of taxation. A value-added tax (VAT) is levied on imports and does not discriminate against exports (taxes on inputs are rebated). A further, and perhaps more powerful, argument is that the VAT has strong administrative advantages, in that to some degree it is self-enforcing. Firm A buying a good from firm B has a strong incentive to show what the good cost, because the tax paid by firm A is deductible against VAT payments, making it harder for firm B to disguise sales. Further, information from VAT administration provides powerful information on incomes (since value added is wages plus profits), and this information can then be used in direct taxation.

Partly because of such advantages, VAT systems have spread across the developing world at a remarkable rate in the past thirty years. More than 120 countries now levy a VAT. In many developing countries VATs have replaced customs duties as the main source of revenue (table 12.3).

A VAT is easiest to administer if the number of rates is kept to a minimum. Nevertheless, a VAT with two rates and appropriate zero rating or exemptions can produce a fairly progressive system in terms of tax burdens at different income levels (as shown, for example, in Ahmad and Stern 1991).

As for other indirect taxes, excise duties on cigarettes, alcohol, and petroleum products can be important sources of revenue. These taxes can be justified on other grounds as well: they reduce demand for products that can have harmful effects on others (that is, negative externalities) or that are nonmerit goods (in that people using them may not fully understand or take account of the damage they do to themselves).

Table 12.3
Comparative VAT rates in selected developing countries (in percent)

	Date VAT introduced	Standard rate	Other rates[a]
Africa			
Côte d'Ivoire	1960	20	
Congo Republic	1997	18	
Kenya	1990	18	16
Madagascar	1994	20	5
South Africa	1991	14	
Zambia	1995	17.5	
Asia			
Bangladesh	1991	15	
China	1994	17	13
Egypt	1991	15	5.0, 10.0, 25.0
Indonesia	1985	10	
Korea	1977	10	2, 3.5
Morocco	1986	20	7.0, 10.0, 14.0
Pakistan	1990	15	
Philippines	1988	10	
Singapore	1994	3	
Sri Lanka	1998	12.5	
Thailand	1992	10	
Tunisia	1988	18	6.0, 10.0, 29.0
Latin America			
Argentina	1975	21	10.5, 27.0
Bolivia	1973	14.9	
Chile	1975	18	
Colombia	1975	15	8.0, 10.0, 20.0
Costa Rica	1975	15	
Ecuador	1970	12	
Mexico	1980	15	10
Nicaragua	1975	15	5.0, 6.0
Panama	1977	5	10
Peru	1973	18	
Uruguay	1968	23	14
Venezuela	1993	15.5	

Notes: VAT rates (in tax-exclusive form, that is, specified as a proportion of the net of tax price) shown are as of April 2001.
[a] Excludes the zero rate on exports.
Source: Ebrill Stotsky, and Gropp (2001).

Direct Taxes   Direct taxes consist mainly of corporate income taxes, personal income taxes, and social security taxes. From the perspective of our proposed development strategy, what can be said about these three types of revenue? Viewed through the lens of the investment climate, the corporate income tax has limited arguments in its favor. There is some argument for using it as a tax on foreign firms or monopoly rents, or as a way to recoup the costs of the protections that incorporation offers firms. But these arguments carry only so much weight. The corporate tax should be seen largely as a device for collecting taxes on personal incomes where these incomes are difficult to measure (or where firms can turn them into capital gains, for example). Indeed, the corporate income tax can be a powerful collection device, particularly in developing countries, where it generally brings in more revenue than the personal income tax (see table 12.2).

It is important, however, to limit the gratuitous distortions caused by the corporate incomes tax—for example, by ensuring that the tax system treats inflation and investment correctly. Burgess and Stern (1993) offer a more detailed discussion of these design and implementation issues than is possible here. But one point worth emphasizing is that countries should be careful about widespread use of tax holidays and corporate tax incentives. Of course, companies often argue that such special treatment is essential for investment. But there is limited evidence that this is true (Tanzi and Zee 2000, Shah 1995), perhaps because companies are uncertain how long tax-favored treatment will last. On the other hand, it is clear that such privileges can erode the tax base, limiting what governments can achieve in crucial sectors such as education and infrastructure. Moreover, special privileges lead to a lobbying and rent-seeking culture that is inimical to competition and productive entrepreneurship.

By contrast, there is powerful evidence of a strong relationship between the investment climate and investment activity. In firm surveys, many entrepreneurs attribute decisions not to invest to punitive levels of taxation (Batra, Kaufmann, and Stone 2003; World Bank 2003b). Governments should focus on improving the investment climate and keeping overall taxation at reasonable levels, rather than providing special tax privileges for some (and imposing much higher tax rates on others who do not qualify for the privileges). Improvements in the investment climate generate benefits throughout the economy, not just for favored sectors. And they improve productivity generally rather than simply stimulating investment that will not necessarily be productive—a particular worry if it is claimed that such investment cannot survive without privileges.

Over time, developing countries should look to build up the personal income tax as a source of revenue. Eventually it will likely generate as much revenue as indirect taxes. Indeed, for developed countries it is usually the most important source of revenue (see table 12.2). But broadening the personal income tax base is a gradual process and will generally not be a priority early in development. An effective personal income tax system depends on having a large share of the workforce employed in the formal sector of the economy, a condition not met by many low-income countries.

In many countries social security taxes are essentially a form of income tax, in that they are related to personal income and the benefit entitlements they bring have only a weak link to future benefit payments. In countries where the links are stronger, however, social security taxes can be seen as a genuinely different revenue instrument from the income tax—not simply as a tax-like contribution to a social security fund. Social security systems in developing countries often offer benefits to a narrow group of privileged workers. As we discussed in chapter 8, "smart" transfer systems are often a more effective way to reach those most in need of support.

This is not the place for a detailed analysis of the principles of income taxation. As with most other taxes, the key issues and principles involve revenue, incentives, income distribution, and administration. It is easier to make income taxes progressive than it is indirect taxes. Exemption limits below which an income tax is not payable are important for ensuring progressivity. In developing countries exemption limits are also important for simplifying tax administration; it would be extremely costly to levy income taxes on millions of poor people with weak income data (see Ahmad and Stern 1991 for further discussion). But it is also the case that the rich taxpayers who can be included in the tax base are typically the most skilled at avoidance and evasion, especially if the tax system is complicated. So to ensure that the system yields substantial revenue and is progressive, governments need to keep the tax structure simple and avoid high marginal rates.

Tax Administration   There are many other important issues for taxation in developing countries, including relationships between levels of government and taxation of natural resources, land, buildings, and agriculture. This is not the appropriate place to go into detail on such issues (see Ahmad and Stern 1991, Burgess and Stern 1993, Bird 1992, Tanzi 1991, and Bird and Oldman 1990 for further discussion). But given its impact on the investment climate in developing countries, the issue of tax administration is of special relevance for our proposed strategy.

The challenge of effective tax administration is to raise revenues without causing excessive economic disincentives or providing opportunities for corruption, harassment, and other predatory behavior by tax authorities. It is about collecting needed revenue while limiting damage to the investment climate and entrepreneurship. While there will always be tensions in responding to this challenge, much can be done to meet it effectively. Tax systems can be designed with simple definitions and rates, limiting the discretion of tax authorities. Such systems also allow for easier audit. Modern information technology can limit direct contact between taxpayers and tax officials. So can self-assessment with random auditing, which also simplifies administration.

As noted, customs administration has been a prominent source of corruption and harm to the investment climate in many countries. In some countries (such as Pakistan in the 1980s and 1990s), customs operations have required inspection of all shipments, leading to considerable delays and providing enormous scope for corruption. In some major Middle Eastern ports with such requirements in the late 1990s, it took an average of sixteen days to clear a container. Not surprisingly, little contraband was officially found—but customs officials probably ended up richer (see Dollar, Hallward-Driemeier, and Mengistae 2003 for survey evidence from more than a dozen countries on this issue).

With customs, as with domestic taxation, self-assessment is now widely used. Customs clearance has been facilitated by the electronic transmission of information, electronic processing of customs declarations, and direct payment of duties through the banking system. As a result cargo can be declared and valued and duties paid well before shipments arrive. With proper risk analysis and random checks, the need to physically inspect cargo and interact with importers (or exporters) has been drastically reduced. In Singapore the average time to clear a container is only a few hours. Faster clearance and reduced inspections need not compromise security. In these streamlined systems, information and energy can be used more intelligently to identify and search high-risk shipments rather than performing perfunctory checks on all cargo.

Possibilities and Ambitions

We have argued that fiscal discipline is crucial in promoting development. We have also argued that our proposed strategy points to a large agenda for government action. We have further discussed the difficulties associated with, and the principles that should guide, the use of different taxes. Some resources can come from external aid, as discussed in chapter 13. But annual aid per capita for low-income countries is only around $8—about 2 percent of their average GDP per capita of around $430. For middle-income countries the figure is also some $8, or just 0.4 percent of their average GDP per capita of $1,860 (World Bank 2003g). Compare this with government spending as a share of GDP, which for most developing countries is at least 20 percent. There is no doubt that aid can and should be expanded substantially. But especially since not all aid will go directly to government, in most countries tax revenue will remain the central mechanism for financing government spending.

Given the arguments and principles laid out in this section, is it feasible for a developing-country government to generate revenue on a scale commensurate with development ambitions and the approach of the proposed strategy? One way of grappling with that question is to look at the potential revenue from each major kind of tax, based on assumptions about the typical developing country's likely tax base relative to GDP and about tax rates. Table 12.4 offers some rough calculations showing the magnitudes that might be involved.

Table 12.4
Illustrative revenue potential in a "typical" developing country

	Effective base as share of GDP	Average rate	Revenue
Trade taxes (imports)	20%	15%	3%
VAT	40	15	6
Excises (on tobacco, alcohol, petroleum products)	10	40	4
Corporate taxes	10	30	3
Income taxes and social security	20	15	3
Total			19

Although the table assumes a developing economy that is fairly typical in terms of its tax bases, the tax bases are moderately ambitious in terms of the assumptions they embody about tax laws and the quality of tax administration. For comparison, the base of the VAT in the United Kingdom is about 50 percent of GDP, compared with 40 percent in table 12.4. The assumed tax base for corporate taxes and income tax and social security contributions is small by the standards of developed countries, but not so small for an economy with substantial agricultural, informal, and small-scale sectors. At the same time, the table omits potentially important tax bases, such as natural resources, land, and buildings. Natural resource taxes can be of enormous importance in some countries but negligible in others, while taxes on land and buildings are a fairly weak source of revenue in most developing countries. The tax rates assumed here may appear moderate, but much higher rates are likely to encounter serious problems of evasion.

The calculations in table 12.4 point to a number of interesting conclusions. First, without a large natural resource base for taxation, it will be difficult to push tax takes much above 20 percent of GDP.[14] Brazil is one of the few exceptions among large countries: by making extensive use of social security contributions, value-added taxes, and direct taxes, it is able to bring in unusually high revenues of around 30 percent of GDP. But few developing countries without significant natural resources achieve a tax take of more than 15 to 20 percent of GDP. For very poor countries, taxes yield even less.

Second, the greatest scope for increasing tax revenues over time is likely to come from growth in income tax bases as a percentage of GDP. Table 12.4 already incorporates fairly optimistic assumptions about bases and rates for trade and indirect taxes, so these are not likely to increase much further. But it is perfectly possible for income tax bases as a share of GDP to double (or more than double) over time, adding perhaps 6 to 9 percent of GDP in revenues. What does this imply for a middle-income country with good tax administration but without substantial natural resources? Once we include other omitted sources of tax revenue, it should not be impossible for such a country to raise revenues of some 30 percent of GDP, in a way that avoids severe damage to incentives.

Third, tax revenues of more than 20 percent of GDP for a low-income country and 30 percent for a middle-income country will not be achieved without contributions from half a dozen or so major tax sources, each of which will need to be administered fairly well.

Fourth, the combination of taxes illustrates that it is not easy to achieve progressivity in the tax system as a whole. Such progressivity that arises in developed countries on the tax side usually comes through the personal income tax—and as we see in table 12.4, the income tax is likely to play only a modest role in developing countries.

Fifth, given the limited possibilities that low-income countries have for raising revenue, external aid equal to 5 percent of GDP—if it raised government resources from, say, 15 to 20 percent of GDP—could have a powerful effect on what it is possible for government to do. This simple calculation hinges on the maintenance of tax effort by the recipient country, since there is a danger that a government will simply reduce its tax collections by 5 percent of GDP once the aid comes in. For that reason donors may want to structure aid so that it supports tax performance through specific tax collection measures and in aggregate. We return to the issue of aid in detail in chapter 13.

Privatization

A government must decide how far it should get involved in the production of goods and services outside the social, administrative, and security sectors. Should it leave everything else to the private sector? How should it go about shifting activities from public to private, if analysis and judgment suggest that is appropriate? To what extent should the private sector be involved in the social, administrative, and security sectors? These big questions cannot be avoided in a discussion of government action to promote development in poor countries.

Over the past decade or so the number of privatizations has increased considerably in developing countries,[15] resulting in fierce public debate about the pros and cons of the process. In determining who is right and who is wrong, much depends on the case at hand and the choice of counterfactuals. Some privatization critics focus on the imperfections in the privatization process—while overlooking the often dreadful performance of former state-owned enterprises. Meanwhile, privatization proponents focus on the improved operating results of privatized companies—and ignore inefficiencies and distributional problems of the privatization process.

When Is Privatization Likely to Be Desirable?

To get a clearer picture of the effects of privatization, it is worth first getting a sector-by-sector picture of the privatization terrain. During the 1990s about one-quarter of infrastructure investment in developing countries involved private participation (World Bank 2003h). Governments still play a large role in directly providing infrastructure in most developing countries, in addition to the regulatory role associated with privatized sectors. Studies have highlighted the efficiency gains from privatization, with telecommunications often noted as an important example. In the electricity sector too, despite some well-publicized difficulties in recent years, substantial efficiency gains have come from privatization. In Argentina labor productivity increased more than 23 percent and electricity losses fell from 18 to 12 percent between 1993 and 1999. In Gabon private operation of the electric company reduced the amount of time the average customer went without electricity by 25 percent in the first two years. And following privatization in Chile, energy losses fell to one-third of historical levels and labor productivity doubled (Gray 2001).

In other sectors where competition is easily established (such as cement production and wheat milling), public ownership neither improves the investment climate nor empowers poor people—even though it has been justified on both grounds. Instead, public ownership is generally associated with bad and expensive products, overstaffing, sinecures for the elite, and wasted fiscal resources. The poor quality and high costs of the goods produced by these firms increase costs for the rest of the economy, reducing returns to investment (for intermediate goods) and restricting access through higher prices and lower quality for poor people (for consumer goods).

Where competition is feasible, privatization introduces choice and so increases efficiency. The main role for government here is competition policy (rather than price regulation): the state should promote competition by ensuring free entry, on the one hand, and by creating reasonable exit options—including orderly but not overly expensive layoffs and a legal bankruptcy regime—on the other. The possibility of exit is important because it allows for innovative risk taking and reduces pressure for government bailouts.

At the same time, government needs to enforce basic property rights if owners are to have the confidence to make investments. In addition, government has an obvious regulatory role in addressing externalities like pollution.[16] Other forms of regulation include sound corporate governance to prevent devious behavior by private managers, and prudential regulation of banking to prevent reckless behavior by bank executives. In short, privatization in competitive sectors (such as cement production) involves nothing very controversial; it requires only that government play its standard role of ensuring competition and addressing market imperfections. These efforts may be challenging for a low-capacity government, but the difficulties are unlikely to justify the costs of government ownership, since many of the same issues arise whether the firm is state owned or private. Further, what is seen as a competitive sector as opposed to a valued monopoly can change with technology—as we have seen with telecommunications, which has moved from the latter to the former.

Natural resource sectors like oil production and mining raise another set of issues. After privatization, many countries require royalty payments from private firms in these sectors, then use the funds to redistribute natural resource rents through government transfers or direct expenditures. A crucial issue for government is to avoid transforming the blessing of resource abundance into a curse by allowing excessive private sector control in natural resources or corrupt hijacking of revenues within government. In a number of countries, including Angola, the Democratic Republic of Congo (formerly Zaire), and Sierra Leone, struggle for control of natural resources has fueled devastating civil conflict (Collier and others 2003).

Finally, in the case of natural monopolies it is less obvious whether privatization is the right strategy. There is no question that managing natural monopolies is a major responsibility. Most natural monopoly sectors, such as roads, water, and electricity transmission, are in the public domain. Before privatization, prices in such sectors are set by government. But even if they are privatized, prices still have to be set—or influenced—by a government regulator.

Because of the cost structures in these sectors, private competition generally does not yield desirable outcomes. Without competition, securing efficiency gains will depend on the quality and expertise of company management, the company's access to finance and technology, the incentives laid out by the regulatory regime, the credibility of that regime, and the actions taken by the regulator. Although we cannot cover these issues in depth here, they are similar to the problems faced by developed-country regulators. Developing countries typically have much less regulatory capacity, and may face serious problems in managing public infrastructure. For example, India's electricity industry is in the public sector, and it is notoriously wasteful and corrupt. We should not jump to the conclusion that everything should be privatized, nor should we assume that certain activities must be in the public sector. We would expect to find different answers for, say, electricity and roads, although the answers will depend on the country context.

In the framework of our proposed strategy, the central questions are whether government ownership of certain companies improves the investment climate and empowers poor people.[17] On the investment climate front, when government-owned enterprises produce poor-quality, costly goods and services, the potential gains from privatization are substantial. Some gains are straightforward: if a private firm gets more output from the same inputs, the static efficiency gains from privatization will likely be obvious and easily measured. But the dynamic gains—the general improvement in the investment climate—are more subtle. If privatization increases the quality and reliability of services while reducing their costs, the returns to investments (new and old) in the wider economy will likely increase and become more predictable. In other words, the climate for entrepreneurship improves.

How Privatization Affects Poor People

What about the impact that privatization can have on poor people? There are several channels. First, as a number of studies have shown, privatization can benefit poor people if it enhances growth. Plane (1997) finds that privatization has a significant, positive impact on growth in a sample of thirty-five developing countries. Tian (2001) finds that Chinese provinces that had ownership structures further along the privatization scale had faster growth rates between 1985 and 1997. Barnett (2000) finds a strong correlation between degrees of privatization and economic growth in a sample of eighteen developing countries.

Second, on the service delivery side, low-income consumers facing public monopolies have little choice or voice in seeking improvements in access or quality. When prices are kept low by government subsidies before privatization, the benefits often accrue to middle-income and rich people rather than poor people. Similarly, while we may fear that traditional cross-subsidies will be difficult after privatization with the introduction of competition, evidence shows that traditional cross-subsidies associated with monopoly state-owned firms (where some consumers are charged a price much further below marginal cost than others) often benefit the better-off more than poor people (Estache,

Gomez-Lobo, and Leipziger 2001; Clarke and Wallsten 2003). In addition, fiscal constraints on subsidized monopolies often lead them to invest too little in expanding or maintaining services—so marginal, usually poorer, neighborhoods have little or no physical access to a variety of public services.

When state enterprises perform badly or cater mostly to middle- and upper-class consumers, privatization can empower poor people. Successful privatization can improve physical and economic access to infrastructure and other goods and services. Physical access to water, telephone, sanitation, and electricity services has improved after privatization in a number of countries, simply through renewed investment in physical networks by the new private owners. Economic access, through affordable prices for poor people, is more complicated because of the more difficult institutional and design issues associated with regulating prices or designing directed subsidies for poor people. In any case, the scope for delivering empowerment through privatization will depend on the success in achieving efficiency gains—some increased surplus—that can be passed on to poor people.

Shirley and Menard (2002) study the effects of water sector privatizations in six cities in developing countries. In general, water and sewerage coverage increased, rates of new connections increased, and water losses declined. Although the results reported are favorable in all the cities, the degree of improvement varied substantially across them, reflecting initial conditions and the quality of reform design. In addition, the authors identify a number of regulatory failings that, if corrected, could lead to far superior outcomes.

To better understand how privatization affected health outcomes in Argentina, Galiani, Gertler, and Schargrodsky (2005) examine the variation of outcomes across a sample of municipalities. They find that child mortality is 8 percent lower in municipalities where water services are provided by a privatized company. The results control for municipality characteristics and for types of cause of death—that is, they restrict the analysis to deaths caused by infectious and parasitic diseases, the diseases associated with poor water quality.

Chile's experience in the electricity sector provides another example. The share of the lowest income decile lacking an electricity connection fell from 29 percent in 1988 to 7 percent in 1998 (World Bank forthcoming). And when Estache, Gomez-Lobo, and Leipziger (2001) examine privatization experiences in Latin America, they conclude that "in

general, competition is good for all consumers, including the poor"
(p. 1191).

Third, a redefined role for the state can enhance empowerment in
terms of greater government focus on delivering direct interventions
to help poor people rather than on administering a public enterprise.
To the extent that privatization increases efficiency in public administration, it can release additional resources that can be used to help
poor people. And to the extent that privatization increases fiscal stability,[18] the reduced risk of macroeconomic crises can also improve poor
people's welfare.

Thus, in principle, from the point of view of our strategy and with
appropriate regulatory institutions, privatization and concession contracts can deliver both improved access to goods and services for poor
people and better financial performance for the company. Still, many
practical difficulties can arise with privatization. First, with limited
government finances, direct subsidies for low-cost services for poor
people may be difficult to finance. So there is a risk that government
will not be able to sustain transparent subsidies after privatization.
These subsidies will compete with other budget demands, while
the indirect subsidy of underpricing—and the accompanying losses
in government-owned utilities prior to privatization—often could be
hidden for years. In addition, there is a risk that the transfer of assets
at the time of privatization could empower rich people rather than
poor. Poorly designed auctions can lead to one-off transfers of wealth
from the public sector (taxpayers) to the new investors (domestic elite
or foreign investors).

If privatized firms are purchased by foreigners, foreign ownership
can provoke a political backlash. Infrastructure services often involve
some degree of necessity, and people may feel particularly vulnerable
to the whims of a private foreign owner. When their government is the
owner, they may feel that they have some leverage, even if low prices
charged by a state-owned firm come with very low quality. Governments sometimes exacerbate consumers' frustration with private
providers, as when they postpone needed price increases until after
privatization—so that private firms, often foreign, get the blame.

Making the Decision to Privatize

Ultimately, proposals for privatization should be examined on a case-
by-case basis; there is no room for doctrinaire responses here. We suggest considering five general groups of criteria or questions.

• *Government failure.* Is government failure occurring in the current situation, and if so, why? Can state-owned enterprise reforms be effective, and what are the costs? Can such reforms be sustained, or are incentives such that the enterprise will ultimately revert to great inefficiencies or corrupt practices?

• *Scope for competition.* What aspects of the good or service can be produced in a competitive setting? What aspects can be unbundled (that is, delivered separately by a private firm)? What complications arise in the commercial relations between unbundled components and remaining monopoly components?

• *Externalities.* What are the externalities in production of the particular good or service? Are there incentives for a private firm to cut costs in ways that impinge on the quality of life or activity of others? Are there positive externalities that will lead to underproduction from a social point of view? Externalities can be an argument for public ownership but, depending on the motivations of government, the state-owned enterprise might not be tackling these issues.

• *Affordability and access.* What prices would ensure efficiency after privatization, and would poor people be able to afford the services? Would cross-subsidies be feasible? Are there enough data to design well-targeted subsidies for poor people? Should these be separated from other social assistance programs? Is the affordability based on limited access to credit to finance connection charges, or is it to do with the consumption of the service itself? Considering these issues in advance can lead to simple changes to privatization design that can have important welfare impacts.

• *Investment, innovation, and access.* What are the incentives for investment and innovation under state ownership? What types of pricing rules and regulations might work best to provide incentives for investment under private ownership? How will these incentives affect coverage in the case of infrastructure sectors?

These questions are interrelated, so this classification of criteria should not be taken too literally. The point is not that a single answer of yes or no to any of the above questions should swing the balance. But making an informed decision depends on weighing the answers to these questions rather than making privatization policy based on slogans or ideology.

Conclusion

Changing institutions and governance is at the heart of the development agenda. But we are only beginning to understand how they can be changed. Let us close with a few words about how to translate knowledge into action to promote this kind of change. The impetus for change can be either top-down or bottom-up. But it has to be both— that is one of the key messages of experience and of this book.

On top-down change, there are strong examples of entrepreneurship in government. Chapter 9 cited the example of Uganda's fight against HIV/AIDS, where strong presidential leadership has helped reverse the tide of the epidemic. India's law requiring representation of women in local government has led to shifts in public investment toward rural infrastructure and other public goods valued by women (Chattopadhyay and Duflo 2004). The household responsibility system originated in China in Anhui province in 1978, the beginning of the reform era. As the system's efficacy and popularity were demonstrated, it was blessed nationally by the government—and led directly to an economywide revolution in agricultural productivity.

In other environments, particularly where government is unable to perform basic functions of governance or is uninterested in trying new approaches, innovations have to come from the grassroots level. This was the case with nongovernmental organizations in Bangladesh, which were the driving force behind the country's dramatic improvements in infant health, girls' education, and family planning. This will likely be even more relevant in low-income countries with the poorest policies, institutions, and governance.

Even in difficult environments, there are always some actions that can contribute to improving governance. Examples include avoiding quotas, licenses, and other policy instruments that require discretion from officials; basing the recruitment of civil servants on transparent, competitive, and scrutinized methods; enhancing transparency, for example by legislating freedom of information acts; and promoting accountability through the involvement of communities in schools, water user associations, and so on, or by using report cards for the provision of public services by municipalities. Such "citizen report cards" on public services—which have been implemented in India, the Philippines, Ukraine, and elsewhere—allow intended beneficiaries of public services to exercise voice on whether the services are reaching them and their quality (World Bank 2003a). Whatever the social and political environment, it should always be possible to trigger institutional change and support innovations in institutions and governance.

Three areas are of particular importance. First, we strongly believe in the power of evidence, information, and analysis as catalysts for change. One way that can happen is through embarrassment where things are going badly. For example, when the *World Development Report 2004* highlighted high rates of doctor absence from public health facilities in Bangladesh, the director general for health responded vigorously: he began making high-profile unannounced visits to government hospitals and transferring truant doctors to less desirable posts (Chaudhury and Hammer 2004, *Daily Star* 2003). Equally important, but less dramatic, can be rigorous analysis of programs and approaches that could work well in a given situation (as described in chapter 6). Good evidence bolsters the constituencies for change.

Second, political action by "policy entrepreneurs" can promote change. Like markets for private goods, markets for policy and institutional innovation are not characterized by spontaneous combinations of inputs. It takes an entrepreneur to recognize an opportunity and exploit it—someone like Muhammad Yunus of the Grameen Bank in Bangladesh, or like Hernando de Soto, who showed in Peru how practical action at the local level can improve property rights and investment opportunities for slum dwellers.

Third, the press and media can goad policymakers to change. The *World Development Report 2002*, on building institutions for markets (World Bank 2001a), and a recent volume on the role of the media (World Bank 2002g) include a host of examples of the media's role in catalyzing changes to policies and institutions. Gandhi, who knew very well how important the media could be, once said that "one of the objects of a newspaper is to understand the popular feeling and give expression to it; another is to arouse among the people certain desirable sentiments; the third is fearlessly to expose popular defects" (Gandhi 1938 [1909], p. 19).

We are beginning to go beyond an understanding of the importance of institutions to an analysis of how to change them. But we have a long way to go.

International Action: Trade
and Aid

This chapter examines international aspects of the partnership required for our strategy. We focus on the role of developed countries in two areas: trade and aid (including debt relief). Both areas have major, complementary roles to play in development. Under the right conditions, trade increases the returns to reforms by offering economies of scale and increasing the competitiveness and innovativeness of domestic producers. At its best, aid helps build the pillars of development by contributing to better policies, governance, and institutions.

When it comes to trade and aid, developed-country governments have the most influence and the greatest responsibility. That does not mean that private capital flows are unimportant. Aid flows are dwarfed by private capital flows (see chapter 2). Although flows of new private portfolio capital to developing countries have slowed to a trickle, flows of foreign direct investment (FDI) remain about three times as large as aid. Cross-border capital flows are increasingly dominated by flows from the private sector to the private sector, and official sector actors—the World Bank, the International Monetary Fund (IMF), other international financial institutions, and individual governments—are minor players when it comes to driving these flows. In most cases these actors have little choice but to step back and let markets operate. When these actors encounter market failures, their job is to nudge, guide, or cajole private capital flows in a way that produces a collectively more desirable outcome. This is the impetus behind recent efforts to improve the international financial architecture, including a proposal to create some kind of bankruptcy mechanism for sovereign debt (Krueger 2002).

Before moving to the discussion of trade and aid policies, we want to make one point about private capital flows. We think that it is time to reconsider the role of external debt flows in financing development.

For much of the past thirty years, development practitioners have tended to think that if a country is creditworthy and has strong growth prospects, then financing development with large amounts of commercial debt is a reasonable strategy. According to this view, as it grows the borrowing country gets all the upside risk—that is, once it has paid its debt, it gets all the gains from growth, which is not the case with equity financing. This approach has paid off for some countries. The Republic of Korea, for example, followed a debt-financed development strategy for more than a generation. Although it suffered debt-related crises in 1980 and again in 1997–1998, one could argue that from a long-term perspective, the strategy of borrowing heavily for development paid off for Korea.

But there are reasons for caution about excessive debt accumulation. Basic risk-sharing principles suggest that it may not be appropriate to finance development, an inherently risky endeavor, with the fixed contractual obligation of debt. Just as start-up companies subject to the vagaries of an uncertain market generally finance themselves with venture capital rather than debt, debt finance often turns out to be far too rigid given the shocks likely to hit many developing countries. Moreover, recent experiences show that commercial debt flows to developing countries are prone to swinging from periods of aggressive overlending (as in East Asia in 1995–1997) to sudden stops (East Asia in 1997–1998). This extreme volatility magnifies the business cycle, hitting poor people in borrowing countries the hardest. Commercial lending to developing countries is not an inherently bad idea. But the development community must take care to keep debt at manageable levels.

By contrast, equity-related finance brings with it the natural benefits of risk sharing. And FDI (though not portfolio capital) has been less volatile than debt flows, partly because investors tend to reinvest a significant portion of retained earnings. There is also the nontrivial point that FDI capital stock depreciates, and thus new inflows are needed to keep the existing capital stock in good shape.[1] Finally, FDI has benefits beyond providing finance: it often contributes new ideas, technologies, and improvements in human capital. There are drawbacks to FDI; for example, it can be costly, and it raises important issues of local accountability. But in current market conditions this type of finance (supplemented by remittances; see chapter 2) seems a firmer capital structure foundation on which to build a development strategy.

What should developing countries do to encourage inflows of private capital, particularly FDI? Answering this question in detail is beyond the scope of this book, but the short answer is: build a good investment climate. The policies that a country takes to make its investment climate conducive to the growth of small and medium-size firms—improving macroeconomic and trade policies, governance, and infrastructure—will generally make it more attractive to foreign firms as well. The reverse need not be true: the tax holidays and enclave infrastructure that developing countries sometimes use to lure foreign firms may do nothing to encourage the growth of small domestic firms. So, countries are best served by building the investment climate from the ground up, with the confidence that it will be strong enough to support FDI as well as domestic firms. They will also find that their own nationals working abroad are likely to respond to an improved investment climate by sending more resources home (World Bank 2003c). Worker remittances now exceed development aid and equal about half of FDI (see chapter 2).

Trade: Breaking Down Barriers

Barriers to developing-country exports remain high in key sectors, making it harder for developing-country entrepreneurs to profit from better domestic investment climates.

Developing Countries and World Trade: Ascendancy and Exclusion

As context for a discussion of trade policy, it is important to understand how trade patterns have changed in recent decades. One prominent development is the developing world's ascendancy in the world trade system. International trade has been a dynamic sector of the global economy: over the past three decades, trade flows have grown more than twice as fast as aggregate GDP. The developing world has more than kept up with this rapid growth: over the past two decades, its share of global trade increased from about one-quarter to one-third. (These data are from World Bank 2003i, on which this section draws heavily; unless otherwise noted, statistics in this section are from that report.)

Developing countries have also achieved a major upgrade in the composition of their exports. For a long time they were exporters of primary commodities and importers of manufactured goods, but over the past two decades they have moved strongly into manufactured exports. Countries that were low income in 1980 managed to raise manufactured exports from roughly 20 percent of their total exports to about 80 percent in 2001, and many have become middle-income countries. The group that was middle income in 1980 has also increased its manufactured exports, though somewhat less rapidly— reaching almost 70 percent of total exports.

Other signs of integration are also heartening. Growth in traditional labor-intensive manufacturing accounts for only part of the gain in manufactured exports; developing countries are also moving into products with high value added, such as electronics. Further, developing countries have expanded their markets: whereas 15 percent of their exports went to other developing countries in 1981, the share had risen to 35 percent by 2001. The constant move to new products and markets helped high-growth exporters like China and India avoid sharp declines in their terms of trade that might have been expected given their rapid export growth. Between 1991 and 2001 every developing region had export growth that was faster than the export growth of developed countries. For sub-Saharan Africa and the Middle East and North Africa, the rate was only marginally faster, but exports from other developing regions grew two to five times as rapidly as developed-country exports.

Why did such rapid and fundamental changes in trade patterns occur? Investments in people and factories both played a role. Average education levels and capital stock per worker rose sharply throughout the developing world, increasing the productivity of developing-country firms. In addition, improvements in transportation and communications, in conjunction with developing-country reforms of their investment climates, allowed the production chain to be broken into components. As a result developing countries came to play an essential role in global production sharing. Policy was no less important. The dramatic liberalization of tariff and nontariff barriers in developing countries after the mid-1980s reduced costs for exporters, increased the competitiveness of developing countries' markets, and further increased the productivity of their firms.

Despite these changes and several rounds of trade liberalization, many developing countries have been unsuccessful in integrating with the world economy. Nearly all the growth in developing-country shares of trade has been driven by middle-income countries. By contrast, the forty-nine least-developed countries, most of which are in

Africa, have gained no market share at all. Moreover, some regions have seen much smaller shifts in the composition of their exports. The manufactured share of merchandise exports is 80 to 90 percent in East and South Asia but only 60 percent in Latin America. Africa and the Middle East have yet to reach the 30 percent mark, and many countries, particularly poor countries, remain dependent on exports of agricultural goods and natural resources. Between 1980 and 2000, forty-three countries had no overall increase in merchandise exports.

Trade barriers in developed countries share the blame for this stagnation. True, in almost all slowly integrating or nonintegrating countries, the investment climate has not been favorable enough—for a range of reasons, including resource depletion, weak infrastructure, and poor economic management—to attract the investments needed to transform export patterns. Steps to strengthen the investment climate need to be a major element of any strategy to promote integration. But developing-country exporters have also faced obstacles to developed-country markets in every major sector—agriculture, manufacturing, and services.

Officially, the international community recognizes these obstacles. Recent international agreements and communiqués have acknowledged that more must be done to remove trade barriers, including those that protect developed-country markets. The Doha development agenda agreed to at the 2001 ministerial meeting of the World Trade Organization (WTO) highlighted the link between trade and poverty reduction and placed development at the core of multilateral trade negotiations. A few months later, the Monterrey consensus (the result of the 2002 United Nations Conference on Financing for Development) committed donors to complementing increased aid with increased market access (see chapter 11). Rapid international integration and rapid growth have tended to go hand in hand for the most economically successful developing countries. Market access and integration increase the returns to investment climate improvements, so the two are strongly complementary.

Sources and Costs of Trade Exclusion
To deliver on the international partnership for development, developed countries must translate their promises into action (see chapter 11). Although many factors have contributed to the disappointingly slow integration of the poorest countries, the trade system is a major determinant, and the current rules of the game discriminate against

developing countries. The negative effects of protection on export activities have declined over successive rounds of multilateral trade negotiations, but the reductions have been larger for manufactured and processed primary products than for agricultural goods and natural resources. Developed and developing countries alike maintain high protection for agriculture, creating a drag on developing countries' agricultural exports.

Developing countries' manufacturing exports also face high barriers in sensitive sectors. Developed-country tariffs on manufactures from developing countries are five times those on manufactures from other developed countries. The barriers that developing countries impose on other developing countries are even higher. Protection takes forms other than ad valorem tariffs, including quotas, specific duties, and antidumping duties. As with tariffs, these measures are used more frequently against labor-intensive products from developing countries. In developed countries average antidumping duties are ten times higher than tariffs, and in developing countries they are five times higher (World Bank 2003i).

Of particular concern are the pockets of protection against products of interest to developing countries. In Canada and the United States, for example, tariff peaks are concentrated in textiles and clothing. In the European Union and Japan they are concentrated in agriculture, food products, and footwear (Hoekman, Matoo, and English 2002). These patterns of protection create hurdles for countries taking their first steps up the technology ladder and penalize the poorest groups in poor countries. About three-quarters of the world's poor people live in rural areas, mostly dependent on agriculture. To export their agricultural goods to OECD countries, they must overcome tariffs at least ten times those on typical intra-OECD exports (of all products).

Moreover, OECD countries provide agricultural subsidies that drive down world prices for agricultural exports, undermining the livelihoods and markets of farmers in developing countries.[2] Including those subsidies, the OECD agriculture sector received $248 billion in support every year on average during the 1999–2001 period. This amount represents 1.3 percent of developed countries' GDP and is about six times the official aid to developing countries—and almost as large as the gross national income of sub-Saharan Africa (which was $311 billion in 2001). The issue here is not the support that developed countries provide for rural development; it is the size and form of that support and its pernicious effects on prices of goods produced by developing countries.

Developed countries have made some efforts to address this problem, introducing preferential schemes that give the poorest countries—primarily those classified as least developed countries—duty-free access to their markets. Examples include the EU Everything But Arms initiative and the U.S. African Growth and Opportunity Act. Although such schemes are a step in the right direction, they have had limited impact. The Everything But Arms initiative grants preferential access to exports from the least-developed countries, but only half of eligible exports are actually granted preferences. Under the African Growth and Opportunity Act, the most generous provisions are granted to apparel exports from sub-Saharan Africa. But 99 percent of apparel exports under the act come from just seven sub-Saharan countries, and only two of these are least developed countries (Madagascar and Malawi). The low coverage of these schemes is primarily the result of complex rules of origin, complicated administrative requirements, and the weak trade capacity of developing countries. Simpler rules of origin would likely increase the impact of trade preferences by improving market access and stimulating export diversification.

More generally, however, assistance is required to build trade capacity in the poorest countries to enable them to take full advantage of these preferential schemes. It is also important to enhance the bargaining capacity of firms in developing countries when confronting large OECD importers. Under the African Growth and Opportunity Act, U.S. apparel importers have been able to capture most of the tariff rents associated with preferential access, with only one-third of the tariff rents accruing to African exporters.

Finally, most of the world's poor people are located outside Africa and the least-developed countries. Thus, preferential market access that targets these countries excludes a large share of the world's poor people—and could even hurt them through the trade diversion that may accompany these schemes. For preferential market access to become an effective tool to achieve the Millennium Development Goals (MDGs), its coverage should be extended as broadly as possible. As noted, special preference schemes involve complex rules of origin and benefit one group of poor people at the expense of others. Moreover, their benefits may be captured by traders and producers in developed countries, and they can conflict with existing World Trade Organization agreements, as well as undermine attempts to institute new agreements. A more open global trade system would be far superior.

A more open trade system could generate enormous benefits for all countries, and particularly for the world's poor people. Removing all trade impediments would mean 300 million fewer people living in income poverty ($1 a day) by 2015, a decline of 13 percent (World Bank 2003i). The bulk of the gains from liberalizing merchandise trade would come from agriculture, not only in OECD countries but also in developing countries, where tariff barriers are often as or even more distorted as in OECD countries (although the degree of distortion on the production side, through subsidies, is generally much lower).

An Agenda for Action on Trade

Realizing the promise of the Doha development agenda will require compromise from all countries. There are enough potential gains from liberalizing trade for everyone to benefit, but so far little cause for optimism about an agreement to do so. Talks have languished in a mire of intransigent positions on agricultural protection, Trade-Related Aspects of Intellectual Property Rights (TRIPs), Special and Differential Treatment, and the so-called Singapore issues—investment, competition, trade facilitation, and transparency in government procurement. The list of missed deadlines is rapidly lengthening. Reenergizing World Trade Organization negotiations is especially important now, with the global economy still trying to recover from the boom and bust of the 1990s and the postwar foundations of multilateralism under question.

While all countries will need to do their part, there are special responsibilities and opportunities for the wealthier developed countries that wrote the rules of the current trade system and continue to dominate global trade flows. Reducing agricultural protection—including trade-distorting tariffs, quotas, other export subsidies, and antidevelopment tariff escalation and tariff peaks—is the most important step for development. Phasing out these measures would attract new investment and, five years after completing the reforms, would increase developing country incomes by $150 to $400 billion. Critical steps toward this goal include converting production subsidies to income subsidies and converting specific duties and tariff rate quotas to more transparent ad valorem tariffs (World Bank 2003i).[3]

Not all developing countries will benefit from liberalization of agriculture. Serious reforms in global agricultural trade policies would lead to higher prices for many products now protected, and these price changes could initially lead to balance-of-payments problems for low-income countries that are net agricultural importers. But if we take out oil exporters and countries with temporary deficits worsened by conflict, only fourteen low-income countries are net food importers.[4] Three of these countries account for 80 percent of the net imports: Bangladesh, the Democratic People's Republic of Korea, and Pakistan. The other eleven countries have a deficit of just $565 million, a small percentage of their trade. These countries would also gain from price increases, because their exports are also predominantly agricultural, as well as from other aspects of multilateral trade negotiations. Still, the international community should be prepared to provide assistance to help countries adjust to and take advantage of new trade opportunities.

The need for action by developed countries is greatest in sugar, cotton, and rice production, where protection is most damaging. Similar stories can be told for dairy, groundnuts, and other products, but here we focus on these three examples because of their importance in world trade and in the lives of poor people.

Sugar is one of the most policy distorted of all commodities. The European Union, Japan, and the United States are all major offenders, protecting their producers at tariff equivalents that often exceed 200 percent—meaning that producers receive more than three times the world market price. Developing-country producers who could provide sugar much more cheaply are excluded from these markets. OECD countries provide their sugar producers with an estimated $6.4 billion a year in support, which is roughly equal to the total value of sugar exports from developing countries. It is absurd that sugar beets are grown in Scandinavian countries at great expense and with large subsidies when sugar from poor countries (such as Mozambique) is excluded from EU markets. Moving to free trade in sugar markets would raise world sugar prices by almost 40 percent, increase sugar trade by 20 percent, and generate $4.7 billion in welfare gains.

U.S. subsidies to cotton growers totaled $3.7 billion during the 2001–2002 season, which is three times U.S. aid to Africa (and large relative to the $20 billion value of world cotton production). Other countries subsidize cotton as well: EU countries provided $0.7 billion during the same season, and a number of developing countries (Brazil, Egypt, Mexico, Turkey) have responded to recent record-low prices by introducing subsidies totaling $0.5 billion. Overall, these subsidies depress world cotton prices by 10 percent, cutting into the incomes of poor farmers in West Africa, Central and South Asia, and other areas. In West Africa alone, where cotton is a critical cash crop for many small-scale and near-subsistence farmers, annual income losses for cotton growers are about $250 million a year. In Benin, where cotton accounts for 40 percent of exports and 7 percent of GDP, a 1 percent increase in the world price of cotton would raise per capita income by 0.5 percent and reduce the incidence of poverty by 1.5 percentage points.

Rice is the world's most important food grain, and rice markets are among the most distorted. The global trade-weighted average tariff on all types of rice is 43 percent (with tariffs on some varieties exceeding 200 percent). Among developed countries, support provided in Japan is especially noteworthy. It amounts to a staggering 700 percent of production value at world prices, stimulating inefficient domestic production, reducing demand, and denying export opportunities to countries like Thailand and Vietnam. In the United States it is extraordinary that subsidies and protection stimulate production of rice, an extremely water-intensive crop, in water-starved California.

Liberalization of services could also yield large gains. In fact, several studies conclude that services liberalization could produce gains three to four times the very large gains from merchandise liberalization. Services are the fastest-growing component of world trade. Developing countries have nearly quadrupled their exports of services in the past decade (at a faster rate than goods exports) and have increased their share of the global market for services to 18 percent, up from 14 percent. Countries are busy pursuing opportunities in different industries. For example, Barbados is increasingly prominent in data processing; China, India, and the Philippines are exporting computer software (the Indian offshore development IT industry has grown from $1.73 billion, or 0.59 percent of GDP, in 1994–1995 to $13.5 billion, or 2.87 percent, in 2001–2002), and South Africa is exporting telecommunications services.

OECD countries could take several steps to promote trade opportunities and investment in services:

• Locking in free trade in cross-border services trade

• Allowing temporary migration of workers supplying services in areas such as construction and health care

• Restraining themselves from seeking "sweetheart" deals and preferential access, and accepting free competition and entry

• Eliminating investment incentives to firms to keep them in OECD countries

Developing countries also need to take action and would benefit from being more aggressive in negotiations on services trade and locking in liberalization of services trade in domestic markets. Too many developing countries still have inefficient state monopolies and low-productivity firms in key sectors—telecommunications, wholesaling and retailing, accounting and other business services, electricity, and even the financial sector—that raise input costs and limit productivity for the entire economy.

Finally, for nonagricultural goods developed countries will need to reduce antidevelopment tariff peaks, tariff escalation, and quotas. Processed foods are particular victims of antidevelopment tariff escalation. For example, fresh tomatoes from Chile enter the United States with a 2.8 percent tariff. If the same tomatoes are dried and packaged, exporters pay 8.9 percent—while U.S. imports of salsa and ketchup face an 11.6 percent tariff. While the EU tariff on cocoa beans is 0.5 percent, the tariff on chocolate is more than 30 percent. These are taxes on development.

Labor-intensive manufacturers face similar escalation. Exporters of cotton T-shirts from China to the United States, for example, face tariff and nontariff barriers many times higher than those on exports from developed countries. In 2001 manufacturers had to pay 95 cents a shirt for the quotas and tariffs needed to reach the U.S. market, leaving only 26 cents to pay workers and meet other costs. These heavy burdens on clothing producers are also another tax on the cotton producers who supply the raw materials.

As suggested above, developing countries also have much to gain from reducing protection and adopting complementary policies to expand trade. Nearly all analyses of the benefits of eliminating global constraints on trade show that 60 to 80 percent of the gains to developing countries come from reforms in those countries. Reducing the 25 percent tariff on cocoa in Turkey, for example, would benefit African cocoa producers, who enjoy much lower tariffs exporting to the European Union and the United States.

Above all, both for the direct gains to themselves and developing countries and to advance the Doha round of trade negotiations, developed countries must make big advances in dismantling agricultural subsidies and protection. It is not just the direct subsidies; border barriers play an even bigger role. Together they drain the treasuries of developed countries, hit their poorest citizens the hardest, and transfer resources mainly to rich farmers and agricultural businesses. There are much better ways to promote rural development in rich countries. The current system is economically illiterate. It is also politically antiquated. It was developed in an era when 20 to 30 percent of the population in these countries worked in agriculture. That figure is now 2 to 3 percent. The system is also environmentally damaging, with excessive fertilizer use and overproduction resulting from distorted prices. And the damage it does to poor people in developing countries is ethically indefensible.

Aid: Increasing Its Amount and Effectiveness

Trade alone will not lead to rapid development. As we have emphasized, private sector growth starts with the domestic investment climate. Although increased integration with the outside world magnifies the benefits of a positive investment climate, the former usually cannot substitute for the latter. Development assistance, or aid, complements trade by helping to build the two pillars of our strategy in recipient countries.

Aid can help create a positive investment climate by financing infrastructure, helping to improve governance, and supporting reform of macroeconomic and trade policies. Some aid is targeted specifically at improving a country's ability to take advantage of trade opportunities—"aid for trade." Many countries need trade assistance to help them take advantage of the opportunities offered by market access. This is particularly the case for countries that face daunting natural barriers to trade, such as landlocked countries surrounded by poor neighbors in Africa and Central Asia.

Aid also has an important role in building the empowerment pillar. Sectors involving human development, most notably health and education, are natural areas for external support. Action in these sectors often yields returns over years, or even decades, making it hard for governments to finance these investments even if they have access to private capital. It is true that money is often fungible, so that a government can borrow in one sector and shift resources to another. But without external support, governments may lack the confidence or incentive to invest for the long term. Aid can also sponsor and help evaluate promising initiatives, then help in scaling them up.

Aid over Time: Declining Levels, Increasing Effectiveness
Despite all the ways that aid contributes to development, it fell from $63 billion in 1992 to $52 billion in 2001, or from 0.34 to 0.22 percent of donors' combined GNP (figure 13.1). In the early 1960s official aid

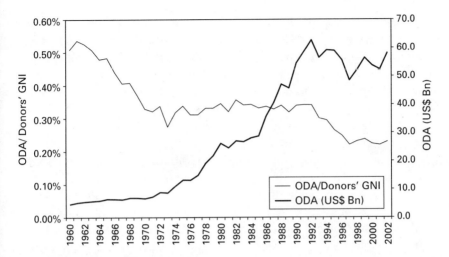

Figure 13.1
Official development assistance (net) has fallen as a share of donor countries' income.
Source: OECD, Development Assistance Committee. *Notes:* ODA = Official development
assistance. GNI = Gross national income.

provided by developed countries was 0.5 percent of their GNP, even
though living standards in those countries were much lower than they
are today. Aid fell through the 1990s even as donor economies surged
and aid effectiveness increased sharply. The main reason for the decline was the end of the Cold War at the beginning of the 1990s, which
reduced governments' geopolitical motivations for providing aid. Fiscal pressures in donor countries exacerbated the situation, strengthening the hand of taxpayers who doubted the efficacy of foreign aid.

Given this decline, it is worth emphasizing the increase in aid effectiveness in the 1990s. The World Bank's 1998 study, *Assessing Aid:
What Works, What Doesn't, and Why,* showed that aid had been productive (in terms of contributing to economic growth) in countries with
relatively good policies and institutions. It also showed that, historically, aid had not been systematically targeted at countries that fit that
description. But for several reasons, that pattern changed markedly in
the 1990s.

The first reason was an improvement in developing countries' policies. Better macroeconomic policies and greater openness have made
these countries' economic environments more conducive to growth.
Inflation, which typically does the greatest harm to poor people,[5]
fell significantly during the 1990s; at the same time, macroeconomic

management improved, exchange rates were more stable, and trade barriers were reduced. In recent years there has also been a moderate increase in the component of the World Bank's Country Policy and Institutional Assessment (CPIA) index that measures governance and the quality of institutions.[6] One illustration of this is the considerable increase in the number of democracies in the world (even if democratic institutions do not always function effectively; see chapter 2 and Zakaria 1997).

Second is an improvement in aid allocations. Although the end of the Cold War reduced aid, it allowed donors to shift aid from recipients that were geopolitically important to those that were developmentally deserving. Aid is increasingly allocated by bilateral donors and multilateral financial institutions on the basis of two criteria: where poor people are and where it can be used effectively. This reallocation was built on research findings, including the *Assessing Aid* report cited above, that showed that aid is more productive in contributing to growth and productivity in a stronger policy and institutional environment. Concerns about aid effectiveness led the Dutch government, for example, to reduce the number of countries receiving its aid from 70 to 17. Similarly, the United Kingdom has taken steps to increase the effectiveness of its aid by allocating it according to the policy environments and needs of recipient countries. U.K. aid has been untied, meaning that recipient countries are no longer required to procure goods and services from U.K. sources. Furthermore, 78 percent of U.K. aid now goes to low-income countries, compared with 71 percent in 1998. The aim is raise this figure to 90 percent by 2006 (DFID 2003). Similar poverty and effectiveness criteria guide allocations by the International Development Association (IDA), the World Bank's instrument for concessional lending.

Third, evidence that project-specific aid is fungible across sectors led donors to place more weight on the overall quality of a country's public spending and less on returns to individual projects (Devarajan and Swaroop 1998). "Fungible" means that a $100 million primary education project does not necessarily translate into a $100 million increase in primary education spending by the recipient country. If the government would have built the primary schools anyway, then the $100 million in aid effectively financed other parts of the government budget. The evidence on fungibility had two implications. First, as noted above, donors focused increasingly on the overall quality of the country's public spending. Second, donors began to recognize that the reason for financing a project was not only the productivity of the investment, but also the knowledge transfer embodied in the project and the learning that would emerge from project innovations. As a result donor projects and programs increasingly focus on providing assistance to shape policy and improve administration in a sector as a whole.

Fourth, traditional conditionality (where aid is made conditional on promises of policy reform) has been recognized to be of limited effectiveness. In recent years the IMF and World Bank have reduced the number and increased the focus of conditions attached to their loans to developing countries—increasing the emphasis on country ownership and jointly monitorable results. The Poverty Reduction Strategy Paper (PRSP) process has proven to be a helpful vehicle for integrating development efforts across sectors and development partners (see chapter 11). As a result some major bilateral donors have shifted from stand-alone projects toward multiyear, multidonor projects and programs with the flexibility to direct resources toward reforms across a significant part of the economy. This is an integral element of the scaling up discussed in chapter 11.

Because of these trends, during the 1990s aid became much more effective at reducing poverty. World Bank research on the impact of aid on growth and poverty (using panel data from a variety of countries) has tried to quantify this change. Though all such efforts are bedeviled by econometric difficulties, even the rough magnitude of the estimates suggests an enormous improvement. In 1990, under existing aid allocation patterns, an additional $10 billion in aid would have lifted 1 million people out of poverty. But improvements in allocations meant that by the end of the decade, the same $10 billion would have enabled nearly 3 million to escape poverty (Collier, Devarajan, and Dollar 2001). Of course, the benefits of aid go well beyond this narrow effect on the number of people moving above the $1 a day poverty line. These poverty-reduction estimates are based on projected increases in overall economic growth, which tends to benefit all income classes. Aid also improves human development outcomes, which are not captured in this summary statistic. The key point here is that aid fell while its productivity increased.

How Much More Aid Is Needed?
Increasing aid is essential to achieving the MDGs. Considerable attention has focused on the cost of attaining the MDGs and the implications

for aid. Yet donor rhetoric and commitment to the MDGs have not been matched by a significant increase in aid to developing countries. Only five donor countries—Denmark, Luxembourg, the Netherlands, Norway, and Sweden—have reached the 0.7 percent of GNP target for aid adopted by the United Nations in 1970. There is nothing magical about the 0.7 percent target; as we have indicated, input measures of aid are often less useful than MDG targets and other more proximate measures of results. But the target does indicate that donor-country efforts fall far short of what was once considered reasonable. Since 2001 there has been a slight reversal in the long-term decline in aid, with aid as a share of donor-country GDP edging up to 0.23 percent. Although this increase is heartening, current aid falls well short of what should be feasible (considering the historical record) and what is needed for the MDGs, or indeed, even for more modest ambitions.

How much aid is needed to enable developing countries to achieve the MDGs by 2015? The World Bank and United Nations—in the latter case, through an expert group headed by former Mexican president Ernesto Zedillo—have made preliminary estimates using a global and sector approach, respectively. Both organizations concluded that aid needs to double to about $100 billion a year. As noted in chapter 11, the World Bank estimates are based on fairly optimistic assumptions about improvements in the policies and institutions of developing countries. If these improvements fail to materialize, much more than an additional $50 billion a year could be needed, and the lower productivity of aid under these circumstances could undermine the argument for aid itself.[7]

Can Extra Aid Be Used Effectively?

Recent estimates indicate that aid must increase by at least $50 billion a year to reach the MDGs. Although these estimates are imprecise in a number of important ways, it is clear that large increases in aid will be required to achieve the MDGs. But some observers, both outside and within international financial institutions, have questioned whether developing countries can make effective use of substantial additional aid.

Before going into details, it is worth noting that even doubling aid would raise the average ratio of aid to GDP to only about 2 percent in developing countries and perhaps 8 percent of total investment. But such ratios are much higher for some developing countries, particularly in sub-Saharan Africa. It is in those countries that the issue of using new aid effectively is likely to be of greatest concern. There are two main concerns: first, that large new aid flows will be macroeconomically disruptive, and second, that administrative and institutional constraints will prevent recipient countries from using new aid well. The rest of this section assesses these concerns.[8]

One macroeconomic concern is that increased aid will reduce recipient countries' medium-term fiscal and debt sustainability. Loans, even if provided on concessional terms, can push a country from a marginally sustainable to an unsustainable fiscal position because of the need to make repayments of principal. Aid can also threaten fiscal sustainability if it finances initial investments but saddles governments with the long-term recurrent costs of investment operations.

Concerns about fiscal sustainability are mitigated to the extent that additional aid takes the form of grants rather than loans. The bulk of the additional aid commitments envisaged in the Monterrey consensus are expected to be in the form of grants. In addition, to the extent that the additional grants are not tied to specific spending, they can be used to reduce and retire debt, which may be especially desirable in developing countries with heavy debt burdens. Thus, the precise implications of additional aid for fiscal sustainability are an empirical matter and should be analyzed for each recipient country.

A second macroeconomic concern is that increased aid will cause an appreciation of the real exchange rate and reduce the recipient country's competitiveness and growth prospects (so-called Dutch disease). Empirical evidence on this effect is mixed, however. Although some studies have found evidence of a Dutch disease effect, including adverse impacts on tradable sectors,[9] in others the findings are less conclusive (Hjertholm and Lauresen 2000, Nyoni 1998).

Though we may not be able to make a general statement about aid and exchange rates, we can identify conditions under which a Dutch disease effect is most likely. The real exchange rate is most likely to be a problem if the increase in aid is rapid and large relative to the economy, if aid-induced spending occurs in nontradable sectors, and if the economy's supply-side response is weak. Thus, whether the impact on the real exchange rate is a serious issue needs to be assessed in the light of the specifics of the case.

Even in cases where the resulting appreciation is likely to be large, the potential Dutch disease effects need to be assessed carefully. Dutch disease alone need not always be a reason to restrain aid increases. First, some appreciation may not harm the economy, especially if aid flows are sustainable.[10] Second, any harm from appreciation should be weighed against the benefits, such as the contribution to productivity and growth, resulting from aid-induced spending. If aid supports policy reforms or infrastructure investments that improve the investment climate and enhance productivity, the recipient country's international competitiveness may improve (perhaps with a lag), notwithstanding some appreciation of the exchange rate. Finally, it might be possible to mitigate the adverse effects of an appreciation through fiscal and monetary policies and through an acceleration of structural reforms that boost the economy's supply response. Ultimately, it is extremely unlikely that extra grant aid, when focused on beneficial uses in the context of, say, a Poverty Reduction Strategy Paper, will cause damage.

Data on official development assistance relative to GDP (measured in purchasing power parity, or PPP, terms) indicate that in the 1991–2000 period, only two developing countries—Zambia and Guinea-Bissau—received more than 10 percent of GDP in aid.[11] Another sixteen countries (thirteen of them in sub-Saharan Africa) received aid equal to between 5 and 10 percent of GDP.[12] Thus there is a limited number of countries where increased aid could seriously threaten macroeconomic stability (that is, countries with poor policies, weak institutions, and relatively high dependence on aid). Even in these cases appropriate macroeconomic policy responses, together with structural reforms, could mitigate some of the potential adverse effects of more aid.

Beyond potential macroeconomic complications, the second concern is that recipient countries will have insufficient structural and institutional capacity to absorb new aid—that is, their economies might lack "absorptive capacity." Whereas with macroeconomic complications it is the quantity of aid and its allocation between the tradable and nontradable sectors that matter, here the issue is the quality of spending. The empirical evidence on this point is less ambiguous: some low-income countries do suffer from capacity constraints. One problem is that a large increase in aid (relative to the size of the economy) can overwhelm the recipient government's administrative capacity.[13] Public expenditure and financial management weaknesses, governance deficiencies, and infrastructure bottlenecks can further constrain absorptive capacity.

This issue is linked to the lesson on aid effectiveness. When aid is more effective because countries have good policies and institutions, they can also absorb larger amounts of aid before the diminishing returns to aid set in strongly.[14] In countries with low capacity, that point arrives much sooner, so additional aid may not be very productive. But arguing that it does damage is less plausible and would require strong evidence.

Beyond these two issues—macroeconomic stability and absorptive capacity—there are potential concerns about the potential moral hazard of increased aid. Aid could reduce the incentive for recipient governments to undertake painful but necessary reforms, such as restructuring the tax system to raise more revenue. In this way aid, some argue, could breed extended aid dependence.

All the issues noted in this section raise questions that require analysis, but they do not justify postponing the large increase in aid needed to achieve the MDGs. Given their improved policies and low aid levels, most developing countries can absorb additional aid. But "most" does not mean all, and donors and international financial institutions will need to tailor aid increases to the capacity of each recipient. The issues raised in this section argue for applying the principles outlined throughout this book: carefully assessing country capacity, carefully allocating and sequencing increased aid, and using the additional aid to support reforms that improve the investment climate and increase the country's administrative capacity.

In weak institutional environments with a high risk of corruption, improving public financial management should be a priority. This may be particularly relevant to grant assistance because, compared with loans, grants are often subject to less strict fiduciary requirements. Where additional aid is focused on certain sectors, such as education, it will be important to embed it within a coherent overall public spending framework and a supportive sector policy.

So how much additional aid can be absorbed? Recent research shows that at the country level, aid eventually reaches a saturation point—defined as the point where additional aid has zero marginal effect on growth (Collier and Dollar 2002), though even at the saturation point, grant aid improves welfare if it is simply consumed. Where this saturation point lies (say, at 5, 10, or 15 percent of GDP) depends on the recipient country's policy and institutional environment. The better is the institutional environment, the higher will be the saturation point (Collier and Dollar 2002).

There is typically considerable scope for expanding aid before reaching the saturation point. One rule of thumb suggested by World Bank research is that the saturation point is two to three times the Bank's Country Policy and Institutional Assessment (CPIA) index for each country, measured as a percentage of GDP (Collier and Hoeffler 2004). The research suggests that returns to aid are particularly high in post-conflict countries where the environment has improved a few years after the conflict; in such cases the saturation point may be even higher, at perhaps five times the CPIA index. With CPIA index scores typically around 3, these saturation points are generally much higher than current aid levels.

At the global level, a recent World Bank (2003k) report evaluates the prospects for accelerating progress toward the MDGs only in countries with good policies, institutions, and governance (see chapter 11). The study uses a country-based approach and takes into account past policy improvements, more effective aid modalities, and greater market access for developing countries. It concludes that these good-policy countries could absorb a substantial increase in aid—initially at least $30 billion, with additional absorption possible as policies and economic performance improve further.

Powerful analyses and arguments tell us that substantial increases in aid would be used well in most countries covering the bulk of the population in developing countries. Arguments to the contrary are usually veils for stinginess. And rigid presumptions against extra aid on macroeconomic grounds (which have occasionally emerged from the IMF) are generally unsound and unacceptable.

Helping Low-Income Countries with Weak Governance

While most countries can use aid well, dozens of others cannot. With the improvements in aid allocations in the 1990s, a smaller share of aid is going to the latter group of countries, which have particularly weak institutions, policies, and governance. This is a hard consequence of the lessons of experience, but it is the right policy. Aid budgets are too constrained, and development needs too vast, to allow the massive waste that can come with misallocations of aid. As a reminder we need only think of Zaire (now the Democratic Republic of Congo). Between 1960 and 2000, when it was ruled mostly by the kleptocratic President Mobutu Sese Seko, Zaire received more than $10 billion in aid—while between 1974 and 1996, income per capita declined by a factor of four. Keeping the aid spigot open did not support long-term poverty reduction in Zaire.

Still, the international community cannot simply abandon people who live in countries that lack the policies, institutions, and governance needed to use aid effectively. Poor people in these countries are among the world's most destitute and face the greatest hurdles in improving their lives. And achieving improvement in these environments is a daunting challenge. Of the two or three dozen countries with the poorest institutions and policies in the late 1980s, only a handful (most notably Ethiopia, Mozambique, and Uganda) have made major advances in the environments for growth and poverty reduction. The rest languish in dire poverty. As noted, external support bears less fruit in these environments. World Bank projects in these countries, for example, have failed at twice the rate for other countries.

Developed countries and international institutions have a responsibility to help these countries, but they must do so wisely. Approaches that work in the typical low-income country may not be appropriate in these countries, because they typically lack the foundation for country leadership of reform, and lending conditionality has not worked well in inducing and supporting reform.[15] Large-scale financial transfers are unlikely to work well, given the limited absorptive capacity in these environments. So what will work? Broadly, the answer is likely to include an intense focus on capacity building, combined with more direct delivery of human development services and humanitarian assistance. We say "broadly" because we recognize that—to paraphrase Tolstoy—each of these countries is unhappy in its own way, and solutions will have to be tailored to each country's circumstances.

First, donors should focus on institution building, capacity building, and knowledge transfer to facilitate change. Given the constraints on government capacity, such efforts should concentrate on a limited reform agenda that is both economically sensible (and mindful of sequencing issues) and sociopolitically feasible. This capacity building is likely to include support for "good examples" located in developing regions with reform-minded governments. In other cases local governments or NGOs may offer the most appropriate arena for these "demonstration" reforms. Only when central governments develop greater capacity, and when early gains demonstrate the benefits of reform, will countries with weak institutions, policies, and governance be able to make better use of large-scale aid.

In these countries there will often be a case for using aid to improve basic health and education services. To be effective, such funding should probably be channeled through entities other than the central government. One possibility is establishing structures in which a donor-monitored wholesaling organization contracts with multiple channels of retail provision from, for example, the private sector,

NGOs, and local governments, where the probability of successful service delivery appears high. While any strategy of engagement with these countries will carry substantial risks of failure, bypassing the central government may be promising.

Some of these countries also require humanitarian aid. A recent example is food aid to Zimbabwe, a country with urgent needs but limited capacity to make effective use of large-scale development assistance.

Adjusting Adjustment Efforts by International Financial Institutions
Also crucial to the aid story—and a key element of how aid is delivered—are the policies and practices of international financial institutions, including the World Bank, IMF, and regional development banks (such as the Asian Development Bank and African Development Bank). Achieving development goals depends on whether these institutions can incorporate into their lending the ideas outlined in these lectures. The evolution of adjustment lending since the early 1980s, which we explore in this section, suggests that they can. The international community has learned from its mistakes (of the 1980s and early 1990s) and begun to incorporate those lessons into current practice.

Adjustment lending emerged in the 1980s to fill a real need. Indeed, the reasons for its emergence presaged some of the themes of these lectures. First, adjustment loans were an attempt to move beyond individual projects—in effect, an early attempt at scaling up. In a highly inflationary global environment, many developing countries suffered from macroeconomic instability and structural problems that undermined growth and made project assistance ineffective. Second, conditionality in adjustment lending was motivated by the desire to create an investment climate in which decisions were made by individuals rather than central planners. Movement toward the market could both improve the investment climate and empower individuals. Finally, adjustment lending was aimed at helping countries undertake reforms and smooth the transition costs of adjusting to economic shocks—in essence, financing the change that is central to development.

Despite these good intentions, the record of adjustment lending by international financial institutions (especially in the 1980s and early 1990s) is mixed at best. To be sure, it includes a number of success stories, such as in Uganda or Vietnam. But it also includes cases where adjustment programs were misguided or not followed. The reasons for poor performance echo other themes of these lectures. First, heavy reliance on conditionality was usually ineffective, with the large number of conditions doing nothing to strengthen borrower ownership of the reforms. Second, while the focus on improving poor policies was understandable, the design of adjustment programs paid inadequate attention to governance and institutional problems, which were major constraints on the investment climate. Finally, there was too little emphasis on equity issues and mitigating the social costs of adjustment—in other words, too little attention to the empowerment pillar. This was probably because many of the poor policies that adjustment lending targeted were both inefficient and biased against poor people. Nevertheless, the lack of specific attention to poverty issues led to progress involving damage to poor people and understandably attracted heavy criticism.

With the help of their critics, for whom adjustment lending has been a lightning rod, international financial institutions have learned from experience and changed course, incorporating many lessons highlighted in this book. First, as with overall lending, international financial institutions increasingly targeted adjustment loans to countries with better track records and greater capacity to use aid well. By 1995–2000 more than 70 percent of World Bank adjustment loans went to countries with above-average performance on a broad range of policies (as measured by the CPIA index). Second, international financial institutions have tried to use conditionality more judiciously, in ways that do not undermine country ownership of reform. In low-income countries this has meant introducing more participatory processes designed to encourage country ownership—most commonly, though the PRSP process, which is now completed or under way in more than fifty countries. Finally, adjustment lending has shifted focus from macroeconomic and trade issues to the governance, institutional, structural, and social issues on which development depend so heavily.

These changes have sharply increased the effectiveness of adjustment lending, as evaluated by the World Bank's Operations Evaluation Department (OED). The OED's outcome ratings measure, in general terms, the extent to which a Bank operation has achieved its objectives. Thus, they provide a useful indicator of the strength of the link between adjustment loans and the implementation of the programs being supported by the loans. The share of operations rated to have satisfactory outcomes increased from 68 percent in fiscal years 1990–1994 to 77 percent for fiscal years 2000–2002 on an unweighted basis. The increase was even more pronounced as a share of lending volumes, rising from 73 percent in fiscal 1990–1994 to 90 percent in fiscal 1999–2000.

OED ratings of long-term sustainability (an assessment of resilience to risk) and institutional development (the contribution of operations to capacity building) also increased over this period. These ratings are not beyond question, because the targets set for operations and the outcome ratings are necessarily somewhat subjective. But anecdotal evidence suggests that international financial institutions have gotten better at taking into account social goals and consequences in their adjustment lending and at embedding their loans in a context of country-owned approaches.

These improvements on the adjustment front are encouraging, suggesting that international financial institutions can learn from experience, change course, and improve outcomes. As part of the development partnership, there is still more that these institutions can do to help countries implement their development strategies and achieve the MDGs. These tasks can be grouped into strategy, country selectivity, type of activity, internal workings, and external role.

In terms of strategy, international financial institutions must guard against the temptation to backslide on their mission and approach. Especially in their rhetoric, and to a considerable extent in their daily activities, the institutions have already incorporated many of the lessons described in these lectures. But there will always be a temptation to return to focusing solely on designing good projects. Such an approach provides a tempting sense of security. But while projects are essential, the scaling-up imperative is such that projects must be embedded in an overall development strategy, and in partnership among donors and with the government. Moreover, projects, and international financial institutions more generally, must be oriented toward learning—creating and exchanging knowledge. These institutions are (and always will be) small relative to the scale of the challenge. But ideas need not be. Good ideas can be scaled up to any challenge. Thus, the learning gained from a project is not a useful add-on, time permitting. It is largely the point of the project.

In terms of country and global support, international financial institutions should continue to move toward selective lending, with aid focused on fighting poverty where it is and where aid can be effective. To a considerable extent, this is likely to mean a greater focus on parts of South Asia and sub-Saharan Africa, a direction the World Bank has moved in already. Not all action will be at the country level; the next section describes global public goods, which international financial institutions should often take the lead in delivering. In becoming more selective in lending, they must also work in partnership to improve policies and governance in countries where they are too weak for strong lending.

In terms of type of activity, international financial institutions could place even more emphasis on governance. In chapter 5 we outlined some of the key elements in fostering good governance: information and transparency, accountability, economic policies that reduce official discretion in poor-governance environments, and civil service professionalism. Because ultimately, it is governance that determines the quality of policies, and in many cases institutions as well, improving governance deserves even more weight in the programs of international financial institutions than it has had in the past several years.

In terms of their internal workings, international financial institutions would benefit from streamlining bureaucratic procedures so that they can act more nimbly and rapidly. Having worked in various government and international financial institution bureaucracies, as well as in academia, Nicholas Stern is struck by the procedural constraints that slow action by the World Bank. The heaviness of the bureaucratic procedures reflects an accumulation of various constraints that were imposed with the best of intentions. But together they add up to an unwieldiness that sometimes makes it difficult to do business at all. They place heavy burdens on partnering countries that can make the World Bank an unattractive lender. The World Bank's current drive to simplify administrative processes is, from this perspective, a welcome development.

Finally, in their external role, international financial institutions will need to speak out more strongly for international responses to international problems, as they have in recent years on trade issues. These institutions were established to embody the international conscience.[16] Indeed, they can be viewed as clubs in which countries bind themselves collectively to goals that rise above their immediate self-interests. Thus, these institutions represent a recognition by all countries—perhaps especially the rich countries that led their founding—that the polities and personalities of nations are divided. A major purpose of international financial institutions and other international institutions is to reinforce the "better angels" in our nature, as they struggle against isolationism, protectionism, and opportunism. They should speak out against trade barriers imposed by developed countries, against the declining levels and destruction of so much of the environment, against the weak response to HIV/AIDS, against restrictive patents on medicines, and so on. These institutions advise developing countries on policies every day. They also have a duty to speak clearly and strongly to developed countries.

Global Public Goods

There is another arena for action by the development community, beyond the level of individual countries. Global development challenges—such as combating the spread of infectious disease, creating a better architecture for international trade and finance, halting deforestation, climate change, and loss of biodiversity, and conducting basic research on agriculture and drugs relevant for developing countries—cannot be handled adequately by individual countries and so require multilateral action. These challenges have key characteristics of global or regional public goods: they have strong cross-border externalities and are nonrival (as with new technology) or nonexcludable (as with clean air) in their consumption, or both.

Three examples illustrate the large returns that such global initiatives can bring:

• West Africa's Onchocerciasis Control Program, a collaborative effort of multilateral agencies, governments, NGOs, and the private sector. Since it was launched in 1974, the program has largely eliminated the scourge of river blindness from eleven countries in West Africa. As a result it has prevented an estimated 600,000 cases of blindness and added 5 million years of productive labor to the eleven countries' economies.

• The Consultative Group for International Agricultural Research (CGIAR), a network of research centers that has created and promoted crop improvements in developing countries over the past thirty years, reducing rural poverty and improving productivity and nutrition. These centers have produced more than 500 varieties of grain now planted in poor countries and have helped increase average yields of target grains by 75 percent.

• The Vienna Convention of 1985 and the subsequent Montreal and London protocols, which committed a large number of nations to address the ozone depletion arising from the widespread use of chlorofluorocarbons (see chapter 2).

Other pressing needs remain for global action today. One area for action is the control of communicable disease, an area that has seen both dramatic successes and major failures. The eradication of smallpox is a vivid example of what is possible, but is offset by the global community's setbacks in combating HIV/AIDS and malaria. The failings on HIV/AIDS, particularly the delayed response, are so great as to require little elaboration, and the decision of some developing-country governments to turn a blind eye to the problem does not exculpate the world community. Malaria is another scourge against which, until recently, there has been too little international response. In the village of Palanpur, India, when Stern did field research in the mid-1970s, it was assumed that malaria would soon go the way of smallpox. A quarter-century later, malaria continues to afflict 300 to 500 million people worldwide each year, killing 1 million of them. Led by the United Nations, the Global Fund to Fight AIDS, Tuberculosis, and Malaria has tried to fill this gap since 2002. But its funding and action have been weak relative to the challenge. In striving toward the MDGs, there can be few higher priorities than global action on this front.

The environment is a second area for global action. Clean water and air, forestation, and biodiversity are all vital global assets, and their loss can be catastrophic, especially for poor people. Tropical countries are particularly vulnerable to the effects of projected climate change and environmental degradation, including losses in food production arising from global warming and an expanding range of tropical diseases. Water scarcity is a looming threat for many poor countries, particularly in Africa and the Middle East. The Nile Basin Initiative, which has brought together the ten riparian states of the Nile river to coordinate efforts to preserve and allocate water supplies, is one example of the type of global or regional response that is needed. To tackle biodiversity loss, Central American countries and their neighbors have banded together to create the Mesoamerican Biological Corridor, which is aimed at preserving substantial contiguous territory in which the region's rich flora and fauna can flourish. Fisheries depletion is another global public goods problem—a classic "tragedy of the commons"—that the international community needs to solve, given the dependence of many poor countries and people on ocean fisheries.

Third, the production of data and information is an important global public good. For example, much of the research discussed in these lectures relies on the purchasing power parity calculations of the International Comparison Project. These data are fundamental: without knowing how prices differ across countries, we could not make international comparisons of living standards and poverty rates or infer the relative effectiveness of different development approaches. Other global public goods in this area include basic development research and mechanisms providing easy access to information and data about the developing world, such as the Development Gateway Web site launched by the World Bank. Finally, as discussed in chapter 11, there is great value in having an impartial arbiter—an international financial institution or NGO—"keep score" by assessing how well countries have lived up to the commitments they made in the development compact reaffirmed at the Monterrey, Johannesburg, and Doha international gatherings. This information is also a public good, since it would be neither practical nor sensible to restrict access to those who are able to pay for these scorecards.

International Debt Forgiveness
New aid is not always enough, no matter how effectively it is allocated and delivered. For countries suffering from severe international debt overhangs, debt forgiveness is a necessary step in building the pillars of development. High debt strains public finances, making it difficult to carry out even minimal government functions, let alone the more ambitious investment climate and empowerment agenda. And fear of debt-induced macroeconomic volatility, combined with a lack of basic government services, discourages entrepreneurs from making long-term plans and investments. Concerns about the costs of rising debt burdens led to the valuable and effective Jubilee 2000 debt forgiveness movement, as well as the heavily indebted poor country (HIPC) debt relief initiative.

The HIPC initiative aims to relieve the onerous debt burdens of the world's poorest countries, conditional on a track record of committed progrowth policy reforms and a commitment to maintain social spending. Countries identified as HIPCs share certain features: they have been heavily indebted for most or all of the past decade; they are poor, with at least half of their populations living on less than $1 a day; and they are highly dependent on development assistance, having received an average of 10 percent of GDP in aid in the 1990s. For this group the HIPC initiative is an important step toward reducing poverty and setting them on a growth path.

By mid-2003, twenty-six countries were benefiting from debt relief under the enhanced HIPC initiative, although only six countries had reached the "completion point" at which the largest debt relief is granted. The debt relief committed so far to these twenty-six countries, together with relief under the traditional mechanism and additional bilateral debt forgiveness, represents a reduction in the outstanding debt stock of around $40 billion in net present value terms.[17] The public debt stock fell substantially in the late 1990s in the first wave of HIPC debt relief; it has since fallen further under the enhanced HIPC initiative, which offers deeper cuts in debt service than the original initiative.

International Action and Development

Foreign governments, foreign donors, and foreign firms cannot themselves build the two pillars of development for a recipient country in the absence of strong domestic efforts. But they can provide very powerful support to development, which can make possible achievements that otherwise would be far out of reach. International action on development is vital if all regions of the developing world are to make advances on the scale indicated by the Millennium Development Goals.

Trade, aid, and other types of international flows raise the returns to country actions that improve the investment climate and empower people. Conversely, by blocking access to their markets—especially the markets for agricultural goods and labor-intensive products and services—developed countries raise further the high hurdles that poor countries must leap to achieve development. And by allowing aid to fall through much of the post–Cold War period, donors have created a situation in which the poorest and most disadvantaged countries in particular may lack the resources necessary to build and strengthen the two development pillars. Rich countries have a moral responsibility to take forward and go beyond recent initiatives that have begun to reverse the aid decline, and to use the opportunity of the current round of trade negotiations to lock in market access for products from the developing world.

If the will is there, then our wealth as a world, our growing understanding of how development happens, and the foundations already laid by many developing countries together provide a historic opportunity to banish poverty from much or all of the planet. History demands that rich countries face up to their moral responsibilities and play their part in building a better world for all.

Conclusion: A Strategy to Guide Policy, a Program for Learning, and a Plan of Action

The world that these lectures envision is one where poor people—indeed, all people—are enabled and equipped to shape their lives. Countries in such a world would have vibrant, innovative market economies complemented by active states. And they would understand the importance of openness to trade and internationalism in their approaches and relationships. It is not the world we are in, but it is a world we can move toward.

The strategy we have offered for creating this world provides a realistic agenda for action. It also helps identify a program for research. If we are to move forward, we must have rigorous evidence and well-founded new ideas—and as students of development, it is our responsibility to provide the evidence and ideas. The agenda sketched out in these lectures is one of development and internationalism, of governance and markets, of idealism in values and down-to-earth experience in methods. It takes a view of capitalism and markets rooted in Schumpeter's emphasis on entrepreneurship and dynamics, and a view of the potency of public policy and internationalism inspired by Keynes. It shares their emphasis on the role of institutions. No challenge is more worthy of their extraordinary legacies than the global fight against poverty.

The past half-century has seen astonishingly rapid change. It has been a period of great achievements, mixed with major disappointments and tragedies. But it has provided lessons about how processes function, about what works and what does not—and these lessons form the basis of the strategy proposed here.

The strategy embodies a view of development as one of structural change, where institutions, while changing along the way, have a powerful influence on the processes themselves. These are dynamic processes where history and learning matter to what happens next. The strategy can be expressed simply in terms of two pillars: building an investment climate for entrepreneurship and growth and empowering and investing in people so that they can participate in and shape that growth. The goal of the strategy is to advance the living standards of all people, but particularly poor people. The interpretation of living standards is broad, covering health and education as well as income— but also the freedom of people to act and participate in society. Thus, it includes the notion of empowerment.

If we can identify the basic dynamic forces of development, then public policy should focus on how to influence them. Public economics becomes the study of how to shape and guide processes of change. This is a program for research that, though it departs from received public economics, is firmly based on the achievements of received theory in this area and those of growth theory and development economics. We are keenly aware that the ideas proposed in these lectures are in their early stages. But if our arguments are accepted, they present both a challenge and a way forward for the economics of policy.

There have already been important steps in this program of research. On the empirical front we are building a set of databases on the investment climate and how public services work that provides valuable insights into the workings of the two pillars. Further, there has been a positive move toward more careful statistical appraisal of the consequences of policies, programs, and projects. Only if we provide serious analysis of what works and what does not can we have any confidence in scaling up our ideas to the economy as a whole or, indeed, internationally. We have also tried to point the way to a theoretical analysis of the question of how the investment climate and empowerment change over time. We have suggested that in both cases there could be virtuous circles at work and that the analysis of public action should be devoted to understanding how to get those moving. We have paid special attention to the role of changing preferences: changes in aspirations, attitudes, perceptions, and goals are part of the essence of development, yet all too often they are left out of economics.

There are real dangers in trying to analyze policy without examining political economy and the role of vested interests. If political action to change the investment climate and empowerment is to be effective, it will face opposition from those who prosper from the status quo. This is a challenge that Machiavelli recognized five centuries ago. He argued that the difficulties were so great that the reformer, or prophet, had to be an "armed prophet." We have tried to suggest that there are ways forward to enact change without necessarily involving the military might that Machiavelli saw as essential.

These lectures close with a call for action. There is a special opportunity to act now, based not only on the achievements and learning of the past fifty years but also on the shared commitments and goals embraced by the international community when it defined the Millennium Development Goals (MDGs) in the autumn of 2000. This was followed by a charting of the way forward on trade (Doha, November 2001), development financing (Monterrey, March 2002), and sustainable development (Johannesburg, August 2002). During those conferences the world's leaders expressed their understanding of and commitment to finding international responses to international problems. And it is clear that trade and environmental issues have to be tackled by the international community, acting together, if there is to be progress on the scale required by the MDGs. Developing countries must take the lead in setting their course—one that will vary with country circumstances. A careful assessment of the role of the state and of the ability to finance it will be at the core of the challenge in every country. And as we argued in detail, there is a tremendous amount that the international community can do by opening up markets and expanding aid. Aid has never before been more productive, but the amount given (as a share of rich countries' income) has never been lower.

The picture of development we have drawn, and the strategy to guide it, places learning at the center. If we are to guide these dynamic processes effectively, we have to be sure that we build learning into our actions. But we must also have the confidence and commitment to act. While we have much to learn, we know enough to act effectively now. We have tried to offer a strategy that both guides action and provides a program for learning. We have also argued that we have today an extraordinary opportunity to act effectively in the fight for development and against poverty. If we accept the moral imperative presented by the poverty challenge, then this opportunity carries a heavy responsibility to act. In these lectures we have tried to set out an analytical framework for action that provides the development community with a firm basis for rising to that responsibility.

Notes

Chapter 1

1. The international poverty line used in World Bank 1990 was set at $1 per day at 1985 purchasing-power parity-adjusted U.S. dollars. The original $1 a day poverty line was chosen as being representative of the poverty lines found among low-income countries. To be consistent, Chen and Ravallion applied the same principle in updating the poverty line to reflect 1993 PPP prices. The resulting poverty line is set at $1.08 a day ($32.74 per month) in 1993 prices; this is the median of the lowest ten poverty lines within the set of countries used in the earlier calculations (Chen and Ravallion 2004).

2. The link here is the "nutritional wage" story: undernourishment and poor health of destitute landless workers lower their marginal product, making them unattractive on the job market even at a lower wage.

3. Senior civil servants in the United Kingdom have longer life expectancies than junior ones, and it has been suggested that this results from the lower stress associated with greater control.

4. The data in this section come from Justino and Litchfield (2003), who survey a large number of studies by the World Bank and other sources.

5. The data in this section come from World Bank (2001d).

6. Shortages of women can also create hazards for them, as some are subjected to new types of violence, such as being kidnapped for marriage.

7. Das Gupta and others (2004) show how divergent government policies toward gender inequalities have led to different outcomes in the three countries in recent decades (see chapter 9, this volume).

Chapter 2

1. It has not always been ignored by practitioners. Consider the views of two chief economists of the World Bank, for example. As we will note later in this chapter, Hollis Chenery's economic models focused on the massive changes to economic structure that came with development. And Stern's immediate predecessor, Joseph Stiglitz, underlined the notion of "development as transformation" in his 1998 Raúl Prebisch Lecture (Stiglitz 1998).

2. Because this book is a series of lectures rather than a statistical yearbook, we will often use phrases such as "rich countries" and "poor countries" without spelling out precisely which countries are included in those categories. "Rich countries" should generally be taken to mean the members of the Organization for Economic Cooperation and Development (OECD), which overlaps considerably with the "upper-income" category used by the World Bank. "Poor countries" will generally mean all developing countries; where we want to make a finer distinction between "low-income" and "middle-income" (again, in the sense used by the World Bank), we will use those more precise terms. Lists of countries by income group can be found in the World Bank's *World Development Indicators* statistical yearbooks.

3. Gros and Steinherr (1995) note that official statistics from the Soviet Union suffered from measurement errors (excluding the underground economy, for instance), over-reporting by plant managers, and political manipulation, though these are hard to document. In addition, there are technical reasons that growth could have been overestimated: the use of net material product accounts; and the use of GDP deflators which, in the light of rationing and poor quality, may have underestimated true price increases and led to overstatements of real GDP growth.

4. Some evidence for the importance of these other factors is provided by World Bank (2000c), which points out that the region's oil exporters such as Nigeria also performed poorly over the 1970–1997 period, despite massive improvements in their terms of trade.

5. Understanding the determinants of growth has a long and noble history going back to Adam Smith, David Ricardo, and Karl Marx, and proceeding through Joseph Schumpeter, Nicholas Kaldor, John Hicks, Robert Solow, and Kenneth Arrow. Following the pioneering work of Kuznets (1956, 1971), Chenery ignited one wave of cross-country regressions in the 1970s. Another wave started in the 1980s when the Summers-Heston data became available (see Kravis, Heston, and Summers 1982, 1983). This wave started with Barro (1991) and Levine and Renelt (1992). Studies often emphasize determinants that most affect long-term economic growth: human capital (Hanushek, Kain, and Rivkin 2004; Krueger and Lindahl 2001, Glewwe 2002), technological innovation (Klenow and Rodriguez-Clare 1997), infrastructure (Canning, Fay, and Perotti 1992), geography and natural resources (Gallup, Sachs, and Mellinger 1999; Engerman and Sokoloff 1997), trade and trade policy (Frankel and Romer 1999, Rodríguez and Rodrik 1999); macroeconomic policies (Fischer 1993), competition policy (Romer 1994, Dutz and Hayri 2000), and institutions (Knack and Keefer 1995, Hall and Jones 1999; Acemoğlu, Johnson, and Robinson 2001). For a recent survey of cross-country growth regressions, see Bosworth and Collins (2003).

6. As noted earlier, there is considerable variation around this mean, but the effect of growth on poverty shares is typically significant and negative. By contrast, the relationship between growth and the income shares for poor people does not even seem to have the same sign in different regions: it is positive in Africa but negative in Latin America. And while growth does improve human development indicators such as infant mortality and primary enrollment, the elasticity (the percentage increase associated with 1 percent growth) is typically much smaller than 1. All these estimates should be taken with caution, because there are so many factors at work—many of them moving in tandem with income growth—that it is difficult to isolate convincingly the effects of income.

7. Inequality tended to fall in Indonesia, Ireland, Italy, Japan, Mauritania, Portugal, Puerto Rico, Singapore, Spain, Taiwan, and Trinidad and Tobago, and tended to rise in Brazil, Chile, China, Gabon, Germany, Hong Kong, Romania, and Thailand.

8. See http://www.worldbank.org/depweb/english/modules/environm/water/.

9. Stark (1991) finds a possible benefit for poor countries from the migration of skilled workers, arguing that the possibility of migration leads to greater investment in human capital.

10. It is difficult to put together a consistent data series on capital flows to developing countries going back to 1970. Only point estimates are available.

11. For example, Fischer (1993), Frankel and Romer (1999), and Dollar and Kraay (2004).

12. The Country Policy and Institutional Assessment (CPIA) index, calculated annually by the World Bank for all its borrowing countries, is a subjective assessment by Bank staff of a particular country's current policy and institutional framework for fostering sustainable growth, poverty reduction, and the effective use of development assistance. It is composed of twenty equally weighted criteria that are grouped in four clusters—economic management, structural policies, policies for social inclusion and equity, and public sector management and institutions. For low-income countries, see http://www.worldbank.org/ida/idalloc.htm.

13. Using the Kaufmann-Kraay index, the evidence on governance and institutions suggests a rather mixed picture. Little average progress in improving important dimensions of governance, controlling corruption, and improving institutional quality worldwide is apparent, though there is significant variance across countries. See Kaufmann (2003).

14. *Democracy* and *autocracy* are ambiguous terms, and different countries have different mixes and qualities of governing institutions. The Polity IV data set rates the levels of democracy and autocracy for each country and each year using information on the general qualities of political institutions and processes: competitiveness of executive recruitment, extent of executive constraints, and openness of political competition. The ratings are combined into a single measure of governance ranging from -10 (fully institutionalized autocracy) to $+10$ (fully institutionalized democracy). See Marshall and Gurr (2003).

15. See Beck and others (2001), which provides a database covering political institutions in 177 countries over 1975–1995. The database was recently updated by Philip Keefer; see http://econ.worldbank.org.

Chapter 3

1. The use of *agents* here is not meant to evoke the concept of principal-agent models. Instead, *agency* here is used in the Aristotelian sense picked up by Sen: the freedom to choose and act and the active exercise of capabilities.

2. Provision for people who are incapacitated is a different matter.

3. Sen is keenly aware of this. For instance, he notes in *Development as Freedom* (1999, p. 253) that "the politics of social consensus calls not only for acting on the basis of given individual preferences, but also for sensitivity of social decisions to the *development* [emphasis in original] of individual preferences and norms. In this context, particular importance has to be attached to the role of public discussion and interactions in the emergence of shared values and commitments."

4. The word *governance*, which is synonymous with the exercise of authority and control, is not new in the English language. In 1470, Sir John Fortescue, chief justice of the Court of King's Bench, published *The Governance of England* (Landes 1998).

5. Atkinson and Bourguignon (2001) offers an explicit statement of the difference between poverty and social exclusion, as well as a proposal for handling both concepts

simultaneously when defining poverty lines. Section 5.3 of Atkinson and Bourguignon's introductory chapter to their *Handbook of Income Distribution* (2000) is also a useful reference.

6. The report *Social Indicators: The EU and Social Inclusion*, prepared under the direction of Tony Atkinson (Atkinson and others 2002), has been influential in defining the European Union's social agenda.

7. *Empowerment* is translated as *insertion* in French and *empoderamiento* in Spanish in the World Bank's *World Development Report 2000/2001* (World Bank 2001c). The Spanish translation is an obvious Anglicism, while the French does not convey the meaning of the empowerment concept in that language.

8. Indeed, there has been some debate about the statistical evidence. Hansen and Tarp (2001) confirm the statistical result that aid is effective, but argue that it is unconditionally effective: that is, even in countries with relatively poor policies and institutions, aid can accelerate growth and reduce poverty. However, our reading of the evidence—statistical as well as case study—is that aid to countries with better policies and institutions typically has a larger growth payoff, with funds less likely to be diverted to nondevelopmental purposes. This is not to say that there is no role for aid in other countries, but to suggest (as we will discuss in chapter 13) that such aid needs to be smaller in scale and more narrowly targeted to specific developmental purposes.

Chapter 4

1. To avoid invidious comparisons with contemporaries, when speaking of foundations and traditions we confine ourselves to scholars born before World War II.

2. The "license raj" or "permit raj" is the term often used to capture the web of bureaucratic requirements that constrained private enterprise during most of India's postindependence period. The name is derived from the numerous permits and licenses that firms had to obtain from often-uncooperative officials. These requirements restricted the dynamism of the private enterprise unnecessarily and were thus a major constraint on India's economic growth rate, which languished well below East Asian levels at the so-called Hindu rate of growth.

3. Jacobs (1969) makes a comparison with the history of ideas about embryos growing. Members of the preformationist school (such as Aristotle) thought the embryo was a tiny version of the mature organism, so that maturation was just "growth." The epigenesis school saw diversification into specialized roles along with growth in size, so that maturation was "development." Aggregate growth theory seems closer to the preformationist idea of quantitative growth, with all the "development" hidden in the black box of growth in "total factor productivity."

4. See Stern (1989, particularly p. 619) for further discussion of this history. Buchanan and Yoon (1994) reprint a number of important papers related to increasing returns.

5. The themes of this tradition have been independently developed with iconoclastic freshness by Jane Jacobs (1969, 1984, 2000) in studies of the oldest and clearest examples of agglomeration due to increasing returns; cities. In Robert E. Lucas's (1988) work on endogenous growth and increasing returns, he noted: "I will be following very closely the lead of Jane Jacobs, whose remarkable book *The Economy of Cities* seems to me mainly and convincingly concerned (although she does not use this terminology) with the external effects of human capital" (p. 37).

Chapter 5

1. Annual inflation is measured here by changes in the GDP deflator (see World Bank 2003i and World Bank database).

2. The Doing Business database (http://rru.worldbank.org/DoingBusiness/default. aspx) provides comparable quantitative data for 110 countries on bankruptcy, contract enforcement, credit markets, entry regulations, and labor regulations. See World Bank (2003b).

3. Indeed, the key ideas were embodied in the strategy adopted by the World Bank in its strategic framework paper of 2001.

Chapter 6

1. Deaton (1997) and Grosh and Glewwe (2000) describe how the systematic collection of household data began more than two hundred years ago with the gathering of family budgets by Reverend David Davies and Sir Frederick Morton Eden in England in the late 1700s. In the 1800s similar data were collected in Belgium, Prussia, Saxony, and the United States. By the mid-1800s generalizations about household behavior were being drawn from the data. For example, Ernst Engel used Edouard Ducpetiaux's 1855 study of 200 Belgian households to derive his classic law that poor families devote a larger share of their household budgets to food. The statistical theory supporting modern survey methods was not developed until the 1920s. Benjamin Seebohm Rowntree did much to validate sampling theory with his own disbelief. Unpersuaded of the reliability of sampling, Rowntree undertook a full census to survey poverty in the city of York, in England, in 1936. He was later able to reproduce most of the results from his full census using samples from his data. The viability of sampling made high-caliber nationwide surveys feasible and led to their appearance in many countries, especially after World War II.

2. Consider the example of estimating changes in mean incomes. If income is positively correlated over time—that is, if households that are poor in one period have a greater-than-average probability of being poor in the next period—panel data will produce estimates of the mean with lower variance. If we are forced to rely on cross-sectional data, the variance of the change in estimated means from two cross-sections would be the sum of the individual variance estimates in each of the two periods, assuming each of the samples is drawn independently. In contrast, since the same households appear in both periods in panel data, the variance of the change in estimated means would be the sum of the variances of the individual estimates of mean income less twice the covariance between the two estimates. Although measurement error complicates the analysis, it is likely to increase the advantage of panel data if the same individuals tend to make the same reporting errors in different periods.

3. This survey work at the European Bank for Reconstruction and Development began when one of this book's authors, Nicholas Stern, was chief economist there in the early 1990s.

4. As of early 2004, Investment Climate Surveys had already been carried out in about fifty developing and transition countries.

5. For example, the ICRG data set contains five indicators: law and order tradition, risk of expropriation, repudiation of contracts by governments, corruption in government,

and quality of bureaucracy. The BERI data set consists of four main indicators: contract enforcement, nationalization potential, bureaucratic delays, and infrastructure quality.

6. The World Database of Happiness (http://www.eur.nl/fsw/research/happiness/), directed by Ruut Veenhoven from Erasmus University in Rotterdam, is an ongoing register of scientific research on subjective appreciation of life. It brings together findings that are scattered throughout many studies and provides a basis for synthetic studies.

7. The distinction suggested by the names of these surveys should not be overemphasized: a PETS typically collects information on much more than just fund flows, while the typical QSDS collects data on expenditure levels and sources.

8. Most QSDS studies have not focused on these issues yet; one notable exception is Reinikka and Svensson (2003).

9. This section draws on Bourguignon, Pereira da Silva, and Stern (2004).

Chapter 7

1. Every *World Development Report* initiated during Nicholas Stern's tenure as chief economist at the World Bank was oriented to the second strain of research. See the 2002 report on building institutions for markets, the 2003 report on sustainable development in a dynamic world, the 2004 report on making services work for poor people, and the 2005 report on the investment climate, growth, and poverty.

2. Of course, it could also lead to pressure for deterioration in the investment climate if higher-income people seek protection of their wealth at the expense of others.

3. A striking example is the great difficulty of starting a firm in Peru due to cumbersome requirements and extensive opportunities for corruption, as described in De Soto (1989). More recent work by the World Bank compares the steps, time, and costs required to register a business in more than 130 countries, as described elsewhere in this book. More cumbersome entry regulation is associated with more corruption, a larger informal sector, and lower productivity and investment but not better public goods (World Bank 2003b, Djankov and others, Porta Lopez-de-Silanes, and Shleifer 2002).

4. The same process is involved when learning about policies and institutions that need to be adapted to local settings. For example, in many developing countries legislation is transplanted from Anglo-Saxon or European countries. But, as shown by Pistor (2000) and Berkowitz, Pistor, and Richard (2001), law enforcement and legality are better in countries that have adapted these transplants to their conditions.

Chapter 8

1. See http://poverty.worldbank.org/files/14660_SEWA-web.pdf and http://www.sewa.org/aboutus/index.htm.

2. See http://poverty.worldbank.org/files/14875_FilipinoReportCard-web.pdf.

3. See http://poverty.worldbank.org/files/14650_Kecamatan-web.pdf and World Bank (2003a).

4. Data from the World Bank SIMA database. The correlation coefficient is an index of the degree to which two variables—in this case, the agricultural and nonagricultural growth rates—move together. It can range from +1 (perfect positive correlation) to −1 (perfect negative correlation).

5. We are gratefully to Abhijit Banerjee for pointing out these references.

6. For further theoretical and empirical evidence on these conclusions, see Ravallion (2003); Aghion, Caroli, and Garcia-Peñalosa (1999); Bardhan and Mookherjee (1998); Broadway and Keen (2000); Kanbur (2000); Dasgupta and Ray (1986); P. Dasgupta (1993); Galor and Zeira (1993); Bowles and Gintis (1996); Bénabou (1996a, 1996b, 2002); McGregor (1995); Hoff and Lyon (1995); Hoff (1996); Aghion and Bolton (1997); Holzmann and Jorgensen (1999); Bourguignon (2002); World Bank (2000a); and Smith and Subbarao (2003).

Chapter 9

1. We are grateful to David Ellerman and Greg Fischer for their collaboration in preparing this chapter and to Michael Walton for comments.

2. This choice parallels the distinction between the neoclassical approach—centered on agents, markets, and efficiency—and the Austrian school approach, which emphasizes markets as processes and arenas in which freedoms can be exercised. Both approaches have something to contribute to this subject, but in our view the Austrian approach is better suited to grappling with preference change.

3. For the United States, Claudia Goldin (1991) casts doubt on this type of preference or norm hysteresis story; there does not seem to have been a permanent increase in women's participation as a result of new behaviors acquired during wartime work.

4. Perhaps the use of the word *capital* is overstretched here, but that is not the main issue. What matters are the influences on preferences, their effects, and how they might change. Cultural capital is a parallel concept to social capital, except that instead of emphasizing social networks, it emphasizes culture. In socially differentiated societies, social and cultural capital can work together in reproducing inequality by preserving differential access to networks, perpetuating symbolic violence that maintains the status quo, and creating a pattern that generates constraining preferences, limiting the hopes and aspirations of the poor and perpetuating adverse "terms of recognition" from dominant groups.

5. It is not clear whether Becker's example is about preferences or about beliefs or information. If his is a story of agents who do not have a taste for discrimination, but simply distasteful (but ultimately self-fulfilling) beliefs about the distribution of skills, then it is not necessarily connected with preferences.

6. These are official figures from Uganda's Ministry of Health.

7. See, for example, the Truth campaign at www.thetruth.com, which combines information about smoking with a presentation that makes use of irony, sleek Web marketing, pop culture references, and guerrilla-style messages about Big Tobacco.

8. What we have in mind here is not primarily an individual's freedom to choose consumer goods or investment vehicles, say, but more fundamental decisions about lives and livelihoods. A recent literature in behavioral economics (such as Iyengar and Lepper

2000) argues that having more options can make decisions too difficult and can in fact reduce utility. This may be meaningful in a consumption or savings context, but the freedoms that we have in mind are unlikely to be welfare reducing—for example, when a woman is given the opportunity to progress on to secondary education or a farmworker has an opportunity to participate in decision making over land use.

9. See, for example, Alexis de Tocqueville (1969 [1848]), John Stuart Mill (1972 [1861]), Walter Bagehot (1948 [1869]), James Bryce (1959 [1888]), John Dewey (1927, 1939), Ernest Barker (1967), Frank Knight (1947), James Buchanan (1954), Jurgen Häbermas (1990), and Gutmann and Thompson (1996), among many others.

10. See Hirschman's (1977) treatment of "doux commerce."

11. This has strong affinities with the grassroots approach to rural development, with its emphasis on building social capital and solving collective action problems through local organizations. See Esman and Uphoff (1984), Hirschman (1984), and Krishna, Uphoff, and Esman (1997) for other cases like the Moroccan village example.

12. There is much room for fruitful interdisciplinary research between economics and management theory (in contrast to the imperialistic forays of economists into organizational theory criticized by Simon). Useful references from the management literature include March and Simon (1958); McGregor (1960), who explores the role of nonpecuniary motivation; Weick (1979), who uses an exploration-exploitation approach based on evolutionary ideas; Senge (1990) and Senge and others (1999), who construct models using positive and negative feedback loops that resonate with the vicious and virtuous circles of the development literature; and Brandenburger and Nalebuff (1996), who use economics and game theory to explore the subtle interplay between competition and cooperation.

13. See http://www.worldbank.org/poverty/strategies/overview.htm.

14. Dudwick and others (2003) is a good example of careful qualitative work that traces the reverse phenomenon: disempowerment that has resulted from poor people's declining participation in social networks in the Kyrgyz Republic and other Central Asian countries over the past decade.

Chapter 10

1. Chang (2002) uses the term "kicking away the ladder" to refer to the interaction between developed and developing countries, but it can also be applied to the interaction between successful elites and those who seek to emulate them in a given country.

2. Murphy, Shleifer, and Vishny (1993) point out that rent-seeking activity is subject to natural increasing returns: the presence of rent seeking breeds more rent seeking, and a high level of rent seeking is self-sustaining. They also point out that public rent seeking (corruption) is particularly damaging for entrepreneurial innovation and sharply reduces economic growth. Their arguments add substance to those of Acemoğlu, Johnson, and Robinson (2001), who focus more on the effects that poor economic institutions have on the dynamics of development.

3. Though not the general phenomenon that Kuznets originally posited, the Kuznets curve—the inverted-U relationship between income inequality and income—appears in the data for a number of Western economies.

4. Ferreira (1996) proposes a model of wealth distribution dynamics with a capital market imperfection and a production function where public capital is complementary to private capital. A unique invariant steady-state distribution is derived, with three social classes: subsistence workers, government-dependent middle-class entrepreneurs, and private infrastructure-owning upper-class entrepreneurs. Increases in untargeted public investment over a certain range lead to unambiguously lower inequality of opportunity, and there is a minimum level of public investment below which the middle class disappears.

5. Shleifer and Treisman (2000) contain a good, but controversial, analysis of the reforms during this period.

Chapter 11

1. The Monterrey declaration makes this partnership explicit: "We commit ourselves to sound policies, good governance at all levels and the rule of law. We also commit ourselves to mobilizing domestic resources, attracting international flows, promoting international trade as an engine for development, increasing international financial and technical cooperation for development, sustainable debt financing and external debt relief, and enhancing the coherence and consistency of the international monetary, financial and trading systems."

2. Bradford (2002) contains a useful account of the history of the MDGs. The development of the MDGs has its roots in the 1990 World Summit for Children, organized by UNICEF. This was followed by a series of UN Summit conferences that set the pace (the education summit in Jomtien in 1990, the environment summit in Rio in 1992, the population and development conference in Cairo in 1995, the social summit in Copenhagen in 1995, the human rights summit in Vienna in 1996, and the summit on women in Beijing in 1996). In parallel, in response to the decline in official development assistance (ODA) after the end of the Cold War and the fall of the Berlin Wall, a high-level meeting of Development Assistance Committee (DAC) ministers of the OECD developed a strategic vision of ODA and issued, in May 1996, a ministerial statement containing seven development goals (on poverty reduction, infant and child mortality, gender equality, universal education, access to reproductive health services and environmental action) as well as plans to achieve them by 2015. These goals came to be known as the International Development Goals (IDGs). They are the precursors for what are now widely known as the MDGs.

The IDGs were endorsed by several OECD ministerials and by the G-7 summits in Denver 1996, Birmingham 1997, and Cologne 1998. There were several developing country consultation conferences, one organized by the Netherlands in The Hague and one held by Japan in Okinawa, among others. The World Bank's new publication of *World Development Indicators* in 1997 featured the IDGs as a framework for assessing progress toward reaching these goals. In 2000, a study was published on progress toward the IDGs by region and by goal called *A Better World for All*. This document, signed by the heads of the World Bank, the IMF, the UN, and the OECD together, represented a milestone in development cooperation with all the major bilateral and multilateral donor agencies agreeing on a common framework of goals and indicators for the development effort. The United Nations Millennium General Assembly in September 2000 was the high point in articulating a consensus on the broad framework for international development cooperation. Some 147 heads of state—and 191 nations in total—adopted the Millennium Declaration. The United Nations Conference on Financing for Development in

Monterrey, Mexico, in March 2002, marked the turning point from consensus building to implementation. The Johannesburg summit on sustainable development in September 2002 reaffirmed each of the Millennium Development Goals (see Bradford 2002; Devarajan, Miller, and Swanson 2002).

3. As discussed below, these targets should not be imposed on countries. However, outside observers might be justified in applying MDG-type criteria to judge the pace of a country's development progress.

4. Tragically, the AIDS epidemic has since reversed much of that progress.

5. There are other reasons that researchers have trouble finding a correlation between health spending and outcomes. First, there are methodological challenges. The cross-country regressions often used to search for a correlation have inherent flaws from a statistical perspective. Most notably, they have a hard time identifying the effects of any particular factor when so many factors are moving together and many stem from unobservable country characteristics. Second, where governance is poor—for example, where a large share of public funding leaks or is stolen outright—there is no reason to expect health spending to lead to better health outcomes. Indeed, research shows that if we focus on countries where governance is relatively good, public spending appears to have a significant effect (Swaroop and Rajkumar 2002). Nevertheless, cross-sector effects likely also tell part of the story.

6. See the conclusions of the Report of the High-Level Panel on Financing for development, chaired by President Zedillo, June 2001: http://www.un.org/reports/financing/summary.htm. The Zedillo report conclusions are consistent with World Bank calculations (see World Bank 2003k).

7. Poverty Reduction Strategy Papers (PRSPs) are prepared by low-income countries through a process involving both domestic stakeholders and external development partners. They describe the country's macroeconomic, structural, and social policies and programs aimed at promoting broad-based growth and reducing poverty in the medium to long term. The IMF and World Bank base their country work programs, concessional assistance, and debt relief (under the heavily indebted poor countries initiative) on these country-owned strategies.

8. During the period 1991–2000, Zambia has had the highest ratio of official development assistance to GDP at purchasing power parity prices (12.4 percent) of all aid recipients. This corresponds to a level of ODA of more than 25 percent of GDP in current U.S. dollars. The experience of Zambia and of nine other African countries is discussed in details in Devarajan, Dollar, and Holmgren (2001).

9. http://www.gdnet.org.

10. "Conflict diamonds" are those that originate from an area in conflict. The sale of diamonds helps finance conflict, and struggle for control of rents from diamonds and other natural resources may provide a motivation for conflict. But diamonds usually have geological features that allow their source to be identified by scientific analysis. Hence it is possible to curtail trade in conflict diamonds and thereby improve the chances of ending the conflict.

11. http://www.cgdev.org/rankingtherich/details.html.

12. http://siteresources.worldbank.org/GLOBALMONITORINGEXT/Resources/DC2003-0013.pdf.

13. http://www.transparency.org/surveys/index.html.

14. While this may seem like an enormous increase, current aid flows represent less than 1 percent of GDP (and less than 4 percent of investment) in developing countries.

Chapter 12

1. See http://siteresources.worldbank.org/IDA/Resources/PBAAR4.pdf for more details.

2. Until the late 1990s, the International Monetary Fund's country macroeconomic assessments, known as Article IV reports, were treated as highly confidential. Yet in a move to increase transparency after the emerging-market financial crises of the 1990s, the IMF decided to release the reports beginning in 1999, conditional on permission of the countries. Glennerster and Shin (2003) recently studied how this policy change has affected twenty-three emerging-market economies, twelve of which had authorized release of the reports. They found, first, that markets rewarded the countries that authorized release by reducing the spreads on their bonds, and second, that markets respond also to the content of the reports. In other words, despite pressures that might lead to a reduction in the accuracy of the reports, they are still seen by market participants as being informative about each country's economic situation. We believe that the same would be true of publicized CPIA ratings.

3. Kharas and Mishra (2001) argue that the conventional story of deficit-driven vulnerabilities and currency crises fits better when "hidden deficits"—driven by such factors as the off-budget costs of implicit guarantees to banking and corporate sectors—are added to the balance sheets of governments in East Asia and elsewhere. Nevertheless, most evidence suggests that the primary drivers of the crisis were currency mismatches and short-term liabilities, combined with open capital markets.

4. These numbers refer to the most recent year for which data are available.

5. It is sometimes difficult to distinguish between the two. In the run-up to the Thai financial crisis that broke in 1997, much of the country's foreign borrowing was going into investment—but firms were making unproductive investments in real estate, leaving them highly vulnerable to a bursting of the speculative bubble.

6. Macroeconomic crises hit poor people hard, and this is one reason a government concerned with promoting growth and fighting poverty must take fiscal discipline seriously. The country studies presented by Bourguignon, de Melo, and Morrisson (1991) contain strong empirical evidence on this view for the 1980s. Poor people are not only more vulnerable to the occurrence of loss of income, they are also much less able to respond and cope. Given the imperfect nature of capital markets, credit and insurance are generally unavailable to poor people, and hence they have limited ability to smooth out consumption (World Bank 1998a). There is also abundant evidence of this for the 1990s. During the 1997–1998 crisis in Indonesia, for example, the poorest quartile of households suffered a much larger drop in per capita spending than did households in the second and third quartiles. The poorest lost most (Thomas and others 1999). How much poor people are actually hit by a crisis varies by country; it differed during Russia's hyperinflation of the mid-1990s and Argentina's crisis in 2001. But in general, even when poor people do not lose proportionately more than other groups, a given decline in income is likely to hit low-income groups much harder than high-income groups (Ferreira, Prennushi, and Ravallion 1999).

7. Only a handful of governments publish consolidated public sector accounts in a timely manner. As a result data on spending by local governments are not published by the International Monetary Fund in its *Government Finance Statistics*.

8. Perotti (1999) presents data on the shares of recurrent and capital spending in the government budget and the budget balance for 133 countries from 1960 to 1999. Government consumption and capital spending on public goods (that is, public investment) are much larger in developing than in developed countries. Comparability is difficult because of differences in accounting definitions and because of the lack of reliable data on spending by subnational governments in many countries.

9. In the case of health, no compelling evidence supports the view that poor health outcomes in developing countries are caused by lack of public health spending. Arbitrary assumptions are made about the links between scaling up expenditures and intervention coverage rates, and no explicit assumptions are made about the links between coverage levels and health outcomes. As a result there is no assurance that incurring the extra public health spending claimed to be necessary would actually reduce mortality, let alone by the proportions required by the Millennium Development Goals (MDGs). This does not mean that the other extreme view is true. Some writers have argued that at the margin public health spending has little effect on health outcomes, once the effects of other determinants have been accounted for, because of the many weak links in the chain running from public spending to health outcomes. This evidence refers simply to child mortality, not to health outcomes in general. While many interventions aimed at reducing child mortality are delivered by households, the same is not true of, say, maternal mortality, which is therefore likely to be more responsive (or elastic) with respect to public health spending than is child mortality. The results are also very general: they indicate what happens to child mortality among the population as a whole in an average country. As a result they hide significant spending effects among specific groups, including the poor, and among specific country types, including well-governed ones. Finally, the results indicate what would happen to child mortality if additional public spending were to take the form of a proportional scaling up of all government health programs. They do not show what would happen if additional spending were focused on specific groups or programs. (For more on this issue, see Wagstaff 2003.)

10. Social funds are mechanisms that provide grants to communities for demand-driven investment projects, largely bypassing traditional government bureaucracies.

11. See also the International Monetary Fund's Code of Fiscal Transparency, at http://www.imf.org/external/np/fad/trans/manual/.

12. See Ahmad, Davies, and Tandberg (2003) for details. In many countries all payments are made through the treasury single account, directly from the treasury to suppliers. In more advanced countries, such as the United States, line agencies are permitted to use zero-balance accounts, with cash being swept into the treasury single account daily (or more often, as needed).

13. Although there will always be a danger that spending will be diverted toward the more powerful and better-off.

14. Tax base refers to the value of economic activity that would be taxable under a given tax, whereas the tax take would be the total tax revenues that the various taxes generated in practice.

15. This section owes much to Rosenblatt and Stern (2003). We define privatization broadly as the transfer to private sector control or administration of government assets,

or the transfer of the provision of a service traditionally provided by the public sector. In the latter sense this includes various forms of concessions or contracting. Many successful forms of privatization, particularly in infrastructure, require appropriate government regulation post-privatization, so in that sense, all the privatization arrangements discussed here involve a public-private partnership to some degree. It would be misleading if we presented privatization solely in terms of private versus public ownership.

16. In some developing and transition economies the pollution from state-owned enterprises has not necessarily been less severe than that from private companies. State-owned companies require regulation and oversight as well.

17. Our discussion in this section is restricted to infrastructure, public utilities, and competitive sectors. Privatization of social services—education, health, and social protection—leads to a much broader set of issues that are beyond the scope of this chapter; some of them have been discussed in chapter 8.

18. Davis and others (2000) find that, on average, privatization receipts are saved rather than spent and that privatization has generally had a positive impact on long-term public finance. But they emphasize that privatization brings risks as well as benefits, and that the way the process is managed is important.

Chapter 13

1. The stock of outstanding FDI in developing countries is about $1.2 trillion. Thus a conservative depreciation rate of 5 percent would imply a net inflow of $60 billion a year.

2. An extensive network of protection and support for domestic agriculture has evolved, particularly in developed countries. This protection takes two main forms: border barriers and subsidies. Border barriers, such as tariffs and quantitative restrictions, are designed to support prices in domestic markets. This form of protection most distorts international markets and harms developing countries, and accounts for about 70 percent of protection in OECD countries. Production-related subsidies given to farmers under different schemes, called direct support, usually take the form of direct budget transfers and are much less distortionary. Agricultural goods produced behind high tariff walls and with production subsidies often require export subsidies to be sold in world markets.

3. *Specific duties* are import taxes set at a specific dollar amount per quantity imported— $50 per ton, say. Unlike ad valorem (percentage of value) tariffs, the specific duties provide larger effective protection against low-valued products. To continue the example, a low-cost producer able to provide the grain (say) at $100 per ton would face a 50 percent equivalent tariff, while a higher-cost (perhaps higher-quality) producer selling at $200 per ton would face only a 25 percent tariff. By the same token, effective protection rises as world prices fall. *Tariff rate quotas* use ad valorem tariff rates, but increase them sharply once a certain amount (the quota) is filled. When that quota level is relatively low and the above-quota tariff rate is high, a tariff rate quota can end up being as restrictive as the quota it replaced.

4. Oil exporters and countries in conflict are omitted because of their special circumstances.

5. Ferreira, Prennushi, and Ravallion (1999) summarize the literature as showing that because there are "barriers to entry in most markets for non-money financial assets," the poor hold more of their financial assets in cash than do the nonpoor during inflationary

periods. This means that proportionately, they will end up being harmed the most by inflation.

6. The evidence on governance and institutions, however, suggests a rather sobering picture: little average progress in improving governance, controlling corruption, and improving institutional quality worldwide is apparent—although there is significant variation across countries (Kaufmann 2003).

7. As country policy and institutional quality declines, it takes more aid to attain a given growth or poverty-reduction goal. And below a certain level of policy quality, no amount of aid is likely to achieve these goals.

8. See Fardoust and Qureishi (2002), on which this section draws heavily.

9. Heller and Gupta (2002) cite several studies that provide evidence of this phenomenon in some low-income countries (such as Burkina Faso, Côte d'Ivoire, Malawi, Senegal, Sri Lanka, and Togo).

10. This argues for aid inflows that are not "lumpy," with infrequent large disbursements, but that instead follow a stable path.

11. If we use market exchange rates to calculate GDP, the number receiving aid greater than 10 percent of GDP is much higher. Economists generally believe that the PPP GDP calculations are a much better reflection of the actual size of the economy, however, so we will stick with those figures here.

12. In order, from highest aid-to-GDP ratio to lowest, this second group included Malawi, Cape Verde, Republic of Congo, Rwanda, Tanzania, Djibouti, Mauritania, Mali, Bosnia and Herzegovina (1995–2000 only), Nicaragua (1991–1998), Mongolia (1993–2000), Equatorial Guinea, Solomon Islands, Sierra Leone, Benin, Senegal, and Burkina Faso. Three small island nations (Vanuatu, Tonga, and Dominica, which had less than 200,000 population in 2000) are excluded from the count. For comparison, consider these aid-to-GDP ratios for some of the large Asian aid recipients: for both India and China, it was a mere 0.1 percent; for Pakistan, 0.5 percent; and for Bangladesh, 1.0 percent.

13. The observed persistent deviation between aid commitments and actual disbursements is at least partly attributable to the administrative and absorptive capacity constraints of recipient countries; see Kanbur, Sandler, and Morrison (1999).

14. For discussions of this perspective on aid effectiveness, see World Bank (1998a) Burnside and Dollar (2000), and Collier, Devarajan, and Dollar (2001). Recent papers that take issue with the result that effectiveness depends on policy and institutional quality include Hansen and Tarp (2001) and Easterly, Levine, and Roodman (2003). As argued above, however, that link between country conditions and aid effectiveness is borne out by case studies of individual countries, as well as evidence on project-level returns (see Goldin, Rogers, and Stern 2002, as well as Devarajan, Dollar, and Holmgren 2001).

15. As we have argued, conditionality is most effective when it serves as a signal of the country's commitment for markets. As a commitment tool to constrain the actions of uncommitted governments, it is typically less productive.

16. See, for example, Skidelsky (2001).

17. The "traditional mechanisms" referred to in this sentence include the so-called Naples terms of the Paris Club of official creditors, which used repayment restructurings or reductions in the stock of debt to reduce the net present value of outstanding debt by a substantial margin.

References

Abraham, Anita, and Jean-Philippe Platteau. 2002. "Participatory Development in the Presence of Endogenous Community Imperfections." Typescript, Centre for Research on the Economics of Development, Faculty of Economics, Namur.

Acemoğlu, Daron. 1997. "Training and Innovation in an Imperfect Labor Market." *Review of Economic Studies* 64:445–464.

Acemoğlu, Daron, Philippe Aghion, and Fabrizio Zilibotti. 2002. "Distance to Frontier, Selection, and Economic Growth." Working paper 9066, National Bureau of Economic Research, Cambridge, Mass.

Acemoğlu, Daron, Simon Johnson, and James A. Robinson. 2001. "The Colonial Origins of Comparative Development: An Empirical Investigation." *American Economic Review* 91:1369–1401.

Acemoğlu, Daron, Simon Johnson, James Robinson, and Yunyong Thaicharoen. 2003. "Institutional Causes, Macroeconomic Symptoms: Volatility, Crises and Growth." *Journal of Monetary Economics* 50(1):49–123.

Acemoğlu, Daron, and James A. Robinson. 1996. "Why Did the West Extend the Franchise? Democracy, Inequality and Growth in Historical Perspective." Discussion paper no. 1797. London: Center for Economic Policy Research.

Acemoğlu, Daron, and James Robinson. 2001. "A Theory of Political Transitions." American Economic Review 91:938–963.

Acs, Zoltan, and D. Audretsch. 1987. "Innovation, Market Structure and Firm Size." *Review of Economics and Statistics* 69:567–574.

Acs, Zoltan, and D. Audretsch. 1991. *Innovation and Technological Change: An International Comparison.* Ann Arbor: University of Michigan Press.

Acs, Zoltan, Randall Morck, and Bernard Yeung. 1999. "Productivity Growth and Firm Size Distribution." In Zoltan Acs, Bo Carlsson, and Charlie Kalsson (eds.), *Entrepreneurship, Small and Medium Sized Enterprises and the Macroeconomy.* Cambridge: Cambridge University Press.

Aghion, Philippe, and Beatriz Armendáriz de Aghion. 2002. "Poverty and Development: A New Growth Perspective." Mimeographed, Harvard University, Department of Economics, August.

Aghion, Philippe, and Patrick Bolton. 1997. "A Theory of Trickle-Down Growth and Development." *Review of Economic Studies* 64:151–172.

Aghion, Philippe, Robin Burgess, Stephen Redding, and Fabrizio Zilibotti. 2003. "The Unequal Effects of Liberalization: Theory and Evidence from India." Mimeo., University College London and London School of Economics.

Aghion, Philippe, Nicholas Bloom, Richard Blundell, Rachel Griffith, and Peter Howitt. 2002. "Competition and Innovation: An Inverted U Relationship." Working paper WP02/04. London: Institute for Fiscal Studies.

Aghion, Philippe, Eve Caroli, and C. Garcia-Peñalosa. 1999. "Inequality and Economic Growth: The Perspective of the New Growth Theories." *Journal of Economic Literature* 37(4):1615–1660.

Aghion, Philippe, and Peter Howitt. 1992. "A Model of Growth through Creative Destruction." *Econometrica* 60:323–351.

Aghion, Philippe, and Peter Howitt. 1996. "The Observational Implications of Schumpterian Growth Theory." *Empirical Economics* 21:13–25.

Aghion, Philippe, and Peter Howitt. 1998. *Endogenous Growth Theory*. Cambridge, Mass.: MIT Press.

Aghion, Philippe, and Peter Howitt. Forthcoming. "Growth with Quality-Improving Innovations: An Integrated Framework." In Philippe Aghion and Steven Durlauf (eds.), *Handbook of Economic Growth*. Amsterdam: North-Holland.

Ahluwalia, Montek. 1976. "Inequality, Poverty and Development." *Journal of Development Economics* 3:307–342.

Ahluwalia, Montek, N. G. Carter, and Hollis Chenery. 1979. "Growth and Poverty in Developing Countries." *Journal of Development Economics* 6:299–341.

Ahmad, Ehtisham, Piyush Desai, Thierry Kalfon, and Eivind Tandberg. Forthcoming. "Reform Strategies for Organizing the Ministry of Finance." In Michael Carnahan, Ashraf Ghani, and Nick Manning (eds.), *Reforming Fiscal and Economic Management in Afghanistan*. Washington, D.C.: World Bank.

Ahmad, Ehtisham, and Nicholas H. Stern. 1991. *The Theory and Practice of Tax Reform in Developing Countries*. Cambridge: Cambridge University Press.

Ajwad, Mohamed Ihsan, and Quentin Wodon. 2002. "Who Benefits from Increased Access to Public Services at the Local Level? A Marginal Benefit Incidence Analysis for Education and Basic Infrastructure." *World Bank Economists' Forum* 2:155–175.

Akerlof, George, and Rachel Kranton. 2002. "Identity and Schooling: Some Lessons for the Economics of Education." *Journal of Economic Literature* 40:1167–1201.

Alesina, Alberto. 1998. "The Political Economy of Macroeconomic Stabilizations and Income Inequality: Myths and Reality." In Vito Tanzi and Ke-young Chu (eds.), *Income Distribution and High-Quality Growth*. Cambridge, Mass.: MIT Press.

Alesina, Alberto, and Allan Drazen. 1991. "Why Are Stabilizations Delayed?" *American Economic Review* 81:1170–1188.

Alesina, Alberto, and Eliana La Ferrara. 2000. "Participation in Heterogeneous Communities." *Quarterly Journal of Economics* 115:847–904.

Alesina, Alberto, and Eliana La Ferrara. 2002. "Who Trusts Others?" *Journal of Public Economics* 85:207–234.

Alesina, Alberto, Sule Özler, Nouriel Roubini, and Phillip Swagel. 1996. "Political Instability and Economic Growth." *Journal of Economic Growth* 1:189–211.

Alesina, Alberto, and Enrico Spolaore. 1997. "On the Number and Size of Nations." *Quarterly Journal of Economics* 112:1027–1056.

Alesina, Alberto, Silvia Ardagna, Giuseppe Nicoletti, and Fabio Schiantarelli. 2003. "Regulation and Investment." Working paper 9560, National Bureau of Economic Research, Cambridge, Mass.

Allen, Carleton Kemp. 1964. *Law in the Making* (7th ed.). Oxford: Oxford University Press.

Anderson, Elijah. 1992. *Streetwise: Race, Class and Change in an Urban Community*. Chicago: University Press of Chicago.

Angrist, Joshua, Eric Bettinger, Erik Bloom, Elizabeth M. King, and Michael Kremer. 2002. "Vouchers for Private Schooling in Colombia: Evidence from a Randomized Natural Experiment." *American Economic Review* 92(5):1535–1558.

Angrist, Joshua, and Alan Krueger. 1999. "Empirical Strategies in Labor Economics." In Orley Ashenfelter and David Card (eds.), *Handbook of Labor Economics*. Amsterdam: North-Holland.

Angrist, Joshua, and Alan Krueger. 2001. "Instrumental Variables and the Search for Identification: From Supply and Demand to Natural Experiments." *Journal of Economic Perspectives* 15(4):69–85.

Appadurai, Arjun. 2004. "The Capacity to Aspire: Culture and the Terms of Recognition." In Vijayendra Rao and Michael Walton (eds.), *Culture and Public Action*. Palo Alto, Calif.: Stanford University Press.

Araujo, Caridad, Alain de Janvry, and Elisabeth Sadoulet. 2004. "Patrones espaciales del crecimiento del empleo no agricola en el Mexico rural en los anos noventa." *Territorio y Economia* 5:11–28.

Arrow, Kenneth J. 1962. "The Economic Implications of Learning by Doing." *Review of Economic Studies* 29:155–173.

Atkinson, Anthony B., and François Bourguignon. 2000. "Income Distribution and Economics." In Anthony B. Atkinson and François Bourguignon (eds.), *Handbook of Income Distribution*. Amsterdam: North-Holland.

Atkinson, Anthony B., and François Bourguignon. 2001. "Poverty and Inclusion from a World Perspective." In Joseph E. Stiglitz and Pierre-Alain Muet (eds.), *Governance, Equity and Global Markets*. Oxford: Oxford University Press.

Atkinson, Anthony B., Bea Cantillon, Eric Marlier, and Brian Nolan. 2002. *Social Indicators: The EU and Social Indicators*. Oxford: Oxford University Press.

Atkinson, Anthony B., and John Hills (eds.). 1998. *Exclusion, Employment and Opportunity*. London: Center for Analysis of Social Exclusion. London School of Economics.

Aw, B. Y., S. Chung, and M. J. Roberts. 2000. "Productivity and the Decision to Export: Micro Evidence from Taiwan and South Korea." *World Bank Economic Review* 14(1):65–90.

Bagehot, Walter. 1948 (1869). *Physics and Politics*. New York: Knopf.

Bailey, Frederick George. 1957. *Caste and the Economic Frontier: A Village in Highland Orissa*. Manchester: Manchester University Press.

Balcerowicz, Leszek. 1995. *Socialism, Capitalism, Transformation*. New York: Central European University Press.

Banerjee, Abhijit, Paul Gertler, and Maitreesh Ghatak. 2002. "Empowerment and Efficiency: Tenancy Reform in West Bengal." *Journal of Political Economy* 110:239–280.

Banerjee, Abhijit, and Lakshmi Iyer. 2005. "History, Institutions and Economic Performance: The Legacy of Colonial Land Tenure Systems in India." *American Economic Review* 95(4):1190–1213.

Banerjee, Abhijit V., and A. F. Newman. 1991. "Risk-Bearing and the Theory of Income Distribution." *Review of Economic Studies* 58:211–235.

Banerjee, Abhijit V., and Andrew F. Newman. 1993. "Occupational Choice and the Process of Development." *Journal of Political Economy* 101(2):274–298.

Bardhan, Pranab, and Dilip Mookherjee. 1998. "Expenditure Decentralization and the Delivery of Public Services in Developing Countries." CIDER Paper C98-104, University of California.

Barker, Ernest. 1967. *Reflections on Government*. Oxford: Oxford University Press.

Barnett, Steven. 2000. "Evidence on the Fiscal and Macroeconomic Impact of Privatization." Working paper WP/00/130, International Monetary Fund, Washington, D.C.

Barro, Robert. 1991. "Economic Growth in a Cross-Section of Countries." *Quarterly Journal of Economics* 56:407–443.

Barro, Robert, and Xavier Sala-i-Martin. 1995. *Economic Growth*. New York: McGraw-Hill.

Batra, Geeta, Daniel Kaufmann, and Andrew H. W. Stone. 2003. *Investment Climate around the World: Voices of the Firms from the World Bank Business Environment Survey*. Washington, D.C.: World Bank.

Bauer, Peter. 1976. *Dissent on Development*. Rev. ed. Cambridge, Mass.: Harvard University Press.

Baumol, William J. 1967. "Macroeconomics of Balanced Growth: The Anatomy of Urban Crisis." *American Economic Review* 57:415–426.

Baumol, William J. 1968. "Entrepreneurship in Economic Theory." *American Economic Review* 58(2):64–71.

Baumol, William J. 1990. "Entrepreneurship: Productive, Unproductive, and Destructive." *Journal of Political Economy* 98:893–921.

Baumol, William J. 1993. *Entrepreneurship, Management and the Structure of Payoffs*. Cambridge, Mass.: MIT Press.

Baumol, William J. 2002. *The Free-Market Innovation Machine*. Princeton, N.J.: Princeton University Press.

Beck, Thorsten, George Clarke, Alberto Groff, Philip Keefer, and Patrick Walsh. 2001. "New Tools and New Tests in Comparative Political Economy: The Database of Political Institutions." *World Bank Economic Review* 15(1):165–176.

Beck, Thorsten, Asli Demirguc-Kunt, and Ross Levine. 2003. "Small and Medium Enterprises, Growth and Poverty: Cross-Country Evidence." Mimeo., World Bank, Washington, D.C., December.

Becker, Gary. 1957. *The Economics of Discrimination*. Chicago: University of Chicago Press.

Becker, Gary. 1996. *Accounting for Tastes*, Cambridge, Mass.: Harvard University Press.

Becker, Gary, Tomas Philipson, and Rodrigo Soares. 2005. "The Quantity and Quality of Life and the Evolution of World Inequality." *American Economic Review* 95(1):277–291.

Becker, Gary, and George J. Stigler. 1977. "De Gustibus Non Est Disputandum." *American Economic Review* 67(2):76–90.

Behrman, Jere R., Alejandro Gaviria, and Miguel Székely (eds.). 2003. *Who's In and Who's Out: Social Exclusion in Latin America*. Washington, D.C.: Inter-American Development Bank.

Bell, Martin, and Keith Pavitt. 1992. "Accumulating Technological Capability in Developing Countries." In L. Summers and S. Shah (eds.), Proceedings of the Annual World Bank Conference on Development Economics 1992, 257–282. Washington, D.C.: World Bank.

Bénabou, Roland. 1996a. "Inequality and Growth." In B. Bernanke and J. Rotemberg (eds.), *NBER Macro Annual 1996*. Cambridge, Mass.: MIT Press.

Bénabou, Roland. 1996b. "Unequal Societies." Working paper 5583, National Bureau of Economic Research, Cambridge, Mass.

Bénabou, Roland. 2002. "Tax and Education policy in a Heterogeneous-Agent Economy: What Levels of Redistribution Maximize Growth and Efficiency?" *Econometrica* 70(2):481–517.

Berkowitz, Daniel, Katharina Pistor, and Jean-François Richard. 2003. "Economic Development, Legality and the Transplant Effect." *European Economic Review* 47(1):165–195.

Berlin, Isaiah. 1977. *The Proper Study of Mankind*. Oxford: Oxford University Press.

Besley, Timothy. 1995. "Property Rights and Investment Incentives: Theory and Evidence from Ghana." *Journal of Political Economy* 103:903–937.

Besley, Timothy, and Robin Burgess. 2001. "Political Agency, Government Responsiveness and Role of Media." *European Economic Review* 45(4–6):629–640.

Besley, Timothy, and Robin Burgess. 2003. "Halving Global Poverty." *Journal of Economic Perspectives* 17(3):3–22.

Besley, Timothy, and Anne Case. 2003. "Political Institutions and Policy Choices: Evidence from the United States." *Journal of Economic Literature* 41(1):7–73.

Besley, Timothy, and Maitreesh Ghatak. 2001. "Government versus Private Ownership of Public Goods." *Quarterly Journal of Economics* 116(4):1343–1372.

Bhagwati, Jagdish. 1998. "The Design of Indian Development." In Isher Judge Ahluwalia and I. M. D. Little (eds.), *India's Economic Reforms and Development: Essays for Manmohan Singh*. Delhi: Oxford University Press.

Bhalla, Surjit. 2002. *Imagine There Is No Country: Poverty, Inequality and Growth in the Era of Globalization*. Washington, D.C.: Institute of International Economics.

Biggs, Tyler. 2002. *Is Small Beautiful and Worthy of Subsidy?* Washington, D.C.: International Finance Corporation.

Bird, Richard, and Luc De Wulf. 1983. "Taxation and Income Distribution in Latin America: A Critical Review of Empirical Studies." *IMF Staff Papers* 20:639–682.

Bird, Richard. 1992. *Tax Policy and Economic Development.* Baltimore: Johns Hopkins University Press.

Bird, Richard, and Oliver Oldman (eds.). 1990. *Taxation in Developing Countries* (4th ed.). Baltimore: Johns Hopkins University Press.

Birdsall, Nancy, and John Williamson. 2002. *Delivering on Debt Relief: From IMF Gold to a New Aid Architecture.* Washington, D.C.: Center for Global Development and the Institute for International Economics.

Blanchard, Olivier, and Francesco Giavazzi. 2002. "Macroeconomic Effects of Regulation and Deregulation in Goods and Labor Markets." Working paper, MIT, Cambridge.

Blanchflower, David G., and Andrew J. Oswald. 2000. "Well-Being Over Time in Britain and the USA." Working paper 7487, National Bureau of Economic Research, Cambridge, Mass.

Bliss, Christopher, and Nicholas Stern. 1978. "Productivity, Wages and Nutrition." *Journal of Development Economics* 5:331–398.

Bobonis, Gustavo, Edward Miguel, and Charu Sharma. 2002. "Iron Supplementation and Early Childhood Development: A Randomized Evaluation in India." Mimeo., University of California, Berkeley.

Boserup, Esther. 1965. *The Conditions of Agricultural Growth.* Chicago: Aldine.

Boserup, Esther. 1991. "Agricultural Growth and Population Change." In J. Eatwell, M. Milgate and P. Newman (eds.), *The New Palgrave: The World of Economics.* New York: Norton.

Bosworth, Barry, and Susan M. Collins. 2003. "The Empirics of Growth: An Update." Typescript, Brookings Institution, Washington, D.C., March.

Botero, Fernando, Simeon Djankov, Rafael La Porta, Florencio Lopez-de-Silanes, and Andrei Shleifer. 2003. "The Regulation of Labor." Working paper 9756, National Bureau of Economic Research, Cambridge, Mass.

Bourdieu, Pierre. 1984. *Distinction: A Critique of the Judgement of Taste.* Cambridge, Mass.: Harvard University Press.

Bourdieu, Pierre. 1990. *The Logic of Practice.* Palo Alto, Calif.: Stanford University Press.

Bourguignon, François. 1998. "Equité et croissance économique: une nouvelle analyse?" *Revue française d'économie* 13(3):25–84.

Bourguignon, François. 1999. "Crime, Violence and Inequitable Development." In B. Pleskovic and J. Stiglitz (eds.), *Annual Bank Conference on Development Economics.* Washington, D.C.: World Bank.

Bourguignon, François. 2002. "The Distributional Effects of Growth: Case Study vs. Cross-Country Regressions." Paper presented at CEPAL, Santiago de Chile, August.

Bourguignon, François. 2003a. "The Growth Elasticity of Poverty Reduction: Explaining Heterogeneity across Countries and Time Periods." In T. Eicher and S. Turnovsky (eds.), *Inequality and Growth: Theory and Policy Implications*. Cambridge, Mass.: MIT Press.

Bourguignon, François. 2003b. "The Poverty-Growth-Inequality Triangle." Paper prepared for a Conference on Poverty, Inequality and Growth, Agence Française de Développement and EU Development Network, Paris, November 13.

Bourguignon, François. 2004. "The Effects of Economic Growth on Social Structures." In Philippe Aghion and Steven Durlauf (eds.), *Handbook of Economic Growth*. Amsterdam: North-Holland.

Bourguignon, François, Francisco Ferreira, and Phillippe Leite. 2003. "Conditional Cash Transfers, Schooling and Child Labor: Micro-Simulating Brazil's Bolsa Escola Program." *World Bank Economic Review* 17(2):229–254.

Bourguignon, François, Francisco Ferreira, and Marta Menéndez. 2003. "Inequality of Outcomes and Inequality of Opportunities in Brazil." Mimeo., World Bank, Washington, D.C., October.

Bourguignon, François, M. Fournier, and G. Gurgand. 2001. "Fast Development with a Stable Income Distribution: Taiwan, 1979–1994." *Review of Income and Wealth* 47(2):139–163.

Bourguignon, François, Jaime de Melo, and Christian Morrison. 1991. "Poverty and Income Distribution during Adjustment: Issues and Evidence from the OECD Project." *World Development* 19(11):1485–1508.

Bourguignon, François, and Christian Morrisson. 2002. "Inequality among World Citizens, 1820–1992." *American Economic Review* 92(4):727–744.

Bourguignon, François, and Luiz Pereira da Silva (eds.). 2003. *The Impact of Economic Policies on Poverty and Income Distribution*. Washington, D.C.: World Bank and Oxford University Press.

Bourguignon, François, Luiz Pereira da Silva, and Nicholas Stern. 2004. "Evaluating the Poverty Impact of Policies: Some Analytical Challenges." In Cathy Pattillo and Ashoka Mody (eds.), *Proceedings of an IMF Conference on Macroeconomic Policies and Poverty*. Washington, D.C.: International Monetary Fund.

Bourguignon, François, and Thierry Verdier. 2000a. "Oligarchy, Democracy, Inequality, and Growth." *Journal of Development Economics* 62:285–313.

Bourguignon, François, and Thierry Verdier. 2000b. "Is Financial Openness Bad for Education? A Political Economy Perspective." *European Economic Review* 44:891–903.

Bowles, Samuel. 1998. "Endogenous Preferences: The Cultural Consequences of Markets and Other Economic Institutions." *Journal of Economic Literature* 36:75–111.

Bowles, Samuel, and Herbert Gintis. 1996. "Efficient Redistribution: New Rules for Markets, States and Communities." *Politics and Society* 24(4):307–342.

Bradford, Colin I. 2002. "Toward 2015: From Consensus Formation to Implementation of the Millennium Development Goals." Typescript, American University, Washington, D.C., December.

Brandenburger, Adam, and Barry J. Nalebuff. 1996. *Co-opetition: The Game Theory That's Changing the Game of Business*. New York: Doubleday.

Braudel, Fernand. 1982. *The Wheels of Commerce: Civilization and Capitalism, 15th–18th Century.* New York: Harper and Row.

Broadway, Robin, and Michael Keen. 2000. "Redistribution." In Anthony B. Atkinson and François Bourguignon (eds.), *Handbook of Income Distribution.* Amsterdam: North Holland.

Bruno, Michael, and Hollis Chenery. 1962. "Development Alternatives in an Open Economy." *Economic Journal* 72(285):79–103.

Bryce, James. 1959 (1888). *The American Commonwealth.* New York: Putnam.

Buchanan, James. 1954. "Social Choice, Democracy and Free Markets." *Journal of Political Economy* 62:114–123.

Buchanan, James, and Yong J. Yoon. 1994. *The Return of Increasing Returns.* Ann Arbor: The University of Michigan Press.

Burchardt, Tania, Julian Le Grand, and David Piachaud. 2002. "Degrees of Exclusion: Developing a Dynamic, Multi-dimensional Measure." In John Hills, Julian Le Grand, and David Piachaud (eds.), *Understanding Social Exclusion.* Oxford: Oxford University Press.

Burgess, Robin, and Nicholas Stern. 1993. "Taxation and Development." *Journal of Economic Literature* 31:762–830.

Burnside, Craig (ed.). Forthcoming. *Fiscal Sustainability in Theory and Practice.* Washington, D.C.: World Bank.

Burnside, Craig, and David Dollar. 2000. "Aid, Policies, and Growth." *American Economic Review* 90(4):847–868.

Busse, Matthias. 2003. "Tariffs, Transportation Costs and the WTO Doha Round: The Case of Developing Countries." *Estey Centre Journal of International Law and Trade Policy* 4(1):15–31.

Canning, David, Marianne Fay, and Roberto Perotti. 1992. "Infrastructure and Growth." *Rivista Di Politica Economica* 82:113–147.

Carvalho Filho, Irineu Evangelista de. 2001. "Household Income as a Determinant of Child Labour and School Enrolment in Brazil: Evidence from a Social Security Reform." Mimeo., MIT, Cambridge, Mass.

Case, Anne. 2001. "The Primacy of Education." Typescript, Research Program in Development Studies, Princeton University, Princeton, N.J., June.

Case, Anne, and Angus Deaton. 1996. "Large Cash Transfers to the Elderly in South Africa." Working paper no. 5572, National Bureau of Economic Research, Cambridge, Mass., May.

Chang, Ha-Joon. 2002. *Kicking Away the Ladder: Development Strategy in Historical Perspective.* London: Anthem Press.

Chattopadhyay, R., and Duflo, E. 2001. "Women as Policy Makers: Evidence from a India-Wide Randomized Policy Experiment." Working paper, Department of Economics, MIT, Cambridge, Mass.

Chaudhury, Nazmul, and Jeffrey S. Hammer. 2004. "Ghost Doctors: Doctor Absenteeism in Rural Bangladeshi Health Facilities." World Bank Economic Review 18(3):423–441.

Chaudhury, Nazmul, Jeffrey Hammer, Michael Kremer, Karthik Muralidharan, and F. Halsey Rogers. Forthcoming. "Missing in Action: Teacher and Health Worker Absence in Developing Countries." *Journal of Economic Perspectives.*

Chen, Shaohua, and Martin Ravallion. 2001. "How Did the World's Poorest Fare in the 1990s?" *Review of Income and Wealth* 47(3):283–300.

Chen, Shaohua, and Martin Ravallion. 2004. "How Have the World's Poorest Fared Since the Early 1980s?" *The World Bank Research Observer*, 19(2):141–169.

Chenery, Hollis, Montek Ahluwalia, Clive Bell, John Dulloy, and Richard Jolly. 1974. *Redistribution with Growth.* Oxford: Oxford University Press.

Chenery, Hollis, Sherman Robinson, and Moshe Syrquin. 1986. *Industrialization and Growth.* Oxford: Oxford University Press.

Clarke, George R. G., and Scott J. Wallsten. 2003. "Universal Service: Empirical Evidence of the Provision of Infrastructure Services to Rural and Poor Urban Consumers." In Penelope J. Brook and Timothy C. Irwin (eds.), *Infrastructure for Poor People: Public Policy for Private Provision.* Washington, D.C.: World Bank.

Coase, R. H. 1960. "The Problem of Social Cost." *Journal of Law and Economics* 3:1–44.

Cochran, Thomas. 1971. "The Entrepreneur in Economic Change." In Peter Kilby (ed.), *Entrepreneurship and Economic Development.* New York: Free Press.

Coleman, James. 1990. *Foundations of Social Theory.* Cambridge, Mass.: Harvard University Press.

Collier, Paul, and David Dollar. 2002. "Aid Allocation and Poverty Reduction." *European Economic Review* 46(8):1475–1500.

Collier, Paul, Shantayanan Devarajan, and David Dollar. 2001. "Measuring IDA's Effectiveness." Typescript, World Bank, Washington, D.C.

Collier, Paul, David Dollar, and Nicholas Stern. 2001. "Fifty Years of Development." In N. Stern (ed.), *A Strategy for Development.* Washington, D.C.: World Bank.

Collier, Paul, Lani Elliott, Haverd Hegre, Anke Hoeffler, Marta Reynal-Querol, and Nicholas Sambanis. 2003. *Breaking the Conflict Trap: Civil War and Development Policy.* Washington, D.C.: Oxford University Press.

Collier, Paul, and Jan Willem Gunning. 1999. "Explaining African Performance." *Journal of Economic Literature* 37(1):64–111.

Collier, Paul, and Anke Hoeffler. 2002. "Aid, Policy, and Growth in Post-Conflict Societies." World Bank Policy Research working paper no. 2902.

Commission on Human Security. 2003. *Human Security Now: Protecting and Empowering People.* Independent Commission chaired by Sadako Ogato and Amartya Sen. New York: Commission on Human Security.

Crafts, Nicholas. 2000. "Globalization and Growth in the Twentieth Century." In E. Prasad (ed.), *World Economic Outlook Supporting Studies.* Washington, D.C.: International Monetary Fund.

Dahms, Harry. 1995. "From Creative Action to the Social Rationalization of the Economy: Joseph A. Schumpeter's Social Theory." *Sociological Theory* 13(1):1–13.

Daily Star (Bangladesh). 2003. "24 of 28 Docs Shunted Out for Absence: DG Health Surprised at Surprise Visit to NICVD." October 2.

Das Gupta, Monica, and Li Shuzhuo. 1999. "Gender Bias in China, South Korea and India 1920–1990: The Effects of War, Famine and Fertility Decline." *Development and Change* 30(3):619–652.

Das Gupta, Monica, Sunhwa Lee, Patricia Uberoi, Danning Wang, Lihong Wang, and Xiaodan Zhang. 2004. "State Policies and Women's Agency in China, the Republic of Korea, and India, 1950–2000: Lessons from Contrasting Experiences." In Vijayendra Rao and Michael Walton (eds.), *Culture and Public Action.* Palo Alto, Calif.: Stanford University Press.

Dasgupta, Partha. 1993. *An Inquiry into Well-Being and Destitution.* Oxford: Oxford University Press.

Dasgupta, Partha, and Debraj Ray. 1986. "Inequality as a Determinant of Malnutrition and Unemployment." *Economic Journal* 96:1011–1034.

Dasgupta, Partha, and Ismail Serageldin (eds.). 2000. *Social Capital: A Multifaceted Perspective.* Washington, D.C.: World Bank.

Datt, Gaurav, and Martin Ravallion. 1992. "Growth and Redistribution Components of Changes in Poverty Measures: A Decomposition with Application to Brazil and India in the 1980s." *Journal of Development Economics* 38(2):275–295.

Datt, Gaurav, and Martin Ravallion. 1996. "Why Have Some Indian States Done Better than Others at Reducing Rural Poverty?" Policy Research working paper no. 1594, World Bank. Washington, D.C.

Datt, Gaurav, and Martin Ravallion. 2002. "Is India's Economic Growth Leaving the Poor Behind?" Research working paper no. 2846, World Bank, Washington, D.C.

Davis, Jeffrey, Rolando Ossowski, Thomas Richardson, and Steven Barnett. 2000. *Fiscal and Macroeconomic Impact of Privatization.* Washington, D.C.: IMF.

Davis, Stephen, and John Haltiwanger. 1999. "On the Driving Forces Behind Cyclical Movement in Employment and Job Reallocation." *American Economic Review* 89(5):1234–1258.

DeLong, Bradford. 2003. "India since Independence: An Analytic Growth Narrative." In D. Rodrik (ed.), *In Search of Prosperity: Analytic Country Studies on Growth.* Princeton, N.J.: Princeton University Press.

Deaton, Angus. 1997. *The Analysis of Household Surveys: A Microeconometric Approach to Development Policy.* Baltimore: John Hopkins University Press.

Deaton, Angus. 2003b. "Randomized or Just Random? Methods of Project Evaluation for Economic Development." Remarks to the World Bank's Seminar on Evaluating Development Effectiveness: Challenges and the Way Forward Conference, Washington, D.C.

Deaton, Angus. 2003c. "Health, Inequality and Economic Development." *Journal of Economic Literature* 41(1):113–158.

Deaton, Angus. 2005. "Measuring Poverty in a Growing World (or Measuring Growth in a Poor World)." *The Review of Economics and Statistics* 87(2).

De Ferranti, David, Guillermo E. Perry, Francisco H. G. Ferreira, and Michael Walton. 2003. *Inequality in Latin America: Breaking with History?* Washington, D.C.: World Bank.

De Ferranti, David, Guillermo E. Perry, Indermit Gill, J. Luis Guasch, William F. Maloney, Carolina Sanchez-Paramo, and Norbert Schady. 2002. *Closing the Gap in Education and Technology*. Washington, D.C.: World Bank.

Dehn, Jan, Ritva Reinikka, and Jakob Svensson. 2003. "Survey Tools for Assessing Performance in Service Delivery." In François Bourguignon and Luiz Pereira da Silva (eds.), *The Impact of Economic Policies on Poverty and Income Distribution*. Washington, D.C.: World Bank and Oxford University Press.

Deininger, Klaus, and Lyn Squire. 1996. "A New Data Set Measuring Income Inequality." *World Bank Economic Review* 10(3):565–591.

Deininger, Klaus, and Lyn Squire. 1998. "New Ways of Looking at Old Issues: Inequality and Growth." *Journal of Development Economics* 57(2):259–287.

De Janvry, Alain, Elisabeth Sadoulet, and Caridad Araujo. 2002. "Geography of Poverty, Territorial Growth and Rural Development." Mimeo., University of California, Berkeley.

DeLong, J. Bradford, and Kevin Lang. 1992. "Are All Economic Hypotheses False?" *Journal of Political Economy* 100(6):1257–1272.

Demombynes, G., Chris Elbers, Jean O. Lanjouw, Peter Lanjouw, Johan A. Mistiaen, and Berk Ozler. Forthcoming. "Producing an Improved Geographic Profile of Poverty: Methodology and Evidence from Three Developing Countries." In Rolph van der Hoeven and Anthony Shorrocks (eds.), *Growth, Inequality and Poverty*. Oxford: Oxford University Press.

Denison, Edward. 1967. *Why Growth Rates Differ: Postwar Experience in Nine Western Countries*. Washington, D.C.: Brookings Institution.

De Soto, Hernando. 1989. *The Other Path: The Invisible Revolution in the Third World*. New York: Harper and Row.

De Soto, Hernando. 2000. *The Mystery of Capital: Why Capitalism Triumphs in the West and Fails Everywhere Else*. New York: Basic Books.

Dethier, Jean-Jacques. 1999. "Governance and Economic Performance: A Survey." ZEF discussion paper on development policy no. 5, Center for Development Research, University of Bonn.

Dethier, Jean-Jacques. 2000. "Governance, Decentralization and Reform: An Introduction." In J.-J. Dethier (ed.), *Governance, Decentralization and Reform in China, India and Russia*. Boston: Kluwer.

Dethier, Jean-Jacques. 2003. "Corruption in the Seven Low Income Countries of the Commonwealth of Independent States." Paper presented at a Conference of the CIS-7 Initiative, Lucerne. Available at http://www.cis7.org/.

Dethier, Jean-Jacques, Peter Lanjouw, Caralee Mcleish, and Renos Vakis. 2003. "Entrepreneurship, Firm Size and Poverty." Typescript, World Bank, Washington, D.C.

Dethier, Jean-Jacques, and Witold Orlowski. 1998. "The Setting: Macroeconomic Policy in Hungary in the 1990s." In L. Bokros and J. J. Dethier (eds.), *Public Finance Reform during the Transition: The Experience of Hungary*. Washington, D.C.: World Bank.

De Tocqueville, Alexis. 1969 (1848). *Democracy in America*. Garden City, N.Y.: Anchor Books.

Devarajan, Shantayanan, David R. Dollar, and Torgny Holmgren. 2001. *Aid and Reform in Africa*. Washington, D.C.: World Bank.

Devarajan, Shantayanan, Margaret Miller, and Eric Swanson. 2002. "Goals for Development: History, Prospects and Costs." Typescript, World Bank, Washington, D.C., April.

Devarajan, Shantayanan, and Vinaya Swaroop. 1998. "The Implications of Foreign Aid Fungibility for Development Assistance." Policy research working paper no. 2022, World Bank, Washington, D.C., December.

Dewey, John. 1927. *The Public and Its Problems*. Chicago: Swallow Press.

Dewey, John. 1939. *Freedom and Culture*. New York: Capricorn.

DFID (Department for International Development), United Kingdom. 2003. "Departmental Report." May.

Diamond, Peter A., and James A. Mirrlees. 1971. "Optimal Taxation and Public Production I: Production Efficiency and II: Tax Rules." *American Economic Review* 61:8–27, 261–278.

Dixit, Avinash K. 1996. *The Making of Economic Policy: A Transaction-Cost Politics Perspective*. Cambridge, Mass.: MIT Press.

Djankov, Simeon, Rafael La Porta, Florencio Lopez-de-Silanes, and Andrei Shleifer. 2002. "The Regulation of Entry." *Quarterly Journal of Economics* 117(1):1–37.

Dollar, David, and Aart Kraay. 2002. "Growth Is Good for the Poor." *Journal of Economic Growth* 7(3):195–225.

Dollar, David, and Aart Kraay. 2004. "Trade, Growth, and Poverty." *The Economic Journal* 114(49):F22–F49.

Dollar, David, Mary Hallward-Driemeier, and Taye Mengistae. 2003. "Investment Climate and Firm Performance in Developing Economies." Typescript, World Bank, Development Research Group, Washington, D.C., November.

Drazen, Allan. 2000. *Political Economy in Macroeconomics*. Princeton, N.J.: Princeton University Press.

Drèze, Jean, and Amartya Sen. 1989. *Hunger and Public Action*. Oxford: Oxford University Press.

Drèze, Jean, and Amartya Sen. 1995. *India: Economic Development and Social Opportunity*. Delhi: Oxford University Press.

Drèze, Jean, and Nicholas Stern. 1990. "Policy Reform, Shadow Prices, and Market Prices." *Journal of Public Economics* 42(1):1–45.

Dudwick, Nora, Elizabeth Gomart, Alexandre Marc, and Kathleen Kuehnast. 2003. *When Things Fall Apart: Qualitative Studies of Poverty in the Former Soviet Union*. Washington, D.C.: World Bank.

Duflo, Esther. 2003. "Grandmothers and Granddaughters: Old-Age Pensions and Intra-Household Allocation in South Africa." *World Bank Economic Review* 17:1–25.

Duflo, Esther, and Michael Kremer. 2003. "Use of Randomization in the Evaluation of Development Effectiveness." Conference paper, World Bank Operations Evaluation Department, Washington, D.C.

Dutz, M. A., and Hayri, A. 2000. "Does More Intense Competition Lead to Higher Growth?" Policy research working paper no. 2320, World Bank, Washington, D.C.

Easterlin, Richard A. 1996. *Growth Triumphant: The Twenty-First Century in Historical Perspective.* Ann Arbor: University of Michigan Press.

Easterly, William. 2001. *The Elusive Quest for Growth.* Cambridge, Mass.: MIT Press.

Easterly, William. 2002. "How Did the Heavily Indebted Poor Countries Become Heavily Indebted? Reviewing Two Decades of Debt Relief." *World Development*, 30(10):1677–1696.

Easterly, William, Michael Kremer, Lant Pritchett, and Lawrence H. Summers. 1993. "Good Policy or Good Luck? Country Growth Performance and Temporary Shocks." *Journal of Monetary Economics* 32(3):459–483.

Easterly, William, and Ross Levine. 1997. "Africa's Growth Tragedy: Policies and Ethnic Divisions." *Quarterly Journal of Economics* 112(4):1203–1250.

Easterly, William, Ross Levine, and David Roodman. 2003. *New Data, New Doubts: A Comment on Burnside and Dollar's Aid, Policies, and Growth.* Working paper 9846, National Bureau of Economic Research, Cambridge, Mass.

Easterly, William, Carlos Rodriguez, and Klaus Schmidt-Hebbel. 1994. *Public Sector Deficits and Macroeconomic Performance.* Oxford: Oxford University Press.

Ebrill, Liam P., Michael Keen, Jean-Paul Bodin, and Victoria Summers. 2001. *The Modern VAT.* Washington, D.C.: IMF.

Ebrill, Liam P., Janet Stotsky, and Reit Gropp. 1999. "Revenue Implications of Trade Liberalization." Occasional paper 180, IMF, Washington, D.C.

Eckersley, Richard. 2000. "The Mixed Blessings of Material Progress: Diminishing Returns in the Pursuit of Happiness." *Journal of Happiness Studies* 1:267–292.

Edwards, Sebastian. 1989. "Structural Adjustment Policies in Highly Indebted Countries." In Jeffrey D. Sachs (ed.), *Developing Country Debt and Economic Performance.* Chicago: University of Chicago Press.

Ehrenberg, Ronald G., Daniel D. Goldhaber, and Dominic J. Brewer. 1994. "D. Teachers' Race, Gender and Ethnicity Matter? Evidence from NELS88." Working paper no. 4669, National Bureau of Economic Research, Cambridge, Mass.

Elbers, Chris, and Peter Lanjouw. 2001. "Intersectoral Transfer, Growth and Inequality in Rural Ecuador." *World Development* 29(3):481–496.

Elbers, Chris, Jean O. Lanjouw, and Peter Lanjouw. 2002. "Welfare in Villages and Towns: Micro-Level Estimation of Poverty and Inequality." Policy research working paper 2911, World Bank, Development Economics Research Group, Washington, D.C.

Ellerman, David, and Vladimir Kreacic. 2002. "Transforming the Old into a Foundation for the New: Lessons of the Moldova ARIA Project." Policy research working paper 2866, World Bank, Washington, D.C.

Elster, Jon. 1984 (1979). *Ulysses and Sirens: Studies in Rationality and Irrationality*. Rev. ed. Cambridge: Cambridge University Press.

Elwan, Ann. 1999. "Poverty and Disability. A Survey of the Literature." Typescript, World Bank, Washington, D.C.

Engerman, Stanley, and Kenneth Sokoloff. 1997. "Factor Endowments, Institutions and Differential Growth Paths among New World Economies." In Stephen Haber (ed.), *How Latin America Fell Behind: Essays on the Economic Histories of Brazil and Mexico, 1800–1914*. Stanford, Calif.: Stanford University Press.

Engerman, Stanley L., and Kenneth Sokoloff. 2002. "Factor Endowments, Inequality, and Paths of Development among New World Economies." Working paper 9259, National Bureau of Economic Research, Cambridge, Mass.

Epstein, T. Scarlett 1973. *South India: Yesterday, Today and Tomorrow*. London: Macmillan.

Esman, Milton, and Norman Uphoff. 1984. *Local Organizations: Intermediaries in Rural Development*. Ithaca, N.Y.: Cornell University Press.

Estache, Antonio, Andres Gomez-Lobo, and Danny Leipziger. 2001. "Utilities Privatization and the Poor: Lessons and Evidence from Latin America." *World Development* 29(7):1179–1198.

Evenson, Robert, and Larry Westphal. 1995. "Technological Change and Technology Strategy." In J. Behrman and T. N. Srinavasan (eds.), *Handbook of Development Economics*. Amsterdam: Elsevier.

Faguet, J. 2004. "Does Decentralization Increase Government Responsiveness to Local Needs? Evidence from Bolivia." *Journal of Public Economics*, 88:867–893.

Fardoust, Shahrokh, and Zia Qureshi. 2002. "Macroeconomic and Structural Policy Implications of Increased Aid: A Guidance Note." Mimeo., World Bank, Washington, D.C., October 22.

Feizioğlu, Tarhan, Vinaya Swaroop, and Min Zhu. 1998. "A Panel Data Analysis of the Fungibility of Foreign Aid." *World Bank Economic Review* 12(1): 29–58.

Fernandez, Raquel, and Dani Rodrik. 1991. "Resistance to Reform: Status Quo Bias in the Presence of Individual-Specific Uncertainty." *American Economic Review* 81:1146–1155.

Ferreira, Francisco H. G. 1996. *Roads to Equality: Wealth Distribution Dynamics with Public-Private Complementarity*. Washington, D.C.: World Bank.

Ferreira, Francisco. 1999. "Inequality and Economic Performance: A Brief Overview to Theories of Growth and Distribution." Available at http://www.econ.puc-rio.br/Fferreira/pdf/inequality.pdf.

Ferreira, Francisco, and Ricardo Paes de Barros. 1998. "Climbing a Moving Mountain: Explaining the Decline of Income Inequality in Brazil from 1976 to 1996." Sustainable Development department paper 10/98, InterAmerican Development Bank, Washington, D.C.

Ferreira, Francisco, Giovanni Prennushi, and Martin Ravallion. 1999. "Protecting the Poor from Macroeconomic Shocks." Policy research working paper no. 2160, World Bank, Washington, D.C.

Field, Erica. 2002. "Entitled to Work: Urban Property Rights and Labour Supply in Peru." Typescript, Economics Department, Princeton University, Princeton, N.J., October.

Fields, Gary. 1980. *Poverty, Inequality, and Development.* Cambridge: Cambridge University Press.

Fields, Gary, and Walter Bagg. 2003. "Long-Term Economic Mobility and the Private Sector in Developing Countries: New Evidence." In G. Fields and G. Pfefferman (eds.), *Pathways out of Poverty: Private Firms and Economic Mobility in Developing Countries.* Boston: Kluwer.

Fields, Gary, and Pfefferman, Guy (eds.). 2003. *Pathways out of Poverty: Private Firms and Economic Mobility in Developing Countries.* Boston: Kluwer.

Filmer, Deon, Jeffrey S. Hammer, and Lant Pritchett. 2000. "Weak Links in the Chain: A Diagnosis of Health Policy in Poor Countries." *World Bank Research Observer* 15(2):199–224.

Fischer, Stanley. 1993. "The Role of Macroeconomic Factors in Growth." *Journal of Monetary Economics* 32(3):485–512.

Fogel, Robert W. 1986. "Nutrition and the Decline in Mortality since 1700: Some Preliminary Findings." Working paper no. 1802, National Bureau of Economic Research, Cambridge, Mass.

Fogel, Robert W. 2004. *The Escape from Hunger and Premature Death, 1700–2100: Europe, America and the Third World.* Cambridge: Cambridge University Press.

Foster, Andrew, and Mark Rosenzweig. 1995. "Learning by Doing and Learning from Others: Human Capital and Technical Change in Agriculture." *Journal of Political Economy* 104:437–467.

Foster, Andrew, and Mark Rosenzweig. 2002. "Democratization, Decentralization and the Distribution of Local Public Goods in a Poor Rural Economy." Working paper no. 010, Bureau for Research in Economic Analysis, Combridge, Mass.

Frankel, Jeffrey, and David Romer. 1999. "Does Trade Cause Growth?" *American Economic Review* 89(3):379–399.

Frankenberg, Elizabeth, James P. Smith, and Duncan Thomas. 2002. "Economic Shocks, Wealth and Welfare." Paper prepared for the HRS/NLS/PSID/ISR Conference on Cross-National Research using Panel Surveys, Ann Arbor, Michigan, Available at http://chd.ucla.edu/IFLS/ppr/wealth.pdf.

Freedom House. 1999. *Freedom in the World 1998–1999: Annual Survey of Political Rights and Civil Liberties.* New York: Freedom House.

Frey, Bruno, and Alois Stutzer. 2002. "What Can Economists Learn from Happiness Research?" *Journal of Economic Literature* 40(2):402–435.

Friedman, Milton. 1976. *Price Theory.* Chicago: Aldine.

Fukuyama, Francis. 1996. *Trust: The Social Virtues and the Creation of Prosperity.* New York: Touchstone Books.

Furubotn, Eirik, and Rudolf Richter. 1998. *Institutions and Economic Theory: The Contributions of the New Institutional Economics.* Ann Arbor: University of Michigan.

Galiani, Sebastian, Paul Gertler, and Ernesto Schargrodsky. 2003. "Water for Life: The Impact of the Privatization of Water Services on Child Mortality." Typescript, Washington, D.C.: World Bank.

Galal, Ahmad. 2001. "Utility Regulation versus BOT Schemes: An Assessment of Electricity Sector Reforms in Arab Countries." Working paper no. 63, Egyptian Center for Economic Studies, Cairo, Egypt.

Galal, Ahmad, Leroy Jones, Pankaj Tandon, and Ing Vogelsang. 1994. *Welfare Consequences of Selling Public Enterprises: An Empirical Analysis.* New York: Oxford University Press.

Gallup, John Luke, Jeffrey Sachs, and Andrew Mellinger. 1998. "Geography and Economic Development." Working paper no. 6849, National Bureau of Economic Research, Cambridge, Mass., December.

Galor, O., and J. Zeira. 1993. "Income Distribution and Macroeconomics." *Review of Economic Studies* 60:35–52.

Gandhi, Mohandas K. 1938 [1909]. *Indian Home Rule or Hind Swaraj.* Ahmedabad: Navajivan Publishing House.

Gauri, Varun. 1998. *School Choice in Chile: Two Decades of Educational Reform.* Pittsburgh: University of Pittsburgh Press.

Gertler, Paul. 2000. "A Preliminary Evaluation of the Impact of PROGRESA on Health and Health Utilization." Washington, D.C.: International Food Research Institute.

Gertler, Paul, and Simone Boyce. 2001. "An Experiment in Incentive-Based Welfare: The Impact of PROGRESA on Health in Mexico." Typescript, Washington, D.C.: World Bank.

Gertler, Paul, and J. Gruber. 2002. "Insuring Consumption against Illness." *American Economic Review* 92(1):51–76.

Ghobarah, H. A., P. Huth, and B. Russett. 2003. "Civil Wars Kill and Maim People—Long after Shooting Stops." *American Political Science Review* 97(2):189–202.

Glennerster, Rachel, and Yongseok Shin. 2003. "Is Transparency Good for You, and Can the IMF Help?" Working paper no. WP/03/132, International Monetary Fund, Washington, D.C.

Glewwe, Paul. 2002. "Schools and Skills in Developing Countries: Education Policies and Socioeconomic Outcomes." *Journal of Economic Literature* 40(2):436–482.

Glewwe, Paul, and Gillette Hall. 1995. "Who Is Most Vulnerable to Macroeconomic Shocks? Hypotheses Tests Using Panel Data from Peru." Living Standards Measurement Survey working paper no. 117, World Bank, Washington, D.C.

Glewwe, Paul, Hanan Jacoby, and Elizabeth King. 2001. "Early Childhood Nutrition and Academic Achievement; A Longitudinal Analysis." *Journal of Public Economics* 81(3):345–368.

Glewwe, Paul, Michael Kremer, and Sylvie Moulin. 2000. "Textbooks and Test Scores: Evidence from a Prospective Evaluation in Kenya." Typescript, Harvard University, Cambridge, Mass.

Goldin, Claudia. 1991. "The Role of World War II in the Rise of Women's Employment." *American Economic Review* 81(4):741–756.

Goldin, Ian, Halsey Rogers, and Nicholas Stern. 2002. "The Role and Effectiveness of Development Assistance: Lessons from World Bank Experience." In I. Goldin, H. Rogers, and N. Stern (eds.), *The Case for Aid*. Washington, D.C.: World Bank.

Gómez-Lobo, Andrés, Vivien Foster, and Jonathan Halpern. 2000. "Better Household Surveys for Better Design of Infrastructure Subsidies." Public Policy for the Private Sector note no. 213, World Bank, Washington, D.C., June.

Gradstein, Mark, and Moshe Justman. 2002. "Education, Social Cohesion, and Economic Growth." *American Economic Review* 92(4):1192–1204.

Gray, Philip. 2001. "Private Participation in Infrastructure: A Review of the Evidence." Washington, D.C.: World Bank, October.

Greif, Avner. 1994. "Cultural Beliefs and the Organization of Society: A Historical and Theoretical Reflection on Collectivist and Individualist Societies." *Journal of Political Economy* 42(5):912–950.

Griliches, Zvi. 1958. "Research Costs and Social Returns: Hybrid Corn and Related Innovations." *Journal of Political Economy* 66(5):419–431.

Grootaert, Christiaan, and Thierry van Bastelaer (eds.). 2002. *The Role of Social Capital in Social Development: An Empirical Assessment*. Cambridge: Cambridge University Press.

Grootaert, Christiaan, Ravi Kanbur, and Gi-Taik Oh. 1995. "Why Some People Escape from Poverty and Others Don't? An African Case Study." Working paper no. 1499, World Bank, Washington, D.C.

Gros, Daniel, and Alfred Steinherr. 1995. *Winds of Change: Economic Transition in Central and Eastern Europe*. New York: Longman.

Grosh, Margaret E., and Paul Glewwe. 2000. *Designing Household Survey Questionnaires for Developing Countries: Lessons from Fifteen Years of Living Standard Measurement Study*. New York: Oxford University Press.

Grossman, Sanford J., and Oliver D. Hart. 1986. "Costs and Benefits of Ownership: A Theory of Vertical and Lateral Integration." *Journal of Political Economy* 94:691–719.

Guasch, J. Luis, and Pablo Spiller. 1999. *Managing the Regulatory Process: Design, Concepts, Issues and the Latin America and Caribbean Story*. Washington, D.C.: World Bank.

Gupta, Sanjeev, Benedict Clements, and Erwin Tiongson. 1998. "Public Spending on Human Development." *Finance and Development* 35(3):10–13.

Gutmann, Amy, and Davis Thompson. 1996. *Democracy and Disagreement*. Cambridge, Mass.: Harvard University Press.

Haberler, Gottfried, and A. Y. C. Koo. 1985. *Selected Essays of Gottfried Haberler*. Cambridge, Mass.: MIT Press.

Habermas, Jürgen. 1990. *Moral Consciousness and Communicative Action*. Cambridge, Mass.: MIT Press.

Haddad, M. 1993. "The link Between Trade Liberalization and Multi-Factor Productivity: The Case of Morocco." Discussion paper no. 4, World Bank, Washington, D.C.

Haddad, M., and A. Harrison. 1993. "Are There Spillovers from Direct Foreign Investment? Evidence from Panel Data for Morocco." *Journal of Development Economics* 42(1):51–74.

Haggard, Stephan, and Robert Kaufman (eds.). 1992. *The Politics of Economic Adjustment.* Princeton, N.J.: Princeton University Press.

Haggard, Stephan, and Robert Kaufman (eds.). 1995. *The Political Economy of Democratic Transitions.* Princeton, N.J.: Princeton University Press.

Hall, Robert, and Charles Jones. 1999. "Why Do Some Countries Produce So Much More Output per Worker Than Others?" *Quarterly Journal of Economics* 114(1):83–116.

Hallberg, Kristin. 2000. "A Market-Oriented Strategy for Small and Medium-Scale Enterprises." IFC discussion paper 40, World Bank, Washington, D.C.

Hansen, Henrik, and Finn Tarp. 2001. "Aid and Growth Regressions." *Journal of Development Economics* 64(2):547–570.

Hanushek, Eric E., John F. Kain, and Steven G. Rivkin. 2001. "Why Public Schools Lose Teachers." Working paper no. 8599, National Bureau of Economic Research, Cambridge, Mass., November.

Harrison, A. 1994. "Productivity, Imperfect Competition, and Trade Reform." *Journal of International Economics* 36(1–2):53–73.

Hart, Oliver. 2003. "Incomplete Contracts and Public Ownership: Remarks, and an Application to Public-Private Partnerships." *Economic Journal* 113:C69–C76.

Hart, Oliver, Andrei Shleifer, and Robert W. Vishny. 1997. "The Proper Scope of Government: Theory and an Application to Prisons." *Quarterly Journal of Economics* 112(4):1127–1161.

Hausmann, Ricardo, and Dani Rodrik. 2003. "Economic Development as Self-Discovery." *Journal of Development Economics* 72(2):603–633.

Hawking, Stephen. 1988. *A Brief History of Time.* New York: Bantam Books.

Hayek, Friedrich. 1984. *The Essence of Hayek.* C. Nishiyama and K. Leube (eds.). Stanford, Calif.: Hoover Institution Press.

He, Baogang. 2003. "How Democratic Are Village Elections in China?" Paper presented at the National Endowment for Democracy, June 10. Available at http://www.ned.org/forum/fellows/presentations/HePresentationSummary.pdf.

Peter S. Heller, and Sanjee V. Gupta. 2002. "Challenges in Expanding Development Assistance." Discussion paper PDP/02/5, International Monetary Fund, Washington, D.C., March.

Heston, Alan, Robert Summers, and Bettina Aten. 2002. Penn World Table Version 6.1. Philadelphia: Center for International Comparisons at the University of Pennsylvania, October.

Hill, Christopher. 1996. *Liberty against the Law: Some Seventeenth-Century Controversies.* Harmondsworth: Penguin Books.

Hill, Kenneth, Rohini Pande, and Gareth Jones. 1997. "Trends in Child Mortality in the Developing World: 1990 to 1995." UNICEF staff working papers, Evaluation, Policy and Planning series, UNICEF, New York.

Hill, Kenneth, et al. 1998. "Trends in Child Mortality in the Developing World: 1990 to 1996." Unpublished report, UNICEF, New York, January.

Hills, John, Julian Le Grand, and David Piachaud (eds.). 2002. *Understanding Social Exclusion*. New York: Oxford University Press.

Hirschman, Albert O. 1958. *The Strategy of Economic Development*. New Haven, Conn.: Yale University Press.

Hirschman, Albert O. 1971. *A Bias for Hope: Essays on Development and Latin America*. New Haven, Conn.: Yale University Press.

Hirschman, Albert O. 1973. *Journeys toward Progress*. New York: Norton.

Hirschman, Albert O. 1977. *The Passions and the Interests*. Princeton, N.J.: Princeton University Press.

Hirschman, Albert O. 1981. *Essays in Trespassing: Economics to Politics and Beyond*. Cambridge: Cambridge University Press.

Hirschman, Albert O. 1984. *Getting Ahead Collectively: Grassroots Experiences in Latin America*. New York: Pergamon Press.

Hjertholm, P., and J. Lauresen. 2000. "Macroeconomic Issues in Foreign Aid." Institute of Economics discussion paper, University of Copenhagen.

Hoekman, Bernard, Aaditya Matoo, and Philip English (eds.). 2002. *Development, Trade, and the WTO: A Handbook*. Washington, D.C.: World Bank.

Hoff, Karla. 1996. "Market Failures and Distribution of Wealth: A Perspective from the Economics of Information." *Politics and Society* 24(4):411–432.

Hoff, Karla, and A. B. Lyon. 1995. "Non-Leaky Buckets: Optimal Redistributive Taxation and Agency Costs." *Journal of Political Economy* 58:365–390.

Holzmann, Robert, and Steen L. Jorgensen. 1999. "Social Protection as Social Risk Management: Conceptual Underpinnings for the Social Protection Strategy Paper." *Journal of International Development* 11:1005–1027.

Holtz-Eakin, Douglas, Harvey Rosen, and Robert Weathers. 2000. "Horatio Alger Meets the Mobility Tables." *Small Business Economics* 14:243–274.

Huntington, Samuel. 1991. *The Third Wave—Democratization in the Late Twentieth Century*. Norman: University of Oklahoma Press.

Huntington, Samuel, and Joan Nelson. 1976. *No Easy Choice: Political Participation in Developing Countries*. Cambridge, Mass.: Harvard University Press.

Husain, Ishrat, and Ishac Diwan (eds.). 1989. *Dealing with the Debt Crisis: A World Bank Symposium*. Washington, D.C.: World Bank.

International Fund for Agricultural Development (IFAD). 2001. *Rural Poverty Report 2001*. Oxford: Oxford University Press.

International Monetary Fund, Fiscal Affairs Department. 2002. *Fiscal Dimensions of Sustainable Development*. Washington, D.C.: International Monetary Fund, September.

International Monetary Fund. 2002. Government Finance Statistics Yearbook. Washington, D.C.: International Monetary Fund.

Iyengar, Sheena S., and Mark R. Lepper. 2000. "When Choice Is Demotivating: Can One Desire Too Much of a Good Thing?" *Journal of Personality and Social Psychology* 76:995–1006.

Jacobs, Jane. 1969. *The Economy of Cities.* New York: Random House.

Jacobs, Jane. 1984. *Cities and the Wealth of Nations: Principles of Economic Life.* New York: Random House.

Jacobs, Jane. 2000. *The Nature of Economies.* New York: Modern Library.

Jayaraj, D., and S. Subramanian. 1999. "Poverty and Discrimination: Measurement and Evidence from Rural India." In B. Harris-White and S. Subramanian (eds.), *Illfare in India: Essays on India's Social Sector in Honour of S. Guhan.* New Delhi, India: Sage.

Jayasuriya, Ruwan, and Quentin Wodon. 2003. "Efficiency in Reaching the Millennium Development Goals." Working paper no. 9, World Bank, Washington, D.C.

Jeffrey, Robin. 1992. *Politics, Women and Well-Being: How Kerala Became "A Model."* Cambridge: Cambridge University Press.

Jimenez, Emmanuel, and Yasuyuki Sawada. 1999. "Do Community-Managed Schools Work? An Evaluation of El Salvador's EDUCO Program." *World Bank Economic Review* 13(3):415–441.

Jones, Leroy, and Il SaKong. 1980. *Government, Business, and Entrepreneurship in Economic Development: The Korean Case.* Cambridge, Mass.: Harvard University Press.

Justino, Patricia, and Julie Litchfield. 2003. "Economic Exclusion and Discrimination: The Experience of Minorities and Indigenous Peoples." International issue paper, Minority Rights Group, London. Available at http://www.minorityrights.org.

Justman, Moshe, and Mark Gradstein. 1999. "The Democratization of Political Elites and the Decline in Inequality in Modern Economic Growth." In Brezis E. S. and P. Temin (eds.), *Elites, Minorities and Economic Growth.* New York: Elsevier, North-Holland.

Kahneman, Daniel, and Amos Tversky. 2000. *Choices, Values and Frames.* Cambridge: Cambridge University Press.

Kaldor, Nicholas. 1960. *Essays on Economic Stability and Growth.* London: G. Duckworth.

Kaldor, Nicholas. 1961. "Capital Accumulation and Economic Growth." In F. A. Lutz and D. C. Hague (eds.), *The Theory of Capital.* New York: St. Martin's Press.

Kaldor, Nicholas. 1967. *Strategic Factors in Economic Development.* Ithaca, N.Y.: New York State School of Industrial and Labor Relations, Cornell University.

Kaldor, Nicholas. 1994. "Interregional Trade and Cumulative Causation." In James Buchanan and Yong J. Yoon (eds.), *The Return to Increasing Returns.* Ann Arbor: University of Michigan Press.

Kanbur, Ravi. 2000. "Income Distribution and Development." In Anthony B. Atkinson and François Bourguignon (eds.), *Handbook of Income Distribution.* Amsterdam: Elsevier.

Kanbur, Ravi T. Sandler, and K. Morrison. 1999. "The Future of Development Assistance." Policy essay 25, Washington, D.C.: Overseas Development Council.

Kaufmann, Daniel. 2003. "Rethinking Governance: Empirical Lessons Challenge Orthodoxy." Typescript, World Bank, Washington, D.C., March.

Kaufmann, Daniel, Aart Kraay, and Pablo Zoido-Lobatón. 1999. "Governance Matters." Policy research working paper no. 2196, World Bank, Washington, D.C.

Kaufmann, Daniel, Aart Kraay, and Pablo Zoido-Lobatón. 2002. "Governance Matters II: Updated Indicators for 2000/01." Policy research working paper no. 2772, World Bank, Washington, D.C.

Kaufmann, Daniel, Aart Kraay, and Massimo Mastruzzi. 2003. "Governance Matters III: Governance Indicators for 1996–2002." Policy research working paper no. 3106, World Bank, Washington, D.C.

Kharas, Homi, and Deepak Mishra. 2001. "Fiscal Policy, Hidden Deficits, and Currency Crises." In Shantayanan Devarajan, F. Halsey Rogers, and Lyn Squire (eds.), *World Bank Economists' Forum, Volume 1*. pp. 31–48.

Khwaja, Asim Ijaz. 2001. "Can Good Projects Succeed in Bad Communities? Collective Action in the Himalayas." Mimeo., Kennedy School of Government, Harvard University, Cambridge, Mass.

King, Stephen, and Rohan Pitchford. 2001. "Private or Public? A Taxonomy of Optimal Ownership and Management Regimes." Mimeo., Australian National University, Canberra.

Kirzner, Israel M. 1973. *Competition and Entrepreneurship*. Chicago: University of Chicago Press.

Kirzner, Israel M. 1979. *Perception, Opportunity, and Profit: Studies in the Theory of Entrepreneurship*. Chicago: University of Chicago Press.

Kirzner, Israel M. 1987. "Austrian School of Economics." In John Eatwell, Murray Milgate, and Peter Newman (eds.), *New Palgrave: A Dictionary of Economics*. New York: Stockton Press.

Klein, Burton H. 1977. *Dynamic Economics*. Cambridge, Mass.: Harvard University Press.

Klein, Burton H. 1984. *Prices, Wages and Business Cycles: A Dynamic Theory*. New York: Pergamon Press.

Klenow, Peter J., and Andrés Rodriguez-Clare. 1997. "Economic Growth: A Review Essay." *Journal of Monetary Economics* 40:597–617.

Knack, Stephen, and Philip Keefer. 1995. "Institutions and Economic Performance: Cross-Country Tests Using Alternative Institutional Measures." *Economics and Politics* 7(3):206–227.

Knack, Stephen, and Philip Keefer. 1997. "Does Social Capital Have an Economic Payoff? A Cross-Country Investigation." *Quarterly Journal of Economics* 112:1251–1288.

Knight, Frank. 1947. *Freedom and Reform*. New York: Harper & Row.

Kravis, Irving B., Alan W. Heston, and Robert Summers. 1978. *International Comparisons of Real Product and Purchasing Power*. Baltimore: Johns Hopkins University Press for the World Bank.

Kravis, Irving B., Alan W. Heston, and Robert Summers. 1982. *International Comparisons of Real Gross Product*. Baltimore: Johns Hopkins University Press for the World Bank.

Kravis, Irving B., Alan W. Heston, and Robert Summers. 1983. *World Product and Income: International Comparisons of Real Gross Product*. Baltimore: Johns Hopkins University Press.

Kremer, Michael. 2003. "Randomized Evaluations of Educational Programs in Developing Countries: Some Lessons." *American Economic Review* 93(2):102–106.

Krishna, Anirudh, Norman Uphoff, and Milton Esman (eds.). 1997. *Reasons for Hope: Instructive Experiences in Rural Development*. West Hartford, Conn.: Kumarian Press.

Krueger, Anne O. 2002. *A New Approach to Sovereign Debt Restructuring.* Washington, D.C.: International Monetary Fund.

Krueger, Alan, and Mikael Lindahl. 2001. "Education for Growth: Why and for Whom?" *Journal of Economic Literature* 39(4):1101–1136.

Krugman, Paul. 1979. "A Model of Balance-of-Payments Crises." *Journal of Money, Credit and Banking* 11:311–325.

Kuczinski, Pedro-Pablo, and John Williamson. 2003. *After the Washington Consensus: Restarting Growth and Reform in Latin America*. Washington, D.C.: Institute for International Economics.

Kuznets, Simon 1956. *Quantitative Aspects of the Economic Growth of Nations*. Chicago: Research Center in Economic Development and Cultural Change, University of Chicago.

Kuznets, Simon. 1971. *Economic Growth of Nations: Total Output and Production Structure*. Cambridge, Mass.: Harvard University Press.

Laffont, Jean-Jacques. 1992. "L'État introuvable" (book review of Nicholas Stern, *Le rôle de l'Etat dans le développement économique*). *Le Monde*, November 3.

La Ferrara, Eliana. 2002. "Inequality and Group Participation: Theory and Evidence from Rural Tanzania." *Journal of Public Economics* 85:235–273.

Landes, David. 1998. *The Wealth and Poverty of Nations*. New York: Norton.

Lanjouw, Jean, and Peter Lanjouw. 2001. "The Rural Non-Farm Sector: Issues and Evidence from Developing Countries." *Agricultural Economics* 26:1–23.

Lanjouw, Peter, and Martin Ravallion. 1999. "Benefit Incidence, Public Spending Reforms and the Timing of Program Capture." *World Bank Economic Review* 13(2):257–273.

Lanjouw, Peter, and Abusaleh Shariff. 2000. "Rural Nonfarm Employment in India: Access, Incomes and Poverty Impact." Mimeo., National Council of Applied Economic Research, New Delhi, December.

Lanjouw, Peter, and Nicholas Stern. 1998. *Economic Development in Palanpur over Five Decades*. New York: Oxford University Press.

La Porta, Rafael, Florencio Lopez-de-Silanes, and Andrei Shleifer. 2000. "Government Ownership of Banks." Working paper no. 7620, National Bureau of Economic Research, Cambridge, Mass.

La Porta, Rafael, Florencio Lopez-de-Silanes, Andrei Shleifer, and Robert Vishny. 1999. "The Quality of Government." *Journal of Law, Economics, and Organization* 15(1):222–279.

Levine, Ross, and David Renelt. 1992. "A Sensitivity Analysis of Cross-Country Growth Regressions." *American Economic Review* 82(4):942–963.

Lewis, W. Arthur. 1954. "Economic Development with Unlimited Supplies of Labour." *Manchester School of Economics and Social Studies* 22:139–191.

Lewis, W. Arthur. 1955. *The Theory of Economic Growth*. Homewood, Ill.: Irwin.

Liles, P. R. 1974. *New Business Ventures and the Entrepreneur*. Homewood, Ill.: Irwin.

Lindert, P., and J. Williamson. 2001. "Does Globalization Make the World More Unequal?" Working paper 8228, National Bureau of Economic Research, Cambridge, Mass.

Lipton, Michael, and Martin Ravallion. 1995. "Poverty and Policy." In J. Behrman and T. N. Srinivasan (eds.), *Handbook of Development Economics*. Amsterdam: North-Holland.

Little, Ian M. D. 1982. *Economic Development: Theory, Policy and International Relations*. New York: Basic Books.

Little, Ian M. D., Tibor Scitovsky, and Maurice F. Scott. 1970. *Industry and Trade in Some Developing Countries: A Comparative Study*. New York: Oxford University Press.

Liu, L., and J. Tybout. 1996. "Productivity Growth in Chile and Colombia: The Role of Entry, Exit, and Learning." In M. Roberts and J. Tybout (eds.), *Industrial Evolution in Developing Countries*. Oxford: Oxford University Press.

Lopez, Ramón. 2002. "The Economics of Agriculture in Developing Countries: The Role of the Environment." In B. Gardner and G. Rausser (eds.), *Handbook of Agricultural Economics*. Amsterdam: Elsevier.

Loury, Glenn C. 1977. "A Dynamic Theory of Racial Income Differences." In P. A. Wallace and A. LeMund (eds.), *Women, Minorities and Employment*. Lexington, Mass.: Lexington Books.

Loury, Glenn C. 1987. "Why Should We Care about Group Inequality?" *Social Philosophy and Policy* 5(1):249–271.

Loury, Glenn C. 1998. "Discrimination in the Post–Civil Rights Era: Beyond Market Interactions." *Journal of Economic Perspectives* 12(2):117–126.

Loury, Glenn C. 2000. "Social Exclusion and Ethnic Groups: The Challenge to Economics." In B. Pleskovic and J. Stiglitz (eds.), *Annual World Bank Conference on Development Economics 1999*. Washington, D.C.

Loury, Glenn C. 2002. *The Anatomy of Racial Inequality*. Cambridge, Mass.: Harvard University Press.

Lucas, Robert E. 1988. "On the Mechanics of Economic Development." *Journal of Monetary Economics* 22(1):3–42.

Lucas, Robert E. 2003. "Macroeconomic Priorities." *American Economic Review* 93(1):1–14.

Lybeck, J. A., and M. Henrekson (eds.). 1988. *Explaining the Growth of Government*. Amsterdam: North-Holland.

Machiavelli, Niccolò. 1940 (1513). *The Prince and the Discourses*. New York: Random House.

Maddison, Angus. 1995. *Monitoring the World Economy, 1820–1992*. Paris: Organization for Economic Cooperation and Development.

Maddison, Angus. 2001. *The World Economy: A Millennial Perspective*. Paris: Organization for Economic Cooperation and Development.

March, J. G., and H. A. Simon. 1958. *Organizations*. New York: Wiley.

Marshall, Alfred. 1961 (1920). *Principles of Economics* (9th ed.), London: Macmillan.

Marshall, Monty G., and Ted Robert Gurr. 2003. *Peace and Conflict 2003: A Global Survey of Armed Conflicts, Self-Determination Movements and Democracy.* University of Maryland, College Park: Center for International Development and Conflict Management.

McClelland, David. 1961. *The Achieving Society.* Princeton, N.J.: Van Nostrand.

McGregor, Douglas. 1960. *The Human Side of Enterprise.* New York: McGraw-Hill.

McGregor, Pat. 1995. "Economic Growth, Inequality, and Poverty: An Analysis of Policy in a Two-Period Framework." *Journal of International Development* 7(4):619–635.

McMillan, John, and Christopher Woodruff. 2000. "Interfirm Relationships and Informal Credit in Vietnam." *Quarterly Journal of Economics* 114:1285–1320.

McMillan, John, and Christopher Woodruff. 2002. "The Central Role of Entrepreneurs in Transition Economies." *Journal of Economic Perspective* 16(3):153–170.

McNamara, Robert S. 1981. *The McNamara Years at the World Bank: Major Policy Addresses of Robert S. McNamara, 1968–1981.* Baltimore: Johns Hopkins University Press.

Messick, Richard. 1999. "Judicial Reform and Economic Development: A Survey of the Issues." *World Bank Research Observer* 14(1):117–136.

Meyer, Bruce D. 1995. "Natural and Quasi-Experiments in Economics." *Journal of Business and Economic Statistics* 13(2):151–161.

Miguel, Edward, and Michael Kremer. 2003. "Worms: Identifying Impacts on Education and Health in the Presence of Treatment Externalities." *Econometrica* 72(1):159–217.

Milesi-Ferretti, Gian Maria, Roberto Perotti, and Massimo Rostagno. 2002. "Electoral Systems and Public Spending." *Quarterly Journal of Economics* 117(2):609–657.

Mill, John Stuart. 1972 (1861). "Considerations of Representative Government." In *J. S. Mill: Utilitarianism, On Liberty and Considerations on Representative Government.* H. B. Acton (ed.). London: J. M. Dent & Sons.

Mirrlees, J. A. 1971. "An Exploration in the Theory of Optimum Income Taxation." *Review of Economic Studies* 38:175–208.

Mitra, Pradeep, and Nicholas Stern. 2002. "Tax Systems in Transition." Mimeo., World Bank, Washington, D.C., August.

Monk, David H. 1994. "Subject Area Preparation of Secondary Mathematics and Science Teachers and Student Achievement." *Economics of Education Review* 13(2):125–145.

Mueller, Dennis. 2003. *Public Choice III.* Cambridge: Cambridge University Press.

Munshi, Kaivan, and Jacques Myaux, 2003. "Development as a Process of Social Change: An Application to the Fertility Transition." Working paper no. 28, Bureau for Research in Economic Analysis of Development, Cambridge, Mass, June.

Murphy, Kevin, Andrei Shleifer, and Robert Vishny. 1989. "Industrialization and the Big Push." *Journal of Political Economy* 97(5):1003–1026.

Murphy, Kevin, Andrei Shleifer, and Robert W. Vishny. 1991. "The Allocation of Talent: Implications for Growth." *Quarterly Journal of Economics* 106(2):503–530.

Murphy, Kevin, Andrei Shleifer, and Robert W. Vishny. 1993. "Why Is Rent-Seeking So Costly to Growth?" *American Economic Review Papers and Proceedings* 83(2):409–414.

Myers, Norman, Russel A. Mittermeier, Cristina G. Mittermeier, Gustavo A. B. Fonseca, and Jennifer Kent. 2000. "Biodiversity Hotspots for Conservation Priorities." *Nature* 403:853–858.

Myrdal, Gunnar. 1968. *Asian Drama: An Inquiry into the Poverty of Nations.* New York: Twentieth Century Fund.

Narayan, Deepa (ed.). 2002. *Empowerment and Poverty Reduction: A Sourcebook for World Bank Staff.* Washington, D.C.: World Bank.

Narayan, Deepa, and Lant Pritchett. 1999. "Cents and Sociability: Household Income and Social Capital in Rural Tanzania." *Economic Development and Cultural Change* 47(4):871–897.

Narayan, Deepa, with P. Raj, K. Schafft, A. Rademacher, and S. Koch-Schulte. 2000. *Voices of the Poor: Can Anyone Hear Us?* New York: Oxford University Press/World Bank.

National Council of Applied Economic Research. 1993/94. Survey data.

Ndulu, Benno J., and Stephen A. O'Connel. 1999. "Governance and Growth in Sub-Saharan Africa." *Journal of Economic Perspectives*, Summer, 13(3):41–66.

Newbery, David, and Nicholas Stern (eds.). 1987. *The Theory of Taxation for Developing Countries.* Oxford: Oxford University Press.

Nicoletti, Giuseppe, and Stefano Scarpetta. 2003. "Regulation, Productivity and Growth: The OECD Evidence." Policy research working paper no. 2944, World Bank, Washington D.C.

North, Douglass. 1981. *Structure and Change in Economic History.* New York: Norton.

North, Douglass. 1990. *Institutions, Institutional Change and Economic Performance.* Cambridge: Cambridge University Press.

Nozick, Robert. 1974. *Anarchy, State, and Utopia.* New York: Basic Books.

Nurkse, Ragnar. 1953. *Problems of Capital Formation in Underdeveloped Countries.* Oxford: Basil Blackwell.

Nurkse, Ragnar. 1967. *Problems of Capital Formation in Underdeveloped Countries and Patterns of Trade and Development.* New York: Oxford University Press.

Nussbaum, Martha, and Amartya Sen (eds.). 1993. *The Quality of Life.* Oxford: Clarendon Press.

Nyoni, T. 1998. "Foreign Aid and Economic Performance in Tanzania." *World Development* 26(7):1235–1240.

Olson, Mancur. 1993. "Dictatorship, Democracy, and Development." *American Political Science Review* 87(3):567–576.

O'Rourke, Kevin H., and Jeffrey G. Williamson. 1997. "Around the European Periphery, 1870–1913: Globalization, Schooling and Growth." *Economic Review of Economic History* 1(2):153–191.

O'Rourke, Kevin H., and Jeffrey G. Williamson. 1999. *Globalization and History: The Evolution of a Nineteenth Century Atlantic Economy*. Cambridge, Mass.: MIT Press.

O'Rourke, Kevin H., and Richard Sinnot. 2003. "Migration Flows: Political Economy of Migration and the Empirical Challenges." Paper presented at the 2003 Annual Bank Conference on Development Economics in Europe, Paris.

Pande, Rohini. 2003. "Can Mandated Political Representation Increase Policy Influence for Disadvantaged Minorities? Theory and Evidence from India." *American Economic Review* 93(4):1132–1151.

Paul, Samuel. 2002. *Holding the State Accountable: Citizen Monitoring in Action*. Bangalore: Books for Change.

Perotti, Roberto. 1996. "Growth, Income Distribution and Democracy: What the Data Say." *Journal of Economic Growth* 1:149–187.

Perotti, Roberto. 1999. "Fiscal Policy in Good Times and Bad." *Quarterly Journal of Economics* 114(4):1399–1436.

Persson, Torsten, and Guido Tabellini. 2002. "Political Institutions and Policy Outcomes: What Are the Stylized Facts?" Mimeo., National Bureau of Economic Research, Cambridge, Mass., August.

Persson, Torsten, and Guido Tabellini. 2000. *Political Economics: Explaining Economic Policy*. Cambridge, Mass.: MIT Press.

Pfeffer, Jeffrey, and Robert Sutton. 1999. *The Knowing-Doing Gap: How Smart Companies Turn Knowledge into Action*. Boston: Harvard Business School Press.

Piketty, Thomas. 1997. "The Dynamics of the Wealth Distribution and the Interest Rate with Credit Rationing." *Review of Economic Studies* 64(2):173–189.

Piore, Michael. 1995. *Beyond Individualism*. Cambridge, Mass.: Harvard University Press.

Pistor, Katharina. 2000. "The Standardization of Law and its Effect on Developing Economies." G-24 discussion paper no. 4, UNCTAD, Geneva, July.

Pistor, Katharina, and Philip Wellons. 1998. *The Role of Law and Legal Institutions in Asian Economic Development, 1960–1995*. New York: Oxford University Press.

Pitt, Mark M., Mark R. Rosenzweig, and Donna M. Gibbons. 1993. "Determinants and Consequences of the Placement of Government Programs in Indonesia." *World Bank Economic Review* 7:319–348.

Plane, Patrick. 1997. "Privatization and Economic Growth: An Empirical Investigation from a Sample of Developing Market Economies." *Applied Economics* 29:161–178.

Platteau, Jean-Philippe. 2000. *Institutions, Social Norms, and Economic Development*. Amsterdam: Harwood Academic Publishers.

Platteau, Jean-Philippe. 2002. "Rushing to Help the Poor through Participation May Be Self-Defeating." Typescript, Center for Research on the Economics of Development, Faculty of Economics, Namur.

Popper, Karl R. 1962. *The Open Society and Its Enemies*. New York: Harper and Row.

Pradhan, Basanta K., and P. K. Roy. 2003. *The Well-Being of Indian Households: MIMAP-India Survey Report*. New Delhi: Tata McGraw-Hill.

Prebisch, Raúl. 1950. *The Economic Development of Latin America and Its Principal Problems.* New York: UN Economic Commission for Latin America.

Pritchett, Lant. 1997. "Divergence, Big Time." *Journal of Economic Perspectives* 11(3):3–17.

Pritchett, Lant. 2002a. "It Pays to Be Ignorant: A Simple Political Economy of Rigorous Program Evaluation." Typescript, Harvard University, Kennedy School of Government.

Pritchett, Lant. 2002b. "When Will They Ever Learn? Why All Governments Produce Schooling." Typescript, Harvard University, Kennedy School of Government.

Pritchett, Lant, and Lawrence H. Summers. 1996. "Wealthier Is Healthier." *Journal of Human Resources* 31(4):841–868.

PROBE Team. 1999. *Public Report on Basic Education in India.* New Delhi: Oxford University Press.

Przeworski, Adam. 1991. *Democracy and the Market: Political and Economic Reforms in Eastern Europe and Latin America.* Cambridge: Cambridge University Press.

Putnam, Robert. 1993. *Making Democracy Work.* Princeton, N.J.: Princeton University Press.

Qian, Yingyi. 1999. "Why Is China Different from Eastern Europe? Perspective from Organization Theory." *European Economic Review* 43:1085–1094.

Rajan, Raghuram, and Luigi Zingales. 2003. *Saving Capitalism from the Capitalists.* New York: Crown Business.

Rao, Vijayendra, and Michael Walton (eds.). 2004. *Culture and Public Action.* Palo Alto, Calif.: Stanford University Press.

Ravallion, Martin. 1997. "Can High-Inequality Developing Countries Escape Absolute Poverty." *Economic Letters* 56(1):51–57.

Ravallion, Martin. 2001. "Growth, Inequality, and Poverty: Looking Beyond Averages." Working paper no. 2558, World Bank, Washington D.C.

Ravallion, Martin. 2002. "Externalities in Rural Development: Evidence from China." Mimeo., World Bank, Washington, D.C., July.

Ravallion, Martin. 2003a. "Measuring Aggregate Welfare in Developing Countries: How Well Do National Accounts and Surveys Agree?" *Review of Economics and Statistics* 85(3):645–652.

Ravallion, Martin. 2003b. "The Debate on Globalization, Poverty and Inequality: Why Measurement Matters." *International Affairs* 79(4):739–754.

Ravallion, Martin. 2003c. "Targeted Transfers in Poor Countries: Revisiting the Tradeoffs and Policy Options." Mimeo., World Bank, Washington, D.C.

Ravallion, Martin, and Shaohua Chen. 1997. "What Can New Survey Data Tell Us about Recent Changes in Distribution and Poverty?" *World Bank Economic Review* 11(2):357–382.

Ravallion, Martin, and Shaohua Chen. 2003. "Measuring Pro-Poor Growth." *Economic Letters* 78(1):93–99.

Ravallion, Martin, and Gaurav Datt. 1999. "When Is Growth Pro-Poor? Evidence from the Diverse Experiences of India's States." World Bank working paper 2263.

Ravallion, Martin, Gaurav Datt, and Dominique Van de Walle. 1991. "Quantifying Absolute Poverty in the Developing World." *Review of Income and Wealth* 37:345–361.

Rawls, John. 1999. *A Theory of Justice* (Rev. ed.), Cambridge, Mass.: Belknap Press of Harvard University Press.

Ray, Debraj. 1998. *Development Economics*. Princeton, N.J.: Princeton University Press.

Reddy, Sanjay, and Thomas Pogge. 2003. "How *Not* to Count the Poor." Working paper, Columbia University. Available at http://www.socialanalysis.org.

Reinikka, Ritva, and Jacob Svensson. 2001. "Explaining Leakage of Public Funds." Policy research working paper no. 2709, World Bank, Washington, D.C.

Reinikka, Ritva, and Jakob Svensson. 2002. "Working for God? Evaluating Service Delivery of Religious Not-for-Profit Health Care Providers in Uganda." Washington, D.C.: World Bank Development Research Group.

Republic of Zambia. 2000. *Interim Poverty Reduction Strategy Paper*. Lusaka: Ministry of Finance and Economic Development.

Reynolds, L. J. 1983. "The Spread of Economic Growth to the Third World: 1850–1980." *Journal of Economic Literature* 21:941–980.

Ritschl, Albrecht O. 1996. "An Exercise in Futility: East German Economic Growth and Decline, 1945–89." In Nicholas Crafts and Gianni Toniolo (eds.), *Economic Growth in Europe since 1945*. Cambridge: Cambridge University Press for the Centre for Economic Policy Research.

Rivera-Batiz, Luis A., and Paul Romer. 1991. "Economic Integration and Long-Run Growth." *Quarterly Journal of Economics* 105(2):531–555.

Roberts, M., and J. Tybout. 1996. *Industrial Evolution in Developing Countries: Micro Patterns of Turnover, Productivity and Market Structure*. New York: Oxford University Press.

Robilliard, Anne-Sophie, François Bourguignon, and Sherman Robinson. 2003. "Examining the Social Impact of the Indonesian Financial Crisis Using a Micro -Macro Model." Paper presented at the Annual Bank Conference on Development Economics, Paris, May 16.

Robinson, James, and Thierry Verdier. 2002. "The Political Economy of Clientelism." Discussion paper no. 3205, Center for Economic Policy Research, London.

Rodríguez, Francisco, and Dani Rodrik. 2001. "Trade Policy and Economic Growth: A Skeptic's Guide to the Cross-National Evidence." Seminar series no. 2000-11, International Monetary Fund, Washington, D.C., April.

Rodrik, Dani. 1994. "The Rush to Free Trade in the Developing World: Why So Late? Why Now? Will It Last?" In S. Haggard and S. Webb (eds.), *Voting for Reform*. Oxford: Oxford University Press.

Rodrik, Dani. 1996. "Understanding Economic Policy Reform." *Journal of Economic Literature* 34:9–41.

Rodrik, Dani. 1997. *Has Globalization Gone Too Far?* Washington, D.C.: Institute for International Economics.

Rodrik, Dani. 1998. "Where Did All the Growth Go? External Shocks, Social Conflict and Growth Collapses." Discussion paper, no. 1789, Centre for Economic Policy Research, London, January.

Rodrik, Dani. 1999. "The Asian Financial Crisis and the Virtues of Democracy." *Challenge* 42(4):44–59.

Rodrik, Dani. 2003a. "Introduction: What Do We Learn from Country Narratives?" In Dani Rodrik (ed.), *In Search of Prosperity: Analytic Narratives in Economic Growth*. Princeton, N.J.: Princeton University Press.

Rodrik, Dani. 2003b. Growth Strategies. In Philippe Aghion and Steven Durlauf (eds.), *Handbook of Economic Growth*. Amsterdam: North-Holland. Available at http://ksghome.harvard.edu/~.drodrik.academic.ksg/growthstrat10.pdf.

Rodrik, Dani, Arvind Subramanian, and Francesco Trebbi. 2002. "Institutions Rule: The Primacy of Institutions over Integration and Geography in Economic Development." Working paper WP/02/189, International Monetary Fund, Washington, D.C., November.

Roemer, John E. 1998. *Equality of Opportunity*. Cambridge, Mass.: Harvard University Press.

Roland, Gérard. 2000. *Transition and Economics*. Cambridge, Mass.: MIT Press.

Romer, Paul M. 1986. "Increasing Returns and Long-Run Growth." *Journal of Political Economy* 94(5):1002–1037.

Romer, Paul M. 1987. "Growth Based on Increasing Returns due to Specialization." *American Economic Review* 77(2):56–62.

Romer, Paul M. 1993. "Two Strategies for Economic Development: Using Ideas and Producing Ideas." In Boris Pleskoric (ed.), *Proceedings of the Annual World Bank Conference on Development Economics*. Washington, D.C.: World Bank.

Romer, Paul M. 1994. "The Origins of Endogenous Growth." *Journal of Economic Perspectives* 8(1):3–22.

Rose-Ackerman, Susan. 1999. *Corruption and Government: Causes and Consequences and Reform*. Cambridge: Cambridge University Press.

Rosenberg, Nathan, and L. E. Birdzell. 1986. *How the West Grew Rich: The Economic Transformation of the Industrial World*. New York: Basic Books.

Rosenblatt, David, and Nicholas Stern. 2003. "Making Privatization Work for Poor People: A Survey of the Issues." Typescript, World Bank Development Research Department, Washington, D.C., September.

Rosenstein-Rodan, Paul. 1943. "Problems of Industrialization of Eastern and South-Eastern Europe." *Economic Journal* 53:202–211.

Rosenzweig, Mark R. 2003. "Payoffs from Panels in Low Income Countries: Economic Development and Economic Mobility." *American Economic Review, Papers and Proceedings* 93(2):112–117.

Rosenzweig, Mark R., and Kenneth I. Wolpin. 1986. "Evaluating the Effects of Optimally Distributed Public Programs: Child Health and Family Planning Interventions." *American Economic Review* 76:470–482.

Rotter, J. B. 1966. "General Expectancies for Internal versus External Control of Reinforcement." *Psychological Monographs* 80(1):1–27.

Sabel, Charles. 1994. "Learning by Monitoring: The Institutions of Economic Development." In N. Smelser and R. Swedberg (eds.), *Handbook of Economic Sociology*. Princeton, N.J.: Princeton University Press and Russell Sage Foundation.

Schelling, Thomas C. 1978. *Micromotives and Macrobehavior*. New York: Norton.

Scherr, Sara. 1999. "Soil Degradation—A Threat to Developing Country Food Security by 2020?" Washington, D.C.: International Food Policy Research Institute.

Schmidt, Klaus M. 1996. "The Costs and Benefits of Privatization: An Incomplete Contracts Approach." *Journal of Law, Economics and Organization* 12(1):1–24.

Schultz, T. Paul. 1987. "School Expenditures and Enrollments, 1960–1980: The Effects of Income, Prices and Population Growth." In D. Gale Johnson and R. Lee (eds.), *Population Growth and Economic Development*. Madison: University of Wisconsin Press.

Schultz, T. Paul. 1998. *Economic Demography*. Northampton, Mass.: Edward Elgar Publications.

Schultz, T. Paul. 2000. "The Impact of *Progresa* on School Enrollments." Washington, D.C.: International Food Policy Research Institute.

Schultz, Theodore W. 1964. *Transforming Traditional Agriculture*. New Haven, Conn.: Yale University Press.

Schumpeter, Joseph. 1934. *The Theory of Economic Development: An Inquiry into Profits, Capital, Credit, Interest, and the Business Cycle*. Cambridge, Mass.: Harvard University Press, 1934.

Schumpeter, Joseph A. 1962. *Capitalism, Socialism and Democracy* (3rd ed.). New York: Harper Torchbooks.

Schumpeter, Joseph. 1989. "The Creative Response in Economic History." In R. V. Clemence (ed.), *Essays: on Entrepreneurs, Innovations, Business Cycles, and the Evolution of Capitalism*. New Brunswick, N.J.: Transaction.

Scott, James C. 1985. *Weapons of the Weak: Everyday Forms of Peasant Resistance*. New Haven, Conn.: Yale University Press.

Scott, James C. 1998. *Seeing Like a State: How Certain Schemes to Improve the Human Condition Have Failed*. New Haven, Conn.: Yale University Press.

Sen, Amartya. 1999. *Development as Freedom*. Oxford: Oxford University Press.

Sen, Amartya. 2000. "Social Exclusion: Concept, Application, and Scrutiny." Social development paper no. 1, Asian Development Bank, Manila.

Sen, Amartya. 2002. *Rationality and Freedom*. Cambridge, Mass.: Harvard University Press.

Senge, Peter. 1990. *The Fifth Discipline: The Art and Practice of the Learning Organization*. New York: Currency Doubleday.

Senge, Peter, Art Kleiner, Charlotte Roberts, et al. 1999. *The Dance of Change: The Challenges to Sustaining Momentum in Learning Organizations*. New York: Currency Doubleday.

Shah, Anwar (ed.). 1995. *Fiscal Incentives for Investment and Innovation.* Washington, D.C.: World Bank.

Shirley, Mary M., and C. Menard. 2002. "Cities Awash: Reforming Urban Water Systems Reform." In M. M. Shirley (ed.), *Thirsting for Efficiency: The Economics and Politics of Urban Water System Reform.* Oxford: Elsevier Press.

Shleifer, Andrei. 1998. "State versus Private Ownership." *Journal of Economic Perspectives* 12(4):133–150.

Shleifer, Andrei, and Daniel Treisman. 2000. *Without a Map: Political Tactics and Economic Reform in Russia.* Cambridge, Mass.: MIT Press.

Shleifer, Andrei, and Robert W. Vishny. 1998. *The Grabbing Hand: Government Pathologies and Their Cures.* Cambridge, Mass.: Harvard University Press.

Simon, Herbert. 1991. *Models of My Life.* New York: Basic Books.

Singer, Hans W. 1950. "The Distribution of Gains between Investing and Borrowing Countries." *American Economic Review* 40:473–485.

Skidelsky, Robert. 2001. *John Maynard Keynes: Fighting for Britain, 1937–1946.* London: Papermac.

Skoufias, Emmanuel, and S. W. Parker. 2001. "Conditional Cash Transfers and Their Impact on Child Work and School Enrollment: Evidence from the *Progresa* Program in Mexico." *Economia* 2(1):45–96.

Smith, James, and Kalanidhi Subbarao. 2002. "What Role for Safety Net Transfers in Very Low Income Countries?" Washington, D.C.: World Bank.

Snodgrass, D., and T. Biggs. 1996. *Industrialization and the Small Firm.* San Francisco: International Center for Economic Growth.

Solow, Robert M. 1956. "A Contribution to the Theory of Economic Growth." *Quarterly Journal of Economics* 70(1):65–94.

Solow, Robert M. 1957. "Technical Change and the Aggregate Production Function." *Review of Economics and Statistics* 39:312–320.

Solow, Robert M. 2000. *Growth Theory: An Exposition* (2nd ed.). New York: Oxford University Press.

Solow, Robert M. 2001. "Applying Growth Theory across Countries." *World Bank Economic Review* 15(2):283–288.

Srinivasan, T. N. 1998. "India's Export Performance." In Isher Judge Ahluwalia and I. M. D. Little (eds.), *India's Economic Reforms and Development: Essays for Manmohan Singh.* Delhi: Oxford University Press.

Srinivasan, T. N. 2004. "Economic Reforms and Global Integration." In Francine R. Frankel and Harry Harding (eds.), *The India-China Relationship: What the United States Needs to Know.* New York: Columbia University Press.

Stark, Oded. 1991. *The Migration of Labor.* Oxford: Basil Blackwell.

Stein, E., and C. Daude. 2002. *Institutions, Integration, and the Location of Foreign Direct Investment.* Washington, D.C.: Inter-American Development Bank Research Department.

Stern, Nicholas. 1989. "The Economics of Development: A Survey." *Economic Journal* 99(397):597–685.

Stern, Nicholas. 1991a. "The Determinants of Growth." *Quarterly Journal of Economics* 101(404):122–133.

Stern, Nicholas. 1991b. "Public Policy and the Economics of Development. Alfred Marshall Lecture." *European Economic Review* 35:241–271.

Stern, Nicholas. 1992. *Le role de l'Etat dans le développement économique.* Lausanne: Editions Payot.

Stern, Nicholas. 1996. "Growth Theories, Old and New, and the Role of Agriculture in Economic Development." FAO Economic and Social Development Paper, Food and Agriculture Organization, Rome.

Stern, Nicholas. 1997. "The World Bank as 'Intellectual Actor.'" In D. Kapur, J. Lewis, and R. Webb (eds.), *The World Bank: Its First Half Century.* Washington, D.C.: Brookings Institution Press.

Stern, Nicholas. 2001. *A Strategy for Development.* Washington, D.C.: World Bank.

Stern, Nicholas. 2002a. "Dynamic Development: Innovation and Inclusion" (Munich Lectures). Lecture delivered at Ludwig Maximilian University, Munich.

Stern, Nicholas. 2002b. "Making Trade Work for Poor People." Lecture delivered in New Delhi, India, November 28. Available at http://econ.worldbank.org/view.php?id=23177.

Stern, Nicholas. 2003. "Investment Climate: Lessons and Challenges." Lecture delivered at the Egyptian Centre for Economic Studies, Cairo, Egypt, January 21.

Stiglitz, Joseph E. 1994. *Whither Socialism?* Cambridge, Mass.: MIT Press.

Stiglitz, Joseph E. 1998. "Towards a New Paradigm for Development." Ninth Raul Prebisch Lecture, delivered at the United Nations Conference for Trade and Development, Geneva, October.

Stiglitz, Joseph, and Jason Furman. 1998. "Economic Crises: Evidence and Insights from East Asia." *Brookings Papers on Economic Activity* 2:1–135.

Summers, Robert, and Alan Heston. 1991. "Penn World Table (Mark 5): An Expanded Set of International Comparisons, 1950–1988." *Quarterly Journal of Economics* 106:327–368.

Summers, Robert, and Alan Heston. 1994. "Differential-Productivity Hypothesis and Purchasing-Power Parities: Some New Evidence." *Review of International Economics* 2:227–243.

Sutton, John. 2002. "Rich Trades, Scarce Capabilities: Industrial Development Revisited." *Economic and Social Review* 33(1):1–22.

Swaroop, Vinaya, and Andrew S. Rajkumar. 2002. "Public Spending and Outcomes: Does Governance Matter?" Policy research working paper no. 2840, World Bank, Washington, D.C., May.

Swartz, D. 2000. *Culture and Power. The Sociology of Pierre Bourdieu.* Chicago: University of Chicago Press.

Syrquin, Moshe, and Hollis Chenery. 1989. "Patterns of Development 1950 to 1983." Discussion paper no. 41, World Bank, Washington, D.C.

Syrquin, Moshe. 1988. "Patterns of Structural Change." In Chenery Hollis and T. N. Srinavasan (eds.), *Handbook of Development Economics*. Amsterdam: Elsevier.

Tanzi, Vito. 1991. *Public Finance in Developing Countries*. Aldershot: Edward Elgar.

Tanzi, Vito, and Howell H. Zee. 2000. "Tax Policy for Emerging Markets: Developing Countries." Working paper WP/00/35, International Monetary Fund, Washington, D.C.

Tawney, Richard H. 1954. *Religion and the Rise of Capitalism*. New York: Mentor Books.

Tawney, Richard H. 1966 (1932). *Land and Labor in China*. Boston: Beacon Press.

Taylor, Alan M., and Jeffrey G. Williamson. 1997. "Convergence in the Age of Mass Migration." *Economic Review of Economic History* 1(1):27–63.

Tendler, Judith. 1997. *Good Government in the Tropics*. Baltimore: Johns Hopkins University Press.

Thaler, Richard H. 1991. *Quasi Rational Economics*. New York: Russell Sage Foundation.

Thomas, Duncan, Elizabeth Frankenberg, Kathleen Beegle, and Graciela Teruel. 1999. "Household Budgets, Household Composition and the Crisis in Indonesia: Evidence from Longitudinal Household Survey Data." Paper presented at the 1999 Population Association Meetings of America, New York.

Tian, Xiaowen. 2001. "Privatization and Economic Performance: Evidence from Chinese Provinces." *Economic Systems* 25(1):65–77.

Turner, John F. C. 1976. *Housing by People: Towards Autonomy in Building Environments*. London: Marion Boyars.

Tybout, J. 1999. "Manufacturing Firms in Developing Countries: How Well Do They Do and Why?" *Journal of Economic Literature* 38(1):11–45.

Tyson, Laura d'Andrea, Tea Petrin, and F. Halsey Rogers. 1994. "Promoting Entrepreneurship in Eastern Europe." *Small Business Economics* 6(3):165–184.

UNAIDS/WHO (United Nations AIDS Programme/World Health Organization). 2003. *AIDS Epidemic Update: December 2003*. Geneva: UNAIDS and World Health Organization.

UNDP (United Nations Development Programme), UNEP (United Nations Environment Programme), World Bank, and WRI (World Resources Institute). 1999. *World Resources 1998–99: A Guide to the Global Environment*. New York: United Nations.

Van de Walle, Dominique, and Dileni Gunewardena. 2001. "Sources of Ethnic Inequality in Viet Nam." *Journal of Development Economics* 65(2001):177–207.

Verdier, Thierry. 2000. "Education as an Engine of Political and Cultural Change?" German Foundation for International Development. Available at http://www.dse.de/ef/instn/verdier.htm.

Vijverberg, Wim, and Jonathan Haughton. 2002. "Household Enterprises in Vietnam: Survival, Growth and Living Standards." Working paper no. 2773, World Bank, Washington, D.C.

Von Weizsacker, Carl Christian. 1971. "Notes on Endogenous Change in Tastes." *Journal of Economic Theory* 3:345–372.

Wacziarg, R. 1998. "Measuring Dynamic Gains from Trade." Policy research working paper no. 2001, World Bank, Washington, D.C.

Wade, Robert. 1990. *Governing the Market: Economic Theory and the Role of Government in East Asian Industrialization*. Princeton, N.J.: Princeton.

Wagstaff, Adam. 2003. *The Millennium Development Goals for Health: Rising to the Challenges*. Washington, D.C.: World Bank.

Wagstaff, A., and E. Van Dooerslaer. 2003. "Catastrophe and Impoverishment in Paying for Health Care, with Applications to Vietnam, 1993–98." *Health Economics* 12(1):921–934.

Weick, Karl. 1979. *The Social Psychology of Organizing*. New York: Random House.

White, Robin, Siobhan Murray, and Mark Rohweder. 2002. "Pilot Analysis of Global Ecosystems (PAGE): Grass Lands Ecosystems." Washington, D.C.: World Resources Institute.

Williamson, John. 1990. *Latin American Adjustment: How Much Has Happened*? Washington, D.C.: Institute for International Economics.

Williamson, John (ed.). 1994. *The Political Economy of Policy Reform*. Washington, D.C.: Institute for International Economics.

Williamson, John. 2002. "Did the Washington Consensus Fail?" Center for Strategic and International Studies, Washington, D.C., November.

Williamson, John. 2003. "The Washington Consensus and Beyond." *Economic and Political Weekly*. Available at http://www.iie.com/publications/papers/williamson1102.htm.

Wood, Adrian. 2003. "A New Definition of Pro-poor Growth." Typescript, UK Department for International Development, London, July 28.

Woolcock, Michael, and Deepa Narayan. 2001. "Social Capital: Implications for Development Theory, Research, and Policy." *World Bank Research Observer* 15(2):225–249.

Wolfensohn, J. D. 1999. "A Proposal for a Comprehensive Development Framework (A Discussion Draft)." Washington, D.C.: World Bank.

World Bank. 1990. *World Development Report 1990: Poverty*. New York: Oxford University Press.

World Bank. 1993. *World Development Report 1993: Investing in Health*. New York: Oxford University Press.

World Bank. 1994. *World Development Report 1994: Infrastructure for Development*. New York: Oxford University Press.

World Bank. 1998a. *Assessing Aid: What Works, What Doesn't, and Why*. Washington, D.C.: World Bank.

World Bank. 1998b. *Global Economic Prospects, 1998/99: Beyond Financial Crisis*. Washington, D.C.: World Bank.

World Bank. 1998c. *World Development Report 1998/99: Knowledge for Development*. Washington, D.C.: Oxford University Press.

World Bank. 2000a. *Reforming Public Institutions and Strengthening Governance*. Washington, D.C.: World Bank.

World Bank. 2000b. *Making Transition Work for Everyone.* Washington, D.C.: World Bank.

World Bank. 2000c. *Can Africa Claim the 21st Century?* Washington, D.C.: World Bank.

World Bank. 2001a. *World Development Report 2002: Building Institutions for Markets.* Washington, D.C.: Oxford University Press.

World Bank. 2001b. *World Development Indicators 2001.* Washington, D.C.: World Bank.

World Bank. 2001c. *World Development Report 2000/2001: Attacking Poverty.* New York: Oxford University Press.

World Bank. 2001d. *Engendering Development: Through Gender Equality in Rights, Resources, and Voice.* New York: Oxford University Press.

World Bank. 2001e. "Environment Strategy Paper: Making Sustainable Commitments." Washington, D.C.: World Bank.

World Bank. 2001f. *Finance for Growth: Policy Choices in a Volatile World.* Washington, D.C.: Oxford University Press.

World Bank. 2001g. *Adjustment Lending Retrospective.* Washington, D.C.: World Bank, Operations Policy and Country Services.

World Bank. 2001h. *Albania Public Expenditure and Institutional Review.* Washington, D.C.: World Bank.

World Bank. 2002a. *Uzbekistan Living Standards Assessment.* Washington, D.C.: World Bank.

World Bank. 2002b. *Global Development Finance: Financing the Poorest Countries.* Washington, D.C.: World Bank.

World Bank. 2002c. *Globalization, Growth and Poverty: Building an Inclusive World Economy.* Washington, D.C.: World Bank.

World Bank. 2002d. *World Development Report 2003: Sustainable Development in a Dynamic World.* New York: Oxford University Press.

World Bank. 2002e. "The Role and Effectiveness of Development Assistance: Lessons from World Bank Experience." Washington, D.C.: World Bank.

World Bank. 2002f. *Transition. The First Ten Years.* Washington, D.C.: World Bank.

World Bank. 2002g. *The Right to Tell: The Role of Mass Media in Economic Development.* Washington, D.C.: World Bank.

World Bank. 2003a. *World Development Report 2004: Making Services Work for Poor People.* Washington, D.C.: Oxford University Press.

World Bank. 2003b. *Doing Business in 2004.* New York: Oxford University Press.

World Bank. 2003c. *Global Development Finance 2003: Striving for Stability in Development Finance.* Washington, D.C.: World Bank.

World Bank. 2003d. *Global Economic Prospects 2003: Investing to Unlock Global Opportunities.* Washington, D.C.: World Bank.

World Bank. 2003e. "Improving the Investment Climate in China." Washington, D.C.: World Bank.

World Bank. 2003f. "Ramping Up Investment Climate Surveys to Spur Change." Washington, D.C.: World Bank.

World Bank. 2003g. *World Development Indicators 2003*. Washington, D.C.: World Bank.

World Bank. 2003h. *Private Participation in Infrastructure: Trends in Developing Countries in 1990–2001*. Washington, D.C.: World Bank.

World Bank. 2003i. *Global Economic Prospects 2004: Realizing the Development Promise of the Doha Agenda*. Washington, D.C.: World Bank.

World Bank. 2003j. *Land Policies for Growth and Poverty Reduction*. Washington, D.C.: World Bank.

World Bank. 2003k. "Supporting Sound Policies with Adequate and Appropriate Financing." Washington, D.C.: World Bank.

World Bank. 2004a. *World Development Report 2005: A Better Investment Climate for Everyone*. Washington, D.C.: Oxford University Press.

World Bank. 2004b. Reforming Infrastructure: Privatization, Regulation, and Competition. World Bank Policy Research Report, Washington, D.C.: World Bank.

World Bank and CII (Confederation of Indian Industry). 2002. "Improving the Investment Climate in India." Washington, D.C.: World Bank, February.

World Health Organization. 2000. *The World Health Report 2000: Health Systems: Improving Performance*. Geneva: WHO.

World Health Organization/UNICEF Joint Monitoring Programme. 2001. DPT Immunization Data. Available at http://www.childinfo.org/eddb/immuni/trends.htm.

Yanikkaya, Halit. 2003. "Trade Openness and Economic Growth: A Cross-Country Empirical Relationship." *Journal of Development Economics* 72:57–89.

Yergin, Daniel, and Joseph Stanislaw. 2002. *The Commanding Heights: The Battle for the World Economy* (rev. ed.). New York: Free Press.

Young, Allyn. 1928. "Increasing Returns and Economic Progress." *Economic Journal* 38:527–542.

Young, Frank. 1971. "A Macroeconomic Interpretation of Entrepreneurship." In Peter Kilby (ed.), *Entrepreneurship and Economic Development*. New York: Free Press.

Zak, Paul, and Stephen Knack. 2001. "Trust and Growth." *Economic Journal* 111:295–321.

Zakaria, Fareed. 1997. "The Rise of Illiberal Democracy." *Foreign Affairs*, November. 76(6):22–43.

Zingales, Luigi. 1998. "Corporate Governance." In P. Newman (ed.), *The Palgrave Dictionary of Economics and the Law*. London: Macmillan.

Index

Abraham, Anita, 151–152
Acemoglu, Daron, 137, 171, 202, 210, 268–271, 281
Acs, Zoltan, 238
Action, xvi–xvii, xxiii–xxiv, xxix–xxxiv, 354–355. *See also* Policy
  accountability and, 319–320, 331–332
  domestic revenue basis for, 333–347
  fiscal discipline and, 321–324, 345–347
  future directions for, 387–389
  good governance and, 317–318
  increased aid and, 368–385
  levels of, 334–335
  macroeconomic stability and, 321–324
  Millennium Development Goals and, 290–313, 385
  physical infrastructure and, 318
  public finances and, 315–317, 324–333
  state's role and, 315–321
  trade policy and, 359–368
  two-pillar strategy and, 136–139 (*see also* Two-pillar strategy)
Afghanistan, 249
Africa, x–xi, 7, 9–10, 85
  aid and, 368, 376–377, 380–381
  Country Policy and Institutional Assessments (CPIAs) and, 321
  decline of, 33, 39–40
  disease and, 17, 22–23
  empowerment and, 100
  government role and, 87–88, 215
  growth patterns in, 39
  HIV/AIDS and, 17, 23
  income distribution and, 46–47
  international trade and, 61–69
  Millennium Development Goals and, 298, 300, 313

New Partnership for Africa's Development and, 289
Onchocerciasis Control Program and, 382
  pensions and, 240
  preferences and, 251
  public spending and, 325
  stagnation in, 33
  subsidies and, 365–366
  tariffs and, 263
  trade policy and, 360–361, *363*
  transition management and, 213
African Development Bank, 321, 378
African Growth and Opportunity Act, 363
Aghion, Phillipe, xx, 114, 202, 204, 276
Agriculture, 110–111, 153, 268, 403n2
  China and, 282
  diffusion effects and, 210–211
  Green Revolution and, 210–211
  off-farm SMEs and, 233–239
  subsidies and, 365–366
  trade policy and, 263, 364–368
Ahluwalia, Montek, 159
Ahmad, Ehtisham, xvi, xix, 335, 340, 343–344
Aid
  amount needed, 371–372
  Cold War effects and, 369–370, 385
  conditionality and, 378–379
  countries with weak governance and, 376–378
  declining levels of, 368–371
  disease and, 381–383
  Dutch disease effects and, 373–374
  effectiveness and, 368–376
  environmental, 383

Aid (cont.)
  fungibilty of, 370–371
  Global Fund to Fight AIDS, Tuberculosis,
    and Malaria, 383
  global public goods and, 382–384
  increasing of, 368–385
  international debt forgiveness and, 384–
    385
  international financial institutions and,
    378–382
  Millennium Development Goals and,
    371–372, 375–376, 380
  NGOs and, 377–378
  OED and, 379–380
Ait Iktel du Développement, 259
Ajwad, Mohamed Ihsan, 231
Akerlof, George, 262
Albania, 312
Alert, Lucie, xix
Alesina, Alberto, 80, 187, 217, 280
Algeria, 133, 136
All India Institute for Public Health and
  Hygiene, 260
Amin, Samir, 94
Anand, Sudhir, xx
Anatomy of Racial Inequality, The (Loury),
  249, 251
Anderson, Elijah, 246, 250–251
Angola, 349
Angrist, Joshua, 196–197
"Animal spirits," 205
Anthropologists, 243, 250
Appadurai, Arjun, 102, 229, 249, 263
Argentina, 201, 216, 324, 351
Armenia, 92
Arrow, Kenneth, 109, 113, 201, 209, 256
Asia, 9–10, 252, 358
  aid and, 368
  Country Policy and Institutional
    Assessments (CPIAs) and, 321
  debt and, 322
  disease and, 22
  financial crisis of, 322
  gender issues and, 28–29
  government role and, 87–88
  green revolution and, 211
  growth patterns in, 38–39
  income distribution and, 46
  inflation and, 131
  international trade and, 61–69
  legal reform and, 90–91
  migration and, 69

  Millennium Development Goals and, 300,
    313
  NGOs and, 151–153, 247
  preferences and, 247
  subsidies and, 365
  trade policy and, 360–361, 365
  transition management and, 213
Asian Development Bank, 321, 378
Asian Drama (Myrdal), 57
Assessing Aid: What Works, What Doesn't,
  and Why (World Bank), 369–370
Aten, Bettina, 201
Atkinson, Tony, xvi, 103
Attrition, 172–173
Audretsch, D., 238
Australia, 330
Austrian school, 89, 209, 255–256, 397n2
Autocracy, 393n14
Aw, B. Y., 96

Backward economy, 210
Bagg, Walter, 237
Bailey, F. G., 145, 273
Balcerowicz, Leszek, 282
Banerjee, Abhijit, xx, 202, 240, 268, 274–
  275
Bangladesh, 5, 94, 312
  female education in, 154
  government inspections in, 138
  Grameen Bank and, 355
  poverty and, 98
  Rural Advancement Committee (BRAC),
    247–248, 252
  trade policy and, 365
Baran, Paul, 94
Barbados, 366
Bardhan, Pranab, 151
Barnett, Steven, 350
Barro, Robert, 209
Batra, Geeta, 176, 212, 338, 342
Bauer, Peter, 157
Baumol, William J., 222
Becker, Gary, 249–251, 254–255
Behavioral factors, 19, 397n8
  entrepreneurship and, 222
  investment and, 214–221 (see also
    Investment)
  preferences and, 243–265
  two-pillar strategy and, 127–145
  vulnerability and, 20–24
Behrman, Jere R., 26
Belarus, 216

Bénabou, Roland, 276
Benin, 366
Berlin, Isaiah, 258
Berlin Wall, x
Besley, Timothy, xx, 154, 217, 230, 232
Bhagwati, Jagdish, 339
Bhalla, Surjit, 11
Bhatt, Ela, 229
Big bang reform, 281–282
Biggs, Tyler, 236
Biodiversity, 56, 383
Bird, Richard, 344
Blanchard, Olivier, 217
Blanchflower, David G., 188
Bliss, Christopher, xiii, 111, 273, 275
Bobonis, Gustavo, 197
Bolivia, 153, 231
Bolsa Escola program, 242
Bolton, Patrick, 276
Boserup, Esther, 109–110, 121, 145
Botero, Fernando, 217
Bourdieu, Pierre, 250
Bourguignon, François, xx, 159, 183, 189,
    194–195
  development policy and, 44, 46–50, 98–99
  living standards and, 9–11, 26–27
  politics and, 271
  public spending and, 328
  redistribution and, 241–242
Boyce, Simone, 154
Braudel, Fernand, 79
Brazil, 154, 183
  Bolsa Escola program, 242
  empowerment and, 101, 231–232, 240
  income distribution and, 49
  living standards and, 26–27, 31
  security and, 189
  taxes and, 336, 346
Bretton Woods system, 38, 70–71
Bribes, 136–138, 311
Bride-prices, 29
British Association for the Advancement
    of Science, 103
Bruno, Michael, 157
Burgess, Robin, xx, 154, 217, 232, 324, 334–
    335, 342, 344
Business Environment Risk Intelligence
    (BERI), 187
Butler, R. A., 283

Cambodia, 249
Canada, 139, 362

Capabilities, 21. *See also* Empowerment
  development economics and, 84–85
  empowerment and, 103–105
  government and, 320–321
  institutional environment and, 186–187
  Millennium Development Goals and, 303
  preferences and, 254, 263–264
Capitalism, 38–39
Capital output ratio, 112–113
Cardoso, Fernando Henrique, 94
Carter, N. G., 159
Carvalho Filho, Irineu Evangelista de, 240
Case, Anne, 230, 240
Caste system. *See* Class systems
Central planning, 117–119, 157, 158
Centre for Economic Studies, ix
Chang, Ha-Joon, 268
Chattopadhyay, R., 230–231, 354
Chaudhury, Nazmul, 151, 355
Chen, Shaohua, 5, 7–9, 11, 46, 48, 168, 184
Chenery, Hollis, xiv, 50, 109, 157–159
Children. *See* Education; Mortality rates
Chile, 96, 280, 348, 351, 367
China, xiii, 5, 25, 40, 44, 111
  bride-prices and, 29
  consumption data and, 170
  Country Policy and Institutional
    Assessments (CPIAs) and, 80
  Cultural Revolution, x
  female infanticides and, 28–29
  fertility and, 29
  governmental changes and, 215
  government corruption and, 138
  household responsibility system and, 354
  infrastructure services and, 133
  integration and, 94–95
  international trade and, 60, 62, 66, 68–69,
    360, 367
  investment and, 202
  migration and, 69
  National Bureau of Statistics and, 180
  politics and, 230
  poverty and, 8–9, 31–32, 98
  preferences and, 246–247
  privatization and, 350
  PRSPs and, 305
  reform and, 91, 282
  SMEs and, 237–238
  technology and, 366
  transition management and, 213
  transparency and, 132
Chinese Communist Party, 230

Chinese National People's Congress, 230
Chlorofluorocarbons (CFCs), 58, 292
Chung, S., 96
Civil war, 93
Clarke, George R. G., 351
Class systems, 13, 142, 145
  Dalit groups and, 226–227
  elitism and, 269–270, 272
  empowerment and, 226
  exclusion and, 25–27, 103–105, 273–277, 359–364
  insurance and, 275–276
  Jatabs and, 227
  preferences and, 249–252
  religion and, 250
  SEWA and, 226–227
Clements, Benedict, 325
Climate change, 58
Clothing, 367
Club of Rome, 57–58
Coase, Ronald, 268
Coasian bargaining, 118
Cochran, Thomas, 222
Cold War, 106, 289, 369–370, 385
Coleman, James, 92, 143
Collective bargaining, 230
Collier, Paul, xix, 39, 94, 108, 349, 375–376
Colombia, 96, 153, 197–198, 216
Commission on Human Security, 23–24, 188
Communism, x, 230
Computers. See Technology
Confederation of Indian Industry (CII), 177
Consultative Group for Agricultural Research (CGIAR), 57, 382
Contract enforcement, 139
Corruption, 136–138, 344–345
Costa Rica, 31, 237, 324
Côte d'Ivoire, 30
Credit, 21, 92, 216, 274–275, 322, 358
Crime, 188–189
Cronyism, 226
Cultural Revolution, x
Customs officials, 344–345

Dahms, Harry, 222
Dalit groups, 226–227
Dasgupta, Monica, xx, 29, 92, 248
Data, xxix–xxxii
  aid and, 383–384
  attrition and, 172–173

collection challenges and, 169
evaluation methods for, 192–198
Family Life Surveys, 191
household surveys and, 6–10, 167–171, 183–184, 191–192
interpretation of, 169
investment climate measurement and, 173–182
Kecamatan Development Project and, 228
Keynesian aggregate theory and, 167
Living Standards Measurement Survey (LSMS) and, 172, 189, 191
Local-Level Institutions Survey, 189
Millennium Development Goals and, 306–312
mortality rates and, 184–185
panel, 171–173
PETSs and, 190–192
QSDSs and, 190–192
randomization and, 196–198
security and, 188–189
social security groups and, 171–172
Social Weather Stations (SWS) and, 227–228
Datt, Gaurav, 5, 11, 44–45
Davis, Jeffrey, 236
Deaton, Angus, xx, 5, 7, 12, 20, 44, 169–171, 184, 197, 240, 395n1
Debt, 322–323, 357–358
  HIPCs and, 294, 330, 384–385
  international forgiveness of, 384–385
Decentralization, 149–152
De Ferranti, David, 99, 203
Deforestation, 56, 383
Dehn, Jan, 190, 192
Deininger, Klaus, 98, 159
DeLong, J. Bradford, 198
Demigurç-Kunt, Asli, xx
Democracy, x, 80, 82, 229–230, 270–271, 393n14
Democratic Republic of Congo. See Zaire
Demombynes, G., 14
Deng, Xiao Ping, x, 8–9
Denison, Edward, 201
Denmark, 372
Dependencia schools, 94
Dependency ratios, 12, 53–54
de Soto, Hernando, 100, 222, 355
Dethier, Jean-Jacques, ix, 14, 93, 129, 282
Devarajan, Shantayanan, xix, 106–107, 312–313, 370

Development
  agriculture and, 110–111
  capabilities and, 84–85
  choice and, 3
  civil war effects and, 93
  cross-border financial flows and, 70–74
  different approaches to, 156–163
  as dynamic process, 86–87
  empowerment and, 99–106 (see also
    Empowerment)
  environmental change and, 55–59
  foreign assistance and, 106–108
  integration and, 59–74, 94–98
  international trade and, 60–69
  living standards and, x–xi, xxiv, 3–32,
    49–59, 90–94, 109, 168–172
  MDGs and, 290–313 (see also Millennium
    Development Goals)
  objectives of, 83–86
  population changes and, 51–53
  post–World War II era and, 34–35, 61–62,
    84
  preferences and, 243–265
  recent global changes and, x–xii, 1
  structural changes to society and, 49–55
  trade barriers and, 359–368
  transition management and, 213
  two-pillar strategy and, 147–163 (see also
    Two-pillar strategy)
  World War II era and, 34–35
Development as Freedom (Sen), 20, 182,
    393n3
Development economics, ix, xvi, 110-112
  different approaches to, 156–163
  future directions for, 387–389
  lessons for, 109-123, 289
Dewey, John, 260
Diamond, Peter, xx, 109
Diamonds, 39
Diffusion, 201, 210–211
"Direct-and-protect" approach, 156
Disability-adjusted life-years (DALYs), 22
Discrimination, 25–27
Disease. See Health issues
Djankov, Simeon, 91, 138, 217
Doha trade talks, xi, xxxiii, 367, 384, 389
Dollar, David, xix, 98, 106–108, 131, 181,
    212, 313, 344, 375
DPT3 immunization, 23
Drèze, Jean, xiii, 4, 111
Drinking, 20
Drugs, 246

Duflo, Esther, 197, 230–231, 240–241, 354
Dupuit, Jules, 116
Dutch disease, 373–374
Dynamic increasing growth, 207–212
Dynamic processes, 86–87
  empowerment and, 225–242
  panel data and, 171–173
  policy and, 119–123
  preferences and, 243–265
  redistribution and, 239–242

Easterlin, Richard A., 88, 188
Easterly, William, 321
Eckersley, Richard, 188
Ecole Polytechnique, xiii
Economic mobility, 29–31
Economics of Discrimination, The (Becker),
    249
Educación con participación de la
    comunidad (EDUCO), 100–101, 152, 192
Education, xxvi, 203, 240, 287
  aid and, 370–371
  bandwagon effect and, 223
  dynamic processes and, 87
  elitism and, 272
  gender issues and, 27–28, 142–143, 164,
    243, 247–248
  income and, 85, 271–272
  increase in, 243
  India and, 331–332
  innovation and, 221–223
  institutions and, 218
  MDGS and, 290 (see also Millennium
    Development Goals)
  panel data and, 171
  parental, 183
  policy agenda and, 317–318
  poverty and, 12, 16–18, 21, 271
  preferences and, 151–153, 246–249
  public spending and, 329
  service delivery and, 149–155
  shocks and, 196
  SMEs and, 238
  surveys and, 168
  trade policy and, 360
  transparency and, 331–332
Egypt, 62, 139
Electoral systems, 229–230
Elitism, 269–270, 272
Ellerman, David, xix, 397n1
El Salvador, 152, 192
Elwan, Ann, 12

Empowerment, xiv–xv, xxiii, xxviii–xix, 394n7
  capabilities and, 21, 84–85, 103–105, 186–187, 254, 263–264, 303, 320–321
  concept of, 85, 99–100, 102, 184–185
  cross-border financial flows and, 70–74
  decentralization and, 149–152
  decision making and, 100
  democratic elections and, 229–230
  determinants of, 102–103
  dynamic processes and, 119–123
  education and, 184 (see also Education)
  enhancement of, 100–102
  environmental issues and, 49–59
  evaluation of, 152–155
  exclusion and, 25–27, 103–105, 273–277, 359–364
  gender issues and, 142–143, 226
  independence and, 184
  indicators for, 184–188
  institutional structure and, 90–94, 100–102, 186–187
  insurance and, 275–276
  international trade and, 60–69
  investment and, 139, 142–145, 148–155
  measurement of, 184–188
  Millennium Development Goals and, 290–313
  mobility and, 183
  obstacle removal and, 226–228
  opportunity and, 182–184
  ownership and, 100
  panel data and, 171
  participation and, 142, 226–231
  PETSs and, 190–192
  politics and, 229–230
  practical steps for, 229–231
  preferences and, 243–265
  privatization and, 347–353
  programs for, 100–101
  QSDSs and, 190–192
  redistribution and, 239–242
  report cards for, 229
  research challenges in, 232–233
  service delivery and, 149–152
  SEWA and, 226–227
  SMEs and, 233–239
  Social Weather Stations (SWS) and, 227–228
  societal structural change and, 49–55
  transparency and, 101–102
Engerman, Stanley L., 269

Entrepreneurship, xxiii, 121, 182
  aggregate, 157–158
  barriers to, 111, 136–139
  education and, 221–223
  ethics and, 136–138
  government and, 87–88, 136–138, 215
  incentives for, 111
  infrastructure services and, 133–136, 219–221
  innovation and, 221–223
  investment and, 179 (see also Investment)
  poverty and, 14, 16
  prestige and, 222
  privatization and, 347–353
  regulatory approaches and, 138–139
  SEWA and, 226–227, 229
  small/medium enterprises and, 233–239
  taxes and, 334–347
  two-pillar strategy and, 128–139, 146–148
Entry regulations, 139
Environmental issues, 39–40, 55, 59, 132
  aid for, 383
  biodiversity loss and, 56
  CFCs and, 58, 292
  CGIAR and, 57
  climate change and, 58
  Club of Rome and, 57–58
  deforestation and, 56, 383
  disaster response and, 90
  fisheries depletion and, 56–57, 383
  legal reform and, 90–91
  MDGs and, 288 (see also Millennium Development Goals)
  Montreal Protocol and, 58, 382
  pollution and, 56, 118
  privatization and, 349
  soil degeneration and, 56
  water and, 56, 293, 296, 366, 383
  World Summit on Sustainable Development and, 288
Epstein, Scarlett, 173, 273
"Equality of agency," 263
Equations, 206
Equilibrium
  aid and, 368–385
  dynamic processes and, 86–87
  exclusion and, 276–277
  incentives and, 321
  macroeconomic stability and, 321–324
  multiple, 210
  Pareto optimality and, 117–118, 255–256

politics and, 271
two-pillar strategy and, 130
Estache, Antonio, 350–351
Ethics, 118–119, 264
  bribes and, 136–138, 311
  cronyism and, 226
  customs and, 344–345
  exclusion and, 103–105, 273–277
  government and, 136–138, 215, 229–230
  preferences and, 257–258
  reform and, 267–283
  Transparency International and, 310–311
Ethiopia, 324, 336, 377
Ethnicity, 142–144
  drugs and, 246
  empowerment and, 226
  living standards and, 25–27
  preferences and, 249–251
Europe, x
  Country Policy and Institutional
    Assessments (CPIAs) and, 321
  Everything But Arms initiative and, 363
  government role and, 87–88
  industrial revolution and, 35
  reform processes and, 211
  trade policy and, 61–69, 263, 362–363,
    365
  transition management and, 213
  unemployment and, 202–203
  Washington consensus and, 162
European Bank for Reconstruction and
  Development
  (EBRD), ix, xiii, 111, 146, 176, 321
Evaluation, 152–155
  effective methods for, 192–198
  in multiple layers, 193–196
  randomization and, 196–198
Everything But Arms initiative, 363
Exclusion, 103–105, 275. See also Inclusion
  costs of, 361–364
  equilibrium and, 276–277
  gender issues and, 273–274
  living standards and, 25–27
  sources of, 361–364
  trade policy and, 359–364
Exercise, 20

Family Life Surveys, 191
Fardoust, Shahrokh, xix
Fernandez, Raquel, 281
Ferreira, Francisco, 26–27, 49, 183, 242,
  275–276, 399n4

Fertility rates, 20, 85, 231
  migration and, 70
  population changes and, 51–53
  poverty and, 29
Field, Erica, 240
Fields, Gary, 5, 237
Filmer, Deon, 149
Firms
  accountability and, 319–320
  adaptability and, 212–213
  data issues and, 171–192
  governments and, 205
  investment and, 214–221 (see also
    Investment)
  privatization and, 347–353
  taxes and, 334–347
Fischer, Greg, xix, 397n1
Fischer, Stanley, 131
Fisheries, 56–57, 383
Fogel, Robert W., 296
Food, 23, 57, 154, 287, 291
Foreign direct investment (FDI), 71, 106–
  108, 132, 358–359
Foster, Andrew, 171, 210
Fournier, M., 271
Frank, André Gunder, 94
Frankel, Jeffrey, 131
Frankenberg, Elizabeth, 171
Freedom House, 80, 187
Frey, Bruno, 188
Friedman, Milton, 159, 244
Fukuyama, Francis, 92
Furman, Jason, 322
Furubotn, Eirik, 261

Gabon, 348
Galiani, Sebastian, 351
Gallup, 75
Galor, O., 274
Gandhi, Mohandas K., 3, 104, 251, 355
Garcia-Thoumi, Ines, xix
Gaviria, Alejandro, 26
Gender issues, xxxi
  bride-prices and, 29
  childbirth and, 23–24
  China and, 248
  education and, 27–28, 142–143, 164, 243,
    247–248
  empowerment and, 142–143, 226
  female infanticides and, 28–29
  India and, 28–29, 248
  Korea and, 28–29, 248

Gender issues (cont.)
  MDGs and, 290 (*see also* Millennium
    Development Goals)
  ownership and, 28
  politics and, 231, 271
  poverty and, 25–29
  preferences and, 246, 253–254, 257–258
  SEWA and, 226–227
  sex industry and, 259–260
  surveys and, 168
  wartime and, 249
General Agreement on Tariffs and Trade
  (GATT), 61
Georgia, 92
Germany, x, 122, 249
Gertler, Paul, 23, 154, 240, 242, 351
Gevers, Coralie, xix
Ghatak, Maitreesh, 240
Ghobarah, H. A., 22
Giavazzi, Francesco, 217
Gibbons, Donna M., 171
Gini coefficient or index, 27, 45, 47, 49
Glewwe, Paul, 23, 168, 171, 196, 395n1
Global Fund to Fight AIDS, Tuberculosis,
  and Malaria, 383
Globalization
  Doha negotiations and, xi, xxxiii, 367,
    384, 389
  economic integration and, 59–74
  environmental issues and, 55–59
  financial flows and, 70–74
  future direction for, 387–389
  global partnerships and, 293–294
  growth patterns and, 39–43
  income distribution and, 46–49
  increased aid and, 368–385
  integration and, 59–74, 94–98
  international debt forgiveness and, 384–
    385
  international financial institutions and,
    311–312
  migration and, 69–70
  MDGs and, 293–294 (*see also* Millennium
    Development Goals)
  population changes and, 51–53
  poverty reduction and, 287–290
  public goods and, 382–384
  structural society change and, 49–55
  trade issues and, 60–69, 359–368
  urbanization and, 53–55
Globalization, Growth, and Poverty (World
  Bank), 60

Goldin, Claudia, 17, 85, 287, 301
Goldin, Ian, xix
Gómez-Lobo, Andrés, 351
Government, xiii–xiv, xvii, xxxii–xxxiii.
    See also Policy
  accountability and, 302–306, 319–320,
    331–332
  aid and, 368–385
  bureaucratic obstacles and, 136–139, 147,
    180, 211, 216–219
  capacity of, 320–321
  changes in, 215–216
  civil war effects and, 93
  conflict of interest and, 280–281
  corruption and, 136–138, 344–345
  cross-country regressions and, 114
  debt and, 322–324, 384–385
  by discussion, 260–261
  domestic revenue and, 333–347
  dynamic processes and, 87
  education and, 249
  elitism and, 269–270
  empowerment and, 229 (*see also*
    Empowerment)
  entrepreneurship and, 87–88
  environmental issues and, 55–59
  ethics and, 136–138, 229–230, 344–345
  failure of, 117
  firms and, 205
  fiscal discipline and, 321–324, 345–347
  gender issues and, 248
  global growth patterns and, 39–43
  importance of, 90–94
  incentive creation and, 89
  institutions and, 78–82, 90–94
  investment and, 136–139
  "kicking away the ladder" and, 268
  legal reform and, 90–91
  macroeconomic stability and, 321–324
  markets and, 87–89
  MDGs and, 288–313 (*see also* Millennium
    Development Goals)
  nation-building and, 92
  "night watchman" view of, 88
  optimal size of, 325
  physical infrastructure and, 318
  preferences and, 245–246
  private sector competition and, 91–92
  privatization and, 347–353
  public spending and, 316, 321–324 (*see
    also* Public spending)
  rent-seeking and, 130

service delivery and, 149–155
state's role and, 315–321
subsidies and, 322, 351, 364–366
trade policy and, 60–69, 131–132, 359–368
two-pillar strategy and, 128–139, 146–148 (*see also* Two-pillar strategy)
village chiefs and, 230
Gradstein, Mark, 270–271
Gradualism, 282
Grass, Martina, xx
Great Depression, 34–35, 61, 156–157
Green Revolution, 210–211
Greif, Avner, 216
Griliches, Zvi, 201, 211
Grootaert, Christiaan, 30, 92
Gros, Daniel, 38, 392n2
Grosh, Margaret E., 168, 171, 395n1
Gross Domestic Product (GDP), 34. *See also* Measurement
China and, 62
integration and, 95
international trade and, 62, 68
public spending and, 324–328
tax policy and, 334–335, 345–347
Growth, xiv–xvi, 392n5
accelerating, 207–212
analysis implications for, 74–82
Country Policy and Institutional Assessments (CPIAs) and, 80, 320–321
Dutch disease and, 373–374
dynamic processes and, 119–123
economic mobility and, 29–31
education and, 85
elitism and, 269–270
empirics of, 212–213
empowerment and, 83–84, 226 (*see also* Empowerment)
environmental issues and, 49–59
exclusion and, 273–277
firm destruction and, 95–96
fiscal discipline and, 321–324
foreign assistance and, 106–108
global capital flow and, 70–74
government role and, 78–82, 87–89
Great Depression and, 34–35, 61, 156–157
historical data for, 34–37, 41–43
industrialization and, 34–35, 269
inequality and, 43–49
innovation and, 201, 204–205
institutions and, 78–82, 90–94, 202

integration and, 59–74, 94–98
inverted U hypothesis, 158–159
"kicking away the ladder" and, 268
lessons for, 112–115
macroeconomic stability and, 321–324
Millennium Development Goals and, 290–313
openness and, 94–98
patterns of, 34–43
poverty and, 43–49 (*see also* Poverty)
reforms and, 107–108, 267–283
relative, 202–203
societal changes and, 49–55
Solow model and, 112–113, 200–201
statistical concerns of, 75–78
technology and, 201, 204–205 (*see also* Technology)
theory of, xvi, 112-115
trade policy and, 60–69, 131–132, 359–368
transition management and, 212–213
transparency and, 131–132
two-pillar strategy for, 127–163 (*see also* Two-pillar strategy)
understanding causes of, 200–213
unemployment and, 202–203
World War II era and, 34–35
Gruber, J., 23
Guatemala, 13, 26
Guinea-Bissau, 374
Gunewardena, Dileni, 25
Gunning, Jan Willem, 39, 108
Gupta, Sanjeev, 325
Gurgand, G., 271
Gurr, Ted Robert, 80, 82

Haberler, Gottfried, 157
Haddad, M., 95
Haiti, 83
Hall, Robert, 75, 137, 171, 202
Hallward-Driemeier, Mary, 181, 212, 344
Haltiwanger, John, 236
Hammer, Jeffrey S., 149, 355
Hange, Ulrich, xx
Harijans, 104
Harrison, A., 95
Harrod-Domar model, 112–113
Haughton, Jonathan, 237
Hausmann, Ricardo, 218, 339
Hayek, Friedrich, xxvii, 157
He, Baogang, 230

Health issues, 296. *See also* Services
  aid and, 381–383
  DPT3 immunization and, 23
  Global Fund to Fight AIDS, Tuberculosis,
    and Malaria, 383
  HIV/AIDS, xi, 17, 23, 52–53, 221, 251,
    259–260, 292, 299, 354, 381, 383
  life expectancy and, 16–17, 19
  malaria, 52–53, 383
  medicine patents and, 381–382
  Millennium Development Goals and, 292,
    299, 310
  population effects and, 52–53
  poverty and, 20–24
Heavily indebted poor countries (HIPCs),
  294, 330, 384–385
Heckscher-Ohlin analysis, 94
Henrekson, M., 328
Heston, Alan, 160, 201
Heterogeneity, 13–14
Hills, John, 103–104
Hirschman, Albert, xv, 109, 111, 121, 157,
  220
Hitler, Adolf, 249
HIV/AIDS, xi, 17, 23, 221, 381, 383
  ABC campaign and, 251
  Millennium Development Goals and, 292,
    299
  population effects of, 52–53
  sex industry and, 259–260
  Uganda and, 354
Hjertholm, P., 373
Hoeffler, Anke, 376
Hoekman, Bernard, 263
Holland, 370, 372
Holmgren, Torgny, 106–107, 313
Holtz, Paul, xxi
Household surveys, 6–10, 167–171, 183–
  184, 191–192
Howitt, Peter, 114
Human capital, xv, xxiii, xxvi
  behavioral factors and, 19–20
  disabled people and, 12–13
  empowerment and, 84–85, 103–104 (*see
    also* Empowerment)
  environmental issues and, 55–59
  facilitation of, 142
  food and, 57
  increased aid and, 368–385
  integration and, 59–74
  investment in, 139, 142–145 (*see also*
    Investment)

life expectancy and, 16–17, 19 (*see also*
  Health issues)
migration and, xxv, 60–70, 243, 309
population changes and, 51–53
poverty and, 12–13 (*see also* Poverty)
preferences and, 243–265
privatization and, 347–353
program evaluation and, 152–155
service delivery and, 149–155
social exclusion and, 25–27
structural changes to society and, 49–55
Hungary, 282
Huth, P., 22
Hyperinflation, 38, 40

Import substitution model, 35, 37, *158*
Inclusion, 103–105, 273–277. *See also*
  Empowerment, Exclusion, Participation
Income, 395n2
  aggregate, 43–49
  analysis implications for, 74–82
  education and, 85
  evaluation methods and, 192–198
  global distribution of, 46–49, 158
  growth process and, 43–49 (*see also*
    Growth)
  inequality and, 43–49
  international trade and, 60–69
  poverty and, 4–16 (*see also* Poverty)
  productivity and, 113–114, 157–158
  SMEs and, 233–239
India, x, 26, 151, 154, 232, 354
  All India Institute for Public Health and
    Hygiene and, 260
  class systems and, 142, 145, 226–227
  Confederation of Indian Industry and,
    177
  consumption data and, 170
  Country Policy and Institutional
    Assessments (CPIAs) and, 80
  District Primary Education Program and,
    331–332
  education and, 247, 331–332
  entrepreneurship and, 111
  gender issues and, 28–29, 248
  government corruption and, 138
  income distribution and, 46
  infrastructure services and, 136
  integration and, 94–95
  investment and, 176–182, 202
  liberalization and, 204
  Millennium Development Goals and, 312

National Sample Survey and, 168–169
Palanpur, xiii, 5–6, 111, 173, 227, 273, 332, 383
Panchayati Raj Act, 230–231
panel data and, 173
poverty and, 5–9, 11, 31–32, 45, 98
preferences and, 250
PRSPs and, 305
reforms and, 177–178
SEWA and, 226–227
sex industry and, 259–260
SMEs and, 234
technology and, 366
trade policy and, 60, 66, 360
transition management and, 213
transparency and, 96–97, 132
Indian Statistical Institute, xiii
Indonesia, 5, 31, 171, 228, 312
Industrialization, 34–35, 122, 247, 269
Inequality, 203. *See also* Poverty
  Gini coefficient or index and, 45
  growth process and, 43–49
  income distribution and, 46–49
  mobility and, 183
Inflation, 38, 40, 131
Inheritance, 186
Innovation, xxiii. *See also* Technology
  entrepreneurship and, 221–223
  green revolution and, 210–211
  privatization and, 353
  specializing countries and, 218
Institutions, 78–79, 81–82
  aid and, 378–382
  centrality of, 90–94
  cohesion and, 92
  Country Policy and Institutional
    Assessments (CPIAs) and, 80, 320–321
  definition for, 90
  education and, 218
  empowerment and, 100–102
  erosion of, 92
  governance and, 90–94
  growth influences of, 202
  interest groups and, 92–93
  international financial, 311–312, 378–382
  investment and, 136–139
  legal reform and, 90–91
  market building and, 216–219
  Millennium Development Goals and, 298–302
  obstacle reduction and, 219
  panel data and, 171

privatization and, 138, 147–148
service delivery and, 149–155
technology transfer and, 218
transition management and, 213
two-pillar strategy and, 127–163 (*see also* Two-pillar strategy)
Insurance, 21, 275–276
Integration
  China and, 94–95
  firm destruction and, 95–96
  globalization and, 59–74, 94–98
  India and, 94–95
  transparency and, 94–98
Interest rates, 73–74, 161
International Comparison Project, 383
International Country Risk Guide (ICRG), 187
International Development Association (IDA), 370
International Fund for Agricultural Development, 234
International Monetary Fund (IMF), xv, 161, 310, 322, 357, 371, 378, 401n2
International trade
  China and, 60, 62, 66, 68–69
  GATT and, 61
  India and, 60, 66
  liberalization and, 61
  policy issues over, 60–69
  tariffs and, 61, 63–64
  technology and, 60
  World War II era and, 61–62
Interventionism, 40, 88, 296–298. *See also* Millennium Development Goals
Inverted U hypothesis, 158–159, 398n3
Investment, xxiii–xxix
  agenda issues and, 317–318
  aid and, 368–385
  analysis implications for, 74–82
  backward economy and, 210
  bureaucratic obstacles and, 136–139, 147, 180, 211, 217–219
  China and, 176–182
  Country Policy and Institutional
    Assessments (CPIAs) and, 80, 320–321
  dynamic processes and, 86–87, 207–212
  empowerment and, 139, 142–145, 148–155
  equations for, 206
  evaluation methods and, 192–198
  exclusion and, 273–277
  foreign direct, 71, 106–108, 132, 358, 359

Investment (cont.)
  future direction for, 387–389
  global capital flow and, 70–74
  government and, 136–139
  growth models and, 204–207
  improving climate for, 111, 128–139, 146–
    148, 219–221
  India and, 178–182
  infrastructure services and, 133–136, 219–
    221
  institutions and, 136–139
  integration and, 59–74, 94–98
  macroeconomic policy and, 130–132
  measuring climate of, 173–182
  microeconomics of, 202
  mortality rates and, 297
  North/South America and, 269
  obstacle reduction and, 219–221
  participation and, 146–148
  policies for improving, 214–221
  privatization and, 347–353
  reform and, 177–178, 267–283
  SMEs and, 233–239
  spillover effects and, 207–208
  trade policy and, 131–132
  transition management and, 213
  transparency and, 94–98
  types of, 212
Iyer, Lakshmi, 202

Jacobs, Jane, 145, 328
Jacoby, Hanan, 23
Japan, 35, 40, 96–97, 122, 263, 365
Jatabs, 227
Jimenez, Emmanuel, 152, 192
Johannesburg conference, 384, 389
Johnson, Simon, 202, 268–269
Jones, Leroy, 137
Jordan, 324
Jubilee 2000 program, 310, 384–385
Justino, Patricia, 25
Justman, Moshe, 270–271

Kaldor, Nicholas, 70, 112, 120, 201
Kanbur, Ravi, 30
Kaohsiung. See Taiwan
Kaufmann, Daniel, xx, 79, 137, 173, 176,
  212, 338, 342
Kecamatan Development Project, 228–
  229
Keefer, Philip, 75, 92, 173, 202
Kenya, 66, 158, 196, 329

Keynes, John Maynard, xv, xxvii, 167, 205,
  387
Khemani, Stuti, xix
Khmer Rouge, 249
Khwaja, Asim Ijaz, 153
King, Mervyn, xvi, 23
Kirzner, Israel, 89, 222, 254
Klein, Burton, 222–223
Knack, Stephen, 75, 92, 173, 202
Koo, A. Y. C., 157
Korea, Republic of, 40, 90, 178, 201, 358
  gender issues and, 28–29, 248
  industrialization and, 122
  trade policy and, 365
Kraay, Aart, 79, 98, 131, 137, 173
Kranton, Rachel, 262
Kravis, Irving, 160, 201
Kremer, Michael, 196–198, 329
Krueger, Anne O., 75, 196, 357
Kuczinski, Pedro-Pablo, 161
Kuznets, Simon, 46–49, 158–159
Kuznets curve, 271
Kyrgyz Republic, 92

Labor regulations, 139
La Ferrara, Eliana, 187
Laffont, Jean-Jacques, 119
Land and Labor in China (Tawney), 246–247
Lang, Kevin, 198
Lanjouw, Peter, xiii, xix, 5–6, 111, 173, 231,
  234, 236, 273, 275
La Porta, Rafael, 138
Latin America, xi, 9, 40, 205
  debt and, 323
  exports of, 37
  government role and, 87–88
  growth patterns in, 35–38
  market liberalization and, 35
  Mexican default and, 38
  migration and, 69
  poverty and, 99
  private lending and, 38
  privatization and, 351–352
  trade policy and, 61–69, 361
  transition management and, 213
Lauresen, J., 373
Learning-by-doing approach, 201
Learning-by-watching approach, 201
Legal reform, 90–91
Le Grand, Julian, 103–104
Leipziger, Danny, 351
Leite, Phillippe, 242

Lewis, Arthur, 46–49, 158
Li, Shuzhuo, 29
Liberalization, 35, 61, 96, 147, 204
  development strategies and, 160–161
  subsidies and, 364–366
  trade policy and, 131–132, 359–368
Licensing, 217, 381–382, 394n2
Liles, P. R., 222
Lindahl, Mikael, 75
Lindert, P., 60, 69
Lingap Para sa Mahihirap (Caring for the
  Poor) program, 227–228
Lipton, Michael, 12
Liquidity constraints, 272
Litchfield, Julie, 25
Literacy, 85
Little, Ian M. D., 94, 157, 339
Liu, L., 96
Living standards, x–xi, xxiv, 109
  environmental change and, 55–59
  household surveys and, 6–10, 167–171,
    183–184, 191–192
  institution centrality and, 90–94
  poverty and, 3–32 (see also Poverty)
  societal change and, 49–55
  surveys and, 168–172
London Protocol, 58, 382
London School of Economics, xiii, xvi
Lopez-de-Silanes, Florencio, 138
Lorenzetti, Ambrogio, 79
Loury, Glenn, 143, 249
Lucas, Robert E., 113, 209
Ludwig-Maximillian University, ix
Luxembourg, 372
Lybeck, J. A., 328

McClelland, David, 222
Machiavelli, Niccolò, 277–278, 388
McLiesh, Caralee, xix
McMillan, John, 212, 216, 222
McNamara, Robert, 158
Macroeconomic stability
  aid and, 368–385
  domestic action and, 321–324
  poverty effects and, 401n6
Madagascar, 14, 363
Maddison, Angus, 34, 39
Majority rule, 230
Malaria, 52–53, 383
Malawi, 13, 363
Malaysia, 90
Malnutrition, 23

Manual labor, 246
Markets, xiii
  agriculture and, 364–366
  Austrian school and, 89
  building institutions for, 216–219
  bureaucratic obstacles and, 136–139
  corruption and, 138, 344–345
  cross-border financial flows and, 70–74
  customs officials and, 344–345
  degree of competition and, 138
  Doha negotiations and, xi, xxxiii, 367,
    384, 389
  export pessimism and, 157
  failure of, 116
  fundamentalist approach to, xiv, 119,
    159-160
  globalization and, 39–43 (see also
    Globalization)
  Heckscher-Ohlin analysis and, 94
  industrial revolution and, 34–35
  infrastructure services and, 133–136
  integration of, 59–74, 94–98
  international trade and, 60–69
  Latin America, 35–38
  liberalization and, 35, 61, 96, 131–132,
    147, 160–161, 204, 359–368
  macroeconomic policy and, 131–132
  migration and, 69–70
  Millennium Development Goals and,
    304–306, 309
  natural resources and, 39–40
  policy agenda and, 317–318
  privatization and, 347–353
  as processes, 87–89
  securities regulation and, 88
  Solow model and, 112–113
  specializing countries and, 218
  state's role and, 87–89
  subsidies and, 365–366
  tariffs and, xi, 63–64, 263, 338–340, 367,
    403n3
  taxes and, 334–347
  trade policy and, 131–132, 359–368
  transparency and, 94–98, 131–132
  two-pillar strategy for, 127–163 (see also
    Two-pillar strategy)
Marshall, Alfred, 82, 116, 120
Marx, Karl, xxvii, 200
Massachusetts Institute of Technology
  (MIT), xiii
Mastruzzi, Massimo, 137
Mathematics, xiii, 206

Mathur, Priya, xix
Mauritania, 312
Measurement
  aid and, 368–385
  of basic services, 190–192
  budget deficits and, 322
  consumption data and, 170 (*see also* Data)
  effective evaluation and, 192–198
  of empowerment, 184–188
  firm adaptability and, 212–213
  investment climate and, 173–182
  Millennium Development Goals and, 290,
    308–311
  of opportunity, 182–184
  PETSs and, 190–192
  poverty and, 182–190
  public spending levels and, 324–330
  QSDSs and, 190–192
  randomization and, 196–198
  of security, 188–189
  taxes and, 333–337, 345–347
Mellinger, Andrew, 75
Menard, C., 351
Menéndez, Marta, 26–27, 183
Mengistae, Taye, 181, 212, 344
Mesoamerican Biological Corridor, 383
Mexico, 38, 372
  integration and, 95
  international trade and, 62
  migration and, 70
  Monterrey Conference, 287, 289, 373, 384,
    389, 399n1
  Opportunidades program and, 197, 242
  Progresa program and, 153, 197, 242
  redistribution and, 242
  transparency and, 132
Meyer, Bruce D., 196
Migration, xxv, 70, 243, 309
  international trade and, 60–69
Miguel, Edward, 197, 329
Milesi-Ferretti, Gian Maria, 230
Mill, John Stuart, 260–261
Millennium Declaration, 288
Millennium Development Goals, xii,
    xxxii–xiii, 9, 182, 208, 325, 389, 399n2
  Africa and, 298, 300, 313
  aid and, 312–313, 371–372, 375–376, 380,
    385
  Asia and, 300, 313
  capabilities and, 303
  cooperative implementation of, 302–306
  country responsibility and, 302–306

  cross-sectoral effects and, 296–298
  current progress of, 290, 298–302
  data analysis and, 306–312
  disease and, 292, 299, 310
  evaluation and, 306–308, 311–312
  global partnerships and, 293–294
  HIV/AIDS and, 299
  hunger and, 291
  India and, 312
  Indonesia and, 312
  international agreement and, 288
  interpretive cautions for, 295–296
  learning from, 311–312
  markets and, 304–306, 309
  measurement and, 290, 308–311
  migration and, 309
  mortality rates and, 291, 296–297, 306
  PRSPs and, 305
  public spending and, 324–333
  scaling up and, 298–302
  sustainability and, 292–293
  targets of, 288, 291–294, 329
  technology and, 294
  trade and, 304–306, 309, 363
  water and, 293, 296
  World Bank and, 310
Miller, Margaret, 312
Minimalist approach, 88
Minorities, 144. *See also* Ethnicity
Mirrlees, James, xv, 109
Mitra, Pradeep, 30
Mobility, 183, 249–250
Models, 115. *See also* Data
  aggregate, 33, 43–49, 60–69, 74–82, 171–
    173
  exclusion, 274–276
  Ferreira, 399n4
  Harrod-Domar, 112–113
  import substitution, 35, 37
  inverted U hypothesis, 158–159
  investment climate/growth, 204–207
  Justmam-Gradstein, 270–271
  Kuznets, 158–159
  learning, 201
  multiple equilibrium, 210
  preferences, 253–256
  Schumpeter, 114, 209
  S-curve analysis and, 223
  Solow, 112–113, 200–201
  steady state, 33, 114
  unemployment and, 203
Moldova, 92

Mombasa, 66
Monopolies, 90–91, 349, 351
Montreal Protocol, 58, 382
Mookherjee, Dilip, 151
Moral hazard, 276
Morocco, 96, 259
Morrisson, Christian, 9–11, 46
Mortality rates, 184–185, 231, 291, 296–297, 306
Moulin, Sylvie, 196
Mozambique, 365, 377
Msuya, Joyce, xix
Mueller, Dennis, 328
Multicropping, 121
Munshi, Kaivan, 252
Murphy, Kevin, 210–211
Museveni, Yoweri, 251
Myaux, Jacques, 252
Myers, Norman, 56
Myrdal, Gunnar, 57

Nairobi, 158
Narayan, Deepa, 3, 84, 92, 101, 182, 184, 189
Natural resources, 39–40
Ndulu, Benno J., 39
Neoliberalism, 159. See also Markets, fundamentalist approach to
Nepal, 5, 13
Netherlands, 372
Newman, Andrew F., 274–275
New Partnership for Africa's Development, 289
New Zealand, 330
Nicoletti, Giuseppe, 217
Nigeria, 39, 62, 151, 154
Nike, 62
Nile Basin Initiative, 383
Nongovernmental organizations (NGOs), 191, 310–311
  accountability and, 320
  aid and, 377–378, 383–384
  development strategy and, 151–153
  preferences and, 247–248, 259
North, Douglass, 268
Norway, 330–331, 372
Nozick, Robert, 88, 258
Nurkse, Ragnar, 110, 120–121
Nyoni, T., 373

O'Connel, Stephen A., 39
Oh, Gi-Taik, 30

Oldman, Oliver, 344
Oligarchies, 271
Onchocerciasis Control Program, 382
Openness, 94–98, 181. See also Transparency
Opportunidades program, 197, 242
Opportunity, 182–184
Organization for Economic Cooperation and Development (OECD), 7, 38, 176, 178, 217, 392n2
  government role and, 87–88
  Millennium Development Goals and, 294
  tariffs and, 263
  technology and, 366
  trade policy and, 359–368
  transparency and, 94–98
Orlowski, Witold, 282
O'Rourke, Kevin H., 69
Oswald, Andrew J., 188
Outcomes, 182–183
Ownership, 100, 186, 240
Oxford University, xiii

Paes de Barros, Ricardo, 49
Pakistan, 5, 14, 16, 137–138, 247, 344, 365
Pande, Rohini, 231
Panel data, 171–173
Paraguay, 231
Pareto optimality, 117–118, 255–256
Parker, S. W., 242
Participation, 226. See also Empowerment
  concept of, 142
  democracy and, 270–271
  investment climate and, 146–148
  politics and, 229–231
  practical steps for, 229–231
  SMEs and, 233–239
Paternalism, 257–258
Paul, Samuel, 229
Pensions, 21, 240, 280
Peoples University of Beijing, xiii
Pereira da Silva, Luiz, 194–195
Perotti, Roberto, 80, 230
Persson, Torsten, 230
Peru, 145, 151, 171, 240, 355, 396n3
Petrin, Tea, 112
Pfefferman, Guy, 237
Philippines, 62, 171, 354
  Medium Term Development Plan, 228
  Social Weather Stations (SWS) and, 227–228
  technology and, 366

Piachaud, David, 103–104
Pigou, Arthur, 116
Piketty, Thomas, 275–276
Piore, Michael, 261
Pistor, Katharina, 90
Pitt, Mark M., 171
Platteau, Jean-Philippe, 151–152
Pogge, Thomas, 11–12
Poland, 39, 281–282
Policy
  accountability and, 319–320, 331–332
  agenda issues and, 317–318
  analysis implications for, 74–82
  Bretton Woods, 38
  bureaucratic obstacles and, 136–139, 147, 180, 211, 217–219
  capitalism transitions and, 38
  Country Policy and Institutional Assessments (CPIAs) and, 80, 321
  cross-sectoral effects and, 296–298
  democratic effects on, 229–230
  Doha negotiations and, xi, xxxiii, 367, 384, 389
  domestic revenue and, 333–347
  dynamic processes and, 119–123
  economic integration and, 59–74
  elitism and, 269–270, 272
  empowerment and, 229 (see also Empowerment)
  environmental, 55–59
  evaluation methods and, 192–198
  fiscal discipline and, 321–324, 345–347
  foreign assistance and, 106–108
  future directions for, 387–389
  global capital flow and, 70–74
  government role and, 87–89
  incentives and, 321
  income distribution and, 46–49, 239–242
  industrialization and, 247
  infrastructure services and, 133–136, 219–221
  institution centrality and, 90–94
  integration and, 94–98
  international trade and, 60–69
  interventionism, 40
  inverted U hypothesis and, 158–159
  investment climate, 214–221 (see also Investment)
  Kecamatan Development Project and, 228
  "kicking away the ladder" and, 268
  labor regulation and, 204
  lecture guides for, xxvi–xxxiv

  liberalization and, 35, 61, 96, 131–132, 147, 160–161, 204, 359–368
  macroeconomic, 131–132, 321–324
  majority rule and, 230
  management and, 350–351
  measurement inputs and, 182–198
  migration and, 69–70
  MDGs, 290–313 (see also Millennium Development Goals)
  nation-building and, 92
  obstacle reduction and, 219–221
  openness and, 131–132
  paternalism and, 257–258
  poverty reduction and, 31–32, 43–49, 98–99 (see also Poverty)
  preferences and, 243–265
  privatization and, 347–353
  protectionism and, 132
  reform and, 107–108, 112, 121–122, 177–178, 187, 211, 232–233
  responsibility and, 319–320
  SEWA and, 226–227
  Social Weather Stations (SWS) and, 227–228
  state's role and, 315–321
  tax, 116, 118, 136–137, 211 (see also Taxes)
  trade, 131–132, 359–368
  trade-offs in, 189–190
  transition management and, 213
  transparency and, 59–74, 94–98, 131–132
  two-pillar strategy and, 127–163 (see also Two-pillar strategy)
  unsustainable, 280
  Washington consensus and, 161–162
Political economy, 267–283. See also Politics
Politics, 26. See also Government
  as art of the possible, 283
  Cold War and, 106, 289, 369–370
  constituency building and, 277–283
  democracy, x, 80, 82, 229–230, 270–271, 393n14
  economic research level on, 272–273
  economy of growth and, 268–273
  electoral systems and, 229–230
  elitism and, 272
  exclusion and, 103–105, 273–277
  gender issues and, 231, 271
  investment climate and, 206–207 (see also Investment)
  oligarchies and, 271
  Panchayati Raj Act, 230–231

reform and, 230–231, 277–283
village chiefs and, 230–231
voter turnout and, 231
Pollution, 56
Ponchamni, Jean, xix
Popper, Karl, 157
Population changes, 51–53
Populism, 40
Post-World War II era, 34–35, 61–62, 93, 109, 200
Poverty, x, 223
accountability acceptance and, 289
action and, xvi–xvii (*see also* Action; Policy)
aid and, 368–385
analysis implications for, 74–82
behavioral factors and, 19–20
capability assessment and, 21
class systems and, 13 (*see also* Class systems)
consumption and, 4–5, 7
declines in, 7–10
definition for, 3, 5, 7
dependency ratios and, 12
disabled people and, 12–13
discrimination and, 25–27
disease and, 22–23
economic mobility and, 29–31
education and, 12, 16, 18, 21, 271
elasticity and, 45
empowerment and, 84–85, 184–188 (*see also* Empowerment)
evolution over time, 10–11
exclusion and, 103–105
fertility rates and, 29
fiscal discipline and, 321–324
gender and, 25–29
geographical variation in, 13–14
Gini coefficient or index and, 45, 47, 49
growth process and, 43–49
health issues and, 20–24
historical achievements on, 288–289
HIV/AIDS and, 17, 23
household surveys and, 6–10, 167–171, 183–184, 191–192
income distribution and, 46–49
institution centrality and, 90–94
insurance and, 275–276
international commitment on, 288
Kecamatan Development Project and, 228
lesson set for, 289
life expectancy and, 16–17, 19

measurement of, 4–12, 182–190, 391n1
MDGs and, 290–313 (*see also* Millennium Development Goals)
mobility and, 183
moral issues of, 4
multidimensional factors of, 4, 189–190, 288
non-income factors for, 16–20
opportunity and, 182–184
post-World War II levels and, 10
preferences and, 250 (*see also* Preferences)
privatization and, 350–352
public spending and, 320–321 (*see also* Public spending)
reduction of, 31–32, 43–49, 98–99
regional profiles for, 12–16
relativist approach to, 6–7
rent-seeking and, 130
report cards for, 229
security and, 188–189
service delivery and, 149–155
SEWA and, 226–227
shared recognition of, 287
SMEs and, 14–15, 233–239
social exclusion and, 25–27, 103–105
Social Weather Stations (SWS) and, 227–228
spatial heterogeneity in, 13–14
statistics for, 3, 8–10, 14–15, 17–18
subsidies and, 322, 351, 364–366
surveys and, 168–171
trade policy and, 131–132, 359–368
two-pillar strategy and, 127–163 (*see also* Two-pillar strategy)
urban/rural areas and, 13, 31
vulnerability and, 20–24
wage employment and, 14
World Development Report, and, 3, 5, 158
Poverty Reduction Strategy Papers (PRSPs), 305, 371, 374
Prebisch, Raú, 35, 157
Preferences, 243, 265
aggregation rule for, 261
Asia and, 247
Austrian School and, 255–256
capabilities and, 254, 263–264
China and, 246–247
class systems and, 249–251
conceptual challenges and, 244–245
constraining, 250
consumer prices and, 255
decision making and, 258–264

Preferences (cont.)
development effects of, 245–253
education and, 151–153, 246–249
"equality of agency" and, 263
ethics and, 264
ethnicity and, 246, 249–251
gender issues and, 246, 253–254, 257–258
government and, 245–246, 260–261
identification of, 251–253
industrialization and, 247
information and, 252
leadership and, 251
mobility and, 249–250
Morocco and, 259, 262
NGOs and, 151–153, 247–248, 259
paternalism and, 257–258
policy approaches for, 257–258
sex industry and, 259–260
shifting economies and, 245–246
wartime and, 249
well-being assessment and, 253–256
Prince, The (Machiavelli), 277–278
Pritchett, Lant, 92, 149, 198, 249
Privatization, 138, 147–148, 402n15
access and, 353
affordability and, 353
competition scope and, 353
decision making and, 352–353
desirability of, 347–350
externalities and, 353
innovation and, 353
Latin America and, 351–352
monopolies and, 349, 351
natural resources and, 349
poverty effects of, 350–352
productivity and, 348
subsidies and, 351
PROBE Team, 150
Productivity, xxiii, xxv, 115
aggregate function for, 113–114
analysis implications for, 74–82
degree of competition and, 138
disease and, 52–53
infrastructure services and, 133, 136
integration and, 59–74, 94–98
international trade and, 60–69
investment and, 199 (see also Investment)
Latin America and, 35–38
privatization and, 348
public spending and, 320–330
rent seeking and, 118–119
SMEs and, 233–239

two-pillar strategy and, 127–163 (see also Two-pillar strategy)
Progresa program, 153–154, 242
Property rights, 160–161, 216, 218–219, 364
Protectionism, 94–98, 132
Przeworski, Adam, 230
Psychologists, 222, 243
Public economics, 109–110, 161. See also Policy
development dynamics and, 119–123
government failure and, 117–119
incentives and, 115
market failure and, 116–118
program evaluation and, 152–155
standards for, 115–116
Public Expenditure Tracking Surveys (PETSs), 190–192
Public goods, 382–384
Public spending
accountability and, 319–320, 331–332
agenda issues and, 317–318
domestic revenue and, 333–347
education and, 329
fiscal discipline and, 321–324, 345–347
global data of, 324–328
levels of, 324–330, 334–335
macroeconomic stability and, 321–324
management and, 330–331
physical infrastructure and, 318
reform and, 332–333
responsibility and, 319–320
state's role and, 315–321
transparency and, 331–332
Purchasing power parity (PPP), 201, 374
Putnam, Robert, 92, 143

Qian, Yingyi, 202
Quantitative Service Delivery Surveys (QSDSs), 190–192
Quasi-tax, 195
Quirk, Kerrie, xix

RAND Corporation, 191
Randomization, 196–198
Rao, Vijayendra, 250, 255, 263
Ravallion, Martin, xix, 231, 242
developmental change and, 44–46, 48, 168, 170, 184
living standards and, 5, 7–9, 11–12
Rawls, John, 91–92, 183
Ray, Debraj, 275
Reddy, Sanjay, 11–12

Redistribution, 239–242
Redistribution with Growth (Chenery, et al.),
  158, 271
Reform, 211
  barriers to, 279–283
  big bang, 281–282
  conflict of interest and, 280–281
  constituencies and, 277–279
  cost-benefit ratio of, 280
  credit and, 274–275
  democracy and, 270–271
  elitism and, 269–270, 272
  insurance and, 275–276
  legal, 90–91
  Machiavelli on, 277–278
  Millennium Development Goals and,
    290–313
  oligarchies and, 271
  public spending and, 332–333
  Russia and, 277–279
  Transparency International and, 310–311
Reinikka, Ritva, 150, 190, 192
Religion, 142, 191, 226, 250, 310
Rent seeking, 118–119, 130, 211, 268–269,
  398n2
Report cards, 229
Reynolds, L. J., 79
Ricardo, David, 200
Richter, Rudolf, 261
Roberts, M. J., 96
Robilliard, Anne-Sophie, 194
Robinson, James, 50, 150, 194, 202, 268–
  269, 271, 281
Rodríguez, Francisco, 321
Rodrik, Dani, 40, 75, 97, 202, 280–281, 339
Roemer, John E., 104, 183
Rogers, Halsey, ix, 17, 85, 112, 287, 301
Roland, Gérard, 211, 281
Romer, Paul, 113, 131, 201, 209
Rosenblatt, David, xix
Rosenstein-Rodan, Paul, 109–110, 120, 157,
  210
Rosenzweig, Mark R., 171, 173, 210
Rossel, Carlos, xxi
Rostagno, Massimo, 230
Rotter, J. B., 222
Russett, B., 22
Russia. *See also* Soviet Union
  government role and, 87–88
  oligarchs and, 229–230
  reform and, 277–279, 282
  security and, 189

Sabel, Charles, 262
Sachs, Jeffrey, 75
Safety, 136–137
SaKong, 112
Sala-i-Martin, Xavier, 209
Samuelson, Paul, 109
Sawada, Yasuyuki, 152, 192
Scarpetta, Stefano, 217
Schargrodsky, Ernesto, 351
Schelling, Thomas, 211
Scherr, Sara, 56
Schleifer, Andrei, 211
Schmidt-Hebbel, Klaus, 321
Schultz, Theodore, 109–110, 242
Schumpeter, Joseph, xv, xxvii, 109–111,
  114, 121, 209
Scitovsky, Tibor, 94, 339
Scott, James C., 94, 145, 277, 339
S-curve analysis, 223
Security, 188–189, 344–345
Self-Employed Women's Association
  (SEWA), 226–227, 229
Sen, Amartya, xv, xxiv, 182–183
  Development and Freedom and, 20
  development policy and, 84, 109–110
  living standards and, 3–4
  preferences and, 255–256, 258
Senegal, 62
Serageldin, Ismail, 92
Services, 217, 354–355, 400n5, 402n9
  accountability and, 232, 319–320
  delivery of, 149–155, 186–187
  infrastructure, 219–221
  Kecamatan Development Project and, 228
  measurement of, 190–192
  MDGs and, 297–298 (*see also* Millennium
    Development Goals)
  obstacles to, 219–221
  organization of, 318
  PETSs and, 190–192
  physical infrastructure and, 318
  privatization and, 347–353
  public spending and, 318 (*see also* Public
    spending)
  QSDSs and, 190–192
  randomization and, 196–198
  reform of, 232–233
  report cards for, 229
  SWS survey and, 227–228
  taxes and, 334–347
Sese Seko, Mobuto, 376
Sex industry, 259–260

Shah, Anwar, 342
Shariff, Abusaleh, 236
Sharma, Naresh, xiii, 197
Shirley, M. M., 351
Shleifer, Andrei, 138, 210, 268
Shocks
  Bretton Woods and, 38
  education and, 196
  insurance and, 275–276
  oil prices and, 38, 62, 93, 203
  panel data and, 171–173
  poverty and, 20–24
  SMEs and, 236
  Zambia and, 93
Sierra Leone, 349
Simon, Herbert, 262
Singapore, 344, 364
Singer, Hans, 157
Sinn, Hans-Werner, xx
Sinnot, Richard, 69
Skoufias, Emmanuel, 242
Slavery, 269
Slovak Republic, 216–218
Small and medium enterprises (SMEs),
  xxiii, 14–15, 233–239
Smith, James, 171
Smith, Adam, 200
Smoking, 20
Social security, 171–172
Social Weather Stations (SWS), 227–228
Society. *See also* Human capital
  class systems and, 142, 145 (*see also* Class
    systems)
  disease and, 52–53
  empowerment and, 103–104
  environmental issues and, 55–59
  exclusion and, 103–105, 273–277
  fertility rates and, 20, 29, 51–53, 70, 85
  fiscal discipline and, 321–324, 345–347
  governance issues and, 78–82
  increased aid and, 368–385
  institution centrality and, 90–94
  migration and, 69–70
  MDGs and, 291 (*see also* Millennium
    Development Goals)
  population effects and, 51–53
  preferences and, 243–265
  program evaluation and, 152–155
  role perceptions and, 143–145
  service delivery and, 149–155
  state's role and, 315–321
  structural changes to, 49–55

surveys and, 168–171
urbanization and, 53–55
Sociologists, 243, 250
Soil degradation, 56
Sokoloff, Kenneth, 269
Solow, Robert, 109, 200–201
Solow model, 112–113, 200–201
Soviet Union, xiii–xv, 9, 121, 157, 159, 205,
  249
  Cold War and, 106, 289, 369–370, 385
  government role and, 89, 215
  income distribution and, 47–48
  institution centrality and, 93
  reform and, 211, 277–279
  transition management and, 213
  Washington consensus and, 162
Special and Differential Treatment, 364
Specialization, 121
Spillover effects, 207–208
Squire, Lyn, 98, 159
Srinivasan, T. N., 339
Stalin, Joseph, 249
Stanislaw, Joseph, 89
Steinherr, Alfred, 38, 392n2
Stern, Nicholas, xii–xvi, 83, 85, 160, 287
  aid and, 381
  disease and, 383
  education and, 75, 332
  entrepreneurship and, 111–112
  government and, 89
  growth determinants and, 120, 211
  living standards and, 17, 30
  Millennium Development Goals and, 301,
    304
  political reform and, 273, 275
  public spending and, 334
  SMEs and, 234
  surveys and, 173
  taxes and, 324, 335, 340, 342–344
Stigler, George J., 255
Stiglitz, Joseph, 322, 391n1
Stone, Andrew H. W., 176, 212, 338, 342
Structural adjustment, 160. *See also*
  Liberalization
Stutzer, Alois, 188
"Stylized facts," 112
Subsidies, 322, 351, 364–366
Summers, Robert, 160, 201
Sundberg, Mark, xix
Sutton, John, 96
Svensson, Jakob, 150, 190, 192
Swanson, Eric, 312

Swaroop, Vinaya, 107, 370
Sweden, 330–331, 372
Syrquin, Moshe, 50
Székely, Miguel, 26

Tabellini, Guido, 230
Taiwan, 31, 60, 66, 90
  income distribution and, 271–272
  SMEs and, 237
  transparency and, 96–97
Tajikistan, 92
Taliban, 249
Tanzania, 5
Tanzi, Vito, 342, 344
Tariffs, xi, 63–64, 263, 338–340, 367, 403n3
Tawney, Richard H., 214, 246–247
Tax policy, 117–118, 211, 230, 316, 323–324
  administration of, 343–345
  as aggregate expenditure, 334
  corruption and, 344–345
  direct taxes and, 342–343
  fiscal discipline and, 345–347
  GDP measurement of, 345–347
  indirect taxes and, 340–341
  structure of, 335–338
  tariffs, xi, 63–64, 263, 338–340, 367, 403n3
  value-added tax (VAT), 340–341, 346
Taylor, Alan M., 69
Technology, 113, 366
  agriculture and, 110
  diffusion effects and, 210–211, 218
  dynamic processes and, 86–87
  elitism and, 269
  growth and, 201, 204–205
  international trade and, 60
  Millennium Development Goals and, 294
  surveys and, 168
  tariffs and, 263
Tendler, Judith 87, 154, 231
Thailand, 5, 95, 178, 336
Theill index, 47
Thomas, Duncan, 171
Tian, Xiaowen, 350
Tiongson, Erwin, 325
Tocqueville, Alexis de, 260
Trade policy, 5, 131–132, 203, 403nn3
  agenda for, 364–368
  agriculture and, 263, 364–368
  Doha negotiations and, xi, xxxiii, 367, 384, 389
  Everything But Arms initiative and, 363
  exclusion and, 359–364

international politics and, 60–69
Millennium Development Goals and, 363
subsidies and, 364
tariffs and, 263
Trade-Related Aspects of Intellectual Property Rights (TRIPs), 364
Transparency, 131–132, 181
  accountability and, 319–320
  firm destruction and, 95–96
  growth and, 94–98
  Heckscher-Ohlin analysis and, 94
  Kecamatan Development Project and, 228–229
  obstacle reduction and, 220
  public spending and, 331–332
  reform and, 103–105, 277–283, 332–333
    (see also Reform)
  SEWA and, 226–227, 229
  SWS and, 227–228
Transparency International, 187, 310–311
Tunisia, 5
"Two Concepts of Liberty" (Berlin), 258
Two-pillar strategy
  accountability and, 319–320
  bureaucratic obstacles and, 136–139
  decentralization and, 149–152
  different approaches and, 156–163
  empowerment and, 139–145, 148–155
  equilibrium and, 130
  future directions for, 387–389
  good governance and, 317–318
  government corruption and, 136–138
  implementation of, 145–155
  inflation and, 131
  infrastructure services and, 133–136
  investment climate and, 128–139, 146–148
  macroeconomic factors for, 130–132
  openness and, 131–132
  policy agenda and, 317–318
  political reform and, 267–283
  program evaluation and, 152–155
  public spending and, 317–318 (see also Public spending)
  rent-seeking and, 130
  responsibility and, 319–320
  service delivery and, 149–155
  structure of, 129–131, 133, 136
  surveys and, 146–148, 160
Tybout, J., 96
Tyson, Laura d'Andrea, 112

Uganda, 154, 232, 354
  aid and, 377–378
  empowerment and, 101
  poverty and, 98
  preferences and, 251
  transparency and, 132
Ukraine, 354
United Kingdom, 6, 103, 157, 252
  aid and, 370
  consumption data and, 170
  gender issues and, 271
  industrialization and, 122
  public spending and, 330
  taxes and, 346
  Treasury, ix
  wartime and, 249
United Nations
  aid and, 372
  Conference on Financing for
    Development, xii, 287, 361
  Development Programme, 182, 186
  Global Fund to Fight AIDS, Tuberculosis,
    and Malaria, 383
  Millennium Declaration, xi–xii
United States, 252, 365
  Cold War and, 106, 289, 369–370, 385
  consumption data and, 170
  industrialization and, 122
  migration and, 69–70
  mobility and, 183
  securities regulation and, 88
  subsidies and, 366
  tariffs and, 263
  unemployment and, 202–203
University of Warwick, xiii
Urbanization, 53, 55
Utility functions, 254, 258
Uzbekistan, 14

Value-added tax (VAT), 340–341, 346
van Bastelaer, Thierry, 92
van de Walle, Dominique, 5, 25
Van Dooerslaer, E., 23
Verdier, Thierry, 150, 271–272
Vienna Convention, 57–58, 382
Vietnam, 25, 62
  aid and, 378
  poverty and, 98
  SMEs and, 237–238
  subsidies and, 366
  transparency and, 132
Vijverberg, Wim, 237

Village chiefs, 230
Vishny, Robert W., 210–211, 268
von Hayek, Friedrich, 157
Von Weizsacker, Carl Christian, 253
Voting, 231
Vulnerability, 20–24

Wacziarg, R., 96
Wagner's law, 328
Wagstaff, Adam, 22–23, 296–297, 329
Wallsten, Scott J., 351
Walton, Michael, xx, 250, 255, 263, 397n1
Washington consensus, xv, 125, 161–162
Water, 56, 293, 296, 366, 383
Wellons, Philip, 90
West Bengal, 240
Wicksell, Knut, 116
Williamson, John, xv, 60, 69, 161
Wodon, Quentin, 231
Wolfensohn, James, xx
Wolpin, Kenneth I., 171
Woodruff, Christopher, 212, 216, 222
World Bank, ix, xiv–xv, xxx, 12, 25, 80,
    146, 154, 176
  aid and, 371–372, 378–381
  Assessing Aid: What Works, What Doesn't,
    and Why and, 369–370
  bureaucracy of, 381
  Country Policy and Institutional
    Assessments (CPIAs), 80, 320–321, 370,
    375–376, 379, 393n12
  Development Gateway Web, 384
  environmental issues and, 56–57
  foreign assistance and, 71, 106–108
  Globalization, Growth, and Poverty, 60
  Living Standards Measurement Survey
    (LSMS) and, 172, 189, 191
  Local-Level Institutions Survey, 189
  McNamara and, 158
  Millennium Development Goals and, 300,
    310
  Operations Evaluation Department
    (OED), 379–380
  policy quality index and, 93
  privatization and, 148
  regulation benchmarks of, 216–217
  surveys and, 168
  Washington consensus and, 161
  World Development Report and, 3, 5, 59, 92,
    149–151, 158, 181–182, 222, 233, 264,
    324, 355, 396n1
World Business Environment Survey, 180

World Health Organization (WHO), 22
World Summit on Sustainable
    Development, xii, 288
World Trade Organization (WTO), xi,
    287–288, 361, 363–364

Yergin, Daniel, 89
Young, Allyn, 120, 222
Yugoslavia, 39
Yunus, Muhammad, 355

Zaire, 349, 376
Zak, Paul, 92
Zakaria, Fareed, 82, 370
Zambia, 5, 39, 62, 83, 93, 305, 313, 374
Zedillo, Ernesto, 372
Zee, Howell H., 342
Zeira, J., 274
Zilibotti, Fabrizio, 202
Zingales, Luigi, 129
Zoido-Lobatón, Pablo, 79, 173